Fodor's 2009

D0196976

PARIS

Where to Stay and Eat
for All Budgets

Must-See Sights
and Local Secrets

Ratings You Can Trust

Fodor's Travel Publications   New York, Toronto, London, Sydney, Auckland
www.fodors.com

FODOR'S PARIS 2009
Editor: Caroline Trefler

Editorial Production: Astrid deRidder
Editorial Contributors: Jennifer Ditsler-Ladonne, Linda Hervieux, Simon Hewitt, Rosa Jackson, Lisa Pasold, Nicole Pritchard, Heather Stimmler-Hall
Maps & Illustrations: Mark Stroud, Henry Colomb and David Lindroth, *cartographers*; William Wu, *information graphics*; Rebecca Baer and Bob Blake, *map editors*
Design: Fabrizio LaRocca, *creative director*; Guido Caroti, Siobhan O'Hare, *art directors*; Tina Malaney, Chie Ushio, Ann McBride, *designers*; Melanie Marin, *senior picture editor*; Moon Sun Kim, *cover designer*
Cover Photo: Terry Vine/Stone/Getty Images
Production/Manufacturing: Angela McLean

ISBN 978–1–4000–1948–9

ISSN 0149–1288

SPECIAL SALES

This book is available at special discounts for bulk purchases for sales promotions or premiums. Special editions, including personalized covers, excerpts of existing books, and corporate imprints, can be created in large quantities for special needs. For more information, write to Special Markets/Premium Sales, 1745 Broadway, MD 6-2, New York, New York 10019, or e-mail specialmarkets@randomhouse.com.

AN IMPORTANT TIP & AN INVITATION

Although all prices, opening times, and other details in this book are based on information supplied to us at press time, changes occur all the time in the travel world, and Fodor's cannot accept responsibility for facts that become outdated or for inadvertent errors or omissions. So **always confirm information when it matters,** especially if you're making a detour to visit a specific place. Your experiences—positive and negative—matter to us. If we have missed or misstated something, **please write to us.** We follow up on all suggestions. Contact the Paris editor at editors@fodors.com or c/o Fodor's at 1745 Broadway, New York, NY 10019.

PRINTED IN THE UNITED STATES OF AMERICA
10 9 8 7 6 5 4 3 2 1

Be a Fodor's Correspondent

Your opinion matters. It matters to us. It matters to your fellow Fodor's travelers, too. And we'd like to hear it. In fact, we need to hear it.

When you share your experiences and opinions, you become an active member of the Fodor's community. That means we'll not only use your feedback to make our books better, but we'll publish your names and comments whenever possible. Throughout our guides, look for "Word of Mouth," excerpts of your unvarnished feedback.

Here's how you can help improve Fodor's for all of us.

Tell us when we're right. We rely on local writers to give you an insider's perspective. But our writers and staff editors—who are the best in the business—depend on you. Your positive feedback is a vote to renew our recommendations for the next edition.

Tell us when we're wrong. We're proud that we update most of our guides every year. But we're not perfect. Things change. Hotels cut services. Museums change hours. Charming cafés lose charm. If our writer didn't quite capture the essence of a place, tell us how you'd do it differently. If any of our descriptions are inaccurate or inadequate, we'll incorporate your changes in the next edition and will correct factual errors at fodors.com immediately.

Tell us what to include. You probably have had fantastic travel experiences that aren't yet in Fodor's. Why not share them with a community of like-minded travelers? Maybe you chanced upon a beach or bistro or B&B that you don't want to keep to yourself. Tell us why we should include it. And share your discoveries and experiences with everyone directly at fodors.com. Your input may lead us to add a new listing or highlight a place we cover with a "Highly Recommended" star or with our highest rating, "Fodor's Choice."

Give us your opinion instantly at our feedback center at www.fodors.com/feedback. You may also e-mail editors@fodors.com with the subject line "Paris Editor." Or send your nominations, comments, and complaints by mail to Paris Editor, Fodor's, 1745 Broadway, New York, NY 10019.

You and travelers like you are the heart of the Fodor's community. Make our community richer by sharing your experiences. Be a Fodor's correspondent.

Bon Voyage!

Tim Jarrell, Publisher

CONTENTS

PARIS IN FOCUS

ABOUT THIS BOOK

Our Ratings

Sometimes you find terrific travel experiences and sometimes they just find you. But usually the burden is on you to select the right combination of experiences. That's where our ratings come in.

As travelers we've all discovered a place so wonderful that its worthiness is obvious. And sometimes that place is so experiential that superlatives don't do it justice: you just have to be there to know. These sights, properties, and experiences get our highest rating, **Fodor's Choice,** indicated by orange stars throughout this book.

Black stars highlight sights and properties we deem **Highly Recommended,** places that our writers, editors, and readers praise again and again for consistency and excellence.

By default, there's another category: any place we include in this book is by definition worth your time, unless we say otherwise. And we will.

Disagree with any of our choices? Care to nominate a place or suggest that we rate one more highly? Visit our feedback center at www.fodors.com/feedback.

Budget Well

Hotel and restaurant price categories from ¢ to $$$$ are defined in the opening pages of the respective chapters. For attractions, we always give standard adult admission fees; reductions are usually available for children, students, and senior citizens. Want to pay with plastic? **AE, DC, MC, V** following restaurant and hotel listings indicate if American Express, Diners Club, MasterCard, and Visa are accepted.

Hotels

Hotels have private bath, phone, TV, and air-conditioning and operate on the European Plan (aka EP, meaning without meals), unless we specify that they use the Continental Plan (CP, with a Continental breakfast), Breakfast Plan (BP, with a full breakfast), or Modified American Plan (MAP, with breakfast and dinner) or are all-inclusive (AI, including all meals and most activities). We always list facilities but not whether you'll be charged an extra fee to use them, so when pricing accommodations, find out what's included.

Restaurants

Unless we state otherwise, restaurants are open for lunch and dinner daily. We mention dress only when there's a specific requirement and reservations only when they're essential or not accepted—it's always best to book ahead.

Many Listings

★	Fodor's Choice
★	Highly recommended
✉	Physical address
✛	Directions
⬠	Mailing address
☎	Telephone
🖷	Fax
⊕	On the Web
✍	E-mail
🕮	Admission fee
☉	Open/closed times
Ⓜ	Metro stations
▭	Credit cards

Hotels & Restaurants

🏨	Hotel
⇲	Number of rooms
☖	Facilities
⑩	Meal plans
✕	Restaurant
☖	Reservations
⬎	Smoking
⑰	BYOB
✕🏨	Hotel with restaurant that warrants a visit

Outdoors

⅄	Golf
⛺	Camping

Other

☾	Family-friendly
⇨	See also
✉	Branch address
☞	Take note

Experience Paris

Tourists watching the Eiffel Tower from the Trocadéro

WORD OF MOUTH

". . . take the metro to the Trocadero and walk down toward the river. The view of the Eiffel Tower from there is breathtaking both day and night, and you know that you are really in Paris. From there you can walk down toward the Eiffel Tower. Just below the bridge you can catch the boat ride on the Seine (about 1 hour) that is another easy activity on your first day there."

—Leburta

PARIS TODAY

Bienvenue à Paris! Although it may seem as if time stands still in this city—with its romantic, old buildings and elegant 19th-century parks and squares—there's an undercurrent of small but significant changes happening here that might not be immediately obvious.

Today's Paris...

...is less smoky. The image of the intellectual sitting in a café, cigarette in hand, may have been as much a part of the French identity as wine and cheese, but as of 2008, that all changed. Following the lead of Spain, Italy, and Ireland, the French government banned smoking in offices and public buildings, including hotels, bars, cafés, and restaurants. For all those who smirk that the French have never been known to respect laws they don't like, this one seems to be working. There may have been a bit of grumbling, but Parisians have adapted quickly.... There's still smoke, but it's outside: the smokers have pretty much taken over the café terraces (many are enclosed and heated in winter) as their own little smoking lounges.

...is cleaner. Paris has had a bit of a brushing-up: those who haven't been to the city in a decade or two will notice that streets have been returned to their pre-1970s cobblestoned charm and are cleaner, and that the façades of landmarks have received a healthy washing down. Much of this is thanks to the city's mayor, socialist Bertrand Delanoë, elected in 2001. Parisians praise him for reducing pollution in this congested city. There are more bus, bike, and pedestrian lanes now, and he introduced the city's lighthearted ad campaigns urging residents to pick up after their dogs.

...is diverse. A steady flow of immigrants from former French colonies in African and Arab countries—as well as people from China and Russia—make up a large part of Paris's vibrant multicultural community. Yet these same populations—and their France-born children and grandchildren—are also some of the city's most disadvantaged groups, posing a problem to already overstretched social programs. With fewer resources to go around, it's no surprise that the nation's multicultural youth feel they're not getting their fair share of the Liberté, Égalité et Fraternité that the French hold so dear. The suburban riots that took place during the fall of 2005 reminded politicians that although

WHAT'S HOT IN PARIS NOW

Tecktonik dancing—a mix of techno, hip-hop, and rave—is the latest craze to hit the mainstream in Paris, with dancers "battling" to outdo each other on the Esplanade at Trocadéro or at techno clubs. Young and suburban, Tecktonik fans can be spotted in skinny jeans with fluorescent accessories and punk'd-out hair. • Parisian ladies have begun to openly embrace the joys of female-friendly **adult toys**, which have recently become the rage and are more visibly available at boutiques around town as well as at Au Printemps. There's even a cheeky bimonthly magazine on the newsstands now, called S'Toys. • Two historic Parisian promenades have undergone a shift in character recently. Travel agencies along the **Champs-Elysées** have been replaced by big-name brands

things are improving in la capitale, racial tension still remains a serious issue. The average visitor may see little evidence of this, as even the protest marches that got out of hand outside the Sorbonne were tightly contained, but these issues are very real.

...is friendlier. One area where fraternité has evolved is with French service: although North Americans, raised on the principle that the customer is always right, may find servers and store clerks a bit curt (and not always so efficient), Paris has become friendlier than it once was. This can be chalked up to necessity, as the service industry scrambled to compete for tourism dollars after the post-9/11 slump in business. And many of Paris's waiters have discovered that happy American tourists tip better than unhappy ones—even when the 15% service fee is already included in the bill. That's not to say that service is delivered with a smile everywhere, and some visitors' perceptions of idyllic Paris are still dashed when met with huffy abruptness à la française. In 2006, reports recounted that Japanese tourists were suffering from "Paris Syndrome" and were rushed home because they were traumatized by the rudeness of those Parisians they encountered. Perhaps they would have suffered less had they not taken it so personally—a Parisian certainly wouldn't.

...is becoming more globalized. It's what the French call *mondialisation, en français,* and it's happening in Paris, as international chains and country-specific favorites are slowly seeping into Parisian culture. There are now 34 Starbucks in the city, including the location under the Pyramide in the Louvre. And if challenging their traditional cafés isn't enough, the Italian-owned gelato chain Amorino has opened several new Paris locations after the runaway success of their Ile St-Louis gelateria—a few feet from the famous (and French) Berthillon ice-cream shop! A fitting trend that the country's new First Lady, the Italian-born model-musician Carla Bruni, would surely approve.

such as Adidas, Lacoste, and Esprit. Nearby, shops in the **Palais-Royal** are transforming from vintage- and antiques-only to *au courant*, with the Marc Jacobs flagship store and boutiques from high-fashion designers such as Rick Owens and Jerôme l'Huillier. • **Green is the new gold** in Paris, and what's organic (*bio*) and environmentally friendly is not only trendy but becoming the norm. Health-food stores are popping up everywhere, and major supermarkets carry products with certified "ethical" labels. • The city's low-cost **bike-rental** system for short trips around town has been wholeheartedly adopted by Parisians, and visitors lucky enough to have a European credit card with the microchip necessary for payment. For €5 per week or €1 per day (payable by card at any of the 600 bike-rental stations), you can rent bikes for 30-minute stints, with each additional half hour costing €4. See the "Bicycling in Paris" box in chapter 3.

PARIS PLANNER

Getting Around

Paris is without question best explored on foot, and thanks to Baron Haussmann's mid-19th-century redesign, the City of Light is a compact wonder of wide boulevards, gracious parks, and leafy squares. When you want a lift, though, public transportation is easy and inexpensive. The métro (subway) goes just about everywhere you're going for €1.50 a ride (a carnet, or "pack" of 10 tickets, is €11.10); tickets are good for the vast bus network, too.

Paris is divided into 20 *arrondissements* (or neighborhoods) spiraling out from the center of the city. The numbers reveal the neighborhood's location and its age, the 1er arrondissement at the city's heart being the oldest. The *arrondissements* in central Paris—the 1er to 8^{e}—are the most visited.

It's worth picking up a copy of *Paris Pratique*, the essential map guide, available at bookstores and souvenir shops.

Paris Temps

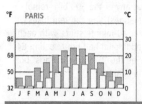

Saving Time & Money

Paris is one of the world's most visited cities—with crowds to prove it—so it pays to be prepared. Buy tickets online when you can: most cultural centers and museums offer advance-ticket sales, and the small service fee you'll pay is worth the time saved waiting in line. Investigate alternative entrances at popular sites (there are three at the Louvre, for example), and check when rates are reduced, often during once-a-week late openings. Also, most major museums—including the Louvre and the Musée d'Orsay—are free the first Sunday of each month.

A Paris Museum Pass can save you money if you're planning serious sightseeing, but it might be even more valuable because it allows you to bypass the lines. It's sold at the destinations it covers and at airports, major métro stations, and the tourism office in the Carrousel du Louvre (two-, four-, or six-day passes are €30, €45, and €60 respectively; for more info visit www.parismuseumpass.com).

Stick to the omnipresent ATMs for the best exchange rates; exchanging cash at your hotel or in a store is never going to be to your advantage.

Hours

Paris is by no means a 24/7 city, so planning your days beforehand can save you aggravation. Museums are closed one day a week, usually Tuesday, and most stay open late at least one night each week, which is also the least crowded time to visit. Store hours are generally 10 AM to 7:30 PM, though smaller shops may not open until 11 AM, only to close for several hours during the afternoon. Some retailers are still barred by law from doing business on Sunday, but exceptions include the shops along the Champs-Elysées, the Carrousel du Louvre, and around the Marais, where most boutiques open at 2 PM.

Eating Out

Restaurants follow French mealtimes, serving lunch from noon to 2:30 PM and dinner from 7:30 or 8 PM on. Some cafés serve food all day long. Always reserve a table for dinner, as top restaurants book up months in advance. When it comes to the check, you must ask for it (it's considered rude to bring it unbidden). In cafés you'll get a register receipt with your order. Gratuities (*servis*) are almost always included in the bill, but it's good form to leave some small change on the table: a few cents for drinks, or €2–€3 at dinner.

What to Wear

When it comes to dress, the French reserve athletic-type clothing for sports. Sneakers are fine as long as they're not "gym shoes" (think urban hip). You'll feel comfortable wearing jeans just about anywhere as long as they're neat, although it can't hurt to check if the restaurant you're heading to has a specific no-jeans dress code.

When to Go

The City of Light is magical all year round, but it's particularly gorgeous in June, when the long days (the sun doesn't set until 10 PM) stretch sightseeing hours and make it ideal to linger in the cafés practicing the city's favorite pastime—people-watching.

Winter can be dark and chilly, but it's also the best time to find cheap airfares and hotel deals.

April in Paris, despite what the song says, is often rainy.

Summer is the most popular (and expensive) season, and at the height of it, in July, Paris can feel like a city under siege, bursting at the seams as crowds descend *en masse*. Keep in mind that, like some other European cities, Paris somewhat shuts down in August—some restaurants are closed for the entire month, for example—though there are still plenty of fun things to do, namely free open-air movies and concerts, and the popular *Paris Plage*, the "beach" on the right bank of the Seine.

September is gorgeous, with temperate weather, saner airfares, and cultural events timed for the *rentrée* (or return), signifying the end of summer vacation.

Paris Etiquette

The Parisian reputation for rudeness is undeserved. In fact, Parisians are sticklers for politesse and exchanging formal greetings is the rule. Informal American-style manners are considered impolite. Beginning an exchange with a simple "Do you speak English?" will get you off on the right foot. Learning a few key French words will take you far. Offer a hearty *bonjour* (bohn-zhoor) when walking into a shop or café and an *au revoir* (o ruh-vwahr) when leaving, even if nobody seems to be listening (a chorus may reply). When speaking to a woman over age 16, use *madame* (ma-dam), literally "my lady." For a young woman or girl, use *mademoiselle* (mad-mwa-zel). A man of any age goes by *monsieur* (muh-syuh). Always say please, *s'il vous plaît* (seel-voo-play), and thank you, *merci* (mair-see).

WHAT'S WHERE

The following numbers refer to chapters.

2 Ile de la Cité & Ile St-Louis. Also known as "the Islands," although they're just a few quick steps from the "mainland," the Ile de la Cité and Ile St-Louis are the heart of Paris. This is where you'll find Notre-Dame and Sainte-Chapelle.

3 The Tour Eiffel and Invalides. With the Eiffel Tower and Champs de Mars, and the Seine nearby, there are many lovely strolls that give you lovely views of the Paris's ultimate monument.

4 The Champs-Elysées. The Champs-Elysées and Arc de Triomphe attract the tourists, but there are also several excellent museums here, well worth checking out.

5 The Faubourg St-Honoré. The Faubourg, with its well-established shops and cafés, has always been chic, and probably always will be.

6 The Grands Boulevards. Use the Opera Garnier as your orientation landmark and set out to do some power shopping. There are some intriguing small museums in the neighborhood, too.

7 Montmartre. Like a small village within a big city, Montmartre feels distinctly separate from the rest of Paris—but it's prime tourist territory, with Sacré-Coeur as its main attraction.

8 The Marais. The Marais, what used to be Paris's Jewish neighborhood, is now one of the city's hippest destinations. While away the afternoon at the Place des Vosges or shop to your heart's content.

9 Canal St-Martin, Bastille & Oberkampf. If it's new and happening in Paris, this is where you'll find it: trendy restaurants, funky galleries, and cutting-edge boutiques are popping up everywhere.

10 The Quartier Latin. Leave yourself lots of time to wander the Latin Quarter, known for its vibrant student life.

11 St-Germain. Fabulous cafés and two of the city's best museums (the d'Orsay and Musée Rodin) are here, but make sure you also leave yourself time to wander the Jardin du Luxembourg.

12 Montparnasse. Once the haunt of writers and artists—Picasso and Hemingway included—this neighborhood is now known for its contemporary-art scene as well as the Catacombs.

13 Western Paris. The Bois de Boulogne and the Musée Marmottan–Claude Monet are two great reasons to trek out here.

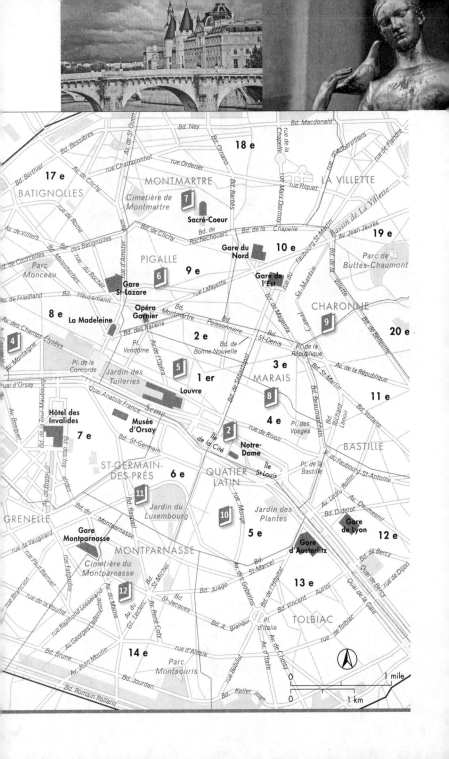

TOP PARIS ATTRACTIONS

Eiffel Tower

(**A**) Originally built as a temporary exhibition for the 1889 World's Fair, today there's no other monument that symbolizes Paris better than Gustave Eiffel's world-famous Iron Lady. It's breathtaking, whether you see it sparkling from your hotel window after dark or join the millions of annual visitors to brave the glass-bottom elevator trip to the top.

Notre-Dame

(**B**) It took almost 200 years to finish this 12th-century Gothic masterpiece immortalized by Victor Hugo and his fictional hunchback. Climb the spiral staircase of the bell towers for a close-up gander at the gargoyles, or have a peek at relics such as the Crown of Thorns in the cathedral treasury.

Jardin du Luxembourg

(**C**) This is one of the prime leisure spots on the Left Bank for urban-weary Parisians. Relax in a reclining park chair with a picnic lunch or a book and watch a game of *boules* while the kids enjoy a marionette show.

Jardin des Tuileries

(**D**) The 17th-century formal French landscape of these gardens behind the Louvre is punctuated by contemporary sculptures, a café, and two noteworthy museums: the Musée du Jeu de Paume and the Musée de l'Orangerie. In summer there's a small amusement park and Ferris wheel.

Arc de Triomphe

(**E**) The 164-foot-tall Arc de Triomphe has served as the backdrop to official military parades since its completion in 1836. Use the underground passageway to reach the monument, where you can visit the Tomb of the Unknown Soldier beneath the arch or climb the stairs for amazing panoramic views of the city.

Sacré-Coeur

(F) This wedding-cake white basilica dominates Montmartre's hilltop. Most visitors are content with the views overlooking the city from the basilica stairs, but ambitious sight seekers can climb to the bell tower for an even higher vantage point.

Opéra Garnier

(G) Opulent, stunning, and magnificently over-the-top, Charles Garnier's opera house is one of the outstanding jewels of the Second Empire. Its illustrious marble staircase and ruby-red box seats have been featured in films from *Dangerous Liaisons* to *Marie-Antoinette,* and its backstage corridors are famously haunted by the Phantom of the Opera.

Centre Georges Pompidou

(H) Still visually shocking three decades after its opening in 1977, the Pompidou Centre's groundbreaking "inside-out" design is the top destination for modern-art lovers in Paris.

Musée d'Orsay

(I) After a stunted lifespan as a train station constructed for the 1900 World's Fair, this beautiful Belle Époch building is filled with Art Nouveau objects, Impressionist paintings, vintage photography, and realist sculptures. Don't miss the scale model of the Opéra Garnier or the views of the Seine from the grand ballroom now housing the museum's restaurant.

Louvre

(J) The grandest museum in the world started out as a humble fortress in the 12th century, growing in size and prestige as a sumptuous royal palace until the French Revolution gave it a new lease on life as home to the young Republic's art collection. The Big Three—*Mona Lisa, Winged Victory,* and *Venus de Milo*— should not be missed.

PARIS LIKE A LOCAL

To appreciate the City of Light as the locals do, you can start by learning some of the daily rituals of Paris life. These simple, fun pleasures will quickly get you into the swing of being Parisian.

Shop Like a Parisian

Parisians prefer the boisterous atmosphere of bustling street markets to the drab *supermarchés*. Even if you're just buying picnic fixings, you can follow suit. For a full listing of Paris's markets, check out the city hall Web site at www.paris.fr, but these are some of our faves. **Le Marché d'Aligre,** just off the Rue du Faubourg Saint-Antoine beyond the Opéra Bastille, dates back to the 18th century. Open Tuesday through Sunday, the market has fruit, vegetables, cheese, meat, fish, and poultry, as well as a host of other products. The best selection is on the weekend. And if flea markets are your thing, Paris has three that can satisfy any bargain hunter. At **Les Puces de Montreuil** (Saturday, Sunday, and Monday, 9 AM to 7:30 PM, métro Porte de Montreuil) dig through the heaps of old clothes until you make a find, probably for less than €3. **Les Puces des Vanves** (weekends, 9 AM to 7:30 PM, métro Porte de Vanves; Avenue de le Porte de Vanves and Rue Marc Sangnier), is two in one: in the morning, collectors revel among old furniture, stamps, postcards, and almost everything else imaginable; in the afternoon, merchants of new and vintage clothing take over. **Les Puces de Saint-Ouen** (Saturday, Sunday, and Monday 9 AM to 7:30 pm, métro Clignancourt), otherwise known as the Clignancourt flea market, is a little more expensive, but a real treasure trove. Bypass the noisy stands near the métro in favor of the buildings beyond the elevated highway, where antiques dealers and vin-

tage-clothing boutiques provide a real blast from the past. You might not *need* to buy flowers, but the flower markets are lovely for wandering, and you can cheer up a budget hotel room with a few daisies in a water glass. Try one of the **Les Marchés aux Fleurs:** at Place de la Madeleine (Tuesday to Sunday, 8 AM to 7:30 PM), Place des Ternes (Tuesday to Sunday, 8 AM to 7:30 PM), or Place Lépine (Monday to Saturday 8 AM to 7:30 PM, with the bird market Sunday morning).

Drink Coffee Like a Parisian

Le café in Paris isn't simply a drink that begins the day: it's a way of life. Though Parisians do stop at the counter to order a quick *café expresse, bien serré, s'il vous plaît* ("good and strong, please"), more often people treat the café as an extension of their apartments, with laptops precariously balanced, cell phones ringing, and business being done; in Paris the café is the place to work, read, and chat with friends, any time of the day. Think of Simone de Beauvoir, who spent more time at the **Café de Flore** (*172 bd. St-Germain, 6ᵉ, 01–45–48–55–26*) than in her chilly apartment. Choose a café with a patio or good windows for people-watching, or pause at the nearest counter, and you're in for a dose of Parisian café culture. Most locals have their own favorites, and we've listed some of our top choices on the neighborhood Getting Oriented pages; you're bound to find your own preferred haunt(s).

Walk Like a Parisian

Paris was made for wandering, and the French have coined a lovely word for a person who wanders the streets: le flâneur, one who strolls or loiters, usually without a destination in mind. In Paris the streets beckon, leading you past mon-

uments, down narrow alleyways, through arches, and into hidden squares. As a *flâneur,* you can become attuned to the city's rhythm and, no matter how aimlessly you stroll, chances are you'll end up somewhere magical. Some of our suggestions for wandering are along the Seine, into the poetic streets of **St-Germain**, or into the tangled lanes around the **Bastille** and **Canal St-Martin** area. Strolling is a favorite Sunday pastime for the locals—but you're on vacation, so you can be a *flâneur* any day of the week.

Eat Baguettes Like a Parisian

The Tour Eiffel might be the most famous symbol of Paris, but perhaps the true banner of France is the *baguette,* the long, caramel-color bread brandished at every meal. Locals take inordinate pride at finding the best *baguette* in the neighborhood. To find a worthy *boulangerie*—a bakery that specializes in bread, as opposed to a *pâtisserie,* specializing in pastries—look for a line outside on weekend mornings. Three faves in Paris are **Arnaud Delmontel** (39 rue des Martys, 01–48–78–29–33), **Jean-Pierre Cohier** (270 rue du Faubourg St-Honoré, 01–42–27–45–26), and **Boulanger de Monge** (123 rue Monge, 01–43–37–54–20). Note that some *boulangeries* follow the traditional three-step customer service protocol: first you place your order at the counter and receive a receipt; then you pay at the *caisse* and get your receipt stamped; finally, you return to the first counter to exchange the stamped receipt for your package of edible art. As you're leaving the bakery, do as many Parisians do—nibble the end of the crust to taste the bread while it's still warm.

Eat Pastries Like a Parisian

High prices are making luxury all the more elusive in Paris, but there's one indulgence most people can still afford, at least occasionally—fine pastries. As you'll see when you stop in at any of Paris's extraordinary pâtisseries (pastry shops) a whole different and wonderful array of French treats await. Tops on our list are the deliciously airy and intense *macarons*—nothing like the heavy American macaroons you might be familiar with. **Ladurée** (16 rue Royale, 8e, 01–42–60–21–79) claims to have invented these ganache-filled cookies, but two Left Bank pâtissiers also have particularly devoted fans of their macarons: the flavors at **Gérard Mulot** (76 rue de Seine, 6e, 01–43–26–85–77) include pistachio, caramel, and terrific orange-cinnamon, and **Pierre Hermé** (72 rue Bonaparte, 6e, 01–43–54–47–77) has exotic ones like peach-saffron, olive oil, and white truffle. The classic opera pastry—almond cake layered with chocolate and coffee cream—can be found at **Lenôtre** (61 rue Lecourbe, 15e, 01–42–73–20–97), but devotees also flock to the fine-food emporium **Fauchon** (26 pl. de la Madeleine, 8e, 01–47–42–60–11). Another traditional pastry is the mont-blanc, a mini-mountain of chestnut purée capped with whipped cream, best rendered by **Jean-Paul Hévin** (3 rue Vavin, 6e, 01–43–54–09–85). And those really in the know watch for anything from the Tokyo-born **Sadaharu Aoki** (35 rue Vaugirard, 6e, 01–45–44–48–90); look for his green-tea madeleines and black-sesame éclairs. Many of the sweet spots mentioned here have multiple locations; only the original store is listed.

PARIS WITH KIDS

Paris is often promoted as an adult destination, but there's no shortage of children's activities to keep the young 'uns busy, not to mention the fact that many of the city's top attractions have carrousels parked outside them in summer. Make sure to buy a *Pariscope* (found at most newsstands) and check the *enfants* section for current children's events. In addition to what's listed below, sites of particular interest to children are marked with a rubber-ducky icon.

Museums

Paris has a number of museums that cater to the young, and the young at heart. They're a great place to occupy restless minds, especially if the weather is bad. The **Cité des Sciences et de l'Industrie** (the Museum of Science and Industry), at the Parc de la Villette, is an enormous science center, and the children's area is divided into two main sections: one for children from 3 to 5 years of age; another for those from 5 to 12. Interactive exhibits allow kids to do everything from building a house and comparing their body to that of a favorite animal, to learning about communications systems throughout history, from the tom-tom to the satellite. The **Musée de la Poupée** (the Doll Museum) is a cozy museum in the heart of the Marais, with a collection of more than 500 dolls dating back to the 1800s, complete with costumes, furniture, and accessories. Labels might be in French, but they're not really the point anyway, and the museum features a "Doll Hospital," where "sick" dolls and plush toys come to be repaired; the doctor is in on Thursday, but free estimates are offered throughout the week. The **Palais de la Découverte** (the Palace of Discovery) has high-definition, 3-D exhibits covering everything from chemistry, biology, and physics, to the weather, so there's bound to be some interesting dinner conversation when the day is done. Many of the displays are in French, but that doesn't stop most kids from having a blast; hands down, the choice between this and the Louvre is a no-brainer.

Sites & Shows

A zoo is usually a good bet to get the kids' attention—although you might want to keep in mind that most European zoos aren't as spacious as American zoos. The **Ménagerie** at the Jardin des Plantes is an urban zoo dating from 1794 and home to more than 240 mammals, 400 birds, 270 reptiles, and a number of insects. The huge **Parc Zoologique**, in the Bois de Vincennes, is the largest zoo in Paris, although parts are closed for renovation; the bonus of taking the métro out here, though, is the park's two lakes, both with rentable rowboats. When it comes to spectacles, what child would pass up the circus? There are several in the city (see the *Performing Arts* chapter), and the **Cirque de Paris** has a special feature called a "Day at the Circus"—your kids (and you) can learn some basics like juggling and tightrope walking, then you'll lunch with the artists and see a performance in the afternoon. Less interactive are **Les Guignols,** French puppet shows: the original Guignol was a marionette character created by Laurent Mourguet, supposedly in his own likeness, celebrating life, love, and wine. Today the shows are primarily aimed at children, and are found in open-air theaters throughout the city in the warmer months. Check out the Champs-Elysées, Parc Montsouris, Buttes Chaumont, Jardin du Luxembourg, and the Parc Floral in the Bois de Vincennes.

Even if they don't understand French, kids are usually riveted. Of course, the best sight in Paris is the city itself, and a **boat ride** on the Seine is a must for everyone. It's the perfect way to see the sights, rest weary feet, and, depending on which option you choose, lunch or dinner may be part of the treat.

Expending Energy

Most kids are thrilled (at least more than the grown-ups) at the prospect of climbing innumerable stairs to be rewarded with cool views: the **Eiffel Tower** is the quintessential Paris climb, but **Notre-Dame** gets extra points for the gargoyles, and the **Arc de Triomphe** is a good bet, since it's centrally located at the end of the Champs-Elysées. When it comes to open spaces for running around, Paris has lots of park options, with extra attractions in summer when kids can work off steam on the trampolines or ride ponies at the **Jardin des Tuileries**. The **Jardin du Luxembourg** has a playground and a pond where kids can rent miniature boats, and the **Bois de Boulogne** has a zoo, rowboats, bumper cars, and lots of wide-open spaces. Ice-skating is seasonal but always a thrill, and from mid-December through February, several outdoor Paris sites are turned into spectacular ice-skating rinks with Christmas lights, music, and instructors. The rinks are free to the public; skate rental for adults costs €5. The main rink is at **Place de l'Hôtel de Ville** (the square in front of City Hall), but the rink on the **Eiffel Tower**'s first level, though small, has prime novelty value.

Underground Paris

There's something about exploring underground that seems to fascinate kids, at least the older ones. **Les Egouts,** the Paris sewer system, has a certain gross factor but isn't actually that disgusting. Keep in mind, though, that the smell is definitely ranker in the summer months. At the **Catacombs,** in Montparnasse, dark tunnels filled with bones are spookily titillating—at least for those not prone to nightmares. For some cheap underground entertainment without the ick factor, the **métro** itself can be its own sort of adventure, complete with fascinating station art such as the submarine decor at Arts-et-Metiers, the colorful Parisian timeline murals at Tuileries, or the Egyptian statues of the Louvre-Rivoli station. A good tip: the Météor (Line 14), is the only driverless métro that lets you sit at the very front; it's hard to resist the feeling that you're driving.

And for Treats

All that fun will no doubt bring on an appetite, and there's no shortage of special places to stop for a snack in Paris. **Angelina** (226 rue de Rivoli), near the Jardin des Tuileries, is world famous for its hot chocolate—deliciously thick and yummy, unlike what American children are usually used to. **Berthillon,** renowned for its decadent ice cream, has outposts around town, including on the Ile St-Louis—though the **Amorino** gelaterias give it a run for its money. And when in need, a pâtisserie selling chocolate croissants is never hard to find. French children adore the pastel clouds of *meringue* (which resemble hardened whipped-cream puffs) that decorate almost every bakery's window, and there are all sorts of cookies to tempt a smile from a tired tot.

GREAT ITINERARIES

Paris is a treasure of neighborhoods and history, and a visit to this glorious city is never quite as simple as a quick look at a few landmarks. These one-day itineraries are mix and match: follow the ones that intrigue you—and leave yourself time to just walk and explore.

Monumental Paris

Begin your day at the Trocadéro métro, where you can get the best views of the Tour Eiffel from the esplanade of the Palais de Chaillot. If you absolutely must ride to the top, now is the best time to get in line. Otherwise, get a Seine-side view of the city's other noteworthy monuments from the Bateaux-Mouches, moored below the Pont d'Iéna. Hour-long cruises loop around the Ile de la Cité, with multilingual commentary on the sights along the way. Afterward you can take the RER to the Musée d'Orsay for lunch in the museum's Belle Époque dining room before tackling the late-19th-century works of art. Then it's a short walk to the imposing Hôtel des Invalides, the French military museum built as a retirement home for wounded soldiers under Louis XIV. The emperor Napoléon Bonaparte rests beneath the golden dome. If the weather's nice, have tea next door in the sculpture gardens of the Musée Rodin (entrance to the gardens €1). If your feet are still happy, cross the gilded Pont Tsar Alexandre III to the Champs-Elysées, passing the Belle Époque art palaces known as the Grand et Petit Palais. You can take Bus 73 from the Assemblée Nationale across the bridge to the Place de la Concorde and all the way up the Avenue des Champs-Elysées to the Arc de Triomphe. Open until 11 PM, its panoramic viewing platform is ideal for admiring the City of Light.

Alternative: Instead of the traditional Seine cruise, try the Batobus, which allows you to hop on and hop off through the day with one ticket. The seven Batobus ports include Notre-Dame, Hôtel de Ville, Louvre Museum, and Musée d'Orsay. Note that there's no commentary on these tours.

Old Paris

Start at the Pont Neuf for excellent views off the western tip of the Ile de la Cité, then explore the island's magnificent architectural heritage, including the Conciergerie, Sainte-Chapelle, and Notre-Dame. The brave can climb the corkscrew staircase to the towers for a gargoyle's-eye view of the city. Then detour to the neighboring Ile St-Louis for lunch before heading into the medieval labyrinth of the Latin Quarter: its most valuable treasures are preserved in the Cluny Musée National du Moyen-Age, including the reconstructed ruins of 2nd-century Gallo-Roman steam baths. At the summit of the hill above the Sorbonne university is the imposing Panthéon, a monument (and mausoleum) of French heroes. Don't miss the exquisite Eglise St-Etienne-du-Mont next door, where the relics of the city's patron Saint Geneviève are displayed. Follow the Rue Descartes to the Rue Mouffetard for a *café crème* on one of the oldest market streets in Paris. If the sun's still shining, visit the Gallo-Roman Arènes de Lutèce.

Alternative: A different look at the Latin Quarter (Old Paris) can include a visit to the sleek Institute du Monde Arabe, then a relaxing afternoon at the authentic steam baths and tearoom of the nearby Mosquée de Paris.

Royal Paris

Begin at the Place de la Concorde, where an Egyptian obelisk replaces the guillotine

where Louis XVI and Marie-Antoinette met their bloody fate during the French Revolution, then escape the traffic in the formal Jardin des Tuileries, which once belonged to the 16th-century Tuileries Palace, destroyed during the Paris Commune of 1871. Pass through the small Arc du Carrousel to the modern glass pyramid that serves as the main entrance to the Louvre, the world's grandest museum, once a 12th-century fortress. When you've built up an appetite, cross the street to the peaceful gardens of the Palais Royal for lunch at a café beneath the stone arcades. From here take métro Line 1 to station St-Paul. To the south you can find the Hôtel de Sens, home to King Henry IV's feisty ex-wife Queen Marguerite, and one of the few surviving examples of late-medieval architecture. Around the corner on Rue Charlemagne is a preserved section of the city's 12th-century fortifications built by King Philippe-Augustus. Cross the busy Rue St-Antoine to the Marais and enter the Hôtel de Sully, a fine example of the elegant private mansions built here by aristocrats in the early 17th century. Pass through the gardens to the doorway on the right, which leads to the lovely symmetrical town houses of the Place des Vosges, designed by King Henry IV. Many of the old aristocratic mansions in the Marais have been turned into museums, including the Musée Carnavalet and the Musée Picasso.

Power-Shopping Paris

Get an early start to avoid crowds at Au Printemps and Galeries-Lafayette, two of the city's grandest historic department stores conveniently side by side behind the Opéra Garnier. Refuel at the Place de la Madeleine, where gourmet food boutiques such as Hédiard and Fauchon

LOGISTICS & TIPS

Save time and money with a Paris Museum Pass. Some museums have reduced fees on Sunday and on extended-hour days if you go in the evening.

Keep closing days in mind. Most museums are closed one day a week, usually Monday or Tuesday.

offer light deli foods for shoppers on the move. If the luxury boutiques on the Rue Royale aren't rich enough for you, head down the Rue du Faubourg St-Honoré and the Avenue Montaigne (via Avenue Matignon), where the exclusive couture houses of Chanel, Dior, Hermès, and Yves St-Laurent hold court. ■TIP→ If you plan on spending more than €175 in one store, bring your passport to get the détaxe forms for your Value Added Tax rebate. Department stores are closed on Sunday, but open late on Thursday. Most small boutiques are closed Sunday and Monday. The Marais and the Champs-Elysées are the best bets for shopping on Sunday.

Alternative: For a more genteel shopping experience, head to the Left Bank's chic Bon Marché department store, then work your way through the fashion and home décor boutiques around the Eglise St-Sulpice and St-Germain-des-Prés. Shops get less expensive between métro Odéon and the Latin Quarter.

REAL PARISIAN EXPERIENCES

Sometimes, it's not enough to see the sights, shop the boutiques, and sample the regional delicacies: there is the compulsion to really immerse yourself. Taking part in some of Paris's quintessential experiences will allow you to learn more about French culture, and you'll get to meet and mingle with locals and like-minded travelers, creating a far more enriching trip to Paris, whether it's your first or fortieth visit! Below are some experiences that we recommend.

Food

Nothing is more French than fine wine and gourmet cuisine. So why not enjoy them hands-on, with cooking classes to perfect your *magret de canard* (duck breast) or to master the art of the soufflé. There are many options, from full-day courses in a Parisian home (in English) that include a market tour, to quick lunch lessons with the locals where everyone dines together afterward. In English except as noted: Paule Caillat's Promenades Gourmandes (☎01–48–04–56–84 ⊕*www.promenades gourmandes.com*). Food Unites the World (☎01–45–00–08–31 ⊕ *www.foodunites theworld.com*). Marguerite's Elegant Home Cooking (☎ 01–42–04–74–00 ⊕ *www.elegantcooking.com*). Les Coulisses du Chef (☎ 01–40–26–14–00 ⊕ *www. coursdecuisineparis.com*). Atéliers des Chefs (⊕ *www.atelierdeschefs.com*), group classes in French.

Wine

And it's no secret that appreciating your wine is greatly enhanced when you know what you're drinking and where it came from. Wine-tasting classes range from fun and casual lessons in English for absolute beginners to more formal dégustations of the finest vintages by seasoned sommeliers. There's something to fit all budgets and experience levels. O-Château (☎ 01–44–73–97–80 or 0–800–801–148 toll-free in France ⊕*www.o-chateau. com*) does wine-tasting lessons in English, vineyard tours, and Champagne cruises on the Seine. Legrand Filles & Fils (☎01–42–60–07–12–12 ⊕ *www.caves-legrand. com*) conducts Tuesday night Soirées Dégustation with a bilingual presentation of carefully chosen wines. Wine Dinners (☎ 01–41–83–80–46 ⊕ *www.wine-dinners.com*) is a French group hosted by bilingual François Audouze; it organizes gourmet meals (in Michelin-starred restaurants) with a selection of 10 wines.

21st-century Salons

Parisian salons—where a select group of connoisseurs gathered in a private home to discuss the artistic, literary, political, and philosophical ideas of the time—flourished in past centuries. They're back, in English, and open to anyone who calls to reserve a place. It's an experience not to be missed, and a great way to meet interesting people. Jim Haynes (☎ 01–43–27–17–67) hosts an international crowd for Sunday night dinner: informal "standing room only" affairs in his converted artist atelier. Patricia Laplante-Collins (☎ 01–43–26–12–88 ⊕ *http://parissoireesevents. blogspot.com/*)has guest speakers at her twice-weekly dinners on the Ile St-Louis, including writers, artists, chefs, or other personalities. Teatime = Talktime (☎01–43–25–86–55 ⊕ *http://language.meetup. com/59/*)is a weekly language gathering hosted in a Latin Quarter home by Michael and Veronique. Guests sip tea and munch snacks while mingling, with half the evening reserved for French conversation, the other half in another language (usually English).

BEATING THE EURO IN PARIS

Paris has never been cheap but with a weak dollar and a strong euro, traveling seems more and more daunting. We think that shouldn't stop you from going to Europe, but we know you're going to be looking for some tips on how not to break the bank, and who better to ask than travelers on www.Fodors.com Travel Talk forums?

■TIP➜Paris is definitely a walking city—take the opportunity to learn the word flaneur (one who strolls)—but when your feet get tired, take the métro instead of a taxi.

"As far as money saving tips, we did not take a single taxi—we bought books of 10 subway tickets at a time and used those. The Metro goes EVERYWHERE and is very efficient, safe, etc. We took the RER and Metro to/from both Orly and Charles de Gaulle airport, no problem." —poodle13905

"You can buy the 'Carte Orange' week pass for the metro/bus for 16-17€ pp; it is good Monday-Sunday." —travelnut

■TIP➜There are so many ways to eat well in Paris but still save money: eat picnics, spend your restaurant euros at lunch instead of dinner, have your latté at the counter instead of at a table…You'll save money and probably have a more authentic Parisian experience, too.

"I would second the suggestion to 'reste au comptoir' in a cafe, vs. sitting at a table. You will save a few coins, and it's a great experience." —petitepois

"Paris is a city where you can be master of your food expense. I rent an apartment to be able to have breakfast, store picnic fixings and snacks. Lunch menus are less expensive than evening meals… fixed price menus are less expensive than

ordering directly from the menu. If you enjoy wine…order the house carafe of wine rather than a bottle it is usually cheaper. Eating cheap can be a fun challenge. Visit the markets, enjoy the onion soup, the crepes, wonderful cheeses and breads." —jhaskell

"Buying a picnic and a bottle of wine would be about 1/2 the price of lunching at a resto." —ira

■TIP➜Save money on lodging. Why not rent an apartment instead of shelling out large sums on a hotel? The built-in perk is the money you'll save if you use the kitchen—even just for breakfast. And if you do opt for a hotel, choose your neighborhood with budget in mind.

"People will get much more for their money by staying away from the exact center of the city. It is all very well to want to see the Eiffel Tower from your hotel window or to be a 5-minute walk from the Louvre or Notre Dame, but that adds a lot of money to the travel expenses." —kerouac

"Having breakfast and snacks at home [in your rented apartment] will also save quite a bit." —nytraveler

■TIP➜Note that the jury's still out on whether a Museum Pass will save you money—but everyone agrees it'll save you time because with it, you don't have to wait in lines.

"A two day pass will cost you 30E. If you plan on visiting more than 3 or 4 places in the two days, you will break even. Even if you don't break even, (in my opinion) the advantage is you get to skip the long lines."—Dejais 04/08

FREE & ALMOST FREE

It's easy to break the bank in Paris, but those acquainted with the city know where to find the free (or almost free) stuff. Here are some tips.

Free Art

Thanks to the City of Paris's dedication to promoting culture, access to the permanent collections in the city's municipal museums is free, so you can learn about the city's rich history, the characters who contribute to its aura of romance, and the warriors who fought for France's liberation—all without dropping a cent. Setting the example, the **Hôtel de Ville** de Paris (City Hall) in the Marais regularly runs several expositions at a time, most of which focus on French artists. Past expos have included the "Life of Edith Piaf" and the works of photographers Wally Ronis and Robert Doisneau. The **Maison Européene de la Photographie,** also in the Marais, is a favorite among flash-bulb-poppers and amateur photography buffs alike—and every Wednesday evening, from 5 to 8, this museum opens its doors free of charge. Expositions can cover everything from the history of the camera and the evolution of printing, to selections from some of the world's most famous photographers. It's a perfect prelude to cocktail hour. The **Musée Carnavalet**—yup, this is in the Marais also, near Place des Vosges—puts Paris's history on display with a collection of old signs, relics from bars and cafés, paintings of what the city looked like before it was fully developed (Montmartre was all farmland!), and old keepsakes and letters. It's an excellent place to get a feel for Paris past and present. More free art throughout the year can be found at the **Maison de Balzac,** the **Maison de Victor Hugo, Musée d'Art Moderne de la Ville de Paris,** and

the **Petit Palais,** also known as the **Musée des Beaux-Arts de la Ville de Paris.**

Free Music

For free classical music in an ethereal setting, many of Paris's churches host free or almost-free concerts at lunchtime and in the evening. For popular venues like **Sainte-Chapelle,** reserve well in advance. Flyers are posted around the city and outside the churches, or check weekly events listings. Also free are *l'Heure Musicale,* medieval music concerts at the **Musée du Moyen-Age** every Friday at 12:30 and Saturday at 4, between October and July. In summer and fall there are free concerts in the city's parks, including the **Jardin des Luxembourg** (classical music), **Parc de la Villette** (world music and jazz), and the **Parc Floral** in the Bois de Vincennes (classical and jazz). During **Paris Plage,** in late summer, there are free nightly pop and rock concerts on the quays of the Seine. When the weather's nice, you're also likely to find would-be, wannabe, and even a few real musicians along the *quai* of the **Canal St-Martin,** or in the **Place des Vosges,** guitars in hand for spontaneous song.

Free Serenity

If the hustle and bustle of Paris is getting to you, opt for a free session of **Qi gong** at the **Parc des Buttes-Chaumont** in the 19e arrondissement. Every day at 9 AM instructor Thoi Tin Cau leads classes, free of charge, at 7 rue Botzaris, métro Botzaris, on the patch of grass in the middle of the park. Parisians also like to recharge their batteries with an afternoon **catnap** in one of the handy reclined chairs scattered throughout the city's gardens. This is the cheapest option for relaxation, reading, and postcard writing—just make sure your possessions are secure if you're actually going to grab some shut-eye.

Perennial favorites for parking yourself, or weary companions, are the **Jardin des Luxembourg** and the **Jardin du Tuileries,** but one of the most serene venues, buffered from the traffic by the arcaded shops, is the garden at the **Palais Royal,** not far from the Louvre. Any perch along the Seine will also do in a pinch if the busy streets are getting to you: it's amazing how serene a spot by the water can be, so close to the frenetic workings of the city, especially if you find yourself on the incomparably charming **Ile de la Cité.**

Cheap Souvenirs
Perfect for yourself or friends back home, what souvenir retails for just about €0.10 each? The postcard, of course. Go retro (snail mail!) and send some quintessential scenery home with a "J'aime Paris" scribbled on the back, or just bring back a little packet of choice images. For the best prices, check out the news kiosks along Rue de Rivoli and the Grands Boulevards, or visit the bookstore **Mona Lisait** (9 rue St-Martin, 4e, 01–42–74–03–02). For more unusual cards, pop into **Images de Demain** (141 rue St-Martin, 4e, 01–44–54–99–99), opposite the Pompidou. **Mondial Art** (10 rue St-André des Arts, 6e, 01–55–42–19–00) has racks of stylish choices, including cards quoting famous French authors. Keep an eye out for vintage postcards, too, sold by the *bouquinistes* along the Seine and by collectors inside Passage des Panoramas. You can buy stamps at any *tabac* as well as at post offices.

(Almost) Free Sightseeing Tours
Imagine passing the Louvre as part of your daily commute. Some of the city's public bus routes are fantastically scenic; hop on the right one and you can get a great tour for just €1.50—sans squawk-ing commentary. The **No. 29** route reaches from the Gare St-Lazare, past the Opéra Garnier, to the heart of the Marais, crossing the Place des Vosges before ending up at the Bastille. This is one of the few lines that run primarily on small streets, not major arteries. Hop the **No. 69** bus at the Champ de Mars (by the Tour Eiffel) and ride through parts of the Quartier Latin, across the bridge to the Rive Droite near the Louvre, and on to the Bastille. The **No. 72** bus follows the Seine from the Hôtel de Ville west past the Louvre and most of the big-name Rive Droite sights, also giving you views of the Rive Gauche, including the Tour Eiffel. Bus **No. 73** is the only line that goes along the Avenue des Champs-Elysées, from the Arc de Triomphe through the Place de la Condorde and ending at Musée d'Orsay.

Free Wine (Tastings)
Here's a tip for getting tipsy: wine stores sometimes offer free or inexpensive wine tastings, generally on the weekends. Check out La Derniere Goutte (6 rue de Bourbon le Château, 6e, 01–46–29–11–62) on Saturday afternoons. La Cave du Panthéon (174 rue Saint-Jacques, 5e, 01–46–33–90–35), touted for its conviviality, is another destination where wine lovers congregate on Saturday afternoons to learn about—and indulge in—their favorite beverage. If you're lucky, the winemaker hailing from the featured winery of the day may be among those taking part in the tasting.

PARIS MUSEUMS, AN OVERVIEW

There's no shortage of museums in Paris, so it's a good idea to formulate a plan. This overview includes all the museums listed elsewhere in the book; check the index for full listings.

Major Museums

Ambitious art goers will focus on the Big Three—the **Louvre**, the **Musée d'Orsay**, and **Centre Georges Pompidou**. The Louvre's collection spans from about 7,000 BC until 1848, and has its own Big Three: the *Mona Lisa,* the *Venus de Milo,* and *Winged Victory.* The d'Orsay's collection picks up where the Louvre's leaves off and continues until 1914. The Pompidou has art from the early 20th century to the present.

One-Man Shows

Three major must-sees are **Musée Rodin**, with its lovely sculpture garden; **Musée Picasso**; and **Musée Marmottan–Claude Monet**. There's also **Musée Gustave Moreau**, **Musée Delacroix**, and **Musée Maillol**. Dalí enthusiasts will appreciate **Espace Salvador Dalí**.

New & Improved

The **Musée de l'Orangerie**'s recent renovations make Monet's stunning *Water Lilies* even more stunning. The newly redone **Musée des Arts Decoratifs** inside **Les Arts Décoratifs** (which includes **Musée de la Publicité** and **Musée de la Mode**) has one of the world's greatest decorative-art collections. The new **Musée du Quai Branly** features African, Asian, and Oceanic art.

House Museums

A house museum is two treats in one: the art, and the house itself. **Maison de Victor Hugo** and **Maison de Balzac** are the former homes of writers. **Musée Jacquemart-André** has an intriguing collection of Italian art, and **Musée Nissim de Camondo** has deco-rative art, mostly from the 18th century. **Musée de la Vie Romantique** was the elegant town house of Dutch-born painter Ary Scheffer, and **Musée Cognacq-Jay** was the home of Ernest Cognacq, founder of the now closed *La Samaritaine* department store. The **Palais Galliera** opens for exhibits on costume and clothing design.

Contemporary Art

Excellent venues for modern art include the **Palais de Tokyo** and **Musée d'Art Moderne de la Ville de Paris**. There's also **Fondation Cartier pour l'art contemporain** to see emerging artists' work, and **La Maison Rouge**, which shows private collections. The **Pinacothèque de Paris** is a private museum dedicated solely to temporary exhibits.

French History

Musée National du Moyen-Age has the well-known tapestry *Lady and the Unicorn.* **Musée d'Art et d'Histoire du Judaïsme** documents Jewish history in France. For Parisian history, don't miss **Musée Carnevalet**. Montmartre has its own museum, **Musée de Montmartre**, and the history of one of Paris's most-visited churches can be absorbed at **Musée de Notre-Dame** (although the church's archaeological crypt is more interesting). The new **Cité de l'Architecture et du Patrimoine** presents a history of French architecture, and maritime history is the subject of the **Musée de la Marine** (both are in the Palais Chaillot). The **Musée de la Légion d'Honneur** is an exploration of French and foreign military decoration, and the **Musée de l'Armée**, at the Hotel des Invalides, is a phenomenal military museum. There's also the **Musée Jean-Moulin** in the Jardin Atlantique, focusing on the life of the famous leader of the French Resistance. The **Musée de la Monnaies**, in the Hôtel des

Monnaies (the mint), is impressive for its coin collection.

Best for Kids

Kids will love the hands-on science and technology displays at **Cité des Sciences et de l'Industrie**, and the **Musée de la Musique**, both in Parc de la Villette. The **Grande Galerie d'Evolution** and **Musée de la Chasse et de la Nature** have stuffed animals in natural surrounds. The **Palais de la Découverte**, a planetarium, and **Musée Grévin**, a wax museum, are perennial favorites. The fabulous **Musée des Art et Metiers** has neat scientific instruments and inventions. For doll lovers, there's the **Musée de la Poupée**.

Photography & Design

For a mix of photographs from different artists, your best bet is the **Maison Européenne de la Photographie**. **Fondation Henri Cartier-Bresson** features works by the well-known French photographer in a building that was also his atelier. The **Musée du Jeu de Paume,** in the Tuileries, showcases modern photography exhibits. For modern design, the **Fondation Le Corbusier** is well worth the trip to the western edge of the city. The **Fondation Pierre Bergé-Yves Saint Laurent** is the designer's atelier as well as an archive and gallery of his work. For architecture, sit in on a workshop (in French) at the **Maison de l'architecture d'Ile de France-Les Recollets**.

African, Asian & Islamic Art

There are two places in town to see Asian art: the **Musée Guimet** is not to be missed and the **Musée Cernuschi is a small house museum that holds the personal Asian art collection of Enrico Cernuschi.** For Arab and Islamic art and architecture, visit the impressive **Institut du Monde Arabe**, and for African art, try **Musée Dapper**.

Etc.

There are some museums that can't easily be classified. The **Musée de l'Erotisme** is a seven-story building dedicated to everything associated with erotic fantasy, the **Manufacture des Gobelins** traces the history of weaving and tapestry, and the **Musée de l'Art Naïf Max-Fourny**, inside Halle St-Pierre, focuses on folk art, and *art brut* (raw art). **Maison de Baccarat** has gorgeous glass creations, and **Maison de Radio France** presents the history of French radio. The **Musée du Vin** is a history of wine making, that also has wine tastings; the **Musée du Parfum rue Scribe** is dedicated to the art of perfume. The **La Musée de la Prefecture de Police** is, you guessed it, a museum of the Paris police.

Art Galleries

You'll find several contemporary-art galleries near the Centre Georges Pompidou, the Musée Picasso, and the Bastille Opéra. The city's hottest avant-garde art scene is on and around Rue Louise Weiss near the Bibliothèque François-Mitterrand in the 13e. Around St-Germain and the Place des Vosges the galleries are more traditional; works by old masters and established modern artists dominate the galleries around Rue du Faubourg St-Honoré and Avenue Matignon. Carré Rive Gauche, around Rue du Bac in St-Germain, has dozens of art and antiques galleries on its narrow streets.

The Association des Galeries (*www.associationdesgaleries.org*) lists exhibits in more than 100 galleries throughout the city. Paris-art.com (*www.paris-art.com*) focuses on contemporary art, with reviews, exhibition calendars, and interviews, in French only.

ROMANTIC PARIS

It isn't hard to stumble across a romantic moment in Paris. Couples kiss on park benches, dine by candlelight in cozy neighborhood bistros, and walk arm-in-arm in the rain.

At the top of our list for romantic moments is a trip to the top of the quintessential Paris monument, the **Tour Eiffel**. You get extra points for making a reservation at the elegant (and pricey) Jules Verne restaurant, which lets you bypass the crowds for a VIP elevator ride. And if your sweetheart isn't with you in Paris, you can send a soulful missive from the Tower's exclusive mailbox; it'll arrive with the Eiffel Tower postmark.

If seeing the Eiffel Tower in the skyline is part of your romantic vision, there are choice spots throughout Paris from which to gaze upon it. Montmartre's **Sacré-Coeur**, the second-highest point in the city (after the Tower itself), has breathtaking vistas, as well as a lovely green space to throw down a blanket and snuggle. Or head to the top of **Center Georges Pompidou** for a glass of champagne at the restaurant while gazing out at the Tower and the silvery Parisian rooftops. Although somewhat more prosaic, don't rule out **Au Printemps**'s top-floor terrace for views: the café atop the department store has stunning 360-degree panoramas.

Speaking of shopping, some of the world's best lingerie can be found in Paris; wear it for romance, but enjoy shopping for it, too. Department stores have entire floors dedicated to underthings, and there are fabulous boutiques throughout the city where you can find styles and materials to suit every personality and budget.

Romance in Paris? Well, there's always something sexy about a hotel room, but why does it seem that Paris hotels have a little something extra? It might be the gorgeous old buildings and the unique, often family-owned, accommodations. Or maybe it's the history—the ghost of Oscar Wilde or Henry Miller wandering through what used to be a *pavillon d'amour*? At any rate, it seems to us that if you're going to splurge on luxury accommodations, Paris is the place to do it.

Big spending, of course, isn't always necessary, no matter what you're up to. An expensive meal is one thing, but snacking at a corner crêperie can be just as romantic as a sit-down dinner. Indeed, a picnic by the Seine, or at one of the marvelous *jardins* (gardens) is one of the ultimate romantic, and generally inexpensive, Parisian experiences (unless you buy a €2,000 bottle of Château Lafite to wash it down). Feed your love with bites of chocolate and cheese in the manicured **Jardin du Luxembourg** or at the intimate **Place des Vosges**.

If art fuels your passions, Paris is home to romantic museums aplenty—for starters, visit the **Musée Rodin** and its elegant gardens, and make sure to see the sculpture of *The Kiss*.

If you just love to stroll, hand in hand, Paris is your place. Any of the windy streets will do, but a walk along **the Seine** is assured to create romantic memories—especially if you pick a bridge for a sunset kiss. For a straight-from-the-movies moment, pretend you're Audrey Hepburn and Cary Grant in *Charade* and take a nighttime boat tour, making sure to time it so that you see the Eiffel Tower sparkle at the top of the hour.

THE SEINE

No matter how you approach Paris—historically, geographically, or emotionally—the Seine flows through its heart, dividing the City of Light into two banks, the *Rive Droite* (Right Bank) and the *Rive Gauche* (Left Bank).

The Seine has long been used as a means for transportation and commerce and although there are no longer any factories along its banks, all manner of boats still ply the water. You'll see tugboats, fire and police boats, the occasional bobbing houseboat, and many kinds of tour boats; it might sound hokey, but there's really no better introduction to the City of Light than a boat cruise, and there are several options, depending on whether you want commentary on the sights or not. Many of the city's most famous attractions can be seen from the river, and are especially spectacular at dusk, as those celebrated lights of Paris glint against the sky.

FROM ILE DES CYGNES TO THE LOUVRE

Musée d'Orsay clock

Petit Palais

Pont de l'Alma

Grand Palais

Assemblée Nationale

Pont Alexandre III

Eiffel Tower

Bir Hakeim Bridge

Ile des Cygnes

The Zouave of the Pont de l'Alma, sole survivor of the bridge's four original stone soldiers, is used by Parisians to judge water levels.

Whether you hop on a boat cruise or stroll the quays at your own pace, the Seine comes alive when you get off the busy streets of Paris. At the western edge of the city on the **Ile des Cygnes** (literally the Isle of Swans), a small version of the Statue of Liberty stands guard. Auguste Bartholdi designed the original statue, given as a gift from France to America in 1886, and in 1889 a group of Americans living in Paris installed this ¼ scale bronze replica—it's 37 feet, 8 inches tall.

You can get to the Ile des Cygnes via the **Bir Hakeim** bridge—named for the 1942 Free French battle in Libya—whose lacy architecture horizontally echoes the nearby **Eiffel Tower**. You might recognize the view of the bridge from the movie *Last Tango in Paris*.

As you make your way downstream you can drool in envy at the houseboats docked near the bronze lamp–lined **Pont Alexandre III**. No other bridge over the Seine epitomizes the fin-de-siècle frivolity of the Belle Epoque: It seems as much created of cake frosting and sugar sculptures as of stone and iron, and makes quite the backdrop for fashion shoots and weddings. The elaborate decorations include Art Nouveau lamps, cherubs, nymphs, and winged horses at either end. The bridge was built, like the Grand Palais and Petit Palais nearby, for the 1900 World's Fair.

Strollers by the water

Along the banks of the Seine

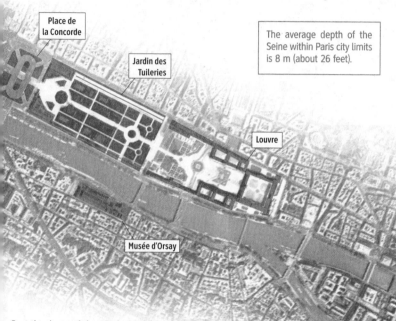

Place de la Concorde

Jardin des Tuileries

Louvre

Musée d'Orsay

The average depth of the Seine within Paris city limits is 8 m (about 26 feet).

Past the dome of the Hôtel des Invalides, is the 18th-century neoclassical façade of the **Assemblée Nationale**, the palace that houses the French Parliament. Across the river stands the **Place de la Concorde**. Also look for the great railway station clocks of the Musée d'Orsay that once allowed writer Anaïs Nin to coordinate her lovers' visits to her house-boat, moored below the Tuileries. The palatial **Louvre** museum, on the Right Bank, seems to go on and on as you continue up the Seine.

PERFECT PICNIC PLACES

Paris abounds with romantic spots to pause for a picnic or a bottle of wine, but the Seine has some of the best.

Try scouting out a place on the point of Ile St-Louis; at sunset you can watch the sun slip beneath receding arches of stone bridges.

The long, low quays of the Left Bank, with its public sculpture work, are perfect for an al-fresco lunch.

FROM PONT DES ARTS TO JARDIN DES PLANTES

At the water's edge.

The Institut de France

Parisians love to linger on the elegant **Pont des Arts** footbridge that streches between the palatial Louvre museum and the Institut de France. Napoléon commissioned the original cast-iron bridge with nine arches; it was rebuilt in 1984 with seven arches.

Five carved stone arches of the **Pont Neuf**—the name means "new bridge" but it actually dates from 1605 and is the oldest bridge in Paris—connect the Left Bank to the Ile de la Cité. Another seven arches connect the Ile and the Right Bank. The pale gray curving balus-

trades include a row of stone heads; some say they're caricatures of King Henry IV's ministers, glaring down at the river.

On the Right Bank at the end of the Ile de la Cité is the **Hôtel de Ville (City Hall)**—this area was once the main port of Paris, crowded with boats delivering everything from wood and produce to visitors and slaves.

Medieval turrets rise up from **Ile de la Cité**, part of the original royal palace; the section facing the Right Bank includes the **Conciergerie**, where Marie Antoinette was imprisoned in 1793 before her execution.

PARIS PLAGE

Paris Plage, literally Paris Beach, is Mayor Bertrand Delanoë's summer gift to Parisians and visitors. In August the roads along the Seine are closed, tons of sand are brought in and decorated with palm trees, and a slew of activities are organized, from free early morning yoga classes to evening samba and swimming (not in the Seine, but in the fabulous Josephine Baker swimming pool). Going topless is discouraged but hammocks, kids' playgrounds, rock-climbing, and cafés keep everyone entertained.

Pont des Arts

Paris Plage

Notre-Dame

Ile St-Louis

Jardin des
Plantes

Bibliothéque
Francois
Mitterand

Also on the Ile de la Cité is the cathedral of **Notre-Dame,** a stunning sight from the water. From the side it looks almost like a great boat sailing down the Seine.

As you pass the end of the island, you'll notice a small grated window: this is the evocative Deportation Memorial.

Next to the Ile de la Cite is the lovely residential **Ile St-Louis**; keep an eye out for the "proper" depth measuring stick on Ile St-Louis, near the Tour d'Argent restaurant.

Sightseeing boats turn near the public sculpture garden at the **Jardin des Plantes**, where you'll get a view of the huge national library, **Bibliothèque François Mitterrand**—the four towers look like opened books. Moored in the Seine near the bibliothèque is the Josephine Baker swimming pool with its retractable roof. Paris used to have several floating pools, including the elaborate Piscine Deligny, which was used in the Paris Olympics in 1924; it inexplicably sank in 1993.

PLANNING A BOAT TOUR ON THE SEINE

■ Most boat tours last about an hour; in the winter, even the interior of the boats can be cool, so take an extra scarf or sweater.

■ It never hurts to book ahead since schedules vary with the season and the (unpredictable) height and mood of the Seine.

■ As you float along, consider that Parisians used similar boats as a form of public transportation until the 1930s. Not really like Venice; more like the Staten Island ferry.

■ For optimal Seine enjoyment, combine a boat tour with a stroll—walk around Ile St-Louis, stroll along the Left Bank quays near the Pont Neuf, or start at the quay below the Louvre and walk to the Eiffel Tower, past the fabulous private houseboats.

WHICH BOAT IS FOR YOU?

If you want... lots of information	☎ 01-40-76-99-99 ⊕ www.bateaux-mouches.fr 🎫 €9 Ⓜ Alma-Marceau	
	The massive, double-decker **Bateaux Mouches,** literally "fly boats," offer prerecorded commentary in seven languages.	Departs from the Pont de l'Alma (Right Bank) daily April to September: every half hour from 10 AM to 11 PM; daily: October through March approximately every three hours from 11 AM to 9 PM.
If you want... to do your own thing	☎ 08-25-05-01-01 ⊕ www.batobus.com 🎫 €12, €14 for 2 consecutive days	
	The commentary-free **Batobus** boat-bus service allows you to hop on and off at any of the eight stops along the river. (Note: there's no service early January through early February.)	Departs from 8 locations: Eiffel Tower, Champs Elysées, Musée d'Orsay, Louvre, St. Germain-des-Pres, Notre-Dame, Hotel de Ville, and Jardin des Plantes.
If you want... to impress a date or client	☎ 01-44-54-14-70 ⊕ www.yachtsdeparis.fr 🎫 €165 for dinner cruise Ⓜ Bastille	
	The **Yachts de Paris** specialize in gorgeous boats—expensive, yes, but glamorous as all get-out, with surprisingly good meals.	Departs from Quai de Javel (west of the Eiffel Tower); dinner cruises leave from Port Henri IV (near Bastille).
If you want... the Seine, with music	☎ 01-43-54-50-04 ⊕ www.calife.com 🎫 €49 and up for dinner cruise Ⓜ Louvre-Rivoli	
	Le Calife is the Aladdin's lamp of the Seine, moored across from the Louvre. Jazz, piano music, and evenings devoted to French song makes this a quirky and charming choice.	Departs from the Quai Malaquais, opposite the Louvre and just west of the Pont des Arts footbridge.

Ile de la Cité & Ile St-Louis

2

Sidewalk café, Ile de la Cité near Notre-Dame

WORD OF MOUTH

"Strolling on the Ile St-Louis should absolutely be included during your trip. Even if it's cold out, don't miss a trip to Berthillon (on Ile St-Louis). It was the best ice cream/sorbet I've ever, ever had."

—tara3056

GETTING ORIENTED

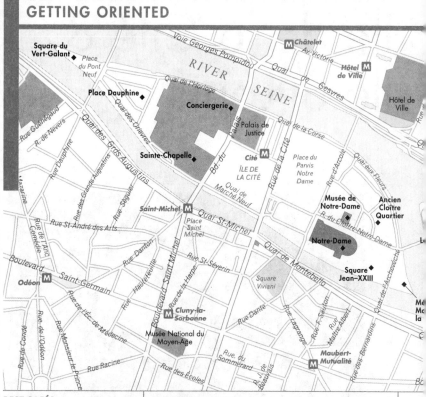

Square du Vert-Galant
Place du Pont Neuf
M Châtelet
Av. Victoria
Hôtel **M** de Ville
RIVER
Voie Georges Pompidou
Quai de Gesvres
Place Dauphine
Quai de l'Horloge
Quai des Orfèvres
SEINE
Hôtel de Ville
Rue Guénégaud
R. de Nevers
Rue Dauphine
Quai des Grands Augustins
Concergerie
Palais de Justice
Quai de la Corse
Rue
Rue de la Cité
Sainte-Chapelle
Bd. du Palais
Cité **M**
ÎLE DE LA CITÉ
Place du Parvis Notre Dame
Quai aux Fleurs
Quai d'Arcole
Rue d'Arcole
Rue des Grands Augustins
Rue de Séguier
Quai de Marché Neuf
Musée de Notre-Dame
Ancien Cloître Quartier
Saint-Michel **M**
Quai St-Michel
R. du Cloître-Notre-Dame
Rue de l'Anc. Comédie
Rue St-André des Arts
Place Saint Michel
Notre-Dame
Le
Boulevard
Rue Danton
Rue St-Séverin
Quai de Montebello
Square Jean–XXIII
Quai de l'Archevêché
Odéon **M**
Saint-Germain
Rue Hautefeuille
Boulevard Saint Michel
Rue de la Harpe
Square Viviani
Mé Mo la
Rue de l'Éc. de Médecine
Cluny-la-Sorbonne **M**
Rue Dante
Rue Lagrange
Rue F. Sauton
Rue Maître Albert
Rue de Condé
Rue Monsieur le Prince
Rue de l'Odéon
Musée National du Moyen-Âge
Rue du Sommerard
Rue J. de Beauvais
Maubert-Mutualité **M**
Rue des Bernardins
Rue Racine
Rue des Écoles
Bo

BEST CAFÉS

La Charlotte en l'Ile. The witch from *Hansel and Gretel* might take a fancy to this spot, set with fairy lights and carnival masks. They have more than 30 varieties of tea, thick hot chocolate, and wickedly good cakes. *Open 2–8 PM, Thurs.–Sun.* ✉ *24 rue St-Louis-en-l'Ile, Ile St-Louis* ☎ *01-43-54-25-83* Ⓜ *Pont Marie.*

Le Flore en l'Ile. At this café on the Ile St-Louis you can find Berthillon ice cream and a magnificent view of the Seine. The terrace looks onto the back of Notre-Dame. ✉ *42 quai d'Orléans, Ile St-Louis* ☎ *01-43-29-88-27* Ⓜ *Pont Marie.*

TOP REASONS TO GO

Notre-Dame. This Gothic cathedral has always been the spiritual heart of Paris. Go inside to gaze at its famed rose windows, climb the towers to talk with the gargoyles, or go around back to contemplate the stunning architecture from the quiet Square Jean-XXIII.

Sainte-Chapelle. Visit on a sunny day to best appreciate the exquisite stained glass in this 13th-century chapel built for King Louis IX (St-Louis) and now often used for choral concerts (try to get a ticket in advance).

Strolling the islands. Start with the oldest bridge in Paris, the Pont Neuf, incongruously called "the new bridge," and give a nod to the statue of Henry IV, who once proudly said, "I make love, I make war, and I build"—this is one of the things he had built during his too-short reign. From here, walk to Place Dauphine and stroll wherever whim takes you—every inch of these two islands begs for a photo. You might have a hard time deciding whether to stop for an ice cream at Berthillon or a gelato from Amorino.

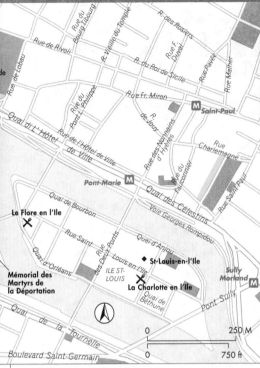

ICE CREAM VS. GELATO

Cafés all over sell this haute couture brand of ice cream, but the headquarters of **Berthillon** (⊠ *31 rue St-Louis-en-l'Ile, Ile St-Louis* ☎ *01–43–54–31–61*) is *the* place to come for this amazing treat. It features more than 30 flavors that change with the seasons, including scrumptious *chocolat au nougat* and mouthpuckering *cassis* (black currant). Expect to wait in line. The shop and adjacent tea salon is open Wednesday to Sunday 10–8 but closed during the peak summer season, from July 15 to September 1.

Also popping up all over Paris—there were 22 outlets at this writing, including Ile St-Louis (⊠ *47 rue St-Louis-en-l'Ile, Ile St-Louis* ☎ *01–44–07–48–08*)—and winning converts faster than you can finish a double scoop, is the **Amorino** chain of gelaterias. Popular flavors include rich *Bacio* (dark chocolate and hazelnuts) and *spécialités* such as amaretto laced with crunchy biscuits and almonds. The shop is open every day, noon to midnight.

MAKING THE MOST OF YOUR TIME

This little area of Paris is easily walkable and packed with sites and stunning views, so give yourself as much time as possible to explore. With Notre-Dame, the Conciergerie, and Sainte-Chapelle, you could spend a day wandering, but the islands are easily combined with St-Germain—the Rue de Buci is a perfect place to pick up a picnic lunch you can enjoy at the leafy Square du Vert-Galant at the tip of Ile de la Cité. If you have limited time in the area, just make sure you see Notre-Dame and go for a stroll.

GETTING HERE

Ile de la Cité and Ile St-Louis are in the 1er and 4er arrondissements (the Boulevard du Palais is the dividing line between the 1er and 4er arrondissements on Ile de la Cité). If you're too far away to get here on foot, take the métro to St-Michel station or La Cité.

Sightseeing
★★★★
Dining
★★
Lodging
★★★
Shopping
★★
Nightlife
★

At the heart of Paris, linked to the banks of the Seine by a series of bridges, are two small islands: Ile de la Cité and Ile St-Louis. They're the perfect place to start exploring the city. The Ile de la Cité is anchored by mighty Notre-Dame, which casts her shadow on curving streets dating back to the city's founding. Farther east lies the exclusive Ile St-Louis, a tiny enclave dotted with charming hotels, cozy restaurants, and small shops.

At the western tip of Ile de la Cité is regal Place Dauphine, one of Paris's oldest squares. The impressive Palais de Justice (Supreme Court) sits between **Sainte-Chapelle**, the exquisite medieval chapel of Mad King Louis IX, and the **Conciergerie**, the prison where Marie-Antoinette and other bluebloods awaited their slice of history at the guillotine.

> ### WORD OF MOUTH
>
> "We went to an instrumental performance at Sainte-Chapelle, and that was a wonderful and restful way to see the chapel and enjoy the music."
>
> –maryantex

The Gothic powerhouse that is **Notre-Dame** originally loomed over a medieval huddle of buildings that were later ordered razed by Baron Haussmann, the 19th-century civic planner who transformed Paris into the city we see today. In front of the cathedral is now the Place du Parvis, also known as kilomètre zéro, the point from which all roads in France are measured. On the north side of the square is the **Hôtel-Dieu** (translated nonliterally as "general hospital"), immortalized by Balzac as the squalid last stop for the city's most unfortunate but which today houses a modern hospital. Just behind the cathedral lies Rue du Cloître-Notre-Dame, which cuts through the **Ancien Cloître Quartier**, along whose narrow streets you can imagine the medieval quarter as it once was, densely packed and teeming with activity. At 10 rue Chanoinesse, a plaque commemorates the tragic, 12th-century love affair between the philosopher Peter Abélard and his young conquest, Héloïse.

At the farthest eastern tip of Ile de la Cité is the **Mémorial des Martyrs de la Déportation,** all but hidden in a pocket-size park. A set of stairs leads down to the impressive and moving memorial to the 200,000 French citizens who died in Nazi concentration camps.

The nearby Pont St-Louis, seemingly always occupied by an accordion player or group of musicians, leads to the Ile St-Louis, one of the city's best places to wander. There are no cultural hot spots, just a few streets that may make you think you've stumbled into a village, albeit an unusually tony one. Small hotels, restaurants, art galleries, and shops selling everything from cheese to pâté to silk scarves line the main drag, Rue St-Louis-en-l'Ile. There were once two islands here, the Ile Notre-Dame and the Ile aux Vaches ("Cow Island," a former grazing pasture), both owned by the church. Speculators bought the islands, joined them, and sold the plots to builders who created what is today some of the city's most elegant and expensive real estate. Baroque architect Louis Le Vau (who later worked on Versailles) designed fabulous private homes for aristocrats, including the majestic mansions, the Hôtel Lambert and the Hôtel de Lauzun on the lovely quai d'Anjou.

> **MONSIEUR GUILLOTIN**
>
> Beheading was a popular means of punishment long before the French Revolution, but it was Dr. Joseph-Ignace Guillotin who suggested that there was a more humane way of effecting decapitation than by use of a sword or ax. Not surprisingly, Dr. Guillotin's descendants changed their surname.

MAIN ATTRACTIONS

Updated by
Linda Hervieux

Conciergerie. Much of Ile de la Cité's medieval buildings fell victim to wunderkind planner Baron Georges-Eugène Haussmann's ambitious rebuilding program of the 1860s. Among the rare survivors are the jewel-like Sainte-Chapelle, a vision of shimmering stained glass, and the Conciergerie, the former city prison where Marie-Antoinette and other victims of the French Revolution spent their last days.

Built by Philip IV in the 13th and 14th centuries, the Conciegerie was part of the original palace of the kings of France, before the royals moved into the Louvre (in 1358) and this palace was turned into a prison (in 1391). During the French Revolution, the old palace famously imprisoned Queen Marie-Antoinette as she awaited her fatal trip to the guillotine. You can still visit Marie-Antoinette's cell, and learn about some of Paris's more infamous criminals. The chapel's stained glass is emblazoned with the initials M. A.; it was commissioned after the queen's death by her daughter. Outside, in the courtyard, victims of the Terror spent their final days playing piquet, writing letters to loved ones, and waiting for the dreaded climb up the staircase to the Chamber of the Revolutionary Council to hear its final verdict. The building takes its name from the palace's *concierge,* or high-level keeper of the palace. ✉ *1 quai de l'Horloge, Ile de la Cité* ☎ *01–53–40–60–97 3* ⊕ *www. monum.fr* 🎫 *€6.50, joint ticket with Sainte-Chapelle €10.50* ☯ *Mar.–*

Oct., daily 9:30–6; Nov.–Feb. 9–5. daily Ⓜ *Cité.*

Mémorial des Martyrs de la Déportation *(Memorial of the Deportation)*. On the eastern tip of the Ile de la Cité lies this extraordinary monument to the 200,000 men, women, and children who died in Nazi concentration camps during World War II. The evocative memorial was intentionally designed to be claustrophobic; a light at the end of the long, narrow tunnel that is the main part of the installation symbolizes hope. The walls are studded with 200,000 pieces of quartz crystal. ⊠ *Ile de la Cité* ✆ *Free* ⊙ *Mar.–Oct., daily 10–noon and 2–7; Nov.–Feb., daily 10–noon and 2–5* Ⓜ *Maubert Mutualité.*

> ### THE FLOWER MARKET
>
> Every day of the week except Monday, you can find the flower market facing the entrance to the imposing Palais de Justice (Supreme Court) on Boulevard du Palais. It's a fragrant detour from the Ile de la Cité, and the Guimard-designed métro entrance to the Cité métro station seems to blend with the greenery on display. On Sunday, the place is chirping with birds and other small pets for sale.

Fodor's Choice   **Notre-Dame**
★   *See the highlighted listing in this chapter.*

Fodor's Choice   **Sainte-Chapelle**
★   *See the highlighted listing in this chapter.*

ALSO WORTH SEEING

Fodor's Choice   **Ancien Cloître Quartier.** Hidden in the shadows of Notre-Dame is this
★   magical, often-overlooked tangle of medieval streets. Through the years lucky folk, including Ludwig Bemelmans (who created the beloved *Madeleine* books) and the Aga Khan have called this area home, but back in the Middle Ages this was the domain of cathedral seminary students. One of these was the celebrated Peter Abélard (1079–1142)— philosopher, questioner of the faith, and renowned declaimer of love poems. Abélard boarded with Notre-Dame's clergyman, Fulbert, whose 17-year-old niece, Héloïse, was seduced by the compelling Abélard, 39 years her senior. She became pregnant and the vengeful clergyman had Abélard castrated; amazingly, he survived and fled to a monastery, while Héloïse took refuge in a nunnery. The poetic, passionate letters between the two cemented their fame as thwarted lovers, and their story inspired a devoted following during the romantic 19th century. The clergyman's house at 10 rue Chanoinesse was redone in the 1800s, but a plaque commemorates the lovers; the Ancien Cloître just might have you reciting love poems despite yourself. ⊠ *Rue du Cloître-Notre-Dame north to quai des Fleurs, Ile de la Cité* Ⓜ *Cité.*

Palais de Justice. The city's law courts were built by Baron Haussmann in his characteristically weighty neoclassical style in about 1860. ⊠ *Bd. du Palais, Ile de la Cité* Ⓜ *Cité.*

Continued on page 45

NOTRE-DAME

Notre-Dame is the symbolic heart of Paris and, for many, of France itself. Napoléon was crowned here, and kings and queens exchanged marriage vows before its altar. There are a few things worth seeing inside the Gothic cathedral, but the real highlights are the exterior architectural details and the unforgettable view of Paris, framed by stone gargoyles, from the top of the south tower.

OUTSIDE NOTRE-DAME

Begun in 1163, completed in 1345, badly damaged during the Revolution, and restored by the architect Eugène Viollet-le-Duc in the 19th century, Notre-Dame may not be France's oldest or largest cathedral, but in beauty and architectural harmony it has few peers. The front entranceways seem like hands joined in prayer, the sculpted kings on the facade form a noble procession, and the west (front) rose window gleams with what seems like divine light.

The most dramatic approach to Notre-Dame is from the Rive Gauche, crossing at the Pont au Double from quai de Montebello, at the St-Michel métro or RER stop. This bridge will take you to the open square, place du Parvis, in front of the cathedral. (The more direct metro stop is Cité.)

THE WEST (FRONT) FACADE
The three front entrances are, left to right: the Portal of the Virgin, the Portal of the Last Judgment (*above*), and the Portal of St. Anne, the oldest of the three.

THE STONE GARGOYLES
Notre-Dame's gargoyles were designed by Eugène Viollet-le-Duc, the architect who oversaw the cathedral's 19th-century renovations. Technically they're chimeras, not gargoyles, as they're purely ornamental; a true "gargoyle" is a carved sculpture that functions as a waterspout.

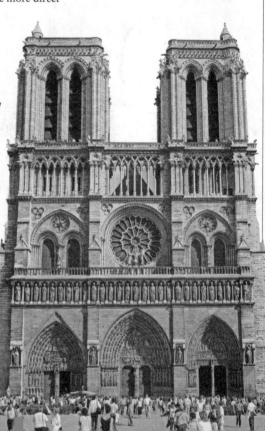

THE GALLERY OF KINGS
Above the three front entrances are the 28 restored statues of the kings of Israel, the Galerie des Rois.

INSIDE THE CATHEDRAL

① **The Pietà**, behind the choir, represents the Virgin Mary mourning over the dead body of Christ.

② **The biblical scenes** on the north and south screens of the choir represent the life of Christ and the apparitions of Christ after the Resurrection.

③ **The north rose window** is one of the cathedral's original stained-glass panels; at the center is an image of Mary holding a young Jesus.

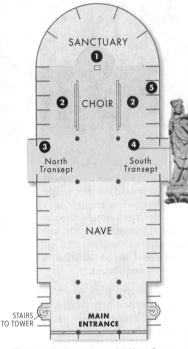

SANCTUARY
①
⑤
② CHOIR **②**
③ ④
North Transept   South Transept
NAVE
STAIRS TO TOWER
MAIN ENTRANCE

④ At the south (right) entrance to the choir, you'll glimpse the haunting 12th-century statue of **Notre-Dame de Paris**, "Our Lady of Paris," the Virgin, for whom the cathedral is named.

⑤ **The treasury**, on the south side of the choir, holds a small collection of religious garments, reliquaries, and silver- and gold-plate.

■ TIP➜ The best time to visit Notre-Dame is early in the morning, when the cathedral is at its brightest and least crowded.

MAKING THE CLIMB

A separate entrance, to the left of the front facade if you're facing it, leads to the 387 stone steps of the south tower. These steps take you to the bell of Notre-Dame (as tolled by the fictional Quasimodo). Looking out from the tower, you can see how Paris—like the trunk of a tree developing new rings—has grown outward from the Ile de la Cité. To the north is Montmartre; to the west is the Arc de Triomphe, at the top of the Champs-Elysées; and to the south are the towers of St-Sulpice and the Panthéon. ■ TIP➜ **Lines to climb the tower are shortest on weekday mornings.**

SOMETHING TO PONDER

Do Notre-Dame's hunchback and its gargoyles have anything in common other than bad posture? Quasimodo was created by Victor Hugo in the novel *Notre-Dame de Paris*, published in 1831. The incredible popularity of the book made Parisians finally take notice of the cathedral's state of disrepair and spurred Viollet-le-Duc's renovations. These included the addition of the gargoyles, among other things, and resulted in the structure we see today.

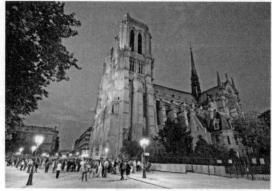

Place du Parvis

Flying buttresses

Notre-Dame was one of the first Gothic cathedrals in Europe and one of the first buildings to make use of **flying buttresses**—exterior supports that spread out the weight of the building and roof. At first people thought they looked like scaffolding that the builders forgot to remove.

■**TIP→** The most tranquil place to appreciate the architecture of Notre-Dame is from the lovely garden behind the cathedral, Square Jean-XXIII. By night, take a boat ride on the Seine for the best view—the lights at night are magnificent.

Place du Parvis is *kilomètre zéro*, the spot from which all distances to and from the city are officially measured. A polished brass circle set in the ground, about 20 yards from the cathedral's main entrance, marks the exact spot.

The Archaeological Crypt (entrance down the stairs in front of the cathedral) is a quick visit but very interesting, especially for kids and archaeology buffs. It gives an "under the city" view of the area, with remains from previous churches that were built on this site, scale models charting the district's development, and artifacts dating from 2,000 years ago. The **Musée de Notre-Dame**, on the other hand, has little to interest the average visitor.

☎ 01-53-10-07-00

✕ www.monum.fr

💳 Cathedral free. Towers: €7.50. Crypt €3.30. Treasury €2.50. Museum €2.50.

🕐 Cathedral daily 8–6:45. Towers Apr.–June and Sept., daily 10 AM–6:30; July and Aug., weekdays 10 AM–6:30, weekends 10 AM–11 PM; Oct.–Mar., daily 10–5:30. Note: towers close early when overcrowded. Treasury Mon.–Fri. 9:30–6 PM, Sat. 9:30–6:30, Sun. 1:30–6:30. Crypt Tues.–Sun. 10–6. Museum Wed. and weekends 2:30–6.

TIMELINE

1160	Notre-Dame is conceived by Bishop Maurice de Sully, the bishop of Paris.	c. 1200–1245	The western facade and towers are completed.	1345	Construction of the original cathedral is completed.
1163	Construction begins.	1208	The Nave is completed.	1699–1723	The original Gothic choir is replaced with a Baroque one.
1182	Choir is completed; the main altar is consecrated.	1235–1250	A series of chapels are added to the nave.	c 1790	The church is plundered during the Revolution.
1196	Bishop de Sully dies.	1250–1270	The High Gothic–style north and south Rose windows are installed.	1845	Viollet-le-Duc's restoration begins, lasting 23 years.
		1296–1330	A series of chapels are added to the apse.		

Place Dauphine. The Surrealists loved Place Dauphine, which they called "le sexe de Paris" because of its suggestive V shape. Its origins were much more proper: it was built by Henry IV, who named the square in homage to his successor, called the dauphin, who became Louis XIII when Henry was assassinated. ■TIP→ Snag a table at one of the restaurant terraces here to enjoy one of the best places in Paris to dine en plein air. ⊠ *Ile de la Cité* Ⓜ *Cité*.

> **DINING AT A GLANCE**
>
> For full reviews ⇨ Ch. 17
>
> Inexpensive Dining
> **Mon Vieil Ami,** *Modern French,* 69 rue St-Louis-en-l'Isle
>
> Moderate Dining
> **Brasserie de l'Ile St-Louis,** *Brasserie,* 55 quai de Bourbon

Square du Vert-Galant. The equestrian statue of the Vert Galant himself—amorous adventurer Henry IV—keeps a vigilant watch over this leafy square at the western end of the Ile de la Cité. The dashing but ruthless Henry, king of France from 1589 until his assassination in 1610, was a stern upholder of the absolute rights of monarchy, and a notorious womanizer. He is probably best remembered for his cynical remark that *"Paris vaut bien une messe"* ("Paris is worth a mass"), a reference to his readiness to renounce Protestantism to gain the throne of predominantly Catholic France. To ease his conscience, he issued the Edict of Nantes in 1598, according French Protestants (almost) equal rights with their Catholic countrymen. The square is a great place to picnic—you can almost dangle your feet in the Seine. ■TIP→It's also the departure point for the Vedette tour boats on the Seine (at the bottom of the steps to the right). ⊠ *Ile de la Cité* Ⓜ *Pont Neuf*.

St-Louis-en-l'Ile. You can't miss the unusual lacy spire of this church as you approach the Ile St-Louis; it's the only church on the island and there are no other steeples to compete with it. It was built from 1652 to 1765 to the Baroque designs of architect François Le Vau, brother of the more famous Louis, who designed several mansions nearby—as well as the Palace of Versailles. St-Louis's interior was essentially stripped during the Revolution, as were so many French churches, but look for the bizarre outdoor iron clock, which dates from 1741. ⊠ *Rue St-Louis-en-l'Ile, Ile St-Louis* Ⓜ *Pont Marie*.

SAINTE-CHAPELLE

- ✉ 4 bd. du Palais, Ile de la Cité
- ☎ 01–53–40–60–97
- 🌐 www.monum.fr
- 🎟 €7.50, joint ticket with Conciergerie €10.50
- 🕑 Mar.–Oct., daily 9:30–6; Nov.–Feb., daily 9–5
- Ⓜ Cité

TIPS

■ To avoid waiting in killer lines, plan your visit for a weekday morning, the earlier the better, though be aware that sunset is the best time to see the rose window.

■ Come on a sunny day to appreciate the full effect of the light streaming in through all that beautiful stained glass.

■ You can buy a joint ticket with the Conciergerie; buy the ticket there, where the lines are shorter.

■ The chapel is especially magical during the regular concerts held here; call for the schedule.

Built by the obsessively pious Louis IX (1226–70), this Gothic jewel is home to the oldest stained-glass windows in Paris. The chapel was constructed over three years, at phenomenal expense, to house the king's collection of relics acquired from the impoverished emperor of Constantinople. These included Christ's Crown of Thorns, fragments of the Cross, and drops of Christ's blood—though even in Louis's time these were considered of questionable authenticity. Some of the relics have survived and can be seen in the treasury of Notre-Dame, but most were lost during the Revolution.

HIGHLIGHTS

The upper chapel is where the famed beauty of Sainte-Chapelle comes alive: 6,458 square feet of stained glass is delicately supported by painted stonework that seems to disappear in the colorful light streaming through the windows. The lowest section of the windows was restored in the mid-1800s, but otherwise this chapel presents intact, incredibly rare stained glass. Deep reds and blues dominate the background glass, noticeably different from later, lighter medieval styles such as those in Notre-Dame's rose windows. This chapel is essentially an enormous magic lantern illuminating the 1,130 figures from the Bible, to create—as one writer poetically put it—"the most marvelous colored and moving air ever held within four walls."

You'll no doubt be transfixed by the stained glass in the upper chapel, but don't miss the detailed carvings on the columns and the statues of the apostles.

The lower chapel is a bit gloomy and plain, but notice the low vaulted ceiling decorated with fleurs-de-lis and cleverly arranged Ls for Louis. The dark spiral staircase near the entrance takes you upstairs.

The Tour Eiffel & Les Invalides

A view of the Eiffel Tower, from Palais de Chaillot.

WORD OF MOUTH

"They light the Eiffel Tower up in the evening and it is an especially amazing feeling when you happen to be at the top of it when they do so."

—Swoop

GETTING ORIENTED

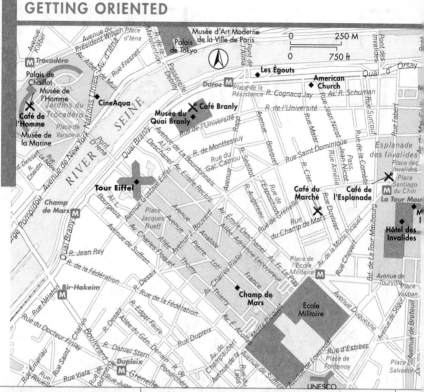

This neighborhood covers the 7th arrondissement. The most romantic way to get to the Tour Eiffel is by boat—see the Seine In-Focus section for details. Otherwise, you can head for RER C, station Champs de Mars/Tour Eiffel or Invalides.

TOP REASONS TO GO

Tour Eiffel. No question: you must visit this ultimate symbol of Paris at least once in your life.

The Pont Alexandre. This glittering bridge connects the Grand and Petit Palais on the Right Bank with Invalides on the Left—but it's worth a stop on its own to admire all its cherubs, golden horses, and nymphs. Opened in 1900, its single span was the engineering marvel of its time.

Napoléon's tomb. The golden domed Hôtel des Invalides is a strikingly fitting place for Napoléon's remains. After you pay your respects to the emperor, visit the adjoining Musée de l'Armée.

A boat ride. Whether you choose a guided tour on the Bateaux Mouches or the unguided Batobus (which lets you off at different stops along the river), a boat tour along the Seine is a trip through the lifeblood of the city, allowing you to enjoy the marvelous monuments far from maddening traffic noise and jostling museum groups.

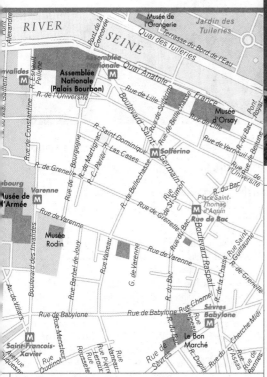

BEST CAFÉS

Café de l'Esplanade. This reliable restaurant (part of the Costes tribe) has a fabulous view over Invalides and boasts an exuberantly tasteful interior by Jacques Garcia. Reserve ahead for a sidewalk seat. 52 rue Fabert, Invalides ☎01–47–05–38–80 Ⓜ Invalides

Café Branly. This café underneath the Quai Branly museum is best in warm weather, when you can sit in the interesting contemporary garden. It's good for a quick light lunch (there's also a high-end restaurant upstairs). 27 quai Branly, Tour Eiffel ☎01–47–53–68–00 Ⓜ Alma-Marceau

MAKING THE MOST OF YOUR TIME

This neighborhood is focused on the ultimate symbol of France: the Eiffel Tower. If you're pressed for time, take the métro to the Hôtel des Invalides (La Tour-Maubourg station), admire the outside of the building, then walk along the Rue St. Dominique for some fabulous window-shopping (especially the bakeries!) en route to the Eiffel Tower. After visiting the tower, stroll along the river (don't cross the bridge) until you get to the Quai Branly. When the weather's nice, this walk makes for a perfect afternoon of sightseeing.

If you have more time, take a picnic to the Champs de Mars and camp out on a bench with a book; there's something very satisfying about just sitting back and contemplating life in the shadow of the Eiffel Tower.

Sightseeing
★★★★★

Dining
★★★

Lodging
★★★★★

Shopping
★★★★

Nightlife
★★★

This is Paris at its monumental best, with the ultimate symbol of France, the Tour Eiffel, as well as the Palais Bourbon, home of the French Parliament and the grand dome of the Hôtel des Invalides.

The **Tour Eiffel** lords over the southwest part of the city, and for most of the world, it's quintessential Paris, even if the locals thought it was a monstrosity when it was first erected. Today, it's beloved, especially for its stunning nighttime illumination (which one wag called a "Marilyn Monroe shimmy"), topped by a sweeping lighthouselike beacon that's visible for 80 km (50 mi) around. Often overlooked, the park behind the tower offers a lovely spot for picnics (the wonderful foodie shopping strips Rue Saint-Dominique and Rue Cler are nearby). There is also a wide walkway along the Seine on this side of the river, at street level—a bit dusty for picnics but a nice relief after all those cobblestones if you're pushing a stroller or want to be near the water. Walk west (away from the center of town) from the Tour Eiffel and you'll find yourself at the fascinating **Quai Branly** museum.

You can't miss the massive dome of the **Hôtel des Invalides,** where you'll find Napoléon's tomb and the Musée de l'Armée—a fascinating stop even if you're not a military-history buff. The museum has lots of information and artifacts about Bonaparte—including his dog (now stuffed). The tomb is one of the only sites that Hitler felt he absolutely had to visit during his extraordinarily brief tour of Paris during World War II. And gruesome history aside, the building is a phenomenal example of Baroque architecture. Along the Seine is the **Palais Bourbon,** home of the Assem-

> ### WORD OF MOUTH
>
> "Don't assume you won't like something. I had been in Paris a few times having absolutely no interest in Napoleon's Tomb. Then, on a cold rainy day I was near Les Invalides so I decided to go inside just to have a quick lunch, see the 'tomb' and get warm. Boy was I ever wrong about this place. Les Invalides is now high, high on my list of must-sees!"
>
> —cchottel

blée Nationale—also known as the French Parliament. Keep an eye out for outdoor photo exhibits on the fence surrounding the Palais.

MAIN ATTRACTIONS

Updated by
Lisa Pasold

Fodor's Choice

★

Hôtel des Invalides. Les Invalides, as it is widely known, is probably the world's grandest rest home. The sprawling building was designed by architect Libéral Bruant in the 1670s at the request of Louis XIV's minister of finance, Colbert, to house wounded soldiers. Along the façade are eerie dormer windows shaped like 17th-century armor. When it was finished, some 4,000 residents lived here. No more than a handful of aging veterans reside at the Invalides today, but the military links remain in the form of the **Musée de l'Armée,** one of the world's foremost military museums. The collection of arms, armor, uniforms, banners, and military paintings is staggering.

Paris's most impressive dome covers Paris's largest ego: Napoléon's tomb is here—his body protected by a series of no fewer than six coffins, one inside the next (sort of like a Russian nesting doll), within a bombastic memorial of red porphyry, and ringed by a dozen statues symbolizing his campaigns. Among others commemorated in the church are French World War I hero Marshal Foch; Napoléon's brother Joseph, an erstwhile king of Spain; and military architect Sébastien de Vauban. The dome itself, over the Eglise du Dôme (Church of the Dome), at the back of the Invalides, is the second-tallest building in Paris, after the Eiffel Tower. For the 200th anniversary of the French Revolution, in 1989, the dome was regilded—using more than half a million gold leaves, or more than 20 pounds of gold. A variety of historical, thematic, and general tours of the premises are offered, at an additional cost. The great lawns in front of the building are often used for pickup soccer and Frisbee games, sunbathing, and dog walking—despite extensive signage asking you to stay off the grass. ⊠*Pl. des Invalides, Tour Eiffel* ☎*01–44–42–37–72 Army and Model museums* ⊕*www.invalides.org* ▧*€7* ☉*Eglise du Dôme and museums Apr.–Sept., daily 10–6; Oct.–Mar., daily 10–5. Closed 1st Mon. of every month* Ⓜ*La Tour–Maubourg/Invalides.*

Musée du Quai Branly. Also known as the Musée des Arts Premiers, this controversial new museum (it opened in 2006) displays state-held troves of African, Asian, and Oceanic art, including anthropological collections previously shown in the Louvre. The collection is phenomenal, arranged according to geographic zone and mapped out by differently colored floor tiles, although some critics complain that the museum focuses too much on visual ingenuity at the expense of explanation and context. The temporary exhibits, however, pull in astonishing objects from all over the world, making cross-cultural connections. Make sure to get the telephone-style audioguide, as printed information is limited, and don't miss the "living wall" on part of the exterior of the building: there are about 1,500 species of plants on the vertical surface. Architect Jean Nouvel (he was awarded the Pritzker Architecture Prize in 2008) meant for the long, low outline of the museum to sug-

Continued on page 54

la TOUR EIFFEL

If the Statue of Liberty is emblematic of New York, Big Ben is London, and the Kremlin is Moscow, then the Eiffel Tower is the symbol of Paris. French engineer Gustave Eiffel—already famous for building viaducts and bridges—spent two years working to erect this monument for the World Exhibition of 1889. And after it was built, many Parisians felt it was an iron eyesore and called it the Giant Asparagus, agreeing with designer William Morris, who, explaining why he had been spending so much time at the tower, said "Why on earth have I come here? Because it's the only place I can't see it from." Gradually, though, the Tour Eiffel became part of the Parisian landscape, entering the hearts and souls of Parisians and visitors alike.

Total height: 1,063 feet

■ The 200 millionth visitor went to the top of the Eiffel Tower in 2002.

■ To get to the first viewing platform, Gustave Eiffel originally used avant-garde hydraulic cable elevators designed by American Elisha Otis for two of the curved base legs of the tower. French elevators with a chain-drive system were used in the other two legs. During the 1989 renovation, all the elevators were rebuilt by the Otis company.

Jules Verne

■ An expensive way to beat the queue is to dine at the **Jules Verne** restaurant on the second level. You ascend on a private elevator to the dining room. It's run by chef Alain Ducasse and open for lunch and dinner (☎ 08–25–56–66–62 for reservations). **Attitude 95** on level one is slightly less pricey.

The base formed by the tower's feet is 410 by 410 feet.

■ You can take the stairs as far as the third level (check out the fantastic ironwork), but if you want to go to the very top you'll have to take the elevator.

■ Every 7 years the tower is repainted. The job takes 15 months and uses 60 tons of "Tour Eiffel Brown" paint in three shades—lightest on top, darkest at the bottom.

The Eiffel Tower contains 12,000 pieces of metal and 2,500,000 rivets.

■ The tower almost became scrap iron in 1909, when its concession expired, but its use as a radio antenna saved the day.

■ The tower is most breathtaking at night, when every girder is illuminated. The light show, conceived to celebrate the turn of the millennium, was so popular that the 20,000 lights were reinstalled for permanent use in 2003. It does its electric shimmy for 10 minutes every hour on the hour until 1 AM in winter and 2 AM in summer.

3

IN FOCUS LA TOUR EIFFEL

☎ 01–44–11–23–23

⊕ www.tour-eiffel.fr

✉ By elevator: 2nd fl., €4.50, 3rd fl. €7.80, 4th fl. €11.50. Climbing: 2nd and 3rd fl. only, €4.00

☼ June–late Aug., daily 9 AM–midnight; late Aug.–May, daily 9 AM–11 PM, stairs close at dusk in winter

Ⓜ Bir-Hakeim, Trocadéro, Ecole Militaire; RER Champ de Mars

■ TIP➜ A **Museums and Monuments Pass** will let you skip long lines but might not be worth the investment.

DINING ON A BUDGET

Looking for an inexpensive option near the tower? Head to nearby **Café du Marché** (✉ 38 rue Cler, Trocadéro/Tour Eiffel, ☎ 01–47–05–51–27), a relaxed restaurant where drinks are cheap, the salads gigantic, and the daily specials truly special.

Bicycling in Paris

You've seen those 1930s photographs of Paris—men in berets bicycling the streets, carefully balancing baguettes; women in elegant hats gliding past the Eiffel Tower on two wheels. But until recently, it was difficult for visitors to use a bike in the city unless they signed up for a specific bike tour. That changed in the summer of 2007, when the City of Paris introduced Vélib—a city-run rent-a-bike system.

You'll see the silver-and-purple bike stands all over the city. There are several right near the Eiffel Tower—one on Quai Branly and Avenue de la Bourdonnaise—and if you walk down the avenue, you'll find another at the corner of Avenue Rapp, and a third at Rue de Grenelle. This arrondissement is ideal for cycling: the roads are wide, there are several bicycle lanes, and most important, this part of Paris is gloriously flat. Try a relaxing ride across the Champs de Mars, along Rue St-Dominique, and around Invalides, for starters.

The rental bikes have been a resounding success with locals as well as tourists. French drivers haven't stopped screeching up the Champs-Elysées in their Citroëns, but in the first month of the new Vélib system, the city estimates there were 1.7 million users of the clunky yet iconic bikes, or vélos, as they're called here.

Don't worry about getting correct cycling gear: the French ride bicycles in high-heeled boots and miniskirts, tight business suits and well-laced oxfords, overalls and work boots, and even shorts and sneakers—but you'll never see them in Lycra cycling gear unless they're training for the Tour de France. (They also don't wear helmets—except for kids.)

To use Vélib, you pay a temporary membership fee of 1€ a day, or 5€ for a seven-day pass. If you ride for less than 30 minutes at a time, there's no other charge (you get a code to use through the day, getting a bike whenever you need one). If you keep a bike for more than 30 minutes, you pay about a euro per half hour. The system is designed to complement public transit: to get to work or visit a museum, borrow a bike, ride to where you're going, and park at a central meter. If you have the annual métro and bike pass (you can get a métro pass, a separate bike pass, or a combination métro/bike pass), there's no daily fee. For visitors, the system requires that you have a bank or credit card that can be read by the French system, and only some American cards have the necessary code; unfortunately, there's currently no way to check before you leave home. If your card doesn't work, don't despair: Fat Tire Bikes also rents inexpensive bikes for the city (www.fattirebiketoursparis.com or 01–56–58–10–54; rates start at 2€ per hour).

Remember to obey traffic signals, don't cycle on the sidewalk, and be warned—cycling on cobblestones takes some getting used to: they're very bumpy!

Visit www.velib.paris.fr/ (click "autres langues" for English—not everything is translated, though). The bike-parking meters have some English directions.

gest the Tour Eiffel's shadow—you can see the Tour towering above the classy museum restaurant and the less expensive main-floor café. ✉ *Quai Branly, Trocadéro/Tour Eiffel* ☎ *01–56–61–70–00* ⊕ *www. quaibranly.fr* 🎫 *€8.50* ۞ *Tues., Wed., and Sun. 11–7, Thurs.–Sat. 11–9* Ⓜ *Iéna, Alma-Marceau.*

Fodor's Choice **Tour Eiffel**
★ *See the highlighted listing in this chapter.*

ALSO WORTH SEEING
American Church. The staff of this Rive Gauche neo-Gothic church, built in 1927–31, welcomes English-speaking foreigners. The church hosts free classical music concerts on Sunday from September to June at 6 PM. ✉ *65 quai d'Orsay, Trocadéro/Tour Eiffel* ☎ *01–40–62–05–00* ⊕ *www.acparis.org* ۞ *Mon.–Sat. 9–noon and 1–10* Ⓜ *Alma-Marceau; RER: Pont de l'Alma.*

Champ de Mars. This long, formal garden, landscaped at the start of the 20th century, lies between the Tour Eiffel and Ecole Militaire. It was previously used as a parade ground and was the site of the world exhibitions of 1867, 1889 (when the tower was built), and 1900. Today the park is a bit dusty, but it's a great spot for pickup soccer, outdoor concerts, a picnic, or just some time on a bench admiring the view of Lady Eiffel. There's also a playground where kids can let off steam. Ⓜ *École Militaire; RER: Champ de Mars.*

☺ **Les Egouts** *(the Sewers).* Everyone visits the Louvre, so surprise your friends back home by telling them you toured the infamous 19th-century sewers of Paris. Brave their unpleasant though tolerable smell (it's worse in the height of summer) to follow an underground display describing the passages and footbridges famously immortalized as the escape routes of Jean Valjean in *Les Misérables* and the Phantom of the Opera. Signs indicate the streets above you, and detailed panels illuminate the history of waste disposal in Paris, whose sewer system is the second largest in the world, after Chicago's. ✉ *Opposite 93 quai d'Orsay, Trocadéro/Tour Eiffel* ☎ *01–53–68–27–81* ⊕ *www.egouts.idf. st* 🎫 *€4.10* ۞ *May–Sept., Sat.–Wed. 11–5; Oct.–Apr., Sat.–Wed. 11–4; closed last 3 wks of Jan.* Ⓜ *Alma-Marceau; RER: Pont de l'Alma.*

Palais Bourbon. The most prominent feature of the Palais Bourbon—home of the **Assemblée Nationale,** the French Parliament since 1798—is its colonnaded façade, commissioned by Napoléon to match that of the Madeleine, across the Seine. Jean-Pierre Cortot's sculpted pediment portrays France holding the tablets of Law, flanked by Force and Justice. There are sometimes outdoor photo exhibitions here, on the Assemblée's railings, and there are always fine views across the Seine to Place de la Concorde and the church of the Madeleine. ✉ *Pl. du Palais-Bourbon, St-Germain-des-Prés* ۞ *During temporary exhibits only* Ⓜ *Assemblée Nationale.*

> **WORD OF MOUTH**
>
> "Didn't go to the collections or the restaurant, but the building is astonishing…the facade is partly screened by glass and partly composed of a vertical garden. Yes, the front of the building is planted with a lush garden that completely obscures the underlying structure. Simply wonderful."
>
> —Ackislander

3

Dining at a Glance

For full reviews
⇨ Ch. 17

INEXPENSIVE DINING

Afaria, *Bistro,* 15 rue Desnouettes

Le Café Constant, *Bistro,* 139 rue St-Dominique

Les Cocottes de Christian Constant, *French,* 135 rue St-Dominique

Thoumieux, *Bistro,* 79 rue St-Dominique

MODERATE DINING

Le 144 Petrossian, *French Fusion,* 18 bd. de La Tour–Maubourg

L'Agassin, *Bistro,* 8 rue Malar

Chez L'Ami Jean, *Basque,* 27 rue Malar

Chez les Anges, *Bistro,* 54 bd. de la Tour-Maubourg

Le Soleil, *Bistro,* 153 rue de Grenelle

EXPENSIVE DINING

L'Arpège, *Haute French,* 84 rue de Varenne

Au Bon Accueil, *Bistro,* 14 rue de Montttessuy

Jules Verne, *Haute French,* Tour Eiffel

Il Vino, *French Fusion,* 13 Bd. de La Tour–Maubourg

Le Violon d'Ingres, *Haute French,* 135 rue St-Dominique

L'Os à Moelle, *Bistro,* 3 rue Vasco-de-Gama

Le Troquet, *Haute French,* 21 rue François-Bonvin

The Champs-Elysées

4

Champs-Elysées

WORD OF MOUTH

"Walk from the Arc de Triomphe down the Champs Elysées . . . There
is a tomb of the unknown soldier memorial at the Arc de Triomphe
[and] down the Champs Elysées there are lots of designer shops,
fabulous restaurants where you can sit and people watch for a bit,
maybe have a crepe along the way."

—freeman0819

GETTING ORIENTED

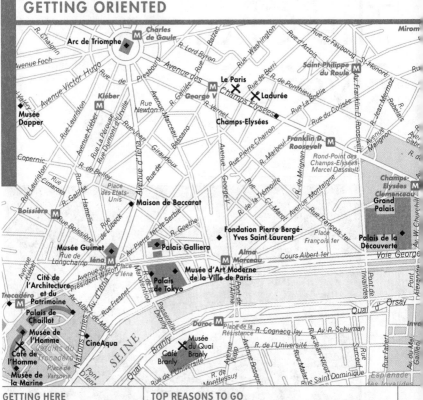

This neighborhood covers the 8th and 16th arrondissements. The best way to get here is by boat; get off at Grand Palais, Champs-Elysées, or Pont d'Alma, depending on the boat company (see the "Seine In-Focus" section for details). Otherwise, head for métro Franklin D. Roosevelt (at the bottom of the Champs) or métro/ RER A station Charles-de-Gaulle-Étoile (at the top of the Champs). To head directly to the museums, go to métro Trocadéro.

TOP REASONS TO GO

The Champs-Elysées. A stroll along the most famous avenue in the world after dusk is mesmerizing, with spectacular lights and great people-watching.

Palais de Chaillot. Beloved by fashion photographers worldwide, this statue-lined plaza has a phenomenal view of the Tour Eiffel and the Trocadéro.

Musée Guimet. Step out of contemporary Paris and into another world by visiting this stunning collection of Asian art (including rare Khmer sculpture from Cambodia); the soaring sculptures and gemlike upstairs rooms exude a contemplative calm.

A macaron from Ladurée. For a memorable pause in your wanderings, step into this over-the-top tea shop midway down the Champs. The pastry company was founded in 1862 and offers more than 20 flavors of their signature macaron cookies—to eat here, or in lovely gift boxes.

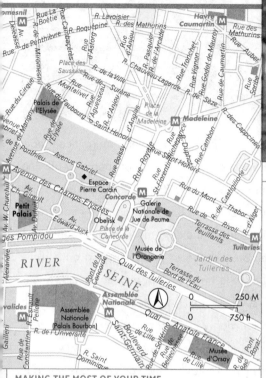

BEST CAFÉS

Le Café de l'Homme. With good food, fair prices, and a drop-dead view of the Tour Eiffel, this restaurant is a splendid reason (we'd say the only reason) to step into the outdated Musée de l'Homme, in the Palais de Chaillot. ⊠ *17 pl. du Trocadéro, Champs-Elysées* ☎ *01– 44–05–30–15* Ⓜ *Trocadéro*

Ladurée. This branch of the café– pastry shop is especially opulent. The *macarons* (meringue cookies) come in seemingly every feasible flavor; word is they helped inspire the color scheme of Sofia Coppola's film Marie Antoinette. ⊠ *75 av. des Champs-Elysées, Champs-Elysées* ☎ *01–40–75– 08–75* Ⓜ *George V*

Le Paris. This buzzy little café with a cool crowd and decor is a sign that the Champs-Elysées is back in fashion. Service can be chilly, but it's worth it for the interesting crowd and good food. ⊠ *93 av. des Champs-Elysées, Champs-Elysées* ☎ *01–47–23– 54–37* Ⓜ *Georg e V*

MAKING THE MOST OF YOUR TIME

This neighborhood is essential for every visitor to Paris— whether you're spending only a couple of days in the city or enjoying a leisurely month. This is where you can stroll the Champs-Elysées, see astonishing art in the museums around Trocadéro, drool at haute couture on Avenue Montaigne, and swan around at night. Although these streets are touristy by day, locals throng the area in the evening—the Champs- Elysées is known for its late-night shopping, movie theaters (often playing in original English with subtitles), bars for all tastes, and swank nightclubs. If your time in Paris is limited, give yourself an hour or two to walk the Champs and pause for a pastry—save shopping for another time. Or, make a quick visit at night: hail a cab at Invalides and ask the driver to go across the Pont Alexandre and up the Champs.

Sightseeing
★★★★★

Dining
★★★

Lodging
★★★★★

Shopping
★★★★

Nightlife
★★★★★

This is see-and-be-seen Paris, with several magnificent boulevards and roundabouts designed for people-watching and promenading. The ultimate Right Bank experience, this neighborhood is where you'll find the gigantic Arc de Triomphe, standing at the top of the city's most famous avenue, the Champs-Elysées. Unless it's four in the morning on a rainy night, these streets will be crowded with sightseers, haute-couture shoppers, and wealthy Parisians going about their daily lives in this enviably elegant *quartier*. Museums dedicated to every kind of art can be found within easy walking distance of Trocadéro. The only thing you can't easily find in this neighborhood is an ordinary bakery—instead, savor a pastry in a café, linger in a museum, and admire the incredible views from Trocadéro and the grandiose boulevards.

Updated by
Lisa Pasold

If you're an architecture buff, start your visit at the **Cité de l'Architecture et du Patrimoine** in the **Palais de Chaillot**. If you're traveling with wannabe pirates, try the **Musée de la Marine** next door. Farther on, the exquisite **Musée Guimet** offers a phenomenal Asian arts collection. For 20th-century art, visit the **Musée d'Art Moderne de la Ville de Paris**, and if you're a contemporary-arts observer, you won't want to miss the trendy **Palais de Tokyo**. Both these museums are a vestige of the 1930 Universal Exposition, and are impressive simply for their monumental façades. If you're more interested in wearable art, head over to the **Palais Galliera**, a former private palace that's now a fashion museum on Avenue du Président-Wilson.

Nearby, at the foot of that most famous avenue, the **Champs-Elysées**, the splendidly restored **Grand** and **Petit Palais** offer even more for art lovers. A small garden here offers the footsore a pleasant break before taking in the Champs: this greatest of streets surges with visitors and locals at all times of day. There are chic restaurants with fun sidewalk cafés (pricey, but you are on the most famous boulevard in the world!), but don't be shocked by the presence of car showrooms, megastore chain outlets like Virgin (music, video, and books) and Sephora (makeup and perfume), cinemas, and the inevitable fast-food outlets like the humongous McDonald's. For a concentrated dose of high style, turn down nearby Avenue Montaigne, with its great haute-couture houses such as Dior, Chanel, Christian Lacroix, Prada, and Louis Vuitton. At the top of the Champs is the **Arc de Triomphe**.

> **DID YOU KNOW?**
>
> The monument at the Place de l'Alma, at the bottom of the Champs-Elysées, has become Princess Diana's unofficial shrine, where bouquets and messages are still placed by her admirers— city workers regularly clean up flowers, graffiti, and photographs. The truth, however, is that this replica of the Statue of Liberty's flame was donated by Paris-based U.S. companies in 1989 in honor of the bicentennial of the French Revolution.

MAIN ATTRACTIONS

Fodor's Choice **Arc de Triomphe**
★ *See the highlighted listing in this chapter.*

Champs-Elysées. Marcel Proust lovingly described the elegance of the world's most famous avenue, the Champs-Elysées, during its Belle Époque heyday, when its cobblestones resounded to the clatter of horses and carriages. Today, despite the constant surge of cars up and down the "Champs" (as Parisians casually call the boulevard) and the influx of chain stores, there's still a certain *je ne sais quoi* about strolling up the avenue, especially at dusk as the refurbished street lamps are just coming on. The bustle means the café tables are always good for people-watching, and the cinemas, nightclubs, and late-hour shopping ensure the parade continues well into the night. Fouquets, across from the Lido, is where the famous folk used to hang out—including Orson Welles and James Joyce—but today it's more of photo op than a destination. The grand avenue is also the last leg of the Tour de France bicycle race, on the third or fourth Sunday in July, as well as the site of major ceremonies on Bastille Day (July 14) and Armistice Day (November 11). The 2-km- (1¼-mi-) long Champs-Elysées, originally cattle-grazing land, was laid out in the 1660s by the landscape architect André Le Nôtre as a park. Traces of its green origins remain in the lower section of the avenue, where elegant 19th-century park pavilions house the historic restaurants Ledoyen, Laurent, and Le Pavillon Elysées. Ⓜ *Champs-Elysées–Clemenceau, Franklin-D.-Roosevelt, George V, Etoile.*

Grand Palais. With its curved-glass roof and gorgeous restored Belle Époque ornamentation, you can't miss the Grand Palais whether you're approaching from the Seine or the Champs-Elysées. It forms a volup-

Hemingway's Paris

There is a saying: "Everyone has two countries, his or her own—and France." For the Lost Generation after World War I, these words rang particularly true. Lured by favorable exchange rates, free-flowing alcohol, and a booming arts scene, many American writers, composers, and painters moved to Paris in the 1920s and 1930s, Ernest Hemingway among them. He arrived in Paris with his first wife, Hadley, in December 1921 and made for the Rive Gauche—the Hôtel Jacob et d'Angleterre, to be exact (still operating at 44 rue Jacob). To celebrate their arrival the couple went to the Café de la Paix for a meal they nearly couldn't afford.

Hemingway worked as a journalist and quickly made friends with expat writers such as Gertrude Stein and Ezra Pound. In 1922 the Hemingways moved to 74 rue du Cardinal Lemoine, a bare-bones apartment with no running water (his writing studio was around the corner, on the top floor of 39 rue Descartes). Then, in 1924, the couple and their baby son settled at 113 rue Notre-Dame des Champs. Much of *The Sun Also Rises*, Hemingway's first serious novel, was written at nearby café La Closerie des Lilas. These were the years in which he forged his writing style, paring his sentences down to the pith. As he noted in *A Moveable Feast*, "hunger was good discipline." There were some especially hungry months when Hemingway gave up journalism for short story writing, and the family was "very poor and very happy."

They weren't happy for long: in 1926, as *The Sun Also Rises* made him famous, Hemingway left Hadley and the next year wed his mistress, Pauline Pfeiffer, then moved to 6 rue Férou, near the Musée du Luxembourg, whose collection of Cézanne landscapes (now in the Musée d'Orsay) he revered.

For gossip and books, and to pick up his mail, Papa would visit Shakespeare & Co., at 12 rue de l'Odéon, owned by Sylvia Beach, who became a trusted friend. For cash and cocktails Hemingway usually headed to the upscale Rive Droite. He collected the former at the Guaranty Trust Company, at 1 rue des Italiens. He found the latter, when he was flush, at the bar of the Hôtel Crillon, or, when poor, at the Caves Mura, at 19 rue d'Antin, or Harry's Bar, still in brisk business at 5 rue Daunou. Hemingway's legendary association with the Hôtel Ritz was sealed during the Liberation in 1944, when he strode in at the head of his platoon and "liberated" the joint by ordering martinis all around. Here Hemingway asked Mary Welsh to become his fourth wife, and here also, the story goes, a trunk full of notes on his first years in Paris turned up in the 1950s, giving him the raw material to write *A Moveable Feast*.

---

tuous duo with the Petit Palais, on the other side of Avenue Winston-Churchill: both stone buildings, adorned with mosaics and sculpted friezes, were built for the World's Fair of 1900, and, like the Tour Eiffel, no one expected them to be permanent. Parisians flock to the special exhibitions and events held here. ■ TIP→**To avoid long lines, try to reserve your ticket more than 24 hours in advance, although prices are less expensive without reservations.** ✉ *Av. Winston-Churchill, Champs-Elysées* ☎ *01–44–13–17–30* ⊕ *www.rmn.fr/galeriesnationalesdugrand*

palais ☒€11.10 with reservation; €10 no reservation ☉Thurs.–Mon. 10–8, Wed. 10–10 Ⓜ Champs-Elysées–Clemenceau.

Musée d'Art Moderne de la Ville de Paris *(Paris Museum of Modern Art).* Although the city's modern-art museum hasn't generated a buzz comparable to that of the Centre Georges Pompidou, it can be a more pleasant museum-going experience. ■TIP➔Like the Pompidou, the Musée d'Art Moderne shows temporary exhibits of painting, sculpture, and installation and video art, plus it has a permanent collection of top-tier 20th-century works from around the world—but it happily escapes the Pompidou's overcrowding. The building reopened in February 2006, and its vast, white-wall galleries are an ideal backdrop for the bold statements of 20th-century art. The museum takes over, chronologically speaking, where the Musée d'Orsay leaves off; among the earliest works are Fauvist paintings by Maurice Vlaminck and André Derain, followed by Pablo Picasso's early experiments in Cubism. Other highlights include works by Robert and Sonia Delaunay, Chagall, Matisse, Rothko, and Amedeo Modigliani. ☒11 av. du Président-Wilson, Trocadéro/Tour Eiffel ☎01–53–67–40–00 ⊕www.paris.org ☒Permanent collection free, temporary exhibitions €7–€12, depending on the exhibition ☉Tues.–Sun. 10–5:20 Ⓜ Iéna.

★ **Musée Dapper.** A well-curated museum dedicated to African art, the Dapper is famous for its stunning temporary mask exhibitions. It's a relatively new museum to the Paris scene—created by Christiane Falgayrettes-Leveau and her husband, Michel Leveau, in 1986—and as a result, often a calm place to visit. Unfortunately most of the visitor information is still only in French. ☒35 rue Paul Valéry, Champs-Elysées ☎01–45–00–91–75 ⊕www.dapper.com.fr ☒€6–€9 ☉Wed.–Mon. 11–7 Ⓜ Charles-de-Gaulle–Etoile.

FodorśChoice **Musée Guimet.** This seemingly small building is the surprise treasure of
★ the museum neighborhood; here you can find an Asian art collection founded by Lyonnais industrialist Emile Guimet, who traveled around the world in the late 19th century amassing priceless Indo-Chinese and Far Eastern objets d'art. In the entrance area you can see the largest collection of Khmer art outside Cambodia, including astonishingly lifelike yet serene 12th-century portrait heads. Each floor has something fascinating; be sure to peer into the delicate round library (where you'd swear Guimet has just stepped out for tea) and toil up to the top floor's 18th-century ivory replica of a Chinese pavilion. A separate building up the street (included in the entry ticket) displays a vast collection of Buddhas and occasionally holds traditional Japanese tea ceremonies. You can pick up an English-language brochure and free audioguide at the entrance. ☒6 pl. d'Iéna, Trocadéro/Tour Eiffel ☎01–56–52–53–00 ⊕www.museeguimet.fr ☒€6.50 ☉Wed.–Sun. 10–5:30 Ⓜ Iéna, Boissiére.

Palais de Chaillot. This honey-color Art Deco cultural center was built in the 1930s to replace a Moorish-style building constructed for the World Exhibition of 1878. It contains the Institut Français d'Architecture; the Chaillot School, which trains architects as restor-

ARC DE TRIOMPHE

✉ Pl. Charles-de-Gaulle, Champs-Elysées

☎ 01–55–37–73–77

⊕ www.monum.fr

💳 €8, free under 18

🕐 Apr.–Sept., daily 10 AM–11 PM; Oct.–Mar., daily 10 AM–10:30 PM

Ⓜ Métro or RER: Etoile

TIPS

■ France's Unknown Soldier is buried beneath the arch; the flame is rekindled every evening at 6:30, which is the most atmospheric time to visit. To beat the crowds, though, come early in the morning.

■ Be wary of the traffic circle that surrounds the arch. It's infamous for accidents—including one several years ago that involved the transport minister of France (oh, the irony!). Use the underground passage from the northeast corner of the avenue des Champs-Elysées.

Inspired by Rome's Arch of Titus, this colossal, 164-foot triumphal arch was planned by Napoléon—who liked to consider himself the heir to the Roman emperors—to celebrate his military successes. Unfortunately, Napoléon's strategic and architectural visions were not entirely on the same plane, and the Arc de Triomphe proved something of an embarrassment: although the emperor wanted the monument completed in time for an 1810 parade in honor of his new bride, Marie-Louise, the arch was still only a few feet high, and a dummy arch of painted canvas was strung up to save face. Empires come and go, but Napoléon's had been gone for more than 20 years before the Arc de Triomphe was finally finished, in 1836.

HIGHLIGHTS

The Arc de Triomphe is known for its magnificent sculptures by François Rude, including *The Departure of the Volunteers in 1792*, better known as *La Marseillaise*, to the right of the arch when viewed from the Champs-Elysées. Names of Napoléon's generals are inscribed on the stone façades—the underlined names identify the hallowed figures who fell in battle.

The traffic circle around the Arc is named for Charles de Gaulle, but it's known to Parisians as "L'Etoile," or the Star—a reference to the streets that fan out from it.

Climb the stairs to the top of the arch and you can see the star effect of the 12 radiating avenues and the vista down the Champs-Elysées toward Place de la Concorde and the distant Louvre.

There is a small museum halfway up the arch, devoted to its history.

ers; and three large museums: the **Musée de l'Homme,** the **Musée de la Marine,** and the new **Cité de l'Architecture et du Patrimoine.** The latter two are worth visiting, but the only reason to visit the first is for its café. The garden leading to the Seine has sculptures and dramatic fountains and is the focus for fireworks demonstrations on Bastille Day. The palace terrace, flanked by gilded statuettes, offers a wonderful picture-postcard view of the Tour Eiffel. ⊠ *Pl. du Trocadéro, Trocadéro/Tour Eiffel* Ⓜ *Trocadéro*

Palais de Tokyo. In a space that was derelict for more than a decade, this Art Nouveau twin of the Musée d'Art Moderne reopened in 2002 as a trendy, stripped-down space for contemporary arts with unorthodox, ambitious programming. There is no permanent collection; instead, dynamic temporary exhibits spread over a large, open area reminiscent of a construction site, with a trailer for a ticket booth. Instead of traditional museum guards, young art students—most of whom are at least semifluent in English—are on hand to help explain the installations. As if the art exhibits weren't adventurous enough, the cultural programming extends to debates, DJ-driven concerts, readings, and fashion shows; there is also a cafeteria, a funky restaurant, and a bookstore. ■ **TIP→** **Until at least the end of 2008, the art installation/hotel room "Everland" by Swiss artists L/B is available on the roof ($463 for the night, with one heck of a view (** ⊕www.everland.ch/en/info/). ⊠ *13 av. du Président-Wilson, Trocadéro/Tour Eiffel* ☎ *01–47–23–54–01* ⊕ *www. palaisdetokyo.com* ▣€6 ☉ *Tues.–Sun. noon–midnight* Ⓜ *Iéna.*

NEED A BREAK?

For an inexpensive bite, check out the Palais de Tokyo restaurant, Tokyo Eat (⊠ *13 av. du Président-Wilson, Trocadéro/Tour Eiffel* ☎ *01–47–20–00–29*), the only museum café in town whose tables are filled with hip locals, especially at lunch.

ALSO WORTH SEEING

CineAqua. An aquarium and an animation studio might not seem like the most likely roommates, but there's a good story behind this bizarre establishment. Empty for years, this part of the Palais is historically designated as an underground aquarium, which forced the new owner, a Japanese investor who wanted to open an animation studio, to include fish in his floor plan. So now there are 16 screens with constantly running animated cartoons, interspersed with fish tanks and shark pools (9,000 fish, at last count, along with more than 20 sharks). Great for kids, CineAqua is surreal for adults—for whom the Aqua lounge opens after 8 PM for late-night drinks, DJs, and special events. There's a Japanese restaurant overlooking the largest tank…Sushi, anyone? ⊠ *2 av. des Nations Unies, Champs-Elysées* ☎ *01–40–69–23–23* ⊕ *www. cineaqua.com* ▣€19.50 ☉ *Daily 10–8* Ⓜ *Trocadéro.*

Cité de l'Architecture et du Patrimoine (formerly the French Monuments Museum). Dedicated to France's phenomenal architectural heritage, this museum also encompasses the present and future, with the cutting-edge Institut Français d'Architecture along with the Chaillot School, which trains architects in restoration. The original institute was founded in 1879 by architect-restorer Viollet-le-Duc (the man mainly responsible for the extensive renovation of Notre-Dame and countless other Gothic cathedrals), and, in 2007, the monuments collection finally reopened, with cutting-edge virtual visits to complement its vast repository of copies of statues, columns, archways, and frescoes. ⊠*1 pl. du Trocadéro, Trocadéro/Tour Eiffel* ☎*01–58–51–52–00* ⊕*www.citechaillot.fr* ☑*€19.50* ⊘*Fri.–Mon. and Wed. 11–7, Thurs. 11–9* Ⓜ*Trocadéro.*

DID YOU KNOW?

Did you know that the former residents of the Baccarat Museum financed Luis Buñuel's first movie, *L'Age d'Or*? Marie-Laure, Vicomtesse de Noailles (nicknamed "Countess Bizarre"), and her husband lived in the magnificent mansion that is now the Baccarat showroom; Marie-Laure was a great supporter and friend of the Surrealists, including Buñuel, Jean Cocteau (whom she considered marrying), and Man Ray.

Fondation Pierre Bergé–Yves Saint Laurent. With his business partner, Pierre Bergé, iconic fashion designer Yves Saint Laurent reopened his former atelier in 2004—this time as a gallery and archive of his work. Temporary exhibits, some fashion related, rotate roughly every six months. The first, a show of Saint Laurent's art-inspired clothing, including his Mondrian dress, was a knockout; a more recent exhibit was devoted to fashionista doyenne Nan Kempner. ⊠*1 rue Léonce Reynaud, Trocadéro/Tour Eiffel* ☎*01–44–31–64–31* ⊕*www.ysl-hautecouture.com* ☑*€5* ⊘*Tues.–Sun. 11–6* Ⓜ*Alma-Marceau.*

Maison de Baccarat. Designer Philippe Starck brought an irreverent *Alice in Wonderland* approach to the HQ of the venerable Baccarat crystal firm. Opened in 2003, the Baccarat museum plays on its building's Surrealist legacy; Cocteau, Dalí, Buñuel, and Man Ray were all frequent guests of the mansion's onetime owner, Countess Marie-Laure de Noailles. At the entrance, talking heads are projected onto giant crystal urns, and a lighted chandelier is submerged in an aquarium. Not all the marvels come from Starck though; Baccarat has created exquisite crystal pieces since Louis XV conferred his seal on the glassworks in 1764, and many of the company's masterworks are on display, from the soaring candlesticks made for Czar Nicholas II to the perfume flacon Dalí designed for Schiaparelli. ∎**TIP→The museum's Cristal Room café attracts an appropriately glittering crowd, so book well in advance for lunch or dinner.** ⊠*11 pl. des Etats-Unis, Trocadéro/Tour Eiffel* ☎*01–40–22–11–00* ⊕*www.baccarat.fr* ☑*€7* ⊘*Mon. and Wed.–Sat. 10–6* Ⓜ*Trocadéro.*

☉ **Musée de la Marine** *(Maritime Museum).* After an intensive and ambitious renovation, France's most important maritime history museum is fully rigged and readied—a must-see for fans of Patrick O'Brian's nautical *Master and Commander* books, or anyone who has dreamed of running away to sea. One of the best parts of this little-known collection is the boat models, from 17th-century flagships up through 20th-century naval war machines. Video works by contemporary artists are shown alongside the early navigational equipment and original restored boats that form the bedrock of the collection. There are excellent explanatory panels in English throughout, and there's a changing roster of special exhibits. ✉ *17 pl. du Trocadéro, Trocadéro/Tour Eiffel* ☎ *01–53–65–69–69* ⊕ *www.musee-marine.fr* 💶€9 ⊙ *Wed.–Mon. 10–6* Ⓜ *Trocadéro.*

Palais de la Découverte *(Palace of Discovery)*. A planetarium, working models, and scientific and technological exhibits on such topics as optics, biology, nuclear physics, and electricity make up this science museum behind the Grand Palais. There are some hands-on exhibits, but most of the explanations are in French only. ✉ *Av. Franklin-D.-Roosevelt, Champs-Elysées* ☎ *01–56–43–20–20* ⊕ *www.palais-decouverte.fr* 💶€7, *planetarium additional €3.50* ⊙ *Tues.–Sat. 9:30–6, Sun. 10–7* Ⓜ *Champs-Elysées–Clemenceau.*

Palais Galliera. This luxurious mansion, built in 1888 for the Duchesse de Galliera, opens only for special exhibitions on costume and clothing design. Although the generous Duchesse, who donated her mansion to the city, might not recognize the exhibition rooms, the mansion's garden was restored to its 19th-century style in 2005. Thanks to its aggressive curatorial team, this museum has quickly won attention; its Marlene Dietrich show, for instance, influenced many fashion-designer collections. Unfortunately, the museum has been closed for more than a year for renovations, so check before you go. ✉ *10 av. Pierre-1ᵉʳ-de-Serbie, Trocadéro/Tour Eiffel* ☎ *01–56–52–86–00* ⊕ *www.paris.fr/musees/* 💶€8 ⊙ *Tues.–Sun. 10–6* Ⓜ *Iéna.*

Petit Palais. The smaller counterpart to the Grand Palais, just off the Champs-Elysées, has a permanent collection of French painting and furniture, with splendid canvases by Courbet and Bouguereau. There are often inventive temporary exhibitions here, but the building itself—a 1902 cream puff of marble and gilt, with huge windows over-looking the Seine—is worth a look. Outside, as you admire the architecture, keep an eye out for two excellent sculptures: French World War I hero Georges Clemenceau, facing the Champs-Elysées; and Jean Cardot's resolute image of Winston Churchill, facing the Seine. ✉ *Av. Winston-Churchill, Champs-Elysées* ☎ *01–42–65–12–73* ⊕ *www.paris.fr/musees/* 💶*Permanent collection free, temporary exhibit entry fees vary* ⊙ *Tues.–Sun. 10–6; Tues. until 8 for temporary exhibits* Ⓜ *Champs-Elysées–Clemenceau.*

Trocadéro (Place du Trocadéro et du 11 novembre). Named for an 1823 Spanish battle, this hilltop became the site of glittering international exhibitions from 1867 to 1937; the Art Deco buildings are still standing. By the end of the 1800s, the most daring aristocrats of Paris were living around this hilltop. It was here, in the Palais de Chaillot, that the United Nations adopted the Universal Declaration of Human Rights in 1948. The Passy Cemetery (where painter Manet is buried) is just to the west. Today, the Place is essentially a traffic circle much like Place de la Concorde; the area remains alluring because museums like the Musée d'Art Moderne have taken over former World's Fair buildings as well as several magnificent mansions. The Trocadéro métro station is a popular beginning point for visitors; to rest your feet, join the locals at the traditional café terrasses on the far side of the traffic circle

Dining at a Glance

For full reviews
⇨ Ch. 17

INEXPENSIVE DINING

Chez Savy, *Bistro,* 23 rue Bayard

La Maison de l'Aubrac, *Brasserie,* 37 rue Marbeuf

Le Petit Rétro, *Bistro,* 5 rue Mesnil

MODERATE DINING

Au Petit Verdot du 17e, *Bistro,* 9 rue Fourcroy

La Butte Chaillot, *Bistro,* 110 bis, av. Kléber

La Fermette Marbeuf 1900, *Brasserie,* 5 rue Marbeuf

Le Graindorge, *Bistro,* 15 rue de l'Arc-de-Triomphe

La Grande Armée, *Brasserie,* 3 av. de la Grande Armée

Kifuné, *Japanese,* 44 rue St-Ferdinand

Rech, *Seafood,* 62 Av. des Ternes

La Table de Joël Robuchon, *Modern French,* 16 av. Bugeaud

La Table de Lauriston, *Bistro,* 129 rue de Lauriston

EXPENSIVE DINING

Alain Ducasse au Plaza Athénée, *Haute French,* Hôtel Plaza Athénée, 25 av. Montaigne

Les Ambassadeurs, *Haute French,* Hôtel de Crillon, 10 pl. de la Concorde

L'Astrance, *Haute French,* 4 rue Beethoven

Au Petit Colombier, *Bistro,* 42 rue des Acacias

Le Bristol, *Haute French,* Hôtel Bristol, 112 rue du Faubourg St-Honoré

Le Cinq, *Haute French,* Hôtel Four Seasons George V, 31 av. George V

Le Cristal Room, *Haute French,* 11 pl. des Etats-Unis

Dominique Bouchet, *Bistro,* 11 rue Treilhard

Guy Savoy, *Haute French,* 18 rue Troyon

Hiramatsu, *French Fusion,* 52 rue de Longchamp

Ledoyen, *Haute French,* 1 av. Dutuit, on Carré des Champs-Elysées

Maison Blanche, *Modern French,* 15 av. Montaigne

Market, *Modern French,* 15 av. Matignon

L'Os à Moelle, *Bistro,* 3 rue Vasco-de-Gama

Pierre Gagnaire, *Haute French,* 6 rue de Balzac

Les Saveurs de Flora, *Haute French,* 36 av. George V

Spoon, Food & Wine, *Modern French,* 14 rue de Marignan

Stella Maris, *French Fusion,* 4 rue Arsène-Houssaye

La Table de Babette, *Trocadero,* 32 rue de Longchamp

La Table du Lancaster, *Haute French,* Hotel Lancaster, 7 rue de Berri

Taillevent, *Haute French,* 15 rue Lamennais

---

from the Palais. ⊠*Pl. du Trocadéro et du 11 novembre Trocadéro* Ⓜ*Trocadéro.*

The Faubourg St-Honoré

WITH THE LOUVRE

Place de la Concorde

WORD OF MOUTH

"At the end of Tuileries Garden, you cross the street and you're in Place de la Concorde. It's basically a plaza type of place, with statues and fountains. It's pretty impressive!"

—lmlweb

GETTING ORIENTED

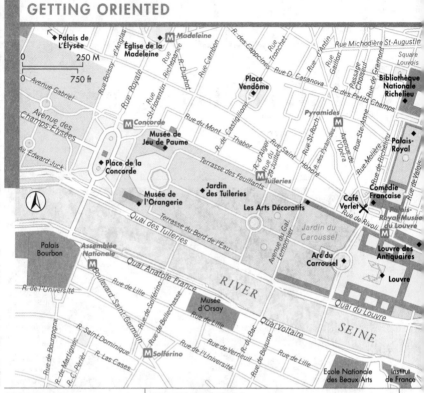

GETTING HERE

The Faubourg St-Honoré includes the 1ᵉʳ and 2ᵉ arrondissements. There are several métro stations in this neighborhood. If you're heading to the Louvre, use the Louvre/Rivoli or the Palais-Royal/Musée du Louvre stops, both on the 1 line. For the Tuileries, use the Tuileries stop, also on the 1 line. For Place de la Concorde, use the Concorde stop on lines 1 and 12. Wherever you choose to begin, be prepared to be overwhelmed by architecture and traffic; once you get used to the scale of the neighborhood, though, you should be able to pause and admire all that surrounds you.

TOP REASONS TO GO

Galerie Vivienne. Before department stores there were 19th-century shopping arcades, and this is one of the prettiest remaining in Paris. Stop for a cup of tea or a glass of wine and contemplate a more elegant era.

Palais-Royal. Visit these arcades and understand why the French writer Colette called the view from her window "a little corner of the country" in the heart of the city.

Place de la Concorde. Maybe it's the way the light glints off the gold tip of the obelisk, but you haven't really seen Paris until you've walked through the regal Jardin des Tuileries and admired the view toward Place de la Concorde.

Rue Saint-Honoré. Well-established staples of fashion, as well as trendy duds, vie for place in shop windows along Paris's most prestigious shopping street.

5

MAKING THE MOST OF YOUR TIME

This neighborhood can easily take an entire day, as shopping, stargazing, and admiring the historic architecture will keep you entertained for hours. Don't be intimidated by the poshness, though: alongside the grandeur, this is a functioning neighborhood like any other in Paris with local cafés, great bakeries, and hidden quiet streets. The area is certainly more crowded on weekends, but don't think visiting on a weekday will mean you can sail down Rue St-Honoré without getting jostled. The Faubourg has foot traffic at almost all hours, with the exception of late nights.

The Louvre could almost be considered a neighborhood unto itself, and so large as to be daunting, so we recommend having a plan of action before you enter. And head to the underground entrance, Carrousel Du Louvre, where there's almost never a line for entry tickets.

BEST CAFÉS

Le Fumoir. This café-restaurant has passed from red-hot chic to favored mainstay. Its location just across from the Louvre helps, but ultimately what makes it work is the high quality of its food, not to mention the notably good brunches. Its salons seem variously inspired by Vienna, Edward Hopper, and Scandinavia. ✉ Pl. du Louvre, 6 rue de l'Amiral-Coligny Louvre/Tuileries ☎ 01–42–92–00–24 Ⓜ Louvre.

Au Père Tranquille. In a neighborhood swarming with all sorts—tourists, Parisian teens, street musicians—this café's popular terrace is a particularly prime spot for people-watching. ✉ 16 rue Pierre Lescot, Beaubourg/Les Halles ☎ 01–45–08–00–34 Ⓜ Les Halles.

Café Verlet. Many Parisians think this compact coffee roaster crowded with wooden tables and fashionable shoppers serves the best coffee in town—you might find unusual beans from Rwanda or India. You can also get sandwiches and lustrous tarts. ✉ 256 rue St-Honoré, Louvre/Tuileries ☎ 01–42–60–67–39 Ⓜ Tuileries.

Sightseeing
★★★★
Dining
★★
Lodging
★★★★
Shopping
★★★★★
Nightlife
★★

Fashions change, but the Faubourg St-Honoré has been a chic shopping strip since the days of Louis XIV. At one time the place to stay when visiting Paris, here you'll find the presidential palace and former royal residences, cheek by jowl with famous design shops, renowned jewelers, and exclusive perfume shops—where kings' mistresses once shopped. The Faubourg is still the place to stay for fashionistas—who love the Ritz on Place Vendôme, and the more recent celebrity mainstay, Hotel Costes—and it remains the symbol of luxury across the world, so be sure to visit when the shops are open! Keep an eye out for Colette (at 213 rue St-Honoré), the must-visit shop for 21st-century trendsetters.

Updated by
Lisa Pasold

This neighborhood includes all that's elegant in Paris, from architecture to fashion to food. The biggest nearby attraction, of course, is the massive **Louvre** museum with the lovely **Jardin des Tuileries** next door. At the southwest corner of the Tuileries you'll find the recently renovated **Musée de l'Orangerie**, which houses Monet's Water Lilies. **Les Arts Décoratifs** Center, attached to the Louvre but with a separate entrance, houses its own three separate museums, including the **Musée des Arts Décoratifs**, with its impressive period rooms and rotating exhibits for design aficionados.

Posh Rue St-Honoré is a block up from the museum and gardens, running parallel to the Seine. Alongside the Louvre, there's also the **Louvre des Antiquaires**, a former hotel that's been gutted and divided into innumerable high-end antiques shops—a fun browse, especially if you're a connoisseur.

Tucked behind the **Comédie Francaise** is the unobtrusive entrance to the **Palais-Royal**, a former palace built around a gorgeous garden. Look for Jean-Michel Othaniel's psychedelic Palais-Royal métro entrance to find the alley that leads into the royal arcades. The Palais-Royal includes an astonishingly peaceful garden, very different from the crowded yet spectacular Tuileries. The city's first restaurants came into being here and were popular with the aristocrats and, later, the Revolutionary politicians. You can peek in the window at Le Grand Véfour to admire the original Directoire-period interior, and there are often wonderful singers busking under the arches, farthest from the Louvre. The existence of the restaurants meant that some of the city's finest food shops also sprang up here, and still call the area home. E. Dehillerin at 18-20 rue Coquillière is a chef's shop that has been around since 1820 and sells everything a well-dressed kitchen needs. The nearby massive food market of **Les Halles** (pronounced lay-ahl) fed the city until 1969. The famed 19th-century buildings, once called "the Louvre of the people," were torn down to make way for a 1970s shopping mall and garden, and Parisians are currently arguing about what kind of redevelopment might beautify the area, update the crumbling mall, and make it safer at night. Everyone has an opinion—just ask!

MAIN ATTRACTIONS

★ **Les Arts Décoratifs.** A must for those with an eye for design, the decorative arts center, with its own separate entrance, in the northwestern wing of the Louvre building houses three famously chic museums. The **Musée de la Mode,** with its archives of clothing and accessories dating back to the 18th century, has rotating special exhibits plus a glittering permanent jewelry display. Some descriptive info is available in English. The changing exhibits of advertising and posters in the **Musée de la Publicité** compete for attention with Jean Nouvel's brash decor. The **Musée des Arts Décoratifs,** the main wing of the center, reopened in late 2006 after a 10-year renovation, with a spectacular arrangement of furniture, tapestries, glassware, paintings, toys, and other necessities of life from the 1300s until today. Now you can gawk at Napoléon's over-the-top throne, admire the bed of Valtesse (the courtesan who inspired Zola's novel Nana), and fantasize about living in period rooms that range from a bedroom Catherine de Medici might recognize, to the Art Deco boudoir of designer Jeanne Lanvin. ⊠ *107 rue de Rivoli, Louvre/Tuileries* ☎ *01–44–55–57–50* ⊕ *www.lesartsdecoratifs.fr* ☎ *€8–€16.50, depending on which museums you wish to visit* ☉ *Tues., Wed., and Fri. 11–6, Thurs. 11–9, weekends 10–6* Ⓜ *Palais-Royal.*

Bibliothèque Nationale Richelieu. France's longtime national library, named for 17th-century prime minister Cardinal Richelieu, now hosts photography exhibits featuring prints culled from its collection. Holdings range from the work of early daguerreotypists, to that of legendary practitioners of the *sixième art* like Nadar, Atget, Cartier-Bresson, Doisneau, and Man Ray, to contemporary French photographers such as Sophie Calle. Though the books have mostly been moved to the Bibliothèque Nationale François-Mitterand, researchers still consult original manuscripts, engravings, coins, and prints here; parts of these collections go on display from time to time. Display information is available in French only. ⊠ *58 rue de Richelieu, Opéra/Grands Bou-*

levards ☎ *01–53–79–59–59* ⊕ *www.bnf.fr* ☒ *Free–€8.50, depending on show* ⊙ *Tues.–Sat. 10–7, Sun. 1–7* Ⓜ *Bourse.*

★ **Galerie Vivienne.** Once upon a time Paris shoppers flocked to covered arcades to sate their consumer lust. Of the city's remaining *galeries*, Vivienne has best survived the fickle winds of fashion. Admire the elegant, well-worn marble mosaics and neoclassical bas-reliefs, which frame shop windows from designers like Gaultier alongside quirky individual artisan shops. It's the perfect place to buy gifts, whether you're looking for a vintage cognac glass for your boyfriend or a hand-woven French scarf for your mother-in-law, or are just browsing to get out of the rain. ☒ *6 rue Vivienne, enter on rue des Petits-Champs, Louvre/Tuileries* Ⓜ *Palais-Royal/Bourse.*

NEED A BREAK?

A Priori Thé (☒ *35 Galerie Vivienne, Louvre/Tuileries* ☎ *01–42–97–48–75*) has been comforting travelers for more than 20 years with its teas and sweets. The reassuringly familiar menu includes brownies and crumbles, a combination of French and Anglo traditions dreamed up by American owner Peggy Ancock. Another option is the family-run *épicerie* (grocery store) and wineshop Legrand Filles et Fils (☒ *1 rue Banque, Louvre/Tuileries* ☎ *01–42–60–07–12*), in business since 1880. A wine bar in the back serves simple, delicious fare and a superb selection of wines. (Wine tastings are held most Tuesday nights—call to reserve or visit their Web site, www.caves-legrand.com.)

★ **Jardin des Tuileries.** *See the highlighted listing in this chapter.*

Louvre des Antiquaires. This "shopping mall" of superelegant antiques dealers opposite the Louvre is a minimuseum in itself. Pretty bibelots that would have gladdened the heart of Marie-Antoinette vie for shelf space alongside vases by Art Deco master Lalique and the shoes worn by dancer Josephine Baker, and don't miss the Louis XVI *boiseries* (wainscoting). These stylish glass-walled corridors deserve a browse whether you intend to buy or not. ☒ *Main entrance: Pl. du Palais-Royal, Louvre/Tuileries* ⊙ *Tues.–Sun. 11–7* Ⓜ *Palais-Royal.*

★ **Musée de l'Orangerie.** People line up for hours for a glimpse of Claude Monet's huge, meditative *Water Lilies* displayed inside what was once a winter greenhouse for the Tuileries' citrus trees. The 2006 renovation has allowed more light to pour into this small museum, with its selection of early-20th-century paintings by Renoir, Paul Cézanne, Henri Matisse, and Marie Laurencin, among other masters.

> **WORD OF MOUTH**
>
> "If you're not big into museums, stay outside of the Louvre and opt instead for the Orsay and most definitely the Orangerie, where the huge, gorgeous Monet water lily panels are."
>
> —aliced

☒ *Pl. de la Concorde, Louvre/Tuileries* ☎ *01–44–77–80–07* ⊕ *www.musee-orangerie.fr* ☒ *€7.70–€4.50, free 1st Sun. of month* ⊙ *Wed., Thurs., and Sat.–Mon. 12:30–7, Fri. 12:30–9* Ⓜ *Concorde.*

FodorsChoice
★ **Palais-Royal.** In one of the most quintessentially Parisian sights, it's not inconceivable to imagine whiling away an afternoon having lunch at Le Grand Véfour in the very room where Josephine dined, wandering into Didier Ludot's vintage couture boutiques, sizing up displays of old military medals, or buying the latest frock from Marc Jacobs. If you're in Paris with your sweetheart—especially in spring—do as the locals do and lock lips on a stone bench under one of the majestic, manicured trees in the garden. The *Palais* dates from the 1630s (parts of the original building still remain) and is *royal* because Cardinal Richelieu (1585–1642) bequeathed it to Louis XIII. In his early days as king, Louis XIV lived with his mother and brother here, in relative intimacy, instead of in the scandal-drenched intimidating splendor of the Louvre—of course, he soon decided that his own intimidating splendor warranted a more majestic home, hence Versailles. Other famous residents of the Palais-Royal include Jean Cocteau and Colette, who wrote while looking out over her *province à Paris*. Today the Palais-Royal contains the French Ministry of Culture—closed to the public—a block of apartments, and the most refined sandbox in the city. ⊠*Pl. du Palais-Royal, Louvre/Tuileries* Ⓜ*Palais-Royal.*

Place de la Concorde. This square—actually more of a traffic circle these days—at the foot of Champs-Elysées was originally consecrated to and named after Louis XV. During the Revolution, crowds watched Louis XVI, Marie-Antoinette, and more than 2,000 others lose their heads here to Madame Guillotine. After the blood washed away, it was renamed Concorde, and in 1833 the politically neutral 107-foot pink granite obelisk originally quarried in the 8th century bc (making this Paris's oldest monument) was erected; it was a present from the viceroy of Egypt. Among the handsome 18th-century buildings facing the square is the Hôtel Crillon, originally built by Gabriel—architect of Versailles's Petit Trianon—as a home for three of France's wealthiest families. ⊠*Champs-Elysées* Ⓜ*Concorde.*

Place Vendôme. Property laws have kept the cafés and shops away from this snobbish but gorgeous plaza, leaving it stately and refined—and the perfect home for the rich and famous. Chopin lived and died at No. 12, and today's celebs camp out at the Hotel Ritz at No. 15, where Hemingway's Bar serves up some of the best martinis in Paris.

With its granite pavement and Second Empire street lamps, Jules-Hardouin Mansart's perfectly proportioned example of 17th-century urban architecture shines in all its golden-stone splendor. To maintain a uniform appearance, Mansart first built only the façades of the *hôtels particuliers* (mansions), and the lots behind were then sold to buyers who custom-tailored their palaces. In the square's center, a statue of Napoléon tops the massive column, which was knocked over (into a pile of manure, no less) and shattered in 1871 by painter Gustave Courbet and his band of Revolutionary hooligans. The Third Republic stuck the pieces together again and sent him the bill. Ⓜ*Opéra.*

St-Eustache. Built as the market neighborhood's answer to Notre-Dame, this massive Gothic and early-Renaissance church is decidedly squeezed

JARDIN DES TUILERIES

✉ Bordered by Quai des Tuileries, Pl. de la Concorde, Rue de Rivoli, and the Louvre

Ⓜ Tuileries or Concorde

☎ 01–40–20–90–43

🕐 April–end of September daily 7 AM–9 PM; rest of year daily 7:30–7

🍴 Open-air café

🎟 Free

😊 Good for kids

The Tuileries may be a typical French garden—formal, with statues, rows of trees, fountains with gaping fish, and gravel paths—but the grand scale and location make coming here anything but a typical experience. The name comes from the fact that roof tiles were once made from clay dug here (tuileries were the kilns used to fire the tuiles, or tiles). The gardens were designed by André Le Nôtre in the 17th century for Louis XIV. He didn't spend much time here, but the gardens quickly became the place to see and be seen in Paris. Claude Monet and Auguste Renoir captured the Tuileries with paint and brush, and it's no wonder the Impressionists loved it so—the gray, austere light of Paris's famous overcast days makes the green trees look even greener.

HIGHLIGHTS

It's still one of the loveliest places to stroll in the city. Walking through you'll see the Louvre at one end and the Place de la Concorde at the other, the Musée d'Orsay on the Seine side, and the Eiffel Tower from several vantage points (although the best is from the top of the west end's staircase). What was once the formal royal greenhouse used to store the Tuileries' citrus trees in winter is now a reason to visit the garden in its own right. At the end of the Tuileries overlooking Place de la Concorde on the Rue de Rivoli side is the **Musée de l'Orangerie,** which now contains the largest display of Claude Monet's lovely *Water Lilies* series, as well as a sizable collection of early-20th-century paintings. On the opposite side is the **Musée du Jeu de Paume,** which holds photography exhibits.

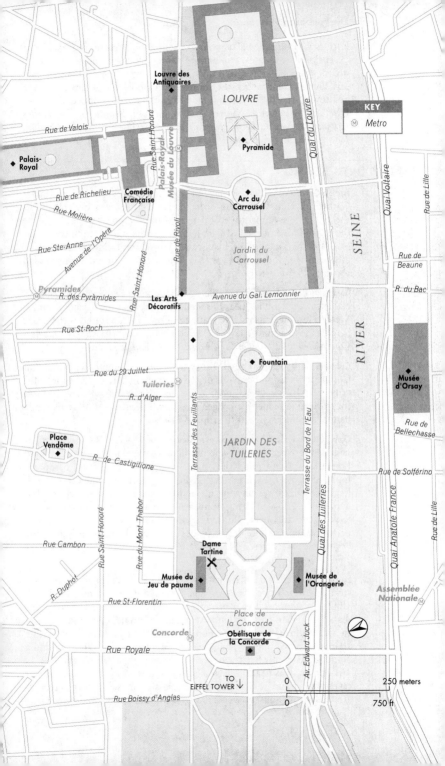

into its surroundings. The church itself, completed in 1637 with the exception of the late-18th-century façade, contains classical column orders, rounded arches, and thick, comparatively simple window tracery. Outside, check out the impressive Gothic flying buttresses, the bell tower, and the gigantic stone head with a hand cupped to its ear: *L'Ecoute* by Henri de Miller. ⊠*2 rue du Jour, Beaubourg/Les Halles* ⊕*www.saint-eustache.org for concert info* ⊙*Daily 8–7* Ⓜ*Les Halles; RER: Châtelet Les Halles.*

ALSO WORTH SEEING

Arc du Carrousel. When Napoléon I stole the bronze horses of St. Mark's Cathedral from Venice, he ordered this commemorative arch built: the horses were positioned on top (where Napoléon could admire them from his Louvre bedroom), and the pink marble arch was dedicated to the victories of his Grand Army. The horses were eventually returned, and replaced with a statue of a quadriga, a four-horsed chariot. Ⓜ*Palais-Royal.*

Bourse du Commerce. The circular, shallow-domed 18th-century commercial exchange building near Les Halles began life as the Corn Exchange; Victor Hugo waggishly likened it to a jockey's cap without the peak. Step inside to admire the 1889 stained-glass dome. ⊠*Rue de Viarmes, Opéra/Grands Boulevards* Ⓜ*Métro or RER: Les Halles.*

Colonne de Ruggieri. The 100-foot-tall column behind the Bourse du Commerce is all that remains of a mansion built here in 1572 for Catherine de' Medici. The column is said to have been used as a platform for stargazing by her astrologer, Ruggieri. Legend has it that his shade haunts the metal cage at the top. Ⓜ*Les Halles.*

Comédie Française. Mannered productions of Molière, Racine, and Corneille appear regularly on the bill here—enjoyable if you understand French and don't mind declamatory formal acting. This company, founded in 1680 by Louis XIV, who was more interested in controlling theater than promoting it, finally opened its doors in 1799, but it burned almost to the ground a hundred years later; what you're looking at dates from 1900. The *comedienne* Sarah Bernhardt, who performed everywhere, from palaces in St. Petersburg to tents in Texas, began her career here. ⊠*2 rue de Richelieu, Louvre/Tuileries* ☎*08–25–10–16–80* Ⓜ*Palais-Royal.*

Église de la Madeleine. With its rows of uncompromising columns, this sturdy neoclassical edifice—designed in 1814 but not consecrated until 1842—looks more like a proudly inflated version of a Greek temple than a Christian church. The resemblance is no fluke; changing political winds during the construction meant that the building was literally a Greek basilica one day, a temple to Napoléon's glory another, and a National Assembly hall the next. At one point, in fact, La Madeleine, as it is known, was nearly selected as Paris's first train station. A simpler crypt offers intimate weekday masses; classical music and organ recitals are held throughout the week, though acoustics can be muddy. ⊠*Pl. de* *la Madeleine, Faubourg* ⊕*www.eglise-lamadeleine.com* ⊙*Mon.–Sat. 7:30–7, Sun. 8–7* Ⓜ*Madeleine.*

Forum des Halles. Plans are under way to remodel Les Halles yet again, using a design by French architect David Mangin. Until construction gets going, there are two reasons to visit. First, the boutiques of up-and-coming young designers are worth a look. Second, the Forum des Images offers inexpensive screenings of rare, foreign, and historic films, often accompanied by excellent lectures (in French). But if you see a late film and are here after dark, watch your wallet.

Les Halles was Paris's legendary central food market from 1168 until 1969, though aside from the energy on Rue Montorgueil few traces of the market's rambunctious 24-hour community remain. The range of food sold here helped French cuisine to develop, and over the centuries different buildings evolved to house the food stalls. The best known, the stunning iron-and-glass halls built during the Second Empire, were tragically destroyed in the 1970s, when the wholesale market was moved out to the suburbs. ⊠*Main entrance: Rue Pierre-Lescot, Beaubourg/Les Halles* ⊕*www.forum-des-halles.com* ⊙*Mon.–Sat. 10–7:30* Ⓜ*Les Halles; RER: Châtelet Les Halles.*

Musée du Jeu de Paume. At the entrance to the Jardin des Tuileries stands this 19th-century building that was once used for jeu de paume (literally, "palm game," a forerunner of tennis) but has been given another lease on life as an ultramodern, white-walled photography showcase. The museum's holdings include some national photography archives, but the real standouts are the temporary shows. Basement rooms are dedicated to photography-themed videos and movies. ⊠ *1 pl. de la Concorde, Louvre/Tuileries* ☎ *01–47–03–12–50* ⊕*www. jeudepaume.org* ⊠ *€6* ⊙ *Tues. noon–9, Wed.–Fri. noon–7, weekends 10–7* Ⓜ *Concorde.*

Palais de l'Elysée. Madame de Pompadour, Napoléon, Joséphine, the Duke of Wellington, and Queen Victoria all stayed at this palace, today the official home of the French president. Originally built as a private mansion in 1718, the Elysée (note that when Parisians talk about "L'Elysée," they mean this, the president's palace, whereas the Champs-Elysées is known simply as "Les Champs") has housed presidents only since 1873. Unfortunately, although you can peer at the palace forecourt and façade through the Rue du Faubourg St-Honoré gateway, it's difficult to get much of an idea of the building's size, or of the extensive gardens that stretch back to the Champs-Elysées, because it's closed to the public. ⊠*55 rue du Faubourg St-Honoré, Champs-Elysées* Ⓜ*Miromesnil.*

Passage du Grand-Cerf. Built around 1835, this pretty glass-roof *passage* (gallery) was renovated in 1990, emerging as a nexus for design. A ramble through its dozen or so shops turns up everything from a Mies van der Rohe chair to a bustier made of distressed safety pins. The passage also hosts the twice-yearly Les Puces du Design, a sort of street fair, which spills out onto surrounding sidewalks as vintage-furniture dealers and up-and-coming designers show off their wares.

Continued on page 92

THE LOUVRE

Try to wrap your mind around this: The Louvre has about 35,000 pieces of art in its collection, with representations from nearly every civilization on earth, and more than 645,000 square feet of exhibition space. It's gone through countless cycles of construction and demolition, expansion and renovation, starting as a medieval fortress, then becoming a royal residence before opening its doors as the Museum Central des Arts at the end of the 18th century.

Left: Michelangelo's *Dying Slave*

Below: The Louvre's iconic Pyramide, designed by I. M. Pei.

Don't make the mistake of thinking that you'll be able to see the Louvre's entire collection in one visit and still enjoy—or remember—what you've seen. The three most popular pieces of art here are, of course, the *Mona Lisa*, the *Venus de Milo*, and *Winged Victory*. Beyond these must-sees, your best bet is to focus on highlights that interest you personally—and don't despair if you get lost, for you're bound to stumble into something fascinating. When you arrive, pick up a copy of the museum's excellent color-coded map to get your bearings. The Louvre is comprised of three wings—the Richelieu, the Sully, and the Denon—arranged like a horseshoe, with I.M. Pei's striking *Pyramide* nestled outside in the middle.

For more on touring and other general information on the Louvre ⇨ pg. 90

HISTORY OF THE LOUVRE

Evolution of the Building

1527. François I (left) expands the palace, demolishing many original buildings and rebuilding in the new Renaissance style.

1655-58. The Queen Mother, Anne of Austria, orders up private apartments and imports Italian artists to decorate it.

1672. Sun King Louis XIV moves the royal court to Versailles and the Louvre is abandoned.

1756. Louis XV (right) resumes construction. After a century, the Cour Carrée finally gets a roof.

12TH C.	13TH C.	14TH C	15TH C	16TH CENTURY	17TH CENTURY	18TH CENTURY
FORTRESS		▲		ROYAL PALACE		▲ ROYAL ARTS ACADEMY ▲

1190. Philippe Auguste builds a fortress to protect Paris..

1364. Charles V converts it into a royal palace.

Henry IV adds the Grand Gallery and begins the passage to the adjacent Tuileries Palace. Work halts upon his death in 1610.

1660. Architect Louis LeVau is hired to finish the Louvre. Erasing all medieval traces, he adds pavilions, rebuilds facades and doubles the palace's width.

1699. Royal Academy of Painting and Sculpture stages first exhibition.

1791. Revolutionary government declares the Louvre a national museum.

1793. Doors open to the public. Admission is free.

Acquisition of Art

17TH CENTURY
18TH CENTURY

Mona Lisa Leonardo da Vinci, 1503-06.

Purchased by Francois I under unknown circumstances. It later adorned Napoléon I's bedroom wall.

The Slaves Michelangelo 1513-1515.

From François I's collection. **Entered the Louvre in 1794.**

Pilgrimage to Cythera 1717, Watteau.

Acquired in 1793.

Coronation of Napoléon 1806-07, Jacques Louis David.

Commissioned by Napoléon, whose collection fell into state hands after his defeat in 1815.

Venus de Milo (Aphrodite) Late 2nd century BC.

Found on the Greek island of Milos in 1820 and purchased by the French ambassador to Turkey, who presented it to Louis XVIII. **Placed in the Louvre in 1821.**

The Raft of the Medusa 1819, Géricault.

Purchased after the artist's death, 1824.

18TH CENTURY
19TH CENTURY

1803. Renamed Musée Napoléon and stocked with booty from the emperor's many conquests.

1852. Napoléon III (right) lays the cornerstone of the New Louvre.

1939. Artwork is hidden as World War II erupts.
1940. Near-empty museum reopens.

1989, I.M. Pei's controversial glass *Pyramide* rises over the new entrance in the Cour Napoléon.
1993. Renovated Richelieu Wing reopens.

19TH CENTURY   **20TH CENTURY**   **21ST CENTURY**

NATIONAL MUSEUM

1815. Artworks plundered by **Napoléon**, returned to their native countries after his defeat.

1852-1861. Collection expands with works acquired from Egypt, Spain and Mexico. Cour Napoléon completed.

1871. Mob sets fire to Tuileries Palace. Louvre is damaged.

1945. Asian collection sent to the new Musée Guimet.

1981. President François Mitterrand (above) kicks off Grand Louvre project to expand and modernize the museum.

2000. Non-French works destined for the future Musée de Quai Branly shown at Louvre.

2009. New Islamic art wing is projected to open.

Louis XV's Coronation Crown 1793. Apollo Gallery

Acquired in 1852. Original stones replaced with paste in 1729.

The Turkish Bath Ingres, 1862.

Gift to the Louvre, 1911. Commissioned by Napoléon but deemed too shocking to display. Revealed to the public in 1905.

Gabrielle d'Estrées and One of Her Sisters Unknown artist, 1594.

Purchased in 1937. This (nipple-pinching) scene could represent sisterly teasing related to the pregnancy of Gabrielle, the favorite mistress of Henri IV.

Winged Victory of Samothrace Around 190 BC.

Discovered on the Greek island of Samothrace in 1863 by a French archaeologist who sent the pieces to be reassembled at the Louvre. Her right hand (in nearby glass case) was discovered in 1950.

Seated Scribe Around 2500 BC.

Discovered in Saqqara, Egypt in 1850. **Given to France by the Egyptian government in 1854.**

The Lacemaker Vermeer, 1669-70.

Purchased at auction in Paris, 1870.

19TH CENTURY   20TH CENTURY   20TH CENTURY   21ST CENTURY

RICHELIEU WING

COLLECTIONS

Near East Antiquities
Islamic Arts
French Painting
French Sculpture
Northern Schools
Decorative Arts

Below Ground & Ground Floor. Entering from the Pyramide, head upstairs to the sculpture courtyards, Cour Marly and Cour Puget. In Cour Marly you'll find the **Marley Horses** (see right). Salle 2 has fragments from Cluny, the powerful Romanesque abbey in Burgundy that dominated 11th-century French Catholicism. Salles 4–6 follows the evolution of French sculpture, and in Salles 7–10 you'll find funerary art. In Cour Puget, products from the Académie Royale, the art school of 18th-century France, fill Salles 25–33. Behind this is the Near East Antiquities Collection. Salle 3's centerpiece is the Codex of Hammurabi, an 18th-century BC black-diorite stela containing the world's oldest written code of laws. In Salle 4, you'll find **Lamassu** (see right).

First Floor. Head straight through Decorative Arts to see the magnificently restored **Royal Apartments of Napoléon III** (see right).

Second Floor. Much of this floor is dedicated to French and Northern School paintings. At the entrance is a 14th-century painting of John the Good—the oldest-known individual portrait from the north of Italy. In Salle 4 hangs *The Madonna of Chancellor Rolin*, by the 15th-century Early Netherlandish master Jan van Eyck (late 14th century–1441). Peter Paul Rubens's (1577–1640) the *Disembarkation of Maria de' Medici at the Port of Marseille* is in Salle 18. In Salle 31 are several paintings by Rembrandt van Rijn (1606–69). The masterpiece of the Dutch collection is Vermeer's *The Lacemaker* (see right).

Also worth noting are three private collections displayed in Salles 20–23. The terms of the legacies prevent these collections from being broken up, and they cover a stunning range of work, from Canaletto to Degas.

TIPS

■ The Passage Richelieu entrance, reserved for ticket holders, is an easy way into the museum—or out for a lunch break. (Hold onto your ticket!)

■ Enjoy a different perspective on I.M. Pei's pyramid from the terrace of Café Richelieu on the first floor.

■ Take a second-floor detour: on your way to the bathrooms near Salle 19, don't miss Salle 18 and the 25 works by Rubens ordered up by Maria de Medici for her Luxembourg Palace. (You can see Maria in all her finery in Salle 15.)

■ Café Marly, attached to the Richelieu wing but only accessible from outside, has a terrace with a gorgeous view of the *Pyramide*. The food is pricey and unremarkable, so stick to the basics.

DON'T MISS

LAMASSU, 8TH CENTURY   SALLE 4

With their fierce beards and gentle eyes, these massive winged beasts are benevolent guardians straight from the dreamworld. Magical for children and adults, the strangely lifelike sculptures are located in the Near Eastern antiquities collection. The winged bull demigods are part of the Cour Khorsabad, a re-creation of the temple erected by Assyrian king Sargon II.

Lamassu

THE LACEMAKER, 1669-1671   SALLE 38

This is a small but justifiably famous gem of Dutch optical accuracy (and a must-see for fans of the movie and book, Girl With a Pearl Earring, to see how his style evolved over a 5-year period.) Here, Jan Vermeer (1632—75) painted the red thread in the foreground as a slightly blurred jumble, just as one would actually see it if focusing on the girl. The lacemaker's industriousness represents domestic virtue, but the personal focus of the painting is far more engaging than a simple morality tale.

The Lacemaker

MARLY HORSES, 1699-1740   COUR MARLY

During the dramatic 1989 reorganization of the Louvre, two courtyards were elegantly glassed-over to match the entrance pyramid. The dramatic glass-roofed Marly sculpture court houses several sculptures from Louis XIV's garden at Marly, including two magnificent winged horses by Antoine Coysevox. Later, the artist's nephew Guillaume Coustou created two accompanying earthbound horse sculptures for Louis XV; their fame was such that, during the Revolution, these sculptures were moved to the Tuileries gardens for public viewing. Now the four original horses greet visitors to the Richelieu Wing, ready to gallop off into the museum; replicas stand guard in the Tuileries.

The Marly Horses

ROYAL APARTMENTS
OF NAPOLEON III, 1860s   SALLE 87

These dozen reception rooms, hung with crystal chandeliers, elaborate mirrors, and imperial velour, are a gilt-covered reminder that the Louvre was a palace for centuries, regally designed to impress. En route, you'll pass decorative items like the solid-crystal Restoration dressing table (Salle 77) that prepare you for the eye-popping luxury of the Second Empire.

Royal Apartments of Napoleon

SULLY WING

Below Ground & Ground Floor. The entrance into the Sully Wing is more impressive than the entrances to the others—you get to walk around and through the 13th century foundations and the **Medieval Moat** (see right). In Salle 12 you'll find **Ramses II** (see right). Salles 14 and 15 will delight mummy enthusiasts, and there are rare examples of Egyptian funerary art.

Upstairs, the northern galleries of the Sully continue the ancient Iranian collection begun in the Richelieu Wing. To the right is the Greek collection home to the famous 2nd-century **Venus de Milo** (see right).

First Floor. The northern galleries of the first floor continue with the Decorative Arts collection including works from all over Europe, and connect with the Napoléon III apartments.

Second Floor. Sully picks up French painting in the 17th century where the Richelieu leaves off. The Académiciens are best exemplified by Nicolas Poussin (1594–1665, Salle 19), who was the first international painting star to come from France. The antithesis of this style was the candlelighted modest work by outsider Georges de La Tour (Salle 28) such as in his Magdalene of Night Light.

The Académie Royale defined the standards of painting through revolution, republic, and empire. Exoticism wafted in during the Napoleonic empire, as seen in **Turkish Bath** (see right) paintings of Jean-Auguste-Dominique Ingres (1780–1867). Fresh energy crackled into French painting in the 18th century. Antoine Watteau (1684–1721), was known for his theatrical scenes and fêtes galantes, portrayals of well-dressed figures in bucolic settings. In Pilgrimage to the Island of Cythera (Salle 36), he used delicate brushstrokes and soft tones to convey the court set, here depicted arriving on (or departing from) Cythera, the mythical isle of love.

TIPS

■ Don't miss the Sleeping Hermaphrodite at the entrance to Salle 17 on the ground floor.

■ Be sure to look up as you make your way up Escalier Henri II. It took four years to complete this 16th-century vaulted ceiling.

■ Need a bathroom? There are some tucked between Salles 22 and 23 on the 1st floor. (And admire the colorful, 4,000-year-old Seated Scribe in Salle 22.)

■ For a breather, duck into this nook off Salle 49 on the 2nd floor, between the two Vernets. Sit on the bench and enjoy a view of the Cour Carrée, one of the oldest parts of the Louvre.

DON'T MISS

RAMSES II APPROX. 1200 BC   SALLE 12

The sphinx-guarded Egyptian Wing is the biggest display of Egyptian antiquities in the world after the Cairo museum—not surprising, considering that Egyptology as a Western concept was invented by a Frenchman, Champollion, founder of the Louvre's Egypt collection and translator of the hieroglyphics on the Rosetta Stone. This statue from the site of Tanis, presumed to be Ramses II, never fails to stop visitors' breath with its gleaming stone, beatific expression, and perfect proportions.

Ramses II

VENUS DE MILO, APPROX. 120 BC   SALLE 12

After countless photographs and bad reproductions, the original Aphrodite continues to fascinate those who gaze upon her. The armless statue, one of the most reproduced and recognizable works of art in the world, is actually as beautiful as they say—and worth the trouble to push past the lecturing curators and tourist groups to get a closer look at the incredible skill with which the Greeks turned cold marble into something vibrant and graceful. She was unearthed on the Greek island of Milos in the 19th century and sold for 6,000 francs to the French ambassador in Constantinople, who presented her to King Louis XVIII.

Venus de Milo

MEDIEVAL MOAT, 13TH BC   MEDIEVAL LOUVRE

Wander around the perimeter of the solidly-built original moat (no longer filled with water) to reach the remarkable Salle Saint-Louis with its elegant columns and medieval artifacts. Keep an eye out for the parade helmet of Charles VI, which was dug up in 169 fragments and astonishingly reassembled.

Medieval Moat

THE TURKISH BATH, 1862   SALLE 60

Though Jean-August-Dominique Ingres' (1780–1867) long-limbed women hardly look Turkish, they are singularly elegant and his polished immaculate style was imitated by an entire generation of French painters. This painting is a prime example of Orientalism, where Western artists played out fantasies of the Orient in their work. Popular as a society portrait painter, Ingres returned repeatedly to langorous nudes—compare the women of the *Turkish Bath* with the slinky figure in his *La Grande Odalisque,* in the Denon Wing.

The Turkish Bath

THE DENON WING

COLLECTIONS

Ancient Egypt
Greek, Roman, & Etruscan Antiquities
French Painting
Italian & Spanish Painting
Graphic Arts
Italian, Spanish, & Northern Sculpture
African, Asian, Oceanic, & American Arts

Below Ground & Ground Floor. To the south and east of the *Pyramide* entrance are galleries displaying early Renaissance Italian sculpture, including a 15th-century Madonna and Child by the Florentine Donatello (1386–1466). Before going upstairs, it's worth walking through the galleries of Etruscan and Roman works. In Salle 18 you'll find the 6th-century Etruscan Sarcophagus from Cerveteri, showing a married couple pieced together from thousands of clay fragments.

Drift upstairs to Italian sculpture on the ground level, concluding with Salle 4, where you'll find Michelangelo's Slaves (1513–15).

First Floor. Walk up the marble Escalier Daru to discover the sublime **Winged Victory of Samothrace** (see right). Then head to the Gallerie d'Apollon, reopened in 2004 after a stunning renovation. Built in 1661 but not finished until 1851, the hall was a model for Versaille's Hall of Mirrors.

Back out and into Paintings, you'll find four by Leonardo da Vinci (1452–1519). His enigmatic, androgynous St-John the Baptist hangs here, along with more overtly religious works such as the 1483 Virgin of the Rocks. Take a close look at the pretty portrait of La Belle Ferronnière, which Leonardo painted a decade before the **Mona Lisa** (see right); it will give you something to compare with Mona when you finally get to meet her in the Salle des Etats, near Salles 5 and 6. Head across to Salle 75 for an artistic 180°: the gleaming pomp and circumstance of a new empire with the **Coronation of Napoléon** (see right) by French classicist Jacques-Louis David (1748–1825).

In Salle 77 is the gruesome 1819 **The Raft of the Medusa**, (see right) by Théodore Géricault (1791–1824).

TIPS

■ Don't skip the coat check on the ground floor tucked behind the stairs. Much of the museum is hot and stuffy.

■ Need a break? Snag an outdoor table at cozy Café Denon on the lower ground floor, which has a little outdoor garden seating area.

■ For an easy escape, duck out the Porte de Lions at the end of the wing. On your way out, check out the Goyas in Salle 32 on the first floor. (But don't forget your coat!)

■ See history in the making. As you mount the stairs leading to the Winged Victory of Samothrace, look to the right and spy the museum's new Islamic arts wing taking shape. (Projected opening 2009.)

DON'T MISS

MONA LISA, 1503   SALLE 7
The most famous painting in the world, La Gioconda (*La Joconde* in French) is tougher than she looks: the canvas was stolen from the Louvre by an Italian nationalist in 1911, recovered from a Florentine hotel, and survived an acid attack in 1956. She is believed to be the wife of Francesco del Giocondo, a Florentine millionaire, was probably 24 when she sat for this painting; some historians believe the portrait was actually painted after her death. Either way, she has become immortal through da Vinci's ingenious "sfumato" technique, which combines glowing detail with soft, depth-filled brushwork.

Mona Lisa

THE RAFT OF THE MEDUSA, 1819   SALLE 77
Théodore Géricault was inspired by the grim news report that survivors of a wrecked French merchant ship were left adrift on a raft without supplies. Géricault interviewed survivors, visited the morgue to draw corpses, and turned his painting of the disaster into a strong indictment of authority, the first time an epic historical painting had taken on current events in this way. Note the desperate energy from the pyramid construction of bodies on the raft and the manipulation of greenish light.

The Raft of the Medusa

WINGED VICTORY OF SAMOTHRACE, 305 BC   STAIRS
Poised for flight at the top of the Escalier Daru, this exhilarating statue was found on a tiny Greek island in the northern Aegean. Depicted in the act of descending from Olympus, Winged Victory, or Nike, to the Ancient Greeks, was carved to commemorate the naval victory of Demetrius Poliorcetes over the Turks.

Winged Victory of Samothrace

CORONATION OF NAPOLEON, 1805   SALLE 75
Classicist Jacques-Louis David (1748–1825) was the ultimate painter-survivor: he began his career under the protection of the King, became official designer of the Revolutionary government, endured two rounds of exile, and became one of the greatest of Napoléon's painters. Here, David avoided the politically fraught moment of December 2, 1804—when Napoléon snatched the crown from the hands of Pope Pius VII to place it upon his own head—choosing instead the romantic moment when the new emperor turned to crown Joséphine.

Detail from the Coronation of Napoleon

PLANNING YOUR VISIT

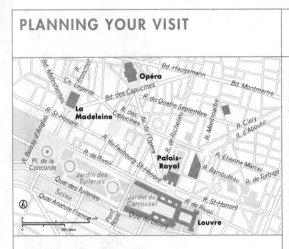

TOURS

The underground entrance to each wing has audio rentals; for €5 (with picture ID) you get information about the entire museum.

Formal Louvre guided tours are available from the front desk, which also has thematic leaflets to self-guide through a particular trail—some designed especially for kids. The Louvre has a phenomenal program of courses and workshops (mostly in French); see Web site for details.

ACCESSIBILITY

Wheelchair visitors can skip the long entry line and use the marvelous cylinder lift inside the entrance pyramid.

WITH KIDS

Begin your tour in the Sully Wing at the Medieval Moat, which leads enticingly to the sphinx-guarded entrance of the Egyptian Wing, a must for mummy enthusiasts.

For a more in-depth visit, you can reserve private kid-centric family tours such as the Paris Muse Clues (www.parismuse.com) Don't forget the Tuileries is right next door (with carnival rides in summer).

ENTRY TIPS

Those in the know head straight for the entrance in the underground mall, Carrousel du Louvre, which has automatic ticket machines. Another time-saving option is to book tickets online and have them mailed to you before you even leave home. Be sure to hold onto your ticket. You can come and go as often as you like during one day. The shortest entry lines tend to be around 1 P.M. Prices drop after 6 P.M. for the late-night Wednesday and Friday openings; crowds thin out in the evening. Remember that the Louvre is closed on Tuesday!

A WHIRLWIND TOUR

If you've come to Paris and feel you must go to the Louvre to see the Big Three—**Venus de Milo, Winged Victory,** and **Mona Lisa**—even though you'd rather be strolling along the Champs-Elysees, it can be done in an hour or less if you plan well. Start in Denon and head upstairs through Estruscan and Greek antiquities, walking down the long hall of sculptures until you see the Winged Victory in front of you. Take a right and head up the staircase through French painting to the Mona Lisa. Then go back down under the Pyramide to Richelieu to see the Venus de Milo.

✉ Palais du Louvre, Louvre/Tuileries

☎ 01-40-20-53-17 (information)

⊕ **www.louvre.fr**

🎟 €9, 6 after 6 PM Wed. and Fri., free 1st Sun. of month, under 18 (anytime), under 26 on Fri. after 6 PM; €9.50 for Napoléon Hall exhibitions

🕐 Mon., Thurs., and weekends 9–6; Wed. and Fri. 9 AM–10 PM

Ⓜ Palais-Royal

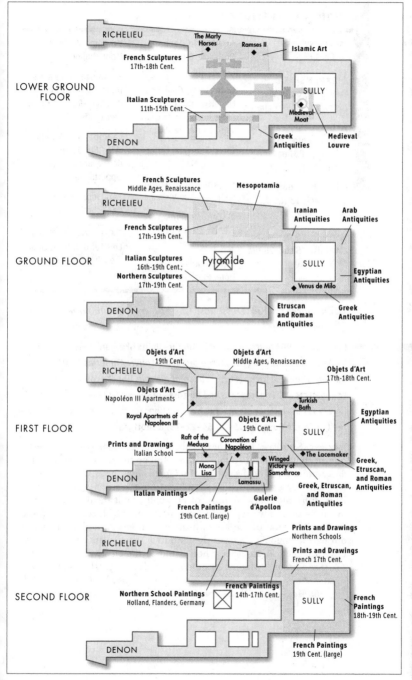

AT A GLANCE

Dining at a Glance

For full reviews
⇨ Ch. 17

INEXPENSIVE DINING

La Bourse ou la Vie, *Bistro,* 12 rue Vivienne

Le Georges, *Modern French,* Centre Pompidou, 6th fl., Rue Rambuteau

Willi's Wine Bar, *Modern French,* 13 rue des Petits-Champs

MODERATE DINING

L'Ardoise, *Bistro,* 28 rue du Mont Thabor

Au Pied de Cochon, *Brasserie,* 6 rue Coquillière

Café Marly, *Café,* Cour Napoléon du Louvre, enter from Louvre courtyard, 93 rue de Rivoli

Chez Georges, *Bistro,* 1 rue du Mail

Le Grand Colbert, *Brasserie,* 2–4 rue Vivienne

Macéo, *Modern French,* 15 rue des Petits-Champs

Pinxo, *Modern French,* Hôtel Plaza Paris

Vendôme, 4 rue du Mont Thabor

Restaurant du Palais-Royal, *Bistro,* Jardins du Palais-Royal, 110 Galerie Valois

La Robe et le Palais, *Wine Bar,* 13 rue des Lavandières-Ste-Opportuneen

Zen, *Japanese,* 8 rue de l'Echelle

EXPENSIVE DINING

Le Grand Véfour, *Haute French,* 17 rue Beaujolais

✉*Entrances on Rue Dussoubs, Rue St-Denis, Beaubourg/Les Halles* Ⓜ*Etienne Marcel.*

NEED A BREAK? Founded in 1903 and patronized by literary lights like Marcel Proust and Gertrude Stein, Angélina (✉*226 rue de Rivoli, Louvre/Tuileries* ☎*01–42–60–82–00*) is beloved for its (€6.50) *chocolat africain,* hot chocolate topped with whipped cream. The frescoes and mirrors are showing the tearoom's age, so finicky Proust might now reserve his affections for *macaron* served at Ladurée (✉*16 rue Royal* ☎*01–42–60–21–79*) a short walk away.

Tour Jean Sans Peur. If you have kids, the turret alone is worth a visit, offering a window into a murky time. Toil up the seven flights of stairs and admire the carved vaulting of sculpted vines, hops, and hawthorn, but first pick up the English pamphlet from the front desk. Jean Sans Peur (John the Fearless), duke of Burgundy, built the defensive turret in 1409—and he wasn't simply being paranoid. He'd recently arranged the assassination of the king's brother and was an ambitious player during the ongoing chaos of the Hundred Years' War. The turret was once attached to an elegant house and to the city walls, now gone. ✉*20 rue Etienne Marcel, Beaubourg/Les Halles* ☎*01–40–26–20–28* ⊕*www.tourjeansanspeur.com* 🎫*€5* 🕑*Nov.–Apr., Wed. and weekends 1:30–6; May–Sept., Wed.–Sun. 1:30–6* Ⓜ*Etienne Marcel.*

The Grands Boulevards

Shoppers along boulevard Haussmann in front of Printemps

WORD OF MOUTH

"Walk past the Paris Opera. It is really an impressive building. You can either see this after walking around Galleries Lafayette and Printemps or after wandering around Le madeleine area just walk up Blvd des Capucines to the Opera."

—richardab

GETTING ORIENTED

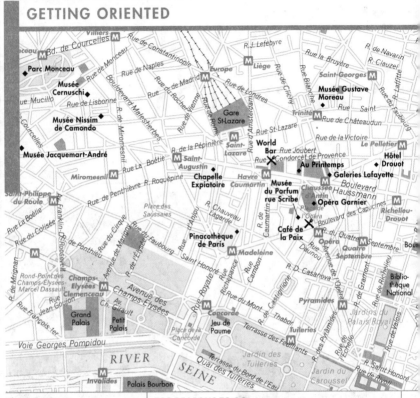

GETTING HERE

This neighborhood covers parts of the 2nd, 3rd, 8th, and 9th arrondissements. For shopping, take the métro to Chaussée d'Antin station—you'll be at Galeries Lafayette. Au Printemps is just down the street, along with all the usual chain shops. For a grander entrance, get off at Opéra station and admire Haussmann's elegant city boulevards from the steps of the opulent Opéra Garnier. This architectural showpiece is just south of the *grands magasins* (literally "big shops," or department stores), and it's a good landmark by which to orient yourself.

TOP REASONS TO GO

Opéra Garnier. Over-the-top with gilt and colorful marble inside and out—it's no wonder the Phantom haunted this building. Pause on the steps to watch the world rush by.

Parc Monceau. Join the well-dressed children of wealthy Parisians and frolic on the prettiest lawns in the city.

Musée Cernuschi. A superb Asian art collection is housed in this magical mansion just off the Parc Monceau; imagine you're a Belle Époque millionaire with impeccable taste as you stroll rooms of exquisite ceramics and artifacts.

Musée d'Arts et Métiers. The brilliant displays of flying machines, nautical instruments, and all other manner of technical achievements, from the Middle Ages to today, are a hit with all ages.

Les Grands Magasins. Be seduced by a silk cravat in Au Printemps' menswear department, drool over delicacies in Galeries Lafayette's food courts, or linger under one of the stained-glass ceilings, scenting your skin with perfume.

BEST CAFÉS

Few cafés are as grand as the **Café de la Paix**. Once described as the "center of the civilized world," it was a meeting place for the glitterati of the Belle Époque. These days few Parisians eat here and prices are steep, but the view is still beyond compare. ⊠ *5 pl. de l'Opéra, Opéra/Grands Boulevards* ☎ *01-40-07-30—10.*

When your shopping feet can take no more, put down your parcels at the **World Bar,** on the fifth floor of the men's department of Au Printemps. Enjoy superb coffee (or lunch), relax, and gaze out at the rooftops. With international newspapers available for patrons, this is a good place to park nonshoppers. ⊠ *At Rue de Caumartin and Rue de Provence, behind main Au Printemps Bldg., Opéra/Grands Boulevards* ☎ *01-42-82-78-02.*

To join the latest generation of trendy *flaneurs* (wanderers), take a break opposite the Rex Cinema, at **De la Ville Café**. Look for the Belle Époque details—this was once a high-end bordello—but choose a seat facing the boulevard, so you can watch the passersby. ⊠ *34 bd. Bonne Nouvelle, Opéra/Grands Boulevards* ☎ *01-48-24-48-09.*

MAKING THE MOST OF YOUR TIME

This neighborhood is perfect for a long afternoon's visit: spend an hour or two in one of the museums near Parc Monceau (in the heart of one of the most exclusive residential neighborhoods), wander over to the shops, then finish with an evening at the opera or a cocktail at a sidewalk café—in the past few years, the boulevards have once again come into their own for people-watching. The neighborhood is focused around the main avenue that runs west to east from Parc Monceau to Place de la République (whose very name symbolizes the downfall of the imperial regime). Be forewarned: the name of the avenue changes six times along its way (it is, variously, Boulevard Monceau, Haussmann, des Capucines, etc.), which is why Parisians refer to it, in the plural, as "Les Grands Boulevards."

Sightseeing
★★★

Dining
★★★

Lodging
★★★★★

Shopping
★★★★★

Nightlife
★★★★★

Famously immortalized in the canvases of Monet, Renoir, and Camille Pissarro, the Grands Boulevards are the long chain of avenues that join the Parc Monceau to the Opéra and continue all the way to Place de la République and Bastille. From the mid-18th century through the Belle Époque, the Grands Boulevards hummed with activity, as theaters, cafés, music halls, and *passages* (glass-roofed, gaslighted shopping arcades) appeared. Although the east end of the avenues (toward République) has always been slightly seedy, the area around the Opéra continues to attract glamorous French shoppers, serious theatergoers, and "see-and-be-seen" barflies.

Updated by
Lisa Pasold

The area is best known for the extravagant **Opéra Garnier** opera house, showpiece of the Second Empire and named for its architect Garnier—its multicolor marbles and gilt are visible all the way from the Louvre—and for the renowned French department stores **Au Printemps** and **Galeries Lafayette.** The streets around the department stores are crammed with chain shops and specialty clothing boutiques. Crowded at Christmas, this area is also chaotic (but fun) during the state-controlled *soldes* (sales) period in January and early February—prices go down percentage by percentage the longer the sale lasts, driving Parisians into a frenzy.

The Grands Boulevards aren't only about commerce, though: the neighborhood also encompasses the superb Parc Monceau and a variety of small but spectacular museums, all originally private collections—from the exquisite Asian arts of the **Musée Cernuschi** to the 18th-century elegance of the **Musée Nissim de Camondo.** A visit to the area isn't really complete without a stroll in the refreshingly lush **Parc Monceau**—the heart of a posh residential area once called home by the

Street scene in the Quartier Latin.

(top left) The Pompidou Center. (top right) A detail of the facade of Notre-Dame Cathedral.
(bottom) Postcards for sale, against the backdrop of Notre-Dame.

(top) At the Marché d'Aligre. (bottom) I.M. Pei's glass pyramid in front of the Louvre.

(top left) The Musée Rodin. (top right) The Tour Eiffel. (bottom) Jardin des Tuileries.

The Seine River at dusk.

(top) A modern-art exhibition at the Pompidou Center. (bottom left) Inside Sainte-Chapelle. (bottom right) Pastries at Ladurée, the 19th-century tearoom.

(top) Inside the Musée d'Orsay. (bottom) The Bateau Lavoir, where Picasso once had his studio.

Sacré-Coeur.

likes of "the Divine" Sarah Bernhardt, actress and *monstre sacrée* of the Belle Époque.

Just below the triumphal arches of **Porte St-Denis** and **Porte St-Martin** is the easily missed Rue Blondel: it's here, at No. 32, that you can find the red tiles of a former brothel once patronized by literary voyeurs Henry Miller and Anaïs Nin. (Be aware that Rue Blondel continues to attract ladies of the night of varying genders and their clientele.)

MAIN ATTRACTIONS

Au Printemps. The Belle Époque green-and-gold domes of this vast department store have been luring shoppers for more than a century. Founded in 1865 by Jules Jaluzot, a former employee of Au Bon Marché (nothing like giving one's old boss some new competition), Au Printemps was the inspiration for Emile Zola's novel *Au Bonheur des Dames*. The top floor café has splendid views. ⊠*64 bd. Haussmann,* ☎*01–42–82–50–00 Opéra/Grands Boulevards* Ⓜ*Havre Caumartin.*

Galeries Lafayette. This turn-of-the-20th-century department store has a vast glass-dome roof that can be seen only if you venture inside to the perfume counters—it's worth a look even for perfume haters. The food hall next door (upstairs from menswear) is guaranteed to make even the fussiest eaters drool. ⊠*40 bd. Haussmann, Opéra/Grands Boulevards* ☎*01–42–82–30–25* Ⓜ*Chaussée d'Antin; RER: Auber.*

OFF THE BEATEN PATH

Musée Gustave Moreau. A visit to this town house and studio of painter Gustave Moreau (1826–98), high priest of the Symbolist movement, is one of the most distinctive artistic experiences in Paris. The Symbolists strove to convey ideas through images, but many of the ideas Moreau was trying to express were so obscure that the artist had to provide explanatory texts, which rather confuses the point. It's easy to admire his extravagant colors and flights of fantasy, though, influenced by Persian and Indian miniatures. The museum tour (in French only) includes the artist's studio, some personal ephemera, and a significant collection of his drawings, paintings, watercolors, and sculptures. From Galeries Lafayette (or the Chaussée D'Antin métro stop), follow Rue de la Chaussée d'Antin up to the Trinité church, turn right on Rue St-Lazare and left on Rue de la Rochefoucald. The museum is a block up on the right. ⊠*14 rue de la Rochefoucald, Opéra/Grands Boulevards* ☎*01–48–74–38–50* ⊕*www.musee-moreau.fr* ☑*€5* ۞ *Wed.–Mon. 10–12:45 and 2–5:15* Ⓜ*Trinité.*

Fodor's Choice ★

Musée des Arts et Métiers *(National Technical Museum).* Prepare to be astounded. This museum of scientific instruments and inventions is a treasure trove, where 16th-century astrolabes share shelf space with jeweled celestial spheres, and models of locomotives give way to Edison's early phonographs and early film-camera prototypes from the Frères Lumière. The building was originally the medieval church and priory of St-Martin des Champs, built between the 11th and 13th century. Confiscated during the Revolution, it was used first as an educational institution, then as an arms factory, before becoming, in 1799,

Continued on page 103

C'EST *SUPER* CHIC:
HOW NOT TO LOOK LIKE AN AMERICAN IN PARIS

It's hard to imagine a trip to Paris that doesn't include, at the very least, an afternoon of shopping. But the question is what to wear *while* you're shopping—and sightseeing, and eating at a café—as high fashion reigns supreme in the City of Light.

No matter where you live or what your style, from the moment you step off the plane you'll obsess over how to achieve the relaxed, elegant way Parisian women dress. You'll marvel at how they casually toss a scarf around their neck and have it look amazing, or how they can make a 15-year-old cashmere cardigan fresh with a skinny belt. Suddenly, virtually all the clothes in your suitcase may feel outdated, frumpy, and wrong.

But fret not, *ma chère amie*. You're not destined to walk around Paris feeling less-than. We've given you a fail-safe guide that promises to keep you looking fabulous as you stroll down the Champs-Elysées or around the Marais. But we can't promise that once you hit the streets of this fashion-obsessed city, that your credit card won't max out faster than you can say *oh la la*.

LA JEUNE FEMME

She's that young wisp of a thing standing on rue Oberkampf, chatting with her friends, cigarette in-hand, looking as if she's had less than her eight hours—and whatever she has on, she wears it well.

Denim mini

Repetto ballet flats

L'Autre Cafe, Oberkampf

Audrey Tautou

Antoine & Lili

Vanessa Bruno tote

Converse high top

INSPIRATION: Audrey Tautou

BEST ACCESSORY: The huge, costume cocktail ring you found at the bar last night.

FAVORITE PARTS OF TOWN: Canal St-Martin, Oberkampf, the Bastille.

BIGGEST SPLURGE: Are those 200 euro jeans from Colette really considered a splurge when you wear them every day?

CHIC BOUTIQUE: Thank goodness the designers have secondary lines! Now you'll only spend one paycheck at Paul & Joe Sister.

CHAIN STORE KNOCKOFF: Never underestimate the genius that is H&M.

FAVORITE PICK ME UP: A croque madame and side of *frites*.

MODE OF TRANSPORT: Get thee a boyfriend with a Vespa! Otherwise, it's the métro for you.

WON'T LEAVE THE HOUSE WITHOUT: Your trendy new cell phone.

MUST-HAVE ITEM: Nearly-destroyed high-top Converse. Hands down.

LA DAME ELEGANTE

How's she so stunning at the Sunday market, children in tow, no make-up, hair up in a knot? Easy—she's meticulous about skincare, has in-laws with a house in the south, and is carrying the latest bag from Lamarthe.

Cartier necklace

agnès b.

Longines watch

Lamarthe bag

Café L'Etoile Manquante

Cacharel perfume

Juliette Binoche

INSPIRATION: Juliette Binoche

BEST ACCESSORY: The 400 euro cashmere Chanel sweater you just scored from that fabulous consignment shop on rue St-Honoré. It retailed for more than double the price!

FAVORITE PARTS OF TOWN: The Marais, Rive Gauche.

BIGGEST SPLURGE: It's hard to resist those new platform sandals from Dior.

CHIC BOUTIQUE: You can't get enough of Chloé, but you'll settle for anything from Vanessa Bruno.

CHAIN STORE KNOCKOFF: How is it that you ever survived without agnès b.?

FAVORITE PICK ME UP: Lentil and poached egg salad and sparkling water.

MODE OF TRANSPORT: You take the métro, but chances are you have an Audi that'll get you and the kids out of town.

WON'T LEAVE THE HOUSE WITHOUT: The scarf your grandmother bought you for Christmas.

MUST-HAVE ITEM: Every elegant woman needs a trench coat.

LA GRANDE DAME

You can't miss her walking down the Champs-Elysées — she's still turning heads, with her Chanel suit, Hermès scarf, and her near-perfect posture. Something to aspire to...

Cartier earrings

Les Ambassadeurs, Place de la Concorde

Roger Vivier flats

Catherine Deneuve

Place Vendome Square

Cartier tank watch

INSPIRATION: Catherine Deneuve

BEST ACCESSORY: Your favorite companions: your two french poodles.

FAVORITE PARTS OF TOWN: The Faubourg St-Honoré and the Grand Boulevards to name a few...but definitely not the Rive Gauche.

BIGGEST SPLURGE: Does it really have to be just one? If so, a private jet will do.

CHIC BOUTIQUE: Only the standards—that's Chanel and Hermès, darling...

CHAIN STORE KNOCKOFF: What's a knockoff?

FAVORITE PICK ME UP: Foie gras or steak tartare...plus champagne.

MODE OF TRANSPORT: Having a driver is really the only way to get around with all those shopping bags.

WON'T LEAVE THE HOUSE WITHOUT: Your Chanel No. 5.

MUST-HAVE ITEM: A Kelly bag, of course!

SCARF—TYING 101

THE FRENCH KNOT
Wrap around once so both ends are behind your neck; bring ends forward and tie double-knot to the side, under chin.

THE NECK WRAP
With a square scarf, make a triangle. Bring to neck with point facing downward; wrap long ends around back and bring forward; tie loose double-knot, just off-center.

THE SQUARE KNOT
Tie around neck with ends in front. Alternate wrapping ends up and through neck loop until they reach the back. Tie end tips and tuck in knot.

DO'S & DON'TS OF DRESSING IN PARIS

■ When in doubt, DO wear black.

■ DON'T overdo jewelry. A minimalist look is better.

■ For those on the smaller side, DO go braless—they're decidedly optional.

■ DON'T get a french manicure (the French don't!). Your best bet is to keep nails short with clear polish.

■ DO wear your glasses if they're funky and colorful. Bonus for not having to schlep solution on the plane!

■ If you visit in summer, DON'T dress like you're going to camp.

■ DO bring a scarf or two. You'll look instantly chic with one wrapped loosely around your neck.

■ DON'T match your shoes to your bag—or spend time worrying about matching too much at all.

■ DO carry a backpack—but only if it's small, sleek, and doesn't say college student.

■ DO rock your best t-shirt and a pair of Chucks with just about anything—even a skirt!

home to its blossoming collection. All displays have information in English. ⊠*60 rue Réaumur, Opéra/Grands Boulevards* ☎*01–53–01–82–00* ⊕*www.arts-et-metiers.net* ⊠*€6.50* ⊗*Tues., Wed., and Fri.–Sun. 10–6, Thurs. 10–9:30* Ⓜ*Arts et Métiers.*

NEED A BREAK?

A tiny Chinatown exists around Rue au Maire near Arts et Métiers. Chinese and Vietnamese restaurants are everywhere; most are unremarkable, but you can slurp delicious *phô* (beef noodle soup) at tiny Shun Da (⊠*16 rue Volta/Grands Boulevards* ☎*01–42–72–71–11*), a five-table Vietnamese restaurant in a 14th-century timbered building on Rue Volta. Stroll through this tiny *quartier* for its lively vibe and crooked medieval buildings.

Musée Cernuschi. Italian banker Enrico Cernuschi came to Paris for his Republican democratic ideals, only to be arrested during the 1871 Paris Commune; he subsequently decided to wait out the unrest of the Commune by traveling the world—and collecting Asian art. On his return, he had a special mansion built to house his treasures, including a two-story bronze Buddha from Japan. Cernuschi loved bronze, but he also had a stunning eye for everything from Neolithic pottery (3rd millennium BC) to funeral statuary, painted 8th-century silks, and contemporary paintings. ⊠*7 av. Velasquez, Parc Monceau* ☎*01–53–96–21–50* ⊕*www.paris.fr/musees/* ⊠*Free* ⊗*Tues.–Sun. 10–6* Ⓜ*Monceau.*

★ **Musée Jacquemart-André.** Often compared to New York City's Frick Collection, this was one of the grandest private residences of 19th-century Paris. Built between 1869 and 1875, it became a showcase for the art collections of its owners, Edouard André and his wife, Nélie Jacquemart. The couple felt little connection to their contemporary art scene and instead sought out Italian Renaissance masterpieces. During repeated trips to Italy they amassed outstanding Venetian and Florentine paintings; these were supplemented by choice 18th-century French portraits and a few Rembrandts. The Jacquemart-Andrés always intended to make their home a museum, and one of the distinctive pleasures of a visit here is the balance between great art and intimate setting. While walking through (free English-language audioguides are available), you'll be able to see the private rooms as well as the grand formal spaces. Tiepolo frescoes waft up a stunning double staircase and across the dining-room ceiling. In the salons, done in the Louis XVI–Empress style, you'll find Uccello's *Saint George Slaying the Dragon*, Rembrandt's *Pilgrims of Emmaus*, and Jacques-Louis David's *Comte Antoine-Français de Nantes*. ■TIP➔The Jacquemart's former dining room, with its Tiepolo ceiling, now contains a café, where you can lunch on salads named after some of the painters you've seen upstairs. The terrace is open in nice

6

DID YOU KNOW?

Around the corner from the Musée Jacquemart-André, at No. 45 rue de Courcelles, is the former apartment of French writer Marcel Proust, whose epic *Remembrance of Things Past* was reputedly inspired by the smell of a madeleine cookie. You can buy your own delicious madeleines at Fauchon's behind Place de la Madeleine (although the name has nothing to do with the cookie).

weather. ✉ *158 bd. Haussmann, Parc Monceau* ☎ *01–45–62–11–59* ⊕ *www.musee-jacquemart-andre.com/jandre/* 🖼️ *€9.50* 🕙 *Daily 10–6* Ⓜ️ *St-Philippe-du-Roule or Miromesnil.*

Fodor's Choice
★

Opéra Garnier. Haunt of the Phantom of the Opera, the real-life setting for some of Edgar Degas's famous ballet paintings, and still the most opulent theater in the world, the Paris Opéra building was begun in 1862 by Charles Garnier at the behest of Napoléon III. Expenses slowed the work, and it wasn't finished until 1875, five years after the emperor's abdication. Awash with Algerian colored marbles and gilded putti, the building is the ultimate Second Empire statement: a hodgepodge of styles with as much subtlety as a Wagnerian cymbal crash.

To see the theater and lobby, you don't have to attend a performance: after paying the €7 entry fee, you can view the Grand Foyer, which is almost as big as the auditorium itself: together they fill 3 acres. This was a theater for Parisians who came to the opera primarily to be seen; on opening nights you can still see Rothschilds and rock stars preen on the grand staircase. If the crimson-and-gilt auditorium seems small, it's because the stage is so enormous—more than 11,000 square yards, with room for up to 450 performers. Illuminated by a giant chandelier, the fluid pastel figures of Marc Chagall's 1964 ceiling painting might seem incongruous. This addition was part of André Malraux's scheme to mesh contemporary art with French tradition. Today the Opéra is the home of the Paris Ballet. (One or two operas per season are presented here; the rest are performed at the Opéra de la Bastille.) A small, nondescript on-site museum contains a few paintings and theatrical mementos. ■**TIP➔Guided tours are a bit dry, focusing on the building's history and architecture, and don't offer much of a glimpse into the current backstage world, but the building is so fantastic it's worth it.** ✉ *Pl. de l'Opéra, Opéra/Grands Boulevards* ☎ *08–92–89–90–90* ⊕ *www.opera-de-paris.fr* 🖼️ *€12 for guided visit; €8 for solo visit* 🕙 *Daily 10–4:30* Ⓜ️ *Opéra.*

> ### DID YOU KNOW?
>
> The inspiration for the mysterious lake underneath the Opéra Garnier in *The Phantom of the Opera* came about because construction of the gorgeous building was delayed while the marshy site was pumped out (Paris is naturally swampy and has several natural springs). Rumors began to circulate that an underground river ran below the Opéra, far below the elegant dressing rooms, and from there, it was only a small leap for Gaston Leroux to invent the original Phantom, sailing on a creepy underground waterway.

★ ☺ **Parc Monceau.** This exquisitely landscaped park began in 1778 as the Duc de Chartres's private garden. Though some of the parkland was sold off under the Second Empire (creating the exclusive real estate that now borders the park), the refined atmosphere and some of the fanciful faux-ruins have survived. Immaculately dressed children play, watched by their nannies, while lovers picnic on the grassy lawns. In 1797 André Garnerin, the world's first-recorded parachutist, staged a landing in the park. The rotunda—known as the Chartres Pavilion—is surely the city's grandest public restroom; it started life as a tollhouse. ✉*Entrances on Bd. de Courcelles, Av. Velasquez, Av. Ruysdaël, Av. van Dyck, Parc Monceau* Ⓜ*Monceau.*

NEED A BREAK?

Opened by superchef Alain Ducasse and renowned baker Eric Kayser, Be (✉*73 bd. de Courcelles, Parc Monceau* ☎*01–46–22–20–20), a boulange-rie-épicerie,* **is a hybrid bakery and corner store stocked with gastronomic grocery items like candied tomatoes and walnut oil from the Dordogne. You can pick up a superlative sandwich to eat in nearby Parc Monceau or, if the weather's not cooperating, grab a seat in the back and order soup.**

ALSO WORTH SEEING

Chapelle Expiatoire. Built in 1815, this small temple marks the original burial site of Louis XVI and Marie-Antoinette. After the deposed monarchs took their turns at the guillotine on Place de la Concorde, their bodies were taken to a nearby mass grave. A loyalist marked their place, and their remains were eventually retrieved by Louis XVI's brother, Louis XVIII, who then ordered the monument. The neoclassical mausoleum now emerges defiantly from the lush undergrowth of Square Louis-XVI off Boulevard Haussmann. Two stone tablets are inscribed with the last missives of the doomed royals, including touching pleas to God to forgive their Revolutionary enemies. This surprisingly subtle and moving tribute is in sharp contrast to Napoléon's splashy memorial at Les Invalides. ✉*29 rue Pasquier, Opéra/Grands Boulevards* ☎*01–44–32–18–00* 🎫*€2.50* 🕐*Thurs.–Sat. 1–5* Ⓜ*St-Augustin.*

Hôtel Drouot. Hidden away in a grid of narrow streets not far from the Opéra is Paris's central auction house, selling everything from stamps and toy soldiers to Renoirs and Art Nouveau commodes. You can walk in off the street and browse through the open salesrooms—there's no obligation to bid. The mix of ladies in fur coats with money to burn, penniless art lovers desperate to unearth an unidentified masterpiece, and scruffy dealers trying to look anonymous makes up Drouot's unusually rich social fabric. Anyone can attend the sales and viewings. For centuries the French government refused to allow foreign firms to stage auctions, but that changed in 2001, and Drouot faces stiff competition from Sotheby's and Christie's, who are now established in Paris. ✉*9 rue Drouot, Opéra/Grands Boulevards* ☎*01–48–00–20–00* ⊕*www.gazette-drouot.com* 🕐*Viewings mid-Sept.–mid-July, Mon.–Sat. 11– noon and 2–6, with auctions starting at 2* Ⓜ*Richelieu Drouot.*

🕐 **Musée Grévin.** Founded in 1882, this waxworks museum in the passage Jouffroy ranks in scope and ingenuity with Madame Tussaud's in London. The grotto-like entrance leads up to an Opéra-inspired staircase into the Palais des Mirages, a small mirrored *salon* from the 1900 Paris Exposition. After this classy beginning, wax takes center stage with renderings of 250 historic and contemporary celebrities, from Charlemagne and Jean-Paul Marat to Ernest Hemingway, and a huge assortment of French pop singers. ✉*10 bd. Montmartre, Opéra/Grands Boulevards* ☎*01–47–70–85–05* ⊕*www.grevin.com* 🎫*€18.50* 🕐*Daily 10–6:30* Ⓜ*Grands Boulevards.*

Spas for Paris Pampering

After an afternoon of shopping along the Grands Boulevards, nothing can revive you quite like spending time at a Parisian spa. A few can be found right inside department stores, but walking through the streets of the city you'll notice an *institut de beauté* on just about every corner. Many Parisians consider a massage or a stint in a sauna to be as healthful as a work-out—and French women have ritualized steaming, polishing, and plucking since Marie-Antoinette took milk baths. You don't have to spend all day (and more than your plane ticket) being royally pampered; make like a local and devote an hour or two to your *bien-être* (well-being). Reserve at least a month in advance, two months for a weekend appointment. Tax and service charges are generally included in listed prices, but you may tip extra for outstanding service.

The Zen **Cinq Mondes** (⊠ *6 sq. de l'Opera Louis Jouvet, 9ᵉ, Opéra/Grands Boulevards* ☎ *01–42–66–00–60* ⊕ *www.cinqmondes.com* Ⓜ *Opéra*) blends techniques from five ancient schools. The "urban ritual" includes a ceremonial Japanese bath in a cedar tub afloat with rose petals and essential oils. Treatments start at €48.

At **Labullekenzo** (⊠ *1 rue du Pont Neuf, 1ᵉʳ, Louvre/Tuileries* ☎ *01–73–04–20–04* ⊕ *www.labullekenzo.com* Ⓜ *Pont Neuf*), choose from a series of New-Age-meets-space-age massages from their "tactile experience

menu"—choices include the "sensitive caresses from head to waist" massage. You guessed it, this is Paris's hippest spa, featuring Kenzo's four lines of Kenzoki beauty products. The ambience and design alone almost make it worth a visit.

Nickel (⊠ *48 rue des Francs-Bourgeois, 4ᵉ, Le Marais* ☎ *01–42–77–41–10* ⊕ *www.nickel.fr* Ⓜ *St-Paul*) specializes in treatments for men. Get the hands of a croupier with a manicure for €14, or a one-hour love-handle liquidation for €60.

Spa Nuxe (⊠ *32 rue Montorgueil, 1ᵉʳ, Beaubourg/Les Halles* ☎ *01–55–80–71–40–10* ⊕ *www.nuxe.com* Ⓜ *Les Halles*) is the hip spa by the creators of the Nuxe line of skin-care products. The ancient cellar with its arched corridors, exposed cream stone, and hush-hush atmosphere is smack in the middle of one of the busiest areas in Paris. Try the *rêve de miel* (honey dream), a spectacular, nourishing 1½-hour body treatment, for €140.

Mediterranean-style **Villa Thalgo** (⊠ *218–220 rue du Faubourg St-Honoré, 8ᵉ, Champs-Elysées* ☎ *01–45–62–00–20* ⊕ *www.thalgo.com* Ⓜ *Charles-de-Gaulle–Etoile*) has massages and a heated swimming pool that uses ozone instead of chlorine. Facials and body packs filled with trace sea minerals promote rejuvenation (note: closed three weeks in August).

Musée Nissim de Camondo. Molière made fun of the *bourgeois gentil-homme,* the middle-class man who aspired to the class of his royal betters, but the playwright would have been in awe of Comte Moïse de Camondo, whose sense of style, grace, and refinement could have taught the courtiers at Versailles a thing or two. After making a fortune in the late 19th century, the businessman built this grand *hôtel particulier* (mansion) in the style of the Petit Trianon and proceeded to furnish it with some of the most exquisite furniture, boiseries (wainscoting), and bibelots of the mid- to late 18th century. But the promising family tragically unraveled: the wife ran off and the son, Nissim, was killed in World War I. Upon Moïse's death in 1935, the house and its contents were left to the state as a museum named for the lost son. A few years later the daughter and her family were deported and murdered in Auschwitz. Today the house remains an impeccable tribute to its founder's life, from the gleaming salons to the refined private rooms, including the 1912 state-of-the-art kitchen. You can even see the condolence letter written by Marcel Proust, a family friend, after Nissim's death. There are background materials available in English. ■**TIP→if you understand French, don't miss the fascinating video on the second floor.** ⊠ *63 rue de Monceau, Parc Monceau* ☏ *01–53–89–06–50* ⊕ *www. ucad.fr* ☏ *€6* ☉ *Wed.–Sun. 10–5:30* Ⓜ *Villiers.*

Passage Jouffroy. Built in 1846, as its giant clock will tell you, this covered arcade contains everything from the waxworks at the **Musée Grévin** to funky shops and cafés. Such passageways were the favorite haunt of 19th-century dandies like the bohemian poet Gérard de Nerval, who strolled here in top hat and tails with a large lobster on a pink-ribbon leash. Cross Boulevard Montmartre to connect with the Passage des Panoramas, famous for its 1817 panoramic scenes (now gone); for a bit of time-warp shopping, stop at Stern engravers, which has been here since the passage opened. ⊠ *Entrances on Bd. Montmartre, Rue de la Grange-Batelière, Opéra/Grands Boulevards* Ⓜ *Richelieu Drouot.*

Pinacothèque de Paris. The latest incarnation of Marc Restellini's vision for a private museum in Paris is off Place de la Madeleine. Many have been skeptical about the need for another museum in a city already packed with world-class destinations. The Pinacothèque is dedicated solely to temporary exhibitions; the recent Chaïm Soutine exhibit was excellent and is to be followed by a show of Man Ray work and a traveling exhibit of several terra-cotta army figures from China. Be wary of the overactive security guards—don't try to take photographs in here! ⊠ *28 pl. de la Madeleine, Opéra* ☏ *01–53–96–21–50* ⊕ *www.paris. fr/musees/* ☏ *€9* ☉ *Daily 10:30–6, Christmas Day and New Year's Day 2–6* Ⓜ *Madeleine.*

Porte St-Denis. Not as grandiose as the Arc de Triomphe, but triumphant nonetheless, Paris's second-largest arch (76 feet) was erected by François Blondel in 1672 to celebrate the victories of Ludovico Magno (as Louis XIV is here styled) on the Rhine. The bas-reliefs by François Girardon include campaign scenes and trophies stacked on shallow pyramids. The arch faces Rue St-Denis, formerly the royal processional route into Paris from the north. Last used as such a route by Queen Victoria in 1855, it's now known primarily for its sidewalk queens of the night. ⊠ *Bd. St-Denis, Opéra/Grands Boulevards* Ⓜ *Strasbourg St-Denis.*

Porte St-Martin. This 56-foot triumphal arch, slightly smaller and younger than the neighboring Porte St-Denis, was designed in 1674. Louis XIV's

Dining at a Glance

For full reviews
⇨ Ch. 17

INEXPENSIVE DINING
Chartier, *Bistro,* 7 rue du Faubourg-Montmartre

Chez Casimir, *Bistro,* 6 rue de Belzunce

La Ferme Opéra, *Café,* 55–57 rue St-Roch

Goupil le Bistro, *Bistro,* 4 rue Claude Debussy

Higuma, *Japanese,* 32 and 32 bis, rue Ste-Anne

Julien, *Brasserie,* 16 rue du Faubourg St-Denis

Le Vaudeville, *Brasserie,* 29 rue Vivienne

MODERATE DINING
Aux Lyonnais, *Bistro,* 32 rue St-Marc

Drouant, *Modern French,* 16–18 pl. Gaillon

Racine, *Wine Bar,* 8 passage des Panoramas

EXPENSIVE DINING
Senderens, *Haute French,* 9 pl. de la Madeleine

---

victories at Limburg (in Flanders) and Besançon in Franche-Comté get bas-relief coverage from Martin Desjardins. ⊠*Bd. St-Denis, Opéra/ Grands Boulevards* Ⓜ*Strasbourg St-Denis.*

Musée du Parfum rue Scribe. The famous parfumier Fragonard runs this interesting small museum dedicated to the art of perfume and housed in a 19th-century mansion. The focus is on decorative objects associated with perfume—not only crystal bottles but also gloves and other bibelots. This is essential sniffing for perfume connoisseurs (and of course there's a shop in case you feel inspired to purchase). ⊠*9 rue Scribe, Opéra* ☎*01–47–42–04–56* ⊕*www.fragonard.com* ✉*Free* ☉*Mar. 15–Oct. 15 and Dec. 15–Jan. 15, Mon.–Sat. 9–6, Sun. 9:30–4* Ⓜ*Madeleine.*

Montmartre

Dancers of the Moulin Rouge cabaret

WORD OF MOUTH

"If you like to walk, you can easily walk from the Gare du Nord to Sacré-Coeur and the seedy (but fun) area of the Moulin Rouge. I stayed in a little hotel near the Gare du Nord, and I had 48 hours in Paris one Thanksgiving weekend that I will never forget."

—Magellan 5

GETTING ORIENTED

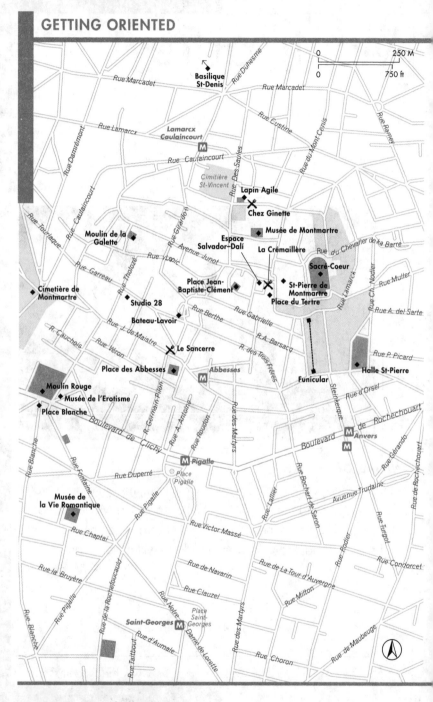

Rue Marcadet

Rue Duhesme

Basilique
St-Denis

Rue Marcadet

0   250 M

0   750 ft

Rue Lamarcx

Rue Custine

Rue Dammémont

Rue Caulaincourt

Lamarcx
Caulaincourt

Ⓜ

Rue Caulaincourt

Rue du Mont-Cenis

Rue Ramey

Cimitière
St-Vincent

Rue Des Saules

Lapin Agile

Chez Ginette

Rue Tourtaque

Rue Caulaincourt

Musée de Montmartre

Rue Girardon

Moulin de la
Galette

Avenue Junot

Rue Vécrc

Rue Tholozó

Espace
Salvador–Dalí

La Crémaillère

Rue du Chevalier de la Barre

Sacré-Coeur

Rue Ch. Nodier

Rue Muller

Rue Garreau

Place Jean-
Baptiste-Clément

St-Pierre de
Montmartre

Rue Lamarck

Rue A. del Sarte

Cimetière de
Montmartre

Studio 28

Place du Tertre

Bateau-Lavoir

Rue Berthe

Rue Gabrielle

R. Cauchois

Rue J. de Maistre

R.A.-Barsacq

Rue Véron

Le Sancerre

R. des Trois Frères

Rue P. Picard

Place des Abbesses

Abbesses

Ⓜ

Halle St-Pierre

Moulin Rouge

Rue Germain-Pilon

Rue A.-Antoine

Rue Roudon

Rue des Martyrs

Funicular

Steinkerque

Rue d'Orsel

Musée de l'Erotisme

Place Blanche

Boulevard   de   Clichy

Boulevard   de   Rochechouart

Ⓜ

Anvers

Rue Blanche

Rue Fontaine

Ⓜ   Pigalle

Place
Pigalle

Rue Duperré

Rue Ch. de Séron

Rue Lallier

Ⓜ

Rue Gérando

Rue de Rochechouart

Musée de
la Vie Romantique

Rue Pigalle

Avenue Trudaine

Rue Chaptal

Rue Victor Massé

Rue Rodier

Rue Turgot

Rue Condorcet

Rue la Bruyère

Rue de Navarin

Rue de La Tour d'Auvergne

Rue Milton

Rue Pigalle

Rue de la Rochefoucauld

Rue Clauzel

Rue Blanche

Rue Taitbout

Saint-Georges   Ⓜ

Place
Saint-
Georges

Rue Notre Dame de Lorette

Rue d'Aumale

Rue des Martyrs

Rue Choron

Rue de Maubeuge

TOP REASONS TO GO

Bateau-Lavoir. The original artist ateliers burned down, but if you go around the corner to Rue Orchampt, you can find some of the old atmosphere lingering in the twisting street's quirky studio apartments and lonesome mansion (which once belonged to French torch singer Dalida).

Carré Roland Dorgelès. Overlooking the historic Montmartre vineyard, this tiny square is tucked just across from the famous cabaret Lapin Agile. With three small benches, the elevated square is perfect for a picnic or a photo op. Just beyond the ivy-covered stone wall is the atmospheric Cimetière St-Vincent, where the painter Utrillo is buried.

Lapin Agile. Montmartre became a magnet for writers and artists at the turn of the 20th century, and this bar-cabaret is where they gathered. More than 150 years later, it has still managed to preserve a piece of its nostalgic past.

Sacré-Coeur. You haven't really seen Paris until you've viewed it from these famous steps high above the city—especially at twilight when the city lights spread out in a magnificent panorama below the hill of Montmartre.

MAKING THE MOST OF YOUR TIME

If you're pressed for time, take the funicular straight up to Sacré-Coeur; after your visit, walk down the steps to the métro. If you have a bit more time, start your visit at the métro station Abbesses and from here, explore the cobblestone alleyways and narrow staircases nearby to discover the "real" Montmartre, as you make your way to Sacré-Coeur. Be warned that this is a neighborhood that suffers from crowds every day of the week and especially on weekends, so keep your eye out for quiet streets that aren't lined with postcard shops. By getting gently lost, you'll be able to give the hordes the slip.

GETTING HERE

Montmartre is in the 18ᵉ arrondissement. Take line 2 to Anvers métro station, then take the funicular up to Sacré-Coeur. Or, take line 12 to Abbesses station and stroll through Montmartre en route to the basilica. For a scenic tour for the cost of a simple métro ticket, hop the local city-run Monmartrobus at station Jules-Joffrin: the bus winds through the old village streets of Montmartre, with a convenient stop in front of Sacré-Coeur.

BEST CAFÉS

Chez Ginette. There are few attractive food options around Place du Tertre, but this neighborhood favorite is the perfect place to sit with a coffee and rest your feet. ✉ *101 rue Caulain Ct., down the street from Lapin Agile, Montmartre* ☎ *01–46–06–01–49* Ⓜ *Lamarck Caulaincourt.*

La Crémaillère. Alphonse Mucha frescoes decorate the walls at this veritable monument to 19th-century fin-de-siècle art. ✉ *15 pl. du Tertre, Montmartre* ☎ *01–46–06–58–59* Ⓜ *Anvers.*

Le Sancerre. Sit on the terrace sipping a coffee or a beer and watch the ebb and flow of artists, hipsters, and tourists and guess how many people are on an *Amélie* quest. ✉ *35 rue des Abbesses, Montmartre* ☎ *01–45–58–08–20* Ⓜ *Abbesses.*

7

Residents of Montmartre often talk about "going down into Paris," and after spending time here, you'll start to understand why. Topped by its "sculpted cloud," the Sacré-Coeur basilica, and set on a dramatic rise above the city, Montmartre retains an independent spirit. It may be *in* the city, but it's not entirely *of* it, and its sometimes scruffy streets have an intriguing, timeless quality—once you get away from the swarms of tourists, that is.

Updated by
Lisa Pasold

Aside from **Sacré-Coeur**, its biggest draw, Montmartre has market streets, bustling squares—like the lovely **Place du Tertre** and **Place de Abbesses**—and dreamy old houses and private apartments with gardens, untouched by the long arm of Haussmann. Until 1860, the area was a separate village, bristling with windmills, and at more than 300 feet, it's Paris's highest ground, and the sweeping views of the city below are phenomenal.

Always a draw for bohemians and artists, many of whom had studio space at **Bateau-Lavoir** and **Musée de Montmartre**, Montmartre's resident painters have included Géricault, Renoir, Suzanne Valadon, Picasso, van Gogh, and of course Henri Toulouse-Lautrec, who famously painted the **Moulin Rouge**. In 1928, the first cinema built expressly for experimental films opened—now called **Studio 28**—and the area has continued in the movie tradition, with indie favorite *Amélie* and the blockbuster *Moulin Rouge* taking their inspiration here.

One of the best reasons to visit Montmartre, though, is to experience the surviving village life and get in tune with its leisurely, countrified pace. Stop into local bars to see pastis-drinking elders, stroll slowly down winding cobblestone streets to admire ancient trees and painters with easels, and spend time marketing, choosing the best baguette and cheese for a picnic to be had once you reach the top of the hill.

MAIN ATTRACTIONS

★ **Bateau-Lavoir** *(Wash-barge).* Montmartre poet Max Jacob coined the name for the original building here, which reminded him of the laundry boats that used to float in the Seine. He joked that the warren of paint-splattered artists' studios needed a good hosing down. (Wishful thinking, since the building had only one water tap.) It was in the original Bateau-Lavoir that, early in the 20th century, Pablo Picasso, Georges Braque, and Juan Gris made their first bold stabs at Cubism; Picasso painted the groundbreaking *Les Demoiselles d'Avignon* here in 1906–07. The experimental works of the artists didn't meet with complete acceptance, even in liberal Montmartre. Writer Roland Dorgèles, in teasing protest against the Bateau-Lavoir team, once tied a loaded paintbrush to the tail of a donkey belonging to the Lapin Agile cabaret and sold the resulting oeuvre for 400 francs. But poet Guillaume Apollinaire, also on board the Bateau, set the seal on the movement's historical importance by writing *The Painters of Cubism* in 1913. The building that replaces the original Bateau contains art studios, like the original, and is quite modest; a window in the front details the site's history. ⊠ *13 pl. Emile-Goudeau, Montmartre* Ⓜ *Abbesses.*

♺ **Halle St-Pierre.** This elegant iron-and-glass 19th-century market hall at the foot of Sacré-Coeur houses a children's play area, a café, an interesting bookstore, and the **Musée de l'Art Naïf Max-Fourny** (Max Fourny Museum of Naive Art), with its psychedelic collection of outsider and folk art and *art brut* (raw art). The exhibits focus on mainly contemporary artists who for various reasons work outside the fine-art tradition. ⊠ *2 rue Ronsard, Montmartre* ☎ *01–42–58–72–89* ⊕ *www.hallesaintpierre.org* ⊠ *Museum €7.50* ⊙ *Daily 10–6. Closed weekends in Aug.* Ⓜ *Anvers.*

★ **Lapin Agile.** This bar-cabaret, which still manages to preserve something of its original flavor today, got its curious name—the Nimble Rabbit—when humorist André Gill created its sign (now in the Musée du Vieux Montmartre) showing a laughing rabbit jumping out of a saucepan and clutching a bottle of wine. Once the sign went up, locals rechristened it the *Lapin à Gill.* In 1902 the place was bought by the most celebrated cabaret entrepreneur of them all, Aristide Bruand, portrayed by Toulouse-Lautrec in a series of famous posters, and soon thereafter Picasso painted his famous *Au Lapin Agile* (sold at auction in the 1980s for nearly $50 million and on view at New York City's Metropolitan Museum of Art). ⊠ *22 rue des Saules, Montmartre* ☎ *01–46–06–85–87* ⊠ *€24 (includes first drink)* ⊙ *Tues.–Sun. 9 PM–2 AM* Ⓜ *Lamarck Caulaincourt.*

Moulin de la Galette. On a hillock shrouded by shrubbery, this is one of the two remaining windmills ("moulin") in Montmartre; it's privately owned and can be admired only from the street. Its name comes from the inexpensive *galettes* made from leftover flour ground at the mill. It was once the focal point of an open-air cabaret, which soon had competition from another mill: le Moulin Rouge. ⊠ *Rue Tholozé, Montmartre* Ⓜ *Abbesses.*

A Scenic Walk in Montmartre

One of the prettiest walks in Paris begins just outside the Lamarck-Caulaincourt (line 12) métro station, where you'll find two flights of stone stairs. Take a moment to sit on one of the benches on the way up.

At the top is Place Dalida, named for the late, dramatic French songstress of the 1960s. The winding Rue Abreuvoir (one of the most-photographed in Paris) leads you past the Maison Rose (famously painted by Utrillo), and if you turn left at Rue des Saules you'll find Montmartre's very own vineyard and the famous **Lapin Agile**, originally one of the area's raunchiest haunts. The vineyard produces 125 gallons of wine per year (which

is aged in the mairie, or "town hall," of the 18th and sold for charity)—it's hardly grand cru, but the harvest celebration and parade in early October is great fun.

Savor the view from **Carré Roland Dorgelès** before returning up Rue Abreuvoir to Rue Cortot, where you'll find the **Musée de Montmartre**. Composer Eric Satie, who played piano at the Chat Noir, lived a few doors down at No. 6, in a closet-apartment 6 feet by 4 feet (with a 9-foot ceiling and skylight). Follow the curving street past the water tower and you'll come upon the Byzantine-style white domes of **Sacré-Coeur**.

Moulin Rouge. The world-famous cabaret opened in 1889, and aristocrats, professionals, and the working class all came to watch the scandalous performers, such as the dancer La Goulue (the Glutton, so called for her habit of draining leftover glasses). The cancan, by the way—still a regular sight here—was considerably raunchier when Toulouse-Lautrec was around (girls used to kick off their knickers while dancing). ⊠ *82 bd. de Clichy, Montmartre* ☏ *01–53–09–82–82* ⊕ *www.moulin-rouge.fr* Ⓜ *Blanche.*

Place des Abbesses. This triangular square is typical of the countrified style that has made Montmartre famous. Now a hub for shopping and people-watching, the place is surrounded by trendy boutiques, sidewalk cafés, and shabby-chic restaurants—a prime habitat for the young, neo-bohemian crowd and a sprinkling of expats. The entrance to the Abbesses métro station, designed by the great Hector Guimard as a curving, sensuous mass of delicate iron, is one of the two original Art Nouveau entrance canopies left in Paris. Ⓜ *Abbesses.*

Place du Tertre. This tumbling square (*tertre* means "hillock") regains its village atmosphere only late at night or in deepest winter, when the branches of the plane trees sketch traceries against the sky. At any other time of year you'll be confronted by crowds of tourists and a swarm of artists clamoring to do your portrait. If one of them produces a picture of you without your permission, you're under no obligation to buy. Ⓜ *Abbesses.*

Fodor'sChoice **Sacré-Coeur**
★ *See the highlighted listing in this chapter.*

ALSO WORTH SEEING

OFF THE
BEATEN
PATH

Basilique de St-Denis. Built between 1136 and 1286, the St-Denis basilica is in some ways the most important Gothic church in the Paris region. It was here, under dynamic prelate Abbé Suger, that Gothic architecture (typified by pointed arches and rib vaults) arguably made its first appearance. The kings of France soon chose St-

WORD OF MOUTH

"I can't imagine why it took us years of visits to Paris before we went to the Basilica at St-Denis; it was wonderful! Lots to see and absorb, and it helps to have some sense of French history to keep the various monarchs straight."
—shellio

Denis as their final resting place, and their richly sculpted tombs—along with what remains of Suger's church—can be seen in the choir area at the east end of the church. The basilica was battered during the Revolution; afterward, Louis XVIII reestablished it as the royal burial site by moving the remains of Louis XVI and Marie-Antoinette here to join centuries' worth of monarchial bones. The vast 13th-century nave is a brilliant example of structural logic; its columns, capitals, and vault are a model of architectural harmony. The façade, retaining the rounded arches of the Romanesque that preceded the Gothic style, is set off by a small rose window, reputedly the earliest in France. You can also check out the extensive archaeological finds, such as a Merovingian queen's grave goods; there's information in English. ⊠ *1 rue de la Légion d'Honneur, St-Denis* 🕾*01–48–09–83–54* 🖃*Choir and tombs €6.50* ⊘*Easter–Sept., Mon.–Sat. 10–6, Sun. noon–6; Oct.–Easter, Mon.–Sat. 10–4:30, Sun. noon–4:30. Guided tours daily at 11 and 3* Ⓜ*St-Denis Basilique.*

Cimetière de Montmartre. Although not as large as the better-known Père-Lachaise, this leafy cemetery is just as moving and evocative. Incumbents include painters Jean-Honoré Fragonard and Degas; Adolphe Sax, inventor of the saxophone; dancer Vaslav Nijinsky; composers Hector Berlioz and Jacques Offenbach; and La Goulue, the Belle Époque cabaret dancer. The florid Art Nouveau tomb of novelist Emile Zola (1840–1902), who died in nearby Rue de Clichy, lords over a lawn near the entrance—though Zola's mortal remains were removed to the Panthéon in 1908. ⊠*20 av. Rachel, Montmartre* ⊘*Mar. 15–Nov. 6, Mon.–Sat. 8–6, Sun. 9–6; Nov. 7–Mar. 14, Mon.–Sat. 8–5:30, Sun. 9–5:30* Ⓜ*Blanche.*

Espace Salvador-Dalí *(Dalí Center).* Some of the mustached man's less familiar works are among the 25 sculptures and 300 signed etchings and lithographs housed in this Dalí museum. The "ambience" is meant to approximate the Surreal experience, with black walls, low lighting, and a new age-y musical score—punctuated by recordings of Dalí's own voice. There's plenty of information in English, including an audioguide. ⊠*11 rue Poulbot, Montmartre* 🕾*01–42–64–40–10* 🖃*€10* ⊕*www.daliparis.com* ⊘*Daily 10–6* Ⓜ*Abbesses.*

Musée de l'Erotisme. The seven-story Museum of Eroticism, at the foot of Montmartre, claims to provide "a prestigious showcase for every kind

SACRE-COEUR

✉ Pl. du Parvis-du-Sacré-Coeur, Montmartre

☎ 01–53–41–89–00

🕑 Basilica daily 6 AM–10:30 PM; dome and crypt Oct.–Mar., daily 9–6; Apr.–Sept., daily 10–5

💲 Free; dome €5

Ⓜ Anvers, plus funicular

TIPS

■ The best time to visit Sacré-Coeur is at sunrise, long after sunset, and preferably not on a Sunday. If you want to see Sacré-Coeur in action, come just before a service takes place.

■ If you seek perfect photo ops, try to pick a perfectly clear, blue-sky day—although it's difficult to assess what the weather will be like from the top will be like from the streets of central Paris.

■ The funicular, recommended for those short on time and energy, costs one métro ticket each way.

It's hard to not feel as if you're actually climbing your way up to heaven—either on foot or by funicular—when you visit Sacré-Coeur, as this basilica is the city's white castle in the sky, perched atop butte Montmartre. Meant to symbolize the return of self-confidence to late-19th-century Paris after the Commune and Franco-Prussian War, the French government decided to build Sacré-Coeur in 1873. It was designed by architect Paul Abadie, using elements from Romanesque and Byzantine architectural styles. Construction lasted until World War I, and the church wasn't consecrated until 1919.

HIGHLIGHTS

Many people come to Sacré-Coeur to admire the superlative view from the top of the 271-foot-high dome, the second-highest point in Paris after the Eiffel Tower. If you opt to skip the climb up the spiral staircase, the view from the front steps is still well worth the trip.

Don't miss spending some time inside the basilica gazing at the massive golden mosaic set high above the choir: it was created by Luc Olivier Merson, and is titled *Christ in Majesty*. Completed in 1922, it shows Christ, arms outstretched with a golden heart, surrounded by various figures, including the Virgin Mary and Joan of Arc. It remains one of the largest mosaics of its kind and is meant to represent France's devotion to the Sacred Heart. There are also the seemingly endless vaulted arches in the basilica's crypt, the portico's bronze doors—decorated with biblical scenes, including the Last Supper—and the stained-glass windows, which were installed in 1922, destroyed by bombing during World War II, and later rebuilt in 1946. In the basilica's 262 foot-high campanile hangs La Savoyarde, one of the world's heaviest bells, weighing about 19 tons.

of erotic fantasy." Its collection includes Peruvian potteries, African carvings, Indian miniatures, Chinese ivories, Japanese prints, racy Robert Crumb cartoons, and a really peculiar chair. Don't miss the "forbidden film" section (mostly old-style pornography, which looks pretty darn wholesome these days). Three floors are devoted to temporary exhibitions of painting and

> **PICASSO LIVED HERE**
>
> Picasso lived at three different addresses in Montmartre: on Rue Gabrielle when he first arrived; at Bateau-Lavoir; and at No. 11 boulevard de Clichy. The area is virtually littered with "Picasso Lived Here" plaques.

photography. ⊠ *72 bd. de Clichy, Montmartre* ☎ *01–42–58–28–73* ⌨ *€8* ⊙ *Daily 10* AM*–2* AM Ⓜ *Blanche.*

Musée de Montmartre. In its turn-of-the-20th-century heyday, the building now used for Montmartre's historical museum was a studio block for painters, writers, and cabaret artists. Foremost among them was Renoir—he painted the *Moulin de la Galette,* an archetypal scene of sun-drenched revelers, while he lived here—and Utrillo, Montmartre painter par excellence. The museum recaps the area's history; the collection's strong points are its many Toulouse-Lautrec posters, original Eric Satie scores, and its view of the tiny vineyard—the only one in Paris—on Rue des Saules. There's some basic info available in English. ⊠ *12 rue Cortot, Montmartre* ☎ *01–46–06–61–11* ⊕ *www.musee demontmartre.fr* ⌨ *€7* ⊙ *Wed.–Sun. 11–6* Ⓜ *Lamarck Caulaincourt.*

Place Blanche. Today this boulevard is crammed with tourist buses and sex shops, but the side streets are worth exploring for their cafés, nightclubs, edgy boutiques, and tiny, treasure-packed antiques shops. The name—White Square—comes from the clouds of chalky dust that used to be churned up by carts carrying plaster of Paris down from quarries. Crushed wheat and flour from the nearby windmills added to the powdery atmosphere. The Boulevard de Clichy, which intersects the square, was virtually an artists' highway at the turn of the 20th century; Degas lived and died at No. 6, Picasso lived at No. 11, and art supply stores and dealers lined the street. Ⓜ *Blanche.*

OFF THE
BEATEN
PATH
Musée de la Vie Romantique. This tranquil, countrified town house, set in a little park at the foot of Montmartre (head down Rue Blanche from Place Blanche; the third left is Rue Chaptal), was for years the site of Friday-evening salons hosted by the Dutch-born painter Ary Scheffer. Guests included Ingres, Delacroix, Turgenev, Chopin, and George Sand. The memory of author Sand (1804–76)—real name Aurore Dudevant—haunts the museum. Portraits, furniture, and household possessions, right down to her cigarette box, have been moved here from her house in the Loire Valley. There's also a selection of Scheffer's competent artistic output on the first floor. You can sip tea in the garden café. ⊠ *16 rue Chaptal, Montmartre* ☎ *01–55–31–95–67* ⊕ *www.paris.fr/musees/* ⌨ *Free for permanent collection, exhibitions €6* ⊙ *Tues.–Sun. 10–5:40* Ⓜ *St-Georges.*

Dining at a Glance

For full reviews
⇨ Ch. 17

INEXPENSIVE DINING
Kastoori, *Indian*, 4 pl.
Gustave Toudouze

Rose Bakery, *British*,
46 rue des Martyrs

MODERATE DINING
Chez Toinette, *Bistro*,
20 rue Germaine Pilon

Le Ch'ti Catalan, *Bistro*,
4 rue de Navarin

La Famille, *Modern
French*, 41 rue des
Trois-Frères

La Mascotte, *Brasserie*,
52 rue des Abbesses

Velly, *Bistro*, 52 rue
Lamartine

EXPENSIVE DINING
**Bistrot des Deux
Théâtres**, *Bistro*,
18 rue Blanche

Place Jean-Baptiste-Clément. Clément, a singer, was "Mayor of Montmartre" during the heady 70 days of the 1871 Commune, when this area actually seceded from Paris. Painter Amedeo Modigliani (1884–1920) had a studio here at No. 7, and Picasso lived around the corner at 49 rue Gabrielle. Look for the octagonal tower at the north end of the square; it's all that's left of Montmartre's first water tower, built around 1840 to boost the area's feeble water supply. ⊠*Pl. Jean-Baptiste-Clément, Montmartre* Ⓜ*Abbesses.*

St-Pierre de Montmartre. Sitting beneath the brooding silhouette of Sacré-Coeur is one of the oldest churches in Paris. Built in the 12th century as the abbey church of a substantial Benedictine monastery, it has been remodeled on a number of occasions through the years; thus the 18th-century façade built under Louis XIV clashes with the mostly medieval interior. Check out the excellent 20th-century stained-glass windows. ⊠*Off Pl. du Tertre, Montmartre* Ⓜ*Anvers.*

Studio 28. What looks like no more than a generic little movie theater has a distinguished dramatic history: when it opened in 1928. it was the first theater in the world purposely built for *art et essai,* or experimental film. Over the years the movies of directors like Jean Cocteau, François Truffaut, and Orson Welles have been shown here before their official premieres. Today it's a repertory cinema, showing first-runs, just-runs, and previews, usually in their original language. ⊠*10 rue Tholozé, Montmartre* ☎*01–46–06–58–40* Ⓜ*Abbesses.*

The Marais

Cafe L'Etoile Manquante in the Marais

WORD OF MOUTH

"I love the Marais and on my last visit, stayed there on my own. I was completely comfortable walking around late at night by myself, going to restaurants, etc. . . . There are plenty of people around until late, lots of shops, restaurants and cafes, and it's pretty convenient to public transit."

—waldrons

GETTING ORIENTED

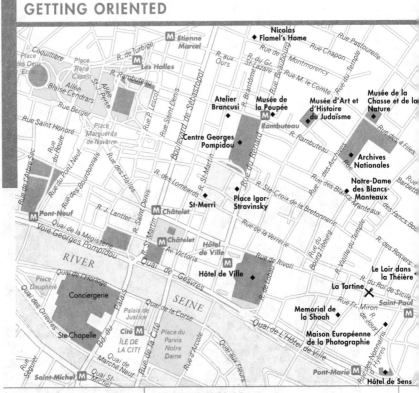

GETTING HERE

The Marais includes the 3e and 4e arrondissements. It's a pleasant walk around Centre Georges Pompidou—into the Marais. Rue Rambuteau turns into Rue de Francs Bourgeois, which runs right past the Place des Vosges. If you're going by métro and plan to wander around the streets of the Marais, the closest stop is St-Paul on the 1 line. If you're just going to the Musée Picasso, the closest stop is St-Sébastien Froissart on the 8 line.

TOP REASONS TO GO

Centre Georges Pompidou. This outrageously designed building is more than just a museum—it has excellent theater and dance performances, a superb library, and a fabulous piazza for people-watching.

Hôtels Particuliers (private mansions). The Marais is one of the best areas of Paris for strolling, in part because of the gorgeous Baroque mansions, such as Hôtel de Sully, that line the streets. Keep your eyes open.

Maison Européenne de la Photographie. A must for photography enthusiasts, this is the space that put Paris on the map for contemporary photo exhibits.

Musée d'Art et d'Histoire du Judaïsme. Dedicated to Jewish culture and history, this fascinating collection includes not only religious objects and historic artworks, but also contemporary artists' installations.

Place des Vosges. Visiting this magical Renaissance square is like walking into a soignée Parisian drawing room.

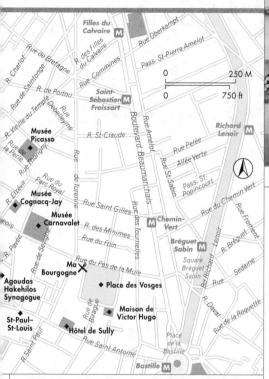

BEST CAFÉS

Le Loir dans la Théière. Sink into one of the comfortably shabby armchairs of this wonderful tea-room in the heart of the Marais and indulge in a fabulous pastry, most memorably a sky-high lemon-meringue tart. ✉ *3 rue des Rosiers, Le Marais* ☎ *01–42–72–90–61* Ⓜ *St-Paul.*

Ma Bourgogne. On the Place des Vosges, this is a calm oasis for coffee or a light lunch away from the noisy streets. In summer, aim for a terrace seat under the arcades fringing the square. The specialty is steak tartare. ✉ *19 pl. des Vosges, Le Marais* ☎ *01–42–78–44–64* Ⓜ *St-Paul.*

La Tartine. This café has an impressive wine list, most of which can be ordered by the glass. Cheerful and quiet, it's a great refuge after a long day of shopping. ✉ *24 rue de Rivoli, Le Marais* ☎ *08–99–78–21–55* Ⓜ *St-Paul.*

8

MAKING THE MOST OF YOUR TIME

The Marais is an area that you'll want to visit every time you're in Paris, but even if you're in town only for a long weekend, try to dedicate at least a day to being here, more if you plan to spend a chunk of time in the Picasso Museum. It's not a hurry-up-and-see-the-sites kind of place, so choose a café and make sure to linger over a proper Parisian lunch—or grab something to go (traditionally very un-Parisian) and have a picnic in one of the neighborhood's lovely tucked-away parks. Sunday afternoons are when the Marais is at its liveliest—the streets teem with shoppers, and the Place des Vosges is so packed that you can barely see the grass—and it can be fun to place yourself in the middle of it all. If you truly can't stand crowds, pick a weekday. Be sure to leave yourself lots of time to wander down the crooked residential streets and peek into private courtyards.

Sightseeing
★★★★★

Dining
★★★★

Lodging
★★★★

Shopping
★★★★★

Nightlife
★★★★

Visiting the Marais is like being in a place where it's always a lazy Sunday afternoon. There's an abundance of restaurants, shops, tiny parks, and museums to wander in and out of, all nestled close together along the winding, charming streets. This is prime people-watching territory, so find a corner café that suits your taste and pass away the afternoon ogling the young and the fabulous.

Updated by
Lisa Pasold

Much of the hanging out in this neighborhood happens in and around one of the most eye-pleasing squares in Paris: the **Place des Vosges**, in the far east corner of the 3e arrondissement. Another popular spot is the wide, sloping piazza in front of **Centre Georges Pompidou**, in the western part of the 3e. The Pompidou is certainly the largest (and most striking-looking) of the Marais museums, but there are several others, including **Musée Carnavalet, Maison Européenne de la Photographie, Musée Picasso,** and **Musée Carnavalet,** all within a stone's throw of one another.

This neighborhood has managed to keep a strong identity within the city, and is home to three distinct Parisian communities: Jewish, gay, and haute couture. In the heart of the Marais is Paris's **Jewish quarter,** which has existed in one form or another since the 12th century. The narrow streets around Rue des Rosiers are loaded with Jewish bookshops, synagogues, delis, and falafel shops. The out-and-about center of the gay community is Rue St. Croix de la Bretonnerie, where you'll find trendy cafés, fascinating shops, and cool nightspots. As for haute couture, although there are several designers' ateliers here, most are closed to the public—but don't despair, you'll still have the chance to shell out plenty of cash if your goal is to spend the afternoon popping in and out of boutiques—which you can do on a Sunday, unlike in the rest of Paris. Head for Rue des Francs-Bourgeois and Rue Vielle-du-Temple as well as Rue Charonne—the latter starts off running parallel to Vielle-du-Temple but ends up leading into Bastille; it's one of the up-and-coming shopping streets in the Marais.

The upper part of the Marais, north of Rue des Quatres-Fils, is becoming increasingly exciting for strolling. There are hip boutiques, charming cooking classes (check out L'Atelier de Fred at 6 rue des Vertus), and the wonderful Marche des Enfants Rouges on Rue de Bretagne—the oldest covered market in Paris, recently restored with fabulous deli-type food as well as raw ingredients (open Tuesday through Sunday). Nearby, clustered around Rue Charlot, you'll find some of the most exciting private art galleries in the city, wedged ingeniously into tiny former industrial spaces and aristocratic mansions.

FREE IN THE MARAIS

The **Maison Européenne de la Photographie** is free on Wednesday after 5; the **Mémorial de la Shoah** and the **Maison de Victor Hugo** are always free, as are the extensive permanent collections of the **Musée Carnavalet** and the **Musée Cognacq-Jay.** There's a small, free exhibition space inside the **Centre Georges Pompidou**, and the nearby **St-Merri** church has twice-weekly, free, classical music concerts.

MAIN ATTRACTIONS

Fodor'sChoice **Centre Georges Pompidou**

★ *See highlighted listing in this chapter.*

Hôtel de Sully. There's an excellent bookshop featuring innumerable publications in French and English about Paris (be sure to look up at the shop's original Louis XIII ceiling) inside this mansion, built in 1624, which is the best surviving example of early Baroque in Paris. Like much of the area, this *hôtel particulier* fell into ruin until the 1950s, when it was rescued by the administration of French historic monuments, **Caisse Nationale des Monuments Historiques.** There are also regular photography exhibitions. ⊠*62 rue St-Antoine, Le Marais* ☎*01–44–61–20–00* ☉*Tues.–Sun. 10–6:30* Ⓜ*St-Paul.*

Hôtel de Ville. Overlooking the Seine, City Hall is the residence of the mayor of Paris; the building was rebuilt after a looting in 1873, and its elaborate nighttime lighting makes it a knockout. The building includes an exhibition space (just look for the long line along Rue Rivoli) and occasionally opens its reception halls for public events. Parisians come here for the elegant public square in front of the building, often filled with tents for free temporary exhibits. In August there's a beach volleyball court set up here; in winter an open-air ice rink appears with inexpensive skate rental—it's particularly romantic at night. These days, most locals feel almost fond of City Hall, with the popularity of Mayor Bertrand Delanoë. ⊠*Pl. de l'Hôtel-de-Ville, Le Marais* ☉*For special exhibitions* Ⓜ*Hôtel de Ville.*

★ **Maison Européenne de la Photographie** *(MEP; European Photography Center).* Much of the credit for photography's current perch in the city's cultural scene can be given to MEP (whose director, Jean-Luc Monterosso, also founded Paris's hugely successful Mois de la Photographie festival held in November in even-numbered years). This terrific center hosts up to four exhibitions every three months, and they include photographers from around the world in their selection. A show on a Magnum photographer could overlap with an Irving Penn display or a collection of 19th-century images. Programs and guided tours are available in English. ⊠*5 rue de Fourcy, Le Marais* ☎*01–44–78–75–00* ⊕*www.mep-fr.org* ☑*€6, free Wed. after 5* PM ⊙ *Wed.–Sun. 11–8* Ⓜ*St-Paul.*

Maison de Victor Hugo. The workaholic French author famed for *Les Misérables* and the *Hunchback of Notre-Dame* lived in a corner of beautiful Place des Vosges between 1832 and 1848. The memorabilia here includes several of his atmospheric, horror-movie-like ink sketches—a tribute to Hugo's unsuspected talent as an artist—along with illustrations for his writings by other artists, including Bayard's rendition of Cosette (which has graced countless *Les Miz* T-shirts). Upstairs, in Hugo's original apartment, you can see the tall desk where he stood to write, along with furniture from several of his homes—including the Chinese-theme panels and woodwork he created for his mistress. ⊠*6 pl. des Vosges, Le Marais* ☎*01–42–72–10–16* ☑*Free* ⊙ *Tues.–Sun. 10–5:45* Ⓜ*St-Paul.*

Mémorial de la Shoah *(Memorial to the Holocaust).* This memorial honors, name by name, the 6 million Jews who died "without graves" at the hands of the Nazis. The entrance is a deeply moving installation of names on tall plinths (often marked with flowers, stones, and candles left to commemorate relatives). This is a crucial part of the commemoration of the Jewish presence in the Marais. France's Jewish population sank from 300,000 to 180,000 during World War II, but has since grown to around 700,000—the largest in Europe—bolstered by a wave of Sephardic Jews from North Africa who arrived in the 1960s. This memorial is committed to showcasing the diverse communities' history and culture; the center has archives, a library, and a gallery that hosts temporary exhibitions about Jewish history; on the second Sunday of every month at 3 PM there is a free English guided tour. ⊠*17 rue Geoffroy-l'Asnier, Le Marais* ☎*01–42–77–44–72* ⊕*www. memorialdelashoah.org* ☑*Free* ⊙ *Sun.–Wed. 10–6, Thurs. 10–10, Fri. 10–6* Ⓜ*Pont Marie.*

Musée d'Art et d'Histoire du Judaïsme. Exhibits at this museum of Jewish art and history—housed in what was once the Hôtel St-Aignan, a gorgeous mansion built in 1650—have good explanatory texts in English, and there are free audioguides. Highlights include 13th-century tombstones excavated in Paris; wooden models of destroyed Eastern European synagogues; a roomful of early paintings by Marc Chagall; and Christian Boltanski's stark, two-part tribute to Shoah (Holocaust) victims in the form of plaques on an outer wall naming the (mainly Jewish) inhabitants of the Hôtel St-Aignan in 1939, and canvas hangings with the personal data of the 13 residents who were deported and died in concentration camps. ⊠*71 rue du Temple, Le Marais* ☎*01–53–01–86–60* ⊕*www.mahj.org* ☑*€6.80* ⊙ *Weekdays 11–6, Sun. 10–6* Ⓜ*Rambuteau or Hôtel de Ville.*

★ **Musée Picasso**
See highlighted listing in this chapter.

Fodor'sChoice **Place des Vosges**
★ *See highlighted listing in this chapter.*

St-Merri. This church near the Centre Pompidou, completed in 1552, has a turret containing the oldest bell in Paris (cast in 1331) and an 18th-century pulpit supported on carved palm trees. Parisians whisper that this was once a center of black witchcraft; nowadays, you can drop by on the weekend for rather magical free concerts. ⊠*Rue de la Verrerie, Beaubourg/Les Halles* Ⓜ*Hôtel de Ville.*

ALSO WORTH SEEING

Agoudas Hakehilos Synagogue. Art Nouveau genius Hector Guimard built this unique synagogue in 1913 for a Polish-Russian Orthodox association. The façade resembles an open book: Guimard consciously used the motif of the Ten Commandments to inspire the building's shape and its interior, which can only rarely be visited. Knock on the door and see if the caretaker will let you upstairs to the balcony, where you can admire Guimard's well-preserved interior decor. Like other Parisian synagogues, the front door of this address was dynamited by the Nazis on Yom Kippur 1940. The Star of David over the door was added after the building was restored, symbolizing the renaissance of the Jewish community here. ⊠*10 rue Pavé, Le Marais* ☏*No phone* Ⓜ*St-Paul.*

NEED A
BREAK?
Detour off Rue Sévigné to Place Marché Ste-Catherine and Pitchi Poï (⊠ 7 rue Caron, Le Marais ☏01–42–77–46–15) for a Jewish feast—perhaps some gefilte fish (a chopped fish patty)—appropriate to the Marais's layered history.

Archives Nationales. The National Archives are a history buff's fantasy; they hold thousands of historical documents dating from the Merovingian period to the 20th century. The highlights are the Edict of Nantes (1598), the Treaty of Westphalia (1648), the wills of Louis XIV and Napoléon, and the Declaration of Human Rights (1789). Louis XVI's diary is also here, containing his sadly ignorant entry for July 14, 1789, the day the Bastille was stormed and when, for all intents and purposes, the French Revolution began: "*Rien*" ("Nothing"). Even if you're not into history, the buildings themselves are worth seeing. The Archives are housed in two elegant mansions built in 1705 by trendsetting architect Alexandre Delamair: the **Hôtel de Soubise,** once the grandest house in all of Paris, and the **Hôtel de Rohan,** built for Soubise's son, Cardinal Rohan. As you enter the main courtyard, check out the medieval turrets to the left: this is the Porte de Clisson, all that remains of a 15th-century mansion. Decorative-arts mavens flock to this museum for special exhibits and to see the apartments of the Princess de Soubise. Her rooms were among the first examples of the rococo, the light-filled, curving style that followed the heavier Baroque opulence of Louis XIV. ⊠*60 rue des Francs-Bour-*

8

CENTRE GEORGES POMPIDOU

✉ Pl. Georges-Pompidou,
Beaubourg/Les Halles

Ⓜ Rambuteau

☎ 01–44–78–12–33

🌐 www.centrepompidou.fr

💶 €12, including Atelier
Brancusi; €8–€10 for tem-
porary exhibits; free 1st
Sun. of month

🕐 Wed.–Mon. 11–10

🧸 Good for Kids

The Pompidou is definitely a unique-looking building. Most people love it and can't help but giggle with
childish glee at the spaceship-like exterior that scan-
dalized all of Paris when it was built in 1977; some
people still think it's ugly. Named after French president
Georges Pompidou (1911–74), it was designed by then-
unknowns Renzo Piano and Richard Rogers. The architects' claim to fame with this museum is that they put
all the building's guts on the outside and color-coded
them: water pipes are green, air ducts are blue, electrics
are yellow, and things like elevators and escalators are
red. Art from the 20th century to the present day is
what you'll find inside.

TIPS

■ The Pompidou's perma-
nent collection takes up a
relatively small amount of the
space here: a free reference
library and temporary exhibit
galleries with a special wing
for design and architecture
are also here, and the basement includes two cinemas, a
theater, a dance space, and a
small, free exhibition space.

■ On your way up the esca-
lator, you'll have spectacular
views of Paris, ranging from
the Tour Montparnasse, to
the left, around to the hilltop
Sacré-Coeur on the right.

■ The trendy rooftop res-
taurant, Georges (01–44–78–
47–99) is great for romantic
dinners. Make sure to reserve
a table near the window.

■ There are public toilets in
the basement that don't have
the long lines of those on the
ground floor.

HIGHLIGHTS

The **Musée National d'Art Moderne** (*Modern Art
Museum*, entrance on Level 4) occupies the top two levels. Level 5 is devoted to modern art, including major
works by Matisse, Modigliani, Marcel Duchamp, and
Picasso; level 4 is dedicated to contemporary art from
the '60s on, including video installations. Outside, next
to the museum's sloping piazza—where throngs of teen-
agers hang out (and there's free Wi-Fi)—is the **Atelier
Brancusi** (*Brancusi Studio*). This small, airy museum
contains four rooms reconstituting Brancusi's studios
with works from all periods of his career. Around the
corner in the **Place Igor-Stravinsky** is the zany, colorful
Stravinsky fountain. On the opposite side of Rue Rambuteau, on the wall at the corner of Rue Clairvaux and
Passage Brantô, is the appealingly bizarre mechanical
brass-and-steel clock, **Le Défenseur de Temps**.

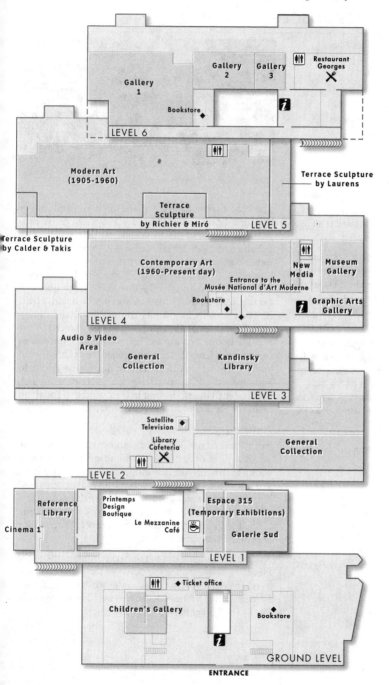

LEVEL 6

Gallery 1

Gallery 2

Gallery 3

Restaurant Georges

Bookstore

LEVEL 5

Modern Art (1905-1960)

Terrace Sculpture by Laurens

Terrace Sculpture by Richier & Miró

Terrace Sculpture by Calder & Takis

LEVEL 4

Contemporary Art (1960-Present day)

New Media

Museum Gallery

Entrance to the Musée National d'Art Moderne

Bookstore

Graphic Arts Gallery

LEVEL 3

Audio & Video Area

General Collection

Kandinsky Library

LEVEL 2

Satellite Television

Library Cafeteria

General Collection

LEVEL 1

Reference Library

Printemps Design Boutique

Le Mezzanine Café

Espace 315 (Temporary Exhibitions)

Cinema 1

Galerie Sud

GROUND LEVEL

Ticket office

Children's Gallery

Bookstore

ENTRANCE

8

PLACE DES VOSGES

- ⊠ Off Rue des Francs Bourgeois, near Rue de Turenne
- Ⓜ Bastille or St-Paul
- 🎫 Free
- 🕙 Open year-round
- 🖐 Good for Kids

TIPS

■ Unlike so many parks in Paris, one of the best things about the Place des Vosges is that you're allowed to sit on the grass.

■ There is no better location for a picnic in the Marais. Drop by the street market of Richard Lenoir on Thursday and Saturday mornings to pick up great lunch snacks.

■ The way you'll most likely approach the Place des Vosges is off Rue des Francs Bourgeois, as it's the main shopping street. However, for a grander entrance, you can walk along Rue Saint Antoine until you get to Rue de Birague, which leads directly into the square.

The oldest monumental square in Paris—and one of hypnotic beauty—the Place des Vosges's precise proportions give it a placid regularity that will inspire a feeling of calm for all those who visit. But things weren't always so calm in this nearly 400-year-old square. A royal palace—the Palais des Tournelles—once stood here, lived in by the Italian-born queen of France, Catherine de' Medici, and her husband, Henri II. The couple held jousting tournaments, and during one of them, in 1559, Henry was fatally lanced in the eye. Catherine abandoned her palace afterward, and years later Henry IV commissioned the Place Royal, inaugurated in 1612. Napoléon decided it ought to be named the Place des Vosges to honor the French département Vosges, the first in the country to cough up taxes for the Revolutionary government.

HIGHLIGHTS

At the base of the 36 redbrick-and-stone houses—nine on each side of the square—is an arcaded, covered walkway where you can shop, stroll, or sit at a café. There's also an elementary school, a synagogue (whose barrel roof was designed by Gustav Eiffel), and several chic hotels. The formal, gated garden's perimeter is lined with chestnut trees; inside are a children's play area and a fountain.

Aside from hanging out in the park, people come to the Place des Vosges to see the house of the man who once lived at No. 6—Victor Hugo, the workaholic, famed French author of Les Misérables and Notre-Dame de Paris (The Hunchback of Notre-Dame).

geois, Le Marais ☎*01–40–27–60–96* ⊕*www.archivesnationales. culture.gouv.fr* ✉*€3* ⊗*Mon. and Wed.–Fri. 10–5:30, weekends 2–5:30* Ⓜ*Rambuteau.*

Hôtel de Sens. Though much restored, this medieval mansion still shows its rich Gothic lines. Built for the Archbishop of Sens in 1474, the building

developed a decidedly more secular side while Henri IV's first wife lived here after her marriage was annulled. Marguerite was renowned for her lovers (she supposedly collected locks of their hair to make wigs for herself) and launched the style for heavy powdering because her face bore terrible smallpox scars. She named this street after the fig tree she had cut down, as it was inconveniencing her carriages. (Notice the fig tree defiantly planted in the back garden.) Today the building houses occasional exhibits and a fine-arts library, the **Bibliothèque Forney.** ✉*1 rue du Figuier, Le Marais* ☎*01–42–78–14–60* ✉*Exhibitions €3* ⊗*Tues.–Sat. 1:30–8* Ⓜ*Pont Marie.*

Fodor'sChoice **Musée Carnavalet.** If it has to do with Paris, it's here. This collection is a fascinating hodgepodge of Parisian artifacts, from the prehistoric canoes used by Parisii tribes to the furniture of the bedroom where Marcel Proust wrote his evocative, legendarily long novel. The museum fills two adjacent mansions, the Hôtel Le Peletier de St-Fargeau and the Hôtel Carnavalet. The latter is a Renaissance jewel that in the mid-1600s became the home of writer Madame de Sévigné. The long-lived Sévigné wrote hundreds of letters to her daughter, giving an incomparable view of both public and private life during the time of Louis XIV. The museum offers a glimpse into her world, but the collection covers far more than just the 17th century. The exhibits on the Revolution are especially interesting, with scale models of guillotines and a downright weird cast-iron stove in the shape of the Bastille. You can also walk through an amazing assortment of reconstructed interiors from the Middle Ages through rococo and into Art Nouveau—showstoppers include the Fouquet jewelry shop and the Café de Paris's original furnishings. Information in English is on hand. ✉*23 rue de Sévigné, Le Marais* ☎*01–44–59–58–58* ⊕*www. paris.fr/musees/musee_carnavalet/* ✉*Free for permanent collection, €6 for exhibits* ⊗*Tues.–Sun. 10–5:40* Ⓜ*St-Paul.*

NEED A BREAK? **Le Loir dans la Théière** (✉ *3 rue des Rosiers, Le Marais* ☎ *01-42-72-90-61*) **(the dormouse in the teapot) is named for the dormouse who fell asleep at Alice in Wonderland's tea party. It's the perfect place to recover from museum overload—cozy into a leather chair, order a silver pot of tea, and choose a homemade cake.**

Musée de la Chasse et de la Nature. Installed in the gorgeous Hôtel de Guénégaud, which was designed around 1650 by François Mansart, this collection of items on hunting and nature is one of the more

MUSEE PICASSO

✉ 5 rue de Thorigny,
Le Marais

☎ 01-42-71-25-21

🌐 www.musee-picasso.fr

🎫 €9.50; free 1st Sun. of
month

🕐 Winter, Wed.-Mon. 9:30-
5:30; summer, Wed.-Mon.
9:30-6

Ⓜ St-Sébastien

TIPS

■ If you're here to see
the entire collection, pace
yourself—the museum doesn't
appear large when you look
at the floor plan, but there's a
lot of art packed inside.

■ If you'd rather not see
the museum in chronological
order and would like to split
it up into two digestible parts,
see the second floor first and
take a break in the lovely
café. Afterward, see the basement and the ground floor,
which together should take
about as long to see as the
second floor.

■ The line outside the
museum in the courtyard can
seem pretty long when you
arrive, but don't get put off—it
tends to move quickly.

The Picasso museum opened in 1985 and shows no
signs of losing its immense popularity. This is the largest
Picasso collection in the world—and these are "Picasso's Picassos," not necessarily his most famous works
but rather the paintings and sculptures the artist valued
most. Arranged chronologically, the museum gives you
a great snapshot (with descriptions in English) of the
painter's life. It also covers Picasso's personal collection of work by friends and influences such as Matisse,
Braque, Cézanne, and Rousseau. The building itself,
erected in the 17th century, became a permanent home
for Picasso's work after much of it was given to the government by the artist's heirs after the painter's death in
1973 in lieu of death duties. The Hôtel Salé is showing
some wear and tear from being one of the city's most
popular museums; on peak summer afternoons this
place is more congested than the Gare du Lyon.

HIGHLIGHTS

The collection spans Picasso's entire life's work, from the
Blue period all the way to Surrealism, when he painted
what's arguably his most famous painting, *Guernica*,
which hangs in the Museo Reina Sofia in Madrid. But
there's still plenty to see, and we advise setting aside an
entire morning or afternoon to spend here. For those
who are short on time and want a whirlwind tour, the
three don't-miss paintings, listed in chronological order
(which is how you'll see them if you run through the
museum) are *Self Portrait* (1901), *Two Women Running on the Beach* (1922), and *The Kiss* (1969).

The ground floor of the museum is a lovely sculpture
garden, where you'll find *The Bathers* (1956), and in
the basement there's a collection of Picasso's ceramics,
which are stunningly colorful.

bizarre in the Marais and features taxidermy, historic weaponry, and contemporary artists' works on the theme of the hunt. After an extensive remodeling, the collection also has an impressive new permanent exhibition based on the tracks and habits of wild animals. It's worth a quick visit for the elegant rooms alone. ⊠*60 rue des Archives, Le Marais* ☎*01–42–72–86–42* 🎟*€6, free first Sun. of the month* ⊙*Weekdays 11–6* Ⓜ*Rambuteau.*

Musée Cognacq-Jay. Another rare opportunity to see how cultured rich Parisians once lived, this 16th-century rococo-style mansion contains an outstanding collection of 18th-century artwork in its *boi-*

seried (wainscoted) rooms. Ernest Cognacq, founder of the department store La Samaritaine, and his wife, Louise Jay, amassed furniture, porcelain, and paintings—notably by Fragonard, Watteau, François Boucher, and Tiepolo—to create one of the world's finest private collections of this period. Some of the best displays are also the smallest, like the tiny enamel portraits showcased on the third floor, or, up in the attic, the glass vitrines filled with exquisite inlaid snuff boxes, sewing cases, pocket watches, perfume bottles, and cigar cutters. English-language guides are available. ⊠*8 rue Elzévir, Le Marais* ☎*01–40–27–07–21* ⊕*www.paris.fr/musees/cognacq_jay/* 🎟*Free for permanent collection, €4.60 for exhibits* ⊙*Tues.–Sun. 10–5:40* Ⓜ*St-Paul.*

☾ **Musée de la Poupée** (*Doll Museum*). If you love dolls, make a detour to this quaint, low-ceiling house in a cul-de-sac near the Centre Pompidou to admire this rarefied collection that spans the 1800s through the Mattel era. Bisque-head dolls with enamel eyes were a Paris specialty; here the well-labeled (in French only) displays show dolls in original costumes. Don't miss the miniature greyhound made of rabbit fur, growling at an alarmed cat figure. ⊠*Impasse Berthaud, Le Marais* ☎*01–42–72–73–11* ⊕*www.paris.fr/musees/musee_carnavalet/* 🎟 *€7* ⊙*Tues.–Sun. 10–6* Ⓜ*Rambuteau or Hôtel de Ville.*

OFF THE BEATEN PATH

Nicolas Flamel's Home. Harry Potter fans, take note: Nicolas Flamel, the alchemist whose sorcerer's stone is the source of immortality in the popular book series, really existed. He was a wealthy merchant and left his home at 51 rue Montmorency to the city as a dormitory for the poor (it's no longer used as such), on the condition that boarders pray daily for his soul. He may not have been immortal, but the building is one of the oldest in Paris, built in 1407. The interesting carvings on the front were added at least a century after Flamel's death, but they add appropriate atmosphere.

Dining at a Glance

For full reviews
⇨ Ch. 17

INEXPENSIVE DINING

Au Bourguignon du Marais, *Bistro*, 52 rue François-Miron

Breizh Café, *French*, 109 rue Vieille du Temple

Chez Marianne, *Middle Eastern*, 2 rue des Hospitalières-St-Gervais

L'Ambassade d'Auvergne, *Bistro*, 22 rue du Grenier St-Lazare

L'As du Fallafel, *Israeli*, 34 rue des Rosiers

MODERATE DINING

Bu Bar, *Wine Bar*, 3 rue des Tournelles

Le Dôme du Marais, *Bistro*, 53 bis, rue des Francs-Bourgeois

Le Rouge Gorge, *Wine Bar*, 8 rue St-Paul

EXPENSIVE DINING

Benoît, *Bistro*, 20 rue St-Martin

Le Murano, *Modern French*, 13 bd. du Temple

Notre-Dame des Blancs-Manteaux. The Blancs Manteaux were white-robed 13th-century mendicant monks whose monastery once stood on this spot; their late-17th-century church gave the street its name. There's a pocket-size park here, with a playground for small children, a Ping-Pong table, and convenient benches for picnics. The community center at the foot of the street was once a covered market (with horns of plenty carved over the door). ⊠Rue des Blancs-Manteaux, *Le Marais* ⊕*http://www.notre-dame-des-blancs-manteaux.org/* Ⓜ*Rambuteau.*

St-Paul–St-Louis. The leading Baroque church in the Marais, its dome rising 180 feet above the crossing, was begun in 1627 by the Jesuits and modeled on their Gesù church in Rome. Check out the trompe l'oeil painting of sculpted figures in the highest part of the dome, and look for Delacroix's dramatic *Christ on the Mount of Olives* in the transept. The beautifully split clamshell at the entrance was donated by Victor Hugo, who lived in nearby Place des Vosges. ⊠*Rue St-Antoine, Le Marais* Ⓜ*St-Paul.*

Canal St-Martin, Bastille & Oberkampf

WORD OF MOUTH

"I think that seeing the Canal is worth it—especially if a boat is going through the locks. On Sundays, the roads along the canal are closed to cars—lots of pedestrians strolling along. On the side streets around the canal are some funky shops for window shopping."

—ParisEscapes

GETTING ORIENTED

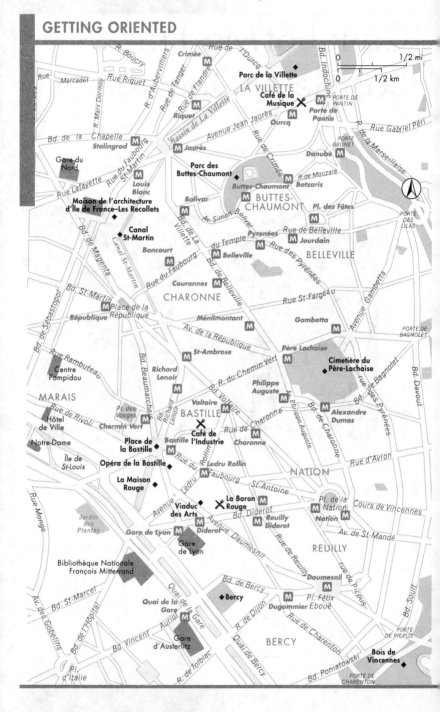

TOP REASONS TO GO

Canal St-Martin. The scenic canal has become the ideal hangout for hipsters, artists, and young families—galleries, charming shops, and chic cafés abound.

Cimetière du Père Lachaise. This is the best-known and largest cemetery in Paris, filled with history, huge trees, and elaborate tombs that resemble small houses. It's especially interesting on November 1, All Saint's Day, when it seems every Parisian in the city turns out with bouquets of mums for their favorite dead celebrity. It's not exactly Halloween, but the mood is much more festive than you might expect.

Parc de la Villette. If you're traveling with kids or simply young at heart, this is an essential stop, whether you want to listen to samba bands in the park, play pickup soccer, or visit the submarine.

Place de la Bastille. An excellent place to visit if you're planning to overthrow a monarchy, the Place is also a great jumping-off point for lunch (especially with the Richard Lenoir street market on Thursday and Sunday mornings).

Viaduc des Arts. A surprisingly successful urban renovation along a disused rail line has turned into a wonderful shopping strip at street level and a lovely walkway aboveground.

MAKING THE MOST OF YOUR TIME

Much of eastern Paris is generally neglected by visitors but beloved by residents. You can easily dedicate a day here, having a long lunch at a café and enjoying the laid-back ambience of the canal. If you're on a shorter trip or if it's your first time in Paris, you might want to just check the area out to shop and experience the nightlife.

GETTING HERE

Canal St-Martin, Bastille, and Oberkampf include the 10e, 11e, and 19e arrondissements. The Bastille métro stop, where you can get the 1, 5, and 8 lines, is a good place to start—the station is directly below Place de la Bastille, so keep an eye out for the few remaining stones of the Bastille prison (most visible in the foundation of line 5). For Canal St-Martin, use the Gare de l'Est stop and walk along Rue des Recollets to reach the canal, or the Jacques-Bonsergeant stop on the 5. For Oberkampf, use the Oberkampf stop on the 5 and 9 or the Parmentier stop on the 3.

BEST CAFÉS

Le Baron Rouge. This friendly wine bar is the perfect spot to pair a glass of your favorite Bordeaux with some bread and sausage after strolling the Marché d'Aligre. ✉1 rue Théophile Roussel, Bastille ☎01-43-43-14-32 Ⓜ Ledru Rollin.

Café de la Musique. Next to the Cité de la Musique in Parc de La Villette is this vast café. It's often filled with people going to, or coming from, a concert, but the free jazz on Wednesday nights and the interesting crowd make it worth the trip. ✉214 av. Jean-Jaurès, La Villette ☎01-48-03-15-91 Ⓜ Porte de Pantin.

Café de l'Industrie. The warm yellow rooms of this Bastille hangout make it an inviting spot for a late-afternoon coffee or beer. ✉16 rue St-Sabin, Bastille ☎01-47-00-13-53 Ⓜ Bastille.

9

Sightseeing ★★	It might be a bit off the beaten path from central Paris, but there's a lot going on out here, and it's certainly worth the
Dining ★★★★	trip. Canal St-Martin, Bastille, and Oberkampf are Paris's
Lodging ★★	hippest hoods, brimming with bars, new and well-priced res-
Shopping ★★★★	taurants, busy cafés, and cutting-edge clothing boutiques—
Nightlife ★★★★★	and the trendiness has begun to radiate outward even more, pushing far into the 18e, 19e, and 20e arrondissements.

Updated by
Lisa Pasold

The making of a hot neighborhood is cyclical: first come the artists and the hip factor, then comes gentrification, then the artists move on. In the early 1980s, the Marais was restored to glory as the latest cool 'hood to hang out, then the artists moved east, finding studio space in former ateliers and derelict 18th-century buildings along **Canal St-Martin**. It's funky and flourishing, and full of character. North and east of the canal, things have begun to sprout up in **Ménilmontant** and **Belleville**, too. South of **Bastille**, you'll find the enormously successful **Viaduc des Arts**, an urban renewal project that turned an old elevated rail line into an arcaded, tree-lined walkway filled with crafts studios. Bring your shopping basket for nearby Marché d'Aligre—a traditional covered market, open Tuesday through Sunday, that's a popular haven for foodies. From the Bastille all the way up to **Cimetière du Père Lachaise**, there are intriguing pockets of busy streets as well as several impressive movie houses run by the MK2 chain. The cemetery itself, known as the final resting place of Proust, Oscar Wilde, Colette, Jim Morrison, and many other famous figures, should not be missed.

Those traveling with kids also love this part of Paris for its parks: whether they're roaring up and down the quays of the canal, or letting off steam in the gorgeous **Parc de la Villette, Bois de Vincennes,** or the **Parc Buttes-Chaumont,** this is a good area to help them recover from museum overload. If you're without kids and it's nightlife you're after, Rue **Oberkampf,** Rue St-Maur, and Rue Jean-Pierre-Timbaud beg for barhopping.

MAIN ATTRACTIONS

☺ **Bercy.** Bercy is a testament to the French genius for urban renewal. Tucked away south of the Gare de Lyon in the 12^e arrondissement, stone buildings that were once used to store wine from the provinces have become the shops and restaurants of **Bercy Village**, also known as Cour St-Emilion. Close by is a quirky Cubist building designed by Frank Gehry, who described the work as "a dancing figure in the park." It houses the new and improved **Cinémathèque Française** (⊠*51 rue de Bercy, Bercy/Tolbiac* ☎*01–71–19–33–33* ⊕*www.cinematheque. fr* ⊠*Depending on combination of exhibits, €4–€18* ☉*Mon.–Sat. noon–7, Thurs. until 10, Sun. 10–8* Ⓜ*Bercy or Cour St-Emilion*), a film-buff's paradise with theaters as well as a cinema museum. To your right is a contemporary garden named for Nobel peace prize-winner Yitzhak Rabin. Immediately across from Bercy is the fabulous new floating aquatic center, **Piscine Josephine Baker** (⊠*Port de la Gare, Bibliothèque* ☎*01–56–61–96–50* ⊕*www.paris.fr/portail/sport* Ⓜ*Quai de la Gare*), named after the American dancer who sang so convincingly of her two loves—her native country and Paris. The pool offers inexpensive swimming lessons, a glamorous deck for sunbathers, and a stellar view—all for €5.

Fodor's Choice   **Canal St-Martin.** Walking along the canal, pausing to check out the
★   trendy shops and lingering over a sunny lunch, it's hard to believe that this water link was built by Napoléon to provide the city with drinking water. When the Industrial Revolution kicked in, all kinds of industry set up shop on its banks—which means that nowadays, 21st-century artists are enjoying converted studios and gallery spaces in this area. The scenic quays, locks, and footbridges are magnificent for strolling, especially on Sunday when cars are blocked from the core area. There are €15 **barge rides** (⊠*Embarkation at 13 quai de la Loire, La Villette*) in which the 2½-hour cruise takes you through the canal's nine locks along the once-industrial Bassin de la Villette to the nearby Parc de la Villette. Ⓜ*Jacques Bonsergent (southern end) or Porte de Pantin (northern end).*

NEED A BREAK? Despite its unassuming white façade, the Hôtel du Nord (⊠*102 quai de Jem-mappes, République* ☎*01-40-40-78-78* Ⓜ*Jacques Bonsergent*) is a local star. Newly revamped into a trendy café-restaurant serving basic French fare, the hotel is famous for its role in Marcel Carné's 1938 namesake movie. The film's star, actress-icon Arletty, claimed to be unmoved by the romantic canal-side setting in her classic line, loosely translated as "Atmosphere, atmosphere, I've had it with atmosphere!"

★ **Cimetière du Père Lachaise**
See highlighted listing in this chapter.

La Maison Rouge. Former gallery owner Antoine de Galbert established this exciting contemporary-art foundation, where three shows a year bring private collections to the public eye. All are curated with a real flair for contemporary trends—a rarity for Paris galleries. The building

CANAL FLÂNEUR

The Canal St-Martin has become the hippest place to stroll and people-watch on weekend afternoons, and the best place to party at night—which means there are now some excellent cafés and bars in this neighborhood, just waiting for flâneurs, or "strollers." Start with a coffee or beer at Chez Prune (71 quai de Valmy), then drift north along the canal, with a detour along Rue de Lancry for great food shops and a constantly shifting bar scene. Métro station Jacques Bonsergeant is the best bet for public transportation. Along the canal, there are lots of boutiques—including the Antoine & Lili chain—and innumerable French and South Asian restaurants. As you head up the canal, don't miss the Point Ephémère (200 quai de Valmy)—a café, art gallery, club, and DJ scene in a converted warehouse. At Stalingrad, you'll pass a former tax collection point, and you'll hit the enormous MK2 cinemas—be sure to take the little canal ferry that's included in your movie ticket. And if you keep going toward Parc de la Villette, you'll find a tapas bar on a boat and two floating theaters (near Rue Riquet).

itself is a treat: an industrial space cleverly redone and anchored by the original courtyard building, now painted bright red (hence the foundation's name). So far the only flaw is a comparative lack of information about the art being displayed—a problem you can partly remedy by browsing in the gallery's excellent bookshop. There are free guided tours on Saturday at 4, but only in French. ⊠ *8 bd. de la Bastille, Bastille* ☎ *01–40–01–08–81* ⊕ *www.lamaisonrouge.org* ☜ *€4.50–€6.50* ⊙ *Wed.–Sun. 11–7, Thurs. 11–9* Ⓜ *Quai de la Rapée/Bastille*.

Opéra de la Bastille. Locals joke that Uruguay-born architect Carlos Ott was channeling the old Bastille prison when he designed this high-tech Opéra on the south side of the Place de la Bastille. Opened on July 14, 1989, in commemoration of the bicentennial of the French Revolution, the acoustics of the steeply sloping, stylish auditorium have earned more plaudits than the gray curved façade, which is plagued with falling marble panels. The guided tour includes part of backstage, but you'll have more fun simply buying a ticket to whatever's on. Shows are consistently spectacular, and inexpensive same-day tickets are often available. ⊠ *Pl. de la Bastille, Bastille/Nation* ☎ *01–40–01–19–70* ⊕ *www.opera-de-paris.fr* ☜ *Guided tours €11* Ⓜ *Bastille*.

NEED A BREAK? If you work up an appetite looking at the food stalls in Marché Aligre, duck around the corner to the friendly, bustling Petit Porcheron (⊠ *3 rue de Prague, Bastille/Nation* ☎ *01-43-47-39-47*) It's both hip and committed to taking advantage of the neighborhood markets, the perfect spot to join the locals for a bite.

ⓒ **Parc de la Villette.** This 130-acre ultramodern park was once an abattoir, but don't let its history put you off: today it's the perfect place to entertain sightseeing-weary kids, with futuristic gardens, an excellent science museum, a music complex, and a cinema. You could easily spend a whole day here.

The park itself was designed in the 1980s by postmodern architecture star Bernard Tschumi, who successfully incorporated industrial elements, children's games (don't miss the dragon slide), lots of green space, and dreamlike light sculptures along the canal into one vast yet unified playground. A great place for a picnic, the lawns of La Villette attract rehearsing samba bands and pickup soccer games. In summer there's a free outdoor cinema festival—people gather at dusk to picnic and watch movies on a huge inflatable screen.

In cold weather, visit the museums, the submarine, the circus tent (which features superb contemporary acrobatic theater performances), and **La Géode**—it looks like a huge silver golf ball but is actually an Omnimax cinema made of polished steel, with an enormous hemispherical screen. The ambitious Cité des Sciences et de l'Industrie (⊠*30 av. Corentin-Cariou, La Villette* ☎*01–40–05–80–00* ⊕*www.cite-sciences.fr*)tries to do for science and industry what the Pompidou does for modern art. There are 60 or so colorful interactive contraptions, and the multilingual children's workshops are perfect ways to while away rainy afternoons. The museum is open Tuesday through Sunday 10–6; admission ranges from €3 to €15, depending on whether you visit the planetarium and the submarine, take a workshop, or see an exhibition. If you're with very young children, don't miss the fish-tank wall in the basement. The postmodern **Cité de la Musique** is a music academy designed by geometry-obsessed Christian de Portzamparc. It has a state-of-the-art concert hall and the spectacular **Musée de la Musique** (⊠*221 av. Jean-Jaurès, La Villette* ☎*01–44–84–44–84* ⊕*www.cite-musique.fr*). The music museum contains a mind-tingling array of 900 instruments; their sounds and story are evoked through wireless headphones (ask for English commentary). It's open Tuesday through Saturday noon–6, and Sunday 10–6; during the current renovation, admission is free (renovations should be finishing in late 2008, at which point ticket prices will change).

All that remains of the slaughterhouse is **La Grande Halle** (Great Hall), a magnificent iron-and-glass building now used for exhibitions, performances, and trade shows.

Place de la Bastille. Nothing remains of the infamous Bastille prison destroyed at the beginning of the French Revolution, and until the late '80s there was little more to see here than a huge traffic circle and

9

BASTILLE AT NIGHT

From Place de la Bastille, go up Rue de la Roquette and turn right onto Rue de Lappe, the Parisians' answer to Bourbon Street. Lappe has long been a favorite for artists and writers, including Henry Miller. In the early 1900s, Auvergne immigrants brought *bal musette*, accordion-driven popular music, with them, and many later collaborated with gypsy jazzman Django Reinhardt. One of its anchors is the Balajo dance club, established in 1930 and still going strong. Postgentrification, these tangled streets have added unusual shops, theaters, and galleries to the constantly evolving bar lineup.

✉ Entrances on Rue des Rondeaux, Bd. de Ménilmontant, and Rue de la Réunion, Père Lachaise

⊕ www.pere-lachaise.com

⊘ Easter–Sept., daily 8–6; Oct.–Easter, daily 8–dusk

Ⓜ Gambetta, Philippe-Auguste, Père-Lachaise

TIPS

▪ Buy a map at the entrance on Boulevard de Ménilmontant—you're still likely to get lost, but that's part of the pleasure of wandering here. On a hot day, don't be surprised to see many locals simply sitting on the benches, reading or feeding the many feral cats. Just resist the urge to picnic in this calm oasis, as it's considered disrespectful.

▪ Note that the two biggest draws are Jim Morrison's grave (with its own guard to keep Doors fans under control) and the life-size bronze figure of Victor Noir, whose alleged fertility-enhancing power accounts for the patches rubbed smooth by hopeful hands.

▪ One of the best days to visit Père-Lachaise is on All Saints' Day (November 1), when everyone in Paris brings flowers to adorn the graves of favorite dead celebrities.

Press a lipsticked kiss to Oscar Wilde's tombstone or bring a red rose for "the little sparrow" Edith Piaf—the cobblestone avenues and immense trees make the 118-acre cemetery a worthwhile trip. Named for Père François de la Chaise, Louis XIV's confessor, it has some political history attached to it—it was the site of the Paris Commune's final battle on May 28, 1871, when the rebel troops were lined up against the Mur des Fédérés (*Federalists' Wall*) in the southeast corner and shot.

HIGHLIGHTS

Aside from the sheer aesthetic beauty of the cemetery, the main attraction is what (or who, more accurately) is belowground. Here's a list of grave sites you won't want to miss:

1. **Pierre Abélard** (1079 –1142), French philosopher, lover of Heloise.
2. **Honoré de Balzac** (1799–1850), French writer
3. **Sarah Bernhardt** (1844–1923), French actress
4. **Georges Bizet** (1838 –1875), French composer
5. **Maria Callas** (1923–77), Greek-American opera singer
6. **Frédéric Chopin** (1810–49), Franco-Polish composer
7. **Sidonie-Gabrielle Colette** (1873–1954), French writer
8. **Jacques-Louis David** (1748 –1825) French painter
9. **Eugène Delacroix** (1798–1863), Romance painter
10. **Max Ernst** (1891–1976) German painter
11. **Théodore Géricault** (1791 –1824) French painter
12. **Stéphane Grappelli** (1908 –1997) French jazz violinist
13. **Baron Haussmann** (1809–91), French civic planner
14. **Sedegh Hedayat** (1903–51), Iranian writer
15. **Heloïse** (1101-1162) scholar, lover of Pierre Abelard
16. **Jean Auguste-Dominique Ingres** (1780-1867) French painter

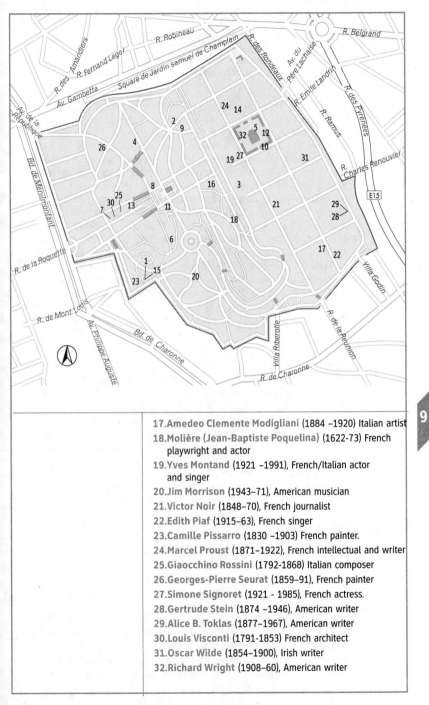

17. **Amedeo Clemente Modigliani** (1884 –1920) Italian artist
18. **Molière (Jean-Baptiste Poquelina)** (1622-73) French playwright and actor
19. **Yves Montand** (1921 –1991), French/Italian actor and singer
20. **Jim Morrison** (1943–71), American musician
21. **Victor Noir** (1848–70), French journalist
22. **Edith Piaf** (1915–63), French singer
23. **Camille Pissarro** (1830 –1903) French painter.
24. **Marcel Proust** (1871–1922), French intellectual and writer
25. **Giaocchino Rossini** (1792-1868) Italian composer
26. **Georges-Pierre Seurat** (1859–91), French painter
27. **Simone Signoret** (1921 - 1985), French actress.
28. **Gertrude Stein** (1874 –1946), American writer
29. **Alice B. Toklas** (1877–1967), American writer
30. **Louis Visconti** (1791-1853) French architect
31. **Oscar Wilde** (1854–1900), Irish writer
32. **Richard Wright** (1908–60), American writer

the **Colonne de Juillet** (*July Column*), a memorial to the victims of the uprisings in 1830 and 1848. When the Opéra de la Bastille came along in 1989, though, the surrounding streets were reenergized with art galleries, funky clubs, and Spanish-style tapas bars, especially along Rue de Lappe—once a haunt of Edith Piaf—and Rue de la Roquette.

The original building here, the ominous Château de la Bastille, was protected by eight immense towers and a wide moat. (Its ground plan is marked by hard-to-find paving stones set into the modern square.) Built by Charles V in the late 14th century, it was a fortress intended to guard the city's eastern entrance. By Louis XIII's reign (1610–43), it was used almost exclusively to house political prisoners. Voltaire, the Marquis de Sade, and the mysterious Man in the Iron Mask were among many incarcerated here. The Bastille's political symbolism and its location between the city center and an impoverished working-class neighborhood made it an obvious target for the largely unarmed mob that broke into the prison on July 14, 1789. They killed the governor, stole firearms, and freed the seven remaining prisoners. Later that year, the prison was knocked down. Original stones from the building were carved into facsimiles of the Bastille and sent to each of the French provinces as a memento of royal oppression. The key to the prison was given to George Washington by Lafayette, and has remained at Mount Vernon ever since. Of course, July 14—Bastille Day—is now the national holiday of France. If you're in town for it, don't miss the gut-rattling sight of high-tech tanks speeding down the Champs-Elysées. Ⓜ*Bastille.*

★ **Viaduc des Arts.** This redbrick viaduct once brought trains to the edge of the canal at Bastille; today it's brought a swath of greenery and a jolt of energy to the neighborhood. The elevated tracks have been transformed into a stylish promenade with upscale boutiques and artisans' workshops sheltered in its arches. The only hardship is deciding whether to stay up on the garden path or browse the shops down at street level (stairways regularly connect the two levels). You can detour down Rue de Lyon, which will lead you to the **Gare de Lyon**; inside, walk up the grand staircase to gape at Le Train Bleu, a hallucinatory Belle Époque restaurant and bar that was once Salvador Dalí's favorite Paris hangout. ✉*Av. Daumesnil, Bastille* Ⓜ*Gare de Lyon, Daumesnil, Bel-Air.*

ALSO WORTH SEEING

☾ **Bois de Vincennes.** The Vincennes Woods in east Paris are often considered the poor man's Bois de Boulogne, but the comparison is unfair: the Bois de Vincennes is no more difficult to get to and has equally illustrious origins. It, too, was landscaped under Napoléon III, although Louis XV had already created a park here in 1731. The park has several lakes, notably **Lac Daumesnil**, with two islands, and **Lac des Minimes**, with three; rowboats can be hired at both. There's also a zoo, the **Hippodrome de Vincennes** (a cinder-track racecourse), a castle, a flower garden, and several cafés. In spring there's also an amusement park, the **Foire du Trône**. Bikes can be rented from the Château de Vincennes de Vincennes métro station for €4 an hour or €14 a day. To reach the park, take the métro to Porte Dorée or Château de Vincennes.

The impressive **Château de Vincennes** (⊠ *Av. de Paris, Bois de Vincennes* ☎ *01–48–08–31–20* ⊕ *www.chateau-vincennes.fr* ⊠ *€7.50* ⊗ *May–Aug., daily 10–*

6; Sept.–Apr., daily 10–5 Ⓜ *Château de Vincennes*) is on the northern edge of the Bois. Built in the 15th century by various French kings, the castle is France's medieval Versailles, an imposing, high-walled castle surrounded by a dry moat and dominated by a 170-foot keep. The royal residence eventually became a state prison, with illustrious convicts such as philosopher Diderot. Parts of the chateau have been reopened to the public after a lengthy and spectacular renovation.

An exceptional Art Deco building that once held an African art museum now teems with fish instead of artifacts. The **Palais de la Porte Dorée Tropical Aquarium** (⊠ *293 av. Daumesnil, Bois de Vincennes* ☎ *01–44–74–84–80* ⊠ *€5.70* ⊗ *Tues.–Sun. 10–5:15* Ⓜ *Porte Dorée*) fills the basement with tanks of colorful tropical fish, crocodiles, and turtles, but the building itself is even more captivating; built for the Colonial Exhibition in 1931, it has an ornate façade depicting France's erstwhile overseas empire. Sharing the building is the new **Cité Nationale de l'Historie de l'Immigration** (⊠ *293 av. Daumesnil, Bois de Vincennes* ☎ *01–53–59–58–60* ⊠ *€3* ⊗ *Tues.–Fri. 10–5:15, weekends 10–7* Ⓜ *Porte Dorée*), which focuses on the history of immigration in France—a controversial subject in today's political climate.

*[e]*The **Parc Floral de Paris** (⊠ *Rte. de la Pyramide, Bois de Vincennes* ☎ *01–55–94–20–20* ⊠ *€3* ⊗ *Apr.–Sept., daily 9:30–8; Oct.–Mar., daily 9:30–5* Ⓜ *Château de Vincennes*) is the Bois de Vincennes's 70-acre flower garden. It includes a lake and water garden and is renowned for its seasonal displays of blooms. It also contains a miniature train, a game area, and an "exo-tarium" with tropical fish and reptiles; in summer, an outdoor jazz festival makes this the most popular weekend picnic site in the city.

Some 1,200 mammals and birds can be seen at the 33-acre **Parc Zoologique**, (⊠ *53 av. de St-Maurice, Bois de Vincennes* ☎ *01–44–75–20–10* ⊠ *€5* ⊗ *Daily 9–5* Ⓜ *Porte Dorée*), the largest zoo in France. Parts of the zoo are closed for rehabilitation through 2008. The most striking element is the 210-foot steel-and-concrete Grand Rocher, an artificial rock built in 1934, inhabited by wild mountain sheep and penguins.*[e]*

Maison de l'architecture d'Ile de France–Les Recollets. If you're heading to Canal St-Martin, pause at this elegant Renaissance monastery, created by Marie de' Medici. After stints as a military hospital (in the 1800s) and an artists' squat (in the 1980s), the site has become a center for architecture workshops and an international artists' residence. Walk

9

Dining at a Glance

For full reviews
⇨ Ch. 17

INEXPENSIVE DINING

Astier, *Bistro,* 44 rue Jean-Pierre Timbaud

Bofinger, *Brasserie,* 5–7 rue de la Bastille

Chai 33, *Modern French,* 33 Cour St-Emilion

Dong Huong, *Vietnamese,* 14 rue Louis-Bonnet

Le Martel, *North African,* 3 rue Martel

Le Passage des Carmagnoles, *Bistro,* 18 passage de la Bonne Graine

Sardegna a Tavola, *Italian,* 1 rue de Cotte

MODERATE DINING

Au Boeuf Couronné, *Brasserie,* 188 av. Jean-Jaurès

La Boulangerie, *Bistro,* 15 rue des Panoyaux

Chez Jenny, *Brasserie,* 39 bd. du Temple

Chez Omar, *North African,* 47 rue de Bretagne

Le Baron Bouge, *Wine Bar,* 1 rue Théophile Roussel

Jacques Mélac, *Wine Bar,* 42 rue Léon-Frot

L'Oulette, *Bistro,* 15 pl. Lachambeaudie

Le Repaire de Cartouche, *Bistro,* 8 bd. des Filles du Calvaire

Le Square Trousseau, *Bistro,* 1 rue Antoine Vollon

Le Temps au Temps, *Bistro,* 13 rue Paul Bert

Unico, *Latin American,* 15 rue Paul-Bert

Wok, *Chinese,* 25 rue des Taillandiers

EXPENSIVE DINING

Au Trou Gascon, *Bistro,* 40 rue Taine

La Cave Gourmande, *Bistro,* 10 rue du Géneral-Brunet

down Rue des Recollets to see the yellow day-care center created by Frédéric Borel (a rising star in the modern "architectural hedonism" movement in Paris), or take a break in the small garden behind the Recollets, which leads to the canal—a great place for people-watching on the weekend. ⊠ *148 rue du Faubourg St-Martin, République* ☎ *01–53–26–10–70* ⊕ *www.maisonarchitecture-idf.org* ⊠ *Free* ⊙ *Tues.–Fri. 10–7, weekends 2–7* Ⓜ *Gare de l'Est.*

☮ **Parc des Buttes-Chaumont.** The 19e arrondissement doesn't have many tourist attractions, but locals flock to this hilly park, part of Napoléon III's "greening" of Paris (the emperor had spent years in exile in London and loved that city's public parks). Built on abandoned gypsum quarries and a former gallows, Haussmann managed to transform the mess into elegant apartments ringing a steep-sloped romantic escape; there are waterfalls, grottoes, mysterious pathways, a lake filled with swans, and even a pseudo-Greek temple. When downtown Paris is stifling, this is a nice retreat; there's even a Guignol de Paris (an open-air puppet theater) on the northern side of the park; shows start at 3:30 PM Wednesday and weekends (€2.50 charge; weather permitting, closed in winter). ⊠ *Rue Botzaris, Buttes-Chaumont* Ⓜ *Laumière, Buttes-Chaumont, Botzaris.*

The Quartier Latin

Quartier Latin

WORD OF MOUTH

"Today was market day and the market at Place Monge was in full swing so we headed there to soak up the atmosphere...then to rue Mouffetard, watching the singing and dancing and enjoying a crowded street scene. People don't look that happy while shopping at home. We wandered up the street washing in the wonderful food stores and restaurants. This street always feels more vibrant with the influx of young people, students, and their joie de vivre."

—AGM_Cape_Cod

GETTING ORIENTED

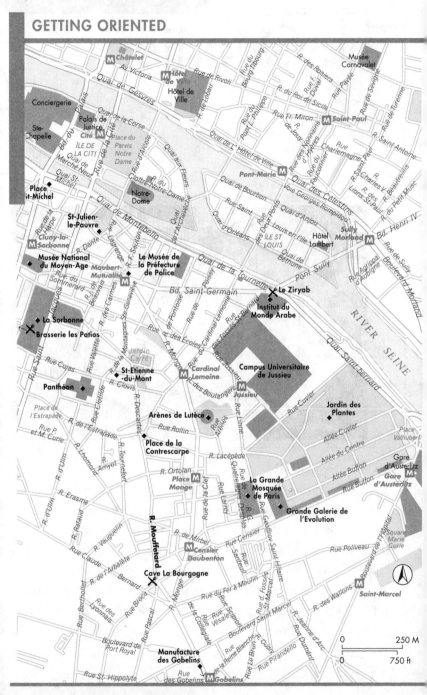

Châtelet

Av. Victoria

Hôtel de Ville

Hôtel de Ville

Quai de Gesvres

Rue de Rivoli

Musée Carnavalet

Concergerie

Quai de la Corse

Palais de Justice

Ste-Chapelle

Place du Parvis Notre Dame

ÎLE DE LA CITÉ

Quai de Marché Neuf

Quai St-Michel

Place St-Michel

Saint-Paul

Pont-Marie

Quai de l'Hôtel de Ville

Notre-Dame

St-Julien-le-Pauvre

Cluny-la-Sorbonne

Musée National du Moyen-Age

Maubert-Mutualité

Le Musée de la Préfecture de Police

Quai de Montebello

Quai d'Orléans

ÎLE ST LOUIS

Hôtel Lambert

Sully Morland

Bd. Saint-Germain

Le Ziryab

Institut du Monde Arabe

La Sorbonne

Brasserie les Patios

Jardin Carré

St-Etienne-du-Mont

Panthéon

Campus Universitaire de Jussieu

Jussieu

RIVER SEINE

Quai Saint-Bernard

Cardinal Lemoine

Arènes de Lutèce

Jardin des Plantes

Place de l'Estrapade

Place de la Contrescarpe

Allée Cuvier

Allée du Centre

Allée Buffon

Rue Buffon

Gare d'Austerlitz

Place Valhubert

Place Monge

La Grande Mosquée de Paris

Grande Galerie de l'Evolution

Square Marie Curie

R. Mouffetard

Censier Daubenton

Cave La Bourgogne

Saint-Marcel

Boulevard Saint Marcel

Manufacture des Gobelins

Boulevard de Port Royal

Rue St-Hippolyte

Gobelins

0   250 M

0   750 ft

TOP REASONS TO GO

Musée National du Moyen-Age. On the site of an ancient Roman bath, this former abbey is home to the famous Lady and the Unicorn tapestries; the building, tranquil garden, and extensive collection have the hush of a medieval monastery.

Shakespeare & Company. This legendary English-language bookstore is more than a shopping destination; it's a meeting place for young expats and curious travelers alike.

Rue Mouffetard. Stroll down this winding market street to construct a picnic à la française with fresh breads, deliciously smelly cheeses, and briny fresh oysters.

Jardin des Plantes. This is a great spot to picnic or to rest your tired feet on one of the many shaded benches.

La Grande Mosquée de Paris. Enjoy a mint tea in the lovely leafy courtyard of Paris's most beautiful mosque.

MAKING THE MOST OF YOUR TIME

The Quartier Latin is the perfect place to wander sans itinerary, though there is no shortage of sites worth seeing. Shopping here is generally more affordable, though less original, than in other neighborhoods, and there are lots of new- and used-book stores, many of which stock English-language titles. Pick up a picnic at the many food shops along Rue Mouffetard (closed Monday), or head to the open-air market at Place Monge (Wednesday, Friday, and Sunday mornings), then savor your booty on a bench at the Jardin de Plantes. Sip mint tea either in the courtyard café at the lovely Grande Mosquée (Mosque) de Paris or take in a terrific view on the roof of the Institut du Monde Arabe (closed Monday). Stroll the hilly streets around the Panthéon on your way to see the treasures at the Musée National du Moyen-Age (closed Tuesday). Finish with a sunset apéritif on one of the barge cafés (open spring to fall) along the Seine, across from Notre-Dame.

GETTING HERE

The Quartier Latin is the 5ᵉ arrondissement. Take line 4 to métro St-Michel for the Musée National du Moyen-Age or for a walk along the river toward Shakespeare & Company. The Place Monge stop on line 7 puts you near the winding streets around the Panthéon and Rue Mouffetard, the Mosquée de Paris, and the Jardin des Plantes. Les Gobelins neighborhood straddles the 5e, 13e, and 14e arrondissements, but is considered part of the 5e because of the Manufacture des Gobelins.

BEST CAFÉS

Le Ziryab. This outdoor café/terrace on the top floor of the Institut du Monde Arabe is a great place to enjoy an affordable Lebanese lunch or dinner, with fantastic views. It's closed Monday. ⊠ *Institut du Monde Arabe, 1 rue des Foss-St-Bernard, Quartier Latin* ☎ *01—55—42—55—42.*

Brasserie les Patios. You may need a student ID to get into the Sorbonne, but all you need is a newspaper or a fat novel to fit right in at this brasserie. The large outdoor terrace is perfect for people-watching. ⊠ *5 pl. de la Sorbonne, Quartier Latin* ☎ *01–43–54–34–43.*

Cave La Bourgogne. Settle in at this bustling old-school bistro for a morning coffee, or take a seat at the zinc bar for a glass of wine. ⊠ *144 rue Mouffetard, Quartier Latin* ☎ *01–47–07–82–80.*

10

The Quartier Latin is the heart of student Paris—and has been for more than 800 years. France's oldest university, *La Sorbonne*, was founded here in 1257, and the neighborhood takes its name from the fact that Latin was the common language of the students, who had come from all over Europe. Today the area is full of cheap and cheerful cafés, bars, and shops.

Updated by
Linda Hervieux

The main drag, Boulevard St-Michel, is a bustling maw where bookshops have given way to chain clothing stores and fast-food joints—but don't let that stop you! There are (almost) as many French people wandering the streets here as there are tourists. At **Place St-Michel**, the symbolic gateway to the quartier, notice the 19th-century fountain depicting St. Michael slaying the dragon, a symbolic warning to rebellious locals from Napoléon III. Today the fountain serves as a meeting spot and makes a rather fine metaphor for the boulevard it anchors: a bit grimy but very popular.

When you've had enough of the crowds, turn off the boulevard and explore the side streets, where you'll find quirky boutiques and intimate bistros. Or stop for a demi (a half pint of draft beer) at one of the many cafés on the Place de la Sorbonne, ground zero for students (and their many noisy demonstrations). Around the winding streets behind the **Panthéon**, where French luminaries are laid to rest, you'll still find plenty of academics arguing philosophy while sipping espresso, but today the 5e arrondissement is also one of Paris's most charming and sought-after (read: expensive) places to live.

Shop along **Rue Mouffetard** as Parisians do—all the while complaining about the high prices—for one of the best selections of runny cheeses, fresh breads, and charcuterie. Grab a seat in a bustling café—or do as the locals do and stand at the bar, where drinks are always cheaper. Film buffs won't have to look far to find one of the small cinema revival houses showing old American films in English (look for V.O. for version originale). Not far from Rue Mouffetard is the gorgeous white La

Grande **Mosquée de Paris** with its impressive minaret. Just beyond the mosque is the **Jardin des Plantes**—a large, if somewhat bland, botanical garden that is home to three natural-history museums, notably the **Grande Galerie de l'Evolution**. Inside, kids can marvel at enormous whale skeletons, along with all sorts of taxidermy. Some of Paris's most intriguing sites are in this neighborhood, including the **Musée National du Moyen-Age** and the innovative **Institut du Monde Arabe**. And see ancient history mingling with modern life at the **Arènes de Lutèce,** a Roman amphitheater and favorite soccer pitch for neighborhood kids.

MAIN ATTRACTIONS

☾ **Grande Galerie de l'Evolution** *(Great Hall of Evolution).* With a parade of taxidermied animals ranging from the tiniest dung beetle to the tallest giraffe, this museum in the Jardin des Plantes is an excellent break for kids who have been trudging, sourpussed, around the Louvre. The flagship of the three natural-history museums in the Jardin des Plantes, it is easily the most impressive. The original 1889 building was renovated in 1994, and has a ceiling that changes color to suggest storms, twilight, or the hot savanna sun. Don't miss the gigantic skeleton of a blue whale, and the stuffed royal rhino—he came from the menagerie at Versailles, where he was a pet to Louis XV. There are some English-language information boards available, but not many. ■TIP➜Hang on to your ticket; it'll get you a discount at the other museums within the Jardin des Plantes. ⊠*36 rue Geoffroy-St-Hilaire, Quartier Latin* ☎*01–40–79–54–79* ⊕*www.mnhn.fr* 🎟*€8* ☉ *Wed.–Mon. 10–6* Ⓜ*Pl. Monge or Jussieu.*

★ **Institut du Monde Arabe.** Jean Nouvel is a master of glass construction; here, at the *Institute of the Arab World* (IMA), he tempers transparency with a beautiful façade of variable, irislike apertures that control the light entering the building, evoking a Moorish-style screen. The IMA's layout reinterprets the traditional enclosed Arab courtyard. Inside, items largely on loan from Syria and Tunisia help present Arab culture from prehistory to the present day, with an emphasis on painting and medicine, but the temporary exhibitions tend to be a bigger draw than the permanent collection. The museum also includes performance spaces, a sound-and-image center, a vast library, and a permanent collection of Arab-Islamic art, textiles, and ceramics. Information in English is limited, but temporary exhibitions usually have English audioguides. ■TIP➜Glass elevators whisk you to the ninth floor, where you can sip mint tea in the rooftop café, Le Ziryab, while feasting on one of the best views in Paris. ⊠*1 rue des Fossés-St-Bernard, Quartier*

10

DID YOU KNOW?

French architect Jean Nouvel made news when the Quai Branly museum opened in 2006, but in 1987 he was already wowing Parisians with the Institut du Monde Arabe, an intriguing fusion of Arabian and French styles. His new Orchestra Hall, which won't open until 2012, is sure to get attention, too. In the meantime, he was awarded the Pritzker Architecture Prize in 2008.

Shakespeare & Company

In the shadow of Notre-Dame across the Seine, this English-language bookstore is one of Paris's most eccentric and lovable literary institutions. Founded by George Whitman, this maze of new and used books has offered a sense of community (and often a bed) to wandering writers since the 1950s. The store takes its name from Sylvia Beach's original Shakespeare & Company, which opened in 1919 on Rue d'Odeon, welcoming the likes of Ernest Hemingway, James Baldwin, and James Joyce. Beach famously bucked the system when she published Joyce's *Ulysses* in 1922, but her original store closed in 1941. After the war Whitman picked up the gauntlet, naming his own bookstore after its famous predecessor.

Today, Shakespeare & Company welcomes a new generation of Paris dreamers. Walk up the almost impossibly narrow stairs to the second floor and you'll see laptop computers and sleeping bags tucked between the aging volumes and under dusty daybeds; it's sort of like a hippie commune. A revolving cast of characters helps out in the shop or cooks meals for fellow residents. They're in good company; Henry Miller, Samuel Beckett, and William Burroughs are among the famous writers to benefit from Whitman's hospitality.

Shakespeare & Company (at 37 rue de la Bûcherie, 01–43–25–40–93) is open daily 10 am to 11 pm and has readings most Monday evenings. Check the Web site (www.shakespeareco.org) for a schedule of events.

Latin ☎01–40–51–38–38 ⊕www.imarabe.org ✉Exhibitions €9, museum €3 ⊙Tues.–Sun. 10–6 Ⓜ Cardinal Lemoine.

☾ **Jardin des Plantes** (*Botanical Gardens*). Bordered by the Seine, Gare d'Austerlitz, and the ugly, utilitarian Jussieu University campus, this swath of greenery is much loved by residents but hardly the most impressive of Parisian gardens. Come to picnic or, if you have kids, take them to the excellent **Grande Galerie de l'Evolution** (⇨*above*) **or one of the other** two other natural-history museums here: the **Musée Paléontologique, which has some dinosaurs, and the Musée Minéralogique** with rocks and minerals. Plant lovers will enjoy the botanical garden, the rose garden, and the several greenhouses from the 1930s that are filled with tropical and desert plants. The garden is also home to the Ménagerie, one of the world's oldest zoos, founded by Napoléon. It's a small, rather sad zoo by North American standards, and is utterly forgettable, but if your kids are bored, take them to see the two notable inhabitants: Kiki, an ancient Seychelles tortoise, and an alligator abandoned in a Paris hotel room. ■TIP➔**Keep your ticket: entrance to any of these sites will get you a discount to other museums within the gardens.** ✉*Entrances on Rue Geoffroy-St-Hilaire, Rue Cuvier, Rue de Buffon, and Quai St-Bernard, Quartier Latin* ☎01–40–79–54–79 ⊕www.mnhn.fr ✉*Museums and zoo €6–€8 (free, 4 and under), greenhouses €2.50* ⊙*Museums Wed.–Mon. 10–5 or 6. Zoo June–Aug., daily 9–6; Sept.–May, daily 9–5. Garden daily 7:30* AM*–sunset* Ⓜ *Gare d'Austerlitz, Jussieu.*

Fodor'sChoice **Musée National du Moyen-Age**
★ *(National Museum of the Middle Ages, nicknamed the Musée Cluny).* Built on the ruins of Lutecia's Roman Baths, the **Hôtel de Cluny** has been a museum since medievalist Alexandre Du Sommerard established his collection here in 1844. The over-the-top mansion was a choice location for such a collection; the 15th-century building

was created for the abbot of Cluny, leader of the most powerful monastery in France. Symbols of the abbot's power literally surround the building, from the crenellated walls that proclaimed his independence from the king, to the carved Burgundian grapes, symbolizing his valuable vineyards, twining up the entrance. The scallop shells *Coquilles-Saint-Jacques* covering the façade are a symbol of religious pilgrimage, another important source of income for the abbot; the well-traveled pilgrimage route to Spain, Rue St-Jacques, once ran just around the corner. The highlight of the collection is the world-famous *Dame à la Licorne* (*Lady and the Unicorn*) tapestry series, woven in the 15th or 16th century, probably in Belgium. The tapestries are an allegorical representation of the five senses. In each, a unicorn and a lion surround an elegant lady against an elaborate millefleur (literally, 1,000 flowers) background. The enigmatic sixth tapestry, *Mon seul désir,* is thought to symbolize love or understanding. The collection also includes the original sculpted heads of the *Kings of Israel and Judah* from Notre-Dame, discovered in 1977: the statues were decapitated off the cathedral during the Revolution and the heads hidden by a nobleman near today's Galeries Lafayette. You can also visit the remnants of the city's Roman baths—hot (*caldarium*) and cold (*frigidarium*), the latter containing the *Boatmen's Pillar,* Paris's oldest sculpture. A charming garden is laid out in the medieval style, using the flora depicted in the unicorn tapestries. ✉ *6 pl. Paul-Painlevé, Quartier Latin* ☎ *01–53–73–78–00* ⊕ *www.musee-moyenage.fr* ✇ *€7.50, free 1st Sun. of month, otherwise €4 on Sun.* ☽ *Wed.–Mon. 9:15–5:45* Ⓜ *Cluny–La Sorbonne.*

10

NEED A BREAK? **Place de la Contrescarpe.** This intimate square behind the Panthéon doesn't start to swing until dusk, when its cafés and bars fill up. Café Delmas, at 2 place de la Contrescarpe (01–43–26–51–26), has a large terrace and comfy club chairs that attract a mix of students and professionals. During the day the Place de la Contrescarpe has something of an intimate, small-town feel to it as people haggle over produce at the daily market at the bottom of Rue Mouffetard. ✉ *Quartier Latin* Ⓜ *Monge.*

Panthéon. Rome has St. Peter's, London has St. Paul's, and Paris has the Pantheon, whose enormous dome dominates the Left Bank. Built as a church, it has long been the resting place of a virtual who's who of France's cultural and political elite, including Voltaire, Zola, Dumas, Victor Hugo, Rousseau, and Marie Curie. Begun in 1764, the building was almost complete when the French Revolution erupted; meanwhile, Soufflot, the architect, had died, supposedly from worrying that the dome would collapse. He needn't have fretted: the dome is so perfect that Foucault used this space to test his famous pendulum. The best view is had from outside, however, as the vast neoclassical interior looks more like an abandoned wine cellar than a hallowed burial ground. It's entirely empty except for the 19th-century murals lining the walls and a model of Foucault's pendulum hanging from the center of the dome. The famous residents are in the crypt. There is little info in English—and none on the people buried here, so if you're a history buff, do your homework before you come. ⊠*Pl. du Panthéon, Quartier Latin* ☎*01-44-32-18-00* ⊕*http://pantheon.monuments-nationaux.fr/en/* ⊡*€7.50* ⊙*Apr.–Sept., daily 10–6:30; Oct.–Mar., daily 10–6* Ⓜ*Cardinal Lemoine; RER: Luxembourg.*

Fodor'sChoice
★
Rue Mouffetard. This winding cobblestone street is one of Paris's oldest—it was once a Roman road leading south from Lutecia (the Roman name for Paris) to Italy. The upper half of the street is dotted with restaurants that can get rather touristy; the lower half is home to a lively market, open daily—the highlight of the street, though, is the stretch in between, where, as your nose will tell you, the shops are literally spilling over into the street with luscious offerings such as roasting chickens and potatoes, rustic saucisson, pâtés, and pungent cheeses, especially at Androuët (No. 134). You can find everything you'll need for a picnic as well as gifts to bring home to your favorite foodie. If you're here in the morning, Le Mouffetard Café (No. 116) is a good place to stop for breakfast (for about €8). For one of the best baguettes in Paris detour to the nearby Boulanger de Monge at 123 rue Monge. Note that most of the shops are closed on Monday.

ALSO WORTH SEEING

☯ **Arènes de Lutèce** *(Lutetia Amphitheater).* This Roman amphitheater, designed as a theater and circus, was almost completely destroyed by barbarians in AD 280. The site was rediscovered in 1869, and you can still see part of the stage and tiered seating. Along with the remains of the baths at Cluny, the arena constitutes rare evidence of the powerful Roman city of Lutetia that flourished on the Rive Gauche in the 3rd century. Today it's a favorite spot for picnicking, or a pickup game of soccer or *boules.* ⊠*Entrance at Rue Monge or Rue de Navarre, Quartier Latin* ⊡*Free* ⊙*Daily 8–sunset* Ⓜ*Pl. Monge.*

Manufacture des Gobelins. Tapestries have been woven on this spot in southeastern Paris, on the banks of the long-covered Bièvre River, since 1662. Guided tours combine historical explanation with the chance to admire both old tapestries and today's weavers at work in their airy workshops. To get here from the Place de la Contrescarpe, go south on Rue Mouffetard and continue down Rue de Bazeilles, which becomes Avenue des Gobelins (about a 15-minute walk). Call ahead to check that the guide on duty speaks English. ⊠*42 av. des Gobelins, Les Gobelins*

☎01–44–08–52–00 🎫€8 🕐Tues.–
Thurs., guided tours at 2 and 2:45
Ⓜ Les Gobelins.

★ **La Grande Mosquée de Paris.** This
beautiful white mosque was built
between 1922 and 1925 and has
tranquil arcades and a minaret
decorated in the style of Moorish
Spain. Enjoy a sweet mint tea and
an exotic pastry in the charming
courtyard tea salon or tuck into
some couscous in the restaurant.
Prayer rooms are not open to the
public. There are inexpensive ham-
mams, or Turkish steam baths,
here with scrubs and massages
on offer—but be warned that the
facilities are extremely rustic. ✉2
pl. du Puits de l'Ermite; entrance
to tea salon and restaurant at
39 rue Geoffroy Saint-Hillaire,
Quartier Latin ☎01–43–31–18–
14 🎫Guided tour €3 🕐Guided tours in French, daily 9–noon and
2–8 Ⓜ Pl. Monge.

**THE 13E
ARRONDISSEMENT**

The friendly villagelike neighborhood of La Butte aux Cailles, in
the 13ᵉ arrondissement, south of
the Place d'Italie, is a funky destination with a hip crowd, not far
from the Latin Quarter if you want
a break from the tourists. The
many bars and cafés buzz until
well after the last métro stops
running. You can settle in for bistro fare at the crowded, fun, and
cooperatively run **Les Temps des
Cerises** (✉18–20 rue de la Butte
aux Cailles, La Butte aux Cailles
☎01–45–89–69–48), whose
name recalls a song made famous
by the Paris Commune.

Place St-Michel. This square was named for Gabriel Davioud's grandiose
1860 fountain sculpture of St. Michael slaying the dragon—a loaded
political gesture from Napoléon III's go-to guy, Baron Haussmann,
who hoped St. Michael would quell the Revolutionary fervor of the
neighborhood. Today the fountain is a good starting point for a walking tour. ✉Quartier Latin Ⓜ Métro or RER: St-Michel.

St-Etienne-du-Mont. This beautiful church has been visited by several
popes, owing to the fact that Ste-Geneviève, the patron saint of Paris, is
buried here. The chaotic combination of the building's Gothic, Renaissance, and early Baroque styles contrasts with the cold and pure clas-
sicism of the Pantheon. St-Etienne contains the only rood screen in
Paris—a masterwork of carved knot work dating from 1525—and the
church's organ is the oldest in the city, from 1631. An archbishop of
Paris was stabbed to death here in 1857 by a defrocked priest angry
over church celibacy laws. Look for the marker in the floor near the
entrance. ✉30 rue Descartes, Quartier Latin Ⓜ Cardinal Lemoine.

St-Julien-le-Pauvre. This tiny shrine in the shadow of Notre-Dame is
one of the three oldest churches in Paris. Founded in 1045, it became
a meeting place for university students in the 12th century. This was
Dante's church when he was in Paris writing his *Divine Comedy* in
1300. Today's structure dates mostly from the 1600s, but keep an eye
out for older pillars, which crawl with carvings of demons. The church
holds classical and gospel concerts, or you can simply perch on a bench

Dining at a Glance

For full reviews
⇨ Ch. 17

INEXPENSIVE DINING
L'Avant-Goût, *Bistro,*
26 rue Bobillot

La Chine Massena,
Chinese, Centre Commercial Massena, 13 pl. de Venetie

Mirama, *Chinese,* 17 rue St-Jacques

L'Ourcine, *Bistro,*
92 rue Broca

Le Pré Verre, *Modern French,* 8 rue Thénard

Ribouldingue, *Bistro,* 10 rue St-Julien-le-Pauvre

MODERATE DINING
Anacréon, *Bistro,* 53 bd. St-Marcel

Au Petit Marguery, *Bistro,* 9 bd. de Port Royal

Le Balzar, *Bistro,* 49 rue des Ecoles

Le Buisson Ardent, *Bistro,* 25 rue Jussieu

Chez René, *Bistro,*
14 bd. St-Germain

Les Papilles, *Wine Bar,* 30 rue Gay-Lussac

Toustem, 12 rue de l'Hôtel Colbert

EXPENSIVE DINING
La Tour d'Argent, *Haute French,* 15 quai de la Tournelle

in the garden to enjoy the view of Notre-Dame. ⊠*1 rue St-Julien-le-Pauvre, Quartier Latin* Ⓜ*St-Michel.*

La Sorbonne. You can't get into Paris's most famous university without a student ID, although you can try to talk your way past a friendly guard. If you succeed, enter on Rue Victor Cousin, cross the cobbled courtyard where students have gathered for nine centuries, and peek into the muraled lecture halls. Today, La Sorbonne remains the heart and soul of the Quartier Latin, though it is also known as Paris IV, one of several campuses that make up the public Université de Paris. ⊠*1 rue Victor Cousin, Quartier Latin* Ⓜ*Cluny-La Sorbonne.*

OFF THE
BEATEN
PATH

Le Musée de la Préfecture de Police. Crime buffs will enjoy this museum hidden on the second floor of the 5e arrondissement's police station. Although the exhibits are in French only, the photographs, letters, drawings, and memorabilia of some of the city's most sensational crimes are easy enough to follow. Relics include a guillotine, old uniforms, and remnants of the World War II occupation, including what's left of a firing post, German machine guns, and the star insignias worn by Jews. ⊠*4 rue de la Montagne Ste-Geneviève, Quartier Latin* ☎*01–44–41–52–50* Free ⊘Weekdays 9–5 Ⓜ*Maubert-Mutualité.*

St-Germain

Place St Sulpice

WORD OF MOUTH

"We headed back toward the hotel, but opted to get off the metro at St-Germain-des-Prés for an easy (and early) dinner...then followed up with a short walk to Place St-Sulpice—the fountain was illuminated, some kids were kicking a ball around, and the terrace at Café de la Mairie was full of outward-facing customers."

—travelnut

GETTING ORIENTED

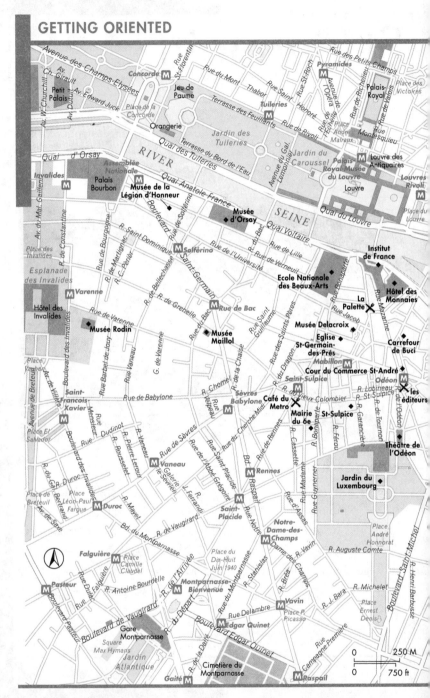

11

TOP REASONS TO GO

Musée d'Orsay. The graceful vaulted ceiling and abundance of natural light in this train-station-turned-museum is a reminder of why the Impressionist painters thought that train stations were the cathedrals of the 19th century.

Jardin du Luxembourg. Take in a puppet show, meander past the palace, or just laze by the fountain at this most elegant of Parisian gardens.

Musée Rodin. Stroll the garden of this elegant mansion; it's a lovely and intimate setting for the emotionally charged sculptures of Auguste Rodin.

Blvd. St-Germain. Window-shop along the avenue, then plunge into the warren of streets on the south side for a crash course in Paris chic.

Cafés, cafés, cafés. This is excellent people-watching territory. Take a seat at one of the many cafés, hang out, and watch the world go by.

MAKING THE MOST OF YOUR TIME

Aim for an early start—have a *café crème* at a café along the river and get to the Musée d'Orsay early, when crowds are thinner. Leave some time for window-shopping around the Boulevard St-Germain on your way to the Jardin du Luxembourg. You might want to plan to visit this area on a day other than Monday, when Musée d'Orsay, Musée Rodin, and many of the local art galleries and shops are closed. The Delacroix and Maillol museums are closed on Tuesday.

GETTING HERE

The St-Germain neighborhood is the 6ᵉ arrondissement. Take line 10 to métro Solferino or the RER to the Musée d'Orsay stop for direct access to the Orsay. To get to the heart of the shopping district take line 4 to métro St-Germain or St-Sulpice—and when you're tired of window-shopping, it's just a short walk to the Jardin du Luxembourg.

BEST CAFÉS

La Palette. This café with a terrace, on the corner of Rue de Seine and Rue Callot, has long been a favorite haunt of local gallery owners and Beaux Arts students. One of the students painted the ungainly portrait of the patron, François, that presides with mock authority. Closed Sunday. ⌂43 rue de Seine, St-Germain-des-Prés ☎01-43-26-68-15.

les éditeurs. This trendy café favored by the Parisian publishing set is a perfect place to sip a kir (white wine with black currant syrup) from a perch on the skinny sidewalk or at an inside table shadowed by book-lined walls. ⌂4 *carrefour de l'Odéon, St-Germain-des-Prés* ☎01–43–26–67–76.

Café du Métro. Settle in at this convivial café-brasserie for hot chocolate or French onion soup after an exhausting round of shoe shopping around the Rue de Rennes. Linger over coffee and a book, or use their Wi-Fi connection to get some work done. Closed Sunday. ⌂67 rue de Rennes, St-Germain-des-Prés ☎01-45-48-58-56.

Shanghai Café. Secreted away in the Maison de la Chine, this sleek little-known oasis of calm serves lunch and a nice afternoon tea. To find it, head to the back and pass through a small outpost of the upscale Hong Kong boutique Shanghai Tang. Closed Sunday. ⌂ *76 rue Bonaparte, St-Germain-des-Prés* ☎ *01–40–51–95–17* ⊕ *www.maisondelachine.fr.*

Sightseeing
★★★★★

Dining
★★★

Lodging
★★★★★

Shopping
★★★★★

Nightlife
★★

Updated by
Linda Hervieux

If you had to choose the most classically parisien neighborhood in Paris, this would be it. St-Germain-des-Prés has it all: genteel blocks lined with upscale art galleries, storied cafés, designer boutiques, and a fine selection of museums. Cast your eyes upward after dark and you may spy a frescoed ceiling in a tony apartment. These historic streets can get quite crowded, so mind your elbows and plunge in.

This *quartier* is named for the oldest church in Paris, **St-Germain-des-Prés**, and it's become a prized address for Parisians and expats alike. Despite its pristine façade, though, this wasn't always silver-spoon territory. Claude Monet and Auguste Renoir shared a cramped studio at 20 rue Visconti, and the young Picasso barely eked out an existence in a room on the Rue de Seine. By the 1950s St-Germain bars bopped with jazz, and the likes of Albert Camus, Jean-Paul Sartre, and Simone de Beauvoir puffed away on Gaulois while discussing the meaninglessness of existence at Café Flore.

The star attraction of the neighboring 7e arrondissement is the **Musée d'Orsay**, which houses a world-class collection of Impressionist paintings in a converted Belle Époque rail station on the Seine. Farther along the river is the realm of select, discreet *vieille France,* where aristocrats lived in gracious apartments and *maisons particuliers* (town houses). The splendid **Musée Rodin** in the beautifully landscaped Hôtel Biron—one of the few houses here where you can explore the grand interior and gardens—is a short walk away. Several smaller museums, including the **Musée Maillol**, dedicated to the work of sculptor Aristide Maillol, and the **Musée Delacroix** are also in the neighborhood.

Paris is a city for walking, and St-Germain is one of the most enjoyable places to practice the art of the *flaneur,* or stroller. Make your way to the busy crossroads of **Carrefour de Buci**, dotted with cafés, flower markets, and shops. Rue de l'Ancienne is so named because it was the first home of the legendary Comédie Française; it cuts through to busy Place de l'Odéon and Rue St-André des Arts. Along the latter you can find the historic **Cour du Commerce St-André** (opposite No. 66), a magnificently cobbled pedestrian street lined with cafés, including, halfway down on the left, Paris's oldest, Le Procope.

Make sure you save some energy for the delightful **Luxembourg Gardens,** with its tree-lined promenades, frolicking children, and unex-

CLOSE UP

Dueling Cafés

Les Deux Magots, at 6 place St-Germain-des-Prés, and the neighboring **Café de Flore,** at 172 boulevard St-Germain, have been duking it out on this bustling corner in St-Germain for more than a century. Les Deux Magots, the snootier of the two, is named for the two Chinese figurines, or *magots*, inside, and has hosted the likes of Oscar Wilde, Hemingway, James Joyce, and Richard Wright. Jean-Paul Sartre and Simone du Beauvoir frequented both establishments, though they are claimed by the Flore.

The two cafés remain packed, though these days you're more likely to rub shoulders with tourists than with philosophers Still, if you're in search of that certain *je ne sais quoi* of the Rive Gauche, you can do no better than to station yourself at one of the sidewalk tables—or at a window table on a wintry day—to watch the passing parade. Stick to a croissant and an overpriced coffee or an early-evening apéritif; the food is expensive and nothing special.

pected modern art. Fortunately there are lots of chairs for resting those weary feet.

MAIN ATTRACTIONS

Fodor's Choice ★ **Carrefour de Buci.** This colorful crossroads (carrefour is French for "intersection") was once a notorious Rive Gauche landmark: during the 18th century it contained a gallows, and during the French Revolution the army used the site to enroll its first volunteers. Many royalists and priests lost their heads here during the bloody course of the Terror. There's certainly nothing sinister about the carrefour today; brightly colored flowers are for sale alongside take-out ice-cream and snack kiosks. Devotees of the superb, traditional bakery Carton (at No. 6) line up for pastries (try their *tuiles* cookies). ■ TIP→**Rue de Buci has several good épiceries and boulangeries stocked with the fixings for a perfect picnic.** Ⓜ *Mabillon.*

Eglise St-Germain-des-Prés. Paris's oldest church was built to shelter a simple shard of wood, said to be a relic of Jesus' cross brought back from Spain in AD 542. Vikings came down the Seine and sacked the church, and Revolutionaries used it to store gunpowder, yet the elegant building has defied history's abuses: its 11th-century Romanesque tower continues to be the central symbol of the neighborhood. The colorful 19th-century frescoes in the nave are by Hippolyte Flandrin, a pupil of the classical master Ingres. The church stages superb organ concerts and recitals. Step inside for spiritual nourishment, or pause in the square to people-watch—there's usually a street musician tucked against the church wall, out of the wind. ⊠ *Pl. St-Germain-des-Prés, St-Germain-des-Prés* ⊘ *Daily 8–7:30* Ⓜ *St-Germain-des-Prés.*

Fodor's Choice ★ **Jardin du Luxembourg**
See the highlighted listing in this chapter.

Fodor'sChoice **Musée d'Orsay**
★ *See the highlighted listing in this chapter.*

Fodor'sChoice **Musée Rodin**
★ *See the highlighted listing in this chapter.*

St-Sulpice. Dubbed the Cathedral of the Rive Gauche, this enormous 17th-century church has entertained some unlikely christenings—among them the Marquis de Sade and Charles Baudelaire—as well as the nuptials of novelist Victor Hugo. The church's most recent appearance was a supporting role in the best-selling novel *The Da Vinci Code*. The 18th-century façade was never finished, and its unequal towers add a playful touch to an otherwise sober design. The interior is oddly impersonal, despite the two magnificent Delacroix frescoes. The congregation makes for good people-watching on days of confirmation and wedding parties, and Catherine Deneuve and other St-Germain celebrities are occasionally spotted in the square's Café de la Mairie, once the haunt of existentialist author Albert Camus. ⊠*Pl. St-Sulpice, St-Germain-des-Prés* ☉ *Weekdays 7:30–7:30* Ⓜ*St-Sulpice.*

NEED A BREAK?
If you need a break, head to the small upstairs tea salon at La Bonbonnière de Buci (⊠*12 rue de Buci, St-Germain-des-Prés* ☎*01–43—26—97–13*) and order a flaky millefeuille pastry.

ALSO WORTH SEEING

Fodor'sChoice **Cour du Commerce St-André.** Like an 18th-century engraving come to life,
★ this exquisite, cobblestone street arcade is one of Paris's loveliest sights. Famed for its Revolutionary inhabitants—journalist Jean-Paul Marat ran the Revolutionary newspaper *L'Ami du Peuple,* at No. 8, and the agitator Georges Danton lived at No. 20—it's also home to Le Procope, Paris's oldest café. This passageway also contains a turret from the 12th-century wall of Philippe-Auguste (visible through the windows of the Catalogne tourist office). ⊠*Linking Bd. St-Germain and Rue St-André-des-Arts, St-Germain-des-Prés* Ⓜ*Odéon.*

Ecole Nationale des Beaux-Arts. Occupying three large mansions near the Seine, the national fine-arts school—today the breeding ground for painters, sculptors, and architects—was once the site of a convent founded in 1608 by Marguerite de Valois, the first wife of Henri IV. After the Revolution the convent was turned into a museum for works of art salvaged from buildings attacked by the rampaging French mobs. In 1816 the museum was turned into a school. Today its peaceful courtyards harbor some contemporary installations and exhibits, and the school staff includes international art stars like Christian Boltanski and Annette Messager. You can wander into the courtyard and galleries of the school to see the casts and copies of the statues stored here for safekeeping during the Revolution. ⊠*14 rue Bonaparte, St-Germain-des-Prés* ☉ *Daily 1–7* Ⓜ*St-Germain-des-Prés.*

Hôtel des Monnaies. Louis XVI transferred the royal mint to this imposing mansion in the late 18th century; then it was moved to Pessac, near

Bordeaux, in 1973. Weights and measures, medals, and limited-edition coins are still made here, though, and the **Musée de la Monnaie** has an extensive collection of coins, documents, engravings, and paintings. If those offerings don't thrill, you can watch the coin-metal craftsmen at work in their ateliers overlooking the Seine, each Wednesday and Friday at 2:15 PM; advance reservations are necessary (you can e-mail . ✉*11 quai de Conti, St-Germain-des-Prés* ☎ *01–40–46–55–35* ⊕*www.monnaieparis.fr/musee* ≤*€8, includes audioguide in English, €3 for atelier visit by reservation only* ☉*Tues.–Fri. 11–5:30, weekends noon–5:30* Ⓜ*Pont Neuf, Odéon.*

Institut de France. The *Institute* is one of France's most revered cultural institutions, and its golden dome is one of the Rive Gauche's most impressive landmarks. The site once held the Tour de Nesle, which formed part of Philippe-Auguste's medieval fortification wall along the Seine; the tower had many royal occupants, including Henry V of England. In 1661 the wealthy Cardinal Mazarin willed 2 million French *livres* (pounds) for the construction of a college. It's also home to the Académie Française: protectors of the French language. The edicts issued by this fusty group of 40 "perpétual" (lifelong) members are happily ignored by the French public, who prefer to send an e-mail rather than the Académie-approved *courriel*. The Institute is off-limits to visitors except for tours arranged by private guides. Check for guided visits in the weekly listings in Pariscope and L'Officiel des Spectacles magazines ✉*Pl. de l'Institut, St-Germain-des-Prés* Ⓜ*Pont Neuf.*

Musée Delacroix. The final apartment of artist Eugène Delacroix (1798–1863) contains only a small collection of his sketches and drawings, but you can see the studio he had specially built in the large garden at the back. From here you can pay homage to France's foremost Romantic painter, who had the good luck to live on **Place Furstenberg**, one of the tiniest, most romantic squares in Paris. ✉*6 rue Furstenberg, St-Germain-des-Prés* ☎*01–44–41–86–50* ⊕*www.musee-delacroix.fr* ≤*€5* ☉*Wed.–Mon. 9:30–5* Ⓜ*St-Germain-des-Prés.*

Musée de la Légion d'Honneur. A must for military-history buffs only, the modern Legion of Honor Museum housed in a neoclassical mansion is dedicated to homegrown and foreign military leaders and features a vast collection of military decorations and related paintings. There are video tributes to various luminaries, including U.S. General Dwight Eisenhower, a Légion member who led the Allied liberation of France in 1944. Entrance is free, and there are free English audioguides. ✉*2 rue de Bellechasse, St-Germain-des-Prés* ☎*01–40–62–84–25* Ⓜ*Solférino; RER: Musée d'Orsay.*

Mairie du 6ᵉ. The "town hall" of the 6ᵉ arrondissement often plays host to impressive free art exhibitions and other cultural offerings. Stop by the accueil (reception desk) on the ground floor to see what's on or to pick up information on other timely happenings around this artsy district. ✉*78 rue Bonaparte, St-Germain-des-Prés* ☎*01–40–46–76–60* ⊕*www.mairie6.paris.fr* ≤*Free.*

JARDIN DU LUXEMBOURG

✉ Bordered by Bd. St-Michel
and rues de Vaugirard,
de Medicis, Guynemer,
and Auguste-Comte,
St-Germain-des-Prés

🎫 Free

🕓 Open daily 7:30 or
8:15–sunset (hours vary
depending on the season)

Ⓜ Odéon; RER: B Luxembourg

TIPS

■ So you can't sit in the
grass—feel free to move the
green chairs around to create
an ideal picnic spot or people-
watching perch.

■ If you're eager to burn
off that breakfast *pain au
chocolat*, the Jardin du
Luxembourg has a well-
maintained trail around the
perimeter frequented by a
surprising (for France) number
of joggers—mostly groups of
buff cops. It is one of the few
public places where you'll spy
the French clad in (perfectly
matching) athletic wear.

■ If you're looking for a
familiar face, one of the original (miniature) casts of the
Statue of Liberty was installed
in the gardens in 1906.

The Luxembourg Gardens has all that is charming,
unique, and befuddling about Parisian parks: cookie-
cutter trees, ironed-and-pressed walkways, sculpted
flower beds, and immaculate emerald lawns meant
for admiring, not for lounging. The tree- and bench-
lined paths are, however, a marvelous reprieve from
the bustle of the Quartier Latin. Beautifully austere
during the winter months, the garden becomes intoxi-
cating as spring fills the flower beds with daffodils,
tulips, and hyacinths, and the circular pools teem with
boats nudged along by children. The park's northern
boundary is dominated by the Palais du Luxembourg,
home of the Musée du Luxembourg and the Sénat
(Senate), which is one of two chambers making up
the Parliament.

HIGHLIGHTS

The original inspiration for the gardens came from
Marie de Medici, nostalgic for the Boboli gardens of
her native Florence. She is commemorated by the **Fontaine de Medicis.**

One of the great attractions of the park is the **Théâtre
des Marionnettes,** where on weekends at 11 and 3:30,
and on Wednesday at 3:30, you can catch one of the
classic *guignols* (marionette shows) for a small charge.
The wide-eyed kids might be the real attraction; their
expressions of utter surprise, despair, and glee have
fascinated the likes of Henri Cartier-Bresson and François Truffaut. The park also has a merry-go-round,
swing sets, and pony rides; older visitors should look
out for the bandstand, which hosts free concerts on
summer afternoons.

Check out the rotating photography exhibits hanging
on the perimeter fence near the entrance on the Boulevard St-Michel.

MUSEE D'ORSAY

✉ 1 rue de la Légion d'Honneur, St-Germain-des-Prés

☎ 01–40–49–48–14

🌐 www.musee-orsay.fr

🎟 €8; €5.50 after 4:15 except Thurs. after 6; free 1st Sun. of every month

🕐 Tues.–Sun. 9:30–6, Thurs. 9:30 AM–9:45 PM

Ⓜ Solférino; RER: Musée d'Orsay

TIPS

■ Lines at the d'Orsay are some of the worst in Paris. Book ahead on the Internet or buy a Museum Pass; then go directly to entrance C.

■ Thursday evenings the museum is open until 9:45 PM and less crowded.

■ The elegant **Musée d'Orsay Restaurant** once served patrons of the 1900 World's Fair; there's also a café and a self-service cafeteria on the top floor just after the Cézanne galleries. Don't miss the views of Sacré-Coeur from the balcony—this is the Paris that inspired the Impressionists.

■ The d'Orsay is closed Monday, unlike the Pompidou and the Louvre, which are closed on Tuesday.

■ English audioguides are available just past the ticket booths; pick up a free color-coded map of the museum here, too.

Opened in 1986, this gorgeous, renovated Belle Époque train station has a world-famous collection of Impressionist and Postimpressionist paintings. The museum is arranged on three floors; to visit the exhibits in a roughly chronologic manner, start on the first floor, take the escalators to the third, and end on the second. If you came to see the biggest names on display here, head straight for the top floor and work your way down.

HIGHLIGHTS

Ground floor: **Salle 7** has Courbet's masterpieces *L'Enterrement à Ornans* and *Un Atelier du Peintre*. His realist painting influenced the Impressionists, whose work is upstairs. There are also works by lesser-known academic painters here, showing the prevailing artistic atmosphere of the period. More experimental visions, including Gustave Moreau's myth-laden decadence and Puvis de Chavanne's surprisingly modern lines, make the leap into Impressionism easier to understand. In **Salle 14** is Edouard Manet's *Olympia*. The artist is poking fun at the fashion for all things Greek and Roman; this young lady is a 19th-century courtesan, not a classical goddess. Photography exhibits are also on the ground floor.

Top floor: Impressionism really gets going here, with works by Degas, Monet, Pissarro, Sisley, and Renoir. Postimpressionist galleries include work by van Gogh, Gauguin, Toulouse-Lautrec, and Odilon Redon.

Second floor: An exquisite collection of sculpture as well as Art Nouveau furniture and decorative objects are housed here. There are rare surviving works by Hector Guimard (designer of the swooping green Paris métro entrances), as well as Lalique and Tiffany glassware.

11

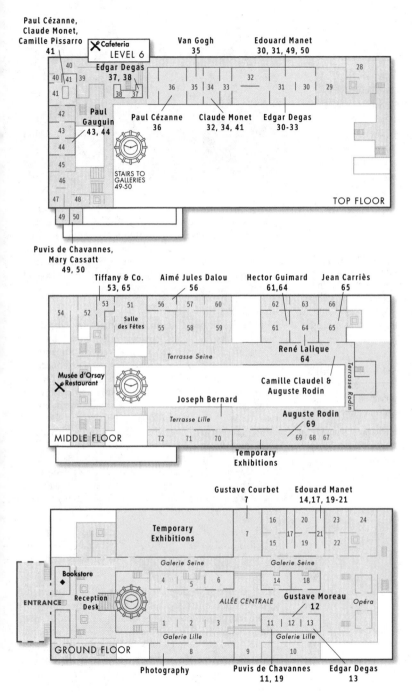

**Paul Cézanne,
Claude Monet,
Camille Pissarro
41**

Cafeteria
LEVEL 6

**Van Gogh
35**

**Edouard Manet
30, 31, 49, 50**

**Edgar Degas
37, 38**

40
40 | 41 | 39
41
42
43
44
45
46
47 | 48
49 | 50

36
38 | 37
35 | 34 | 33
32
31 | 30 | 29
28

**Paul
Gauguin
43, 44**

**Paul Cézanne
36**

**Claude Monet
32, 34, 41**

**Edgar Degas
30-33**

STAIRS TO
GALLERIES
49-50

TOP FLOOR

**Puvis de Chavannes,
Mary Cassatt
49, 50**

**Tiffany & Co.
53, 65**

**Aimé Jules Dalou
56**

**Hector Guimard
61,64**

**Jean Carriès
65**

54
52
53
51
Salle
des Fêtes
56 | 57 | 60
55 | 58 | 59
62 | 63 | 66
61 | 64 | 65

Terrasse Seine

**René Lalique
64**

**Musée d'Orsay
Restaurant**

Terrasse Rodin

**Camille Claudel &
Auguste Rodin**

Joseph Bernard

Terrasse Lille

**Auguste Rodin
69**

MIDDLE FLOOR

72 | 71 | 70

69 | 68 | 67

**Temporary
Exhibitions**

**Gustave Courbet
7**

**Edouard Manet
14,17, 19-21**

**Temporary
Exhibitions**

7

16
15
17
20
19
21
23
22
24

Galerie Seine

Galerie Seine

Bookstore

ENTRANCE

Reception
Desk

4 | 5 | 6
1 | 2 | 3

14 | 18

ALLÉE CENTRALE

11 | 12 | 13

**Gustave Moreau
12**

Opéra

Galerie Lille

8

Galerie Lille

9

10

GROUND FLOOR

Photography

**Puvis de Chavannes
11, 19**

**Edgar Degas
13**

MUSEE RODIN

✉ 79 rue de Varenne, Trocadéro/Tour Eiffel

☎ 01-44-18-61-10

🌐 www.musee-rodin.fr

🎟 €6; gardens only, €1; free 1st Sun. of month

🕐 Apr.–Oct., Tues.–Sun. 9:30–5:45; Nov.–Mar., Tues.–Sun. 9:30–4:45

Ⓜ Varenne

TIPS

■ For just €1, you can enjoy the 7 acres of gardens.

■ If you want to linger, Cafétéria du Musée Rodin serves drinks and light meals in the shade of the garden's linden trees. It's much lovelier than the word cafeteria implies.

■ The small chapel on your right as you enter the gardens is now used for temporary exhibitions. A combination ticket is €9 at the main entrance.

■ An English audioguide (€4) is available for the permanent collection.

This grand 18th-century *hôtel particulier* (private mansion) was Auguste Rodin's (1840–1917) studio and now houses a museum dedicated to his work. He died rich and famous, but many of the sculptures that earned him his place in history were first met with contempt by the public, who weren't quite ready for his powerful brand of sexuality and raw physicality.

HIGHLIGHTS

Most of Rodin's well-known sculptures are outside in the gardens. The front garden is dominated by *The Gates of Hell* (circa 1880). Inspired by the monumental bronze doors of Italian Renaissance churches, Rodin set out to illustrate stories from Dante's *Divine Comedy.* He worked on the sculpture for more than 30 years, and it serves as a "sketch pad" for many of his later works. If you look carefully, you can see miniature versions of *The Kiss* (bottom right), his most celebrated work *The Thinker* (top center), and *The Three Shades* (top center). *The Thinker* (circa 1881) is a seated male nude caught in a moment of deep contemplation. Look at the flexing toes and the way the figure seems to bite his hand. Rodin wants us to feel the physical effort of creativity.

Inside the house are early works, including *The Bronze Age,* inspired by a pilgrimage to Italy and the sculptures of Michelangelo; the work was so realistic, critics accused Rodin of having cast a real body in plaster.

The museum also displays works by Rodin's student and longtime mistress Camille Claudel (1864–1943). A remarkable sculptor in her own right, her torturous relationship with Rodin eventually drove her out of his studio—and out of her mind. In 1913 she was packed off to an asylum, where she remained until her death.

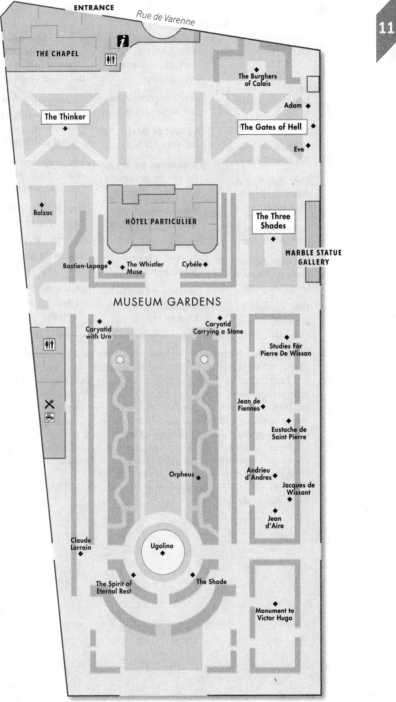

ENTRANCE

Rue de Varenne

THE CHAPEL

The Burghers
of Calais

Adam ◆

The Thinker
◆

The Gates of Hell

Eve ◆

Balzac
◆

HÔTEL PARTICULIER

**The Three
Shades**
◆

MARBLE STATUE
GALLERY

Bastien-Lepage ◆   The Whistler
Muse ◆   Cybéle ◆

MUSEUM GARDENS

Caryatid
with Urn
◆

Caryatid
Carrying a Stone
◆

Studies For
Pierre De Wissan
◆

Jean de
Fiennes ◆

Eustache de
Saint Pierre
◆

Orpheus ◆

Andrieu
d'Andres ◆

Jacques de
Wissant
◆

Jean
d'Aire
◆

Claude
Lorrain
◆

Ugolino
◆

The Spirit of
Eternal Rest ◆

◆ The Shade

Monument to
Victor Hugo
◆

Dining at a Glance

For full reviews
⇨ Ch. 17

⇨ Ch. 17

INEXPENSIVE

Boucherie Roulière,
Bistro, 24 rue des
Canettes

Le Bouillon Racine,
Brasserie, 3 rue Racine

Chez Maître Paul,
Bistro, 12 rue
Monsieur-le-Prince

La Ferrandaise, *Bistro,*
8 rue de Vaugirard

Fògon St-Julien,
Spanish, 45 quai des
Grands-Augustins

Yen, *Japanese*, 22 rue
St-Benoît

MODERATE DINING

Alcazar, *Brasserie*, 62
rue Mazarine

Au Sauvignon, *Wine
Bar*, 80 rue des St-Péres

La Bastide Odéon, *Bistro,* 7 rue Corneille

Brasserie Lipp, *Brasserie,* 151 bd. St-Germain

**Le Comptoir du Relais
Saint-Germain,** *Bistro,*
9 carrefour de l'Odéon

Huîtrerie Régis,
Seafood, 3 rue de
Montfaucon

Josephine Chez Dumonet, *Bistro,* 117 rue du
Cherche-Midi

Ze Kitchen Galerie,
Modern French, 4 rue
des Grands-Augustins

EXPENSIVE DINING

L'Atelier de Joël Robuchon, *Modern French*,
5 rue Montalembert

Les Bouquinistes,
Bistro, 53 quai des
Grands-Augustins

Gaya Rive Gauche,
Modern French, 44 rue
du Bac

Hélène Darroze, *Haute
French*, 4 rue d'Assas

Lapérouse, *Bistro,*
51 quai des Grands
Augustins

★ **Musée Maillol.** Bronzes by Art Deco sculptor Aristide Maillol (1861–1944), whose voluptuous, stylized nudes adorn the Tuileries gardens, can be admired at this handsome town house lovingly restored by his former model and muse, Dina Vierny. The museum is particularly moving because it's Vierny's personal collection. She met Maillol when she was a teenager and he was already an old man. The stunning life-size drawings upstairs are both erotic and tender—age gazing on youth with fondness and longing. Popular temporary exhibits of 20th-century painters such as Jean-Michel Basquiat and Francis Bacon often trigger long lines; they're worth the wait. ⊠ *61 rue de Grenelle, St-Germain-des-Prés* ☎ *01–42–22–59–58* ⊕ *www.museemaillol.com* ⊠ *€8* ☽ *Wed.–Mon. 11–6* Ⓜ *Rue du Bac.*

Montparnasse

Boulevard Montparnasse

WORD OF MOUTH

"The neighborhood is filled with movie theaters, restaurants, cafes, creperies. There is a street market around the corner on Edgar Quinet on Wednesday and Saturday. It turns into an arts and crafts market on Sunday. The small and very good restaurant La Cerisaie is around the corner on Edgar Quinet."

—Nikki

GETTING ORIENTED

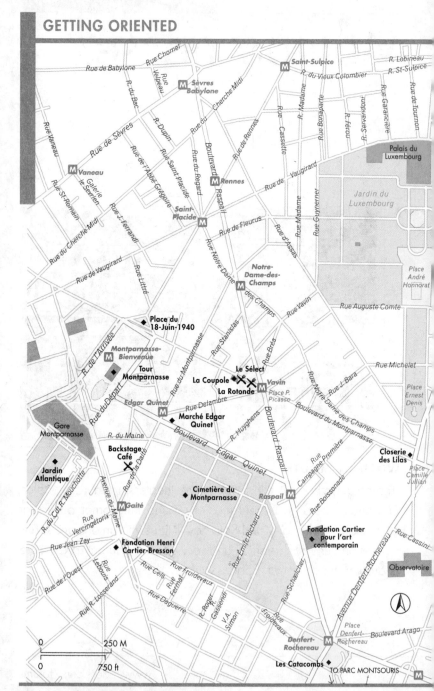

OSSEMENTS DU
CIMETIERE DES
INNOCENTS
DÉPOSÉS EN

TOP REASONS TO GO

Catacombs. It's not a great place to visit if you're claustrophobic or uncomfortable about the macabre, but if you're into the history of underground Paris, you won't want to miss this underground mecca of skin and bones.

Fondation Cartier pour l'art contemporain. If cutting-edge art is what you're after, don't miss what's on view at this exhibition space that was once a cultural landmark. The building was designed by Jean Nouvel, the darling of Paris architecture.

Fondation Henri Cartier-Bresson. No photography fan should pass up the chance to see Cartier-Bresson's restored atelier, which features a small collection of his work as well as photographs from young, contemporary artists.

The Tour Montparnasse. Even though this 680-foot black behemoth of a skyscraper is one of the most hated buildings in Paris, the view from the open-air roof terrace is one of the best spots to see the City of Light.

MAKING THE MOST OF YOUR TIME

If you can get to the top of the Tour Montparnasse on a clear day, you will be rewarded with the best view in all of Paris. The viewing deck is open until 10:30 PM, so you can watch the lights sparkle on the Eiffel Tower at the top of the hour. The Catacombs and the Fondation Henri Cartier-Bresson are closed on Monday. The Cimetière du Montparnasse is open daily. Le Coupole is perfect for a celebratory evening, but make reservations for this famous brasserie well in advance.

GETTING HERE

Montparnasse includes the 14ᵉ and 15ᵉ arrondissements. Take line 4 to the Montparnasse-Bienvenue métro stop for the Tour Montparnasse and walk along the Boulevard du Montparnasse to hit the cafés. You can also take line 4 to the Raspail métro stop to get to the Cimetière du Montparnasse as well as to Fondation Henri Cartier-Bresson. To visit the Catacombs, take the 4 one stop farther and get off at Denfert-Rochereau. Other nearby métro stops include the Edgar Quinet stop on the 6 line and the Gaîté stop on the 13 line.

BEST CAFÉS

La Rotonde. The café, a second home to foreign artists and political exiles in the 1920s and '30s, has a less exotic clientele today, but it's still very pleasant to have coffee on the sunny terrace. ⊠ *105 bd. Montparnasse, Montparnasse* ☎ *01–43–26–68–84* Ⓜ *Montparnasse.*

Le Sélect. Isadora Duncan and Hart Crane used to hang out here; now it's a popular spot for a post-cinema beer or a well-made cocktail. ⊠ *99 bd. Montparnasse, Montparnasse* ☎ *01–45–48–38–24* Ⓜ *Vavin.*

Backstage Café. Settle into a comfy chair and order a creation from the extensive cocktail list; this is one of Montparnasse's most lively streets, aptly named Rue de la Gaité (or "Cheerful Street"). ⊠ *31 bis, rue de la Gaité, Montparnasse* ☎ *01–43–20–68–59* Ⓜ *Edgar Quinet.*

12

Sightseeing
★★★
Dining
★★★
Lodging
★★
Shopping
★
Nightlife
★★

Once a warren of artist studios and swinging cafés, much of Montparnasse was leveled in the 1960s to make way for a gritty train station and Paris's only—and much maligned—skyscraper, Tour Montparnasse. Over the years, this neighborhood has evolved into a place where Parisians can find more reasonable rents, well-priced cafés, and the kind of real-life vibe lost in some of the trendier parts of the city.

Despite the soulless architecture, the modernity of **Tour Montparnasse** has its advantage: the rooftop terrace has the best panoramic view of Paris. It's okay to feel smug during your ascent, as you consider yourself savvy for avoiding long lines at Tour Eiffel. And you can reward yourself with a fancy cocktail at Le Bar Américain on the 56th floor.

The other star attraction of Montparnasse is belowground. The mazelike tunnels of the Paris **Catacombs** contain the bones of centuries' worth of Parisians, moved here when disease, spread by rotting corpses, threatened the city center.

The café society that flourished in the early 20th century—Picasso, Modigliani, Hemingway (where *didn't* he drink?), Man Ray, and even Leon Trotsky raised a glass here—is still evident along the Boulevard du Montparnasse. The Art Deco interior of **La Coupole** attracts diners seeking piles of golden *choucroute*.

Along the Boulevard Raspail you can see today's cutting-edge art stars at the **Fondation Henri Cartier-Bresson** or the **Fondation Cartier pour l'art contemporain**, or pay your respects to Baudelaire, Alfred Dreyfus, or Simone du Beauvoir in the **Cimetière du Montparnasse**.

MAIN ATTRACTIONS

★ **Les Catacombes.** Perhaps the most interesting parts of the catacombs are the ones you *won't* see. *Cataphiles,* mostly art students with a macabre twist, have found alternate entrances into the 300 km (186 mi) of tunnels where they make art, hold parties, and generally raise hell. What you will see after a descent through dark, clammy passages is Paris's principal ossuary. Bones from the defunct Cimetière des Innocents were the first to arrive in 1786, when decomposing bodies started seeping into the cellars of the market at Les Halles, bringing swarms of ravenous rats with them. The legions of bones dumped here are

12

arranged not by owner but by type—rows of skulls, stacks of tibias, and piles of spinal disks. Be prepared for stairs and a long underground walk; the floor can be damp, so wear appropriate shoes. Note that you won't be shrouded in tomblike darkness: the tunnels are well lighted. Among the nameless 6 or so million are the bones of Madame de Pompadour (1721–64), laid to rest with the riffraff after a lifetime spent as the mistress to Louis XV. ✉ *1 pl. Denfert-Rochereau, Montparnasse* ☎ *01-43-22-47-63* ⊕ *www.paris.fr/musees* ⊠ *€7* ⊙ *Tues.–Sun. 10–5* Ⓜ *Métro or RER: Denfert-Rochereau.*

Cimetière du Montparnasse. Many of the neighborhood's most illustrious residents are buried here at the Montparnasse Cemetery, only a stone's throw from where they lived and loved: Baudelaire, Bartholdi (who designed the Statue of Liberty), Alfred Dreyfus, Guy de Maupassant, and, more recently, photographer Man Ray, playwright Samuel Beckett, writers Marguerite Duras, Sartre, and de Beauvoir, actress Jean Seberg, and singer-songwriter Serge Gainsbourg. ✉ *Entrances on Rue Froidevaux, Bd. Edgar-Quinet, Montparnasse* ⊙ *Mid-Mar.–mid-Nov., weekdays 8–6, Sat. 8:30–6, Sun. 9–6; mid-Nov.–mid-Mar., weekdays 8–5:30, Sat. 8:30–5:30, Sun. 9–5:30* Ⓜ *Raspail, Gaîté.*

★ **Fondation Cartier pour l'art contemporain.** There's no shortage of museums in Paris, but this eye-catching contemporary-art gallery may be the city's best place to view cutting-edge art. Funded by luxury giant Cartier, the foundation is at once an architectural landmark, a corporate collection, and an exhibition space. Architect Jean Nouvel's 1993 building is a glass house of cards layered seamlessly between the boulevard and the garden. The nearly self-effacing building highlights a cedar of Lebanon planted 180 years ago by French writer Chateaubriand, who once lived at this address. Along with high-quality exhibitions of contemporary art, the foundation hosts performance nights (contemporary dance, music, film, fashion) on Thursday evenings, some in English. These "Nuits Nomades" start at 8:30. ✉ *261 bd. Raspail, Montparnasse* ☎ *01-42-18-56-50* ⊕ *http://fondation.cartier.com* ⊠ *€6.50* ⊙ *Tues. 11–10; Wed.–Sun. 11–8* Ⓜ *Raspail.*

★ **Fondation Henri Cartier-Bresson.** Photography has deep roots in Montparnasse, as great experimenters like Louis Daguerre and Man Ray lived and worked here. In keeping with this spirit of innovation, Henri Cartier-Bresson, legendary photographer and creator of the Magnum photo agency, opened this foundation supporting contemporary photography in 2003. The restored 1913 artists' atelier holds three temporary exhibitions each year. Be sure to go up to the top floor to see a small gallery of Cartier-Bresson's own work. ⊠*2 impasse Lebouis, Montparnasse* ☎*01–56–80–27–00* ⊕*www.henricartierbresson.org* ✉*€6, free on Wed. 6:30 PM–8:30 PM* ⊗*Tues.–Sun., 1–6:30; Sat. 11–6:45; free on Wed. 1–8:30* Ⓜ *Gaîté.*

Tour Montparnasse. Continental Europe's tallest skyscraper offers visitors a stupendous view of Paris from its 56th-floor observation desk, renovated in 2005, or you can climb another three flights to the open-air roof terrace. Completed in 1973, the 680-foot building attracts 800,000 gawkers each year; on a clear day you can see for 40 km (25 mi). A glossy brochure, "Paris Vu d'en Haut" ("Paris from on High"), explains what to look for. Have a cocktail with your view at Le Bar Américain on the 56th floor in Le Ciel de Paris restaurant, which serves lunch and dinner daily with a moderate fixed-price menu. ⊠*Rue de l'Arrivée, Montparnasse* ☎*01–45–38–52–56 Le Ciel de Paris, 01–40–64–77–64* ⊕*www.tourmontparnasse56.com* ✉*€9.50* ⊗*Apr.–Sept., daily 9:30 AM–11:30 PM; Oct.–Mar., daily 9:30 AM–10:30 PM; last elevator 30 mins before closing.* Ⓜ*Montparnasse Bienvenüe.*

ALSO WORTH SEEING

Closerie des Lilas. Now a pricey bar-restaurant, the Closerie remains a staple of all literary tours of Paris. Commemorative plaques are bolted to the bar like so many name tags—as if they were still saving seats for their former clientele—an impressive list of literati including Zola, Baudelaire, Rimbaud, Apollinaire, Beckett, and, of course, Hemingway. (Hemingway wrote pages of *The Sun Also Rises* here; he lived around the corner at 115 rue Notre-Dame-des-Champs.) Although the lilacs that graced the garden are gone—they once shaded such habitués as Ingres, Whistler, and Cézanne—the terrace still opens onto a garden wall of luxuriant evergreen foliage. ⊠*171 bd. du Montparnasse, Montparnasse* ☎*01–40–51–34–50* Ⓜ*Vavin; RER: Port Royal.*

La Coupole. One of Montparnasse's most famous brasseries, La Coupole opened in 1927 and soon became a home-away-from-home for Apollinaire, Max Jacob, Cocteau, Satie, Stravinsky, and (again) Hemingway. In the 1980s the brasserie was bought by the Flo chain, which preserved the superb Art Deco interior, including pillars by Chagall and Brancusi. The place retains its hustle and bustle—with scurrying waiters and the overwhelming noise of clinking glasses and clattering silverware. A visit here is a great way to sample what Paris must have been like in the good ol' days. ⊠*102 bd. du Montparnasse, Montparnasse* ☎*01–43–20–14–20* ⊗*Daily 8:30 AM–1 AM* Ⓜ*Vavin.*

Jardin Atlantique (Atlantic Garden). Built above the tracks of Gare Montparnasse, this park nestled among tall modern buildings is named for its

CLOSE UP

Artists, Writers & Exiles

12

Paris became a magnet for the international avant-garde in the mid-1800s and remained Europe's creative capital until the 1950s. It all began south of **Montmartre** when Romantics, including writers Charles Baudelaire and George Sand (with her lover, Polish composer Frédéric Chopin), moved into the streets below Boulevard de Clichy. Impressionist painters Claude Monet, Edouard Manet, and Mary Cassatt had studios here, near Gare St-Lazare, so they could commute to the countryside. In the 1880s the neighborhood dance halls had a new attraction: the cancan, and in 1889 the **Moulin Rouge** cabaret was opened. Toulouse-Lautrec designed posters advertising the neighborhood stars, and sketched prostitutes in his spare time.

The artistic maelstrom continued through the Belle Époque and beyond. In the early 1900s Picasso and Braque launched Cubism from a ramshackle hillside studio, the **Bateau-Lavoir,** and a similar beehive of activity was established at the south end of the city in a curious studio building called La Ruche (the beehive, at the Convention métro stop). Artists from different disciplines worked together on experimental productions. In 1917 the modernist ballet Parade hit the stage, danced by impresario Sergei Diaghilev's Ballet Russes, with music by Erik Satie and costumes by Picasso—and everyone involved was

hauled off to court, accused of being cultural anarchists.

World War I shattered this creative frenzy, and when peace returned, the artists had moved. The narrow streets of **Montparnasse** had old buildings suitable for studios, and the area hummed with a wide, new, café-filled boulevard. At No. 27 rue Fleurus, Gertrude Stein held court with her partner, Alice B. Toklas. Picasso drew admirers to **La Rotonde,** and F. Scott Fitzgerald drank at the now-defunct Dingo. In the '30s **La Coupole** became a favorite brasserie of Henry Miller, Anaïs Nin, and Lawrence Durrell.

The Spanish Civil War and World War II brought an end to carefree Montparnasse. But the literati reconvened in **St-Germain-des-Prés. Café de Flore** and **Deux Magots** had long been popular with an alternative crowd. Expat writers Samuel Beckett and Richard Wright joined existentialists Jean-Paul Sartre, Simone de Beauvoir, and Albert Camus in the neighborhood, drawn into the orbit of literary magazines and publishing houses.

Although Paris can no longer claim to be the epicenter of Western artistic innovation, pockets of outrageous creativity still bubble up. The galleries on Rue Louise Weiss in **Tolbiac** and open-studio weekends in **Belleville** and **Oberkampf** reveal the city's continuing artistic spirit.

assortment of trees and plants found in coastal regions near the Atlantic Ocean. At the far end of the garden, you'll find twin small museums devoted to World War II: the Mémorial du Maréchal-Leclerc, named for the liberator of Paris, and the adjacent Musée Jean-Moulin, devoted to the leader of the French Resistance. Both feature memorabilia and share a common second floor showing photo and video footage (with English subtitles) of the final days of the war and the liberation of Paris. Entrance is free. In the center of the park, what looks like a quirky piece of metallic sculpture is actually a meteorological center, with a battery of flickering lights reflecting temperature, wind speed, and monthly rainfall. ✉ *1 pl. des Cinq-Martyrs-du-Lycée-Buffon, Montparnasse* ☎ *01–40–64–39–44* ⊕ *www.paris.fr/musees* ⊘ *Jardin 8–sunset; musée Tues.–Sun. 10–5* Ⓜ *Montparnasse Bienvenüe.*

Place du 18-Juin-1940. Next to Tour Montparnasse, this square commemorates Charles de Gaulle's famous radio broadcast from London urging the French to resist the Germans after the Nazi invasion of May 1940. It was in this square that German military governor Dietrich von Choltitz surrendered to the Allies in August 1944, ignoring Hitler's orders to destroy the city as he withdrew. Ⓜ *Montparnasse Bienvenüe.*

Marché Edgar Quinet. This excellent street market sells everything from fresh fruit to hot crêpes to wool shawls on Wednesday and Saturday. This is a good place to pick up lunch to go before strolling through Cimetière du Montparnasse just across the street. ✉ *Bd. du Edgar Quinet at métro Edgar Quinet.,/SI.*

Western Paris

Bust of Honoré de Balzac at Balzac house museum

WORD OF MOUTH

"...the pedestrian rue de l'Annonciation is very near the Balzac House museum. That has free entry now...you could get out at Passy metro stop, see the Musee du Vin and Balzac's House and then go shopping on rue de l'Annonciation and meander up to rue de Passy and the Muette metro stop. There is some good shopping up there, also, but then you can just keep walking to the west past a lovely park, Jardin du Randelagh, (with ponies!!!!) towards the Marmottan museum."

—Christina

GETTING ORIENTED

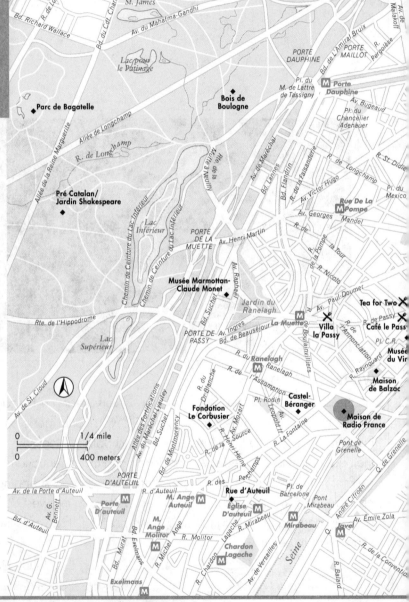

La Défense
Bd. A. M. Maurois

PORTE
MAILLOT

Jardin d'Acclimatation
Bras de Neuilly
R. de Longchamp la Ferme
Mare
St. James
Bd. Richard Wallace
R. de Longchamp la Ferme
Av. du Cdt. Charcol

Av. du Mahatma-Gandhi

PORTE
DAUPHINE

Lac pour
le Patinage

Bd. de L'Amiral Bruix
PORTE
MAILLOT
Av. de Malakoff
R. Pergolèse

Av. du Maréchal

Bois de
Boulogne

Parc de Bagatelle

Allée de la Reine Marguerite

Allée de Longchamp

R. de Longchamp

Route de la Muette à Neuilly

Pl. du
M. de Lattre
de Tassigny

M Porte
Dauphine
Av. Bugeaud
Pl. du
Chancelier
Adenauer
Pl. C.R.

Bd. Lannes
Bd. Flandrin
R. de la Faisanderie
R. de Longchamp
R. St-Didier

Pré Catalan/
Jardin Shakespeare

Av. Victor Hugo
Av. Georges Mandel
Pl. du
Mexico

Rue De La
M Pompe

Lac
Inférieur

Chemin de Ceinture du Lac Inférieur
Chemin de Ceinture du Lac Inférieur

PORTE
DE LA
MUETTE

Av. Henri Martin

R. de la Pompe
R. de la Tour
R. de la R. Nicolo

Rte. de l'Hippodrome

Av. Raphaël

Musée Marmottan-
Claude Monet

Jardin du
Ranelagh

Bd. Suchet

Av. Paul-Doumer

Av. Ingres
La Muette M
Rue Boulainvilliers

Tea for Two ✕
R. de Passy
Café le Pass ✕
Villa
la Passy ✕
R. de l'Annonciation
Musée
du Vir

PORTE DE
PASSY

Bd. de Beauséjour

Lac
Supérieur

R. du Ranelagh
R. du
Dr. Blanche
R. de Ranelagh
R. de l'Assomption
Av. Mozart

Pl. C.R.
R. Raynouard
Maison
de Balzac

Av. de St. Cloud

0   1/4 mile
0   400 meters

Pl. Rodin
Fondation
Le Corbusier
R. Henri Heine
R. de la Source

Castel-
Béranger
Av. Léopold II
R. La Fontaine

Maison de
Radio France

Allée des fortifications
Bd. Suchet
Bd. de Montmorency
Allée du Maréchal Lyautey

Pont de
Grenelle

Q. de Grenelle

PORTE
D'AUTEUIL

R. des Perchamps

Av. de la Porte d'Auteuil
Av. G. Bennett
Porte
D'auteuil M

R. d'Auteuil
M. Ange
Auteuil M
Bd. Murat
R. Michel Ange
M. Ange Molitor
M
R. Molitor

Rue d'Auteuil
Église
D'auteuil M

Pl. de
Barcelone
Pont
Mirabeau
Mirabeau M
André Citroën
Av. Émile Zola
Javel M
Q. de la Convention
R. Balard

Chardon
Lagache M
Av. de Versailles
Seine

Bd. d'Auteuil
Av. de la Porte d'Auteuil
Bd. Exelmans

Exelmans M

TOP REASONS TO GO

Musée Marmottan–Claude Monet. If you're a fan of Monet, don't miss this gem of a museum tucked away deep in the 16e.

Bois de Boulogne. Whether you spend your afternoon in a rowboat on one of the two lakes or wander through gardens covered with foliage from Shakespeare's plays, the Bois is the perfect escape from the city.

Jardin d'Acclimatation. There's not a child under the age of five who won't love this amusement park on the northern edge of the Bois de Boulogne.

Fondation Le Corbusier. The iconic designs of Swiss master Le Corbusier are in this small, gorgeous museum.

MAKING THE MOST OF YOUR TIME

If this isn't your first time in Paris, or even if it is and you've had enough of the touristy central part of the city, this neighborhood is a great choice and can be treated like a day trip. Spend the morning admiring the Monets at the uncrowded Musée Marmottan–Claude Monet (closed Monday), then take in some of the Art Nouveau architecture on Rue la Fontaine. If your goal is to leave the city lights behind altogether, pack a picnic, and spend the day in the Bois de Boulogne.

GETTING HERE

Western Paris includes the 16e and 17e arrondissements. Take line 9 to La Muette métro stop for the Musée Marmottan–Claude Monet, or to the Jasmin stop (also line 9) to explore Rue de la Fontaine. Take line 6 to the Passy stop for the Musée du Vin or to reach the main drag, Rue de Passy. For the Bois de Boulogne, take line 2 to the Porte Dauphin stop or RER C to Avenue Foch. For the Jardin d'Acclimatation enter the park from the Porte Maillot métro stop on line 1. If you're heading out to La Défense, it's the end of the line on the 1.

13

BEST CAFÉS

Tea for Two. Despite the name, this thoroughly French café is a must for an inexpensive lunch. Try a savory brick (pronounced breek), a flaky pastry stuffed with luscious fillings such as seasoned chicken or salmon. Or enjoy afternoon tea with a slice of homemade tarte du citron. Closed evenings and Sunday. ⊠ *4 rue de la Tour, Trocadero–Tour Eiffel* ☎ *01–40–50–90–46* Ⓜ *Passy.*

Villa La Passy. The leafy courtyard of this café just off Rue de Passy may make you think you've stumbled into a small village. Sit outside on a cushioned banquette shaded by ivy and order the plat du jour, prepared with fresh market ingredients. The €20 Sunday brunch is a good value. ⊠ *4 impasse des Carrières, Trocadéro–Tour Eiffel* ☎ *01–45–27–68–76* Ⓜ *Passy.*

Café le Passy. The plush chestnut-and-cream decor of this café is the work of one of Givenchy's nephews. Cocktails are classy, the food—such as grilled lamb with tarragon—is good, and candlelight makes everyone look that much more glamorous. Closed Sunday. ⊠ *2 rue de Passy, Trocadéro–Tour Eiffel* ☎ *01–42–88–31–02* Ⓜ *Passy.*

Sightseeing
★★
Dining
★
Lodging
★
Shopping
★

Welcome to Paris at its most prim and proper—but hardly stodgy. This genteel area is a study in smart urban planning, with classical architecture and newer construction commingling as easily as the haute bourgeoisie inhabitants mix with their American expat neighbors. There is no shortage of celebrities here seeking some peace and quiet, but you're just as likely to find well-heeled families who decamped from the center of the city in search of a spacious apartment.

A walk along the main avenues here will give you a sense of Paris's finest Art Nouveau and Modernist buildings, including **Castel-Béranger**, by Hector Guimard, and the **Foundation Le Corbusier** museum, a prime example of the Swiss architect's style. This neighborhood is also home to one of the city's best and most overlooked museums—the **Musée Marmottan–Claude Monet**—with its wonderful collection of Impressionist art. Enjoy a dégustation (tasting) at the Musée du Vin or simply find a café on Rue de Passy and savor a moment in one of the city's most exclusive enclaves. If it's a leafy landscape you're after, spend an afternoon at the **Bois de Boulogne,** especially if you have kids. At *Le Bois*, you can explore the Pré Catelan and Bagatelle gardens, both meticulously landscaped and surrounded by woods. Head to the amusement park at the Jardin d'Acclimatation or take a boat out on one of the park's two gorgeous lakes. You can also rent a bike and hit the 14 km (9 mi) of marked trails.

MAIN ATTRACTIONS

FodorsChoice   **Bois de Boulogne**
★   *See highlighted listing in this chapter.*

Castel-Béranger. It's a shame you can't go inside this house, considered the city's first Art Nouveau structure, dreamed up in 1898 by Hector Guimard. The wild combination of materials and the grimacing grillwork led neighbors to call this the Castle Dérangé (Deranged), but this private commission cata-pulted Guimard into the public eye, leading to his famous métro commission. After admiring the sea-inspired front entrance, go partway down the alley to admire the inventive treatment of the tradi-tional Parisian courtyard, complete with a melting water fountain. Just up the road at No. 60 is the **Hotel Mezzara**, designed by Guimard in 1911 for textile designer Paul Mezzara. You can trace Guimard's evolution by walking to the sub-tler Agar complex at the end of the block (at the corner of Rue la Fon-

WORD OF MOUTH

"The Musee Marmottan in the 16th is not as well-known as many museums, but it's well worth a visit. It has the largest collection of Monets in the world, a beautiful collection of illumi-nated manuscripts and it's located in a beautiful mansion with park views on the western edge of the 16th arrondissement."

—Kate W

13

taine and Rue Gros). Tucked beside the stone entrance at the corner of Rue Gros is a tiny café-bar with an Art Nouveau glass front and furnishings. ⊠*14 rue la Fontaine, Passy-Auteuil* Ⓜ*Ranelagh; RER: Maison de Radio France.*

NEED A BREAK? It seats just 15, but charming Café-Bar Antoine (⊠*17 rue la Fontaine, Passy-Auteuil* ☎*01–40–50–14–30*) warrants a visit for its Art Nouveau façade, floor tiles, and carved wooden bar. Count on €3 for a meal or stick to a snack and coffee.

Fondation Le Corbusier *(Le Corbusier Foundation).* Built in 1923, the Villa Laroche is a well-preserved example of Swiss architect Le Corbusier's innovative construction techniques based on geometric forms, recherché color schemes, and an unblushing use of iron and concrete. The sloping ramp that replaces the traditional staircase is one of the most eye-catching features. ⊠*10 sq. du Docteur Blanche, Passy-Auteuil* ☎*01–42–88–41–53* ⊕*www.fondationlecorbusier.asso. fr* ⊠*€3* ⊙*Tues.–Fri. 10–12:30 and 1:30–6, Mon. 1:30–5* Ⓜ*Jasmin.*

Fodor'sChoice
★ **Musée Marmottan–Claude Monet.** A few years ago the underrated Mar-mottan tacked CLAUDE MONET onto its official name—and justly so, as this may be the best collection of the artist's works anywhere. Monet's works occupy a specially built basement gallery in this elegant 19th-century mansion, where you can find such captivating works as the *Cathédrale de Rouen* series (1892–96) and *Impression: Soleil Levant (Impression–Sunrise, 1872),* the work that helped give the Impression-ist movement its name. Other exhibits include letters exchanged by Impressionist painters Berthe Morisot and Mary Cassatt. Upstairs the mansion still feels like a graciously decorated private home. Empire fur-nishings fill the salons overlooking the Jardin de Ranelagh on one side and the hotel's private yard on the other. There's also a wonderful room of illuminated medieval manuscripts. To best understand the collec-tion's context, buy an English-language catalog in the museum shop on your way in. ⊠*2 rue Louis-Boilly, Passy-Auteuil* ☎*01–44–96–50–33* ⊕*www.marmottan.com* ⊠*€8* ⊙*Tues.–Sun. 10–5* Ⓜ*La Muette.*

ALSO WORTH SEEING

OFF THE BEATEN PATH

La Défense. First conceived in 1958, this Modernist suburb just west of Paris was inspired by Le Corbusier's dream of high-rise buildings, pedestrian walkways, and sunken vehicle circulation. Built as an experiment to keep high-rises out of the historic downtown, the Parisian business hub has survived economic uncertainty to become a surprising success. Visiting La Défense gives you a crash course in contemporary skyscraper evolution, from the solid blocks of the 1960s and '70s to the curvy fins of the '90s and beyond. Today 20,000 people live in the suburb, but 150,000 people work here, and many more come to shop in its enormous mall. While riding the métro line 1 here, you'll get a view of the Seine, then emerge at a pedestrian plaza studded with some great public art, including César's giant thumb and one of Calder's great red "stabiles." The **Grande Arche de La Défense** dominates the area; it was designed as a controversial closure to the historic axis of Paris (an imaginary line that runs through the Arc de Triomphe, the Arc du Carrousel, and the Louvre glass pyramid). Glass bubble elevators whisk you 360 feet to the viewing platform. ⊠*Parvis de La Défense, La Défense* ☎*01–49–07–27–55* ⊕*www.grandearche.com* ▢*Grande Arche €9* ☉*Daily 10–8* Ⓜ*Métro or RER: Grande Arche de La Défense.*

Maison de Balzac. The Paris home of the great French 19th-century novelist Honoré de Balzac (1799–1850) contains exhibits charting his tempestuous yet prolific career. Balzac penned the nearly 100 novels and stories known collectively as *The Human Comedy,* many of them set in Paris. You can still feel his presence in his study and pay homage to his favorite coffeepot—his working hours were fueled by his tremendous consumption of the "black ink." There's some English-language information available. ⊠*47 rue Raynouard, Passy-Auteuil* ☎*01–55–74–41–80* ⊕*www.paris.fr/musees/* ▢*Free, except during temporary exhibitions, then €4* ☉*Tues.–Sun. 10–6* Ⓜ*Passy.*

Maison de Radio France. Headquarters to France's state radio, this imposing circular building was completed in 1962. More than 500 yards in circumference, it's said to have more floor space than any other building in France. Its 200-foot tower overlooks the Seine. Tours were offered but have been discontinued during renovations, and there is no word on whether they will resume. ⊠*116 av. du Président-Kennedy, Passy-Auteuil* ☎*01–56–40–15–16* ⊕*www.radiofrance.fr* Ⓜ*Ranelagh; RER: Maison de Radio France.*

Musée du Vin. Fans of wine making will enjoy this quirky museum housed in a 15th-century abbey, a reminder of Passy's roots as a pastoral village. Though hardly exhaustive, the collection includes old wine bottles, glassware, and ancient wine-related pottery excavated in Paris. Wine-making paraphernalia shares the grottolike space with hokey figures retired from the city's wax museum, including Napoléon appraising a glass of Burgundy, but you can partake in a thoroughly nonhokey wine tasting, or bring home one of the 200-plus bottles for sale in the tiny gift shop. If you call ahead, the staff will arrange a guided tour in English.

BOIS DE BOULOGNE

Ⓜ Porte Dauphine for the main entrance; Porte Maillot for northern end; Porte d'Auteuil for southern end

🕿 Parc de Bagatelle: 01–53–64–53–80; Jardin d'Acclimatation: 01–40–67–90–82

🕑 Daily; hours vary according to time of year but are generally around 9 AM to dusk

🎫 Parc de Bagatelle free except during temporary exhibitions; otherwise: adults €3, children €1.50, under 7 free; Jardin Shakespeare: €1; Jardin d'Acclimatation: €2.70, workshops €4.50.

🧒 Good for kids

13

TIPS

▪ The main entrance to the Bois de Boulogne is off Avenue Foch near the Porte Dauphine métro stop on the 2 line, best for accessing Pré Catelan and Jardin Shakespeare off Route de la Grande-Cascade. For Jardin d'Acclimatation, off Boulevard Des Sablons, take the 1 line to Porte Maillot. The Parc de Bagatelle, off Route de Sèvres-à-Neuilly, can be accessed from either Porte Dauphine or Porte Maillot.

▪ You'll definitely want to get out of the park by dusk, as the Bois becomes a distinctly adult playground after the sun goes down.

When Parisians need a day in the great outdoors close to home, they head to the Bois de Boulogne. The Bois is not a park in the traditional sense—more like a tamed forest, as it was once a royal hunting ground. On nice days the park is filled with cyclists, rowers, joggers, strollers, riders, *pétanque* players, and picnickers enjoying the elegant promenades, romantic lakes, and formal gardens.

HIGHLIGHTS

The **Parc de Bagatelle** is a floral garden of irises, roses, tulips, and water lilies, at its most colorful between April and June. **Pré Catelan** contains one of Paris's largest trees: a copper beech more than 200 years old. The romantic Le Pré Catelan restaurant, where *le tout Paris* of the Belle Époque used to dine on the elegant terrace, still lures diners and wedding parties, especially on weekends. The **Jardin Shakespeare** inside the Pré Catelan has a sampling of the flowers, herbs, and trees mentioned in Shakespeare's plays. The **Jardin d'Acclimatation**, on the northern edge of the park, is a fabulous amusement park where it seems every child under the age of five in Paris spends his or her summer Sunday afternoons. Highlights include boat trips along an "enchanted river," and a zoo. A miniature railway shuttle runs from Porte Maillot on Wednesday and weekends beginning at 1:30; tickets cost €1. Also here is the Musée en Herbe (literally, "Museum in the Grass"). Rent rowboats or bikes for a few euros at **Lac Inférieur**. There are two popular horse-racing tracks here, the Hippodrome de Longchamp and the Hippodrome d'Auteuil. Fans of the French Open can visit its home base, Stade Roland-Garros, and true devotees can check out the Tenniseum (tennis museum).

You can book ahead for lunch, too. ✉*Rue des Eaux/5 sq. Charles Dickens, Passy-Auteil* ☎*01–45–25–63–26* ⊕*www.museeduvinparis.com* 🎫*€8.90 with glass of wine; €2 for English audioguide; wine tastings €14–€20, includes admission* ⏱*Tues.–Sun. 10–6* Ⓜ*Passy.*

DINING AT A GLANCE

For full reviews ⇨ Ch. 17

EXPENSIVE DINING
Le Pré Catelan, *Haute French*;
Rue de Surèsnes

Rue d'Auteuil. This narrow, crooked shopping street escaped Haussmann's urban renovations and today still retains the country feel of old Auteuil. Molière once lived on the site of No. 2; Racine was on nearby Rue du Buis; the pair met up to clink glasses and exchange drama notes at the Mouton Blanc Inn, now a brasserie, at No. 40. Numbers 19–25 and 29 are an interesting combination of 17th- and 18th-century buildings, which have evolved into a mixture of private housing and shop fronts. At the foot of the street, the scaly dome of the **Eglise d'Auteuil** (built in the 1880s) is an unmistakable small-time cousin of the Sacré-Coeur. Rue d'Auteuil is at its liveliest on Wednesday and Saturday mornings, when a much-loved street market crams onto Place Jean-Barraud. Ⓜ*Michel-Ange Auteuil, Eglise d'Auteuil.*

Nightlife

Chez Justine, 96 Rue Oberkampf

WORD OF MOUTH

"Nightlife in Paris can be as flashy or low-key as desired. From west to east, the city moves from A-list (Champs Elysées) to artsy (Marais/Canal St. Martin), and the locals are great at pointing you towards the best vibe."

—PetiteBrigitte

Updated
by Nicole
Pritchard

There's no question that you can fill your days to the brim in Paris, whether you're shopping, sightseeing, or lazing your time away in a café—but make sure you save some energy for the evenings. Paris by night is spectacular, and there is a range of activities to keep everyone from party animals to families entertained: the offerings can be as glamorous or as simple as desired, from fashion-week parties to rides on Ferris wheels.

Parisians love to go out...weekends and weeknights, late and early. And they tend to frequent the same place once they've found something they like: it could be a wine bar, corner café, or hip music club, but you'll often find a welcoming "the-gang's-all-here" atmosphere. A wise way to spend an evening is to pick an address in a neighborhood that interests you, then give yourself time to browse. Parisians love to barhop and the energy shifts throughout the evening, so be prepared not to stay in one place all night.

Nightlife is spread out among neighborhoods, with each offering a unique vibe. For those who prefer clinking drinks with models and celebrities, check out the Champs-Elysées area, where the posh surroundings will be met with expensive drinks and often surly bouncers. More laid-back, bohemian-chic revelers can be found in the northeastern districts like Canal St-Martin and Belleville. Students tend to infiltrate the Bastille and Latin Quarter, and gays and fun-loving types can find a wild party nearly every night in the Marais. Grands Boulevards and Rue Montorgueil, just north of Les Halles, are quickly turning into party central for young professionals and the fashion crowd, and the Pigalle/Montmartre area is increasingly lively with plenty of theaters, cabarets, bars, and concert venues. Warmer months bring the allure of the floating clubs and bars, moored along the Seine from Bercy to the Eiffel Tower.

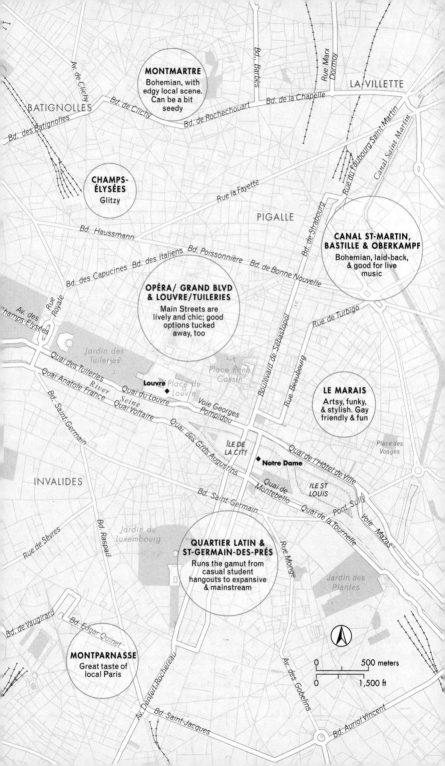

NIGHTLIFE PLANNER

Hours

Bars tend to stay open until between midnight and 2 AM, with no specific last call. Clubs often stay open until 4 AM, and many until dawn.

If you want to hit bars at a relatively quiet hour, go for an *apéritif* around 6 PM. Many places offer drink specials at this time, and it's also when Parisians congregate to decide where they want to go later. Many bars charge slightly higher prices after 10.

Wine Bars

Wine bars are different from regular bars in that they serve simple meals and snacks (charcuterie, cheese) as well as wine; they usually close earlier than full-fledged bars—somewhere between 10 and midnight. *For reviews of bars à vins, see the Wine Bars section in the Where to Eat chapter.*

Table service, or non?

Some bars have table service; at others (designated by SERVICE AU BAR signs), you must fetch your own drinks.

Getting Past the Bouncer

It shouldn't surprise any nightlife lover that the more *branché* (literally, "plugged-in" or trendy) the spot, the knottier the door-entry problem will be. Most bars aren't a problem, but when it comes to clubbing, like in any other big city, don't assume you're going to get in just because you show up. This is particularly true at the hot spots near the Champs Elysées. A limo at your disposal and global fame aren't essential to pass muster, but you absolutely must have a cocky-yet-somehow-simultaneously-polite attitude and look fabulous. Having a high female quotient in your party helps, too (fashion models are a particular plus). Solo men—or, worse, groups of men—are going to have a tougher time, unless they are high rollers and have reserved a table (bottle purchase obligatoire).

Late-Night Transportation

The last métro runs between 12:30 AM and 1 AM Monday through Sunday, but there is new late-night service on Friday and Saturday until 2:15 AM. After that, you can take a cab, but it can be difficult to find one in the wee hours. Even the taxi stands boast long lines for few cabs, and calling Taxi Bleu (01–49–36–10–10) or Taxi G-7 (01–47–39–47–39) is unpredictable on weekends. Another option is the Noctilien, the sometimes rowdy night-bus system *(see By Bus in Paris Essentials)*. A new option is the Velib, for those staying within biking distance of where they want to go, though after a few champagnes it may be better to do like the Parisians and just stay out until the métro starts running again at 5:45 AM.

What to Wear

Parisians are chic, so if you want to blend in (and get into clubs), dress up. Men, you can wear your jeans—designer jeans, that is—but leave the sneakers at your hotel and try adding a blazer. Ladies, dressing up doesn't necessarily mean a dress and heels—Parisian girls manage to look like a million in jeans and a chic top.

BARS

★ **Alcazar** (✉62 *rue Mazarine, 6ᵉ, St-Germain-des-Prés* ☎01–53–10–19–99 Ⓜ *Odéon*) is Sir Terence Conran's first makeover of a Parisian landmark, and this restaurant has a stylish mezzanine-level bar under a huge glass roof. The vibe changes from Wednesday to Saturday, moving as various DJs spin records and revelers enjoy post-dinner drinks.

★ **American Bar at La Closerie des Lilas** (✉171 *bd. du Montparnasse, 6ᵉ, Montparnasse* ☎01–40–51–34–50 Ⓜ *Montparnasse*) lets you drink in the swirling action of the adjacent restaurant and brasserie at a bar hallowed by plaques honoring such former habitués as Man Ray, Jean-Paul Sartre, and Samuel Beckett. It's a must for certain tony Parisians.

Andy Wahloo (✉69 *rue des Gravilliers, 3ᵉ, Le Marais* ☎01–42–71–20–38 Ⓜ *Arts et Métiers*) draws a mixed crowd, many from the fashion industry, who come primarily to smoke hookahs and drink ginger-rum "Wahloo spéciales" beneath silk-screened Moroccan coffee ads. Background music tends toward Raï remixes (Arabic lounge music).

★ **Apicius** (✉20 *rue d'Artois, 8ᵉ, Champs-Elysées* ☎01–43–80–19–66 Ⓜ *George V*) is all about elegance and pampering. Wander through the unbelievable front garden into this veritable palace of a restaurant, where the bartender will mix you a couture cocktail based on your stated tastes. Closed Saturday and Sunday.

Bar du Marché (✉16 *rue de Buci, 6ᵉ, St-Germain/Buci* ☎01–43–26–55–15 Ⓜ *Mabillon/Odeon*) is a local legend where waiters wearing red overalls and revolutionary "Gavroche" hats serve drinks every day of the week, with particular zeal around happy hour. With bottles of wine at about €25, it draws a quintessential Left Bank mix of expat locals, fashion-house interns, and even some professional rugby players. Sit outside on the terrace and enjoy the prime corner location.

Bar Fleur (✉3 *rue des Tournelles, 4ᵉ, Marais* ☎01–42–71–04–51 Mi *Bastille*) may be the only bar where you're surrounded with huge bouquets of fresh-cut flowers while you sip top-shelf champagne or vodka. Enchanting.

Barramundi (✉3 *rue Taitbout, 9ᵉ, Opéra/Grands Boulevards* ☎01–47–70–21–21 Ⓜ *Richelieu Drouot*) is a hub of Paris nouveau-riche chic. The lighting is dim and the copper bar is long. During the week relaxing electro-lounge and world music plays.

Barrio Latino (✉46–48 *rue du Faubourg St-Antoine, 12ᵉ, Bastille* ☎01–55–78–84–75 Ⓜ *Bastille*) is a large dance club–tapas bar that will have you shaking to the salsa beat all night. It can get pricey on weekend nights, but the €20 entrance fee includes a drink.

Bar Sans Nom (✉49 *rue de Lappe, 12ᵉ, Bastille* ☎01–48–05–59–36 Ⓜ *Bastille*) is one of the loveliest bars in Paris, perfect for a cozy rendez-vous. Candlelight and ornate decor give a sultry glow, and hip lounge music add to the charm. Try the flaming Kucaracha shot to get things heated up.

14

La Belle Hortense (⊠*16 rue Vielle-du-Temple, 4ᵉ, Le Marais* ☎*01–48–04–71–60* Ⓜ*St-Paul*) is heaven for anyone who ever wished they had a book while in a bar (or wished they had a drink in a bookstore).

Le Bilboquet (⊠*13 rue St-Benoît, 6ᵉ, St-Germain-des-Prés* ☎*01–45–48–81–84* Ⓜ*St-Germain-des-Prés* is one of Paris's premier jazz hangouts, though it was closed for renovations at this writing. Sip a cocktail or dine in the ritzy Belle Époque salon while a jazz combo sets the mood.

Bound Bar (⊠*49–51 av. George V, 8ᵉ, Champs-Elysées* ☎*01–53–67–84–60* Ⓜ*George V*) is the former home of Barfly. It's now a dark, popular place with a long, long bar and lounge music. It draws a mix of classy tourists and after-work professionals, and its location right off the Champs-Elysées makes it convenient for an evening *apéritif.*

At **Buddha Bar** (⊠*8 rue Boissy d'Anglas, 8ᵉ, Champs-Elysées* ☎*01–53–05–90–00* Ⓜ*Concorde*) a towering gold Buddha holds court over expanses of Chinese screens and colorful *chinoiserie*, and a spacious mezzanine bar overlooks the dining room. Though past its prime, it fills up nightly with an eclectic bunch.

★ **Café Charbon** (⊠*109 rue Oberkampf, 11ᵉ, Oberkampf* ☎*01–43–57–55–13* Ⓜ*St-Maur, Parmentier*) is pure Paris glory, a beautifully restored 19th-century institution whose trendsetting clientele gossips against a jazz background. It gets livelier after 11 when a DJ takes over.

Café le Fourmi (⊠*74 rue des Martyrs, 18ᵉ, Montmartre* ☎*01–42–64–70–35* Ⓜ*Pigalle*) is Pigalle's trendiest address: an inviting bar-café where cool locals hang out.

Le Café Noir (⊠ *65 rue Montmartre, 1ᵉʳ, Les Halles* ☎*01–40–39–07–36* Ⓜ*Etienne Marcel*), a centrally located "bobo" (bourgeois bohemian) favorite, has globe sculptures hanging from the ceiling. Two words describe this place: guaranteed fun.

La Chaise au Plafond (⊠*10 rue du Trésor, 4ᵉ, Le Marais* ☎*01–42–76–03–22* Ⓜ*St-Paul*) has the feel of a traditional bistro with a few offbeat, contemporary touches. Never overcrowded, it's the perfect place for an excellent glass of wine and people-watching.

★ **Chao Ba** (⊠*22 bd. de Clichy, 18ᵉ, Montmartre* ☎*01–46–06–72–90* Ⓜ*Pigalle*) is a classy lounge in the midst of Pigalle. The glamorous evocation of colonial French Indochina has exotic drinks, two levels (with comfy bamboo chairs), a mellow atmosphere, and a sleek bar.

Chez Felix (⊠*23 rue Mouffetard, 5ᵉ, Rue Mouffetard* ☎*01–47–07–61–16* Ⓜ*Place Monge*), a fun newcomer to the Mouffetard scene, has glowing red lighting, wild DJs, and a young crowd.

Chez Georges (⊠*11 rue de Canettes, 6ᵉ, St-Germain-des-Prés* ☎*01–43–25–32–79* Ⓜ*Mabillon*) has been serving red wine, pastis, and beer for the past 60-odd years in the wonderful "south of Mabillon" area. In Georges's basement, students and locals crowd around tables glowing with candles. World music gets the young on their feet by late night.

CLOSE UP

Canal St-Martin

It's a bit out of the way from the typical tourist track, but the Canal St-Martin area is the latest neighborhood to become something of a cultural hub for young Parisians. It's a funky but beautifully constructed neighborhood of offbeat bars and eclectic shops, and the best spots are clustered around the tree-lined canal built by Napoléon I, where barges still pass under low pedestrian bridges and groups of friends enjoy bottles of wine along the banks. Note that it's not the easiest place to get to by métro—so you might want to plan for a taxi back to your hotel if you're heading out for the evening.

Chez Prune was the groundbreaking establishment here, with a corner location making it perfect for people-

watching. Across the canal, **Hôtel du Nord** is the current bar-restaurant hot ticket where you might find fashion designer Christian Lacroix or graffiti artist André. It's noirishly atmospheric, with a zinc bar and velvet curtains.

The city-sponsored, vast arts center **Point Ephémère** (⊠ *200 quai de Valmy* ☎ *01–40–34–02–48* Ⓜ *Jaurés/Louis Blanc*) hosts late-night electro parties once a month. Housed in a former loading dock and Art Deco warehouse, there are gallery installations, dance performances, and young bands who are hot in every possible sense.The long-established **Opus Café** (⊠ *167 quai de Valmy* ☎ *01–40–34–70–00*) has inexpensive soul concerts and renowned tango soirees twice a month.

14

Chez Prune (⊠ *71 quai de Valmy, 36 rue Beaurepaire, 10ᵉ, République* ☎ *01–42–41–30–47* Ⓜ *Jacques Bonsergent*) is a lively bar with a terrace overlooking one of the wacky-looking footbridges of Canal St-Martin. Open daily until 2 AM.

Culture Biere (⊠ *65 av. des Champs-Elysées, 8ᵉ, Champs-Elysées* ☎ *01–42–56–88–88* Ⓜ *Franklin D. Roosevelt*), with several floors of beer-related everything, is sort of like Drugstore Publicis, but for beer.

Delmas (⊠ *2/4 pl. de la Contrescarpe, 5ᵉ, Rue Mouffetard* ☎ *01–43–26–51–26* Ⓜ *Cardinal Lemoine*), a charming bar-café-resto, is the centerpiece of charming Rue Mouffetard, with fabulous décor, colored straw chairs outside, and comfy leather couches inside.

★ **Drugstore Publicis** (⊠ *133 av. des Champs-Elysées, 8ᵉ, Champs-Elysées* ☎ *01–44–43–79–00* Ⓜ *Charles de Gaulle–Etoile*) is a phantasmagorical, multilevel, open-until-2-AM bar-resto-hipster-shop and generally a gem. The location—facing the Arc de Triomphe—can't be beat.

L'Eclaireur (⊠ *8–10 rue Boissy d'Anglas, 10ᵉ, Louvre/Tuileries* ☎ *01–53–43–09–99* Ⓜ *Concorde*) opened next to the ailing Buddha Bar on this chic shopping block—its creators also run the hip boutiques of the same name. Inside, the spacious venue boasts lavish décor and a refreshing mix of cocktails.

Les Echelles de Jacob (⊠ *10 rue Jacob, 6ᵉ, St-Germain-des-Prés* ☎ *01–43–54–53–53*) adds some Right Bank polish to the laid-back Left Bank. With a sultry ambience and high-quality cocktails, this bar in the heart of the gallery district fills up with everyone from antiques dealers to trendy youngsters. It doesn't really get moving until after midnight.

Experimental Cocktail Club (✉ *37 rue Saint-Sauveur, 2ᵉ, Bourse* ☎ *01–45–08–88–09* Ⓜ *St-Germain*) is the fabulous newcomer whose high-caliber cocktails and original design are the talk of the town. Sit back in your velvet chaise longue and watch the innovative cocktails being served on the zinc bar. Get here early, though: by 11 PM it's packed with a diverse mix of locals, professionals, and fashionable sorts.

★ **La Favela Chic** (✉ *18 rue du Faubourg du Temple, 11ᵉ, République* ☎ *01–40–21–38–14* Ⓜ *République*) was one of the bars that made Oberkampf's hip reputation. Hidden behind gates in a courtyard, this Latin cocktail bar remains popular, offering caipirinhas and mojitos, guest DJs, and a nonstop eclectic party atmosphere.

> ## APÉRITIFS
>
> For *apéritifs* French style, try a *pastis*—anise-flavored liquor such as Pernod or Ricard that turns cloudy when water is added. Ask for "*un petit jaune, s'il vous plait.*" A *pineau* is cognac and fruity grape juice. The *kir* (white wine with a dash of black-currant syrup) is a popular drink, too; a *kir royale* is made with champagne. For the very adventurous, try absinthe, the vivid green, once-outlawed liquor that's making a comeback around town—check out **La Fee Verte** (✉ *108 rue de la Roquette* ☎ *01–43–72–31–24*) in the Bastille area; the food is good, too.

Folie en Tête (✉ *33 rue de la Butte aux Cailles, 13ᵉ, Bercy/Tolbiac* ☎ *01–45–80–65–99* Ⓜ *Corvisart, Place d'Italie*), or "Lunacy in the Head," is a former mainstay of the Paris '70s punk scene. Decorated with colorful African percussion instruments, comic books, and old skis, it's known for its reggae and jazz, not to mention the traffic light in the toilet that says "Free" or "Occupied."

★ **Le Fumoir** (✉ *6 rue Amiral-de-Coligny, 1ᵉʳ, Louvre/Tuileries* ☎ *01–42–92–00–24* Ⓜ *Louvre*) is a charmer: a hot location and chic-yet-friendly spot where the neighborhood gallery owners and professional types meet for late-afternoon wine, early-evening cocktails, or dinner. There's a bar in front, an ample multilingual library in the back, and chess boards for the clientele to use while sipping martinis.

★ **Harry's New York Bar** (✉ *5 rue Daunou, 2ᵉ, Opéra/Grands Boulevards* ☎ *01–42–61–71–14* Ⓜ *Opéra*), a cozy, wood-paneled hangout decorated with dusty college pennants and popular with expatriates, welcomes the ghosts of Ernest Hemingway and F. Scott Fitzgerald. This Paris institution claims to have invented the Bloody Mary—true or not, the bartenders mix a mean one. Gershwin composed "An American in Paris" in the piano bar downstairs.

★ **Hop Hop Hop Bar** (✉ *3 rue Monsieur le Prince, 6ᵉ, Odeon* ☎ *01–46–33–07–17* Ⓜ *Odeon*) is a wacky paradise: two levels' worth of upside-down clocks, Leonardo da Vinci graffiti, barber chairs, and Marilyn

Monroe couches, not to mention an amiable staff and vintage rock and pop music. ■TIP➔Check out the restroom, which boasts a surprise.

Hôtel du Nord (✉*102 quai de Jemmapes, 10ᵉ* ☎*01–40–40–78–78* Ⓜ*Goncourt*) was, in its heyday, the site of the classic Marcel Carne film of the same name. It's been spiffed up as a good restaurant with a vibrant lounge-bar scene and is one of the more upscale spots in the mostly downscale Canal St-Martin district. It's well worth a visit.

Ice Kube (✉*1–5 passage ruelle, 18ᵉ, Montmartre* ☎*01–42–05–20–00* Ⓜ*La Chapelle*) proves that you don't have to be "hot" to be popular. This distinctive theme bar on a Montmartre cul-de-sac ain't cheap—it's €38 for a "session degustation" (entrance fee and free vodkas) and this is the only option—but the fur banquettes, transparent seats dangling from the ceiling, glasses carved from ice, and subzero vodka chamber make for quite the "chill-out" experience.

FodorsChoice ★ **Kong** (✉*1 rue du Pont-Neuf, 1ᵉʳ, Rivoli* ☎*01–40–39–09–00* Ⓜ*Pont-Neuf*) is glorious not only for its panoramic skyline views, but for its exquisite manga-inspired décor, the top-shelf DJs for weekend dancing, and its kooky, disco-ball-and-kid-sumo-adorned bathrooms. It was featured as a chic eatery in Sex and the City; need we say more?

★ **La Perle** (✉*78 rue Vieille-du-Temple, 3ᵉ, Le Marais* ☎*01–42–72–69–93* Ⓜ*Chemin-Vert*) is a masterpiece in the Marais, where straights, gays, and lesbians of all shapes, sizes, colors, and backgrounds come to mingle. The crowd makes this place interesting, not the neon lights or diner-style seats. Its status as a fashion mecca soared even higher when Galliano stopped by, and it continues to pack in some of the city's fashion movers and shakers, from midafternoon onward.

Qui Etes Vous, Polly Magoo (✉*3–5 rue du Petit Pont, 5ᵉ, Latin Quarter* ☎*01–46–33–33–64* Ⓜ*St-Michel*) is a convivial Quarter hangout legendary for having been the student rioters' unofficial HQ during the May '68 uprising. Weekends are wild with live Latino music, and the party goes on until morning, when they serve a breakfast buffet.

Le Rendez-Vous Des Amis (✉*23 rue Gabrielle, 18ᵉ, Montmartre* ☎*01–46–06–01–60* Ⓜ*Abbesses*) is a marvelous midway breather for those mounting the hill of Montmartre by foot, with a jovial staff and a century's worth of previous patrons immortalized in photos.

Step into **Le Rosebud** (✉*11 bis, rue Delambre, 14ᵉ, Montparnasse* ☎*01–43–20–44–13* Ⓜ*Vavin*) through the Art Nouveau front door and you'll find yourself in a dark, moody, fourth dimension of Old Montparnasse, one where white-jacketed servers, red-lacquered tables, and black banquets sweep you into the past.

Le Sancerre (✉*35 rue des Abbesses, 18ᵉ, Montmartre* ☎*01–42–58–08–20* Ⓜ*Abbesses*), a café by day, turns into an essential watering hole for Montmartrois and artist types at night, with Belgian beers on tap and an impressive list of cocktails. It was spruced up in 2007 but still has a traditional old-school vibe.

14

Sanz Sans (⊠*49 rue du Faubourg St-Antoine, 11ᵉ, Bastille/Nation* ☎*01–44–75–78–78* Ⓜ*Bastille*) glows in purple velvet and gilt and has lamp shades fashioned from cymbals, which the staff clang jovially. Arrive early on weekends, when it's heaving with cosmopolitan twentysomethings juicing up for a night of dancing until dawn.

Le Trésor (⊠*7 rue du Trésor, 4ᵉ, Le Marais* ☎*01–42–71–35–17* Ⓜ*St-Paul*) is lively and sophisticated, with mismatched Baroque furnishings and a chill vibe.

> **DID YOU KNOW?**
>
> If you're looking to pay homage to the French hit film *Amélie* in Montmartre (you aren't the only one), stop in at **Café des Deux Moulins** (⊠*15 rue Lepic, 18ᵉ* ☎*01–42–54–90–50*) a '50s-style watering hole with a copper-topped bar where much of the film was shot.

Urbietorbi (⊠*93 rue Montmartre, 1ᵉʳ, Les Halles* ☎*01–40–28–02–83* Ⓜ*Etienne Marcel*), a lusciously decorated Italian "gastronomic bar," has a delicious and free antipasti buffet between 6 and 9 PM.

Fodor'sChoice **De la Ville Café** (⊠*34 bd. Bonne Nouvelle, 10ᵉ, Opéra/Grands Bou-*
★ *levards* ☎*01–48–24–48–09* Ⓜ*Bonne Nouvelle, Grands Boulevards*) maintains a funky, industrial-yet-baroque ambience, with its huge, heated sidewalk terrace, mosaic-tile bar, graffitied walls, and swishy lounge. It's the anchor of the slowly reawakening Grands Boulevards scene, so arrive early on weekends if you want a seat.

HOTEL BARS

Some of Paris's best hotel bars mix historic pedigrees with hushed elegance; others go for a modern, edgy luxe. High prices and the fickle Parisian fashion pack ensure that only the latest, highly hyped bars draw in locals regularly.

★ **L'Hôtel** (⊠*13 rue des Beaux-Arts, 6ᵉ, St-Germain-des-Prés* ☎*01–44–41–99–00* Ⓜ*St-Germain-des-Prés*) has an exquisite, hushed Baroque bar that makes for the perfect discreet rendezvous. Designed in typically gorgeous Jacques Garcia style, it evokes the decadent spirit of Oscar Wilde, a former resident.

Hôtel Le Bristol (⊠*112 rue du Faubourg St-Honoré, 8ᵉ, Champs-Elysées* ☎*01–53–43–43–42* Ⓜ*Miromesnil*) attracts the rich and powerful with a gleaming setting. Cocktails are of the highest quality, and the music is a blend of jazz/lounge. ■TIP➜**Try the famous Crazy Horse cocktail.**

Fodor'sChoice **Hôtel Costes** (⊠*239 rue St-Honoré, 1ᵉʳ, Louvre/Tuileries* ☎*01–42–44–*
★ *50–25*) draws the big names, and not just during fashion week. Despite years on the scene, this place has lost none of its flair, or star clientele. Expect to cross paths with anyone from Kylie Minogue to Bruce Willis, as long as you make it past the chilly greeting of the statuesque hostess. Dressing to kill is strongly advised, especially for newcomers; otherwise expect all the tables to be reserved.

Hôtel de Crillon (⊠*10 pl. de la Concorde, 8ᵉ, Champs-Elysées* ☎*01–44–71–15–39* Ⓜ*Concorde*) seduces visitors with elegance and antique armchairs. The gilded palace bar, designed by sculptor Cesar in 1907, received a major makeover from fashion designer Sonia Rykiel. There is nightly piano music until 1 AM. ■TIP→**Dress smartly and order the signature Duc de Crillon cocktail (Taittinger Champagne with Armagnac).**

Hôtel Meurice (✉228 *rue de Rivoli, 1er, Louvre/Tuileries* ☎01–44–58–10–66 Ⓜ *Tuileries*) converted its ground-floor Fontainebleau library into an intimate bar with wood paneling and huge murals depicting the royal hunting forests of Fontainebleau. With décor updates by Philippe Starck, the bar is set to continue serving its famous Bellinis to its loyal fashion crowd. ■TIP→**Try the Meurice Millenium, a cocktail by the bar's famed bartender, made with champagne, rose liqueur, and Cointreau.**

Hôtel Plaza Athenée (✉25 *av. Montaigne, 8e, Champs-Elysées* ☎01–53–67–66–00 Ⓜ *Champs-Elysées–Clemenceau*) is Paris's perfectly chic chill-out spot, with a sexy, glowing bar designed by Philippe Starck protégé Patrick Jouin. It's the perfect venue for an apéritif before hitting the nearby club scene. ■TIP→**You'll find one of the most inventive cocktail lists in town here: try the acclaimed Rose Royale, with champagne and freshly crushed raspberries.**

★ **Murano Urban Resort** (✉13 *bd. du Temple, 3e, République* ☎01–42–71–20–00 Ⓜ *Filles du Calvaire, République*) is Paris's epitome of space-age-bachelor-pad-hipness *du jour* with a black-stone bar, candy-color walls, and a genuinely friendly staff. It overflows nightly with beautiful Marais culture vultures, and is up-and-coming on the late-night scene with its themed soirées.

★ **Pershing Hall** (✉49 *rue Pierre Charron, 8e, Champs-Elysées* ☎01–58–36–58–36 Ⓜ *George V*) has an überstylish lounge in muted colors and minimalist lines, and an enormous "vertical garden" in the simply stunning courtyard. The chic ambience and hip lounge music make this a neighborhood jewel.

Regina's Bar Anglais (✉2 *pl. des Pyramides, 2e, Louvre* ☎01–42–60–31–10 Ⓜ *Louvre Rivoli*), an oasis of Englishness in the sea of trendy French bars, has comfy leather armchairs and tasteful Belle Époque design. Order a Grand Manhattan and let the peace and quiet have its way with you. The verdant terrace attracts in the warmer months.

Fodor'sChoice **The Hemingway Bar & The Ritz Bar** (✉15 *pl. Vendôme, 1er, Louvre/Tuileries* ☎01–43–16–33–65 Ⓜ *Opéra*) are steps from each other at the luxurious Ritz hotel, and both serve the cocktails of world-famous bartender Colin Field. The Hemingway bar stays true to the old guard of Paris; the reopened Ritz Bar (formerly the Cambon) has its eye on trendy clientele—dark lighting, luxurious seating, and above-average lounge music bring this luxe venue into the 21st century.

CABARETS

Paris's cabarets range from boîtes once haunted by Picasso and Piaf to those sinful showplaces where *tableaux vivants* offer acres of bare female flesh. These extravaganzas—sadly more Las Vegas than the

14

petticoat vision re-created by Hollywood in Baz Luhrmann's *Moulin Rouge*—draw the tourists but are usually shunned by the Parisians. You can dine at many cabarets, but the food isn't the attraction. Prices range from about €30 (admission plus one drink) to more than €130 (dinner plus show).

Fodor'sChoice ★ **Au Lapin Agile** (⊠ *22 rue des Saules, 18ᵉ, Montmartre* ☎ *01–46–06–85–87* Ⓜ *Lamarck Caulaincourt*), a survivor from the 19th century, considers itself the doyen of cabarets. Founded in 1860, it still inhabits a modest house, once a favorite subject of painter Maurice Utrillo. It became the home-away-from-home for Braque, Modigliani, Apollinaire, and Picasso—who once paid for a meal with one of his paintings, then promptly went out and painted another that he named after this place. There are no topless dancers—this is an authentic French cabaret with songs, poetry, and humor in a pub-like setting.

Bobino (⊠ *20 rue Gaîté, 14ᵉ, Montparnasse* ☎ *01–43–27–24–24* Ⓜ *Edgar Quinet Gaîté*) reopened in 2007, and what a buzz it's stirred up. The beautiful renovation turned this onetime concert hall into a glitzy restaurant-cabaret-lounge-club, where the party starts when the cabaret ends at 11:30. It's a feast for the eyes and appetite, reminiscent of Studio 54.

Le Canotier du Pied de la Butte (⊠ *62 bd. Rochechouart, 18ᵉ, Montmartre* ☎ *01–46–06–02–86* Ⓜ *Anvers*) once hosted Piaf, Brel, and Chevalier; today there are several shows nightly with modern-day songsters interpreting the French *chanson* repertoire and magicians performing tricks.

★ **Crazy Horse** (⊠ *12 av. George V, 8ᵉ, Champs-Elysées* ☎ *01–47–23–32–32* Ⓜ *Alma-Marceau*) honed striptease to an art. Founded in 1951 and renovated in 2007, it's renowned for pretty dancers and raunchy routines characterized by lots of humor and few clothes. Burlesque artist extraordinaire Dita von Teese has been known to perform here, elevating the reputation of this haunt to that of the most glamorous cabarets in the city.

Lido (⊠ *116 bis, av. des Champs-Elysées, 8ᵉ, Champs-Elysées* ☎ *01–40–76–56–10* Ⓜ *George V*) stars the supercalifragilisticexpidelicious Bluebell Girls; the owners claim no show this side of Vegas rivals it for special effects.

★ **Le Limonaire** (⊠ *21 rue Bergère, 9ᵉ, Opéra/Grands Boulevards* ☎ *01–45–23–33–33* Ⓜ *Grands Boulevards*), a small restaurant, oozes Parisian charm. At 10 PM, Tuesday–Sunday, food service gives way to the singing of traditional French songs of "expression," with musical accompaniment bien sûr. There's no entrance fee—singers pass a hat around.

Michou (✉*80 rue des Martyrs, 18ᵉ, Montmartre* ☎*01–46–06–16–04* Ⓜ*Pigalle*) is owned by always blue-clad Michou. The men on stage, in extravagant drag, are known as "transformistes," and perform with high camp. The €35 entrance fee to sit at the bar includes a drink.

Moulin Rouge (✉*82 bd. de Clichy, 18ᵉ, Montmartre* ☎*01–53–09–82–82* Ⓜ*Blanche*) offered a circuslike atmosphere when it opened in 1889, and lured Parisians of all social stripes. Think elephants, donkey rides for the ladies, and the incomparable cancan revue. Today, the cancan is still a popular highlight of what is now more a Vegas-y show, starring 100 dancers, acrobats, ventriloquists, and contortionists, and more than 1,000 costumes. Dinner shows start at 7, standard shows at 9 and 11 (arrive 30 minutes early; men should wear a jacket and tie).

★ **Paradis Latin** (✉*28 rue du Cardinal Lemoine, 5ᵉ, Quartier Latin* ☎*01–43–25–28–28* Ⓜ*Cardinal Lemoine*), in a building by Gustav Eiffel, peppers its shows with acrobatics and lighting effects, making it the liveliest and trendiest cabaret on the Rive Gauche. It's closed Tuesday.

CLUBS

Paris's hyped *boîtes de nuit* (nightclubs) are expensive and exclusive—if you're friends with a regular or you've modeled in *Vogue,* you'll have an easier time getting through the door. Cover charges at some spots push the €20 range, with drinks at the bar starting at €10 for a beer. Others are free to enter, but getting past the doorman can still be an issue. Locals looking to dance tend to stick to the smaller clubs, where the cover ranges from free (usually on slower weekdays) to €15 and the focus is on the music and upbeat atmosphere. Club popularity depends on the night or event, as Parisians are more loyal to certain DJs than venues and often hit two or three spots before ending up at one of the many after-parties, which can last until noon the next day.

Le Balajo (✉*9 rue de Lappe, 11ᵉ, Bastille* ☎*01–47–00–07–87* Ⓜ*Bastille*), a casual dance club in an old ballroom, has been around since 1936. Latin groove, funk, and R&B disco are the standards, with salsa on Tuesday and Thursday nights and tango on the last Sunday of the month. Thursday is ladies' night with free entrance before 1 AM.

★ **Le Baron** (✉*6 av. Marceau, 8ᵉ, Champs-Elysées* ☎*01–47–20–04–01* Ⓜ*Alma-Marceau*), formerly a seedy "hostesse" bar, didn't bother to update its decadent cabaret décor (red banquettes, mirror ball, and baronial top-hat sign) when it opened in 2004—and it didn't need to. Models, musicians, and Oscar winners party until morning while indulging in the bar's classic cocktail: a mix of red fruits, champagne, and vodka called the Baron Deluxe. The door policy is notoriously difficult.

★ **Le Batofar** (✉*11 quai François Mauriac, 13ᵉ, Bercy/Tolbiac* ☎*01–53–60–17–30* Ⓜ*Bibliothèque*) is an old tugboat refitted as a bar and concert venue. Music at this trendy yet reasonably priced spot is eclectic,

CLOSE UP

After-Hours Restaurants

Craving steak au poivre after a post-midnight party? Most late-night brasseries and round-the-clock restaurants don't need reservations; here are some of the best.

Le Bienvenu (⊠ *42 rue d'Argout, 2ᵉ, Louvre/Tuileries* ☎ *01–42–33–31–08* Ⓜ *Louvre*) doesn't look like much (notice the kitsch mural on the back wall), but it serves simple French food and couscous in the wee hours of the morning. It's open till 6 ᴀᴍ.

Au Chien Qui Fume (⊠ *33 rue du Pont-Neuf, 1ᵉʳ, Louvre/Tuileries* ☎ *01–42–36–07–42* Ⓜ *Les Halles*), open until 2 ᴀᴍ, is filled with witty, old master–style paintings of smoking dogs. Traditional French cuisine and seafood platters are served until 1 ᴀᴍ.

La Cloche d'Or (⊠ *3 rue Mansart, 9ᵉ, Montmartre* ☎ *01–48–74–48–88* Ⓜ *Place de Clichy*) is a Paris classic, on whose traditional French dishes the likes of the late president François Mitterrand and Moulin Rouge dancers have dined (though not together). It's open until 4 ᴀᴍ every day but Sunday, when it is closed. It's also closed in August.

Les Coulisses (⊠ *1 rue St-Rustique, 18ᵉ, Montmartre* ☎ *01–42–62–89–99* Ⓜ *Abbesses*), near picturesque Place du Tertre, has more character than most late-night restaurants: its red banquettes and 18th-century Venetian mirrors make it look like an Italian theater. The food—traditional French—is served until 2 ᴀᴍ. There's a club in the basement, open Thursday to Saturday, but it's not really much of a destination in itself.

Grand Café des Capucines (⊠ *4 bd. des Capucines, 9ᵉ, Opéra/Grands Boulevards* ☎ *01–43–12–19–00* Ⓜ *Opéra*), whose exuberant pseudo–Belle Époque dining room matches the mood of the neighboring Opéra, serves excellent oysters, fish, and meat dishes at hefty prices, but it's open around the clock.

Le Lup (⊠ *2–4 rue des Sabots, St-Germain-des-Prés* ☎ *01–45–48–86–47*) is the newest lounge-club addition to the late-night scene on the Left Bank. Its candlelit ambience attracts thirtysomething clubbers, the post-opera set, and hungry night owls who duck in for the sultry vibe of red velvet and a bite to eat from the upscale menu. The two-story rococo salon is perfect for drinks or dessert, and a spin along the small dance floor. It's open 10 ᴘᴍ to 5 ᴀᴍ Wednesday to Saturday.

Au Pied de Cochon (⊠ *6 rue Coquillière, 1ᵉʳ, Beaubourg/Les Halles* ☎ *01–40–13–77–00* Ⓜ *Les Halles*) once catered to the all-night workers at the adjacent Les Halles food market. Its Second Empire carvings and gilt have been restored, and traditional dishes like pig's trotters and chitterling sausage still grace the menu. And you haven't tasted pig's trotters until you've tasted them at 6 ᴀᴍ. This place is nothing an institution, and it's open 24 hours daily.

Le Tambour (⊠ *41 rue Montmartre, 2ᵉ, Beaubourg/Les Halles* ☎ *01–42–33–06–90* Ⓜ *Etienne Marcel, Les Halles*) wins hands-down for wackiness, full as it is of flea-market charm. The eye-catching décor includes everything but the proverbial kitchen sink. (Come to think of it, there is a kitchen sink—in the kitchen.) The food's especially fine here—think onion soup, foie gras, steak tartare, and confit de canard. Open 6 ᴘᴍ-5:30 ᴀᴍ; last dinner service at 3:30 ᴀᴍ.

from live world-beat to electronic and techno. ■ TIP→(Stylish) sneakers are recommended on the slippery deck.

Black Calvados (✉ *40 av. Pierre 1er ede Serbie, 8e, Champs-Elysées* ☎ *01–47–20–77–77* Ⓜ *Saint-Philippe-du-Roule*), known as "BC" to its young trendsetters, is a sleek bar where the party starts late (don't bother coming before 1 AM) and lasts until morning. Ring the buzzer out front for the doorman to assess your worth—this is a celebrity hangout. Once inside (let's think positive), try the Black Kiss, a shot of black vodka served on ice with sugar-cube lips. ■ TIP→If all else fails, head upstairs to the smaller but equally sexy bar-restaurant and order a midnight snack of Kobe miniburgers.

Le Cab (✉ *2 pl. du Palais-Royal, 1er, Louvre/Tuileries* ☎ *01–58–62–56–25* Ⓜ *Palais-Royal*) is one of the more popular fashion-centric clubs, where models, photographers, and stylists bypass the lesser beings at the velvet rope. If you make it inside, you'll appreciate the *Space Odyssey* atmosphere. Depending on the night, you'll hear funk, hip-hop, electro, or house.

Castel (aka Chez Castel) (✉ *15 rue Princesse, 6e, St-Germain-des-Prés* ☎ *01–40–51–52–80* Ⓜ *St-Germain-des-Prés, Mabillon*) is the swankiest of private Paris clubs: a three-story gold-and-red-velvet mansion with vaulted ceilings where celebrities like Monica Bellucci and Vincent Cassel cavort far from the St-Germain tourists. Making reservations at the two dining rooms (one more formal than the other) will ease your entry.

La Coupole (✉ *100 bd. du Montparnasse, 14e, Montparnasse* ☎ *01–43–20–14–20* Ⓜ *Vavin*), the gorgeous dance hall beneath the famous brasserie, has "Latin Fever" nights on Friday from 7:45 PM (for beginners) until dawn. Saturday has the popular "Re-Definition" night of hip-hop, R&B, and afro-zouk from 11:30.

Le Djoon (✉ *22 bd. Auriol, 13e, Bibliothèque* ☎ *01–45–70–83–49* Ⓜ *Bibliothèque*) attracts the dance crowd—it's not the place to stand around. With inspiration from the '80s New York house scene, DJ Greg Gauthier mixes afro, disco, and funk. Keep in mind it's a taxi ride away from everywhere, but a fun diversion from the normally cramped clubs.

L'Elysée Montmartre (✉ *72 bd. de Rochechouart, 18e, Montmartre* ☎ *01–44–92–45–47* Ⓜ *Anvers*), the old concert hall with the gorgeous façade, holds popular *bals* (balls) every second and fourth Saturday of the month from 11 PM; music runs the gamut of hits from '40s to '80s (emphasis on the latter), and the DJ is backed by a 10-piece orchestra.

Les Folies Pigalle (✉ *11 pl. Pigalle, 9e, Montmartre* ☎ *01–48–78–55–25* Ⓜ *Pigalle*) is a former cabaret decorated like a '30s-era bordello. The ambience is decadent, and music ranges from house and techno to R&B and electro. After-parties hop on Sunday morning.

Le Gibus (⊠ *18 rue du Faubourg du Temple, 11ᵉ, République* ☏ *01–47–00–78–88* Ⓜ *République*) is one of Paris's most famous music venues. In more than 30 years there have been upward of 6,500 concerts and more than 3,000 performers (including the Police, Deep Purple, and Billy Idol). Today the Gibus's cellars are *the* place for trance, techno, hip-hop, hard-core, and jungle music.

La Java (⊠ *105 rue du Faubourg du Temple, 10ᵉ, République* ☏ *01–42–02–20–52* Ⓜ *Belleville*), where Piaf and Chevalier made their names, has reinvented itself as a dance club with music of the rock/pop genre and frequent live performances by up-and-coming bands.

★ **Mathis Bar** (⊠ *3 rue Ponthieu, 8ᵉ, Champs-Elysées* ☏ *01–53–76–01–62* Ⓜ *Saint-Philippe-du-Roule*) is one of the best-kept secrets on the Paris bar-lounge scene. If you can talk your way past the stern doorwoman, you can mingle with the oligarchs, artists, and visiting American movie stars in a truly posh and decadent atmosphere. It gets cozier on weekends, and the friendly jet-set patrons seated next to you will probably strike up a conversation.

Mix Club (⊠ *24 rue de l'Arrivee, 14ᵉ, Montparnasse* ☏ *01–56–80–37–37* Ⓜ *Montparnasse-Bienvenue*), a massive, self-described "temple of house music" has enough sound-system wattage, blinding lights, and dancing bodies to land you in the ninth circle of Disco Inferno.

Neo (⊠ *23 rue de Ponthieu, 8ᵉ, Champs-Elysées* ☏ *01–42–25–57–14* Ⓜ *Franklin-D.-Roosevelt*) is a ragingly popular new disco with rock-and-roll trimmings, a sleek dance floor, and fashion models cavorting with celebrities.

★ **Le Nouveau Casino** (⊠ *109 rue Oberkampf, 11ᵉ, République* ☏ *01–43–57–57–40* Ⓜ *Parmentier*) is a concert hall and club tucked behind the Café Charbon. Pop and rock concerts prevail during the week, with clubbing on Friday and Saturday from midnight until dawn. Electronic, house, disco, and techno DJs are the standard.

Paris Paris (⊠ *5 av. de l'Opéra, 2ᵉ, Opéra* ☏ *01–42–60–64–45* Ⓜ *Pyramides*) proves that you don't need much in the way of décor to be a success—the patrons, dancing to top-shelf DJs like the duo Justice, are having too much fun to care that there's not much more than black walls and some neon.

Pop-In (⊠ *105 rue Amelot, 4ᵉ, République* ☏ *01–48–05–56–11* Ⓜ *Saint-Sebastien-Froissart*), on a backstreet just off the Boulevard Beaumarchais (which links the Bastille to République), is a dark, hard-partying boho playhouse with a pronounced English-rocker feel. It fills up with a student crowd.

Queen (⊠ *102 av. des Champs-Elysées, 8ᵉ, Champs-Elysées* ☏ *08–92–70–73–30* Ⓜ *George V*), the mythic gay club of the '90s, is not quite as monumental as it once was, but its doors are still difficult to get through, especially—inevitably—on weekends. Proudly hosting a fantastic roster of house DJs from Tiesto to Guetta, it's known for soirees such as "Overkitsch." Queen is no longer a gay mecca and is full of a straight mix of international partygoers eager to dance on podiums.

Le Red Light (⌗ *34 rue du Départ, 15ᵉ, Montparnasse* ☎*01–42–79–94–53* Ⓜ*Montparnasse Bienvenüe*) has two giant dance floors playing mainly house and electronic music by big-name international DJs every Friday and Saturday from midnight until dawn. It draws a casual, mixed crowd, and popular after-parties follow.

★ **Le Rex** (⌗ *5 bd. Poissonnière, 2ᵉ, Opéra/Grands Boulevards* ☎*01–42–36–10–96* Ⓜ*Grands Boulevards*), open Wednesday through Sunday, is the a temple of techno and house, popular with students. France's most famous DJ, Laurent Garnier, is sometimes at the turntables.

La Scène Bastille (⌗ *2 bis, rue des Taillandiers, 11ᵉ, Bastille/Nation* ☎*01–48–06–50–70* Ⓜ*Bastille*) is one of the more refreshing venues in the Bastille club scene, with a laid-back, eclectic crowd and a cozy (if uncreatively decorated) lounge atmosphere. A variety of theme nights keep this place interesting, especially the "Techno Sweet Peak" on the first Friday of the month, and "In Funk We Trust" Saturdays. Gay nights on first and third Sundays also attract a lively crowd.

14

Showcase(⌗ *Pont Alexandre III,8ᵉ, Concorde* ☎*01–45–61–25–43*) takes the gold medal for best location. No one can believe its stunning position under the golden Pont Alexandre bridge. Inside, a long bar, two VIP sections, and a stage that hosts a diverse range of talented groups and DJs makes this a mandatory stop on any night of clubbing, especially around 3 AM when the after-party heats up.

Triptyque (⌗ *142 rue Montmartre, 1ᵉʳ, Grands Boulevards* ☎*01–40–28–05–55* Ⓜ*Bourse*) is a fabulous U-shape downstairs club with a sinsational vibe, a low-key yet hip young following, and some of the most fun (and best-named) theme nights available in Paris—"Chiennes Hi-Fi," "Just One Finger," and "Johnny, Do Me Wrong" are some faves.

WAGG (⌗ *62 rue Mazarine, 6ᵉ, St-Germain-des-Prés* ☎*01–55–42–22–00* Ⓜ*Odéon*) can be found beneath the popular bar-resto Alcazar, in a vaulted stone cellar that was Jim Morrison's hangout back in its '70s incarnation as the Whiskey-a-Go-Go. It's now a welcoming dance club and has state-of-the-art sound, lighting, and guest DJs.

The White Room (⌗ *At Maison Blanche restaurant, 15 av. Montaigne, 8ᵉ Champs-Elysées* ☎*01–47–23–55–99* Ⓜ*Charles de Gaulle–Etoile*) is a very of-the-moment Friday-only hip-hop and disco party in a—you guessed it—white room. It boasts a stellar view from its top-floor vantage, and attracts the St. Tropez set and other VIPs, who buy bottles because the bar is way too small.

GAY & LESBIAN BARS & CLUBS

Gay and lesbian bars and clubs are mostly concentrated in the Marais and include some of the hippest addresses in the city. Keep in mind, however, that many of these sites fall in and out of favor at lightning speed. The best way to find out what's hot is by picking up a copy of

Têtu, 2X, or *Loverboy,* the free "agendas" (listings for hot spots and events), that can be found in any of the bars listed below.

FOR MEN & WOMEN

Amnésia Café (✉ *42 rue Vieille-du-Temple, 4ᵉ, Le Marais* ☎ *01–42–72–16–94* Ⓜ *Rambuteau, St-Paul*) has a dimly lighted bar and Art Deco ceiling murals. It attracts a young-professional mixed crowd. Check out the semiprivate minimezzanine in the back, and don't leave without trying the Coffee Amnesia, a blend of cognac and Chantilly cream that'll zap you.

Banana Café (✉ *13 rue de la Ferronnerie, 1ᵉʳ, Beaubourg/Les Halles* ☎ *01–42–33–35–31* Ⓜ *Châtelet Les Halles*) has a trendy and scantily clad mixed crowd, not to mention show tunes in the cellar, where dancing on tables is the norm. Monday night is the "soirée sans interdit" (where nothing is forbidden)—ooh la la!

Madame Arthur (✉ *75 bis, rue des Martyrs, 18ᵉ, Montmartre* ☎ *01–42–54–49–14* Ⓜ *Pigalle*) stages a wacky burlesque drag show—men dressed as famous French female vocalists—that's not for the faint-hearted. Boys, as they say, will be girls.

★ **Les Neufs Billards** (✉ *17 rue St-Maur, 11ᵉ, Oberkampf* ☎ *01–40–40–05–42* Ⓜ *Saint Maur*) is a popular, somewhat bohemian spot with a mixed clientele and Brazilian and tango nights.

★ **L'Open Café** (✉ *17 rue des Archives, 4ᵉ, Le Marais* ☎ *01–42–72–26–18* Ⓜ *Hôtel de Ville*), with sunny yellow walls, is a Marais favorite, and less of a gay meat market than neighboring Café Cox. In summer the crowd spills out onto the street.

Tango (✉ *11 rue au Maire, 3ᵉ, Le Marais* ☎ *01–42–72–17–78* Ⓜ *Arts et Métiers*) has kept its dance-hall origins and has a cheerful mixed crowd. Before midnight, the DJ plays classic *chansons* (French torch songs)—arrive early to waltz and swing!

MOSTLY MEN

Les Bains-Douches (✉ *7 rue du Bourg-l'Abbé, 3ᵉ, Marais* ☎ *01–48–87–01–80* Ⓜ *Etienne Marcel*) is a clubbing institution that has evolved into one of the hottest gay clubs in the city on Thursday through Saturday nights—think Studio 54 à la français. There are theme nights and guest DJs; be prepared for a wild time.

★ **Bar d'Art/Le Duplex** (✉ *25 rue Michel-Le-Comte, 3ᵉ, Beaubourg/Les Halles* ☎ *01–42–72–80–86* Ⓜ *Rambuteau*) teems with young tortured-artist types who enjoy the frequent art exhibitions, alternative music, and ambient lighting.

Café Cox (✉ *15 rue des Archives, 4ᵉ, Le Marais* ☎ *01–42–72–08–00* Ⓜ *Hôtel de Ville*) is a prime gay pickup joint. Behind the frosted glass windows men line the walls and appraise the talent.

Club 18 (✉ *18 rue de Beaujolais, 3ᵉ, Louvre* ☎ *01–42–97–52–13* Ⓜ *Palais Royale*) takes gay pride to the heart of the Louvre district on the weekends, and this elegant spot bills itself, quite accurately, as the oldest gay club in Paris with a "friendly clubbing party."

Le Dépôt (⊠*10 rue aux Ours, 3ᵉ, Beaubourg/Les Halles* ☏*01–44–54–96–96* Ⓜ*Etienne Marcel*) is a cruising bar, club, and back room. The popular Gay Tea Dance is held here on Sunday (from 2 PM).

Raiddbar (⊠*23 rue du Temple, 3ᵉ, Le Marais* ☏*01–47–27–80–25* Ⓜ*Hôtel de Ville, St-Paul*) is popular and friendly, with a darker downstairs bar and potent drinks. The men are hot, and so is the steamy shower show presented every 20 minutes—not for timid voyeurs.

MOSTLY WOMEN

Chez Moune (⊠*54 rue Pigalle, 18ᵉ, Pigalle* ☏*01–45–26–64–64* Ⓜ*Pigalle*) claims to be the first lesbian cabaret in the city. It showcases singers, transformistes, striptease, and DJs that will keep you dancing until dawn.

Le Nix Café (⊠*30 rue du Roi de Sicile, 4ᵉ, Le Marais* Ⓜ*St-Paul*) is the reincarnation of the famous Bliss KFE, and a happening bar in its own right, at the heart of the gay district. Enjoy their happy hour every evening (6–8) and the DJ in the tiny basement bar on Friday and Saturday evenings. Men are allowed in small numbers on weekdays.

3W (⊠*8 rue des Ecouffes, 4ᵉ, Le Marais* ☏*01–48–87–39–26* Ⓜ*St-Paul*), as in "Women With Women" (formerly called Les Scandaleuses), is a pillar of the lesbian scene, cheerful and friendly.

JAZZ CLUBS

Bar le Houdon (⊠*5 rue des Abbesses, 18ᵉ, Montmartre* ☏*01–42–62–21–34* Ⓜ*Abbesses*) transforms from humdrum café to jazz venue Friday and Saturday. The musicians are top-notch and the price is right.

Caveau de la Huchette (⊠*5 rue de la Huchette, 5ᵉ, Quartier Latin* ☏*01–43–26–65–05* Ⓜ*St-Michel*), one of the few surviving cellar clubs from the 1940s, is a bona fide Paris classic, packing 'em in for swing dancing and Dixieland melodies. It's absolutely charming for everyone but claustrophobics.

Lionel Hampton Jazz Club (⊠*Méridien Hotel, 81 bd. Gouvion–St-Cyr, 17ᵉ, Champs-Elysées* ☏*01–40–68–30–42* Ⓜ*Porte Maillot*), named for the American vibraphonist loved by Parisians, hosts a roster of international jazz musicians in a spacious set of rooms.

Fodor'sChoice **New Morning** (⊠*7 rue des Petites-Ecuries, 10ᵉ, Opéra/Grands Boulevards* ☏*01–45–23–51–41* Ⓜ*Château d'Eau*) is the premier spot for ★ serious fans of avant-garde jazz, folk, and world music. The look is spartan, the mood reverential.

Le Petit Journal (⊠*71 bd. St-Michel, 5ᵉ, Quartier Latin* ☏*01–43–26–28–59* Ⓜ*Luxembourg* ⊠*13 rue du Commandant-Mouchotte, 14ᵉ, Montparnasse* ☏*01–43–21–56–70* Ⓜ*Montparnasse Bienvenüe*), with two locations, has long attracted great French and international jazz names. It specializes in big band (Montparnasse) and Dixieland (St-Michel) jazz, with dinner served from 8:30 to midnight.

14

CLOSE UP

Jazz Clubs

The French fell hard for jazz nearly a century ago, during World War I, but the real coup de foudre—literally "lightning bolt" or figuratively "love at first sight"—came after the war when Yank sax man Sidney Bechet and 19-year-old song-and-dance vamp Josephine Baker of St. Louis joined a European tour of the Revue Nègre musical. Baker, or the "Black Venus that haunted Baudelaire," as she was known by French critics, instantly became the sweetheart of Paris. Note: a larger-than-life picture of Baker wearing only a smile, jewelry, and a thigh-high skirt today adorns a wall of historic photographs along the platform of the Tuileries métro.

By 1934 France had created its own impressive claim to jazz fame, the all-string Quintette du Hot Club de France, which featured Gypsy guitarist Django Reinhardt and his partner, violinist Stéphane Grappelli. They, in turn, influenced string players from country musicians to Carlos Santana. Reinhardt performed throughout much of World War II in the underground French jazz scene. In the 1950s, Paris grew to become a major destination of the bebop diaspora, and expat jazz musicians including Bechet, Bud Powell, and Dexter Gordon played the venues along with such jazz greats as Dizzy Gillespie, Charlie Parker, and Miles Davis. France embraced the evolving jazz sound that many Americans were still struggling to accept and provided a worshipful welcome to musicians battling discrimination at home. In Paris, Davis said, he was "treated like a human being."

Want to experience a night of jazz yourself?

The French obsession with jazz continues to this day, and travelers seeking

a quintessential Parisian experience have the opportunity to hear jazz artists from all over the world nearly any night of the week. Aficionados can choose from traditional jazz to the latest experimental efforts, in clubs ranging from casual to chichi, sedate to hopping. Many venues present a wide range of music: a good option is the double club on Rue des Lombards near Les Halles: Le Sunside specializes in more traditional jazz, and its downstairs sister, Le Sunset, features edgier options.

Music generally begins after 9 PM, so plan accordingly: you can dine at some of the clubs, including Le Petit Journal Montparnasse, or in the Hotel Méridien on the Champs-Elysées, which houses the classy Lionel Hampton Jazz Club.

As everywhere else in the city, the French folks at the clubs tend to dress more stylishly than the average traveler with a limited suitcase, but they're generally a tolerant bunch, particularly in venues frequented by students and in the heart of tourist areas like Caveau de la Huchette, a hot cellar dance club across the river from Notre-Dame. Keep in mind, though, that the French are serious about their jazz: with a few exceptions, the audience is generally focused and quiet during performances.

Recognizable names to watch for include expat Yank flute and sax man Bobby Rangel and singer Sara Lazarus, and much-loved French musicians like the pianists Alain Jean-Marie and Pierre de Bethman, sax man Didier Malherbe, and Oliver Ker Ourio on the harmonica. You might want to check out a jazz style you're less likely to find at home, though, like the latest iteration of Gypsy musette—a distinc-

14

tive, swing-infused interpretation of old Paris dance music—presented by virtuosos like accordionist Richard Galliano, violinist Didier Lockwood, and the guitar-picking Ferre brothers, Boulou and Elios. Look for them at Au Duc Des Lombards.

The best place to find out what's playing and even purchase tickets is at www.infoconcert.com or on club Web sites, some of which offer English versions. *Pariscope, Jazz Magazine,* and *Hot Jazz,* available at newsstands, also have listings in French. Reservations can be critical, especially for leading U.S. jazz musicians.

Entrance charges are rarely more than €20 and often much less. Some venues have free jam sessions, depending on the night, so check listings. Drink prices can be sky-high, but most table staff won't harass budget-conscious customers nursing a single drink.

Another way to experience a variety of top-quality jazz is by attending world-renowned Paris festivals

that run from early spring through September, including the Banlieues Bleues (01–49–22–10–10, www. banlieuesbleues.org), the Paris Jazz Festival (08–92–68–31–12, www. parcfloraldeparis.com), and the Villette Jazz Festival (01–44–84–44–84, www. cite-musique.fr).

Word of Mouth
"OK, if I were hip .. and wanted jazz .. I'd stay in the 10th and find my way to New Morning jazz club." —SuzieC

Le Sunset (✉ *60 rue des Lombards, 1ᵉʳ, Beaubourg/Les Halles* ☎ *01–40–26–46–60* Ⓜ *Châtelet Les Halles*) hosts French and American musicians, with an accent on electronic jazz fusion and groove.

Le Sunside (✉ *60 rue des Lombards, 1ᵉʳ, Beaubourg/Les Halles* ☎ *01–40–26–21–25* Ⓜ *Châtelet Les Halles*), connected to Le Sunset, specializes in contemporary jazz and swing. A featured vocalist takes the mike on Sunday night.

PUBS

Pubs wooing English-speaking clients with selections of British and Irish beers are becoming increasingly popular with Parisians. They're also good places to find reasonably priced food at off hours.

Auld Alliance (✉ *80 rue François Miron, 4ᵉ, Le Marais* ☎ *01–48–04–30–40* Ⓜ *St-Paul*) has Scottish shields adorning the walls and a bar staff dressed in kilts for special events. There are more than 120 malt whiskeys to choose from, Scottish beer, soccer and rugby on TV, and sometimes live music.

★ **Corcoran's Irish Pub** (✉ *23 Grands Boulevards, 1ᵉʳ, Grands Boulevards* ☎ *01–40–39–00–16* Ⓜ *Grands Boulevards*) is a great find: it's roomy (great for conversations), and has an ample menu, a gorgeous bar, and old-timey photos and quotations on the walls—"He who opens his mouth most is the one who opens his purse least."

The **Frog pubs** (✉ *25 cour St-Emilion, 12ᵉ, Bercy/Tolbiac* ☎ *01–43–40–70–71* Ⓜ *Cour St-Emilion* ✉ *116 rue St-Denis, 2ᵉ, Beaubourg/Les Halles* ☎ *01–42–36–34–73* Ⓜ *Etienne Marcel* ✉ *9 rue Princesse, 6ᵉ, St-Germain* ☎ *01–40–51–77–38* Ⓜ *Mabillon* ✉ *114 av. de France, 13ᵉ, Bibliotheque* ☎ *01–45–84–34–26* Ⓜ *Bibliothèque François*) are four fun British-style pubs in Paris.

Kitty O'Shea's (✉ *10 rue des Capucines, 2ᵉ, Opéra* ☎ *01–40–15–00–30* Ⓜ *Opéra*), an ever-popular Irish pub near the Place Vendôme, draws a posh after-work crowd as well as salt-of-the-earth punters. Authentic trimmings like stained glass and Gaelic street signs make up the décor, and there's a hearty restaurant that serves burgers and fish-and-chips.

The Shebeen (✉ *16 rue Pot de Fer, 5ᵉ, Quartier Latin* ☎ *01–47–07–49–13* Ⓜ *Place Monge*) is a stylish but laid-back bar with an open mike on Monday, live music on Thursday, and sports on the TV.

Le Truskel (✉ *12 rue Feydeau, 2ᵉ, Les Halles* ☎ *01–40–26–59–97* Ⓜ *Etienne Marcel*)—what looks and sounds and feels like an English pub but kicks booty like a punk club? Le Trusk, whose basement showcases gigs by the globe's hottest new alternative acts while a loud, happy Parisian rocker crowd staggers around the roomy bar.

Performing Arts

Orchestra with Hugues Reiner at Spring Musical Festival, Sénat Building near Jardin du Luxembourg

WORD OF MOUTH

"There is a summer festival each year that has some concerts in parks. It's usually around the end of July and August…outdoors and lovely."

—Christina

PERFORMING ARTS PLANNER

Where to Get Info

Detailed entertainment listings can be found in the weekly magazines *Pariscope, L'Officiel des Spectacles, Zurban,* and the free *Paris Voice* (⊕*www. parisvoice.com*) found in cafés and English-language bookstores. Also look for *Aden* and the *Figaroscope,* the insert in the *Figaro* newspaper. **Parissi. com** (⊕*www.parissi.com*) has club and concert listings, in French only. Many venues also have their own Web sites.

For theater performances, check out ⊕*www.theatre online.com,* which lists 170 theaters, offers critiques, and provides an online reservation service (in French). You can get theater tickets at the theaters themselves. The 24-hour hotline and the Web site of the **Paris Tourist Office** (☎*08– 92–68–30–00 in English €0.34 minute* ⊕*www.parisinfo.com*) are also excellent resources.

Opera performances are listed on www.opera-de-paris.com or in the Paris Tourist Office's *Saison de Paris* booklet.

Festivals

The music and theater season generally runs from September to June, but in summer there are all sorts of festivals.

There is a Chopin Festival at the picturesque **Orangerie de Bagatelle** (⊠*Parc de Bagatelle, Av. de Longchamp, 16ᵉ, Bois de Boulogne* ☎*01–45–00–22–19* Ⓜ*Porte Maillot, then Bus 244*) in late June and early July. In August and September there are free outdoor classical concerts in the **Parc Floral** (☎*01–49–57–24–84* ⊕*www.parcfloralde-paris.com*) of the Bois de Vincennes on weekends at 4 (entrance to the park is €3). This is also where the **Paris Jazz Festival** is held every weekend in summer. The annual **Villette Jazz Festival** (☎*01–40–03–75–75* ⊕*www.villette. com*) is held at the Parc de La Villette every fall. **The Quartier d'Eté** festival in July and August attracts international stars of dance, classical music, and jazz.

Ticket Prices & Discounts

As anywhere in the world, it's best to buy tickets in advance if you can, especially for popular events.

Tickets for performances range in price from about €5 for standing room (at the Opéra Bastille only) or €7 for a circus performance to upward of €160 for something like a performance at the Opéra Garnier or an elaborate National Opéra production. Most venues, however, are in the €15–€25 range. Discounts are often available for limited-visibility seats, students, and senior citizens. Note that **buying from a scalper is risky: some sell counterfeit tickets.**

Movies cost about €6–€10.50, but many cinemas have reduced rates for Monday or Wednesday.

Half-price tickets for same-day theater performances are available at the **Kiosques Théâtre** (⊠*Across from 15 pl. de la Madeleine, Opéra/Grands Boulevards* Ⓜ*Madeleine* ⊠*Outside Gare Montparnasse, Pl. Raoul Dautry, Montparnasse* Ⓜ*Montparnasse Bienvenüe*), open Tuesday to Saturday 12:30 to 8 and Sunday 12:30 to 4. Half-price tickets are also available at many theaters during the first week of each new show.

Updated by Nicole Pritchard

The performing-arts scene in Paris runs the gamut from highbrow to lowbrow, cheap (or free) to break-the-bank expensive. Venues are indoors and outdoors, opulent or spartan, and dress codes vary accordingly. An added bonus in this city of classic beauty is that many of the venues themselves are worth the visit: views of the inside of the Opéra Garnier can easily wind up being much more spectacular than the sets onstage.

15

One thing that sets Paris apart in the arts world is the active participation of the Ministry of Culture, which sponsors numerous concert halls and theaters, like the Comédie Française, that tend to present less commercial, though artistically captivating productions. Other theaters, like the Théâtre de Marigny, and Palais de Chaillot, are known for sold-out shows and decade-long production runs.

It's worth noting that most performances are in French, although you can find English theater productions; English-language movies are often run undubbed, with subtitles. Of course, you don't need to speak the language to enjoy classical music, dance, or the circus.

CIRCUS

Cirque Alexis Gruss (⊠ *Pelouse de St-Cloud, Bois de Boulogne* ☎ *01–45–01–71–26* ⊕ *www.alexis-gruss.com* Ⓜ *Ranelagh*) is in Paris five months of the year and remains an avowedly old-fashioned production with showy horseback riders, trapeze artists, and clowns.

Cirque Diana Moreno Bormann (⊠ *112 rue de la Haie Coq, 19ᵉ, Porte de La Chapelle* ☎ *01–64–05–36–25* ⊕ *www.cirque-diana-moreno.com* Ⓜ *Porte d'Auberviliers*) is good for all ages; performances are at 3 on Saturday, Sunday, and Wednesday.

Cirque d'Hiver Bouglione (⊠ *110 rue Amelot, 11ᵉ, République* ☎ *01–47–00–28–81* ⊕ *www.cirquedhiver.com* Ⓜ *Filles du Calvaire*) brings together two famous circus institutions: the beautiful Cirque d'Hiver hall, constructed in 1852, and the Bouglione troupe, known for its rousing spectacle of acrobats, jugglers, clowns, contortionists, trapeze artists, crocodiles, and doves.

Cirque de Paris (⊠ *115 bd. Charles-de-Gaulle, Villeneuve-la-Garenne* ☎ *01–47–99–40–40* Ⓜ *Porte de Clignancourt, then Bus 137*) offers a

"Day at the Circus": a peek behind the scenes in the morning, lunch with the artists, and a performance in the afternoon.

Parc de la Villette (⊠*211 av. Jean-Jaurès, La Villette* ☎*01–40–03–75–75* Ⓜ*Porte de Pantin*) has an *Espace chapiteaux*, a high-tech sort of circus tent area, that hosts some of the most innovative French circus performers, focusing on contemporary acrobatics and performance art—not to be missed if you're a fan of "new circus."

> ### CHURCH CONCERTS
>
> There's something majestic about listening to classical music under the airy roof of a gorgeous stained-glass church, and many free or almost-free lunchtime and evening concerts are performed. Check weekly listings and flyers posted at the churches themselves for information.

CLASSICAL MUSIC

Cité de la Musique (⊠*In Parc de La Villette, 221 av. Jean-Jaurès, 19ᵉ, La Villette* ☎*01–44–84–44–84* Ⓜ*Porte de Pantin*) presents a varied program of classical, experimental, and world-music concerts in a postmodern setting.

IRCAM (⊠*1 pl. Igor-Stravinsky, 4ᵉ, Beaubourg/Les Halles* ☎*01–44–78–48–43* Ⓜ*Châtelet Les Halles, Hôtel de Ville*) organizes contemporary classical music concerts in its own theater and at the Centre Pompidou next door.

Maison de Radio France (⊠*116 av. du Président-Kennedy, 16ᵉ, Passy-Auteuil* ☎*01–56–40–15–16* Ⓜ*RER: Maison de Radio France*) is home to France's many state-owned radio stations as well as the Orchestre National de France and Orchestre Philharmonique de Radio France. ∎**TIP**➔ **In addition to the program of orchestral concerts on-site, the public can also attend live broadcasts and recordings for free, space permitting; show up an hour in advance at the Grand Hall for tickets.**

Fodor'sChoice ★ **Salle Cortot** (⊠*78 rue Cardinet, 17ᵉ, Parc Monceau* ☎*01–47–63–80–16* Ⓜ*Malesherbes*) is an acoustic gem built by Auguste Perret in 1918. At the time he promised to construct "a hall that sounds like a violin." Jazz and classical concerts are held here. ∎**TIP**➔ **Free student recitals are at noon and 12:30 on Tuesday and Thursday.**

Salle Gaveau (⊠*45 rue de la Boétie, 8ᵉ, Champs-Elysées* ☎*01–49–53–05–07* Ⓜ*Miromesnil*) is a small gold-and-white hall of only 1,200 seats with a distinctly Parisian allure and fantastic acoustics. It plays host to chamber music, piano, and vocal recitals.

Théâtre des Champs-Elysées (⊠*15 av. Montaigne, 8ᵉ, Champs-Elysées* ☎*01–49–52–50–50* Ⓜ*Alma-Marceau*) was the scene of the famous Battle of the Rite of Spring in 1913, when police had to be called in after the audience started ripping up the seats in outrage at Stravinsky's *Le Sacre du Printemps* and Nijinsky's choreography. Today this elegantly restored and plush Art Deco temple is worthy of a visit if only for its architecture. It also hosts top-notch opera, dance performances, jazz, world music, and chamber concerts.

DANCE

Classical ballet is found in places as varied as the opera house and the sports stadium. More avant-garde or up-and-coming choreographers tend to show their works in the smaller performance spaces in the Bastille and the Marais, and in theaters in nearby suburbs.

Centre National de la Danse (✉ *1 rue Victor Hugo, Pantin* ☏ *01–41–83–98–98* Ⓜ *Hoche or RER: Pantin*), sidelined by politics and budget problems for a decade, finally opened in a former jail in the Pantin suburb of Paris. The space is dedicated to supporting professional dancers, with classes, rehearsal studios, and a multimedia

> ### MUSEUM CONCERTS
>
> Museums also host classical concerts; tickets are usually sold separately from admission. The Auditorium du Louvre presents chamber music, string quartets, and a special series of promising new musicians on Thursday; the Musée du Moyen-Age stages medieval music concerts between October and July, including the free *l'Heure Musicale* on Friday at 12:30 and Saturday at 4; and the Musée d'Orsay often has small-scale concerts in the lower-level auditorium.

dance library. There's also a regular program of performances, expositions, and conferences open to the public.

Maison des Arts de Créteil (✉ *1 pl. Salvador Allende, Creteil* ☏ *01–45–13–19–19* Ⓜ *Créteil Préfecture*), just outside Paris, is a fine venue for dance; it often attracts topflight international and French companies, such as Blanca Li, Bill T. Jones, and the annual EXIT Festival.

FodorśChoice ★ **Opéra Garnier** (✉ *Pl. de l'Opéra, 9ᵉ, Opéra/Grands Boulevards* ☏ *08–92–89–90–90* Ⓜ *Opéra*) is the sumptuous Napoléon III home of the well-reputed Ballet de l'Opéra National de Paris and rarely hosts other dance companies. Note that many of the cheaper seats have obstructed views, more of an obstacle in dance than in opera performances.

Théâtre de la Bastille (✉ *76 rue de la Roquette, 11ᵉ, Bastille/Nation* ☏ *01–43–57–42–14* Ⓜ *Bastille*) merits mention as an example of the innovative activity in the Bastille area; it has an enviable record as a launching pad for tomorrow's modern-dance stars.

Théâtre de la Cité Internationale (✉ *17 bd. Jourdan, 14ᵉ, Parc Montsouris* ☏ *01–43–13–50–50* Ⓜ *RER: Cité Universitaire*) is a complex of three theaters in the heart of the international student residence, the Cité Universitaire. It often stages young avant-garde companies and is also the main venue for the Presqu'Iles de Danse festival in February.

Théâtre de la Ville (✉ *2 pl. du Châtelet, 4ᵉ, Beaubourg/Les Halles* Ⓜ *Châtelet* ✉ *31 rue des Abbesses, 18ᵉ, Montmartre* Ⓜ *Abbesses* ☏ *01–42–74–22–77 for both*) is *the* place for contemporary dance. Troupes like Anne-Teresa de Keersmaeker's Rosas company are presented here. Book early; shows sell out quickly.

MOVIES

The French call movies the *septième art* (seventh art) and discuss the latest releases with the same intensity as they do gallery openings or theatrical debuts. Hence you're as likely to see people standing in line for a Hitchcock retrospective or a hard-hitting documentary as for a Hollywood cream puff. Paris has hundreds of cinemas showing contemporary and classic French and American movies, as well as a tempting menu packed with independent, international, and documentary films. Paris has many theaters in addition to the Cinémathèque Française that show classic and independent films, often found in the Quartier Latin. Showings are often organized around retrospectives.

MOVIE-GOING TIPS

Most theaters run English-language films undubbed, with subtitles. When checking movie listings, note that v.o. means version originale; films that are dubbed are v.f. (*version française*). Some theaters post two showtimes: the *séance*, when the commercials, previews, and, sometimes, short films begin; and the feature presentation, which usually starts 10–25 minutes later. It's worth noting that in France, commercials tend to be more inventive than North American ones, so the séance isn't the time-waster you'd expect.

FIRST-RUN FILMS

First-run cinemas cluster around the principal tourist areas, such as the Champs-Elysées, Boulevard des Italiens near the Opéra, Bastille, Châtelet, and Odéon. If you're looking for a memorable cinema, check out some of the following.

Gaumont Grand Ecran (⊠ *30 pl. d'Italie, 13ᵉ, Chinatown* ☎ *08–92–69–66–96* Ⓜ *Place d'Italie*) boasts the biggest screen in Paris.

MK2 Bibliothèque (⊠ *128–162 av. de France, 13ᵉ, Tolbiac* ☎ *08–92–69–84–84* Ⓜ *Quai de la Gare, Bibliothèque*) is a slick cineplex in the shadow of Mitterrand's National Library, with trademark scarlet-red two-person chairs—they fit two people without a divider; sort of like watching a movie at home on your couch—as well as restaurants, music and DVD shops, and even a DJ bar, the Limelight.

Fodor'sChoice **La Pagode** (⊠ *57 bis, rue de Babylone, 7ᵉ, Trocadéro/Tour Eiffel* ☎ *01–*
★ *45–55–48–48* Ⓜ *St-François Xavier*)—where else but in Paris would you find movies screened in an antique pagoda? A Far East fantasy, this structure was built in 1896 for the wife of the owner of Le Bon Marché department store. In the 1970s it was slated for demolition but saved by a grassroots wave of support spearheaded by director Louis Malle. Though the fare is standard, the surroundings are enchanting. Come early for tea in the garden (summer only).

UGC Ciné-Cité Bercy (⊠ *2 cour St-Emilion, 12ᵉ, Bercy* ☎ *08–92–70–00–00* Ⓜ *Cour St-Emilion*) is a huge 18-screen complex in the Bercy Village shopping area. For sound and seating, it's one of the best.

REVIVAL FILMS & ALTERNATIVE SPACES

Accatone (⊠*20 rue Cujas, 5ᵉ, Quartier Latin* ☎*01–46–33–86–86* Ⓜ*Cluny–La Sorbonne, Luxembourg*) shows European art films.

Action Ecoles (⊠*23 rue des Ecoles, 5ᵉ, Quartier Latin* ☎*01–43–29–79–89* Ⓜ*Maubert Mutualité*) specializes in American classics and cult films.

Le Balzac (⊠*1 rue Balzac, 8ᵉ, Champs-Elysées* ☎*01–45–61–10–60* Ⓜ*George V*) often has directors' talks before screenings.

Cinéma des Cinéastes (⊠*7 av. de Clichy, 17ᵉ, Montmartre* ☎*01–53–42–40–20* Ⓜ*Place de Clichy*) shows previews of feature films, as well as documentaries, short films, and rarely shown movies; it's in an old cabaret transformed into a movie theater and wine bar.

Fodor'sChoice ★ **Cinémathèque Française** (⊠*51 rue de Bercy, 12ᵉ, Bercy* ☎*01–71–19–33–33* Ⓜ*Bercy*) is the main mecca for Francophone cinephiles brought up on Fellini, Bergman, and Alain Resnais. Its new home, in the former American Center designed by Frank Gehry, opened in October 2005 and includes elaborate museum exhibitions as well as four cinemas and a video library.

Le Forum des Images (⊠*Forum des Halles, Porte St-Eustache entrance, 1ᵉʳ, Beaubourg/Les Halles* ☎*01–44–76–63–07* Ⓜ*Les Halles*) organizes thematic screenings, often with the director or a film expert for discussion beforehand, along with archival films and videos. For €5.50 you can watch four films and two hours of video.

La Géode (⊠*At Cité des Sciences et de l'Industrie, Parc de La Villette, 26 av. Corentin-Cariou, 19ᵉ, La Villette* ☎*08–92–68–45–40* Ⓜ*Porte de La Villette*) screens wide-angle Omnimax films—usually documentaries—on a gigantic spherical surface.

Parc de La Villette (Ⓜ*Porte de Pantin, Porte de La Villette*) shows free movies outdoors, July through August. Most people take along a picnic. You can rent deck chairs by the entrance.

St-André-des-Arts (⊠*30 rue St-André-des-Arts, 6ᵉ, Quartier Latin* ☎*01–43–26–48–18* Ⓜ*St-Michel*), one of a number of cinemas near the Sorbonne, is also one of the best cinemas in Paris and generally has an annual festival devoted to a single director, such as Bergman or Tarkovski.

OPERA

Opéra de la Bastille (⊠*Pl. de la Bastille, 12ᵉ, Bastille/Nation* ☎*08–92–89–90–90* ⊕*www.opera-de-paris.fr* Ⓜ*Bastille*), the ultramodern facility designed by architect Carlos Ott and built in 1989, has taken over the role of Paris's main opera house from the Opéra Garnier. Like the building, performances tend to be on the avant-garde side—you're just as likely to see a contemporary adaptation of *La Bohème* as you are to hear Kafka set to music. Tickets for Opéra de Paris productions range from €5 to €150 and go on sale at the box office two weeks before any

15

given show or a month ahead by phone. The opera season usually runs September through July, and the box office is open Monday–Saturday 11–6:30.

Opéra Comique (✉5 rue Favart, 2ᵉ, Opéra/Grands Boulevards ☎08–25–00–00–58 ⊕www.opera-comique.com Ⓜ Richelieu Drouot) is a gem of an opera house run by France's enfant terrible theater director Jérôme Savary. As well as staging operettas, the hall hosts modern dance, classical concerts, and vocal recitals. Tickets cost €7–€90 and can be purchased at the theater, by mail, online, or by phone.

Fodor'sChoice ★ **Opéra Garnier** (✉Pl. de l'Opéra, 9ᵉ, Opéra/Grands Boulevards ☎08–92–89–90–90 ⊕www.opera-de-paris.fr Ⓜ Opéra), the magnificent and magical former haunt of the Phantom, painter Edgar Degas, and any number of legendary opera stars, still hosts occasional performances of the Opéra de Paris, along with a fuller calendar of dance performances, as the auditorium is the official home of the Ballet de l'Opéra National de Paris. The grandest opera productions are usually mounted at the Opéra de la Bastille, whereas the Garnier now presents smaller-scale operas such as Mozart's La Clemenza di Tito and Così Fan Tutte. Gorgeous though the Garnier is, its tiara-shape theater means that many seats have limited sight lines, so it's best to ask specifically what the sight lines are when booking (partial view in French is visibilité partielle). ▪TIP➔ The cheaper seats are often those with partial views. Seats go on sale at the box office two weeks before any given show or a month ahead by phone or online; you must go in person to buy the cheapest tickets. Last-minute discount tickets, if available, are offered 15 minutes before a performance for senior citizens and anyone under 28. The box office is open 11–6:30 daily.

Théâtre Musical de Paris (✉Pl. du Châtelet, 1ᵉʳ, Beaubourg/Les Halles ☎01–40–28–28–40 ⊕www.chatelet-theatre.com Ⓜ Châtelet), better known as the Théâtre du Châtelet, puts on some of the finest opera productions in the city and regularly attracts international divas like Cecilia Bartoli and Anne-Sofie von Otter. It also plays host to classical concerts, dance performances, and the occasional play.

THEATER

A number of theaters line the Grands Boulevards between the Opéra and République, but there is no Paris equivalent to Broadway or the West End. Shows are mostly in French, with a few notable exceptions listed below. English-language theater groups playing in various venues throughout Paris include the **International Players** (⊕www.internationalplayers.info) and the **Lester McNutt Company** (⊕www.colestermcnutt.com). Broadway-scale singing-and-dancing musicals are staged at either the Palais des Sports or the Palais des Congrès.

Bouffes du Nord (✉37 bis, bd. de la Chapelle, 10ᵉ, Stalingrad/La Chapelle ☎01–46–07–34–50 Ⓜ La Chapelle) is the wonderfully atmospheric, slightly decrepit home of English director Peter Brook, who regularly delights with his wonderful experimental productions in French and, sometimes, English, too.

Café de la Gare (⊠*41 rue du Temple, 4ᵉ, Le Marais* ☎*01–42–78–52–51* Ⓜ*Hôtel de Ville*) is a fun spot to experience a particularly Parisian form of theater, the *café-théâtre*—part satire, part variety revue, riddled with slapstick humor, and performed in a café salon. ■TIP→**You'll need a good grasp of French slang and current events to keep up with the jokes.**

La Cartoucherie (⊠*In Bois de Vincennes,* ☎*01–43–74–88–50* or *01–43–74–24–08* Ⓜ*Château de Vincennes, then shuttle bus or Bus 112*), a complex of five theaters (Théâtre du Soleil, Théâtre de l'Aquarium, Théâtre de la Tempête, Théâtre de l'Epée de Bois, and the

15

Théâtre du Chaudron) in a former munitions factory, turns cast and spectators into an intimate theatrical world. The resident director is the revered Ariane Mnouchkine. Go early for a simple meal; the cast often helps serve "in character."

Casino de Paris (⊠*16 rue de Clichy, 9ᵉ, Opéra/Grands Boulevards* ☎*08–92–69–89–26* ⊕*www.casinodeparis.fr* Ⓜ*Trinité*), once a favorite with the immortal Serge Gainsbourg, has a horseshoe balcony, a cramped, cozy music-hall feel, and performances by everyone from whirling dervishes to Young Turk singers.

Comédie des Champs-Elysées (⊠*15 av. Montaigne, 8ᵉ, Champs-Elysées* ☎*01–53–23–99–19* Ⓜ*Alma-Marceau*) has good productions in its small theater. It's next door to the larger Théâtre des Champs-Elysées.

Fodor'sChoice ★ **Comédie Française** (⊠*Salle Richelieu, 2 reu de Richelieu, 1ᵉʳ* ☎*01–44–58–15–15* Ⓜ*Palais-Royal–Musée du Louvre* ⊠*Studio Théâtre, Galerie du Carrousel du Louvre, 99 rue de Rivoli, 1ᵉʳ, Louvre/Tuileries* ☎*01–44–58–98–54* Ⓜ*Palais-Royal* ⊠*Théâtre du Vieux Colombier, 21 rue Vieux Colombier, 6ᵉ, St-Germain-des-Prés* ☎*01–44–39–87–00* Ⓜ*St-Sulpice*) dates from 1680 and is the most hallowed institution in French theater. It specializes in classical French plays by the likes of Racine, Molière, and Marivaux. ■TIP→**Reserve seats in person about two weeks in advance, or turn up an hour beforehand and wait in line for cancellations.**

☺ **Le Lucernaire** (⊠*53 rue Notre-Dame-des-Champs, 6ᵉ, Montparnasse* ☎*01–45–44–57–34* Ⓜ*Notre-Dame-des-Champs*) bats .1000 as far as cultural centers are concerned. With two theaters (six performances per night), three movie screens, an art gallery, a bookstore, a lively bar, and the equally lively surrounding neighborhood of Vavin, it caters to young intellectuals—and thanks to the puppet shows (Wednesday and Saturday), their children, too.

Odéon–Théâtre de l'Europe (⊠*Pl. de l'Odéon, 6ᵉ, St-Germain-des-Prés* ☎*01–44–85–40–00* Ⓜ*Odéon*), once home to the Comédie Française, has today made pan-European theater its primary focus, offering a variety of European-language productions in Paris.

Sudden Theatre (⊠*14 bis, rue Ste-Isaure, 18ᵉ, Montmartre* ☎*01–42–62–35–00* Ⓜ*Jules Joffrin*) is a tiny, contemporary theater and acting academy with regular English-language productions.

Théâtre Darius Milhaud (⊠*80 allée Darius Milhaud, 19ᵉ, La Villette* ☎*01–42–01–92–26* Ⓜ*Porte de Pantin*) shows classics by Camus and Baudelaire as well as occasional productions in English.

Théâtre de la Huchette (⊠*23 rue de la Huchette, 5ᵉ, Quartier Latin* ☎*01–43–26–38–99* Ⓜ*St-Michel*) is a tiny Rive Gauche theater that has been staging the titanic Romanian-French writer Ionesco's *The Bald Soprano and The Lesson* every night since 1950! (The box office is open Monday–Saturday 5 PM–9 PM.)

Théâtre Marigny (⊠*Carré Marigny, 8ᵉ, Champs-Elysées* ☎*01–53–96–70–30* Ⓜ*Champs-Elysées–Clemenceau*) is a private theater where there's a good chance you'll find a big-name French star topping the bill.

Théâtre Mogador (⊠*25 rue de Mogador, 9ᵉ, Opéra/Grands Boulevards* ☎*08–92–70–01–00* Ⓜ*Trinité*), one of Paris's most sumptuous theaters, features musicals and other productions with a pronounced popular appeal.

Théâtre National de Chaillot (⊠*1 pl. du Trocadéro, 16ᵉ, Trocadéro/Tour Eiffel* ☎*01–53–65–30–00* Ⓜ*Trocadéro*) is a cavernous place with two theaters dedicated to drama and dance. Since 2003 it has hosted the groundbreaking duo of Deborah Warner (director) and Fiona Shaw (actress) for several excellent English-language productions. Topflight dance companies like the Ballet Royal de Suède and William Forsythe's Ballet Frankfurt also visit regularly.

Théâtre du Palais-Royal (⊠*38 rue Montpensier, 1ᵉʳ, Louvre/Tuileries* ☎*01–42–97–59–76* ⊕*www.theatrepalaisroyal.com* Ⓜ*Palais-Royal*) is a 750-seat Italian theater bedecked in gold and purple.

Théâtre de la Renaissance (⊠*20 bd. St-Martin, 10ᵉ, Opéra/Grands Boulevards* ☎*01–42–08–18–50* Ⓜ*Strasbourg St-Denis*) was put on the map by Belle Époque star Sarah Bernhardt (she was the manager from 1893 to 1899). Big French stars often perform here.

Shopping

Paris shopping

WORD OF MOUTH

"Great window shopping in the Blvd. St. Germain area of the 6th. Upscale clothing, some designers, great purse shops. If you're a youngster, the Marais might be better: more eclectic."

–JeanneB

Nothing, but nothing, can push you into the current of Paris life faster than a few hours of shopping. Follow the example of Parisians, who slow to a crawl as their eyes lock on a tempting display. Window-shopping is one of this city's greatest spectator sports; the French call it lèche-vitrine — literally, "licking the windows" — which is fitting because many of the displays look good enough to eat.

Updated by Jennifer Ditsler-Ladonne

Store owners in Paris play to sophisticated audiences with voracious appetites for everything from spangly flagship stores to minimalist boutiques to under-the-radar spots in 19th-century glass-roofed passages. Parisians know that shopping isn't about the kill, it's about the chase: walking down cobblestone streets looking for items they didn't know they wanted, they're casual yet quick to pounce. They like being seduced by a clever display and relish the performance elements of browsing. Watching them shop can be almost as much fun as shopping yourself.

And nowhere is the infamous Parisian "attitude" more palpable than in the realm of fine shopping—and the more *haute* the more *hauteur*. Parisians are a proud bunch, and they value decorum. Look good; dress to make an impression. You must say *bonjour* upon entering a shop and *merci, au revoir* when leaving, even if it's to no one in particular. Think of it more as announcing your coming and going. Beyond this, protocol becomes less prescribed and more a matter of good judgment. If a salesperson is hovering, there's a reason; let him or her help you. To avoid icy stares once and for all, confidence and politeness go a long way.

As for what to buy, the sky's the limit in terms of choices. If your funds aren't limitless, however, take comfort in knowing that treasures can be found on a budget. And if you do decide to indulge, what better place to make that once-in-a-blue-moon splurge? When you get home and friends ask where you got those to-die-for shoes, with a shrug you'll casually say, "These? Oh…I bought them in Paris."

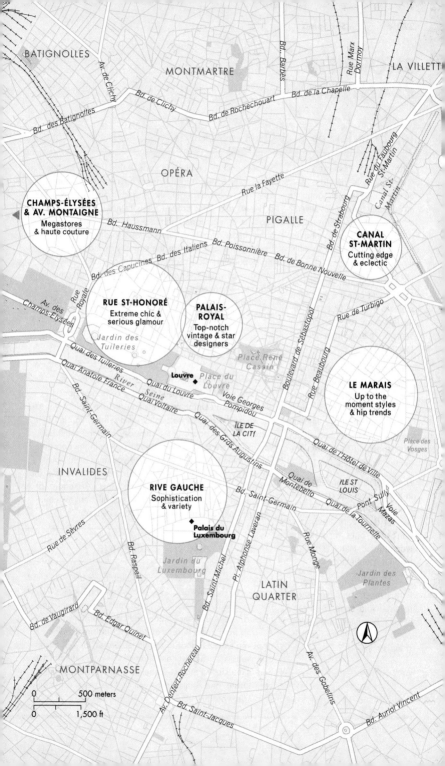

BATIGNOLLES

MONTMARTRE

LA VILLETT

Av. de Clichy

Bd. de Clichy

Rue Marx Dormoy

Bd. des Batignolles

Bd. de Rochechouart

Bd. Barbès

Bd. de la Chapelle

OPÉRA

Rue la Fayette

PIGALLE

Rue du Faubourg St-Martin

Canal St-Martin

Bd. de Strasbourg

**CHAMPS-ÉLYSÉES
& AV. MONTAIGNE**
Megastores
& haute couture

Bd. Haussmann

Bd. des Capucines Bd. des Italiens Bd. Poissonnière Bd. de Bonne Nouvelle

**CANAL
ST-MARTIN**
Cutting edge
& eclectic

Av. des Champs-Élysées

Rue Royale

RUE ST-HONORÉ
Extreme chic &
serious glamour

**PALAIS-
ROYAL**
Top-notch
vintage & star
designers

Rue de Turbigo

Boulevard de Sébastopol

Rue Beaubourg

*Jardin des
Tuileries*

Quai des Tuileries

*Place René
Cassin*

LE MARAIS
Up to the
moment styles
& hip trends

Bd. Saint-Germain

Quai Anatole France

River

Seine

Quai du Louvre

Louvre ◆

*Place du
Louvre*

Voie Georges
Pompidou

*Place des
Vosges*

Quai Voltaire

Quai des Grands Augustins

ÎLE DE
LA CITÉ

Quai de l'Hôtel de Ville

INVALIDES

RIVE GAUCHE
Sophistication
& variety

Bd. Saint-Germain

Quai de
Montebello

ÎLE ST
LOUIS

Quai de la Tournelle

Pont Sully

Voie
Mazas

◆ **Palais du
Luxembourg**

Pl. Alphonse Laveran

Rue de Sèvres

Bd. Raspail

*Jardin du
Luxembourg*

Bd. Saint-Michel

Rue Monge

LATIN
QUARTER

*Jardin des
Plantes*

Bd. de Vaugirard

Bd. Edgar Quinet

Av. des Gobelins

MONTPARNASSE

Av. Denfert-Rochereau

Bd. Saint-Jacques

Bd. Auriol Vincent

0   500 meters

0   1,500 ft

SHOPPING PLANNER

Top Experiences

19th-century Passages. Galerie Vivienne is the oldest and best of Paris's famous shopping arcades, but the city has several other tucked-away gems—filled with everything from antiques to jewelry—for you to stumble upon.

Le Bon Marché. The city's chicest and oldest department store is a great first stop for an overview of the current season's pieces from all the top designers.

Champs-Elysées and Av. Montaigne. Recent years have brought several ho-hum chains, but nothing can beat walking down these famous streets, arms weighed down with shopping bags from the haute houses.

Food Markets. Year-round and in any weather, the city's open-air food markets are an integral part of daily Paris life. A few don't-miss ones include Rue Montorgueil, Marché d'Aligre, and Rue Mouffetard.

The Marais. This is one of Paris's most charming places to stroll and shop, with tons of local boutiques and French-owned chains, along cobblestone streets.

Opening Hours

Store hours can be tricky in Paris. Aside from department stores, which keep slightly longer hours and are usually open late one weeknight, shops tend to open around 10 or 11 AM and close around 7 PM. It's not unusual to find a "back at 3" sign taped on the doors of smaller boutiques at lunchtime. Plan to do most of your foraging between Tuesday and Saturday, as the majority of shops, including department stores, are closed Sunday and some on Monday as well. You can find areas—particularly the Marais—where stores are open on Sunday. However, if you're making a special trip somewhere, always call ahead to check hours.

How to Do Duty-Free

A value-added tax (V.A.T.) of approximately 19.6% (in French, TVA), is imposed on most consumer goods. Non–European Union residents can reclaim part of this tax, known as the *détaxe*. To qualify for a refund, you must purchase €175 of goods in the same shop on the same day, you must have stayed three months or less in the European Union at the time of purchase, and you must have your passport validated by customs within three months after the date of purchase. Don't forget to ask for a détaxe form at the time of purchase; smaller stores will fill it out for you, department stores have special détaxe desks.

Deals Despite the Exchange

Even with the euro trouncing the dollar, there are still sound reasons to shop in Paris. Stay away from the biggies—Chanel, Louis Vuitton, Dior; they'll cost you the same at home. Instead, seek out French-made and other European items. A T-shirt from Petite Bateau in Paris, for instance, will cost about half what it does in the United States, as will a pair of Birkenstocks. Bigger-name French designers still hard to find in the United States—Vanessa Bruno, Paul & Joe, Isabel Marant, and Antik Batik—will cost also less, especially if you get your tax back.

ANTIQUES

Chockablock with antiques shops of every stripe (and offering treasures at every price point), there are really two major antiques neighborhoods in Paris: Carré Rive Gauche and Village St-Paul; both are in lovely, historic districts. From charming French kitchenwares to ancient régime–era artifacts, there's plenty here for everyone. Antiques go through a rigorous evaluation for historical value before they're put on sale, so if you see something in a shop, it's permissible to take it out of the country. Dealers handle all customs forms.

Fodor's Choice **Carré Rive Gauche** (⌧ *Between St-Germain-des-Prés and Musée d'Orsay,*
★ *6ᵉ, St-Germain-des-Prés* Ⓜ *St-Germain-des-Prés, Rue du Bac*) is where you'll find museum-quality pieces. Head to the streets between Rue du Bac, Rue de l'Université, Rue de Lille, and Rue des Sts-Pères to find more than 100 associated shops, marked with a small blue square banner on their storefronts.

Village St-Paul (⌧ *Enter from Rue St-Paul, 4ᵉ, Le Marais* Ⓜ *St-Paul*) is a clutch of streets with many antiques shops, in the beautiful historic netherworld tucked between the fringes of the Marais and the banks of the Seine.

Drouot auction house (⌧ *9 rue Drouot, 9ᵉ, Opéra/Grands Boulevards* Ⓜ *Richelieu Drouot*) is the world-famous auction house that draws all the top dealers as well as savvy novices and those who just love the chase. It's near the Opéra.

BAGS, SCARVES & OTHER ACCESSORIES

Alexandra Sojfer (⌧ *218 bd. St-Germain, 7ᵉ, St-Germain-des-Prés* ☎ *01–42–22–17–02* Ⓜ *Rue du Bac*), the proprietress, is the queen of walking sticks. The late president François Mitterrand used to buy his at this tiny shop, which is also filled with an amazing range of umbrellas.

Goyard (⌧ *233 rue St-Honoré, 1ᵉʳ, Louvre/Tuileries* ☎ *01–42–60–57–04* Ⓜ *Tuileries*) is the choice of royals, blue bloods, and the like (clients have included Sir Arthur Conan Doyle, Gregory Peck, and the Duke and Duchess of Windsor). Parisians swear by the colorful totes because of their durability and longevity; they're copious enough for a mile-long baguette, and durable enough for a magnum of champagne. What's more, they easily transition into ultrachic beach or diaper bags.

★ **Hermès** (⌧ *24 rue du Faubourg St-Honoré, 8ᵉ, Louvre/Tuileries* ☎ *01–40–17–47–17* Ⓜ *Concorde* ⌧ *42 av. Georges V, 8ᵉ, Champs-Elysées* ☎ *01–47–20–48–51* Ⓜ *George V*) was established as a saddlery in 1837 and went on to create the eternally chic Kelly (named for Grace Kelly) and Birkin (named for Jane Birkin) handbags. The silk scarves are legendary for their rich colors and intricate designs, which change yearly. Other accessories are also extremely covetable: enamel bracelets, dashing silk-twill ties, and small leather goods. During semiannual sales, in January and July, prices are slashed up to 50%, and the crowds line up for blocks.

16

★ **Jamin Puech** (⊠*43 rue Madame, 6ᵉ, St-Germain-des-Prés* ☎*01–45– 48–14–85* Ⓜ*St-Sulpice* ⊠*68 rue Vieille-du-Temple, 3ᵉ, Le Marais* ☎*01–48–87–84–87* Ⓜ*St-Paul*) ⊠*26 rue Cambon, 1ᵉ, Louvre/Tuileries* ☎*01–40–20–40–28* Ⓜ*Concord*) thinks of its bags not just as a necessity, but as jewelry. Nothing's

plain Jane here; beaded bags swing from thin link chains, fringes flutter from dark embossed-leather totes, small evening purses are covered with shells, oversize sequins, or hand-dyed crochet. The collections fluctuate with the seasons—some leaning more toward the bohemian than others—but never fail to be whimsical, imaginative, and highly coveted.

Fodor'sChoice
★ **Louis Vuitton** (⊠*101 av. des Champs-Elysées, 8ᵉ, Champs-Elysées* ☎*08–10–81–00–10* Ⓜ*George V* ⊠*6 pl. St-Germain-des-Prés, 6ᵉ, St-Germain-des-Prés* ☎*08–10–81–00–10* Ⓜ*St-Germain-des-Prés* ⊠*22 av. Montaigne, 8ᵉ, Champs-Elysées* ☎*08–10–81–00–10* Ⓜ*Franklin-D.-Roosevelt*) has spawned a voracious fan base from Texas to Tokyo with its mix of classic leather goods and the saucy revamped versions orchestrated by Marc Jacobs. Jacobs's collaborations, such as with Japanese artist Murakami, have become instant collectibles (and knockoffables). This soaring cathedral-esque paean to luxury (and consumption) is unsurpassed.

Loulou de la Falaise ⊠*21 rue Cambon, 1ᵉʳ, Louvre/Tuileries* ☎*01–42– 60–02–66* Ⓜ*Concorde*) was Yves Saint Laurent's original muse: she was at his side for more than 30 years of collections and designed his accessories line, and this paragon of the fashion aristocracy has her own boutique where you can find her much sought-after clothing, accessories, jewelry, scarves, and more.

Marie Mercié (⊠*23 rue St-Sulpice, 6ᵉ, St-Germain-des-Prés* ☎*01–43– 26–45–83* Ⓜ*Mabillon, St-Sulpice*) is one of Paris's most fashionable hat makers. Her husband, Anthony Peto, makes men's hats and has a store at 58 rue Tiquetonne.

Miguel Lobato (⊠*6 rue Malher, 2ᵉ, Le Marais* ☎*01–48–87–68–14* Ⓜ*St-Paul*) is a sweet little boutique with accessories for the woman who wants it all: beautiful high heels by Balenciaga, Chloé, and Pierre Hardy and fabulous bags by Martin Margiela, Alexander McQueen, and Costume National are just the start.

Peggy Huynh Kinh (⊠*11 rue Coëtlogon, 6ᵉ, Quartier Latin* ☎*01–42– 84–83–82* Ⓜ*St-Sulpice*) is a former architect who's now behind the structural line of bags at Cartier. She shows her own line of accessories at this eponymous boutique—understated totes, shoulder bags, wallets, and belts in high-quality leather, as well as a line of office accessories.

Renaud Pellegrino (⊠*14 rue du Faubourg St-Honoré, 8ᵉ, Champs-Elysées* ☎*01–42–65–35–31* Ⓜ*Concorde* ⊠*42 rue de Grenelle, 7ᵉ, St-Germain-des-Prés* ☎*01–45–48–36–30* Ⓜ*Rue du Bac, Sèvres Baby-*

lone) whips satin, calf hair, suede, and beads into totes and shoulder bags, as well as evening bags dainty enough to require an outfit (or date) with pockets for the rest of your things.

DISCOUNT

Accessoires à Soie (✉ *21 rue des Acacias, 17ᵉ, Champs-Elysées* ☎ *01–42–27–78–77* Ⓜ *Argentine*) is where savvy Parisians go for silk scarves and ties in all shapes and sizes. The wide selection includes many big-name designers, and everything costs about half what you'd pay elsewhere.

BEAUTY

When it comes to *maquillage* (makeup), many Parisian women head directly to **Monoprix,** an urban supermarket–dime store that's a gold mine for reasonable, good-quality cosmetics. Brand names to look for are Bourjois, whose products are made in the Chanel factories, and Arcancil. For a great bargain on the best French products, check out the host of "parapharmacies," which have sprung up throughout the city. The French flock here to stock up on pharmaceutical skin-care lines, hair-care basics, and great baby-care necessities normally sold in the more expensive pharmacies. Look for the Roc line of skin products, hair care by Réné Furterer or Phytologie, the popular Caudalíe line of skin care made with grape extracts, or the Nuxe line of body oils and creams infused with a slight gold hue that French actresses swear by, all of which are more expensive back home, if you can find them.

16

Anne Sémonin (✉ *2 rue des Petits-Champs, 2ᵉ, Beaubourg/Les Halles* ☎ *01–42–60–94–66* Ⓜ *Palais-Royal* ✉ *108 rue du Faubourg St-Honoré, 8ᵉ, Champs-Elysées* ☎ *01–42–66–24–22* Ⓜ *Champs-Elysées–Clemenceau*) sells exceptional skin-care products made out of seaweed and trace elements, as well as essential oils that are popular with fashion models.

By Terry (✉ *36 Galerie Véro-Dodat, 1ᵉʳ, Louvre/Tuileries* ☎ *01–44–76–00–76* Ⓜ *Louvre, Palais-Royal* ✉ *1 rue Jacob, 6ᵉ, St-Germain-des-Prés* ☎ *01–46–34–00–36* Ⓜ *St-Germain-des-Prés*) is the brainchild of Terry de Gunzburg, Yves Saint Laurent's former director of makeup. This small, refined store sells her own brand of "ready-to-wear" makeup that's a favorite of French actresses and socialites. Upstairs, specialists create what de Gunzburg calls *haute couleur,* exclusive made-to-measure makeup tailored for each client (very expensive, and you'll need to book an appointment far in advance).

Codina (✉ *24 rue Violet, 15ᵉ, Trocadéro/Tour Eiffel* ☎ *01–45–78–88–88* Ⓜ *Dupleix*) extracts its organic oils using the oldest oil press in Paris. The more than 60 varieties—many exotic—include argan to combat wrinkles, wheat germ and apricot for supple skin, borage and cassis for a detoxified glow, and cherry seed for regeneration. Parisian sylphs adore their exclusive bar shampoos, shea-butter-infused creams, and heavenly soaps. There are also dozens of the purest French-extracted essential oils for less than you'll pay stateside.

Make Up for Ever (⊠*5 rue de la Boétie, 8ᵉ, Champs-Elysées* ☏*01–53–05–93–30* Ⓜ*St-Augustin*), at the back of a courtyard, is a must-stop for makeup artists, models, and actresses. The ultrahip selection has hundreds of hues for foundation, eye shadow, powder, and lipstick.

Sephora (⊠*70 av. des Champs-Elysées, 8ᵉ, Champs-Elysées* ☏*01–53–93–22–50* Ⓜ*Franklin-D.-Roosevelt* ⊠*11 rue de l'Arc en Ciel, in Forum des Halles, 1ᵉʳ, Beaubourg/Les Halles* ☏*01–40–13–72–25* Ⓜ*Châtelet Les Halles*), the leading chain of perfume and cosmetics megastores in the world, sells its own makeup as well as many of the big brands.

Shu Uemura (⊠*176 bd. St-Germain, 6ᵉ, St-Germain-des-Prés* ☏*01–45–48–02–55* Ⓜ*St-Germain-des-Prés*) has enhanced those whose faces are their fortune for decades. Models swear by the cleansing oil; free samples are proffered. A huge range of colors, every makeup brush imaginable, and a no-pinch eyelash curler keep fans coming back.

BOOKS

The scenic open-air *bouquinistes* bookstalls along the Seine are stacked with secondhand books (mostly in French), prints, and souvenirs. French-language bookshops—specializing in art, film, literature, and philosophy—can be found in the scholarly Quartier Latin and the publishing district, St-Germain-des-Prés. For English-language books and magazines, try the following.

Abbey Bookstore (⊠*29 rue de la Parcheminerie, 5ᵉ, Quartier Latin* ☏*01–46–33–16–24* Ⓜ*Cluny–La Sorbonne*) is Paris's Canadian bookstore, with books on Canadian history and new and secondhand Québecois and English-language novels. The Canadian Club of Paris also organizes regular poetry readings and literary conferences here.

Comptoir de l'Image (⊠*44 rue de Sévigné, 3ᵉ, Le Marais* ☏*01–42–72–03–92* Ⓜ*St-Paul*) is where designers John Galliano, Marc Jacobs, and Emanuel Ungaro stock up on old copies of *Vogue, Harper's Bazaar,* and *The Face.* It also sells trendy magazines like *Dutch, Purple,* and *Spoon;* designer catalogs from the past; and rare photo books.

★ **La Hune** (⊠*170 bd. St-Germain, 6ᵉ, St-Germain-des-Prés* ☏*01–45–48–35–85* Ⓜ*St-Germain-des-Prés*), sandwiched between the Café de Flore and Les Deux Magots, is a landmark for intellectuals. French literature is downstairs, but the main attraction is the comprehensive collection of international books on art and architecture upstairs. You can hang out until midnight with all the other genius-insomniacs.

Ofr (⊠*64 rue Tiquetonne, 2ᵉ, Les Halles* ☏*01–42–45–72–88* Ⓜ*Les Halles*) gets magazines from the most fashionable spots in the world before anyone else. The store is messy, but you can rub shoulders with photo and press agents and check out the latest in underground, art, and alternative monthlies.

★ **The Red Wheelbarrow** (⊠22 *rue St-Paul, 4*, *Le Marais* ☎*01–48–04–75–08* Ⓜ*St-Paul*) is *the* Anglophone bookstore: if it was written in English, you can get it here. The store also has a collection of special-edition historical reads, and a great selection of children's books. Check out its flyers for info on English-language readings, given at least once a month; local artists and visiting authors pitch in on events.

Shakespeare & Company (⊠*37 rue de la Bûcherie, 5*, *Quartier Latin* ☎*01–43–25–40–93* Ⓜ*St-Michel*), the sentimental Rive Gauche favorite, is named after the bookstore whose American owner, Sylvia Beach, first published James Joyce's *Ulysses*. Nowadays it specializes in expat literature. You can count on a couple of eccentric characters somewhere in the stacks, a sometimes-spacey staff, the latest titles from British presses, and hidden secondhand treasures in the odd corners and crannies. Poets give readings upstairs on Monday at 8 PM; there are also tea-party talks on Sunday at 4 PM.

Taschen (⊠*2 rue de Buci, 6*, *St-Germain-des-Prés* ☎*01–40–51–79–22* Ⓜ*Mabillon*) is perfect for night owls, as it's open until midnight on Friday and Saturday. The Starck-designed shelves and desks hold glam titles on photography, fine art, design, fashion, and fetishes.

Tea & Tattered Pages (⊠*24 rue Mayet, 6*, *St-Germain-des-Prés* ☎*01–40–65–94–35* Ⓜ*Duroc*) is the place for bargains: cheap secondhand paperbacks plus new books (publishers' overstock) at low prices. Tea and brownies are served, and browsing is encouraged.

Fodor'sChoice **Village Voice** (⊠*6 rue Princesse, 6*, *St-Germain-des-Prés* ☎*01–46–*
★ *33–36–47* Ⓜ*Mabillon*) is a heavy hitter in Paris's ever-thriving expat literary scene. It's known for its excellent current and classic book selections, frequent book signings, and readings by authors of legendary stature along with up-and-comers, all run by a knowledgeable and friendly staff. There's always a fresh stash of English-language periodicals and magazines.

W.H. Smith (⊠*248 rue de Rivoli, 1*, *Louvre/Tuileries* ☎*01–44–77–88–99* Ⓜ*Concorde*) carries a multitude of travel and language books, cookbooks, and fiction for adults and children. It also has the best selection of foreign magazines and newspapers in Paris (which you're allowed to peruse without interruption—many magazine dealers in France aren't so kind).

CLOTHING: CHILDREN'S

Most top designers make minicouture, which usually costs unearthly prices. The following are stores for true children's clothing, as opposed to shrunken versions of adult designer outfits.

Fodor'sChoice **Bonpoint** (⊠*64 av. Raymond Poincaré, 16*, *Trocadéro/Tour Eiffel*
★ ☎*01–47–27–60–81* Ⓜ*Trocadéro* ⊠*15 rue Royale, 8*, *Louvre/Tuileries* ☎*01–47–42–52–63* Ⓜ*Madeleine*) is for the prince or princess in your life (royalty *does* shop here). Yes, prices are high, but the quality is exceptional. Styles range from sturdy play clothes—think a weekend

16

CHAMPS ELYSÉES & AV. MONTAIGNE

Step into your Chanel suit, gird your loins, and plunge into Paris's most elegant and daunting hunting grounds, where royals, jet-setters, starlets, and other glitterati converge in pursuit of the high life.

This elegant triangle—bordered by the avenues Montaigne, Georges V, and Champs-Elysées, with Rue François in between—is home to pretty much all the luxury Goliaths with a few added lesser worthies. Once Paris's most elegant Grand Boulevard, the Champs-Elysées has suffered the blight of megastores, fast food, movie chains, and the like, but once off the avenue, you'll get a sense of what it once was. Palatial old mansions now house embassies and boutiques, all with liveried doormen who will take measure of you—and find you lacking. Not to worry, just hold your head high, flash your platinum card, and don't forget not to smile.

BEST TIME TO GO

Unlike other shopping meccas, these streets never get too wild, even during the biannual sales. Although for most shopping areas in Paris we advise weekday afternoons, when crowds are tame, here you might want to consider a weekend visit.

BEST FIND FOR YOUR SISTER

If there's one place sure to give bang for the buck, it's **Petit Bateau**. Their adorable, soft cotton T-shirts are highly prized among Parisian women, and these and wardrobe staples—including cardigans, wraps, and V-necks—come in colors that change with the season. Stock up—you can afford it!

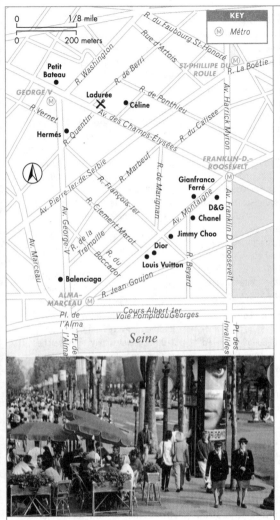

REFUELING

Not only is **Ladurée** one of the world's legendary *pâtisser-ies*, but the Champs-Elysées location also keeps great hours: from early breakfast (doors open at 7:30 AM) to a post-theater snack, just amble over whenever the urge strikes. Whether you desire a cup of their famously rich hot chocolate; a refreshing raspberry, litchee, and rose-petal ice-cream sundae; a melt-in-your-mouth mille-feuille; or a hearty club sandwich, you'll find plenty to choose from at fairly reasonable prices (it's still Paris, dahling), all perfectly scrumptious.

CLASSY COUTURE

Chanel. The best choice for elegant, classic looks and sex appeal with plenty of lasting value.

Gaultier. Only his spectacular garments could outshine this fantasyland boutique.

IN-YOUR-FACE OPULENCE

Balenciaga. Fashion's reigning "it" boy Nicolas Ghesquière does high-concept futurism in nylon and patent leather.

Celine. Feminine dress-for-success styles that appeal to women's sensuality and smarts.

Dior. Don't be fooled by the prim lavender exterior. Inside is pure vixen.

Dolce & Gabbana. Liberate your inner sex goddess: everything here is meant to entice—and succeeds.

Gianfranco Ferré. Crisply tailored, highly stylized clothes that look as pricey as they are.

SHOES & ACCESSORIES

Hermès. The go-to for those who prefer their logo discrete yet still want instant recognition.

Jimmy Choo. Starlets adore his glitzy stilettos and fabulous flats.

Louis Vuitton. The cathedralesque Champs-Elysées megastore houses every line in a drop-dead-gorgeous space.

16

Museum Stores

These days it seems contemporary museum stores hawk their stock-in-trade images on everything from playing cards to neckties. The boutiques below are an antidote to these "mug-and-tote" chains and—dare we say it—are worth the trip, whether you visit the museum or not.

107Rivoli (⊠ *107 rue de Rivoli, 1e, Louvre/Tuileries* ☎ *01–42–60–64–94* Ⓜ *Louvre Rivoli, Châtelet*) is the consummate museum store, located inside the Musée des Arts Décoratifs. The boutique carries books, jewelry, fashion accessories, paper products, toys, tableware, and objects inspired by the past but with an up-to-date design. Some of the contemporary pieces are limited editions.

La Chalcographie du Louvre (⊠ *Louvre museum store, 1e, Louvre/Tuileries* ☎ *01–40–20–59–35* Ⓜ *Palais-Royal/Musée du Louvre*) is an extraordinary find. More than 13,000 prints from the Louvre's collection can be sent to the museum's own print shop for a relatively minor investment. The most popular images are in stock, easy to view, and can walk right out with you.

Musée Baccarat (⊠ *11 pl. des Etats-Unis, 16e, Trocadéro/Tour Eiffel* ☎ *01–40–22–11–00* Ⓜ *Iéna/Boissière*) has a gorgeous gallery filled with contemporary crystal by top-name designers, as well as stemware, vases, tableware, jewelry, chandeliers, and even furniture. It's all here, it's all for sale, and it's all breathtaking.

BlackBlock (⊠ *13 av. du président Wilson 16e, Trocadéro/Tour Eiffel* ☎ *01–47–23–37–04* Ⓜ *Iéna/Alma Marceau*), inside the Palais de Tokyo, has merchandise by contemporary artists and designers as edgy and subversive as the museum's exhibits. There's everything from ultrahip T-shirts, jewelry, bags, and watches to CDs, limited-edition art, and exuberantly colored sex toys. And, if you have a late-night hankering to shop, it's open until midnight.

at the château—to the perfect emerald-green hand-smocked silk dress or a midnight-blue velvet suit for Little Lord Fauntleroy.

Calesta Kidstore (⊠ *23 rue Debelleyme, 3e, Le Marais* ☎ *01–42–72–15–59* Ⓜ *St-Sébastien Froissart*) is Paris's hippest destination for children up to eight years old and their parents. Projected cartoons entrance kids while adults browse racks of the latest clothes and a connoisseur's selection of furniture, toys, strollers, and the leather-and-shearling baby carriers favored by supermodel moms.

Not So Big (⊠ *38 rue Tiquetonne, 2e, Beaubourg/Les Halles* ☎ *01–42–33–34–26* Ⓜ *Etienne Marcel*) has a great selection of original clothes, toys, and accessories for both children and mom. Favorites include a line of fun T-shirts, funky winter coats, sweet slippers, and amber necklaces for baby, said to facilitate the growth of first teeth.

Oona l'Ourse (⊠ *72 rue Madame, 6e, St-Germain-des-Prés* ☎ *01–42–84–11–94* Ⓜ *St-Placide*) racks up tiny classic Shetland and pashmina sweaters, a line of comfy cashmere clothes, one-of-a-kind onesies, and tiny shoes ready for first steps.

Ovale (✉*200 bd. St-Germain, 7ᵉ, St-Germain-des-Prés* ☎*01–53–63–31–10* Ⓜ*St-Germain-des-Prés* ✉*21 rue Marbeuf, 8ᵉ, Champs-Elysées* ☎*01–47–20–00–42* Ⓜ*Franklin Roosevelt*) caters to babies born with the silver spoon—or if not, there are plenty here to choose from. This ebony-and-cream boutique has disposed of color altogether in favor of warm neutrals for their beautifully crafted unisex clothing (newborn to 12 months). All-natural fabrics include undyed linen, cotton, and cashmere.

★ **Petit Bateau** (✉*116 av. des Champs-Elysées, 8ᵉ, Champs-Elysées* ☎*01–40–74–02–03* Ⓜ*George V* ✉*53 bis, rue de Sèvres, 6ᵉ, St-Germain-des-Prés* ☎*01–45–49–48–38* Ⓜ*Sèvres Babylone*) provides a fundamental part of the classic French wardrobe from cradle to teen and beyond: the T-shirt, cut close to the body, with smallish shoulders (they work equally well with school uniforms or vintage Chanel). The high-grade cotton clothes follow designs that haven't changed in decades—onesies and pajamas for newborns, T-shirts that change color for every season, underwear sets, and dresses with tiny straps for summer. Stock up—if you can find this brand back home, the prices are sure to be higher.

Pom d'Api (✉*28 rue du Four, 6ᵉ, St-Germain-des-Prés* ☎*01–45–48–39–31* Ⓜ*St-Germain-des-Prés*) lines up footwear for babies and preteens in quality leathers and vivid colors. Expect well-made, eye-catching fashion—bright gold sneakers and fringed suede boots, as well as classic Mary Janes in shades of silver, pink, and gold. There are also utility boots for boys and sturdy rain gear.

Wowo (✉*11 rue de Marseille, 10ᵉ, République* ☎*01–53–40–84–80* Ⓜ*République*) is an original line of well-made clothes for children from three months to preteen. Designer Elizabeth Relin blends her fashion sensibility and love of color with her respect for the world of childhood—no pop tarts here.

CLOTHING: DISCOUNT

Anna Lowe (✉*104 rue de Faubourg St-Honoré, 8ᵉ, Louvre/Tuileries* ☎*01–42–66–11–32* Ⓜ*Madeleine*) does couture hounds a vital service—offering top-rung, never-worn designer duds at up to half off regular prices. Labels like Chanel, Prada, Missoni, Lacroix, and Armani from one season back are typically 30% off, and certain labels from the latest season—Tricot Chic, Petrovich & Robinson, Scarpa, among others—are slashed 40%. With a large selection and a range of styles that runs the gamut from casual wear to evening gowns, this elegant shop is hugely popular. Tax-free overnight alterations are guaranteed or purchases can be shipped.

Et Vous (✉*17 rue Turbigo, 2ᵉ, Les Halles* ☎*01–40–13–04–12* Ⓜ*Etienne Marcel*) is a great alternative to the regular boutiques because the clothes are still very much in style and are 50% off. You'd never know you were in a stock store if you walked in off the street. There are accessories, too.

Le Dépôt Vente de Passy (⊠*14 rue de la Tour, 16ᵉ, Trocadéro/Tour Eiffel* ☎*01–45–20–95–21* Ⓜ*Passy* ⊠*109 rue de Courcelles, 17ᵉ, Champs-Elysées* ☎*01–40–53–80–82* Ⓜ*Wagram*) specializes in barely worn designer ready-to-wear from big names, including Chanel, Dior, Lacroix, Gucci, and Rykiel. Few can pass up one of last season's outfits at one-third the price, or forgo browsing the vast selection of accessories: bags, belts, scarves, shoes, and costume jewelry.

L'Habilleur (⊠*44 rue de Poitou, 3ᵉ, Le Marais* ☎*01–48–87–77–12* Ⓜ*St-Sébastien Froissart*) is a favorite with the fashion press and anyone looking for a deal. For women there's a great selection from designers like Stefano Mortari, Maria Calderara, and Issey Miyake. Men can find suits from Roberto Collina and Paul & Joe at slashed prices.

Rue d'Alésia (Ⓜ *Alésia*), in the 14ᵉ arrondissement, is the main place to find shops selling last season's fashions at a discount. Be forewarned: most of these shops are much more downscale than their elegant sister shops; dressing rooms are not always provided.

Zadig et Voltaire (⊠*22 rue Bourg Tibourg, 4ᵉ, Le Marais* ☎*01–44–59–39–62* Ⓜ*Hôtel de Ville)* has new unsold stock from last season. You'll find a great selection of beautiful cashmere sweaters, silk slip dresses, rocker jeans, and leather jackets, all in their signature luscious colors for 30% to 50% off.

CLOTHING: MEN'S & WOMEN'S

Agnès b (⊠*2, 3, and 6 rue du Jour, 1ᵉʳ, Beaubourg/Les Halles* ☎*01–42–33–04–13* Ⓜ*Châtelet Les Halles* ⊠*6 rue Vieux Columbier, 6ᵉ, Germain-des-Prés* ☎*01–44–39–02–60* Ⓜ*St-Sulpice* ⊠ *38 av. George V, 8ᵉ, Champs-Elysées* ☎*01–40–73–81–10* Ⓜ *George V*) embodies the quintessential French approach to easy but stylish dressing. There are many branches, and the clothes are also sold in department stores, but for the fullest range go to Rue du Jour, where Agnès takes up most of the street (women's wear at No. 6, children at No. 2, menswear at No. 3), or the newest store at Avenue George V. For women, classics include sleek black-leather jackets, flattering black jersey separates, and trademark wide-stripe T-shirts. Children love the two-tone T-shirts proclaiming their age. And the stormy-gray velour or corduroy suits you see on those slouchy, scarf-clad men? Agnès b.

A.P.C. (⊠*38 rue Madame, 6ᵉ, St-Germain-des-Prés* ☎*01–42–22–12–77* Ⓜ*St-Sulpice* ⊠*112 rue Vieille du Temple, 3ᵉ, Le Marais* ☎*01–42–78–18–02* Ⓜ*Filles du Calvaire*) may be antiflash, but a knowing eye can always pick out their jeans in a crowd. The clothes are rigorously well made; prime wardrobe pieces include dark indigo and black denim, zip-up cardigans, and peacoats.

Balenciaga (⊠*10 av. George V, 8ᵉ, Champs-Elysées* ☎*01–47–20–21–11* Ⓜ*Alma-Marceau*) is now in the hands of Nicolas Ghesquière—guess what inspired him when he designed this boutique? Notice the tile, the wavy line of the store, that slice of turquoise blue, the aloe plants.

The clothes are interesting, sometimes beautiful, as Ghesquière plays with volume (bubbling skirts, superskinny pants) and references (robot, futuristic). The accessories and menswear are often more approachable, like the perfectly tooled leather bags and narrow suits. (You got it, a swimming pool.)

Boutique Renhsen (⊠*22 rue Beaurepaire, 10ᵉ, République* ☎*01–48–04–01–01* Ⓜ*République*) is popular for its jeans: slender, supple, and ultraflattering—but those in the know come for the stylish separates in natural fibers and the range of must-have accessories.

Charvet (⊠*28 pl. Vendôme, 1ᵉʳ, Opéra/Grands Boulevards* ☎*01–42–60–30–70* Ⓜ*Opéra*) is the Parisian equivalent of a Savile Row tailor: a conservative, aristocratic institution famed for made-to-measure shirts, exquisite ties, and accessories; for garbing John F. Kennedy, Charles de Gaulle, and the Duke of Windsor; and for its regal address. Although the exquisite silk ties, in hundreds of colors and patterns, and custom-made shirts for men are the biggest draw, refined pieces for women and girls, as well as adorable miniatures for boys, round out the collection.

Costume Nationale (⊠*5 rue Cambon, 1ᵉʳ, Louvre/Tuileries* ☎*01–40–15–04–13* Ⓜ*Tuileries*) is all about sharp styling and unerring sophistication. Ennio Capasa's flawlessly cut suits confer high-powered status, and teensy dresses with plunging necklines shoot for unabashed allure. Shoes and accessories are surprisingly versatile.

Dolce & Gabbana (⊠*54 av. Montaigne, 8ᵉ, Champs-Elysées* ☎*01–42–25–68–78* Ⓜ*Alma-Marceau* ⊠*3 rue Faubourg St. Honoré, 1ᵉʳ, Louvre/Tuileries* ☎*01–42–78–18–02* Ⓜ*Concorde*) offers a sexy, young-Italian-widow vibe with a side of moody boyfriend. Svelte silk dresses, sharply tailored suits, and plunging necklines are made for drama. Women's clothes are at Avenue Montaigne; men's are at Rue St. Honoré. The secondary (also known as "diffusion") line, **D&G** (⊠*244 rue de Rivoli, 1ᵉʳ, Louvre/Tuileries* ☎*01–42–86–00–44* Ⓜ*Concorde*), rocks the concept of day wear with leather, denim, and splashy florals spiked with lingerie details. There are clothes for men, women, and even kids.

L'Eclaireur (⊠*3 ter rue des Rosiers, 4ᵉ, Le Marais* ☎*01–48–87–10–22* Ⓜ*St-Paul* ⊠*12 rue Mahler, 4ᵉ, Le Marais* ☎*01–44–54–22–11* Ⓜ*St-Paul*) is split with women's wear in one shop, and men's around the corner. It maintains an avant-garde aesthetic, with tastes for designers such as Martin Margiela, Paul Harnden, and Ann Demeulemeester, plus labels such as Chloé and Lanvin.

Gianfranco Ferré (⊠*51 av. Montaigne, 8ᵉ, Champs Elysées* ☎*01–42–89–90–91* Ⓜ*Franklin-D.-Roosevelt*) cultivates an expensive, luxurious look with his highly stylized, meticulously tailored designs. Seasonal collections are punctuated with plenty of fur, leather, and lace.

G-Star Store (⊠*46 rue Etienne-Marcel, 2ᵉ, Beaubourg/Les Halles* ☎*01–42–21–44–33* Ⓜ*Etienne Marcel*) is a haven for fans of raw denim. It, uniquely, stocks the designs of the Dutch-based label G-Star, whose

16

highly desirable jeans have replaced Levi's as the ones to be seen in. There are also military-inspired clothing, bags, and T-shirts.

Kokon To Zaï (⊠ *48 rue Tiquetonne, 2ᵉ, Beaubourg/Les Halles* ☎01–42–36–92–41 Ⓜ*Etienne Marcel*) is a Japanese expression to sum up opposing extremes (such as hot and cold, young and old). It's also a hip boutique selling the work of more than 40 young designers, and now their own label, KZT, as well as jewelry, shoes, and accessories.

Lucien Pellat-Finet (⊠ *1 rue Montalembert, 7ᵉ, St-Germain-des-Prés* ☎01–42–22–22–77 Ⓜ*Rue du Bac*) does cashmere that shakes up the traditional world of cable knits—here, sweaters for men, women, and children come in punchy colors and cheeky motifs. A psychedelic mushroom may bounce across a sky-blue crewneck; a crystal-outlined skull could grin from a sleeveless top. The cashmere's wonderfully soft—and the prices are accordingly high.

Marc Jacobs (⊠ *56–62 Galerie de Montpensier, 1ᵉ, Louvre/Tuileries* ☎01–55–35–02–60 Ⓜ*Palais Royal Musée du Louvre*) remains the darling of American style with his singular take on 20th-century American classics—from flapper-style (big flowers, unstructured lines, drop waists, flounces) to '60s prom (empire waists, copious tulle) with a bit of motorcycle chic thrown in. Metallics appear in most every collection, as do breezy, feminine fabrics and lots of layers.

Maria Luisa (⊠ *19 bis, rue Mont Thabor and 38–40 rue du Mont Thabor, 2 rue Cambon, 1ᵉʳ, Louvre/Tuileries* ☎01–42–96–47–81 Ⓜ*Concorde*) is one of the most important names in town for cutting-edge fashion. The store at No. 38 is considered a "style laboratory" for young designers; No. 2 is the women's shop, stocked with established designers (like Balenciaga and Demeulemeester); No. 19 is the address for *monsieur;* and No. 40 carries top-name accessories and shoes, including Paris's exclusive on Manolo Blahnik.

★ **Martin Margiela** (⊠ *25 bis, rue de Montpensier, 1ᵉʳ, Louvre/Tuileries* ☎01–40–15–07–55 Ⓜ*Palais-Royal* ⊠*23 passage Potier, 1ᵉʳ, Louvre/Tuileries* ☎01–40–15–06–44 Ⓜ*Palais-Royal* ⊠*13 rue de Grenelle, 7ᵉ, St-Germain-des-Prés* ☎01–45–49–06–68 Ⓜ*St-Sulpice*), the famously elusive Belgian designer, has a devoted following for his cut—sometimes oversize but never bulky—and for his innovative technique, from spiraling seams to deconstructed shirts. Be sure to look for Ligne 6, his secondary line of more casual (and less expensive) clothes, and men's at Rue Potier.

Prada (⊠ *10 av. Montaigne, 8ᵉ, Trocadéro/Tour Eiffel* ☎01–53–23–99–40 Ⓜ*Alma-Marceau* ⊠*6 rue du Faubourg St-Honoré, 8ᵉ, Louvre/Tuileries* ☎01–58–18–63–30 Ⓜ*Concorde* ⊠*5 rue de Grenelle, 6ᵉ, St-Germain-des-Prés* ☎01–45–48–53–14 Ⓜ*St-Sulpice*) spins gold out of fashion straw. Knee-length skirts, peacock colors, cardigan sweaters, geometric prints…the waiting lists cross continents. Shoes, bags, and other accessories for men and women perennially become cult items.

Rick Owens (⊠ *130–133 Galerie de Valois, 1ᵉ, Louvre/Tuileries* ☎01–40–20–42–52 Ⓜ*Palais Royal Musée du Louvre*) expertly finessed the jump from L.A. rock-star chic to Paris offbeat elegance. Lately defined more by glamour than grunge, his lush fabrics and asymmetrical designs have evolved to a new level of artistry—and wearability. Owens still loves a paradox (shrouding while revealing), and mixes high luxury with a bit of the tooth and the claw. You'll find shoes, furs and even furniture here.

Sonia Rykiel (⊠*194 bd. St-Germain, 7ᵉ, St-Germain-des-Prés* ☎*01– 45–44–83–19* Ⓜ*St-Germain-des-Prés* ⊠*175 bd. St-Germain, 6ᵉ, St-Germain-des-Prés* ☎*01–49–54–60–60* Ⓜ*St-Germain-des-Prés* ⊠*70 rue du Faubourg St-Honoré, 8ᵉ, Louvre/Tuileries* ☎*01–42–65–20–81* Ⓜ*Concorde*) has been designing insouciant knitwear since the '60s. The women's boutiques tempt with sexy keyhole sweaters, opulent furs, accessories dotted with rhinestones, and soft leather bags. The menswear vibrates with colorful stripes.

Surface to Air (⊠*46 rue de l'Arbre Sec, 1ᵉʳ, Louvre/Tuileries* ☎*01–47– 03–30–98* Ⓜ*Louvre Rivoli* ⊠*68 rue Charlot, 3ᵉ, Le Marais* ☎*01– 44–61–76–27* Ⓜ*Filles du Calvaire*), a garagelike atelier, has an air of counterculture chic. Offbeat items sport glitter bunnies or cheerful, appliquéd skulls; menswear includes unstructured corduroy suits, enigmatic T-shirts, and a small selection of gorgeous shoes. The new Marais store, though still cutting-edge, leans a bit more toward the cool and understated; accessories are here, too.

Yohji Yamamoto (⊠*25 rue du Louvre, 47 rue Etienne Marcel, 1ᵉʳ, Beaubourg/Les Halles* ☎*01–42–21–42–93* Ⓜ*Etienne Marcel*) brings couture and the ready-to-wear Y line for men and women together under one roof, with Y-3 sportswear around the corner at 47 rue Etienne Marcel. A master of the drape, fold, and twist, Yamamoto favors predominantly black clothes that are both functional and edgy. Pleats, florals, and brilliant colors now punctuate each collection.

CLOTHING: VINTAGE

Anouschka (⊠*6 av. du Coq, 9ᵉ, Opéra/Grands Boulevards* ☎*01–48– 74–37–00* Ⓜ*St-Lazare, Trinité*) has set up shop in her apartment (by appointment only, Monday to Saturday) and has rack upon rack of vintage clothing dating from the '30s to the '70s. It's the perfect place to find a '50s cocktail dress in mint condition or a mod jacket for him. A former model herself, she calls this a "designer laboratory," and teams from top fashion houses often pop by looking for inspiration.

★ **Didier Ludot** (⊠*Jardins du Palais-Royal, 20 Galerie Montpensier, 1ᵉʳ, Louvre/Tuileries* ⊠*24 Galerie Montpensier, 1ᵉʳ, Louvre/Tuileries* ⊠*125 Galerie de Valois, 1ᵉʳ, Louvre/Tuileries* ☎*01–42–96–06–56* Ⓜ*Palais-Royal*) is one of the world's most famous vintage clothing dealers and an incredibly charming man to boot. (A tip: be nice to the dogs.) Riffle through French couture from the '20s to the '80s on the racks: wonderful Chanel suits, Balenciaga dresses, and Hermès scarves. He has three boutiques: No. 20 houses his amazing collection of vintage couture, No. 24 the vintage ready-to-wear, and across the way at

16

THE MARAIS

The Marais has just about stolen the show as the city's hottest shopping spot—for sheer volume it can't be beat. Not to mention atmosphere; from the elegant Place des Vosges to the stately Musée Picasso, its irregular streets and hôtels particuliers give it the air of Old Paris.

Rue Francs Bourgeois is the shopping-central spine from which the upper and lower Marais branch out. As the Marais's popularity grows, so, too, do the variety of its attractions. The neighborhood's newest frontier is its northeastern edge—the haut Marais—where ultrastylish boutiques and design ateliers are found amid tiny centuries-old millinery shops. Between Rue de Bretagne and Boulevard du Temple to the east you'll find à la mode boutiques too numerous to list (and still relatively undertouristed). Rue Charlot is one of the area's primary draws, along with upper Rue Vieille du Temple and Rue de Poitou in between. But this is by no means an exhaustive selection. The best idea is to get out there and wander, because in this lovely quartier, everywhere the eye rests, it rests happily.

BEST TIME TO GO

If being jostled by tourists and cranky Parisians isn't your thing, head over between Tuesday and Friday after 11 AM. Remember, the Marais is one of the few places in Paris where shops open up on Sunday. If you're short on time or need a last-minute shopping fix, the Marais is your best bet.

BEST FIND FOR YOUR COWORKER

For those challenged in the gift-finding department, you'll think you've landed in heaven at **Muji**. This store has a flurry of fun, unusual items for the office, home, and bath; many are purse-size, so stuff your suitcase full and *finally* please everyone.

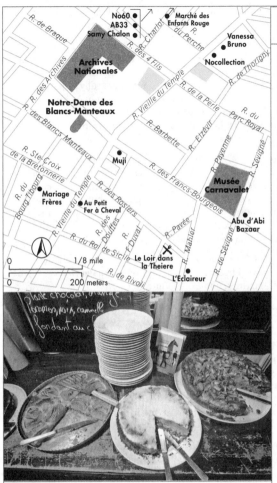

WHAT YOU'LL WANT

SHOWSTOPPING CHIC

No. 60. Slinky tops, avant-garde leather, and bottle-leg jeans add up to flattering rocker chic.

AB33. An A-list of *au courant* designers brings out the beautiful.

Abu d'Abi Bazaar. This is your one-stop outfitter with color-coded racks of the season's standouts.

Antik Batik. Diaphanous silks, resonant colors, and generous beadwork all add up to thrilling pieces that look great day and night.

L'Eclaireur. High-concept fashion for the hip crowd.

Nocollection. Oh-so-pretty silk dresses and separates in soft fabrics and romantic colors.

Samy Chalon. This designer works magic with handmade knitwear.

Vanessa Bruno. Paris's "it" girl combines high style and wearability in her ultrapopular store.

TEATIME

Mariage Frères. Elbow your way in for any and every kind of tea, as well as tea-scented *confitures*, chocolates, and candles. A choice selection of tea ware in porcelain or rainbow-hue glass round out the collection.

REFUELING

Lines are out the door for brunch at **Le Loir dans la Theiere**, so go at teatime instead. It's really what this place is all about—with its comfy, overstuffed chairs, large selection of teas, and glorious pastries, it provides the perfect late-afternoon pick-me-up. Join the Parisians in their favorite activity and grab an outdoor table at **Au Fer à Cheval**—a prime people-watching spot (and the coffee's not so bad either). Nary a tourist lands here at Paris's oldest covered market, **Marché des Enfants Rouge**, where on warm (and not-so-warm) days you can sit in the semi-outdoors under a translucent roof for a satisfying Italian or Japanese lunch or just an espresso.

No. 125 you'll find his own vintage-inspired black dresses and his cof-fee-table book aptly titled *The Little Black Dress*.

Gabrielle Geppert (✉*31–34 Galerie de Montpensier, 1ᵉ, Louvre/Tuile-ries* ☎*01–42–61–53–52* Ⓜ*Palais Royal Musée du Louvre*) carries Cardin, Pucci, a little Chanel, and plenty of classy no-names—what's here is exactly what Gabrielle likes: from a '50s-era fully sequined cape and '60s jet-beaded minidress to an '80s number right at home under the disco ball. Fabulous designer shades, handbags, and jewelry, too. Don't miss the Hermès bags and unique jewelry at the tiny No. 34 boutique just two doors down.

Réciproque (✉*89, 92, 93, 95, and 101 rue de la Pompe, 16ᵉ, Trocadéro/Tour Eiffel* ☎*01–47–04–30–28* Ⓜ*Rue de la Pompe*) is Paris's largest and most exclusive swap shop. Savings on designer wear—Hermès, Dior, Chanel, and Louis Vuitton—are significant, but prices aren't as cheap as you might expect, and there's not much in the way of service or space. The shop at No. 101 specializes in leather goods. Both loca-tions are closed Sunday and Monday.

Scarlett (✉*10 rue Clément-Marot, 8ᵉ, Trocadéro/Tour Eiffel* ☎*01–56–89–03–00* Ⓜ*Alma-Marceau*) offers exceptional vintage couture by the likes of Chanel, Hermès, and Louis Vuitton.

CLOTHING: WOMEN ONLY

CLASSIC CHIC

AB33 (✉*33 rue Charlot, 3ᵉ, Le Marais* ☎*01–42–71–02–82* Ⓜ*Filles du Calvaire*) is like a sleek boudoir—complete with comfy chair and scented candles—and the clothes here are unabashedly feminine: sep-arates in luxury fabrics from top designers, irresistible silk lingerie, dainty jewelry, and a selection of accessories celebrate that certain French *je ne sais quoi*.

Alberta Ferretti (✉*418 rue St-Honoré, 8ᵉ, Louvre/Tuileries* ☎*01–42–60–14–97* Ⓜ*Madeleine/Concorde*) puts out come-hither designs. Sheer, cutout, and structured by turns, these super-feminine creations seek to enchant—and succeed. Lacquered silk dresses in opulent hues resemble molten candies.

Cacharel (✉*64 rue Bonaparte, 6ᵉ, St-Germain-des-Prés* ☎*01–40–46–00–45* Ⓜ*St-Germain-des-Prés*) is the legend that began with a blouse and just got better. Still dedicated to spunky color and youthful styles, with design duo Eley-Kishimoto at the helm, the '60s powerhouse has matured into a fashion contender. Each season brings new takes on their signature prints in luxe fabrics and delicious colors, with themes that range from delicate florals to bold geometrics. Clothes are for sophisticated ladies from birth on up.

Celine (✉*36 av. Montaigne, 8ᵉ, Champs-Elysées* ☎*01–56–89–07–91* Ⓜ*Franklin-D.-Roosevelt*) was venerable and dusty before designer Michael Kors showed up in the late '90s with his version of Jackie O, "the Greek magnate years" and put Celine back on the map. Ivana

Omazic is now at the helm taking the label in an entirely new direction that's both sultry and structured.

Claudie Pierlot (⊠*1 rue Montmartre, 1ᵉ, Louvre/Tuileries* ☎*01–42–21– 38–38* Ⓜ*Etienne Marcel* ⊠*23 rue du Vieux Colombier, 6ᵉ, St-Germain-des-Prés* ☎*01–45–48–11–96* Ⓜ*St-Sulpice*) is deservedly lauded for her smart, urban clothes that unite youthful chic with solid designs; they also successfully transition over several seasons. The irresistible combination of classic looks, good tailoring, and affordability keeps loyal fans coming back year after year.

Comptoir des Cotonniers (⊠*33 rue des Francs-Bourgeois, 4ᵉ, Le Marais* ☎*01–42–76–95–33* Ⓜ*St-Paul* ⊠*59 rue Bonaparte, 6ᵉ, St-Germain-des-Prés* ☎*01–43–26–07–56* Ⓜ*St-Sulpice* ⊠*342 rue St-Honoré, 1ᵉʳ, Louvre/Tuileries* ☎*01–42–60–10–75* Ⓜ*Tuileries*) is a Parisian star for its smart, wearable styles that stress ease and comfort over fussiness. Separates in natural fibers—cotton, silk, and cashmere blends—can be light and breezy or cozy and warm, but are always soft, flattering, and in a range of beautiful colors. Styles for moms and daughters from age four up.

Cotélac (⊠*284 rue St-Honoré, 1ᵉʳ, Louvre/Tuileries* ☎*01–47–03– 21–14* Ⓜ*Tuileries* ⊠*30 rue Montmartre, 1ᵉʳ, Beaubourg/Les Halles* ☎*01–40–28–13–84* Ⓜ*Les Halles* ⊠*17 rue du Cherche Midi, 6ᵉ, St-Germain-des-Prés* ☎*01–42–84–10–25* Ⓜ*Sevres Babylone*) gives feminine shapes an edge in earthy tones from azure to deep aubergine. The figure-skimming and frillier separates beg to be layered.

Et Vous (⊠*6 rue des Francs-Bourgeois, 3ᵉ, Le Marais* ☎*01–42–71– 75–11* Ⓜ*St-Paul* ⊠*69 rue de Rennes, 6ᵉ, St-Germain-des-Prés* ☎*01– 40–49–01–64* Ⓜ*St-Sulpice* ⊠*271 rue St-Honoré, 1ᵉʳ, Louvre/Tuileries* ☎*01–47–03–00–31* Ⓜ*Tuileries*) takes its cue from the catwalk, turning out affordable, extremely well-cut clothing: pants (low waist/slim hip), knee-skimming skirts, chunky sweaters, and classic work wear with individual details.

Jérôme L'Huillier (⊠*138–139 Galerie de Valois, 1ᵉʳ, Louvre/Tuileries* ☎*01–49–26–07–07* Ⓜ*Palais Royal Musée du Louvre*) cut his teeth at the ateliers of Balman and Givenchy, and it shows. A wizard with silk in all its iterations (the joyously colored prints are L'Huillier's own designs), you can find lively, sexy new takes on the wrap dress, along with rainbow-hue blouses, sexy empire-waist dresses, and velvet trench coats in jewel colors.

Massimo Dutti (⊠*24 rue Royale, 8ᵉ, Louvre/Tuileries* ☎*01–53–29–92– 70* Ⓜ*Concorde* ⊠*34 rue Tronchet, 8ᵉ, Louvre/Tuileries* ☎*01–49–24– 19–20* Ⓜ*Concorde*), Zara's upscale, higher-quality cousin, trumps the style-to-price quotient. It hasn't yet made its way to the United States, so you can find bargains your friends won't. Clothes and accessories are ever changing and catwalk inspired, pitched to a polished audience. Women love their bargain-price cashmeres and a line of super-soft sleepwear in sherbet colors.

16

Nocollection (✉96 *rue Vieille du Temple, 3ᵉ, Le Marais* ☎01–40–26–57–80 Ⓜ*Filles du Calvaire*) incorporates ravishing colors with flattering styles and soft fabrics to create a collection friendly to women of every size and shape. Up-to-the moment styles make a statement while still allowing for plenty of sensuality, and, best of all, comfort.

Paul & Joe (✉46 *rue Etienne Marcel, 2ᵉ, Beaubourg/Les Halles* ☎01–40–28–03–34 Ⓜ*Etienne Marcel* ✉2 *Av. Montaigne, 8ᵉ, Champs-Elysées* ☎01–47–20–57–50 Ⓜ*George V* ✉66 *rue des Saints Péres, 7ᵉʳ, St-Germain-des-Prés* ☎01–42–22–47–01 Ⓜ*St-Germain-des-Prés*) is designer Sophie Albou's eclectic, girlish blend of modern trends. There's a retro feel to the diaphanous blouses, A-line jackets with matching short shorts, and swingy felt coats. In summer she'll mix in a little hippie chic. The secondary line, Paul & Joe Sister—with a decidedly younger clientele—brings a slouchy, casual edge to the line: from hipster overalls to minidresses.

Paule Ka (✉20 *rue Malher, 4ᵉ, Le Marais* ☎01–40–29–96–03 Ⓜ*St-Paul* ✉192 *bd. St-Germain, 7ᵉ, St-Germain-des-Prés* ☎01–45–44–92–60 Ⓜ*St-Germain-des-Prés* ✉45 *rue François, 1ᵉ, Champs-Elysées* ☎01–47–20–76–10 Ⓜ*George V* ✉223 *rue St-Honoré, 1ᵉʳ, Louvre/Tuileries* ☎01–42–97–57–06 Ⓜ*Tuileries*) stays youthful yet proper, with knee-skimming dresses in cotton piqué; coats in black, white, or navy with three-quarter-length sleeves; and evening gowns showing just enough décolletage or leg.

Ventilo (✉27 *bis, rue du Louvre, 2ᵉ, Louvre/Tuileries* ☎01–44–76–83–00 Ⓜ*Louvre* ✉13–15 *bd. de la Madeleine, 1ᵉʳ, Louvre/Tuileries* ☎01–42–60–46–40 Ⓜ*Madeleine*) brings cool ethnic style to the city. Where else can you find a bright-orange silk-shantung ball skirt with mirror appliqué or a modern Mongol leather coat lined in fur? There's also room for classics to mix and match, such as handmade wool turtlenecks and zippered riding pants that fit perfectly.

Veronique Leroy (✉10 *rue d'Alger, 1ᵉʳ, Louvre/Tuileries* ☎01–49–26–93–59 Ⓜ*Tuileries*) highlights a woman's silhouette while paying close attention to details like open seam work and perfect draping. Slinky silk-jersey dresses, form-flattering sweaters in dusky hues, and lacy dresses with come-hither necklines help explain her current darling-of-the-fashion-world status.

COUTURE HOUSES

No matter, say the French, that fewer and fewer of their top couture houses are still headed by compatriots. It's the creativity, the workmanship, the *je ne sais quoi* that remains undeniably Gallic. Haute couture, defined by inimitable handwork, is increasingly buoyed by ancillary lines—ready-to-wear, perfume, sunglasses, you name it—that fill the windows of the boutiques. The successes of some houses have spurred the resuscitation of a few more, such as Rochas, now helmed by the young Belgian designer Olivier Theyskens, and Lanvin, with women's wear by Moroccan-born Alber Elbaz. Most of the high-fashion shops are on Avenue Montaigne, Avenue George V, and Rue du Faubourg St-Honoré on the Rive Droite, though St-Germain-des-Prés has also become a stomping ground. The following are a few of Paris's haute couture highlights. Exchange rates being what they are, couture is not in the realm of most of us—but Paris is for dreaming, after all.

★ **Chanel** (✉42 av. Montaigne, 8ᵉ, Champs-Elysées ☎01–47–23–74–12 Ⓜ Franklin-D.-Roosevelt ✉31 rue Cambon, 1ᵉʳ, Louvre/Tuileries ☎01–42–86–26–00 Ⓜ Tuileries) is helmed by Karl Lagerfeld, whose collections are steadily vibrant. The historic center is at the Rue Cambon boutique, where Chanel once perched high up on the mirrored staircase watching audience reactions to her collection debuts. Great investments include all of Coco's favorites: the perfectly tailored tweed suit, a lean, soigné black dress, a quilted bag with a gold chain, or a camellia brooch.

Christian Dior (✉30 av. Montaigne, 8ᵉ, Champs-Elysées ☎01–40–73–54–44 Ⓜ Franklin-D.-Roosevelt ✉16 rue de l'Abbé, 6ᵉ, St-Germain-des-Prés ☎01–56–24–90–53 Ⓜ St-Germain-des-Prés) installed flamboyant John Galliano and embarked on a wild ride. Galliano's catwalks are always the most talked-about *evenements* of the fashion season: they're opulent, crazy shows with strutting Amazons in extreme ensembles, iced champagne, and some of the most beautiful women in the world in attendance (not to mention the men). Despite the theatrical staging and surreal high jinks, his full-length body-skimming evening dresses cut on the bias are gorgeous in whatever fabric he chooses…so what if he pairs them with high-tops and a Davy Crockett raccoon hat? It's fashion, darling.

Christian Lacroix (✉73 rue du Faubourg St-Honoré, 8ᵉ, Louvre/Tuileries ☎01–42–68–79–00 Ⓜ Concorde ✉2 pl. St-Sulpice, 6ᵉ, St-Germain-des-Prés ☎01–46–33–48–95 Ⓜ St-Sulpice) masters color and texture to such an extent that his runway shows leave fans weeping with pleasure—and not just Eddy from *Absolutely Fabulous*. Nubby tweeds might be paired with a fuchsia leopard-print blouse and baroque jewels; a tissue-thin dress could dizzy with vivid paisleys. The Rue du Faubourg St-Honoré location is the Lacroix epicenter; on the ground floor you can find the ready-to-wear line "Bazar"; haute couture is through the courtyard.

FodorśChoice **Galliano** (✉384 rue St-Honoré, 1ᵉʳ, Louvre/Tuileries ☎01–55–35–40–
★ 40 Ⓜ Concorde), fittingly enough, landed an address with Revolutionary history for his first namesake store. What more can be said about John Galliano, a living hyperbole? Well, the boutique pairs glass and stone, a high-tech plasma screen grabs your eye, and a Diptyque candle (see the Diptyque shop listed under Home Décor, below) scents the air. Clothes ricochet between debauchery, humor, and refinement, but look past the wackier distractions to find what he does best: flattering long dresses, structured jackets, and heels that give the best leg.

Jean-Paul Gaultier (✉44 av. George V, 8ᵉ, Champs-Elysées ☎01–44–43–00–44 Ⓜ George V ✉6 rue Vivienne, 2ᵉ, Opéra/Grands Boulevards ☎01–42–86–05–05 Ⓜ Bourse) first made headlines with his celebrated corset with the ironic iconic breasts for Madonna but now sends fashion editors into ecstasy with his sumptuous haute-couture

16

creations. Designer Philippe Starck spun an *Alice in Wonderland* fantasy for the boutiques, with quilted cream walls and Murano mirrors. Make no mistake, though, it's all about the clothes: dazzlers that make Gaultier a must-see.

Loris Azzaro (✉65 *rue de Faubourg St-Honoré, 8ᵉ, Louvre/Tuileries* ☎01–42–66–92–98 Ⓜ*Concorde*) is a master of the dramatic dress: floor-length columns with jeweled collars and sheer gowns with strategically placed sequins. When he saw his 1970s designs, now collector's items, worn by stars like Nicole Kidman and Liz Hurley, he decided to reedit his best sellers.

Ungaro (✉2 *av. Montaigne, 8ᵉ, Champs-Elysées* ☎01–53–57–00–22 Ⓜ*Alma-Marceau*) tempers sexiness with a sense of fun. Ruffled chiffon, daringly draped dresses, and clinging silk jersey radiate exuberance with their bright floral and butterfly prints, polka dots, and tropical colors (like shocking pink, sunset orange).

Yves Saint Laurent (✉38 *and 32 rue du Faubourg St- Honoré, 8ᵉ, Louvre/Tuileries* ☎01–42–65–74–59 Ⓜ*Concorde* ✉6 *pl. St-Sulpice, 6ᵉ, St-Germain-des-Prés* ☎01–43–29–43–00 Ⓜ*St-Sulpice*) revolutionized women's wear in the 1970s, putting pants in couture shows for the first time. His safari jackets, "le smoking" suits, Russian-boho collections, and tailored *Belle de Jour* suits are considered fashion landmarks—and these are big shoes to fill. Stefano Pilati, successor to the ingenious Tom Ford, started his tenure with a mellow hand in color and cut. The menswear collection, at No. 32 rue du Faubourg St-Honoré, can be relied on for Saint Laurent's classic pinstripes and satin-lapel tuxes.

TRENDSETTERS

Abou d'Abi Bazar (✉125 *rue Vieille du Temple, 3ᵉ, Le Marais* ☎01–42–71–13–26 Ⓜ*Filles du Calvaire*) organizes its collection of up-to-the-moment designers on color-coordinated racks that highlight the asymmetrical design of this opulent boutique. Artsy and bohemian all at once, there is plenty to covet here, from frothy Antik Batik silk-organza blouses to sumptuous cashmere-blend tunics and satin shirtwaist dresses. Reasonably priced picks make it a very desirable destination.

Antik Batik (✉20 *rue Mabillon, 6ᵉ, St-Germain-des-Prés* ☎01–43–26–02–28 Ⓜ*Odéon* ✉18 *rue Turenne, 4ᵉ, Marais* ☎01–44–78–93–75 Ⓜ*St-Paul* ✉20 *rue Vaugirard, 6ᵉ, St-Germain-des-Prés* ☎01–43–25–30–22 Ⓜ*Odéon*) has a wonderful line of ethnically inspired clothes. There are row upon row of beaded and sequined dresses, Chinese silk tunics, short fur jackets, flowing organza separates, and some of Paris's most popular handbags. The Rue Vaugirard store features beautiful versions for mothers-to-be and infants.

Antoine & Lili (✉95 *quai de Valmy, 10ᵉ, République* ☎01–40–37–41–55 Ⓜ*Jacques-Bonsergent* ✉90 *rue des Martyrs, 18ᵉ, Montmartre* ☎01–42–58–10–22 Ⓜ*Abbesses*) is a bright fuchsia-color store packed with eclectic objects from the East and its own line of clothing. The fantasy seems to work for the French, because these boutiques are

Notable Neighborhoods, Select Streets

CLOSE UP

Paris's legendary shopping destinations draw people the world over, but perhaps a deeper allure lies in the lesser-known attractions: the city harbors scores of hidden neighborhoods and shopping streets—some well traveled, others just emerging—that brim with treasure. Each carries its own distinct style that reflects the character of the particular quartier. Here are a few of Paris's most satisfying and très branché (very chic) enclaves.

Rue Keller, Rue Charonne (11ᵉ). These streets are a haven for young clothing designers with panache. Stylish housewares, kids' clothes, jewelry, and art galleries augment the appeal. Start at the end of Rue Keller where it intersects with Rue de la Roquette: walk the length of this short street, then make a right onto Rue Charonne and meander all the way to Rue du Faubourg St-Antoine to discover even more great boutiques.

Rue Oberkampf (11ᵉ). At the outer edge of the Marais, this street is well known among young fashionistas for its eclectic atmosphere and bohemian flavor. High-end jewelry and of-the-minute boutiques are clustered amid stylish wine bars and comfy cafés.

Rue des Abbesses, Rue des Martyrs (18ᵉ and 9ᵉ). In the shadow of lofty Sacré-Coeur, the Rue des Abbesses is studded with shops—from vintage jewelry and unique clothing to antiques and upscale gardening. Turn onto the Rue des Martyrs and discover one of Paris's emerging scenes, with trendy boutiques scattered among inviting cafés and pâtisseries.

Rues Etienne Marcel, du Jour, Tiquetonne (2ᵉ). Just around the corner from teeming Les Halles, this area is jam-packed with big names (Yamamoto, Agnès b), but it also boasts multitudes of smaller boutiques (Madame à Paris) popular with hip young Parisians.

Rue du Bac (7ᵉ). After browsing at Le Bon Marché turn the corner at the Grand Epicerie and stroll down this most bountiful of shopping streets. Old and well established, this is where the Paris beau monde finds everything from elegant linens and home furnishings to any item of apparel a grownup or child could possibly want.

Rue Vavin (6ᵉ). One of Paris's epicenters for outfitting those hopelessly chic Parisian children, this street is lined with boutique after boutique for tots. If you have the kids in tow, follow up with a pony ride at the Luxembourg gardens (weekends only). Jewelry, clothing, Savon de Marseille, and J.P. Hevin, one of Paris's top chocolatiers, give adults plenty to love, too.

Rue Pont Louis Philippe (4ᵉ). Long enjoyed for its multitude of elegant paper and stationery shops, here you'll also find antiques, musical instruments, and classy clothing.

Rue Francois Miron (from St. Paul métro to Place St. Gervais, 4ᵉ). Many shoppers overlook this lovely street at the Marais's Seine-side fringes, but there's plenty here to make a wander worthwhile. Parisians in the know head here for spices, top-notch designs for the home, antiques, jewelry, pretty cafés, and much more. Bonus: two of the oldest houses in Paris are here; they're the medieval half-timbered ones.

16

always hopping. There's an ethnic rummage-sale feel, with old Asian posters, small lanterns, and basket upon basket of cheap little doodads, baubles, and trinkets for sale. The clothing itself has simple lines, and there are always plenty of picks in raw silk.

Azzedine Alaïa (✉ *7 rue de Moussy, 4ᵉ, Le Marais* ☎ *01–42–72–19–19* Ⓜ *Hôtel de Ville*) is one of the darlings of the fashion set with his perfectly proportioned "king of cling" dresses. And you don't have to be under twenty to look good in one of his dresses; Tina Turner wears his clothes well, as does every other beautiful woman with the courage and the curves. His boutique/workshop/apartment is covered with artwork by Julian Schnabel and is not the kind of place you casually wander into out of curiosity: the sales staff immediately make you feel awkward in that distinctive Parisian way.

Catherine Malandrino (✉ *10 rue de Grenelle, 6ᵉ, St-Germain-des-Prés* ☎ *01–42–22–26–95* Ⓜ *Sèvres Babylone*) designs for the urban sophisticate, expertly combining glamour, smarts, and allure in her office-to-soirée styles. Dresses caress the body without clinging and incorporate ingenious details—cutout seams, a flattering wide bodice, transparent sleeves—for an ultrastylish look.

Chloé (✉ *54–56 rue du Faubourg St-Honoré, 8ᵉ, Louvre/Tuileries* ☎ *01–44–94–33–00* Ⓜ *Concorde*) is revising its image with Paulo Melim Andersson at the helm; less romantic and feminine than days of yore, the line still features flowing layered dresses but with an asymmetric edge. Bold colors and patterns on lovely diaphanous fabrics made a big splash recently.

★ **Colette** (✉ *213 rue St-Honoré, 1ᵉʳ, Louvre/Tuileries* ☎ *01–55–35–33–90* Ⓜ *Tuileries*) is the place for ridiculously cool fashion par excellence. So the staff barely deigns to make eye contact—who cares! There are ultramodern trinkets and trifles of all kinds: perfumes; an exclusive handful of cosmetics, including Aesop, Kiehls, and François Nars; and loads of superchic jewelry…and that's just the ground floor. The first floor has wares (clothes, shoes, and accessories) from every internationally known and unknown designer with trendy street cred, a small library, the latest out-there CDs, and an art display space. The basement has a water bar (because that's what models eat) and a small restaurant that's good for a quick bite.

Dupleks (✉ *88 quai de Valmy, 10ᵉ, République* ☎ *01–42–06–15–08* Ⓜ *République*) calls itself a boutique for "créateurs éthiques"—and ethical they may be, but they've also got plenty of fashion savvy. Youthful designs range from the whimsical to überchic. The upbeat, friendly atmosphere makes browsing extra enjoyable.

E2 (✉ *15 rue Martel, 10ᵉ, Opéra/Grands Boulevards* ☎ *01–47–70–15–14* Ⓜ *Bonne Nouvelle*), by appointment only, houses a line by designers Michèle and Olivier Chatenet. You'll find their own label of ethnic-influenced fashion inspired by the '30s through the '70s; impeccable vintage couture finds like Chanel, Pucci, Lanvin, and Hermès; plus clothing remade with their own special customizing method. They take tired fashion and transform it—for example, sewing emerald-green sequins into the pleats of an ordinary gray kilt. With one of these creations, you'll definitely be dressed like no one else.

★ **Isabel Marant** (⊠*16 rue de Charonne, 11ᵉ, Bastille/Nation* ☎*01–49–29–71–55* Ⓜ*Ledru-Rollin* ⊠*1 rue Jacob, 6ᵉ, St-Germain-des-Prés* ☎*01–43–26–04–12* Ⓜ*St-Germain-des-Prés* ⊠*47 rue Saintonge, 3ᵉ, Le Marais* ☎*01–42–78–19–24* Ⓜ*Filles du Calvaire*), a young designer, is a honey pot of bohemian rock-star style. Her separates skim the body without constricting: silk jersey dresses, loose sweaters ready to slip from a shoulder, tight little knitwear sets in cool colors. Look for the secondary line, Etoile, for a less-expensive take.

Issey Miyake A-POC-Inside (⊠*47 rue des Francs-Bourgeois, 4ᵉ, Le Marais* ☎*01–44–54–07–05* Ⓜ*St-Paul*) houses the results of the Japanese designer's clothing concept: a fabrication technique that allows for hundreds of pieces to be cut from one piece of tubular cloth, resulting in pieces you can customize. Contrary to first impressions, Miyake's clothes are eminently wearable. A-POC stands for "A Piece of Cloth" (it's also a play on the word *epoch*).

Liza Korn (⊠*19 rue Beaurepaire, 10ᵉ, République* ☎*01–42–01–36–02* Ⓜ*République*) has charming vintage-inspired designs—say, a '60s-style lipstick-pink cashmere coat or a scarf of crimson cock feathers—that blend well with the designer's versatile separates. Bonus: a limited but perfectly adorable line for kids.

16

Maje (⊠*267 rue St-Honore, 2ᵉ, Louvre/Palais-Royal* ☎*01–42–96–84–93* Ⓜ*Palais-Royal-Musée du Louvre* ⊠*9 rue Blancs Manteaux, 4ᵉ, Marais* ☎*01–44–78–03–33* Ⓜ*Hotel de Ville* ⊠*42 rue du Four, 6ᵉ, St-Germain-des-Prés* ☎*01–42–22–43–69* Ⓜ*St-Germain-des-Prés*) brings a certain ease to looking great. So comfortable you could sleep in them, these clothes are designed with real women in mind, not stick figures. Wildly popular dresses feature sensuous draping offset by a bodice, belt, or plunging neckline (or back). Seasonal collections include flirty updates on the shirtwaist, microminis, and lean, peg-leg trousers.

★ **Marni** (⊠*57 av. Montaigne, 8ᵉ, Champs-Elysées* ☎*01–56–88–08–08* Ⓜ*Franklin-D.-Roosevelt*) is an Italian label with a fantastic take on boho chic—retro-ish prints and colors (citron yellow, seaweed green), funky fabrics (striped ticking, canvas), and accessories that suggest wanderlust (hobo bags).

Miu Miu (⊠*219 rue St-Honoré, 1ᵉʳ, Louvre/Tuileries* ☎*01–58–62–53–20* Ⓜ*Tuileries*) is a St. Honoré boutique that dispenses with the designer's Modernist ethos in favor of a neo-Baroque sensibility—and it influences everything from the velvet wallpaper to, perhaps, a lavish pair of ruby slippers. Although the shoes and accessories scream glitz, the clothes still favor sleek refinement, with the designer's notorious tension between minimalism and opulence.

No60 (⊠*60 rue Charlot, 3ᵉ, Le Marais* ☎*01–44–78–91–90* Ⓜ*Filles du Calvaire*) aims for rock-star glamour. Not the tarted-up kind, though: think sophisticated, sexy, and up to the moment. You'll find hot-ticket lines by the likes of Chalayan, Margiela, Anne-Valéry Hash, and a bevy of handpicked designers.

Samy Chalon (✉ *24 rue Charlot, 3ᵉ, Le Marais* 🕾 *01–44–59–39–16* Ⓜ *Filles du Calvaire*) brings hand knits into the 21st century with inspired shapes. Updates on the classics are never bulky and ever flattering. Form-fitting crocheted skirt-and-sweater sets, long mohair wrap coats in deep crimson or indigo, light-as-air scarf-print skirts, and jaunty shrugs with leather insets are a few perennial favorites.

Shine (✉ *15 rue de Poitou, 3ᵉ, Le Marais* 🕾 *01–48–05–80–10* Ⓜ *Filles du Calvaire*) outshines many of the boutiques even in its hip Marais location. Retro and übermodern, you'll find only the sharper edge of chic (with a clientele to match): Marc by Marc Jacobs, See by Chloé, K by Karl Lagerfeld, and 7 For All Mankind.

Stella Cadente (✉ *93 quai de Valmy, 10ᵉ, République* 🕾 *01–42–09–27–00* Ⓜ *République* ✉ *21 rue Beaurepaire, 10ᵉ, République* 🕾 *01–40–40–95–47* Ⓜ *République*) is a touch of schoolgirl, a dash of Wonder Woman, et voilà! Cadente's whimsicality encompasses a graceful chiffon shift as easily as a cropped leather jacket in metallic lavender. Her signature shooting star is emblazoned on the sought-after bags, and her sparkly jewelry is ultrapopular.

★ **Vanessa Bruno** (✉ *12 rue de Castiglione, 1ᵉʳ, Louvre/Tuileries* 🕾 *01–42–61–44–60* Ⓜ *Pyramides* ✉ *25 rue St-Sulpice, 6ᵉ, Quartier Latin* 🕾 *01–43–54–41–04* Ⓜ *Odéon* ✉ *100 rue Vieille du Temple, 3ᵉ, Le Marais* 🕾 *01–42–77–19–41* Ⓜ *St-Sébastien-Froissart*) stirs up a new brew of feminine dressing: some androgynous pieces (skinny pants) plus delicacy (filmy tops) with a dash of whimsy (lace insets). Separates are coveted for their sleek styling, gorgeous colors, and unerring sexiness. Wardrobe staples include perfectly proportioned cotton tops and sophisticated dresses. Athé, the secondary or "diffusion" line, flies off the racks, so if you see something you love, grab it. Bruno's shoes and accessories are the cherry on the cake: her ultrapopular sequin-striped totes inspired an army of knockoffs.

Zadig & Voltaire (✉ *42 rue des Francs Bourgeois, 3ᵉ, Le Marais* 🕾 *01–44–54–00–60* Ⓜ *St-Paul* ✉ *1–3 rue du Vieux Colombier, 6ᵉ, St-Germain-des-Prés* 🕾 *01–43–29–18–29* Ⓜ *St-Sulpice* ✉ *18–20 rue François, 1ᵉ, Champs-Elysées* 🕾 *01–40–70–97–89* Ⓜ *Franklin-D.-Roosevelt*) is the A-list destination for young fashionistas, offering street wear at its funkiest: racy camisoles, cashmere sweaters in gorgeous colors, cropped leather jackets, and form-fitting pants to offset those tiny French derrieres.

DEPARTMENT STORES

For an overview of Paris *mode* (style), visit *les grands magasins,* Paris's monolithic department stores. Size up the sometimes ornate architecture, compare prices, and marvel at the historical value of it all—some of these stores have been around since 1860. Most are open Monday through Saturday from about 9:30 to 7, and some are open until 10 PM one weekday evening.

Au Printemps (⊠ *64 bd. Haussmann, 9ᵉ, Opéra/Grands Boulevards* ☎*01–42–82–50–00* Ⓜ*Havre Caumartin, Opéra, and RER: Auber*) is actually three major stores: Printemps de la Maison (home furnishings), Printemps de l'Homme (menswear—six floors of it), and the brilliant Printemps de la Mode (fashion, fashion, fashion), which has everything from

cutting-edge to the teeny bopper. Be sure to check out the beauty area, with the Nuxe spa, hairdressers, and seemingly every beauty product known to woman under one roof. Fashion shows are held on Tuesday (all year) and Friday (April–October) at 10 AM under the cupola on the seventh floor of La Mode and are free. (Reservations can be made in advance by calling 01–42–82–63–17; tickets can also be obtained on the day of the show at the service desk on the first floor.)

16

BHV (⊠ *52–64 rue de Rivoli, 4ᵉ, Beaubourg/Les Halles* ☎*01–42–74–90–00* Ⓜ*Hôtel de Ville*), short for **Bazar de l'Hôtel de Ville,** houses an enormous basement hardware store that sells everything from doorknobs to cement mixers and has to be seen to be believed. There's even a hardware-theme café, where how-to demos are held. The fashion offerings are limited, but BHV is noteworthy for its huge selection of high-quality household goods, home-décor material, electronics, and office supplies. If you're looking for typically French household items (those heavy, gold-rimmed café sets, gorgeous French linen, or Savon de Marseille), this is your ticket.

Fodor's Choice
★ **Le Bon Marché** (⊠ *24 rue de Sèvres, 7ᵉ, St-Germain-des-Prés* ☎*01–44–39–80–00* Ⓜ*Sèvres Babylone*), founded in 1852, has emerged as the city's chicest department store. Long a hunting ground for linens, table settings, and other home items, the store got a face-lift that brought fashion to the fore. The ground floor sets out makeup, perfume, and accessories; this is where celebs duck in for essentials while everyone pretends not to recognize them. Upstairs, do laps through labels chichi (Burberry, Dries van Noten, Sonia Rykiel) and überhip (Martin Margiela, Comme des Garçons). Menswear, under the moniker Balthazar, keeps pace with designers like Zegna, Yves Saint Laurent, and Paul Smith. Zip across the second floor walkway to the mode section (above the next-door *epicerie*), home to streetwise designers and edgy secondary lines (as well as a funky café). French favorites include Athé by Vanessa Bruno, Mont St. Michel, Zadig & Voltaire, Manoush, Isabel Marant's Etoile line, and Madame à Paris. Best of all, this department store nearly isn't as crowded as those near the Opéra. Don't miss **La Grande Epicerie** right next door; it's the haute couture of grocery stores. Artisanal jams, nougats, olive oils, and much more make great gifts, and the lustrous pastries and fruit beg to be chosen for a snack.

★ **Galeries Lafayette** (✉*35–40 bd. Haussmann, 9ᵉ, Opéra/Grands Bou-levards* ☎*01–42–82–34–56* Ⓜ*Chaussée d'Antin, Opéra, Havre Caumartin* ✉*Centre Commercial Montparnasse, 14ᵉ, Montparnasse* ☎*01–45–38–52–87* Ⓜ*Montparnasse Bienvenüe*) is one of those places that you wander into unawares, leaving hours later a poorer and hum-bler person. The flagship store at 40 boulevard Haussmann bulges with thousands of designers and a Belle Époque stained-glass dome caps the world's largest perfumery. Free fashion shows are held Fridays at 3 PM under the spectacular domed café (advance reservations are a must: call 01–42–82–36–40). A big draw is the delectable comestibles depart-ment, stocked with the best of everything from herbed goat cheese to Iranian caviar. Just across the street at 35 boulevard Haussmann is Galeries Lafayette Maison. The Montparnasse branch is a pale shadow of the Boulevard Haussmann behemoths.

BUDGET

FNAC (✉*Forum des Halles, 1ᵉʳ, Beaubourg/Les Halles* ☎*01–40–41–40–00* Ⓜ*Les Halles* ✉*74 av. des Champs-Elysées, 8ᵉ, Champs-Elysées* ☎*01–53–53–64–64* Ⓜ*Franklin-D.-Roosevelt* ✉*136 rue de Rennes, 6ᵉ, Montparnasse* ☎*01–49–54–30–00* Ⓜ*St-Placide*) is a high-profile French "cultural" department store. Parisians flock here for the huge selection of music and books, as well as photo, TV, and audio equipment.

Monoprix (✉*21 av. de l'Opéra, 1ᵉʳ, Opéra/Grands Boulevards* ☎*01–42–61–78–08* Ⓜ*Opéra* ✉*20 bd. de Charonne, 20ᵉ, Bastille/Nation* ☎*01–43–73–17–59* Ⓜ*Nation* ✉*50 rue de Rennes, 6ᵉ, St-Germain-des-Prés* ☎*01–45–48–18–08* Ⓜ*St-Germain-des-Prés*), with branches throughout the city, is *the* French dime store par excellence, stocking everyday items like toothpaste, groceries, toys, typing paper, and bath mats—a little of everything. It also has a line of relatively inexpensive basic wearables for the whole family and isn't a bad place to stock up on French liqueurs at reasonable prices.

FOOD & WINE

In addition to the establishments listed below, don't overlook La Grande Epicerie next to Le Bon Marché department store.

À la Mère de Famille (✉*35 rue du Faubourg-Montmartre, 9ᵉ, Opéra/Grands Boulevards* ☎*01–47–70–83–69* Ⓜ*Cadet*) is an enchanting shop well versed in French regional specialties and old-fashioned bon-bons, sugar candy, and more.

Les Caves Augé (✉*116 bd. Haussmann, 8ᵉ, Opéra/Grands Boulevards* ☎*01–45–22–16–97* Ⓜ*St-Augustin*), one of the best wineshops in Paris since 1850, is just the ticket, whether you're looking for a rare vintage or a seductive Bordeaux for a tête-à-tête. English-speaking Marc Sibard is a knowledgeable and affable adviser.

Debauve & Gallais (✉*30 rue des Sts-Pères, 7ᵉ, St-Germain-des-Prés* ☎*01–45–48–54–67* Ⓜ*St-Germain-des-Prés*) was founded in 1800.

The two former chemists who ran it became the royal chocolate purveyors and were famed for their "health chocolates," made with almond milk. Test the benefits yourself with ganache, truffles, or *pistols* (flavored dark-chocolate disks).

Fodor'sChoice **La Dernière Goutte** (⊠*6 rue de Bourbon le Château, 6ᵉ, St-Germain-des-★ Prés* ☎*01–46–29–11–62* Ⓜ*Odéon*), an inviting *cave* (literally wine store or wine cellar), focuses on wines by small French producers. Each is handpicked by the owner, along with a choice selection of estate champagnes, Armagnac, and the classic Vieille Prune (plum brandy). The friendly English-speaking staff makes browsing a pleasure. Don't miss the Saturday afternoon tastings.

L'Epicerie (⊠*51 rue St-Louis-en-L'Ile, 4ᵉ, Ile St-Louis* ☎*01–43–25–20–14* Ⓜ*Pont Marie*) sells 90 types of jam (try fig with almonds and cinnamon), 70 kinds of mustard (including one with chocolate and honey), numerous olive oils, caviar, and foie gras.

Á l'Etoile d'Or (⊠*30 rue Pierre Fontaine, 9ᵉ, Opéra* ☎*01–48–74–59–55* Ⓜ*Pigalle*) is the quintessential dream of a candy shop. This whimsical confectionary will delight children of all ages, not to mention chocoholics, as it stocks some of the best-pedigreed chocolates in town (like Bernachon of Lyon). Dedicated to the candies of France, it's a walk back in time, with classic sweets from every Gallic region. Although a tad out of the way, it's well worth the trip.

16

Fauchon (⊠*26 pl. de la Madeleine, 8ᵉ, Opéra/Grands Boulevards* ☎*01–70–39–38–00* Ⓜ*Madeleine*) remains the most iconic of Parisian food stores. It's expanding globally, but the flagship is still behind the Madeleine church. Established in 1886, it sells renowned pâté, honey, jelly, tea, and private-label champagne. Expats come for hard-to-find foreign foods (U.S. pancake mix, British lemon curd); those with a sweet tooth make a beeline for the *macarons* (airy, ganache-filled cookies) in the pâtisserie. There's a café for a quick bite. Prices can be eye-popping—marzipan fruit for €95 a pound—but who can nay-say a Fauchon *cadeau* (present)?

Hédiard (⊠*21 pl. de la Madeleine, 8ᵉ, Opéra/Grands Boulevards* ☎*01–43–12–88–88* Ⓜ*Madeleine*), established in 1854, was famous in the 19th century for its high-quality imported spices. These—along with rare teas and beautifully packaged house brands of jam, mustard, and cookies—continue to be a draw.

Huilerie Artisanale J. Leblanc et Fils (⊠*6 rue Jacob, 6ᵉ, St-Germain-des-Prés* ☎*01–46–34–61–55* Ⓜ*Mabillon*) corrals everything you need for the perfect salad dressing into its small space: aged vinegars, *fleur de sel* (unprocessed sea salt), and more than 15 varieties of oils pressed the old-fashioned way, with a big stone wheel, from olives, hazelnuts, pistachios, or grape seed.

★ **Ladurée** (⊠*16 rue Royale, 8ᵉ, Louvre/Tuileries* ☎*01–42–60–21–79* Ⓜ*Madeleine* ⊠*75 av. des Champs-Elysées, 8ᵉ, Champs-Elysées* ☎*01–40–75–08–75* Ⓜ*George V* ⊠*21 rue Bonaparte, 6ᵉ, Quartier Latin* ☎*01–44–07–64–87* Ⓜ*Odéon*), founded in 1862, oozes period atmo-

RUE ST-HONORÉ

You're just as likely to bump into a Saudi princess as a Japanese DJ on what is unarguably one of the world's great shopping streets. All the big names in luxury rub elbows here, along with scores of independents with loads of fashion cachet.

What really makes this street special, though, is the plenitude of its attractions. Turn the corner and there's the sweeping Place Vendôme, an ex-palace and haven for world-class jewelers. Enter the breathtaking Palais Royal gardens, whose noble mien has been invigorated by the recent arrival of American bad-boy designers Marc Jacobs and Rick Owens, and other gems. With Place de la Concorde and the Tuileries flanking its borders, you'll know you're strolling Paris's most splendid shopping promenade.

BEST TIME TO GO

Weekends can get crowded, especially at the major draws, like Colette. But maybe that's the point: the fabulous seek to mull with their own kind, and aspirants can catch a few of their rays.

BEST FIND FOR THE BABYSITTER

At the oh-so-fabulous **Colette**, head straight for the checkout counter for the adorable tongue-in-chic items in every price range. Cartoon-character key chains and delicate silk-string bracelets (some with tiny diamonds) elate fashionistas—and it's all wrapped up in a Colette bag. *Sigh.*

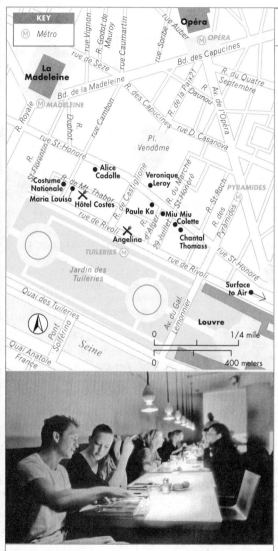

KEY

Ⓜ Métro

La Madeleine

rue Vignon
R. Godot de Mauroy
rue Caumartin
rue de Seze
Bd. de la Madeleine
R. Royale
Ⓜ MADELEINE
R. Duphot
rue Cambon
R. du Marché St-Honoré
rue St-Honoré
R. de Florentin
R. de Mt-Thabor
rue de Rivoli
rue de Castiglione
Pl. Vendôme
rue D. Casanova
R. de la Paix
Av. de l'Opéra
R. Daunou
Bd. des Capucines
rue Scribe
rue Auber
Opéra
Ⓜ OPÉRA
R. du Quatre Septembre
R. des Capucines
29 Juillet
R. d'Alger
R. St-Roch
R. des Pyramides
PYRAMIDES Ⓜ
rue St-Honoré

• Alice Cadolle
• Costume Nationale
• Maria Louisa
✕ Hôtel Costes
• Veronique Leroy
• Paule Ka
✕ Angelina
• Miu Miu
• Colette
• Chantal Thomass

rue de Rivoli

TUILERIES Ⓜ

Jardin des Tuileries

Quai des Tuileries

Pont Solférino

Quai Anatole France

Seine

Av. du Gal. Lemonnier

Louvre

Surface to Air • →

0 ____ 1/4 mile
0 ____ 400 meters

REFUELING

A cocktail at the **Hotel Costes** reassures that you, too, are one of the anointed. Beware: drop-dead-gorgeous waitresses tend to fluster the faint of heart. Chanel-suited dowagers know where to go for a luscious and restorative cup of hot chocolate. **Angelina**, like its quintessentially Parisian clientele, may be a bit frayed at the edges, but that only adds to its charm. Go at teatime for a truly sinful experience.

16

WHAT YOU'LL WANT

GLAMOUR & GLITZ

Costume Nationale. You are the rock star: expensive looks, unbridled sex appeal.

Miu Miu. Shoes and accessories scream opulence, but the clothes favor sleek refinement.

Paule Ka. Movie-stars are her inspiration. Think Audrey—Hepburn & Tautou, that is.

Pierre Hardy. Instantly recognizable ultragorgeous, ultraluxe shoes and bags set the style standard.

Rick Owens. High-concept glamour with an avant-garde edge, these beautiful clothes, furs, and shoes are not for the understated.

Veronique Leroy. Bewitching colors and sexy peekaboo detailing have garnered serious clout among fashion mavens.

FASHION FORECASTERS

Maria Luisa. Edgy designs provide the litmus test for what's to come.

Surface to Air. Without doubt, this place blurs the line between art and fashion with top emerging talent.

LUXE DOWN UNDER

Alice Cadolle. Society brides flock to Rue St-Honoré for bespoke perfection; provocative commoners to Rue Cambon.

The Best Chocolate in Paris

The French take chocolate seriously. Although there are dozens of chocolatiers to choose from, the chocolate purveyors listed below are unusually distinguished for excellence and originality.

La Maison du Chocolat (⊠ *19 rue de Sèvre , 6ᵉ, St-Germain-des-Prés* ☎ *01–45–44–20–40* Ⓜ *Sèvres Babylone* ⊠ *8 bd. de la Madeleine, 9ᵉ, Louvre/Tuileries* ☎ *01–47–42–86–52* Ⓜ *Madeleine* ⊠ *225 rue du Faubourg St-Honoré, 8ᵉ, Louvre/Tuileries* ☎ *01–42–27–39–44* Ⓜ *Ternes*) is chocolate's gold standard. The silky ganaches are unparalleled in subtlety and flavor; the pastries—notably the *macarons*—and in winter the hot chocolate, are icing on the cake.

Michel Chaudun (⊠ *149 rue de l'Université, 7ᵉ, Invalides* ☎ *01–47–53–74–40* Ⓜ *Invalides*) is known for introducing granules of cocoa beans into the chocolates to enhance intensity. His delicate *pavés*—tiny squares of dark-chocolate truffle ganache topped with a dusting of cocoa—are fabulous.

Christian Constant (⊠ *37 rue d'Assas, 6ᵉ, Luxembourg* ☎ *01–53–63–15–15* Ⓜ *St-Placide*) is deservedly praised for his delicate ganaches, perfumed with jasmine, ylang-ylang, or vervain. His famously rich hot chocolate is served by the pitcher at this café (one of Christian Constant's several restaurants), along with his excellent pastries.

Jean-Paul Hévin (⊠ *231 rue Saint-Honoré, 1ᵉʳ, Louvre/Tuileries* ☎ *01–55–35–35–96* Ⓜ *Louvre/Tuileries* ⊠ *3 rue Vavin, 6ᵉ, Luxembourg* ☎ *01–43–54–09–85* Ⓜ *Vavin*) has a formal tearoom at his Rue Saint Honoré boutique, and there are "exhibits" of chocolates and pastries at Rue Vavin—Mr. Hévin hasn't earned his world-class chocolatier status through interiors, though: the 40 different varieties of chocolate each seem more delectable than the last.

Pierre Hermé (⊠ *72 rue Bonaparte, 6ᵉ, Quartier Latin* ☎ *01–43–54–47–77* Ⓜ *Odéon* ⊠ *185 rue de Vaugirard, 15ᵉ, Montparnasse* ☎ *01–47–83–29–72* Ⓜ *Pasteur*) hardly needs an introduction. As Paris's (the world's?) most renowned pâtissier, Hermé's seasonal collections have titles such as "Fetish" or "Emotion." In his tireless quest for the new, the pastries can flounder—but the chocolate never wavers. Assortments of dark and milk chocolate bonbons are well worth the splurge.

Pierre Marcolini (⊠ *89 rue de Seine, 6ᵉ, St-Germain-des-Prés* ☎ *01–44–07–39–07* Ⓜ *Mabillon*) proves it's all in the bean with his specialty *saveurs du monde* chocolates, made with a single kind of cacao from a single location such as Madagascar or Ecuador. Belly up to the wooden bar of this Belgian chocolatier for a selection of chocolates filled with ganache, caramel, or nuts.

sphere—even at the new, large Champs-Elysées branch—but nothing beats the original tearoom on Rue Royale, with its pint-size tables and frescoed ceiling. Ladurée claims a familial link to the invention of the *macaron*, and appropriately there's a fabulous selection of these cookies: classics like pistachio, salted caramel, and coffee, and, seasonally, violet–black currant, chestnut, and lime-basil.

★ **Lavinia** (⊠*3–5 bd. de la Madeleine, 1ᵉʳ, Opéra/Grands Boulevards* 🕿*01–42–97–20–20* Ⓜ*St-Augustin*) has the largest selection of wine in one spot in Europe—more than 6,000 wines and spirits from all over the world, ranging from the simple to the sublime. On-site there are expert sommeliers to help you sort it all out, as well as a wine-tasting bar, a bookshop, and a restaurant.

La Maison du Miel (⊠*24 rue Vignon, 9ᵉ, Louvre/Tuileries* 🕿*01–47–42–26–70* Ⓜ*Madeleine*) takes *miel* (honey) seriously with more than 30 varieties, many sweetly packaged for delicious gift giving.

Mariage Frères (⊠*30 rue du Bourg-Tibourg, 4ᵉ, Le Marais* 🕿*01–42–72–28–11* Ⓜ*Hôtel de Ville* ⊠*13 rue des Grands-Augustins, 6ᵉ, St-Germain-des-Prés* 🕿*01–40–51–82–50* Ⓜ*Mabillon, St-Michel*), with its colonial *charme* and wooden counters, has more than 100 years of tea purveying behind it. Choose from more than 450 blends from 32 countries, not to mention teapots, teacups, books, and tea-flavor biscuits and candies. The tearoom serves high tea and a light lunch.

Le Palais des Thés (⊠*64 rue Vieille du Temple, 3ᵉ, Le Marais* 🕿*01–48–87–80–60* Ⓜ*St-Paul*) is a seriously comprehensive experience—white tea, green tea, black tea, tea from China, Japan, Indonesia, South America, and more. Try one of the flavored teas such as Hammam, a traditional Turkish recipe with date pulp, orange flower, rose, and red berries.

Ryst-Dupeyron (⊠*79 rue du Bac, 7ᵉ, St-Germain-des-Prés* 🕿*01–45–48–80–93* Ⓜ*Rue du Bac*) specializes in fine wines and liquors, with port, calvados, and Armagnacs that date from 1878. A great gift idea: find a bottle from the year of a friend's birth and have it labeled with your friend's name. Personalized bottles can be ordered and delivered on the same day.

Verlet (⊠*256 rue St-Honoré, 1ᵉʳ, Louvre/Tuileries* 🕿*01–42–60–67–39* Ⓜ*Palais-Royal*) is *the* place in Paris to buy coffee. There are more than 20 varieties, from places as far-flung as Hawaii and Papua New Guinea. Also on sale are teas, jams from the Savoie region, and (in winter) a stunning assortment of candied fruits.

HOME DÉCOR

Agatha Ruiz de la Prada (⊠*9 rue Guénégaud, 6ᵉ, Quartier Latin* 🕿*01–43–25–86–88* Ⓜ*Odéon*) is nothing if not prolific. She designs clothing and accessories for the Spanish department store El Corte Inglés, watches for Swatch, and furniture for Amat. In this small store she also sells her own items, from bags and children's fashions to MP4s and digital picture frames.

Alexandre Biaggi (⊠*14 rue de Seine, 6ᵉ, St-Germain-des-Prés* 🕿*01–44–07–34–73* Ⓜ*St-Germain-des-Prés*) specializes in 20th-century Art Deco and also commissions designs from such talented designers as Patrick Naggar and Hervé van der Straeten.

Alter Mundi (✉ *25 rue Beaurepaire, 10ᵉ, République* ☎ *01–42–00–15–73* Ⓜ *République* ✉ *9 rue de Rivoli, 4ᵉ Le Marais* ☎ *01–44–07–22–28* Ⓜ *St Paul*) may be the first "department store" for ethical commerce, but that doesn't mean they can't have fun. They carry great contemporary designs in everything from kitchenware and original artwork to leather-alternative bags and deconstructed scarves.

A. Simon (✉ *48 rue Montmartre, 2ᵉ, Beaubourg/Les Halles* ☎ *01–42–33–71–65* Ⓜ *Etienne Marcel*) is where Parisian chefs come for their kitchen needs—from plates and glasses to pans, dishes, and wooden spoons. The quality is excellent and the prices are reasonable.

Astier de Villatte (✉ *173 rue St-Honoré, 1ᵉʳ, Louvre/Tuileries* ☎ *01–42–60–74–13* Ⓜ *Tuileries*) offers high-style interpretations of 18th-century table settings; live out your Baroque or Empire fancies with milk-white china sets.

Avant-Scène (✉ *4 pl. de l'Odéon, 6ᵉ, Quartier Latin* ☎ *01–46–33–12–40* Ⓜ *Odéon*) is good for original, poetic furniture. Owner Elisabeth Delacarte commissions limited-edition pieces from artists like Mark Brazier-Jones, Franck Evennou, and Hubert Le Gall.

Catherine Memmi (✉ *11 rue St-Sulpice, 6ᵉ, St-Germain-des-Prés* ☎ *01–44–07–02–02* Ⓜ *St-Sulpice* ✉ *61 rue Bonaparte, 6ᵉ, St-Germain-des-Prés* ☎ *01–44–07–22–28* Ⓜ *Odéon*), a trendsetter in pared-down housewares, also sells bath products, lamps, furniture, and home accessories in elegant neutral colors. The Rue Bonaparte location carries her ever-popular luxury products for bath and body.

Christofle (✉ *24 rue de la Paix, 2ᵉ, Opéra/Grands Boulevards* ☎ *01–42–65–62–43* Ⓜ *Opéra* ✉ *9 rue Royale, 8ᵉ, Louvre/Tuileries* ☎ *01–55–27–99–13* Ⓜ *Concorde, Madeleine*), founded in 1830, has fulfilled all kinds of silver wishes, from a silver service for the *Orient Express* to a gigantic silver bed. Come for timeless table settings, vases, jewelry boxes, and more.

Compagnie Française de l'Orient et de la Chine (✉ *163 and 167 bd. St-Germain, 6ᵉ, St-Germain-des-Prés* ☎ *01–45–48–00–18* Ⓜ *St-Germain-des-Prés*) imports ceramics and furniture from China and Mongolia. At No. 167 you can find vases, teapots, and table settings; the basement has straw hats, raffia baskets, and bamboo footstools. Look for unique textiles just down the street at No. 163.

The Conran Shop (✉ *117 rue du Bac, 7ᵉ, St-Germain-des-Prés* ☎ *01–42–84–10–01* Ⓜ *Sèvres Babylone*) is the brainchild of British entrepreneur Terence Conran. The shop carries expensive contemporary furniture, beautiful bed linens, and items for every other room in the house—all marked by a balance of utility with not-too-sober style. Conran makes even shower curtains fun.

Diptyque (✉ *34 bd. St-Germain, 5ᵉ, St-Germain-des-Prés* ☎ *01–43–26–77–44* Ⓜ *Maubert Mutualité*) is famous for its candles and eaux de toilette in sophisticated scents like myrrh, fig tree, and quince. They're delightful but not cheap; the candles, for instance, cost nearly $1 per hour of burn time.

★ **E. Dehillerin** (✉18–20 *rue Coquillière, 1ᵉʳ, Louvre/Tuileries* ☎01–42–36–53–13 Ⓜ*Les Halles*) has been around since 1820. Never mind the creaky stairs; their huge range of professional cookware in enamel, stainless steel, or fiery copper is gorgeous. Julia Child was a regular.

Gien (✉18 *rue de l'Arcade, 8ᵉ, Louvre/Tuileries* ☎01–42–66–52–32 Ⓜ*Madeleine*) has been making fine china since 1821. The faience spans traditional designs, such as those inspired by Italian majolica or blue-and-white delftware, as well as contemporary looks.

16

Idé Co. (✉19 *rue Beaurepaire, 10ᵉ, République* ☎01–42–01–11–11 Ⓜ*République*) offers small items for the home in a riot of color. You'll find staples for the kitchen, espresso sets, and cappuccino bowls in bold primary colors, as well as fabulous rubber jewelry and funky stuff for kids, big and small.

Kaloma (✉32 *rue Beaurepaire, 10ᵉ, République* ☎01–42–00–61–29 Ⓜ*République*) puts you in mind of an exotic bazaar with treasures from around the globe. Sculpted silver jewelry, inlaid boxes, ephemeral silk scarves, candles, and embroidered pillows are some of the items to be found.

Kitchen Bazaar (✉*Galerie des 3 Quartiers, 23 bd. de la Madeleine, 1ᵉʳ, Opéra/Grands Boulevards* ☎01–42–60–50–30 Ⓜ*Madeleine* ✉50 *rue Croix des Petits-Champs, 1ᵉʳ, Louvre/Tuileries* ☎01–40–15–03–11 Ⓜ*Palais-Royal/Musée du Louvre*) gleams with an astonishing array of small culinary essentials. Don't be surprised at the urge to replace every tatty utensil in your kitchen, down to the last pastry brush and pepper mill, with these up-to-the-minute designs.

Laguiole (✉1 *pl. Ste-Opportune, 1ᵉʳ, Beaubourg/Les Halles* ☎01–40–28–09–42 Ⓜ*Châtelet*) is the name of the country's most famous brand of knives. Today designers like Philippe Starck and Sonia Rykiel have created special models for the company. Starck also designed this striking boutique (take note of the animal horn sticking out of the wall).

★ **Maison de Baccarat** (✉11 *pl. des Etats-Unis, 16ᵉ, Trocadéro/Tour Eiffel* ☎01–40–22–11–00 Ⓜ*Trocadéro*) was once the home of Marie-Laure de Noailles, known as the Countess of Bizarre. Now it's a museum and crystal store. Philippe Starck revamped the space with his signature cleverness—yes, that's a chandelier floating in an aquarium and, yes, that crystal arm sprouting from the wall alludes to Jean Cocteau (a friend of Noailles). Follow the red carpet to the jewelry room, where crystal baubles hang from bronze figurines, and to the immense table stacked with crystal items for the home.

★ **Le Monde Sauvage** (✉*11 rue de l'Odéon, 6ᵉ, Quartier Latin* ☎*01–43–25–60–34* Ⓜ*Odéon*) is a must-visit for home accessories—reversible silk bedspreads in rich colors, velvet throws, hand-quilted bed linens, silk floor cushions, Venetian mirrors, and the best selection of hand-embroidered curtains in silk, cotton, linen, or velvet.

★ **Muji** (✉*47 rue des Francs Bourgeois, 4ᵉ, Le Marais* ☎*01–49–96–41–41* Ⓜ*St-Paul* ✉*27 and 30 rue St-Sulpice, 6ᵉ, St-Germain-des-Prés* ☎*01–46–34–01–10* Ⓜ*Odéon*) runs on the concept of *kanketsu,* or simplicity, and the resulting streamlined designs are all the rage in Europe. Must-haves include a collection of mininecessities—travel essentials, wee office gizmos, purse-size accoutrements—so useful and adorable you'll want them all.

Pascal Mutel (✉*6 Carrefour de l'Odéon, 6ᵉ, St-Germain-des-Prés* ☎*01–43–26–02–56* Ⓜ*Odéon*), a stellar florist, also sells the perfect containers to put his flowers in; there are vases in smoked glass and zinc.

R & Y Augousti (✉*103 rue du Bac, 7ᵉ, St-Germain-des-Prés* ☎*01–42–22–22–21* Ⓜ*Sèvres Babylone*) are two Paris-based designers who make furniture and objects for the home from coconut, bamboo, fish skin, palm wood, and parchment. Also for sale are their hand-tooled leather bags, and jewelry made from natural horn and stingray.

★ **Sentou** (✉*24 rue du Pont Louis-Philippe, 4ᵉ, Le Marais* ☎*01–42–71–00–01* Ⓜ*St-Paul* ✉*29 rue Francois Miron, 4ᵉ, Le Marais* ☎*01–42–78–50–60* Ⓜ*Tuileries*) knocked the Parisian world over the head with its fresh designs. Avant-garde furniture, rugs, and a variety of home accessories line the cool showroom at 29 rue Francois Miron. Look for the April Vase, old test tubes linked together to form different shapes, or the oblong suspended crystal vases and arty tableware at 24 rue du Pont Louis-Philippe.

Van der Straeten (✉*11 rue Ferdinand Duval, 4ᵉ, Le Marais* ☎*01–42–78–99–99* Ⓜ*St-Paul*) is the lofty gallery-cum-showroom of Paris designer Hervé van der Straeten. He started out creating jewelry for Saint Laurent and Lacroix, designed a perfume bottle for Christian Dior, and moved on to making rather baroque and often wacky furniture. On show are furniture, jewelry, and startling mirrors.

JEWELRY

Most of the big names are on or near Place Vendôme. Designer semi-precious and costume jewelry can generally be found in boutiques on Avenue Montaigne and Rue du Faubourg St-Honoré.

Agatha (✉*23 bd. de la Madeleine, 1ᵉʳ, Opéra/Grands Boulevards* ☎*01–40–20–90–03* Ⓜ*Madeleine* ✉*45 rue Bonaparte, 6ᵉ, St-Ger-*

main-des-Prés ☎*01–46–33–20–00* Ⓜ*St-Germain-des-Prés*) is the perfect place to buy a moderately priced piece of jewelry just for fun. Agatha's line of earrings, rings, hair accessories, bracelets, necklaces, watches, brooches, and pendants is ever popular with Parisians. Styles change quickly, but classics include nifty charm bracelets and fine gold necklaces with whimsical pendants.

Alexandre Reza (✉*23 pl. Vendôme, 1er, Opéra/Grands Boulevards* ☎*01–42–96–64–00* Ⓜ*Opéra*), one of Paris's most exclusive jewelers, is first and foremost a gemologist. He travels the world looking for the finest stones and then works them into stunning pieces, many of which are replicas of jewels of historical importance.

Anaconda (✉*10 rue de Verneuil, 7e, St-Germain-des-Prés* ☎*01–42–60–18–29* Ⓜ*St-Germain-des-Pres*), designer Monica Rossi's gem of a boutique, displays the ravishing jewels that draw inspiration from antiquity, as well as from land and sea. A delicate choker of smoky rough-cut diamonds, a multistrand bracelet of milky opals with a hand-carved clasp, a whimsical locket, along with rings carved from crimson coral in the likeness of a fish or an octopus, all make a stunning impression.

Arthus-Bertrand (✉*6 pl. St-Germain-des-Prés, 6e, St-Germain-des-Prés* ☎*01–49–54–72–10* Ⓜ*St-Germain-des-Prés*), which dates back to 1803, has glass showcases full of designer jewelry and numerous objects to celebrate births.

L'Atelier Onaya (✉*31 rue Beaurepaire, 10e, République* ☎*01–42–26–07–77* Ⓜ*République*) keeps current with an ever-changing exhibit of unique contemporary jewelry by young designers with fresh ideas. The emphasis is on sleek, wearable (and affordable) designs in unusual materials rather than all-out luxury.

Cartier (✉*23 pl. Vendôme, 1er, Louvre/Tuileries* ☎*01–44–55–32–20* Ⓜ*Tuileries, Concorde* ✉*154 av. des Champs-Elysées, 8e, Champs-Elysées* ☎*01–58–18–17–78* Ⓜ*George V*) flashes its jewels at more than half a dozen boutiques in the city. Longtime favorites such as the Trinity rings and Tank watches have new competition for your attention in the Asian-inspired Baiser du Dragon jewelry and the colorful Délices de Goa collection.

Chanel Jewelry (✉*18 pl. Vendôme, 1er, Opéra/Grands Boulevards* ☎*01–55–35–50–00* Ⓜ*Tuileries, Opéra*) feeds off the iconic design elements of the pearl-draped designer: quilting (reimagined for gold rings), camellias (now brooches), and shooting stars (used for her first jewelry collection in 1932, now appearing as diamond rings).

Fodor'sChoice ★ **Dary's** (✉*362 rue St-Honoré, 1er, Louvre/Tuileries* ☎*01–42–60–95–23* Ⓜ*Tuileries*) brings to realization the best of a Paris shopping experience—a wonderful, family-run, Ali Baba–ish cavern teeming with artists, actors, models, and jewelry lovers. You'll need to take your time though, because the walls are filled with row upon row of antique jewels from every era, more modern secondhand jewelry, and drawer upon drawer of vintage one-of-a-kinds.

16

CANAL ST-MARTIN

"Off the beaten track" aptly describes this up-and-coming neighborhood, dotted with galleries, vintage shops, and iconoclastic boutiques.

Although you're not likely to forget you're in Paris, the pace here is noticeably slower. The canal's cobblestones, plane trees, and arched bridges provide the atmosphere, and its stone embankments make an excellent spot to take in the scene. Or, as Parisians do on temperate evenings, share a bite and a bottle of wine with friends. And the shopping: low-key cool reigns here, none of the high-wattage, high-profile designers that vie for the big bucks in Paris's tony neighborhoods. The area's hipster equivalent of mom-and-pop shops ensure a few choice finds that will be seen on you and only you. Walk along Avenue Beaurepaire, the area's shopping epicenter, toward the canal. From here, you'll want to check out some of the smaller streets, especially Rue Lancry, and meander along the canal—a great way to discover a *quartier* that's still one of Paris's best-kept secrets.

BEST TIME TO GO

If you want to experience the neighborhood at its most tranquil, go on a weekday. If it's the scene you're after, plan on a Saturday afternoon visit.

BEST FIND FOR A PICKY HIPSTER

Cool, colorful bracelets and intricate Gothic-inspired chokers are all in rubber at **Idé Co**. Or, for the best-cut velour jeans this side of the Atlantic, go to **Boutique Renhsen**.

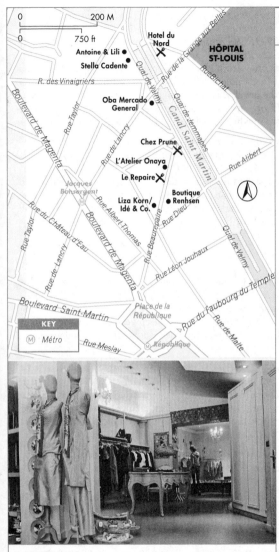

KEY

Ⓜ Métro

REFUELING

To Whom It May Concern: really immerse yourself in the scene, join the young designers and artists at **Chez Prune**. On warm days, its canal-side spot makes it the place to be. Or drop in to **Le Verre Volé** for regional wine, authentic charcuterie, and excellent company. For atmosphere and a little history to boot, lunch at the **Hotel du Nord** (movie buffs will know it from the eponymous 1938 Marcel Carné film).

WHAT YOU'LL WANT

UNDERGROUND CHIC

Antoine & Lili. The whole exuberant universe, with women's, kids, and housewares all on the same block. Tableware and clothes burst with color, imagination, and charm.

L'Atelier Onaya. Original jewelry in sleek, designs and unusual materials.

Boutique Renhsen. Fashionistas swear by the jeans and popular sportswear and accessories.

Dupleks. "Ethical designers" but no lack of design daring. Sexy micro-blazers and form-flattering tunics can be worn in perfectly good conscience.

Liza Korn. Charmingly eccentric and original clothing, shoes, jewelry, and stylish kids' clothes at her boutique-atelier.

Stella Cadente. Ultrafeminine separates and sought-after bags are the rage for bright young things.

HOUSEWARES

Alter Mundi. This department store for equitable commerce champions sleek and chic contemporary designs.

Idé Co. Witty items for the home and updates on all the French staples.

Kaloma. Eclectic selection of artisan-made wares from around the world.

16

Dinh Van (⊠*16 rue de la Paix, 2ᵉ, Opéra/Grands Boulevards* ☎*01–42–61–74–49* Ⓜ*Opéra* ⊠*22 rue François 1ᵉr, 8ᵉ, Champs-Elysées* ☎*01–56–64–09–91* Ⓜ*Franklin-D.-Roosevelt* ⊠*58 rue Bonaparte, 6ᵉ, St-Germain-des-Prés* ☎*01–56–24–10–00* Ⓜ*St-Germain-des-Prés*), just around the corner from Place Vendôme's titan jewelers, thumbs its nose at in-your-face opulence. The look here, both in the boutique's design and in the jewelry, is refreshingly spare. Best sellers include a hammered gold orb necklace and leather-cord bracelets joined with geometric shapes in white or yellow gold, some with pavé diamonds.

Dior Joaillerie (⊠*28 av. Montaigne, 8ᵉ, Champs-Elysées* ☎*01–47–23–52–39* Ⓜ*Franklin-D.-Roosevelt* ⊠*8 pl. Vendôme, 1ᵉr, Opéra/Grands Boulevards* ☎*01–42–96–30–84* Ⓜ*Opéra*) got a big dollop of wit and panache when it signed on young designer Victoire de Castellane to create Dior's first line of fine jewelry. She does oversize rings, hoop earrings, and bracelets swinging with diamonds, and—lest you forget the amped-up spirit at Dior house—white-gold death's-head cufflinks.

LINGERIE

Alice Cadolle (⊠*4 rue Cambon, 1ᵉr, Louvre/Tuileries* ☎*01–42–60–94–22* Ⓜ*Concorde* ⊠*255 rue St-Honoré, 1ᵉr, Louvre/Tuileries* ☎*01–42–60–94–94* Ⓜ*Concorde*) has been selling fine lingerie to Parisians since 1889. Ready-to-wear bras, corsets, and sleepwear fill the Rue Cambon boutique; on Rue St-Honoré, Madame Cadolle offers a made-to-measure service.

Fodor'sChoice
★ **Chantal Thomass** (⊠*211 rue St-Honoré, 1ᵉr, Louvre/Tuileries* ☎*01–42–60–40–56* Ⓜ*Tuileries*), a legendary lingerie diva, is back with this *Pillow Talk*–meets–Louis XV–inspired boutique. This is French naughtiness at its best, striking the perfect balance between playful and seductive. Sheer silk negligees edged in Chantilly lace and lascivious bra-and-corset sets punctuate the signature line.

Erès (⊠*2 rue Tronchet, 8ᵉ, Opéra/Grands Boulevards* ☎*01–47–42–28–82* Ⓜ*Madeleine* ⊠*40 av. Montaigne, 8ᵉ, Louvre/Tuileries* ☎*01–47–23–07–26* Ⓜ*Franklin-D.-Roosevelt*) has the most modern line of swimwear and lingerie in town: streamlined shapes in classic colors uncluttered by lace. This lingerie masters the art of soft sheer tones and is comfortable, flattering, and subtly sexy.

Fifi Chachnil (⊠*231 rue St-Honoré, 1ᵉr, Louvre/Tuileries* ☎*01–42–61–21–83* Ⓜ*Tuileries* ⊠*68 rue Jean-Jacques Rousseau, 1ᵉr, Beaubourg/Les Halles* ☎*01–42–21–19–93* Ⓜ*Etienne Marcel*) girls are real boudoir babes, with a fondness for quilted-satin bed jackets, and lingerie in candy-land colors. The look is cheerfully sexy, with checkered push-up bras, frilled white knickers, and peach-satin corsets.

★ **Les Folies d'Elodie** (⊠*56 av. Paul Doumer, 16ᵉ, Trocadéro/Tour Eiffel* ☎*01–45–04–93–57* Ⓜ*Trocadéro*), a large, lush boutique, can trick you out in anything from a 1950s-style cotton bra and panties à la

Bardot to a risqué sheer-silk nightgown. Everything is handmade, with an emphasis on the grown-up rather than little-girlish.

Princesse Tam Tam (⊠*5 rue Montmartre, 1ᵉʳ, Les Halles* ☎*01–40–41–99–51* Ⓜ*Les Halles* ⊠*53 rue Bonaparte, 6ᵉ, St-Germain-des-Prés* ☎*01–43–29–01–91* Ⓜ*St-Germain-des-Prés* ⊠*20 rue St-Antoine, 4ᵉ, Marais* ☎*01–42–77–32–27* Ⓜ*Bastille*) is the go-to for affordable and beguiling bra-and-panty sets that combine sex appeal and playfulness. Designed for mileage as much as allure, the softer-than-soft cotton wrap tops and nighties, lace-edged silk tap pants, camisoles, slips, and adorable separates for the boudoir are comfortable *and* comely.

Sabbia Rosa (⊠*71–73 rue des Sts-Pères, 6ᵉ, St-Germain-des-Prés* ☎*01–45–48–88–37* Ⓜ*St-Germain-des-Prés*) is a discreet, boudoirlike boutique you could easily walk straight past. It is, however, one of the world's finest lingerie stores and the place where actresses Catherine Deneuve and Isabelle Adjani (and others who might not want to reveal their errand) buy superb French silks.

MARKETS

16

FLEA MARKETS

Fodor'sChoice ★ **Marché aux Puces St-Ouen** (Ⓜ*Porte de Clignancourt* ⊕*www.parispuces.com*), also referred to as **Clignancourt**, on Paris's northern boundary, still attracts the crowds when it's open—Saturday to Monday, from 9 to 6—but its once-unbeatable prices are now a relic of the past. This century-old labyrinth of alleyways packed with antiques dealers' booths and *brocante* stalls sprawls for more than a square mile. Old Vuitton trunks, ormolu clocks, 1930s jet jewelry, and vintage garden furniture sit cheek by jowl. Arrive early to pick up the most worthwhile loot (like old prints). Be warned—if there's one place in Paris where you need to know how to bargain, this is it!

If you're arriving by métro, walk under the overpass and take the first left at the Rue de Rosiers to reach the epicenter of the market. Around the overpass huddle stands selling dodgy odds-and-ends (think pleather, knockoff shoes, and questionable gadgets). These blocks are crowded and gritty; be careful with your valuables. If you need a breather from the hundreds of market vendors, stop for a bite in one of the rough-and-ready cafés. A particularly good pick is **Le Soleil** (⊠*109 av. Michelet* ☎*01–40–10–08–08*).

Porte de Vanvesᵉ & Porte de Montreuil (Ⓜ*Porte de Vanves*), on the southern and eastern sides of the city, are smaller flea markets. Vanves is a hit with the fashion set and specializes in smaller objects—mirrors, textiles, handbags, clothing, and glass—as well as books, posters, and postcards. It's open on weekends only from 8 to 5, but arrive early if you want to find a bargain: the good stuff goes fast, and stalls are liable to be packed up before noon.

FLOWER & BIRD MARKETS

Paris's main **flower market** is in the heart of the city on the Ile de la Cité, between Notre-Dame and the Palais de Justice. It's open every day from 8 until 7:30. There's an eye-popping profusion of cut flowers as well as all manner of plants from the usual suspects to the exotic. On Sunday it also hosts a **bird market**—a great way to spend an hour on an otherwise quiet morning. Parakeets flutter in cages, and you might also spot plumed chickens and exquisite little ducks with teal and mauve markings. What are they for? It's best not to ask. Other colorful flower markets are held beside the Madeleine church (métro Madeleine, open Monday to Saturday, 9 to 9 and alternate Sundays 9:30 to 8:30), and on Place des Ternes (métro Ternes, Tuesday to Sunday).

> **WORD OF MOUTH**
>
> "Le Marché aux Puces St-Ouen is worth the trip!…I do not speak French, but had no trouble going to the markets by myself. If you plan to bargain (and you should!), bring a pen and a small pad of paper…ask for the 'best price' and have the dealer write it down. If you want to go lower, write your number and mention cash.…I don't regret any of my purchases—only those I passed up!" –highledge

FOOD MARKETS

Year-round and in any weather, the city's open-air food markets play an integral part of daily life, attracting the entire spectrum of Paris society, from the splendid matron, her minuscule dog in tow, to the mustachioed regular picking up his daily baguette. Although some markets are busier than others, there's not a market in Paris that doesn't captivate the senses. Each season has its delicacies: *fraises des bois* (wild strawberries) and tender asparagus in spring, squash blossoms and fragrant herbs in summer, saffron-tinted chanterelles in autumn, bergamot oranges in late winter. Year-round you can find pungent *lait cru* (unpasteurized) cheeses, charcuterie, and unfarmed game and fish. Many of the better-known open-air markets are in areas you'd visit for sightseeing. To get a list of market days in your area, ask your concierge or check the markets section on the Web site ⊕*www.paris.fr/EN*.

If you're unused to the metric system, you may find it easier to use the following terms: *une livre* is French for a pound; *une demi-livre,* a half pound. For cheese or meats, *un morceau* will get you a piece, *une tranche* a slice.

Most markets are open from 8 AM to 1 PM three days a week year-round (usually the weekend and one weekday, but never Monday) on a rotating basis. The following are a few of the best.

Boulevard Raspail (⊠*6ᵉ, St-Germain-des-Prés* Ⓜ*Rennes*), between Rue du Cherche-Midi and Rue de Rennes, is the city's major *marché biologique,* or organic market, bursting with produce, fish, and eco-friendly products. It's open Tuesday and Friday.

Rue de Buci (⊠*6ᵉ, St-Germain-des-Prés* Ⓜ*Odéon*) is where vendors often have tastes of their wares to tempt you: slices of sausage, slivers of peaches. It's closed Sunday afternoon and Monday.

Rue Lévis (✉ *17ᵉ, Parc Monceau* Ⓜ *Villiers*), near Parc Monceau, has Alsatian specialties and a terrific cheese shop. It's closed Sunday afternoon and Monday.

Marché d'Aligre (✉ *Rue d'Aligre, 12ᵉ, Bastille/Nation* Ⓜ *Ledru-Rollin*) open until 1 every day except Monday, is arguably the most locally authentic market. Don't miss the covered hall on the Place d'Aligre, where you can stop by a unique olive oil boutique for prebottled oils from top producers.

Rue Montorgueil (✉ *1ᵉʳ, Beaubourg/Les Halles* Ⓜ *Châtelet Les Halles*) has evolved from an old-fashioned market street into a chic *"bobo"* (bourgeois bohemian) zone; its stalls now thrive amid stylish cafés and the oldest oyster counter in Paris.

Rue Mouffetard (✉ *5ᵉ, Quartier Latin* Ⓜ *Monge*), near the Jardin des Plantes, reflects its multicultural neighborhood; it's a vibrant market with a laid-back feel that still smacks of old Paris. It's best on weekends.

STAMP MARKET

Philatelists (and fans of the Audrey Hepburn–Cary Grant 1963 thriller Charade) will want to head to Paris's unique **stamp market** (Ⓜ *Champs-Elysées–Clémenceau*), at the intersection of Avenue Marigny and Avenue Gabriel overlooking the gardens at the bottom of the Champs-Elysées. On sale are vintage postcards and stamps from all over the world. It's open Thursday, weekends, and public holidays from 10 to 5.

16

PERFUME

Annick Goutal (✉ *14 rue de Castiglione, 1ᵉʳ, Louvre/Tuileries* ☎ *01–42–60–52–82* Ⓜ *Concorde*) sells its own line of signature scents, which come packaged in gilded gauze purses. Rose, Tuberose, Violet, and Sable are ones to look for.

L'Artisan Parfumeur (✉ *32 rue du Bourg Tibourg, 4ᵉ, Le Marais* ☎ *01–48–04–55–66* Ⓜ *Hôtel de Ville*) is known for its own brand of scents for the home and perfumes with names like Méchant Loup (Big Bad Wolf).

Comme des Garçons Perfume Shop (✉ *23 pl. du Marché St-Honoré, 1ᵉʳ, Louvre/Tuileries* ☎ *01–47–03–15–03* Ⓜ *Tuileries*) is devoted to the ultraconceptual Japanese label's perfumes, scented candles, and body creams. The shop is worth a visit simply to admire the whiter-than-white store design with pink-tinted lighting.

★ **Editions de Parfums Frédéric Malle** (✉ *37 rue de Grenelle, 7ᵉ, St-Germain-des-Prés* ☎ *01–42–22–76–40* Ⓜ *Rue du Bac* ✉ *140 av. Victor Hugo, 16ᵉ, Trocadéro/Tour Eiffel* ☎ *01–45–05–39–02* Ⓜ *Victor Hugo* ✉ *21 rue du Mont Thabor, 1ᵉʳ, Louvre/Tuileries* ☎ *01–42–22–77–22* Ⓜ *Tuileries*) is based on a simple concept: take the nine most famous noses in France and have them edit singular perfumes. The result? Exceptional,

Worth a Look

There are some stores that are worth visiting, even if there's pretty much no way on earth you're going to make a purchase; check these out for a priceless slice of Parisian life.

Deyrolle (⊠ *46 rue du Bac, 7ᵉ, St-Germain-des-Prés* ☎ *01–42–22–30–07* Ⓜ *Rue du Bac*), for instance, the fascinating 19th-century taxidermist, has long been a stop for curiosity seekers. A fire in early 2008 destroyed much of the shop, though one room is still open and there are plans to rebuild.

Goumanyat & Son Royaume (⊠ *3 rue Charles-François Dupuis, 3ᵉ, Le Marais* ☎ *01–47–78–96–74* Ⓜ *Republique*) is beloved of top French chefs, the proprietors having traveled the world over to furnish this boutique with every spice, herb, and condiment imaginable. Swoon over special spice blends or a saffron-infused calisson. Flower-scented sugars, floral waters, nuts, olives, chocolates, and traditional French sweets and delicacies round out the selection. Upstairs you'll find a sampling of Europe's finest cookware; downstairs is a cave for fine wines and spirits.

Have you always wanted to have something in common with the grand homes of Paris? **Zuber** (⊠ *5 blvd des Filles du Calvaire, 3ᵉ, Le Marais* ☎ *01–42–77–95–91* Ⓜ *Filles du Calvaire*) has operated nonstop for more than two centuries as the world's oldest producer of prestige handprinted wallpapers, renowned for their magnificent panoramic scenes dating as far back as 1804. Warning: with only one scene produced per year, the wait can be nearly ten years long. They appear at Sotheby's, too, from time to time. Opulent Restoration-era wallpapers (including metallics, silks, velvets, and pressed leather) make modern statements and can be purchased in 32-foot rolls for less than a king's ransom.

For elegant decorating on a smaller scale, **Hervé Gambs** (⊠ *9 bis, rue des Blancs-Manteaux, 4ᵉ, Louvre/Tuileries* ☎ *01–44–59–88–88* Ⓜ *Hôtel de Ville* ⊠ *21 rue St-Sulpice, 6ᵉ, St-Germain-des-Prés* ☎ *01–70–08–09–08* Ⓜ *Odéon*) has the chutzpah to vie with Mother Nature. Take home one of his all-silk floral creations—think a no-care stem of orchids or a pristine bouquet of calla lilies—and dazzle your houseguests. Seasonal and holiday-appropriate displays change every few months. Gambs's own sculptural vases styled from natural forms make great gifts.

highly concentrated fragrances. Le Parfum de Thérèse, for example, was created by famous Dior nose Edmond Roudnitska for his wife. Monsieur Malle has devised high-tech ways to keep each smelling session unadulterated. At the Rue de Grenelle store, individual scents are released in glass columns; stick your head in and sniff. The Avenue Victor Hugo boutique has a glass-fronted "wall of scents"; at the push of a button a selected fragrance mists the air.

Guerlain (⊠ *68 av. des Champs-Elysées, 8ᵉ, Champs-Elysées* ☎ *01–45–62–52–57* Ⓜ *Franklin-D.-Roosevelt*) reopened its historic address in 2005 after a spectacularly opulent renovation befitting the world-class perfumer. Still the only Paris outlet for legendary perfumes like

Shalimar and L'Heure Blue, they've added several new signature scents (Rose Barbare, Cuir Beluga), and the perfume "fountain" allows for personalized bottles in several sizes to be filled on demand. Or, for a mere €30,000, a customized scent can be blended just for you. Also here are makeup, scented candles, and a spa featuring their much-adored skin-care line.

Parfums de Nicolaï (⊠*69 av. Raymond Poincaré, 16ᵉ, Trocadéro/Tour Eiffel* ☎*01–47–55–90–44* Ⓜ*Victor-Hugo* ⊠*80 rue de Grenelle, 7ᵉ, Trocadéro/Tour Eiffel* ☎*01–45–44–59–59* Ⓜ*Dupleix* ⊠*28 rue de Richelieu, 1ᵉʳ, Louvre/Tuileries* ☎*01–44–55–02–02* Ⓜ*Palais-Royal*) is run by a member of the Guerlain family: Patricia de Nicolaï. Children's, women's, and men's perfumes are on offer (including some unisex), as well as sprays for the home and scented candles.

Fodor'sChoice **Les Salons du Palais-Royal Shiseido** (⊠*Jardins du Palais-Royal, 142 Gal-*
★ *erie de Valois, 1ᵉʳ, Louvre/Tuileries* ☎*01–49–27–09–09* Ⓜ*Palais-Royal*) douses its old-new *pharmacie* décor in shades of lilac—Aubrey Beardsley would surely feel at home here. Every year Shiseido's creative genius, Serge Lutens, dreams up two new scents, which are then sold exclusively in this boutique. Each is compellingly original, from the strong *somptueux* scents, often with musk and amber notes, to intense florals (Rose de Nuit).

16

SHOES

Berluti (⊠*26 rue Marbeuf, 8ᵉ, Champs-Elysées* ☎*01–53–93–97–97* Ⓜ*Franklin-D.-Roosevelt*) has been making exquisite and expensive men's shoes for more than a century. "Nothing is too beautiful for feet" is Olga Berluti's motto; she even exposes her creations to the moonlight to give them an extra-special patina. One model is named after Andy Warhol; other famous clients of the past include the Duke of Windsor, Fred Astaire, and James Joyce.

Fodor'sChoice **Bruno Frisoni** (⊠*34 rue de Grenelle, 7ᵉ, St-Germain-des-Prés* ☎*01–42–*
★ *84–12–30* Ⓜ*St-Germain-des-Prés*) has an impressive pedigree, most lately as art director for Roger Vivier. His first boutique for women is lined with ultrasexy, ultrasophisticated shoes and bags in vivid colors. The vertiginous tapered heels, lean platforms, and delicately conceived flats mix glamour with a hint of S&M.

Castañer (⊠*264 rue Saint-Honoré, 1ᵉ, Louvre/Tuileries* ☎*01–53–45–96–12* Ⓜ*Palais-Royal/Musee du Louvre*) riffs on all the current trends in footwear to propel the traditional into the 21st century. Espadrille styles include mules, platforms, and traditional flats with ankle ties, in leather, linen, or silk. Some models head into evening with beading or sequins. Rubber-soled ankle boots and leather ballet flats are seasonal hits, along with à la mode straw or linen bags, and the most adorable sun hats this side of the Pyrénées.

★ **Christian Louboutin** (⊠*19 rue Jean-Jacques Rousseau, 1ᵉʳ, Beaubourg/Les Halles* ☎*01–42–36–05–31* Ⓜ*Palais-Royal* ⊠*38–40 rue*

RIVE GAUCHE

Ever since the '60s, when Yves Saint Laurent cashed in on the neighborhood's bohemian-artistic allure, the Rive Gauche has been synonymous with iconoclastic style.

All the major names in French fashion have since taken his lead, transforming the Left Bank into a bastion of Parisian chic. Trendsetters line the jumble of streets in the 6e arrondissement, around Rue Bonaparte, Rue du Four, Rue du Dragon, and Boulevard St-Germain, and tons of exciting boutiques border the charming streets near St. Sulpice. In the 7e arrondissement there is the Rue de Grenelle, the venerable, treasure-lined Rue des Saints Pères, Rue du Bac, and that jewel of a department store, Le Bon Marché. To see it all would take weeks; with a well-drawn-out plan, however, you can see quite a lot in an afternoon or two. There's always the option of doing what Parisians do best: stroll, observe, discover.

BEST TIME TO GO

Although Tuesday through Friday afternoons are recommended, this area covers enough ground never to seem too overcrowded, even on weekends.

BEST FIND FOR A SWEET TOOTH

Ladurée's stylish boxes alone are worth the purchase; filled with their legendary lighter-than-air *macarons*—in flavors like salted caramel, rose, or cassis-violet—they make a celestial offering.

You can take it with you! **Pierre Hermé**, Paris's star *pâtissier*, offers a scrumptious, zesty lemon cake dense enough to survive the trip home. Maybe.

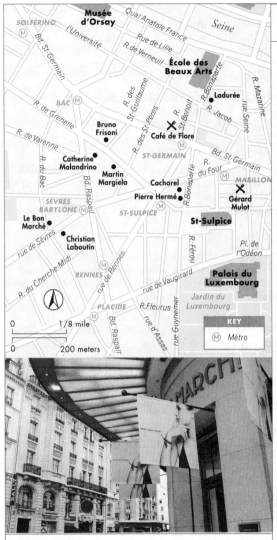

WHAT YOU'LL WANT

CLOTHES À LA MODE

Catherine Malandrino. Feminine dresses, jackets, and skirts go seamlessly from office to evening.

Isabel Marant. Body-caressing shapes in lush colors are perennial favorites.

Martin Margiela. You'll love wearing his soft jersey tops over tailored pants, or, for a little more oomph, the edgier designs.

MOTHERS & DAUGHTERS

Cacharel. An old favorite, with a stellar collection for chic moms and their winsome daughters.

Comptoir des Cotonniers. Comfortable, affordable, and superchic clothes make this boutique chain one of Paris's most popular.

Judith Lacroix. Gorgeous clothes for kids inspired moms who demanded a line of their own.

WELL-SHOD CHIC

Le Bon Marché. A one-stop shop for all the top names in footwear.

Bruno Frisoni. Alluring with more than a hint of naughtiness, each shoe is a work of art.

Christian Louboutin. Sensational, vertiginous styles take glamour (and you) to new heights.

16

REFUELING

With the Luxembourg Gardens nearby, pick up picnic savories and sweets from the excellent pâtisserie-traiteur-chocolatier **Gérard Mulot**. Try a yummy shrimp-salad sandwich or *paté en croute* topped off with a few delectable *macarons*.

If you prefer to be served (however haughtily), the illustrious **Café de Flore** offers better-than-average café fare with excellent opportunities for people-watching—inside and out.

de Grenelle, 7e, St-Germain-des-Prés ☎*01–42–22–33–07* Ⓜ*Sèvres Babylone*) shoes carry their own red carpet with them, in their trademark crimson soles. Whether tasseled, embroidered, or strappy, in Charvet silk or shiny patent leather, these heels are always perfectly balanced. No wonder they set off such legendary legs as Tina Turner's and Gwyneth Paltrow's.

Jimmy Choo (✉*34 av. Montaigne, 8e, Champs Elysées* ☎*01–47–23–03–39* Ⓜ*Franklin-D.-Roosevelt*) is the place for mile-high heels and strappy flats. Bags, evening clutches, and small leather items in metallics, reptile, and colorful canvas with leather accents are seasonal favorites. What more can be said that Sex in the City didn't?

K. Jacques (✉*16 rue Paveé, 4e, Le Marais* ☎*01–40–27–03–57* Ⓜ*St. Paul*) has shod everyone from Brigitte Bardot to Drew Barrymore. The St. Tropez–based maker of strappy flats has migrated to the big time while still keeping designs classic and comfortable. From gladiator-style to demure mules, metallics to neutrals, these perennial favorites never go out of style.

Michel Perry (✉*243 rue St-Honoré, 1er, Louvre/Tuileries* ☎*01–42–44–10–07* Ⓜ*Tuileries*) is known for his polished, slender, mile-high shoes. Napa leather and patent ankle boots in fire-engine red and supersexy python platforms with bags to match punctuate the collection.

Pierre Hardy (✉*156 Galerie de Valois, Palais Royal gardens, 1er, Louvre/Tuileries* ☎*01–42–60–59–75* Ⓜ*Palais Royal Musée du Louvre*) completes the triumvirate (with Frisoni and Louboutin) of anointed Paris shoe designers. Armed with a pedigree—Dior, Hermès, Balenciaga—Hardy opened his own boutique in 2003 and made serious waves. The shoes are unmistakable: sky-scraping platforms and wedges double as sculpture with their breathtaking details. His sensational bags, introduced in 2006, became instant classics.

Robert Clergerie (✉*318 av. Victor Hugo, 16e, Champs Elysées* ☎*01–45–01–81–30* Ⓜ*Charles de Gaulle Etoile* ✉*5 rue du Cherche-Midi, 6e, St-Germain-des-Prés* ☎*01–45–48–75–47* Ⓜ*St-Sulpice*) knows that the shoes make the woman. Styles combine visionary design, first-rate craftsmanship, and wearability with legendary staying power. Plus, they're still a relative bargain on this side of the Atlantic.

Rodolphe Ménudier (✉*14 rue de Castiglione, 1er, Louvre/Tuileries* ☎*01–42–60–86–27* Ⓜ*Tuileries*) spins a hard-edge sexiness, from its interior design—think sleek black windows, metal cupboards, and a wall covered in white crocodile leather—to its pointy-toe high heels. Stilettos with ankle straps? *Mais oui.*

★ **Roger Vivier** (✉*29 rue du Faubourg St-Honoré, 8e, Louvre/Tuileries* ☎*01–53–43–00–85* Ⓜ*Concorde*) was known for decades for his Pilgrim-buckle shoes and inventive heels, and his name is being resurrected through the creativity of über-Parisienne Inès de la Fressange and the expertise of shoe designer Bruno Frisoni. The results are brilliant: leather boots that mold to the calf perfectly, satin evening sandals, and square-toe pumps in crocodile are some of what you might find.

DISCOUNT

In-the-know Parisians flock to the République *quartier* to check out the luxury-shoe-lover-on-a-slender-budget boutiques on **Rue Meslay**. The discount stores are often jam-packed and the service is often rather dodgy, but for more than 50% off on last season's collections from the biggest names, it's well worth the visit.

L'Autre Boutique (✉ *42 rue de Grenelle, 7ᵉ, St-Germain-des-Prés* ☎ *01– 42–84–12–45* Ⓜ *Rue du Bac*) is a mixed bag with reliably great finds: among those unsellable gladiator numbers you might turn up delicate silvery-pink pumps; you have to look to make the finds. Season-old collections of Michel Perry shoes are half off; during sales the store practically gives them away. The staff is helpful and fun.

Mi-Prix (✉ *27 bd. Victor, 15ᵉ, Montparnasse* ☎ *01–48–28–42–48* Ⓜ *Porte de Versailles*) is a jumble of end-of-series designer shoes and accessories from the likes of Alexandra Neel, Michel Perry, Valentino, and Rodolph Ménudier, priced at up to 70% below retail.

SHOPPING ARCADES

16

Paris's 19th-century commercial arcades, called *passages,* are worth a visit for the sheer architectural splendor of their glass roofs, decorative pillars, and mosaic floors. In 1828 they numbered 137, of which only 24 are left. The major arcades are in the 1ᵉʳ and 2ᵉ arrondissements on the Rive Droite.

★ **Galerie Véro-Dodat** (✉ *19 rue Jean-Jacques Rousseau, 1ᵉʳ, Louvre/Tuileries* Ⓜ *Louvre*) was built in 1826. At what is now the Café de l'Epoque, the French writer Gérard de Nerval took his last drink before heading to Châtelet to hang himself. The gallery has painted ceilings and copper pillars and shops selling old-fashioned toys, contemporary art, and leather goods. It's best known, though, for its antiques stores.

Fodor's Choice ★ **Galerie Vivienne** (✉ *4 rue des Petits-Champs, 2ᵉ, Opéra/Grands Boulevards* Ⓜ *Bourse*), between the Bourse and the Palais-Royal, is home base for a range of interesting and luxurious shops as well as the lovely tearoom A Priori Thé and Cave Legrand, a terrific wineshop. Don't leave without checking out the Jean-Paul Gaultier boutique.

Passage du Grand-Cerf (✉ *145 rue St-Denis, 2ᵉ, Beaubourg/Les Halles* Ⓜ *Etienne Marcel*) has regained the interest of Parisians. La Parisette, a small boudoir-pink space at No. 1, sells fun accessories, and Marci Noum, at No. 4, riffs on street fashion. Silk bracelets, crystals, and charms can be nabbed at Eric & Lydie and Satellite.

Passage Jouffroy (✉ *12 bd. Montmartre, 9ᵉ, Grands Boulevards* Ⓜ *Grands Boulevards*) is full of shops selling toys, Oriental furnishings, and cinema books and posters. Try Pain d'Epices, at No. 29, for dollhouse decor, and Au Bonheur des Dames, at No. 39, for all things embroidery.

Passage des Panoramas (⊠*11 bd. Montmartre, 2ᵉ, Grands Boulevards* Ⓜ*Opéra/Grands Boulevards*), opened in 1800, is the oldest arcade extant; it's especially known for its stamp shops.

Passage Verdeau (⊠*4–6 rue de la Grange Batelière, 9ᵉ, Opéra/Grands Boulevards* Ⓜ*Grands Boulevards*), across the street from Passage Jouffroy, has shops carrying antique cameras, comic books, and engravings.

TOYS

Au Nain Bleu (⊠*5 bd. Malesherbes, 8ᵉ, Louvre/Tuileries* ☎*01–42–65–20—00* Ⓜ*Concorde*) is a breathtakingly high-priced wonderland of elaborate dollhouses, miniature sports cars, and hand-carved rocking horses.

Bonton (⊠*82 rue de Grenelle, 7ᵉ, St-Germain-des-Prés* ☎*01–44–39–09–20* Ⓜ*Rue du Bac*) comes from the creators of Bonpoint; check out the selection of music instruments for kids.

Pain d'Epices (⊠*29 Passage Jouffroy, 9ᵉ, Grands Boulevards* ☎*01–47–70–08–68* Ⓜ*Grands Boulevards*) is a thoroughly enchanting shop offering anything you can imagine for the French home (and garden) in miniature, including Lilliputian croissants, wine decanters, Aubusson rugs, and minuscule instruments in their cases. Build-it-yourself dollhouses include a 17th-century town house and a *boulangerie* storefront. Upstairs are do-it-yourself teddy bear kits, lifelike marionettes, and classic toys.

Where to Eat

Le Grand Colbert Brasserie near Palais Royale

WORD OF MOUTH

"Three tastes that I enjoyed on my first trip and always look for now: pain au chocolat (chocolate croissant); chocolat aux poire (chocolate cake with pears);and croque monsieur (grilled cheese sandwich)."
—Dejais

Updated by
Rosa Jackson

A new wave of culinary confidence is running through one of the world's great food cities and spilling over both banks of the Seine. Whether cooking up *grand-mère*'s roast chicken and *riz au lait* or placing a whimsical hat of cotton candy atop wild-strawberry-and-rose ice cream, Paris chefs are breaking free from the tyranny of tradition and following their passions.

Emblematic of this movement is Alain Senderens's eponymous restaurant on the Place de la Madeleine. Swapping turbot for tempura, the renowned chef has transformed what was Lucas Carton, a traditional haute-cuisine restaurant, into something simple and fresh, and he slashed prices so that a dinner for two costs €100 instead of €400. And, in an unprecedented display of radicalism, he tried to give back all three of his prestigious Michelin stars (in 2007 the Michelin gave him two stars).

But self-expression is not the only driving force behind the current changes. A traditional high-end restaurant can be prohibitively expensive to operate. As a result, more casual bistros and cafés, which often have lower operational costs and higher profit margins, have become attractive businesses for even top chefs.

For tourists, this development can only be good news, since it makes the cooking of geniuses such as Joël Robuchon and Pierre Gagnaire more accessible (even if these star chefs rarely cook in their lower-priced restaurants).

Like the chefs themselves, Paris diners are breaking away—albeit cautiously—from tradition. New restaurants and rapidly multiplying sandwich bars recognize that not everyone wants a three-course blow-out every time they dine out. And because Parisians are more widely traveled than in the past, many ethnic restaurants—notably the best North African, Vietnamese/Laotian, Chinese, Spanish, and Japanese spots—are making fewer concessions to French tastes, resulting in far better food.

PLANNER

Dining Strategy

Where should we eat? With thousands of Paris eateries competing for your attention, it may seem like a daunting question. But fret not—our expert writers and editors have done the legwork. The 120-plus selections here represent the best this city has to offer. Search our "Best Bets" for top recommendations by price, cuisine, and experience; sample local flavor in the neighborhood features; or find a review quickly in the alphabetical listings. Delve in, and enjoy!

Reservations

Restaurant staff will nearly always greet you with the phrase *"Avez-vous réservé?"* (Have you reserved?) and a confident *"Oui"* is the best answer, even in a neighborhood bistro. Most wine bars do not take reservations; reservations are also unnecessary for brasserie and café meals at odd hours.

Children

Some restaurants provide booster seats, but don't count on them: be sure to ask when you confirm your reservation.

Tipping & Taxes

According to French law, prices must include tax and tip (*service compris or prix nets*), but pocket change left on the table in cafés, or an additional 5% in better restaurants, is always appreciated. Beware of bills stamped SERVICE NOT INCLUDED in English or restaurants slyly using American-style credit-card slips, hoping that you'll be confused and add the habitual 15% tip.

Hours

Paris restaurants generally serve food from noon to about 2 PM and from 7:30 or 8 PM to about 11 PM. Brasseries have longer hours and often serve all day and late into the evening; some are open 24 hours. Surprisingly, many restaurants close on Saturday as well as Sunday, and Monday closings are also frequent. July and August are the most common months for annual closings, but Paris in August is not quite the culinary wasteland it used to be.

Menus

All establishments must post menus outside so they're available to look over before you enter. Most restaurants have two basic types of menu: à la carte and fixed price (*prix fixe, le menu, or la formule*). Although it limits your choices, the prix fixe is usually the best value. If you feel like indulging, the *menu dégustation* (tasting menu), consisting of numerous small courses, allows for a wide sampling of a chef's offerings. *See the Menu Guide at the back of this book for guidance with common French menu items.*

What to Wear

Casual dress is acceptable at all but the fanciest restaurants—this usually means stylish sportswear, which might be a bit dressier than in the United States. When in doubt, leave the T-shirts and sneakers behind. If an establishment requires jacket and tie, it's noted in the review.

French Restaurant Types

Bistro: The broadest category, a bistro can be a simple, relaxed restaurant serving traditional fare or a chic hot spot where dinner costs more than €50 per person. The bistro menu, often written on a chalkboard, is fairly limited and usually changes with the season.

Brasserie: More informal than a bistro, the brasserie is large, lively, and almost always equipped with a bar. Ideal for relatively quick meals, it often specializes in Alsatian fare, like *choucroute garnie*, a mixed meat dish with sauerkraut and potatoes.

Café: Often an informal neighborhood hangout, the café may also be a showplace attracting a well-heeled crowd. A limited menu of sandwiches and simple dishes is usually available throughout the day. Beware of the prices: a half bottle of mineral water can cost €4.

French Fusion: The French Fusion restaurant possesses discernable influences of both French cuisine and the cuisine of one other region or country.

Haute French: Ambitious and expensive, the Haute French restaurant is helmed by a pedigreed chef who prepares multicourse meals to be remembered.

Modern French: Although not superexpensive or pretentious, the Modern French restaurant boasts a creative menu that showcases a wide span of culinary influences.

Prices

You'll be lucky to find a good bistro meal for €25 or less, even at lunch, so consider economizing on some meals to have more to spend on the others. Slurping inexpensive Japanese noodles on Rue Ste-Anne or having a picnic in a park at lunch will save euros for dinner. Some visitors rent apartments with kitchens, which allow them to shop at the city's wonderful markets.

What It Costs

AT DINNER

¢	$	$$	$$$	$$$$
under €11	€11–€16	€17–€22	€23–€30	Over €30

Price per person for a main course at dinner, including tax (19.6%) and service; note that if a restaurant offers only prix-fixe (set-price) meals, it has been given the price category that reflects the full prix-fixe price.

In this Chapter

17

Smoking

Many Parisians are accustomed to smoking before, during, and after meals, but in January 2008, the national smoking ban was extended to restaurants, bars, and cafés. Many establishments have compensated by adding covered terraces for smokers, but inside, the air is much clearer.

Wine

Most sommeliers are knowledgeable about their lists and will suggest what is appropriate after you've made your tastes and budget known. Simpler spots serve wine in carafes (*en carafe*, or *en pichet*). Many restaurants now sell wine by the glass, but beware of the price.

BEST BETS FOR PARIS DINING

With thousands of restaurants to choose from, how will you decide where to eat? Fodor's writers and editors have selected their favorite restaurants by price, cuisine, and experience in the lists below. You can also search by neighborhood for excellent eating experiences—just peruse the following pages that contain spotlights on specific neighborhoods. Full reviews are listed alphabetically later in the body of this chapter.

FODOR'S CHOICE ★

Les Ambassadeurs, $$$$

L'Ardoise, $$

Aux Lyonnais, $$–$$$

Le Comptoir du Relais Saint-Germain, $$$

Guy Savoy, $$$$

Higuma, ¢

Mon Vieil Ami, $–$$

Rech, $$$

Ribouldingue, $$$

La Table Lauriston, $$–$$$

Le Violon d'Ingres, $$$$

By Price

¢

L'As du Fallafel

Dong Huong

La Ferme Opéra

Higuma

$

L'Ardoise

La Bourse ou la Vie

Le Café Constant

Le Pré Verre

$$

Mon Vieil Ami

Ribouldingue

Le Temps au Temps

Willi's Wine Bar

$$$

L'Atelier de Joël Robuchon

Aux Lyonnais

Drouant

La Table Lauriston

Le Violon d'Ingres

$$$$

Les Ambassadeurs

L'Arpège

L'Astrance

Guy Savoy

Restaurant Pierre Gagnaire

By Type

BISTRO

Au Bon Accueil, $$$–$$$$

Benoît, $$$–$$$$

Café Constant, $

Josephine Chez Dumonet, $$$

Le Soleil, $$–$$$

La Table Lauriston, $$–$$$

BRASSERIE

Au Boeuf Couronné, $$$

Bofinger, $$–$$$

Brasserie de l'Ile Saint-Louis, $$–$$$

La Coupole, $–$$$

Le Grand Colbert, $$–$$$

CAFÉ

Café de Flore, $$

Café Marly, $$

CHINESE, $$

La Chine Massena, $$

Mirama, ¢–$

Wok Cooking, $$

CARIBBEAN

La Table de Babette $$$–$$$$

FRENCH FUSION

Le 144 Petrossian, $$$–$$$$

Hiramatsu, $$$$

Il Vino, $$$$

Stella Maris, $$$$

INDIAN

Kastoori, ¢

JAPANESE

Higuma, ¢

Kifune, $$–$$$

Yen, $–$$

Zen, $–$$

LATIN

Unico, $$–$$$

MIDDLE EASTERN

L'As du Fallafel, ¢–$

Chez Marianne, $–$$

MODERN

L'Atelier de Joël Robuchon, $$$–$$$$
Chez les Anges, $$$
Drouant, $$–$$$
La Famille, $–$$
Ze Kitchen Galerie, $–$$

NORTH AFRICAN

Chez Omar, $$
Le Martel, $–$$

SEAFOOD

Huîtrerie Régis, $$
L'Huîtrier, $$–$$$
Rech $$$

SPANISH

Fogón St-Julien, $–$$

VEGETARIAN

La Bastide Odeon, $$
L'Arpège?, $$$$
L'As du Fallafel, ¢–$
La Butte Chaillot, $$–$$$
Maceo

VIETNAMESE

Dong Huong, ¢

By Experience

CHILD-FRIENDLY

L'As du Fallafel, ¢–$
Bofinger, $$–$$$
La Coupole, $$–$$$
Rose Bakery, $
Le Troquet, $$$–$$$$

DESSERT

Alain Ducasse au Plaza Athénée, $$$$
Les Ambassadeurs, $$$$
Josephine Chez Dumonet, $$$
Restaurant Pierre Gagnaire, $$$$
Taillevent, $$$$

DINNER PRIX FIXE

Bistrot des Deux Théâtres, $$$$
Ribouldingue, $–$$
Le Troquet, $$$–$$$$
Le Vaudeville, $$–$$$
Villa Victoria, $–$$

EXPENSE ACCOUNT

Alain Ducasse au Plaza Athénée, $$$$
La Fermette Marbeuf, $$–$$$
Restaurant Pierre Gagnaire, $$$$

GOOD FOR GROUPS

Bofinger, $$–$$$
Chez Jenny, $$–$$$
La Chine Massena, $$
Les Saveurs de Flora, $$$$

GREAT VIEW

Le Georges, $$–$$$
Lapérouse, $$$–$$$$
Maison Blanche, $$$$
La Tour d'Argent, $$$$

HOT SPOT

L'Atelier de Joël Robuchon, $$$–$$$$
La Famille, $–$$
Le Murano, $$$–$$$$
Le Violon d'Ingres, $$$$

LATE-NIGHT

Au Pied de Cochon, $$–$$$
Bofinger, $$–$$$
La Coupole, $$–$$$
Julien, $$–$$$
Le Vaudeville, $$–$$$

LOTS OF LOCALS

Josephine Chez Dumonet, $$$
La Ferrandaise, $$–$$$
Le Petit Rétro, $–$$
Thoumieux, $$$
Unico, $$–$$$

LUNCH PRIX FIXE

La Boulangerie, $$
Le Pré Verre, $
Le Repaire de Cartouche, $$
Taillevent, $$$$
Willi's Wine Bar, $–$$

MOST ROMANTIC

Chez Toinette, $–$$
Le Pré Catelan, $$$$
Lapérouse, $$–$$$
Restaurant du Palais-Royal, $$$
La Tour d'Argent, $$$$

NEWCOMERS

Afaria, $$
Breizh Café, ¢
Les Cocottes de Christian Constant, $
Il Vino, $$$$
Rech, $$$

OUTDOOR DINING

Au Bourguignon du Marais, $$$
Brasserie de l'Ile St-Louis, $$–$$$
Le Georges, $$–$$$
Restaurant du Palais Royal, $$$
Le Square Trousseau, $$–$$$

WINE LIST

Chai 33, $–$$
Josephine Chez Dumonet, $$$
Macéo, $$$
Le Pré Verre, $
Le Repaire de Cartouche, $$

YOUNG CROWD

La Famille, $–$$
La Grande Armée, $$$–$$$$
Le Murano, $$$–$$$$
Unico, $$–$$$

17

6e, 14e ARRONDISSEMENTS
ST-GERMAIN & MONTPARNASSE

Small bistros are moving into the spotlight in St-Germain, and crêpe stands, fish restaurants, and oyster bars attest to the Breton influence around Montparnasse.

Whether you're sipping rich hot chocolate at Les Deux Magots, diving into a platter of *choucroute garnie* at La Coupole or slurping *fines de claires* at the pristine new oyster bar Régis, it's hard not to feel part of the café culture in St-Germain and Montparnasse. Along the broad boulevards you can find some of the city's classic brasseries. As much fun as these are for their storied settings and buzzy atmospheres, some of the area's best food is found at small bistros on narrow side streets. St-Germain is enjoying a revival as a foodie haunt, with Yves Camdeborde's Le Comptoir du Relais Saint-Germain as the perfect example of the kind of market-inspired bistro that Parisians (and foreigners) adore. For a change of pace, try freshly made *galettes* (buckwheat crêpes) washed down with dry cider at one of Boulevard du Montparnasse's many *crêperies*.

BRINY BLISS

Ever since the first trains from Brittany brought oyster-loving settlers to Montparnasse, the neighborhood has had a proud seafood tradition. The best oysters come from Normandy, Brittany, or Marennes-Oléron on the Atlantic coast. The knobbly shelled *creuses* are more common than the rounder *plates*, which are beloved by connoisseurs. Oysters can be dressed with vinegar and shallots, but a squeeze of lemon—or nothing at all—is probably the best accompaniment. Scoop the raw oyster from its shell with a small fork, slurp the juice, and chew a little before swallowing the taste of the sea.

CLASSIC CAFÉ ITEMS

The Item	Where to get it	Why there?
Omelet	Café de Flore (172 Bd. St-Germain, 01–45–48–55–26), the last classic café that attracts genuine Left Bank intellectuals.	The omelet arrives pale on the outside and slightly runny within – i.e., perfect. Try ham and cheese or, for a splurge, crabmeat.
Chocolat chaud	Les Deux Magots (6 pl. St-Germain des Prés, 01–45–49–31–29), which overlooks the ancient St-Germain des Prés church.	Made with milk and pure chocolate, this hot chocolate is served in a lovely white porcelain pitcher.
Choucroute garnie	Brasserie Lipp (151 bd. St-Germain, 01–45–48–53–91), one of Hemingway's (many) favorites, still favored among some literati.	The "choucroute Lipp" includes mounds of sauerkraut topped with a pork knuckle and smoked sausage.

RESTAURANTS IN THIS AREA

BISTRO

La Bastide Odéon, $$
Bistrot d'Hubert, $$$
Boucherie Roulière, $–$$
Les Bouquinistes, $$$–$$$$
La Cerisaie, $$
Chez Maître Paul, $$–$$$
Le Comptoir du Relais Saint-Germain, $$$
La Ferrandaise, $–$$
Le Timbre, $–$$

BRASSERIE

Alcazar, $$$
La Coupole, $$–$$$
Le Bouillon Racine, $–$$
Brasserie Lipp, $$
Le Dôme, $$$

CAFÉ

Café de Flore, $$

HAUTE FRENCH

Hélène Darroze, $$$$

JAPANESE

Yen, $–$$

MODERN FRENCH

L'Atelier de Joël Robuchon, $$$–$$$$
Gaya Rive Gauche, $$$$

SEAFOOD

Huîtrerie Régis, $$

17

PIQUE-NIQUE IN THE PARC

Everything you need for the perfect Luxembourg gardens picnic is just minutes away from the park. For cheese, **Fromagerie Quatrehomme** (62 rue de Sèvres, 01–47–34–33–45). For cured meats and sparkling water, **Bon Marché's Grande Epicerie** (38 rue de Sèvres, 01–44–39–81–00). For sourdough bread, **Boulangerie Poilâne** (8 rue du Cherche-Midi, 01–45–48–42–59). For something sinfully sweet, **Pâtissier Pierre Hermé** (72 rue Bonaparte, 01–43–54–47–77).

5e, 13e ARRONDISSEMENTS
LATIN QUARTER, GOBELINS & THE ISLANDS

Whether you're seeking a cheap Chinese eatery or a table for two at La Tour d'Argent, the Latin Quarter dishes up something for every taste and budget.

Thanks to its student population, the Latin Quarter caters to those on a budget with kebab shops, crêpe stands, Asian fast-food joints, and no-nonsense bistros. Look beyond the pedestrian streets such as Rue de la Huchette and Rue Mouffetard for less touristy eateries preferred by locals. As you might expect in an area known for its *gauche caviar* (wealthy intellectuals who vote Socialist), the Latin Quarter brims with atmospheric places to linger over a tiny cup of black coffee. Top-notch bistros lurk in the off-the-beaten-track 13^e arrondissement, which is also home to the city's most authentic Chinese, Vietnamese, and Laotian restaurants along Avenue d'Ivry. Wander across the Seine to the Ile St-Louis for a meal in a long-established brasserie or classy bistro.

SECRET CELLAR

Few restaurants in Paris have a more storied history than the Seine-side **Tour d'Argent** *(15 quai de la Tournelle, 01–43–54–23–31)*. It opened in 1780, only to be burned down nine years later by the same Revolutionaries who set the Bastille ablaze. When Paris was occupied by the Germans during World War II, La Tour became a popular dining destination for Nazi officers. Little did they know that the restaurant's laughably large stock of wine was safely hidden behind a brick wall. Today, the wine cellar contains more than 500,000 bottles of the world's finest wines.

UNCOVERING THE QUARTIER

DODGING THE "FAUX BISTRO"

Is it a genuine bistro? It's often hard to tell. Tourist traps can seem thoroughly charming until the food arrives. The Latin Quarter is dangerous rip-off territory, but there are some sure bets: around Notre-Dame, seek out **Le Pré Verre** *(8 rue Thénard, 01–43–54–59–47)*, where Philippe Delacourcelle tinkers successfully with Asian spices, and the recently opened Lyonnais-style bistro **Ribouldingue** *(10 rue St-Julien Le Pauvre, 01–46–33–98–80)*, where the €27 prix fixe is one of the area's best bargains. You'll also find a few honest, old-fashioned bistros like **Au Moulin à Vent ("Chez Henri")** *(20 rue des Fossés St-Bernard, 01–43–54–99–37)* and **La Rôtisserie du Beaujolais** *(19 quai de la Tournelle, 01–43–54–17–47)*, an annex of La Tour d'Argent. Tread carefully on the Ile St-Louis, where star Alsatian chef Antoine Westermann's **Mon Vieil Ami** *(69 rue St-Louis en l'Ile, 01–40–46–01–35)* is the most reliable choice.

THE ANATOMY OF A TABAC

In their primary function, selling cigarettes, *tabacs* play an essential role in the lives of most Parisians, but they're also indispensable to those who don't smoke. At a small counter where customers pick up Gitanes or Marlboros you can buy métro or lottery tickets, phone cards, batteries, and chewing gum. Next to this counter is a bar perfect for a quick drink, like the one Audrey Tautou imbibed at the **Le Verre à Pied** *(118 bis, rue Mouffetard)* in the film *Amélie*. Tabacs often sell newspapers, which you can read while perched at the bar sipping an *express* (strong black coffee). Food is surprisingly palatable in *tabacs*—expect anything from a *jambon-beurre* (a ham sandwich) to hearty dishes such as boeuf Bourguignon. Many *tabacs*, like **Le Québec** *(45 rue Bonaparte, 01–43–26–00–11)*, attract a variety of regulars, from moneyed businessmen to *les sans-abri* (the homeless), who joke and drink together into the wee hours. A reserved bartender in a tattered tuxedo vest often looks on, compulsively wiping beer glasses.

RESTAURANTS IN THIS AREA

BISTRO
Anacréon, $$$
Au Petit Marguery, $$
Le Buisson Ardent, $$–$$$
Chez René, $$–$$$
Lapérouse, $$$–$$$$
L'Ourcine, $
Ribouldingue, $–$$
Toustem, $$$
BRASSERIE
Le Balzar, $$
Brasserie de l'Ile St-Louis, $$–$$$
CHINESE
Mirama, ¢–$
HAUTE FRENCH
La Tour d'Argent, $$$$
MODERN FRENCH
Mon Vieil Ami, $–$$
Le Pré Verre, $
Ze Kitchen Galerie, $–$$
SPANISH
Fogòn St-Julien, $–$$

17

3e, 4e, 12e, 11e, 20e, ARROND.
MARAIS, BASTILLE, NATION

The center of Jewish and gay life in Paris, the Marais serves up the best falafel in town and some great bistro fare, too. Farther east, the Bastille area has attracted more than its share of gifted young chefs.

The once run-down Marais is now the epitome of chic, but you can still find reminders of its down-to-earth past along Rue des Rosiers, where falafel shops and Eastern European delis jostle with designer boutiques. For fantastic people-watching and food to match, pop into Le Petit Fer à Cheval or L'Etoile Manquante on Rue Vieille-du-Temple. Ambitious restaurants are few and far between in the Marais, but Le Dôme du Marais combines a stunning setting with great contemporary cooking, and the new Breizh Café attracts many with its inexpensive and authentic galettes (buckwheat crêpes) made with quality ingredients. The bistro scene gets interesting east of the Bastille, where lower rents have encouraged young chefs to set up shop. Around Père Lachaise, the selection thins, but wander a little farther to multicultural Belleville to find an intriguing mix of Chinese and North African eateries.

TARTE TATIN

For the perfect *tarte tatin*, which is like an upside-down apple pie, take a seat at the horse-shoe-shape bar of **Le Petit Fer à Cheval** (*30 rue Vieille-du-Temple, 01–42–72–47–47*). The restaurant's recipe calls for 11 pounds of juicy Gala apples, which produce a buttery, caramelized tarte that is served warm and pairs perfectly with a glass of hot wine. The *tarte* was first discovered by mistake in the 19th century at the Hôtel Tatin in Lamotte-Beuvron—the product of a botched apple pie recipe. It can be made with other fruit—like pineapple or pears—but nothing beats the classic, faithfully reproduced at this Marais café.

MARAIS NOSHES

	The obvious choice.	Don't forget.
L'As du Fallafel 34 rue de Rosiers	The *fallafel spécial*, a packed pita with chickpea and herb balls, eggplant, harissa, hummus and tahini.	Napkins and a glass of fresh-squeezed lemonade help tame this greasy feast.
Chez Marianne 2 rue Hospitalières St-Gervais	Chopped liver. Who'd have thought that chicken livers and onion fried in melted goose fat could ever taste this good?	A more genteel version of pastrami than the slabs of fatty meat you'll find back home, it'll satisfy any deli devotee.
Korcarz 29 rue de Rosiers	A loaf of shiny, sweet, and delicious challah. For best results, take the bread back to your hotel room and dip in salt and honey.	A *pletzl*, a small onion roll that—surprisingly—tastes great with jam for breakfast.

RESTAURANTS IN THIS AREA

BISTRO
L'Ambassade d'Auvergne, $–$$
Au Bourguignon du Marais, $$$
Au Trou Gascon, $$$–$$$$
Benoît, $$$–$$$$
Le Dôme du Marais, $$
L'Oulette, $$$–$$$$
Le Passage des Carmagnoles, $–$$
Le Repaire de Cartouche, $$
Le Square Trousseau, $$–$$$
Le Temps au Temps, $$
BRASSERIE
Bofinger, $$–$$$
CHINESE
Wok, $$
ISRAELI
L'As du Fallafel, ¢–$
ITALIAN
Sardegna a Tavola, $$$
LATIN AMERICAN
Unico, $$–$$$
MIDDLE EASTERN
Chez Marianne, $–$$
MODERN FRENCH
Breizh Café, ¢
Le Murano, $$$–$$$$

17

FANTASTIQUE FOUR: THE RUE PAUL BERT

This side street between Bastille and Nation is home to four local favorites. **Bistrot Paul Bert** (*18 rue Paul Bert, 01-43-72-24-01*) boasts bistro classics, and its seafood annex, **L'Ecailler du Bistrot** (*22 rue Paul Bert, 01-43-72-76-77*), serves exemplary oysters. The creative **Le Temps au Temps** (*13 rue Paul Bert, 01-43-79-63-40*) is booked nearly every night. And, the Argentinian **Unico** (*15 rue Paul Bert, 01-43-67-68-08*) draws hungry hordes for its charcoal-grilled steaks.

18ᵉ, 19ᵉ, 10ᵉ ARRONDISSEMENTS
MONTMARTRE, CANAL ST-MARTIN, NORTHEAST PARIS

Perched above central Paris, Montmartre is buzzing with a hip vibe, and cutting-edge cafés are springing up along the banks of the Canal St-Martin.

Idyllic as the portrayal of Montmartre might seem in Jean-Pierre Jeunet's film *Amélie*, it's surprisingly close to reality. One of the most desirable areas in Paris, Montmartre seamlessly blends the trendy and the traditional. Less picturesque is the neighborhood around Gare du Nord and Gare de l'Est, but you can still find classic brasseries and tucked-away bistros, as well as the city's most authentic Indian restaurants. Head over to the up-and-coming Canal St-Martin to watch Parisian "*bobos*," or bohemian bourgeois, in action. The area is home to fashion designers, artists, and media folk who make the most of the waterside cafés on sunny days. Restaurants are sparse in the undiscovered Buttes Chaumont area, but you won't have to worry about stumbling onto a tourist rip-off.

GARE GRUB

If you're catching the Eurostar at Gare du Nord, it's worth planning ahead to fit in one last feast. Across the street from the train station, **Terminus Nord** (*23 rue de Dunkerque, 01–42–85–05–15*) is a classic Art Deco brasserie where you can treat yourself to a seafood platter, bouillabaisse, or *sole meunière* before indulging in another house specialty, crêpes Suzette (flambéed in Grand Marnier). Just a few blocks farther, try the acclaimed **Chez Casimir** (*6 rue Belzunce, 01–48–78–28–80*), run by the Breton chef Thierry Breton (above).

CANAL-SIDE CAFÉS

More laid-back than the Seine with its vehicle-clogged *quais,* the Canal St-Martin attracts artsy young professionals who scorn the self-consciously elegant Left Bank. Its once-vibrant live music scene has been quelled somewhat in the last few years by the city's noise restrictions, but that hasn't made the cafés any less entertaining. At the scruffy, long-established **La Patache** *(60 rue de Lancry, 01–42–08–14–35),* the owner provides scraps of paper at each table for note writing, in case customers feel too coy to speak to each other. Bohemian institution **Chez Adel** *(10 rue de la Grange aux Belles, 01–42–08–24–61)* holds live concerts Tuesday to Saturday and avant-garde theater on Sunday. The café of choice on the water is **Chez Prune** *(36 rue Beaurepaire, 10th, 01–42–41–30–47),* whose terrace is overrun with locals as soon as a ray of sunshine emerges.

RESTAURANTS IN THIS AREA

BISTRO
Bistrot des Deux Théâtres, $$$$
Chez Toinette, $–$$
Le Ch'ti Catalan, $–$$
Velly, $–$$
BRASSERIE
La Mascotte, $$–$$$$
BRITISH
Rose Bakery, $
INDIAN
Kastoori, ¢
MODERN FRENCH
La Famille, $–$$

17

THE "NEW MONTMARTRE"

At the Montmartre restaurant **La Famille** *(41 rue des Trois Frères, 01–42–52–11–12),* a DJ spins records in the small, loft-like space while diners puzzle over dishes such as "foie gras milk shake with fresh, powdered, and popped corn." La Famille is typical of the "new Montmartre," which stands in stark contrast to the area's ancient cobbled streets. The district's hip young population occupies the area, perfectly representing 21st-century Paris: nostalgic yet forward thinking. **Café Burq** *(6 rue Burq, 01–42–52–81–27)* is a popular, slightly less ambitious Montmartre hangout. Owned by an architect and an actor, it buzzes with a fashionable crowd that comes for the 1970s décor but also for the satisfying bistro fare. On the other side of the *Butte Montmartre,* the friendly **Café Arrosé** *(123 rue Caulaincourt, 01–42–57–14–30)* proves that even this once-sleepy part of Montmartre is coming to life.

8ᵉ, 16ᵉ, 17ᵉ ARRONDISSEMENTS
CHAMPS-ELYSÉES & WESTERN PARIS

Style often wins out over substance around the Champs-Elysées, but a handful of luxury restaurants continue to defy fashion.

Perma-tans and Botox are de rigueur at fashionable restaurants near the Champs-Elysées, where the St-Tropez set picks at dishes with names like "le tigre qui pleure," the weeping tiger, a Thai-style beef dish. Yet this part of Paris is also home to many of the city's most ambitious chefs, whose restaurants are surrounded by palatial hotels, bourgeois apartments, embassies, and luxury boutiques. Some, such as Eric Frechon at Le Bristol, offer sophisticated updates of French classics, whereas others, like Pierre Gagnaire, constantly push culinary boundaries in the manner of a mad scientist. A few solid bistros survive here, notably the Art Deco Savy. Unlike the uniformly chic 16ᵉ, the 17ᵉ arrondissement has its bourgeois and its bohemian sides. Head over to Batignolles, where an organic market takes place on Saturday, to discover up-and-coming neighborhood bistros.

SPOON-FED

Haute cuisine aside, the Champs-Elysées was something of a restaurant wasteland until Alain Ducasse opened his fusion bistro **Spoon, Food & Wine** (*14 rue Marignan, 01–40–76–34–44*). Ten years later, countless fashionable restaurants have come and gone—Nobu among the defunct—while Spoon has endured. In 2006, the restaurant received a makeover, but its acclaimed menu has not changed dramatically since the beginning. The secret to Spoon's success? Ducasse tacks on a few standards like steak tartare to his mix-and-match, continent-hopping formula. Bubble-gum ice cream, anyone?

LUXE FOR LESS

Hotel Dining Deals
And what they're worth

What if you want to taste the good life on a more modest budget? A dinner for two at one of Paris's superexpensive hotel restaurants like Les Ambassadeurs could easily cost as much your plane ticket. But high prices don't mean you can't catch a glimpse of the gilt. To experience haute hotel cuisine, try our tips for keeping your budget intact.

Breakfast at Les Ambassadeurs, Le Crillon: €47

What you get: An extravagant breakfast buffet (7:30–10 [am]; open to the public weekdays; hotel guests only Saturday and Sunday) amid the Italian marble and Baccarat crystal of an 18th-century ballroom. It's haute cuisine meets all-you-can-eat in an over-the-top setting.

What you could've bought: one ticket to the Disneyland Resort Paris (not including transportation to the park).

Champagne at the Bar Vendôme, Le Ritz: €20

What you get: A glass of Cuvée Ritz Brut in the lush garden of the Bar Vendôme, where a harpist plays in the afternoon and a pianist takes over later on.

You could've bought: Two sodas in a St-Germain café.

Lunch at the Hôtel Bristol: €90

What you get: A four-course meal at the famously discreet Bristol, where the jet set saunters through the lobby bar. If this seems like a lot for a luxe lunch, consider that it's not difficult to spend more than €50 a head in a nearby bistro.

You could've bought: Lunch for two at the kitschy Nos Ancêtres Les Gauloises, a Gallic fantasyland on Ile St-Louis where tourists flock by the busload and foie gras is served in buckets.

Nightcap at the Four Seasons' George V: €24

What you get: A late-night cocktail (maybe a cognac?) at the George V's cozy bar. What would be an indefensible splurge at home is almost a must for rounding out a romantic evening.

You could've bought: A disposable camera at a kiosk by the Sacré-Coeur.

RESTAURANTS IN THIS AREA

BISTRO
Au Petit Colombier, $$$–$$$$
Au Petit Verdot du 17ᵉ, $$–$$$
Chez Savy, $$–$$$,
Dominique Bouchet, $$$–$$$$
Le Graindorge, $$–$$$
BRASSERIE
La Fermette Marbeuf 1900, $$–$$$
La Grande Armée, $$$–$$$$
La Maison de l'Aubrac, $$–$$$
CARIBBEAN
La Table de Babette, $$$–$$$$
FRENCH FUSION
Stella Maris, $$$$
HAUTE FRENCH
Alain Ducasse au Plaza Athénée, $$$$
Les Ambassadeurs, $$$$
Le Bristol, $$$$
Le Cinq, $$$$
Guy Savoy, $$$$
Ledoyen, $$$$
Restaurant Pierre Gagnaire, $$$$
Les Saveurs de Flora, $$$$,
La Table du Lancaster, $$$$
Taillevent, $$$$
JAPANESE
Kifune, $$–$$$
MODERN FRENCH
Maison Blanche, $$$$
Market, $$$–$$$$
Spoon, Food & Wine, $$$–$$$$
SEAFOOD
Rech, $$$

17

7ᵉ, 15ᵉ, ARRONDISSEMENTS
TOUR EIFFEL & INVALIDES

Lively bistros and daring contemporary restaurants bring unexpected exuberance to the otherwise sedate streets around the Eiffel Tower and in the sprawling, residential 15ᵉ.

Eerily quiet as it might sometimes seem, the 7ᵉ arrondissement has a food-loving population of locals and tourists who pack its best restaurants nightly. Since money is rarely an object in this area, you'll find everything from top-notch contemporary restaurants—L'Arpège, 144 Petrossian, Gaya Rive Gauche, and L'Atelier de Joël Robuchon—to nostalgic bistros like Thoumieux and Le Café Constant, which appeal to aristocratic residents with comfort-food cravings. The 15ᵉ arrondissement is known for quaint eateries that provide great value for the money. Even its unlovely outer reaches are filled with warm bistros like L'Os à Moelle and Afaria. Explore the little-known area around Avenue Emile Zola to find the city's best Middle Eastern restaurants.

JOYEUX JOËL

Tomato jelly topped with avocado purée? Thin-crusted mackerel tart? One of the best things about eating at **L'Atelier de Joël Robuchon** *(5 rue Montalembert, 01-42-22-56-56)* is your position on the U-shape bar, which encourages you to share opinions—or even a bite—of this cutting-edge fare with your neighbor. Creative small plates, like a flavor-packed little tower of roasted eggplant, zucchini, and tomato layered with buffalo mozzarella, or smoked foie gras and caramelized eel, make it clear that L'Atelier really is an artist's workshop.

CULINARY TRENDSETTERS

THE LEEK—C'EST CHIC

Vegetarianism was so uncommon in Paris that star chef Alain Passard caused a sensation when he declared a few years ago that he was bored with red meat and would be focusing on vegetables and fish. True to his word, Passard established a small farm outside Paris where he grows heirloom vegetables that are whizzed to his restaurant **L'Arpège** *(84 rue Varenne, 01–45–51–47–33)* by high-speed train. Customers pay the price; a simple yet sensational beet dish costs €45. Though Paris is hardly a vegetarian paradise, Passard's initiative seems to have rubbed off on other chefs in the 7ᵉ. **Le Violon d'Ingres** *(135 rue St-Dominique, 01–45–55–15–05)*, **L'Atelier de Joël Robuchon** *(5 rue Montalembert, 01–42–22–56–56)*, and **Le 144 Petrossian** *(18 bc. De La Tour–Maubourg, 01–44–11–32–32)* all cater, with imagination, to vegetarians.

A CONSTANT CONNECTION

During the 1980s Christian Constant trained a group of young chefs at the Hôtel Crillon who would go on to open their own trendsetting bistros, among them Yves Camdeborde (Le Comptoir), Christian Etchebest (Le Troquet), and Rodolphe Paquin (Le Repaire de Cartouche). Despite cherishing his mentor role, Constant still has a thriving career of his own. In 2006 he did away with the lobster dishes and wall-to-wall carpeting at his **Le Violon d'Ingres** *(135 rue St-Dominique, 01–45–55–15–05)*, transforming it into a happening bistro with a single €45 set menu that doesn't skimp on high-quality ingredients. He also runs three other successful restaurants in the same street: the no-reservations **Café Constant** *(139 rue St-Dominique, 01–47–53–73–34)*, specializing in fabulous, unfussy French food, the reliable fish restaurant **Les Fables de la Fontaine** *(131 rue St-Dominique, 01–44–18–37–55)* with its desirable terrace, and **Les Cocottes** *(135 rue St-Dominique, [note this is the same building as Le Violon d'Ingres] 01–45–50–10–31)*, which serves nonstop all day, at a long counter.

RESTAURANTS IN THIS AREA

BASQUE
Chez L'Ami Jean, $$
BISTRO
Afaria, $$
L'Agassin, $$
Bon Accueil, $$$–$$$$
La Butte Chaillot, $$
Le Café Constant, $
Chez les Anges, $$$
L'Os à Moelle, $$$$
Le Petit Rétro, $–$$
Le Soleil, $$–$$$
La Table de Lauriston, $$–$$$
Thoumieux, $$$
FRENCH FUSION
Le 144 Petrossian, $$$–$$$$
Hiramatsu, $$$$
Il Vino, $$$$
HAUTE FRENCH
L'Arpège, $$$$
L'Astrance, $$$$
Le Cristal Room, $$$$
Le Troquet, $$$–$$$$
Le Violon d'Ingres, $$$$
MODERN FRENCH
Les Cocottes de Christian Constant, $
La Table de Joël Robuchon, $$$–$$$$

17

1er, 2e, 9e ARRONDISSEMENTS

LOUVRE, LES HALLES, OPÉRA

All-night restaurants and hearty bistros continue to thrive around Paris's former wholesale market, creating a boisterous contrast with the elegant streets around the Louvre and Opéra.

Home to the city's wholesale food market until the 1960s, Les Halles is still the place to go for late-night onion soup or steak frites, washed back with gulps of cheap and tasty red wine. The streets grow more subdued around the Louvre and Palais Royal, where you can relax in elegant cafés, slurp oysters at a classic brasserie like Le Vaudeville or Gallopin, or treat yourself to a meal of a lifetime at Le Grand Véfour. Though Madeleine is a food hub, thanks to the gourmet emporiums Fauchon and Hédiard, good restaurants are scarce between here and Opéra. For a quick bite, wander over to Rue Ste-Anne for a cheap and satisfying bowl of Japanese noodles. Quick lunch options are plentiful in this area, since it's crawling with office workers who pack the organic café–juice bar Bioboa and the British-inspired sandwich shop Cojean.

ESCAPE TO ASIA

If you can't face another slab of panfried foie gras, take a stroll down Rue Ste-Anne. The hub of the Japanese community in Paris is lined with noodle shops offering unparalleled value. At the ever-popular, cafeteria-style **Higuma**, *(32 and 32 bis, rue Ste-Anne, 01–47–03–38–59)*, €10 will buy not just a sink-size bowl of ramen but a plate of six *gyoza* (pork-filled dumplings). For udon, squeeze into **Kunitoraya** *(39 rue Ste-Anne, 01–47–03–33–65)*, where these thick wheat noodles are a specialty. Unique in Paris is **Zenzoo** *(2 rue Cherubini, 01–42–96–27–28)*, which serves "bubble tea" made with tapioca, and dim sum–style Taiwanese food.

INSIDE LES HALLES

Faced with the unsightly 1970s shopping mall known as the Forum des Halles, it is hard to conjure up the colors, sounds, and smells of the wholesale market that took place here until the late 1960s. Emile Zola dubbed Les Halles "the belly of Paris," and although the belly has shrunk significantly since the market moved to the suburb of Rungis in 1971, it's not completely empty. The cobblestone street market on Rue Montorgueil (open daily except Sunday afternoons and Monday) is still a feast for the senses. And some area restaurants continue to offer savory, market-inspired fare. Newcomers to Les Halles should tread carefully. A hub for 800,000 daily commuters, the area attracts chain restaurants and street hawkers. With all of the commotion, it's easy to overlook worthy shops and eateries.

FOR SOMETHING SWEET

The scent of butter and almonds has been known to stop traffic outside the bakery and restaurant **Stohrer** *(51 rue Montorgueil, 01-42-33-38-20),* founded in 1730. At the warehouse-style **Dehillerin** *(18 rue Coquillière, 01-42-36-53-13)* nearby, cooks from around the world come searching for gleaming copper pots or silicone madeleine molds. Amateur and professional pastry chefs indulge their fantasies at **Detou** *(58 rue Tiquetonne, 1st, 01-42-36-54-67),* which sells 3-kilogram hunks of Valrhona chocolate.

FOR SOMETHING SAVORY

Hidden in an inconspicuous street, **Chez La Vieille** *(1 rue Bailleul, 01-42-60-15-78)* serves uncompromising French country fare at lunchtime and on Thursday nights. If you're still not convinced that the spirit of Les Halles lives on, visit the brasserie **Au Pied de Cochon** *(see photo below, 6 rue Coquillière, 01-40-13-77-00)* or the boisterous bistro **La Tour de Montlhéry-Chez Denise** *(5 rue des Prouvaires, 1st, 01-42-36-21-82)* and enjoy restorative food in the wee hours, just like the market vendors used to do.

RESTAURANTS IN THIS AREA

BISTRO
Aux Lyonnais, $$–$$$
L'Ardoise, $$
La Bourse ou la Vie, $
Chartier, ¢–$
Chez Georges, $$$
Chez Casimir, $
Restaurant du Palais-Royal, $$$

BRASSERIE
Au Pied de Cochon, $$–$$$
Le Grand Colbert, $$–$$$
Julien, $$–$$$
Le Vaudeville, $$–$$$

CAFE
Café Marly, $$
La Ferme Opéra, ¢

HAUTE FRENCH
Le Grand Véfour, $$$$
Senderens, $$$–$$$$

JAPANESE
Higuma, ¢
Zen, ¢–$

MODERN FRENCH
Drouant, $$–$$$
Le Georges, $$–$$$
Macéo, $$$
Pinxo, $$–$$$
Willi's Wine Bar, $–$$

17

RESTAURANTS (IN ALPHABETICAL ORDER)

$$$–$$$$ **Le 144 Petrossian.** Promising young chef Rougui Dia has injected her
FRENCH FUSION   cosmopolitan style into this contemporary French restaurant with a
Invalides, 7ᵉ   czarist spin. In a conscious decision to opt out of the "star chase," the
restaurant is changing its menu less often and has put an end to the
haute-cuisine flourish of serving "drinkable perfumes" before dessert.
This means that regulars will always find favorite dishes such as agneau
Yagouline, lamb cooked until spoon-tender and served with a Moroc-
can-style fruit tagine (part of the set menu for €35 at lunch and €45 at
dinner), and oeuf Petrossian, a breaded and fried soft-boiled egg topped
with caviar. The à la carte selection is peppered with luxury ingredients
like caviar and smoked salmon, and the indecisive can choose a sampler
of three or five desserts. ⊠ *144 rue de l'Université* ☎ *01–44–11–32–32*
🖃 *AE, DC, MC, V* ⊗ *Closed Sun., Mon., last wk in July, and 3 wks in
Aug.* Ⓜ *La Tour–Maubourg, Invalides.* ✢ *3:E1*

$$ **Afaria.** This otherwise unexciting arrondissement has become home to
BISTRO   yet another promising young chef: Julien Duboué, who worked with
15ᵉ   fellow Basque Alain Dutournier at Le Carré des Feuillants and Daniel
Boulud in New York before settling into this high-ceilinged space near
Porte de Versailles. Basque cooking is known for its bold flavors and
generosity, and the choices at Afaria are no exception: crisp-skinned
duck breast with balsamic-fig vinegar (for two) is served dramatically,
inside a roof tile, with the accompanying potato gratin perched on a
bed of twigs, and big chunks of spoon-tender slow-cooked pork from
Gascony come in an earthenware dish with cubes of roasted celery
root. Though it hasn't been open long, Afaria already has a signature
dish: blood sausage layered with apple and topped with grainy mustard. Tapas are served at a high table near the entrance, and there is
a large-screen TV for rugby matches. ⊠ 15 rue Desnouettes ☎ 01–
48–56–15–36 🖃 *MC, V* ⊗ *Closed Sun. and Aug. No lunch Mon.* Ⓜ
Convention. ✢ *3:C6*

$$ **L'Agassin.** André Le Letty, formerly of L'Anacréon, has transported his
BISTRO   talent to a quiet side street with more than its share of great restau-
Invalides, 7ᵉ   rants. Even if the bare walls and dark-wood tables and chairs make the
dining room feel contemporary, there is something agreeably old-fash-
ioned about a meal here, from the attentive and ever-polite service to
the classic French dishes such as a whole duck *magret* with a fanned-
out pear and side dish of white beans, or skate wing in caper-butter
sauce alongside whole baby potatoes and broad beans. For dessert,
the prune clafoutis with Armagnac ice cream is a must. ⊠ *8 rue Malar*
☎ *01–47–05–94–27* 🖃 *AE, MC, V* ⊗ *Closed Sun., Mon., and Aug.*
Ⓜ *Ecole Militaire.* ✢ *3:1E*

$$$$ **Alain Ducasse au Plaza Athénée.** The dining room at Alain Ducasse's flag-
HAUTE FRENCH   ship Paris restaurant gleams with 10,000 crystals, confirming that this
Champs-Elysées,   is the flashiest place in town for a blowout meal. Clementine-color
8ᵉ   tablecloths and space-age cream-and-orange chairs with pull-out plas-
tic trays for business meetings provide an upbeat setting for the cook-
ing of young Ducasse protégé chef Christophe Moret. Some dishes are

subtle, whereas in others strong flavors overwhelm delicate ingredients. Even so, a meal here is delightfully luxe, starting with a heavenly *amuse-bouche* of langoustine with caviar and a tangy lemon cream. You can continue with a truffle-and-caviar fest, or opt for more down-to-earth dishes like lobster in spiced wine with quince or saddle of lamb with sautéed artichokes. ⊠ *Hôtel Plaza Athénée, 25 av. Montaigne* ☎ *01–53–67–65–00* ⌂ *Reservations essential Jacket required* ▭ *AE, DC, MC, V* ☾ *Closed weekends, 2 wks in late Dec., and mid-July–mid-Aug. No lunch Mon.–Wed.* Ⓜ *Alma-Marceau.* ✛ *1:D6*

$$–$$$$
BRASSERIE
St-Germain, 6ᵉ

Alcazar. When Sir Terence Conran opened this impressive 300-seat restaurant, he promised to reinvent the Parisian brasserie, and he's come close. Alcazar's mezzanine bar is famed for its DJ, and with its slick décor and skylight roof, it feels more like London than the Rive Gauche. If the kitchen started out rather uncertain of what it wanted to accomplish, the food is now resolutely French with the occasional Mediterranean touch. Prices are reasonable: a three-course lunch menu is €30 including a glass of wine and coffee; a dinner menu is €42. The chef seems to have found his groove with dishes such as salmon-and-ginger tataki and veal braised with morels. Lest you forget this is Conran land, there are also very good fish-and-chips and Irish coffee. For dessert, it's hard to pass up the profiteroles, mille-feuille, and baba au rhum. Sunday brunch is popular, and the restaurant has introduced "lyric nights" on Mondays with a set menu. ⊠ *62 rue Mazarine* ☎ *01–53–10–19–99* ▭ *AE, DC, MC, V* Ⓜ *Odéon.* ✛ *4:B2*

$–$$
BISTRO
Le Marais, 3ᵉ

L'Ambassade d'Auvergne. A rare Parisian bistro that refuses to change, the Ambassade claims one of the city's great restaurant characters: the maître d' Francis Panek, with his handlebar mustache and gravelly voice. Settle into the cast-in-amber dining room in this ancient Marais house to try rich dishes from the Auvergne, a sparsely populated region in central France. Lighter dishes such as turbot with fennel are available, but it would be missing the point not to indulge in a heaping serving of lentils in goose fat with bacon or the Salers beef in red wine sauce with *aligot* (mashed potatoes with cheese). Then loosen your belt for the astonishingly dense chocolate mousse. The Auvergnat wines come with appetizing descriptions, but don't expect anything remarkable from this (justifiably) obscure wine region. ⊠ *22 rue du Grenier St-Lazare* ☎ *01–42–72–31–22* ▭ *AE, MC, V* Ⓜ *Rambuteau.* ✛ *4:E1*

$$$$
HAUTE FRENCH
Champs-Elysées,
8ᵉ
Fodor's Choice
★

Les Ambassadeurs. A former star—more of a comet, really—in the Alain Ducasse galaxy, Jean-François Piège has established his own identity in Hôtel Le Crillon's hallowed 18th-century dining room, updated in muted tones that offset the glistening marble. Born in 1970, he's young enough to play with food—deconstructing and reconstructing an egg to look like a square marshmallow, its yolk studded with white truffle—and grown-up enough to serve unabashedly rich classics of French cooking, such as deboned squab stuffed with foie gras. An expert at pairing langoustines and caviar, he has come up with a new version for Le Crillon, wrapping the ingredients in a delicate crêpe. The lunch menu offers lashings of luxe for a relatively reasonable €80. ⊠ *Hôtel de Crillon, 10 pl. de la Concorde* ☎ *01–44–71–16–17* ⌂ *Reservations*

17

essential Jacket required ⊟*AE, DC, MC, V* ⊗ *Closed Sun., Mon., and Aug.* Ⓜ *Concorde.* ✥ *1:G5*

$$
BASQUE
Invalides, 7ᵉ

L'Ami Jean. If you love Yves Camdeborde's southwestern France–inflected cooking at Le Comptoir but can't get a table for dinner, head to this tavernlike Basque restaurant run by Camdeborde's longtime second-in-command, Stéphane Jégo. If his style is remarkably similar to Camdeborde's, it's because he uses the same suppliers and shares his knack for injecting basic ingredients with sophistication. You can go hearty with Spanish *piquillo* peppers stuffed with salt cod paste or *poulet basquaise* (chicken stewed with peppers), or lighter with seasonal dishes that change weekly. The restaurant is popular with rugby fans (a sport beloved of Basques), who create a festive mood. ⊠ *27 rue Malar* ☎ *01–47–05–86–89* ⧠ *Reservations essential* ⊟*MC, V* ⊗ *Closed Sun., Mon., and Aug.* Ⓜ *Métro or RER: Invalides.* ✥ *3:E1*

$$–$$$
BISTRO
Les Gobelins, 13ᵉ

Anacréon. Chef Christophe Accary lures the foodies to this boulevard not known for its gastronomic possibilities. From a deceptively old-fashioned-looking menu, you might start with lemongrass-marinated scallops and baby beets, followed by duck breast cooked with Jerusalem artichoke or a wild mushroom risotto with Nyons olive oil. There are some well-priced Burgundies on the interesting wine list. The €20 lunch menu offers good value but very limited choice, so try to spring for the much more varied €37 menu (you can also order à la carte). The dining room feels a bit soulless, though bright contemporary paintings attempt to liven things up. ⊠ *53 bd. St-Marcel* ☎ *01–43–31–71–18* ⧠ *Reservations essential* ⊟*AE, MC, V* ⊗ *Closed Sat. afternoon, Sun., Mon., and 3 wks in Aug.* Ⓜ *Les Gobelins.* ✥ *4:F6*

$$
BISTRO
Louvre/Tuileries, 1ᵉʳ
Fodor'sChoice
★

L'Ardoise. This minuscule storefront, decorated with enlargements of old sepia postcards of Paris, is a model of the kind of contemporary bistros making waves in Paris. Chef Pierre Jay's first-rate three-course dinner menu for €32 tempts with such original dishes as mushroom and foie gras ravioli with smoked duck; farmer's pork with porcini mushrooms; and red mullet with creole sauce (you can also order à la carte, but it's less of a bargain). Just as enticing are the desserts, such as a superb *feuillantine au citron*—caramelized pastry leaves filled with lemon cream and lemon slices—and a boozy baba au rhum. With friendly waiters and a small but well-chosen wine list, L'Ardoise would be perfect if it weren't often crowded and noisy. ⊠ *28 rue du Mont Thabor* ☎ *01–42–96–28–18* ⊟*MC, V* ⊗ *Closed Mon. and Aug. No lunch Sun.* Ⓜ *Concorde.* ✥ *1:H6*

$$$$
HAUTE FRENCH
Invalides, 7ᵉ

L'Arpège. Breton-born Alain Passard, one of the most respected chefs in Paris, famously shocked the French culinary world by declaring that he was bored with meat. Though his vegetarianism is more theoretical than practical—L'Arpège still caters to fish and poultry eaters—he does cultivate his own vegetables outside Paris, which are then zipped into the city by high-speed train. His dishes elevate the humblest vegetables to sublime heights: salt-roasted beets with aged balsamic vinegar, leeks with black truffles, black radishes, and cardoon with parmigiano-reggiano. Seafood dishes such as turbot cooked at a low temperature for three hours or lobster braised in vin jaune from the Jura are also extraordinary—as are the prices. The understated décor places the emphasis firmly on the food, but try to avoid the gloomy cellar room. ⊠ *84 rue de Varenne* ☎ *01–45–51–47–33* ▭ *AE, DC, MC, V* ⊘ *Closed weekends* Ⓜ *Varenne.* ✛ *3:G2*

¢–$

ISRAELI

Le Marais, 4ᵉ

L'As du Fallafel. Look no further than the fantastic falafel stands on the newly pedestrian Rue de Rosiers for some of the cheapest and tastiest meals in Paris. L'As (the Ace) is widely considered the best of the bunch, which accounts for the lunchtime line that extends into the street. A falafel sandwich costs €5 to go, €7 in the dining room, and comes heaped with grilled eggplant, cabbage, hummus, tahini, and hot sauce. The *shawarma* (grilled, skewered meat) sandwich, made with chicken or lamb, is also one of the finest in town. Though takeout is popular, it can be more fun (and not as messy) to eat off a plastic plate in one of the two frenzied dining rooms. Fresh lemonade is the falafel's best match. ⊠ *34 rue des Rosiers* ☎ *01–48–87–63–60* ▭ *MC, V* ⊘ *Closed Sat. No dinner Fri.* Ⓜ *St-Paul.* ✛ *4:F2*

$

BISTRO

République, 11ᵉ

Astier. There are three good reasons to go to Astier: the generous cheese platter plonked on your table atop a help-yourself wicker tray, the exceptional wine cellar with bottles dating back to the 1970s, and the French bistro fare, even if portions seem to have diminished over the years. Dishes like marinated herring with warm potato salad, sausage with lentils, and baba au rhum are classics on the frequently changing set menu for €31, which doesn't allow you to order fewer than three courses. The vintage 1950s wood-paneled dining room attracts plenty of locals and remains a fairly sure bet in the area, especially since it's open every day. ⊠ *44 rue Jean-Pierre Timbaud* ☎ *01–43–57–16–35* ⚏ *Reservations essential* ▭ *MC, V* Ⓜ *Parmentier.* ✛ *2:H5*

$$$$

HAUTE FRENCH

Trocadéro/Tour Eiffel, 16ᵉ

Fodor's Choice

★

L'Astrance. Pascal Barbot may have risen to fame thanks to his restaurant's amazing-value food and casual atmosphere, but a few years later Astrance has become resolutely haute, with prices to match. The €120 tasting menu (€190 with matching wines), which is compulsory at dinner, unfolds over two to three hours in a series of surprisingly light courses, and Barbot's cooking has such an ethereal quality that it's worth the considerable effort of booking a table (start trying at least six weeks in advance). His dishes often draw on Asian ingredients, as in grilled lamb with miso-lacquered eggplant and a palate-cleansing white sorbet spiked with chili pepper and lemongrass. Wines by the glass offer great value but don't always match the quality of the food. For a tantalizing taste of Barbot's style, order the €70 lunch menu. ⊠ *4 rue Beethoven* ☎ *01–40–50–84–40* ⚏ *Reservations essential* ▭ *AE, DC, MC, V* ⊘ *Closed Sat.–Mon., and Aug.* Ⓜ *Passy.* ✛ *1:B6*

17

$$$–$$$$
MODERN
FRENCH
St-Germain, 7ᵉ

L'Atelier de Joël Robuchon. Famed chef Joël Robuchon retired from the restaurant business for several years before opening this red-and-black-lacquered space with a bento-box-meets-tapas aesthetic. High seats surround two U-shape bars, and this novel plan encourages neighbors to share recommendations and opinions. Robuchon's devoted kitchen staff whip up "small plates" for grazing (€10–€25) as well as full portions, which turn out to be the better bargain. Highlights from the oft-changing menu have included an intense tomato jelly topped with avocado purée and thin-crusted mackerel tart, although his inauthentic (but who's complaining?) take on carbonara with cream and Alsatian bacon, and the *merlan* Colbert (fried herb butter) remain signature dishes. Bookings are taken for the 11:30 AM and 6:30 PM sittings only. ✉ *5 rue Montalembert* ☎ *01–42–22–56–56* ⊟ *MC, V* Ⓜ *Rue du Bac.* ✛ *4:A2*

$$–$$$
BRASSERIE
La Villette, 19ᵉ

Au Boeuf Couronné. La Villette once housed the city's meat market, and this brasserie devoted to fine beef (whether French or Irish) soldiers on as if nothing has changed. If you're beginning to tire of the Flo brasserie formula, it's worth the trek to this far-flung neighborhood to sample one of the 16 takes on the beef theme (plus a gargantuan marrow bone), or very good fish and seafood dishes, such as scallops (in season). You'll find bon vivants from all over Paris in the buzzy dining room. ✉ *188 av. Jean-Jaurès* ☎ *01–42–39–54–54* ⊟ *AE, DC, MC, V* Ⓜ *Porte de Pantin.* ✛ *2:H1*

$$–$$$
BISTRO
Trocadéro/Tour
Eiffel, 7ᵉ

Au Bon Accueil. To see what well-heeled Parisians like to eat these days, book a table at this popular bistro run by Jacques Lacipière as soon as you get to town. The dining room is open and airy, and the sidewalk tables have an Eiffel Tower view; the excellent, well-priced *cuisine du marché* has made this spot a hit. Typical of the sophisticated fare from chef Naobuni Sasaki are milk-fed Pauillac lamb cooked two ways with sautéed vegetables, and roast lobster with mushroom risotto, as well as game in season. Homemade desserts could include citrus terrine with passion-fruit sorbet or caramelized apple mille-feuille with hazelnut ice cream. ✉ *14 rue de Monttessuy* ☎ *01–47–05–46–11* ⌲ *Reservations essential* ⊟ *AE, MC, V* ☉ *Closed weekends and 2 wks in Aug.* Ⓜ *Métro or RER: Pont de l'Alma.* ✛ *3:D1*

$$–$$$
BISTRO
Le Marais, 4ᵉ

Au Bourguignon du Marais. The handsome, contemporary look of this Marais bistro and wine bar is the perfect backdrop for the good traditional fare and excellent Burgundies served by the glass and bottle. Unusual for Paris, food is served nonstop from noon to 11 PM. Always on the menu are Burgundian classics such as *jambon persillé* (ham in parsleyed aspic jelly), escargots, and *boeuf Bourguignon* (beef stewed in red wine). More up-to-date picks include a cèpe-mushroom velouté with poached oysters (though the fancier dishes are generally less successful). The terrace is hotly sought after in warmer months. ✉ *52 rue François-Miron* ☎ *01–48–87–15–40* ⊟ *AE, MC, V* ☉ *Closed weekends, 3 wks in Aug., and 2 wks in Jan.* Ⓜ *St-Paul.* ✛ *4:F2*

$$$–$$$$
BISTRO
Champs-Elysées,
17ᵉ

Au Petit Colombier. This is a perennial favorite among Parisians, who come to eat comforting *cuisine bourgeoise* (traditional cuisine) in the warm dining rooms accented with wood and bright copper. Seasonal specialties include milk-fed lamb chop *en cocotte* (in a small enameled casserole), game in all its guises, and truffles. Order the set menu for €38 or blow your budget à la carte. There is a seafood annex, Au Petit Colombier Côté Mer, next door. Service is friendly and unpretentious. ⊠*42 rue des Acacias* ☎*01–43–80–28–54* ▤*AE, MC, V* ☉*Closed Sun. and Aug. No lunch Sat.* Ⓜ*Charles-de-Gaulle–Etoile.* ✛ *1:B3*

$$
BISTRO
Les Gobelins,
13ᵉ

Au Petit Marguery. As the diorama of a stuffed ferret amid a fairy-tale mushroom forest in the entrance announces, this charming bistro offers some of the earthiest dishes in the French canon. With its historic fin-de-siècle charm, this is the place to head if you're hunting for game: catch it here in late fall, in such dishes as *lièvre à la royale* (hare in wine-and-blood sauce) or the *noisette de biche* (doe). Some dishes are so *authentique* they're topped with pine needles. Watch out, though, for the hefty price supplements to the €23 lunch menu and €30 dinner prix fixe on many seasonal dishes. ⊠*9 bd. de Port Royal* ☎*01–43–31–58–59* ▤*AE, MC, V* ☉*Closed Sun. and Mon.* Ⓜ*Les Gobelins.* ✛ *4:C6*

$
BISTRO
Champs-Elysées,
17ᵉ

Au Petit Verdot du 17ᵉ. Sandwich bars might be threatening the traditional two-hour lunch, but that doesn't stop this old-fashioned neighborhood bistro with a freshly painted façade and wine-themed dining room from flourishing—even though it's open only at lunch, except Thursday and Friday. Businessmen loosen their neckties to feast on homemade pâté, plate-engulfing steak for two, or guinea hen with cabbage, along with one of 40 or so small producers' wines, which are delivered directly to the restaurant. ⊠*9 rue Fourcroy* ☎*01–42–27–47–42* ▤*MC, V* ☉*Closed weekends. No dinner Mon.–Wed.* Ⓜ*Charles-de-Gaulle–Etoile.* ✛ *1:C2*

$$–$$$
BRASSERIE
Beaubourg/Les
Halles, 1ᵉʳ

Au Pied de Cochon. One of the few remnants of Les Halles' raucous all-night past is this brasserie, which has been open every day since 1946. Now run by the Frères Blanc group, it still draws both a French and a foreign crowd with round-the-clock hours and trademark traditional fare such as seafood platters, breaded pigs' trotters, beer-braised pork knuckle with sauerkraut, and cheese-crusted onion soup. It's perfect rib-sticking fare for a winter's day or to finish off a bar crawl. The dining room, with its white tablecloths and little piggy details, feels resolutely cheerful. ⊠*6 rue Coquillière* ☎*01–40–13–77–00* ⊟*AE, DC, MC, V* Ⓜ*Les Halles.* ✛ *2:C6*

$$$–$$$$
BISTRO
Bastille/Nation, 12ᵉ

Au Trou Gascon. This classy establishment off Place Daumesnil—well off the beaten tourist track but worth the trip—is overseen by celebrated chef Alain Dutournier. His wife runs the dining room, which combines contemporary furnishings with beautiful ceiling moldings. He does a refined take on the cuisine of Gascony—a region renowned for its ham, foie gras, lamb, and duck. Most popular with the regulars are the surprisingly light cassoulet (all the meats are grilled before going into the pot) with big white Tarbais beans and a superb duck or goose confit. You can also find an ethereal dessert of raspberries, ice cream, and meringue. With some 1,100 wines and 130 Armagnacs to choose from, this is the place to splurge on vintage. ⊠*40 rue Taine* ☎*01–43–44–34–26* ⊟*AE, DC, MC, V* ⊗*Closed weekends, Aug., and 1st wk. in Jan.* Ⓜ*Daumesnil.* ✛ *4:H4*

$$–$$$
BISTRO
Opéra/Grands
Boulevards, 2ᵉ
Fodor's Choice
★

Aux Lyonnais. With a passion for the old-fashioned bistro, Alain Ducasse has resurrected this 1890s gem by appointing a terrific young chef to oversee the short, frequently changing, and reliably delicious menu of Lyonnais specialties. Dandelion salad with crisp potatoes, bacon, and silky poached egg; watercress soup poured over parsleyed frogs' legs; and fluffy quenelles de brochet (pike-perch dumplings) show he is no bistro dilettante. The décor hews to tradition, too, with a zinc bar, an antique coffee machine, and original turn-of-the-20th-century woodwork. There is a no-choice lunch menu for €28, but the temptation is strong to splurge on the more luxurious à la carte dishes. ⊠*32 rue St-Marc* ☎*01–42–96–65–04* ⊟*AE, MC, V* ⊗*No lunch Sat. Closed Sun. and Mon., 1 wk in July, and 3 wks in Aug.* Ⓜ*Bourse.* ✛ *2:B4*

$
BISTRO
La Butte aux
Cailles, 13ᵉ
☾

L'Avant-Goût. Christophe Beaufront belongs to a generation of gifted bistro chefs who have rejected the pressure-cooker world of haute cuisine for something more personal and democratic. The result: delighted and loyal customers. The three-course dinner prix-fixe costs €31; there's also a lunch menu for €14 (main course, glass of wine, and coffee) and a more elaborate tasting menu for €40. Typical of his market-inspired cooking is his signature pot-au-feu *de cochon aux épices,* in which spiced pork stands in for the usual beef, and the bouillon is served separately. Homemade desserts and a good-value wine list round off a satisfying experience; children get an especially warm welcome here. Drop into his épicerie across the street to browse through his wine selection or order dinner to go, complete with a returnable cast-iron pot. ⊠*26 rue Bobillot* ☎*01–53–80–24–00* ✍*Reservations essential* ⊟*MC, V* ⊗*Closed Sun., Mon., and 3 wks in Aug.* Ⓜ*Place d'Italie.* ✛ *4:G6*

$$
BRASSERIE
Quartier Latin, 5ᵉ
☾

Le Balzar. Regulars grumble about the uneven cooking at Le Balzar, but they continue to come back because they can't resist the waiters' wry humor and the dining room's amazing people-watching possibilities (you can also drop in for a drink on the terrace). It attracts politicians, writers, tourists, and local eccentrics—and remains one of the city's classic brasseries: the perfect stop before or after a Woody Allen film in a local art-house cinema. Don't expect miracles from the kitchen, but stick to evergreens like snails in garlic butter, onion soup, and panfried veal liver with sautéed potatoes. ✉ *49 rue des Ecoles* ☏ *01–43–54–13–67* ⊟ *AE, DC, MC, V* Ⓜ *Cluny–La Sorbonne.* ✛ *4:C4*

\$\$
BISTRO
St-Germain, 6ᵉ

La Bastide Odéon. The open kitchen of this popular Provençal bistro near the Jardin du Luxembourg allows you to watch the cooks at work. Chef Gilles Ajuelos demonstrates an expert, loving, and creative hand with Mediterranean cuisine—expect unusual dishes such as aged Spanish ham with a grilled pepper *pipérade* and artichokes; mushroom-and-pea risotto with arugula; and duck breast with orange sauce, date purée, polenta, and wild asparagus. To finish things off, try the pear poached with lemon and saffron, served with a *fromage blanc* sorbet. Unusual for Paris, an entire section of the menu is devoted to vegetarian dishes. (Ajuelos now also runs the traditional French bistro La Marlotte at 55 rue du Cherche-Midi, 01–45–48–86–79.) ✉ *7 rue Corneille* ☏ *01–43–26–03–65* ⊟ *AE, MC, V* ⊘ *Closed Sun., Mon., and 3 wks in Aug.* Ⓜ *Odéon; RER: Luxembourg.* ✛ *4:C4*

\$\$\$–\$\$\$\$
BISTRO
Le Marais, 4ᵉ
☾

Benoît. If you loved Benoît before it became the property of Alain Ducasse and Thierry de la Brosse—the pair that revived Aux Lyonnais—chances are you'll adore it now. Without changing the vintage 1912 setting, which needed nothing more than a minor dusting, the illustrious new owners have subtly improved the menu with dishes such as marinated salmon, frogs' legs in a morel-mushroom cream sauce, and an outstanding cassoulet served in a cast-iron pot. Hardworking young chef David Rathgeber, formerly of Aux Lyonnais, keeps the kitchen running smoothly, and the waiters are charm incarnate. It's a splurge to be here, so go all the way and top off your meal with tarte tatin that's caramelized to the core or a rum-doused baba. ✉ *20 rue St-Martin* ☏ *01–42–72–25–76* ⊟ *AE, MC, V* ⊘ *Closed Aug.* Ⓜ *Châtelet.* ✛ *4:D1*

\$\$\$
BISTRO
Montparnasse, 15ᵉ

Bistrot d'Hubert. In a studied country-style environment that might have sprung from the pages of *Elle Decor,* this bistro entices with an unusual, oft-changing menu. Once split into two sections—"tradition" and "discovery"—the menu now focuses chiefly on discovery, with complex dishes such as roasted piquillo peppers stuffed with puréed salt cod and served with tomato coulis and pesto, followed by equally elaborate desserts. Culinary experimentation happily works here, and service is friendly. Low-fat recipes are signaled with a double asterisk on the menu. ✉ *41 bd. Pasteur* ☏ *01–47–34–15–50* ⊜ *Reservations essential* ⊟ *AE, DC, MC, V* ⊘ *Closed Sun. No lunch Sat. and Mon.* Ⓜ *Pasteur.* ✛ *3:F5*

\$\$\$\$
BISTRO
Montmartre, 9ᵉ

Bistrot des Deux Théâtres. This theater-lover's bistro with red-velour banquettes, black-and-white photos of actors, and a giant oil painting depicting celebrities is always packed, and with good reason. The prix-fixe menu for €36 includes a *kir royale* (sparkling white wine with cassis), three courses, half a bottle of wine, and coffee, and is a fantastic value. This isn't a place for modest eaters, so have foie gras or escargots to start, a meaty main such as the crackly crusted rack of lamb, and a potent baba au rhum or rustic lemon meringue tart for dessert.

17

Waiters are jokey, English-speaking, and efficient. ⊠*18 rue Blanche* ☎*01–45–26–41–43* ⊟*AE, MC, V* Ⓜ*Trinité.* ✤ *4:A2*

$$$–$$$$
BRASSERIE
Bastille/Nation,
4ᵉ
☾

Bofinger. One of the oldest, loveliest, and most popular brasseries in Paris has generally improved in recent years, so stake out one of the tables dressed in crisp white linen under the glowing Art Nouveau glass cupola and enjoy classic brasserie fare (stick to trademark dishes such as the seafood choucroute, lamb fillet, or smoked haddock with spinach, as the seasonal specials can be hit-or-miss). The prix fixe for €31.50 includes a decent half bottle of red or white wine, and there is a generous children's menu. ⊠*5–7 rue de la Bastille* ☎*01–42–72–87–82* ⊟*AE, DC, MC, V* Ⓜ*Bastille.* ✤ *4:H2*

$–$$
BISTRO
St-Germain, 6ᵉ

Boucherie Roulière. If it's steak you're craving, put your faith in Jean-Luc Roulière, a fifth-generation butcher who opened this long, narrow bistro near St-Sulpice church in 2006. Partner Franck Pinturier is from the Auvergne region, which is also known for its melt-in-the-mouth meat. Start with truffle-scented ravioli or a rich marrow bone before indulging in a generous slab of Limousin or Salers beef, excellent veal kidney, or, for the meat-shy, perhaps lobster or sea bass. The minimalist cream-and-brown dining room with checkerboard floor tiles and black-and-white photos on the walls keeps the focus on the food, and waiters are of the professional Parisian breed. ⊠*24 rue des Canettes* ☎*01–43–26–25–70* ⊟*MC, V* ⊘*Closed Mon. and Aug.* Ⓜ*Mabillon.* ✤ *4:B3*

$–$$
BRASSERIE
St-Germain, 6ᵉ

Le Bouillon Racine. Originally a *bouillon*—one of the Parisian soup kitchens popular at the turn of the 20th century—this two-story restaurant is now a lushly renovated Belle Époque haven with a casual setting downstairs and a lavish upstairs room. The menu changes seasonally: lamb knuckle with licorice, wild boar *parmentier* (like a shepherd's pie, with mashed potatoes on top and meat underneath), and roast suckling pig are warming winter dishes. For dessert, dig into crème brûlée with maple syrup or the *café liégois* (coffee-flavored custard topped with whipped cream), which comes in a jug. This is a good place to keep in mind for a late lunch or an early dinner, since it serves nonstop from noon until 11 PM. ⊠*3 rue Racine* ☎*01–44–32–15–60* ⊟*AE, MC, V* Ⓜ*Odéon.* ✤ *4:C4*

$$
BISTRO
Père Lachaise,
20ᵉ

La Boulangerie. Set in a former bakery spruced up with a bread-theme mural, this bistro in the shabby-chic neighborhood of Ménilmontant dishes up a great-value lunch menu for €17. Dinner costs a still-reasonable €30, and the quality of the ingredients is admirable, even if the cooking can be inconsistent. Expect seasonal dishes such as squash soup with spice-bread croutons, pot-roasted veal with root vegetables, and *cannelés* (eggy, caramelized cakes) with jasmine ice cream made on the premises. If you're exploring the area around Père Lachaise, it would be hard to find a better French eatery. ⊠*15 rue des Panoyaux* ☎*01–43–58–45–45* ⊟*MC, V* ⊘*Closed Sun., Aug., and 1 wk at Christmas. No lunch Sat.* Ⓜ*Ménilmontant.* ✤ *2:H5*

$$$–$$$$
BISTRO
St-Germain, 6ᵉ

Les Bouquinistes. Showcasing the talents of Guy Savoy protégée Magdala de Beaulieu-Caussimon, this is the star chef Savoy's most popular "baby bistro," frequented by art dealers from the nearby galleries and the occasional *bouquiniste* (bookseller) from the quais across the street. Expect to hear more English than French in the

cheery, contemporary dining room looking out onto the Seine, but the sophisticated seasonal cuisine—such as snails and mussels with gnocchi, followed by British Hereford beef with squash-stuffed rigatoni and a nougat crème brûlée—is as authentic as you could hope for. The €28 *retour du marché* (back from the market) lunch menu seems less imaginative than the pricier à la carte options—though it does include three courses, a glass of wine, and coffee. The wine list is extensive, with 180 wines and 12 champagnes. ⊠ *53 quai des Grands-Augustins* ☎ *01–43–25–45–94* ▭ *AE, DC, MC, V* ⊘ *Closed Sun. and 2 wks in Aug. No lunch Sat.* Ⓜ *St-Michel.* ✛ *4:C2*

$
BISTRO
Louvre/Tuileries, 1ᵉʳ

La Bourse ou La Vie. If you've been dreaming of finding the perfect steak frites in Paris, head for this eccentric little place run by a former architect in partnership with two loyal clients. The chairs in this cheerful yellow-and-red dining room appear to have been salvaged from a theater, but they pair nicely with founder Patrice Tatard's theatrical streak; he often refers to first-time diners as "my loves." There is no questioning the threesome's enthusiasm for their new vocation when you taste the steak in its trademark creamy, peppercorn-studded sauce, accompanied by hand-cut french fries cooked to crisp perfection. Aside from steak dishes, there is little else on the menu. ⊠ *12 rue Vivienne* ☎ *01–42–60–08–83* ▭ *MC, V* Ⓜ *Bourse.* ✛ *2:C5*

$$–$$$
BRASSERIE
Ile St-Louis, 4ᵉ

Brasserie de l'Ile St-Louis. Opened in 1870—when Alsace-Lorraine was taken over by Germany and its chefs decamped to the capital—this outpost of Alsatian cuisine remains a cozy, tavern-style cocoon filled with stuffed animal heads, antique fixtures fashioned from barrels, and folkart paintings. Expect rustic country-style fare: coq au Riesling, omelets with muenster cheese, onion tarts, and *choucroute garnie* (sauerkraut studded with ham, bacon, and pork loin). In warm weather the crowds move out to the terrace overlooking the Seine and Notre-Dame. With the famed *glacier* Berthillon so close by, it's best not to bother with the pricey desserts here. ⊠ *55 quai de Bourbon* ☎ *01–43–54–02–59* ▭ *MC, V* ⊘ *Closed Wed., Aug., 3 days at Christmas, and 1 wk in Feb. No lunch Thurs.* Ⓜ *Pont Marie.* ✛ *4:E3*

$$$–$$$$
BRASSERIE
St-Germain, 6ᵉ

Brasserie Lipp. This brasserie, with its turn-of-the-20th-century décor, was a favorite spot of Hemingway's; today television celebrities, journalists, and politicians come here for coffee on the small glassed-in terrace off the main restaurant. Sadly, the kitchen's standards have slipped and a meal in the atmospheric dining room is likely to be disappointing, and expensive—flabby sole meunière is served with soggy boiled

17

potatoes, and even the trademark choucroute is lackluster. ⊠*151 bd. St-Germain* ☎*01–45–48–53–91* ▭*AE, DC, MC, V* Ⓜ*St-Germain-des-Prés.* ✛ *4:A3*

¢
MODERN
FRENCH
Le Marais, 3ᵉ

✕ **Breizh Café.** Eating a crêpe in Paris might seem a bit clichéd, until you venture into this modern offshoot of a crêperie in Cancale, Brittany. The pale-wood, almost Japanese-style décor is refreshing, but what really makes the difference are the ingredients—farmers' eggs, unpasteurized Gruyère, shiitake mushrooms, Valrhona chocolate, homemade caramel, and extraordinary butter from Breton dairy farmer Jean-Yves Bordier. You'll find all the classics among the galettes (buckwheat crêpes), but it's worth choosing something more adventurous like the *cancalaise* (traditionally smoked herring, potato, crème fraîche, and herring roe). You might also slurp a few Cancale oysters, a rarity in Paris, and try one of the 20 artisanal ciders on offer. ⊠ 109 rue Vieille du Temple, ☎*01–42–72–13–77* ▭ *MC, V* ☉*Closed Mon., Tues., and 3 wks in Aug.* Ⓜ*St-Sébastien-Froissart.* ✛ *4:1F*

$$$$
HAUTE FRENCH
Champs-Elysées,
8ᵉ

Le Bristol. After a rapid ascent at his own new-wave bistro, which led to his renown as one of the more inventive young chefs in Paris, Eric Frechon became head chef at the Bristol, the home-away-from-home for billionaires and power brokers. Frechon creates masterworks— say, farmer's pork cooked "from head to foot" with truffle-enhanced crushed potatoes—that rarely stray far from the comfort-food tastes of bistro cooking. The €90 lunch menu makes his cooking accessible not just to the palate but to many pocketbooks. No wonder his tables are so coveted. Though the two dining rooms are impeccable—an oval oak-panel one for fall and winter and a marble-floor pavilion overlooking the courtyard garden for spring and summer—they provide few clues to help the world-weary traveler determine which city this might be. ⊠*Hôtel Bristol, 112 rue du Faubourg St-Honoré* ☎*01–53–43–43–00* ⌖*Reservations essential Jacket and tie* ▭*AE, DC, MC, V* Ⓜ*Miromesnil.* ✛ *1:F4*

$$
BISTRO
Quartier Latin,
5ᵉ

Le Buisson Ardent. Under new ownership since 2006, this charming Latin Quarter bistro with woodwork and murals dating from 1925 is more packed and boisterous than ever. A glance at chef Stéphane Mauduit's €31 set menu makes it easy to understand why. Dishes such as chestnut soup with spice bread, squid with chorizo and creamy quinoa, and quince Tatin (upside-down tart) with mascarpone and pink pralines put a fresh twist on French classics, and service is reliably courteous. Bread is made on the premises, and if you don't finish your bottle of wine, you can take it with you to savor the last drops. ⊠*25 rue Jussieu* ☎*01–43–54–93–02* ▭*MC, V* ☉*Closed Sun. No lunch Sat.* Ⓜ*Jussieu.* ✛ *4:E4*

$$–$$$
BISTRO
Trocadéro/Tour
Eiffel, 16ᵉ

La Butte Chaillot. A dramatic iron staircase connects the two levels of one of the most popular of Guy Savoy's fashionable bistros, done up in warm colors with cushy brown-leather armchairs. Dining here is part theater, as the à la mode clientele demonstrates, but it's not all show. The generally good food includes spit-roasted free-range chicken with potato purée, scallops with spinach and *beurre blanc* sauce, and several vegetarian options such as penne with mushroom fricassée. A wide sidewalk terrace fronts the tree-shaded avenue Kléber. ✉ *110 bis, av. Kléber* ☎ *01–47–27–88–88* ⊟ *AE, DC, MC, V* ⊘ *Closed 3 wks in Aug. No lunch Sat.* Ⓜ *Trocadéro.* ✛ *1:B6*

$
BISTRO
Invalides, 7ᵉ

Le Café Constant. Middle-aged Parisians are a nostalgic bunch, which explains the popularity of this down-to-earth venue from esteemed chef Christian Constant. This is a relatively humble bistro with cream-color walls, red banquettes, and wooden tables. The menu reads like a French cookbook from the 1970s—who cooks veal *cordon bleu* these days?—but with Constant overseeing the kitchen, the dishes taste even better than you remember. There's delicious and creamy lentil soup with morsels of foie gras, and the artichoke salad comes with fresh—not bottled or frozen—hearts. A towering *vacherin* (meringue layered with ice cream) might bring this delightfully retro meal to a close. On weekdays there is a bargain lunch menu for €16 (two courses) or €23 (three courses). ✉ *139 rue St-Dominique* ☎ *01–47–53–73–34* ✍ *Reservations not accepted* ⊟ *MC, V* ⊘ *Closed Sun. and Mon.* Ⓜ *Métro Ecole Militaire, Métro or RER: Pont de l'Alma.* ✛ *3:D2*

$$
CAFÉ
Louvre/Tuileries,
1ᵉʳ

Café Marly. Run by the Costes brothers, this café overlooking the main courtyard of the Louvre and I. M. Pei's glass pyramid is one of the most stylish places in Paris to meet for a drink or a coffee, whether in the stunning dining rooms with their molded ceilings or on the long terrace. Regular café service shuts down during meal hours, when fashion-conscious folks dig into Asian-inspired salads and pseudo-Italian pasta dishes. ✉ *Cour Napoléon du Louvre, enter from Louvre courtyard, 93 rue de Rivoli* ☎ *01–49–26–06–60* Ⓜ *Palais-Royal.* ✛ *4:C2*

$$$$
BISTRO
La Villette, 19ᵉ

La Cave Gourmande. In the space that once housed Eric Frechon, who now heads the kitchens at Le Bristol, chef Mark Singer continues to draw crowds to this out-of-the-way neighborhood with inventive bistro cooking. Wine racks and wooden tables give the room a local bistro feel belied by dishes such as a leek-and-shellfish terrine in a light curry sauce, or pike perch with chorizo. Singer makes astute use of spices and exotic ingredients, and his prix-fixe menu (€36 at lunch and dinner) changes every few weeks. ✉ *10 rue du Général-Brunet* ☎ *01–40–40–03–30* ⊟ *MC, V* ⊘ *Closed weekends, 1 wk in Feb., and 3 wks in Aug.* Ⓜ *Botzaris.* ✛ *2:H1*

$$
BISTRO
Montparnasse,
14ᵉ

La Cerisaie. Cyril Lalanne belongs to a breed of young chefs who like to cook for a privileged few. If you're clever enough to nab a seat in this unremarkable yellow-and-red dining room (be sure to call ahead for lunch or dinner), you can be rewarded with food whose attention to detail restores your faith in humanity. Foie gras makes several appearances on the chalkboard menu, since Lalanne is from southwest France, but you can also find freshly caught fish and perhaps farmer's pork from Gascony, a rarity in Paris. Lalanne does his own variation on baba au rhum—with Armagnac, another nod to his native region—and the wine list is strong on southwestern French bottles. ✉ *70 bd. Edgar Quinet* ☎ *01–43–20–98–98* ✍ *Reservations essential* ⊟ *MC, V* ⊘ *Closed weekends and mid-July–mid-Aug.* Ⓜ *Edgar Quinet.* ✛ *4:A6*

17

$–$$ **Chai 33.** Thierry Begué, one of the names behind the trendsetting night-
MODERN   spots Buddha Bar and Barrio Latino, created something more personal
FRENCH   with this forward-looking dining spot. Appropriately set in a neighbor-
Bercy/Tolbiac,   hood once dedicated to the wine trade, it's a restaurant, bar, and wine-
12ᵉ   shop in one. It aims to make wine unintimidating: instead of regional
listings, wines are classified by style, and you can go into the cellar to
choose a bottle with the help of an expert sommelier. Go for the funky
wine cocktails or the perfectly fine food, which is divided into four
categories: "authentic," "trends," "voyage," and "seasons." In summer there is a pleasant, traffic-free terrace. Good-value prix fixes range
from €16 to €21, and there is brunch on Sunday and holidays for €25.
⊠*33 cour St-Emilion* ☎*01–53–44–01–01* ▭*AE, MC, V* Ⓜ*Cour St-
Emilion.* ✛ *4:H5*

¢–$ **Chartier.** This classic *bouillon* (a term referring to the Parisian soup
BISTRO   kitchens popular in the early 20th century) recently joined the Gérard
Opéra/Grands   Joulie group of bistros and brasseries, which is probably good news
Boulevards, 9ᵉ   since Joulie has pledged to bring a smile back to the staff's faces
☾   and expand the menu without raising prices. People come here more
for the bonhomie and the stunning 1896 interior than the cooking,
which could be politely described as unambitious. This cavernous
restaurant—the only original fin-de-siécle *bouillon* to remain true to
its mission of serving cheap, sustaining food to the masses—enjoys a
huge following, including one regular who has come for lunch nearly
every day since 1946. You may find yourself sharing a table with
strangers as you study the old-fashioned menu of such standards
as pot-au-feu and blanquette de veau. ⊠*7 rue du Faubourg-Montmartre* ☎*01–47–70–86–29* ⚒*Reservations not accepted* ▭*MC, V*
Ⓜ*Montmartre.* ✛ *2:C4*

$ **Chez Casimir.** Thierry Breton's bright, easygoing bistro is popular with
BISTRO   polished Parisian professionals, for whom it serves as a sort of can-
Opéra/Grands   teen—why cook when you can eat this well so affordably? The menu
Boulevards, 10ᵉ   covers lentil soup with fresh croutons, braised endive and andouille
salad, and roast lamb on a bed of Paimpol beans, and there are 12
cheeses to choose from. Good, if not exceptional, desserts include
pain perdu, a dessert version of French toast—here it's topped with
a roasted pear or whole cherries. ⊠*6 rue de Belzunce* ☎*01–48–78–
28–80* ▭*MC, V* ☾*Closed weekends and 3 wks in Aug.* Ⓜ*Gare du
Nord.* ✛ *2:E2*

$$$ **Chez Georges.** If you were to ask Parisian bankers, aristocrats, or
BISTRO   antiques dealers to name their favorite bistro for a three-hour weekday
Louvre/Tuileries,   lunch, many would choose Georges. The traditional fare, described in
2ᵉ   authentically indecipherable handwriting, is good—chicken-liver ter-
rine, curly endive salad with bacon and a poached egg, steak with
béarnaise—and the atmosphere is better, compensating for the rather
steep prices. In the dining room, a white-clothed stretch of tables lines
the mirrored walls and attentive waiters sweep efficiently up and down.
Order one of the wines indicated in colored ink on the menu and you
can drink as much or as little of it as you want (and be charged accord-
ingly); there's also another wine list with grander bottles. ⊠*1 rue du*

Mail ☎*01–42–60–07–11* ▭*AE, MC, V* ⊘*Closed weekends and Aug.* Ⓜ*Sentier.* ✦ *2:C5*

\$\$–\$\$\$
BRASSERIE
République, 3ᵉ

Chez Jenny. This classic two-story brasserie founded in 1932 is famed for its infectious buzz and outstanding choucroute, delivered weekly by a private supplier in Alsace and served with a panoply of sausages and an oversize grilled ham knuckle. If this sounds like too much meat, try the fish choucroute with smoked haddock, salmon, and perch, or slurp your way through an impressive seafood platter. To finish, the perfectly aged muenster cheese and homemade blueberry tart are fine choices. Staff in regional dress and woodwork by Charles Spindler add a charming Alsatian touch. Although reservations aren't required, prepare to stand in line without one. ✉*39 bd. du Temple* ☎*01–44–54–39–00* ▭*AE, DC, MC, V* Ⓜ*République.* ✦ *2:G5*

\$\$\$
BISTRO
Trocadéro/Tour
Eiffel, 7ᵉ

Chez les Anges. In the 1960s and '70s, Chez les Anges served celestial Burgundian cooking; the restaurant went through several incarnations since, but now, under new owner Jacques Lacipière, who runs the popular bistro Au Bon Accueil, it has recovered the original name and spirit. Lacipière has made a few adjustments since opening, warming up the dining room with 1970s-inspired décor and broadening the wine list, and the good-value food from chef Hidenori Kitaguchi is a notch above bistro fare. The menu changes daily according to Lacipière's early-morning purchases at the wholesale market—expect dishes such as suckling pig prepared three ways (lacquered, confit, and breaded). Service is polished and thoughtful. ✉*54 bd. de la Tour-Maubourg* ☎*01–47–05–89–86* ▭*AE, MC, V* ⊘*Closed weekends* Ⓜ*Métro: La Tour-Maubourg.* ✦ *3:E2*

\$\$–\$\$\$
BISTRO
St-Germain, 6ᵉ

Chez Maître Paul. This calm, comfortable spot is a great place to discover the little-known cooking of the Jura and Franche-Comté regions of eastern France. Though sturdy, this cuisine appeals to modern palates, as you'll discover with the *montbéliard,* a smoked sausage served with potato salad, or the veal sweetbreads with morel mushrooms. Also try one of the free-range chicken dishes, either in a sauce of *vin jaune*—a dry wine from the region that resembles sherry—or baked in cream and cheese. The walnut meringue is sinfully wonderful, and there's a regional selection of Arbois wines. Best value is the €35 prix fixe, which brings three courses plus a half bottle of wine per person. ✉*12 rue Monsieur-le-Prince* ☎*01–43–54–74–59* ▭*AE, DC, MC, V* ⊘*Closed Sun. and 2 wks in Aug.* Ⓜ*Odéon.* ✦ *4:C3*

\$–\$\$
MIDDLE
EASTERN
Le Marais, 4ᵉ

Chez Marianne. You'll know you've found Marianne's when you see the line of people reading the bits of wisdom and poetry painted across her windows. The restaurant-deli, with a second cloistered room in the back, serves excellent Middle Eastern and Jewish specialties such as hummus, fried eggplant, and soul-warming chopped liver, which you can match with one of the affordable wines. The sampler platter lets you try four, five, or six items—even the smallest plate makes a filling feast. Falafel sandwiches are served in the restaurant only on weekdays at lunch, though you can get them anytime at the takeout window.

17

Bars à Vin

Bars à vins (wine bars) are perfect for enjoying a glass (or bottle) of wine with a plate of cheese, charcuterie, or tasty hot meal—the food in many wine bars rivals that in very good bistros. Wine bar owners are often true wine enthusiasts, ready to dispense expert advice. With few exceptions, the focus is squarely on French wines, but there is plenty of *terroir* to explore. Hours vary, so check ahead if your heart is set on a particular place; many close around 10 PM.

Au Sauvignon. Edge your way in among the lively tipplers at this homey spot with a terrace. The simple menu makes ordering the right glass a breeze. ⊠ *80 rue des Sts-Pères, 7ᵉ, St-Germain-des-Prés* ☎ *01-45-48-49-02* Ⓜ *Sèvres-Babylone.*

Le Baron Bouge. Formerly Le Baron Rouge, this wine bar near the place d'Aligre market has changed in name only. In winter you can often find an oyster feast in midswing outside the door; inside, expect regulars to welcome you with the same frosty suspicion of cowboys at their local saloon. ⊠ *1 rue Théophile Roussel, 12ᵉ, Bastille/Nation* ☎ *01-43-43-14-32* Ⓜ *Ledru-Rollin.*

Bu Bar. In summer look for the hip professional crowd spilling out the front of this signless wine bar in the Marais. It's named for Jean-Paul, the bartender (*bubar* or *barbu* is French slang for "bearded"). The ever-changing wine menu—with many selections available by the glass—features French wines and (*quelle surprise*) small-batch vintages from South Africa, Chile, Argentina. ⊠ *3 rue des Tournelles, 4ᵉ, Le Marais* ☎ *01-40-29-97-72* Ⓜ *Bastille.*

Jacques Mélac. This wine bar is named after the jolly owner who harvests grapes from the vine outside and bottles his own wines. Cheese is hacked from a giant hunk of Cantal, and the hot dish of the day is always tasty. ⊠ *42 rue Léon-Frot, 11ᵉ, Bastille/Nation* ☎ *01-43-70-59-27* Ⓜ *Charonne.*

Les Papilles. Part wineshop and *épicerie*, part restaurant, Les Papilles has a winning formula—pick any bottle off the shelf and pay a €6 corkage fee to drink it with your meal. The southwestern-inspired bistro fare is delicious. ⊠ *30 rue Gay-Lussac, 5ᵉ, Quartier Latin* ☎ *01-43-25-20-79* Ⓜ *Cluny–La Sorbonne.*

Racines. The food is simple and hearty and the wines are all "natural"—sulfite-free, hand harvested, and unfiltered—at this café in the atmospheric Passage des Panoramas. It's packed at mealtimes, so be sure to reserve. ⊠ *8 passage des Panoramas, 2ᵉ, Opéra/Grands Boulevards* ☎ *01-40-13-06-41* Ⓜ *Grands Boulevards or La Bourse.*

La Robe et le Palais. Come here for the more than 120 wines from all over France, served *au compteur* (according to the amount consumed), as well as the selection of bistro-style dishes for lunch and dinner. ⊠ *13 rue des Lavandières-Ste-Opportune, 1ᵉʳ, Beaubourg/Les Halles* ☎ *01-45-08-07-41* Ⓜ *Châtelet Les Halles.*

Le Rouge Gorge. This sophisticated Marais wine bar attracts discriminating locals who come for unusual wines by the glass, often from obscure regions, and the hearty food with a Moroccan touch. ⊠ *8 rue St-Paul, 4ᵉ, Le Marais* ☎ *01-48-04-75-89* Ⓜ *La Bourse.*

⊠*2 rue des Hospitalières-St-Gervais* ☎*01–42–72–18–86* ▱*MC, V* Ⓜ*St-Paul.* ✛ *4:F2*

$$–$$$
NORTH
AFRICAN
République, 3ᵉ
★

Chez Omar. This is no longer the only trendy North African restaurant in town, but during fashion week you still might see top models with legs like gazelles touching up their lipstick in front of the vintage mirrors—though that doesn't stop them from digging into huge platters of couscous with grilled skewered lamb, spicy *merguez* sausage, lamb shank, or chicken, washed down with robust, fruity Algerian or Moroccan wine. Proprietor Omar Guerida speaks English and is famously friendly to all. The setting is that of a beautifully faded French bistro, complete with elbow-to-elbow seating, so be prepared to partake of your neighbors' conversations. ⊠*47 rue de Bretagne* ☎*01–42–72–36–26* ⌕*Reservations not accepted* ▱*No credit cards* ☾*No lunch Sun.* Ⓜ*Temple, République.* ✛ *2:F6*

$$–$$$
BISTRO
Quartier Latin,
5ᵉ

Chez René. Run by the same family for 50 years, Chez René changed owners in 2007. The new team has wisely preserved the bistro's traditional spirit while brightening the décor and adding chic touches such as valet parking. The menu still consists mainly of Lyonnais classics, but you'll now find some of these grouped into color-themed menus such as "red" (beet salad, coq au vin, and Quincy wine) or "yellow" (Swiss chard gratin, pike-perch in beurre blanc sauce with steamed potatoes, and Mâcon wine). The best sign of the new regime's success is that the old regulars keep coming back, including the former owners, who live upstairs. ⊠*14 bd. St-Germain* ☎*01–43–54–30–23* ▱*AE, MC, VC* ☾*Closed Sun., Mon., Christmas wk, and Aug. No lunch Sat.* Ⓜ*Maubert-Mutualité.* ✛ *4:E4*

17

$$–$$$
BISTRO
Champs-Elysées,
8ᵉ

Chez Savy. Just off the glitzy Avenue Montaigne, Chez Savy occupies its own circa-1930s dimension, oblivious to the area's fashionization. The Art Deco cream-and-burgundy interior looks blissfully intact (avoid the back room unless you're in a large group), and the waiters show not a trace of attitude. Fill up on rib-sticking specialties from the Auvergne in central France—lentil salad with bacon, foie gras (prepared on the premises), perfectly charred lamb with feather-light shoestring frites, and pedigreed Charolais beef. Order a celebratory bottle of Mercurey with your meal and feel smug that you've found this place. ⊠*23 rue Bayard* ☎*01–47–23–46–98* ▱*MC, V* ☾*Closed weekends and Aug.* Ⓜ*Franklin-D.-Roosevelt.* ✛ *1:E5*

$–$$
BISTRO
Montmartre, 18ᵉ

Chez Toinette. Between the red lights of Pigalle and the Butte Montmartre, this cozy bistro with red walls and candlelight hits the romance nail on the head. In autumn and winter, game comes into play in long-simmered French dishes—choose from *marcassin* (young wild boar), venison, and pheasant. Regulars can't resist the crème brûlée and the raspberry tart. With friendly, professional waiters and reasonable prices, Chez Toinette is a rare find for this neighborhood. ⊠*20 rue Germain Pilon* ☎*01–42–54–44–36* ⊕ ▱*MC, V* ☾*Closed Sun. and Aug. No lunch* Ⓜ*Pigalle.* ✛ *2:B1*

$$
CHINESE
Chinatown, 13ᵉ
☾

La Chine Massena. With wonderfully overwrought rooms that seem draped in a whole restaurant-supply catalog's worth of Asiana (plus four monitors showing the very latest in Hong Kong music videos), this is a fun place to come with friends. Not only is the pan-Asian food good and moderately priced, but the place itself has a lot of entertainment value—wedding parties often provide a free floor show, and on weekends Asian disco follows variety shows. Steamed dumplings, lacquered duck, and the fish and seafood you'll see swimming in the tanks are specialties. For the best value come at noon on weekdays for the bargain lunch menus, starting at €13. ⊠ *Centre Commercial Massena, 13 pl. de Vénétie* ☎ *01–45–83–98–88* ⊟ *AE, MC, V* Ⓜ *Porte de Choisy.* ✥ *1:G6*

$–$$
BISTRO
Montmartre, 9ᵉ

Le Ch'ti Catalan. Run by two friends, one from northern France (best known for its potent cheeses and creative use of Belgian endive) and the other from the Catalan-influenced southwest, this bistro has a unique mission in Paris: to combine the two seemingly incompatible styles. Though the restaurant looks a bit scruffy from the outside, the interior is painted in warm ocher tones and the chatty staff will put you at ease. Among the seasonal dishes on the handwritten chalkboard menu, you might come across a wonderful starter of roasted red peppers and fresh anchovies, delicious pork simmered with white beans, Catalan-style salt cod, and steak with potent Maroilles cheese. ⊠ *4 rue de Navarin* ☎ *01–44–63–04–33* ⊟ *MC, V* ⊙ *Closed Sun. and Christmas wk. No lunch Sat.* Ⓜ *Notre-Dame-de-Lorette.* ✥ *2:B2*

$$$$
HAUTE FRENCH
Champs-Elysées,
8ᵉ

Le Cinq. The massive flower arrangement at the entrance proclaims the no-holds-barred luxury on offer here. Painted powder blue, with stucco medallions worked into the ceiling trim, the room is beautiful, though a bit staid. Occasionally, the luxe menu (line-caught turbot with pumpkin-and-grapefruit marmalade, a licorice-infused pear cube with Szechuan pepper ice cream) is brought back down to earth by such selections as grouse and haggis in an aged Scotch whiskey sauce. There is a €75 lunch menu. ⊠ *Hôtel Four Seasons George V, 31 av. George V* ☎ *01–49–52–70–00* ⚖ *Reservations essential Jacket and tie* ⊟ *AE, DC, MC, V* Ⓜ *George V.* ✥ *1:D5*

$
MODERN
FRENCH
Les Invalides, 7ᵉ

✕ **Les Cocottes de Christian Constant.** Chef Christian Constant has an unfailing sense of how Parisians want to eat these days, as proved by the latest addition to his mini-restaurant empire near the Eiffel Tower. At Les Cocottes he's shifted the normally leisurely bistro experience into high gear, which allows him to keep prices moderate. Seated at a long counter on slightly uncomfortable stools that discourage lingering, diners can mix and match from a menu of soups, salads, cocottes (dishes served in cast-iron pots), verrines (starters presented in tapas-style glasses), and comforting desserts, all made from fresh, seasonal ingredients. Food is served nonstop from breakfast onward, but since no reservations are taken, plan on showing up outside peak times to avoid a wait. ⊠ *135 rue St-Dominique* ☎ *01–45–50–10–31* ⚖ *Reservations not accepted* ⊟ *MC, V* Ⓜ *Métro Ecole Militaire, Métro or RER: Pont de l'Alma.* ✥ *3:D2*

$$$
BISTRO
St-Germain, 6ᵉ

Le Comptoir du Relais Saint-Germain. Run by legendary bistro chef Yves Camdeborde, this tiny Art Deco hotel restaurant is booked up several months in advance for the single dinner sitting that comprises a five-course, €48 set menu of haute-cuisine-quality food. On weekends and before 6 PM during the week a brasserie menu is served and reservations are not accepted, resulting in long lineups and brisk service. Start with charcuterie or pâté, then choose from open-faced sandwiches, salads, and a handful of hot dishes such as braised beef

cheek, roast tuna, and Camdeborde's famed deboned and breaded pig's trotter. Sidewalk tables make for prime people-watching in summer and Le Comptoir also runs a down-to-earth snack shop next door that serves crêpes and sandwiches. ⊠*9 carrefour de l'Odéon* ☎*01–44–27–07–50* ⊟*AE, DC, MC, V* Ⓜ*Odéon.* ✛ *4:B3*

$$–$$$
BRASSERIE
Montparnasse,
14ᵉ

La Coupole. This world-renowned cavernous spot with Art Deco murals practically defines the term *brasserie*. La Coupole might have lost its intellectual aura since the Flo group's restoration, but it's been popular since Jean-Paul Sartre and Simone de Beauvoir were regulars, and it's still great fun. Today it attracts a mix of bourgeois families, tourists, and elderly lone diners treating themselves to a dozen oysters. Recent additions to the classic brasserie menu are a tart of caramelized apple and panfried foie gras, beef fillet flambéed with cognac before your eyes, and profiteroles made with Valrhona chocolate. On most days, you can't make a reservation after 8 or 8:30, so be prepared for a wait at the bar. ⊠*102 bd. du Montparnasse* ☎*01–43–20–14–20* ⊟*AE, DC, MC, V* Ⓜ*Vavin.* ✛ *4:A6*

$$$$
HAUTE FRENCH
Trocadéro/Tour
Eiffel, 16ᵉ

Le Cristal Room. The success of this restaurant in the Baccarat museum-boutique stems not only from the stunning décor by Philippe Starck— mirrors, patches of exposed-brick wall, and a black chandelier—but also from the culinary stylings of chef Thierry Burlot. He often plays with textures, as in a dish of hot bouillon poured over jellied oysters, or scallops and langoustines topped with Aquitaine caviar. Plan on reserving a week or two ahead for dinner; lunch requires little advance notice now that the initial fashion feeding frenzy has died down. ⊠*11 pl. des Etats-Unis* ☎*01–40–22–11–10* ⚐*Reservations essential* ⊟*AE, DC, MC, V* ☾*Closed Sun.* ✛ *1:C5*

$$$$
BRASSERIE
Montparnasse,
14ᵉ

Le Dôme. Now a fancy fish brasserie serving seafood delivered fresh from Normandy every day, this place began as a dingy meeting place for exiled artists and intellectuals such as Lenin and Picasso. You can still drop by the covered terrace for just a cup of coffee or a drink. ⊠*108 bd. Montparnasse* ☎*01–43–35–25–81* ⊟*AE, DC, MC, V* Ⓜ*Vavin.* ✛ *4:A6*

17

$$$
BISTRO
Le Marais, 4ᵉ

Le Dôme du Marais. Behind a discreet Marais doorway lies one of the most unusual dining rooms in Paris, under the glass dome of a former chapel that was once used as a municipal auction house. Fortunately, chef Pierre Lecoutre doesn't let the stunning setting steal the show. Whether you opt for one of the set menus starting at €19 (for two courses at lunch) or order à la carte, you can expect carefully considered dishes such as roast saddle of lamb with wild mushrooms and *cocos de Paimpol* (white beans), roast duck with green peppercorns and applesauce, and desserts such as chartreuse soufflé or the lemon and raspberry "diamond" cake. The waiters strike the right balance between friendliness and formality. Meals are also served under the glass atrium at the entrance, but aim for the more impressive main dining room. ⊠ *53 bis, rue des Francs-Bourgeois* ☎ *01–42–74–54–17* 🖃 *AE, MC, V* ☉ *Closed Sun., Mon., 1 wk in Jan., 1 wk in May, and 3 wks in Aug.* Ⓜ *St-Paul or Rambuteau.* ✛ *4:F1*

$$$–$$$$
BISTRO
Champs-Elysées,
8ᵉ

Dominique Bouchet. To taste the cooking of one of the city's great chefs, you no longer need pay for the sumptuous backdrop once provided by the Hotel Crillon: Dominique Bouchet has left that world behind for an elegant bistro where contemporary art brightens cream-painted walls, and he seems all the happier for it. On the menu, refined French technique meets country-style cooking, as in leg of lamb braised in wine with roasted cocoa bean and potato purée, or a chocolate éclair with black cherries and ice cream. Sometimes the dishes can get a touch too complicated, but the warm service makes up for it. ⊠ *11 rue Treilhard* ☎ *01–45–61–09–46* 🖃 *AE, DC, MC, V* ☉ *Closed weekends and 3 wks in Aug.* Ⓜ *Miromesnil.* ✛ *1:F3*

¢
VIETNAMESE
Père Lachaise,
11ᵉ

Dong Huong. Dong Huong isn't a secret, but you wouldn't find it by accident. These two undecorated dining rooms on a Belleville side street are where the local Chinese and Vietnamese come for a reassuring bowl of *pho* (noodle soup) or a big plate of grilled lemongrass-scented meat with rice. Spicy, peanut-y *saté* soup is a favorite, and at this price (€6.50) you can also spring for a plate of crunchy imperial rolls, to be wrapped in accompanying lettuce and mint. Try one of the lurid nonalcoholic drinks, too; they're surprisingly tasty. ⊠ *14 rue Louis-Bonnet* ☎ *01–43–57–18–88* 🖃 *MC, V* ☉ *Closed Tues. and 3 wks in Aug.* Ⓜ *Belleville.* ✛ *2:H4*

$$–$$$
MODERN
FRENCH
Opéra/Les
Halles, 2ᵉ
🕑

Drouant. Best known for the literary prizes awarded here since 1914, Drouant has shed its dusty image to become a forward-thinking restaurant. The man behind the transformation is Alsatian chef Antoine Westermann, who runs the hit bistro Mon Vieil Ami on the Ile St-Louis. At Drouant the menu is more playful, revisiting the French hors d'oeuvres tradition with starters that come as a series of four plates. Diners can pick from themes such as French classics (like a deconstructed *oeuf mayonnaise* and leek salad) or convincing minitakes on Thai and Moroccan dishes. Main courses similarly encourage grazing, with accompaniments that appear in little cast-iron pots and white porcelain dishes. Even desserts take the form of several tasting plates. Pace yourself here, since portions are generous and the cost of a meal quickly adds up. This is the place to bring adventurous young eaters, thanks to the €15 children's menu. The revamped dining room is bright and cheery, though the designer has gone slightly overboard with the custard-yellow paint and fabrics. ⊠ *16–18 place Gaillon* ☎*01–42–65–15–16* ▭*AE, DC, MC, V* Ⓜ*Pyramides.* ✛ *2:B5*

$–$$
MODERN
FRENCH
Montmartre, 17ᵉ

La Famille. Opened by Inaki Aizpitarte, who now runs Le Chateaubriand, this hip restaurant on a street known for its role in the film *Amélie has a new avant-garde chef at the helm.* Jaene Movera's cooking is strongly influenced by that of fellow Spaniard Ferran Adrià: expect dishes like vanilla-scented Jerusalem artichoke "froth" with jellied foie gras, and Thai ravioli with a coconut and galangal soup. The spare space attracts the *bobo* (bohemian bourgeois) neighbors, who are bringing a new energy to Montmartre. ⊠ *41 rue des Trois-Frères* ☎*01–42–52–11–12* ▭*AE, DC, MC, V* ☽*Closed Sun., Mon., and 3 wks in Aug. No lunch* Ⓜ*Abbesses.* ✛ *2:B1*

¢
CAFE
Opéra/Grands
Boulevards, 2ᵉ

☾

La Ferme Opéra. If your arm aches from flagging down café waiters, take a break in this bright, friendly, self-service restaurant near the Louvre that specializes in produce from the Ile-de-France region (around Paris). Inventive salads, sandwiches, and pastas are fresh and delicious, and on the sweeter side, you can find wholesome fruit crumbles, tarts, and cheesecakes. They serve whole-wheat scones and freshly squeezed juices for breakfast, from 8 AM on weekdays and 9 AM on Saturday; breakfast is served from 10 AM on Sunday, when there is also brunch from 11 AM to 4 PM. There's free Wi-Fi access in the barnlike dining room. ⊠ *55 rue St-Roch* ☎*01–40–20–12–12* ▭ *MC, V* Ⓜ*Pyramides.* ✛ *2:A5*

$$–$$$
BRASSERIE
Champs-Elysées,
8ᵉ

La Fermette Marbeuf 1900. Graced with one of the most mesmerizing Belle Époque rooms in town—accidentally rediscovered during renovations in the 1970s—this is a favorite haunt of French celebrities, who adore the sunflowers, peacocks, and dragonflies of the Art Nouveau mosaic. The menu rolls out solid, updated classic cuisine: try the snails in puff pastry, saddle of lamb with *choron* (a tomato-spiked béarnaise sauce), and bitter-chocolate fondant—but ignore the limited-choice €32 prix fixe unless you're on a budget. Popular with tourists and businesspeople at lunch, La Fermette becomes truly animated around 9 PM. ⊠ *5 rue Marbeuf* ☎*01–53–23–08–00* ▭*AE, DC, MC, V* Ⓜ*Franklin-D.-Roosevelt.* ✛ *1:D5*

$–$$
BISTRO
St-Germain, 6ᵉ

La Ferrandaise. Portraits of cows adorn the stone walls of this bistro near the Luxembourg gardens, showing the kitchen's penchant for meaty cooking (Ferrandaise is a breed of cattle). Still, there is something for every taste on the market-inspired menu, which always lists three meat and three fish mains. Dill-marinated salmon with sweet mustard sauce is a typical starter, and a thick, juicy milk-fed veal chop might come with a squash pancake and spinach. The dining room buzzes with locals who appreciate the good-value €32 prix fixe. ⊠ *8 rue de Vaugirard* ☎*01–43–26–36–36* ▭*AE, MC, V* ☽*Closed Sun. and 3 wks in Aug. No lunch Sat.* Ⓜ*Odéon, RER: Luxembourg.* ✛ *4:C4*

17

$–$$
SPANISH
Quartier Latin,
6ᵉ

Fogòn St-Julien. The most ambitious Spanish restaurant in Paris occupies an airy Seine-side space, avoiding tapas-bar clichés. The seasonal all-tapas menu, at €45 per person, is the most creative choice, but that would mean missing out on the paella: saffron with seafood (which could be a bit more generous), inky squid, or Valencia-style with rabbit, chicken, and vegetables. Finish up with custardy crème Catalan and a glass of muscatel. ⊠ *45 quai des Grands-Augustins* ☎ *01–43–54–31–33* ⌕ *Reservations essential* ▭*MC, V* ⊘ *Closed Mon. No dinner weekends* Ⓜ*St-Michel.* ✛ *4:C2*

$$$$
MODERN
FRENCH
St-Germain, 6ᵉ

Gaya Rive Gauche. If you can't fathom paying €200 and up per person to taste the cooking of Pierre Gagnaire, the city's most avant-garde chef, at his eponymous restaurant, book a meal at this, his informal fish restaurant, instead. At Gaya Rive Gauche—aim for the main-floor room, with its fish-scale wall, natural lighting, and bar for solo diners—Gagnaire uses seafood as a palette for his creative impulses. Expect small portions of artfully presented food, as in a seafood gelée encircled by white beans and draped with Spanish ham, or cod "petals" in a martini glass with soba noodles, mango, and grapefruit. Don't miss the desserts, one of Gagnaire's great strengths. ⊠ *44 rue du Bac* ☎ *01–45–44–73–73* ⌕ *Reservations essential* ▭*AE, DC, MC, V* ⊘ *Closed Sun., Aug., and 2 wks at Christmas. No lunch Sat.* Ⓜ*Rue du Bac.* ✛ *3:H2*

$$–$$$
MODERN
FRENCH
Beaubourg/Les
Halles, 3ᵉ

Le Georges. One of those rooftop showstopping venues so popular in Paris, Le Georges preens atop the Centre Georges Pompidou. The staff is as streamlined and angular as the furniture, and at night the terrace has distinct snob appeal. Come snappily dressed or you may be relegated to something resembling a dentist's waiting room. Part of the Costes brothers' empire, the establishment trots out fashionable dishes such as sesame-crusted tuna and coriander-spiced beef fillet flambéed with cognac. It's all considerably less dazzling than the view, except for the suitably decadent desserts (indulge in the Cracker's cheesecake with yogurt sorbet). ⊠ *Centre Pompidou, 6th fl., 19 rue Rambuteau,* ☎ *01–44–78–47–99* ▭*AE, DC, MC, V* ⊘ *Closed Tues.* Ⓜ*Rambuteau.* ✛ *4:E1*

$$–$$$
BISTRO
Parc Monceau
17ᵉ

Goupil le Bistro. The best Paris bistros give off an air of quiet confidence, and this is the case with Goupil, a triumph despite its out-of-the-way location not far from the Porte Maillot conference center. The dining room attracts dark suits at lunch and a festive crowd in the evenings, with a few well-informed English-speakers sprinkled into the mix. The tiny open kitchen works miracles with seasonal ingredients, transforming mackerel into luxury food (on buttery puff pastry with mustard sauce) and panfrying monkfish to perfection with artichokes and chanterelles. Friendly waiters are happy to suggest wines by the glass. ⊠ *4 rue Claude Debussy* ☎ *01–45–74–83–25* ▭*AE, MC, V* ⊘ *Closed weekends and Aug.* Ⓜ*Porte de Champerret.* ✛ *1:B1*

$$–$$$
BISTRO
Champs-Elysées,
17ᵉ

Le Graindorge. Steeped in vintage 1930s character, this restaurant thrives under chef-owner Bernard Broux, who blends the cuisines of southwestern France and his native Flanders. Try the eel terrine in herb aspic (seasonal) or rouget (red mullet) with endive in beer sauce, followed by a small but judicious selection of potent cheeses. If you're counting pennies, go for the €34 set menu at dinner or the €24 menu at lunch. Madame Broux can help you select one of the many fine beers, a rarity in Paris. ⊠*15 rue de l'Arc-de-Triomphe* ☎*01–47–64–33–47* ▤*AE, MC, V* ⊗*Closed Sun. and 2 wks in Aug. No lunch Sat.* Ⓜ*Charles-de-Gaulle–Etoile.* ✛ *1:C3*

$$–$$$
BRASSERIE
Louvre/Tuileries,
2ᵉ

Le Grand Colbert. One of the few independently owned brasseries left in Paris, Le Grand Colbert, with its globe lamps and ceiling moldings, feels grand yet not overpolished. It attracts a wonderfully Parisian mix of elderly lone diners, business lunchers, tourists, and couples, all of whom come for the enormous seafood platters, duck foie gras with Sauternes jelly, and steak tartare, as well as a few southern-influenced dishes. Whet your appetite with one of the "unjustly forgotten" aperitifs, such as bitter Salers or sweet Lillet Blanc. The kitchen does the simple fare best. Finish with profiteroles (choux pastry filled with ice cream and smothered in hot chocolate sauce). It's also a pleasant destination between 3 and 6 pm for rich hot chocolate and cakes, or after the theater for a bowl of soup. ⊠*4 rue Vivienne* ☎*01–42–86–87–88* ▤*AE, DC, MC, V* Ⓜ*Bourse.* ✛ *2:B5*

$$$$
HAUTE FRENCH
Louvre/Tuileries,
1ᵉʳ

Le Grand Véfour. Victor Hugo could stride in and still recognize this place—in his day, as now, a contender for the title of most beautiful restaurant in Paris. Originally built in 1784, it has welcomed everyone from Napoléon to Colette to Jean Cocteau. The mirrored ceiling and early-19th-century glass paintings of goddesses and muses create an air of restrained seduction. Foodies as well as the fashionable gather here to enjoy chef Guy Martin's unique blend of sophistication and rusticity, as seen in dishes such as frogs' legs with sorrel sauce, and oxtail parmentier (a kind of shepherd's pie) with truffles. The outstanding cheese trolley pays tribute to his native Savoie. For dessert, try the house specialty, *palet aux noisettes* (meringue cake with milk-chocolate mousse, hazelnuts, and salted caramel ice cream). Prices are as extravagant as the décor, but there is an €88 lunch menu. ⊠*17 rue de Beaujolais* ☎*01–42–96–56–27* ⌂*Reservations essential Jacket and tie* ▤*AE, DC, MC, V* ⊗*Closed weekends, Aug., 1 wk in Apr., 1 wk at Christmas. No dinner Fri.* Ⓜ*Palais-Royal.* ✛ *2:B5*

17

$$–$$$$
BRASSERIE
Champs-Elysées,
16ᵉ

La Grande Armée. The Costes brothers, of the too-cool Costes hotel, are perpetually in the forefront of whatever's trendy in town. Their brasserie near the Arc de Triomphe is a handy way to sample their cheeky flair, since it's open daily, serves nonstop, and has knockout over-the-top Napoléon III décor dreamed up by superstar designer Jacques Garcia—black-lacquered tables, leopard upholstery, and a carefully tousled clientele picking at seasonal fare that might include smoked salmon, panfried calf's liver, and runny-centered chocolate cake (the menu changes every two months). ⊠*3 av. de la Grande Armée* ☎*01–45–00–24–77* ▤*AE, DC, MC, V* Ⓜ*Charles-de-Gaulle–Etoile.* ✛ *1:B4*

$$$$
HAUTE FRENCH
Champs-Elysées,
17ᵉ
Fodor's Choice
★

Guy Savoy. Revamped with dark African wood, rich leather, cream-color marble, and the chef's own art collection, Guy Savoy's luxury restaurant doesn't dwell on the past. Come here for a perfectly measured haute-cuisine experience, since Savoy's several bistros have not lured him away from his kitchen. The artichoke soup with black truffles, sea bass with spices, and veal kidneys in mustard-spiked jus reveal the magnitude of his talent, and his mille-feuille is an instant classic. If the waiters see you are relishing a dish, they won't hesitate to offer second helpings. Generous half portions allow you to graze your way through the menu—unless you choose a blowout feast for €265 or €320—and reasonably priced wines are available (though beware the cost of wines by the glass). One table is reserved each day for the €100 lunchtime discovery menu, which can be booked only via the Web site (www.guysavoy.com). Best of all, the atmosphere is joyful, because Savoy knows that having fun is just as important as eating well. ⊠ *18 rue Troyon* 🕾 *01–43–80–40–61* ⚲ *Reservations essential Jacket required* ▭ *AE, MC, V* ⊘ *Closed Sun., Mon., Aug., and 1 wk at Christmas. No lunch Sat.* Ⓜ *Charles-de-Gaulle–Etoile.* ✢ *1:C3*

> ## WORD OF MOUTH
>
> "On our day of arrival, it was raining and cold. While getting our bearings we stopped at a crêpe stand. Stood under our umbrellas, lapping up every dripping, hot morsel. It still ranks up there with other 'best meals.'"
>
> –JeanneB

$$$$
HAUTE FRENCH
St-Germain, 6ᵉ

Hélène Darroze. The eponymous chef here has won many followers with her refined take on southwestern French cooking from the lands around Albi and Toulouse. You know it's not going to be *la même chanson*—the same old song—as soon as you see the contemporary tableware, and Darroze's intriguingly modern touch comes through in such dishes as a sublime duck foie gras confit served with an exotic-fruit chutney or a blowout of roast wild duck stuffed with foie gras and truffles. Expect to spend a hefty €350 for two à la carte (with drinks) upstairs. For a more affordable taste of her style, try the relatively casual Salon d'Hélène downstairs; the sultry Boudoir, which specializes in chic finger food; or her new Latin Quarter bistro Toustem. ⊠ *4 rue d'Assas* 🕾 *01–42–22–00–11* ▭ *AE, DC, MC, V* ⊘ *Closed Sun., Mon., and Aug.* Ⓜ *Sèvres Babylone.* ✢ *4:A4*

¢
JAPANESE
Opéra/Grands
Boulevards, 1ᵉʳ
Fodor's Choice
★
☕

Higuma. When it comes to steaming bowls of noodles, this no-frills dining room divided into three sections beats its many neighboring competitors. Behind the counter—an entertaining spot for solo diners—cooks toil over giant flames, tossing strips of meat and quick-fried vegetables, then ladling noodles and broth into giant bowls. A choice of *formules* allows you to pair various soups and stir-fried noodle dishes with six delicious *gyoza* (Japanese dumplings), and the stir-fried dishes are excellent, too. Don't expect much in the way of service, but it's hard to find a more generous meal in Paris at this price. There is a more subdued annex (without the open kitchen) at 163 rue St-Honoré, near the

Louvre. ✉*32 and 32 bis, rue Ste-Anne* ☎*01–47–03–38–59* ▬*MC, V* Ⓜ*Pyramides.* ✛ *2:B5*

$$$$
FRENCH FUSION
Trocadéro/Tour
Eiffel, 16ᵉ
★

Hiramatsu. In fall 2004 Hiramatsu left its Seine-side perch on Ile St-Louis for this spacious Art Deco dining room with just 40 seats. Chef Hajime Nakagawa continues his variations on the subtly Japanese-inspired French cuisine of restaurant namesake Hiroyuki Hiramatsu, who still sometimes works the kitchen. Luxury ingredients feature prominently in dishes such as thin slices of lamb with onion "jam" and truffle-spiked jus, or an unusual pot-au-feu of oysters with foie gras and black truffle. For dessert, a mille-feuille of caramelized apples comes with rosemary sorbet. There is no way to get away cheaply, so save it for a special occasion, when you might be tempted to order a tasting menu for €95 or €130 (lunch menus start at €48). ✉*52 rue de Longchamp* ☎*01–56–81–08–80* ⌖*Reservations essential* ▬*AE, DC, MC, V* ☾*Closed weekends and Aug.* Ⓜ*Trocadéro.* ✛ *1:B6*

$$–$$$
SEAFOOD
St-Germain, 6ᵉ

Huîtrerie Régis. When the oysters are this fresh, who needs anything else? That's the philosophy of this bright 14-seat restaurant with crisp white tablecloths and convenient hours (11 AM–midnight), popular with the area's glitterati. If you find yourself puzzling over the relative merits of *fines de claires, spéciales,* and *pousses en claires,* you can always go with the €21.50 prix fixe that includes a glass of Muscadet, 12 No. 3 (medium) oysters, and coffee—or ask the knowledgeable waiters for their advice. You can supplement this simplest of meals with shrimp and perhaps a slice of freshly made fruit pie. ✉*3 rue de Montfaucon* ☎*01–44–41–10–07* ▬*AE, MC, V* ☾*Closed Mon. and mid-July to end of Sept.* Ⓜ*Mabillon.* ✛ *4:B3*

$$–$$$
SEAFOOD
Parc Monceau,
17ᵉ

L'Huîtrier. If you have a single-minded craving for oysters, this is the place for you. The friendly owner will describe the different kinds available and you can follow with any of several daily fish specials—or opt for a full seafood platter for around €50. Blond-wood and cream tones prevail. If you have trouble getting a table, L'Huîtrier also runs the Presqu'île next door. ✉*16 rue Saussier-Leroy* ☎*01–40–54–83–44* ▬*AE, MC, V* ☾*Closed Sun. Sept.–May; Sun. and Mon. June–Aug.* Ⓜ*Ternes.* ✛ *1:C2*

$$$$
FRENCH FUSION
Invalides, 7ᵉ
Fodor'sChoice
★

Il Vino. It might seem audacious to present hungry diners with nothing more than a wine list, but the gamble is paying off for Enrico Bernardo at his newly opened restaurant with a branch in Courcheval. Winner of the world's best sommelier award in 2005, this charismatic Italian has left the George V to oversee a dining room where food plays second fiddle (in status, not quality). The hip décor—plum banquettes, body-hugging white chairs, a few high tables—has attracted a mostly young clientele that's happy to play the game by ordering one of the blind, multicourse tasting menus for €75 or €100. This might bring you a white Mâcon with saffron risotto, crisp Malvasia with crabmeat and black radish, a full-bodied red from Puglia with Provençal-style lamb, sherrylike *vin jaune* d'Arbois with aged Comté cheese, and sweet Jurançon with berry crumble. You can also order individual wine-food combinations à la carte or pick a bottle straight from the cellar and

17

ON THE RUN

Eating on the run doesn't come naturally to the French, and you can easily spend two hours, albeit pleasantly, having lunch in a Paris café. If you're looking for something a bit quicker, there's no point in trying to make a Parisian waiter move faster than he wants to; instead, head to a new breed of snack shop that puts speed first, without sacrificing quality. Prices can be a bit high for what you get (expect to spend €10–€15 for a meal), but it's still a lot cheaper than eating in most bistros.

Le Pain Quotidien. Part bakery, part café, this Belgian chain with locations throughout the city serves fresh salads and sandwiches at lunch and is one of the best places for breakfast. Try to avoid peak times, though, when it can be overrun with office workers.

Oh Poivrier! Specializing in quirkily named open-face sandwiches, this long-established chain with several locations makes a good alternative to slower-pace cafés, with terraces in some scenic spots.

Cojean. This French-run chain takes an Anglo approach to healthful eating, with premade wraps, salads, and sandwiches plus quick dishes available at the counter. Quality has remained despite its rapid expansion.

Bioboa. Famed for its veggie burger, this organic café also serves seasonal salads, soups, sandwiches, and hot dishes, alongside freshly squeezed juices, milk shakes, and almost-virtuous homemade cakes. It's mobbed with office workers at lunch, so try to come early. ⊠3 rue Danielle Casanova, 1er ☎ 01–48–04–52–56.

Scoop. You can linger in the comfy upstairs room or perch at the counter of this cheerful Anglo-inspired café near the Louvre to tuck into inventive wraps and salads. Ice creams are made on the premises, and the turtle sundae is outstanding. ⊠ 154 rue St-Honoré, 1er ☎ 01–42–60–31–84.

Boost. Once you've built your own super-healthy salad or chosen a warming soup at this minuscule juice bar, grab a table outside or head to the leafy Square du Temple across the street. ⊠16 rue Dupetit-Thouars, 3e ☎ 01–40–27–95–45.

Bob's Juice Bar. If you're strolling along the Canal St-Martin, stop into this funky juice bar run by American Marc Grossman, aka Bob, for uplifting juices, organic salads, and muffins. ⊠ *15 rue Lucien Saimpax*, 10^e ☎ 06–82–63–72–74.

Cosi. Miles from the cardboard panini served at many crêpe stands, this Italian sandwich shop in St-Germain piles fillings onto delicious crusty bread. ⊠ *54 rue de Seine*, 6^e ☎ 01–46–33–35–36.

ask for a meal to match. ⊠ 13 bd. de la Tour-Maubourg Ⓜ*Invalides* ☎01–44–11–72–00 ▭*AE, DC, MC, V* ✛ *3:F2*

$$$
BISTRO
St-Germain, 6^e

Josephine Chez Dumonet. Theater types, politicos, and well-padded locals fill the moleskin banquettes of this venerable bistro, where the frosted-glass lamps and amber walls put everyone in a good light. Unlike most bistros, Josephine caters to the indecisive, since half portions allow you to graze your way through the temptingly retro menu. Try the excellent *boeuf Bourguignon,* roasted saddle of lamb with artichokes, top-notch steak tartare prepared table-side, or anything with truffles in season. For dessert, choose between a mille-feuille big enough to serve three and a Grand Marnier soufflé that simply refuses to sink, even with prodding. The wine list, like the food, is outstanding but expensive. ⊠ *117 rue du Cherche-Midi* ☎ *01–45–48–52–40* ▤ *AE, MC, V* ☉ *Closed weekends* Ⓜ *Duroc.* ✢ *3:G5*

$$$$
HAUTE FRENCH
Tour Eiffel, 7ᵉ

Jules Verne. Alain Ducasse doesn't set his sights low, so it was no real surprise when he took over this prestigious dining room on the second floor of the Eiffel Tower. During months of renovations he did away with the dated black décor, replacing it with designer Patrick Jouin's neo-futuristic look in shades of brown. Sauces and pastries are prepared in a kitchen below the Champ de Mars before being whisked up the elevator to the kitchen, which is overseen by young chef Pascal Féraud. Most accessible is the €75 lunch menu (weekdays only), which brings you à la carte dishes in slightly smaller portions. Spend more (about €150–€200 per person) and you'll be entitled to more lavish dishes such as lobster with celery root and black truffle, and fricassee of Bresse chicken with crayfish. For dessert the kitchen reinterprets French classics, as in an unsinkable pink grapefruit soufflé with grapefruit sorbet. Book months ahead or try your luck at the last minute. ⊠ *Tour Eiffel, south pillar, Av. Gustave Eiffel* ☎ *01–45–55–61–44* ⚓ *Reservations essential Jacket required* ▤ *AE, DC, MC, V* Ⓜ *Bir-Hakeim* ✢ *3:C2*

17

$$–$$$
HAUTE FRENCH
Opéra/Grands
Boulevards, 10ᵉ

Julien. Famed for its 1879 décor—think Art Nouveau stained glass and *La Bohème*–style street lamps hung with vintage hats—this Belle Époque dazzler certainly lives up to its oft-quoted moniker, "the poor man's Maxim's." Look for smoked salmon, stuffed roast lamb, cassoulet, and, to finish, profiteroles or the *coupe Julien* (ice cream with cherries). The crowd here is lots of fun; this place has a strong following with the fashion crowd, so it's mobbed during the biannual fashion and fabric shows. Food is served until midnight, with a late-night menu for €23.50 from 10 PM. ⊠ *16 rue du Faubourg St-Denis* ☎ *01–47–70–12–06* ▤ *AE, DC, MC, V* Ⓜ *Strasbourg St-Denis.* ✢ *2:E4*

¢–$
INDIAN
Montmartre, 9ᵉ

Kastoori. On a pretty little restaurant-strewn square down the hill from Montmartre, Kastoori is something of a miracle. Not only is its terrace (now heated in winter) one of the most agreeable in Paris, but the modest dining room draped with Indian fabrics feels equally relaxing on a rainy day, and the reliably good Indian food offers tremendous value. The best bets at lunch are the €8 or €10 daily-changing *thali* platters—silver trays bearing curried meat (usually chicken or lamb), vegetables, and saffron rice. There's also a €15 dinner menu. You can't go wrong with the Kastoori chicken, braised with yogurt, pistachio, and coriander. Work it all off with a hike up the hill to Sacré-Coeur. ⊠ *4 pl. Gustave Toudouze* ☎ *01–44–53–06–10* ▤ *MC, V* Ⓜ *St-Georges.* ✢ *2:B2*

$$$$
JAPANESE
Champs-Elysées,
17ᵉ

Kifune. It's rare to see a non-Japanese face in the modest dining room of Kifune, where you can sit at the bar and admire the sushi chef's lightning-quick skills or opt for a more intimate table. Crab-and-shrimp salad makes a sublime starter, and the miso soup with clams is deeply flavored. To follow, you can't go wrong with the sashimi. A meal here will leave a dent in your wallet, but some expats say you won't find anything closer to Japanese home cooking in Paris. ✉ *44 rue St-Ferdinand* ☎ *01–45–72–11–19* ⌂ *Reservations essential* ▭ *MC, V* ☾ *Closed Sun. No lunch Mon.* Ⓜ *Argentine.* ✛ *1:A3*

$$$–$$$$
BISTRO
Quartier Latin,
6ᵉ

Lapérouse. Emile Zola, George Sand, and Victor Hugo were regulars, and the restaurant's mirrors still bear diamond scratches from the days when mistresses didn't take jewels at face value. All together, it's hard not to fall in love with this 17th-century Seine-side town house whose warren of intimate, woodwork-graced salons breathes history. The latest chef, Alain Hacquard, has found the right track with a daring (for Paris) spice-infused menu: his lobster, Dublin Bay prawn, and crayfish bisque is flavored with Szechuan pepper and lemon. Game is prominent in the fall, with a selection of southwestern wines to accompany dishes like Scottish grouse. For a truly intimate meal, reserve one of the legendary private *salons* where anything can happen (and probably has). You can also sample the restaurant's magic at lunch, when a prix-fixe menu is served for €35 and the dining room is often quiet. ✉ *51 quai des Grands Augustins* ☎ *01–43–26–68–04* ⌂ *Reservations essential* ▭ *AE, DC, MC, V* ☾ *Closed Sun. No lunch Sat.* Ⓜ *St-Michel.* ✛ *4:C2*

$$$$
HAUTE FRENCH
Champs-Elysées,
8ᵉ

Ledoyen. Tucked away in the quiet gardens flanking the Champs-Elysées, Ledoyen is a slightly faded study in the grandiose style of Napoléon III. Young Breton chef Christian Le Squer's menu is a treat—even if you opt for the relatively affordable lunchtime €88 prix fixe. He uses flawless produce, as seen in *les coquillages* (shellfish), a delicious dish of herb risotto topped with lobster, langoustines, scallops, and grilled ham. The turbot with truffled mashed potatoes is excellent, too, and don't skip the superlative cheese trolley. ✉ *1 av. Dutuit, on Carré des Champs-Elysées,* ☎ *01–53–05–10–01* ⌂ *Reservations essential* ▭ *AE, MC, V* ☾ *Closed weekends and 1 wk at Christmas. No lunch Mon.* Ⓜ *Concorde, Champs-Elysées–Clemenceau.* ✛ *1:F6*

$$$
MODERN
FRENCH
Louvre/Tuileries,
1ᵉʳ

Macéo. Natural light streams through this restaurant, and a broad, curved staircase leads to a spacious upstairs salon. With reasonably priced set menus ranging from €27 (for two courses at lunch) to €38 (for three courses at lunch or dinner), this is an ideal spot for a relaxed meal after a day at the Louvre. It's also a hit with vegetarians, as chef Thierry Bourbonnais whips up a meatless set menu with two starter and three main course options—perhaps a Moroccan-style vegetable *pastilla* (phyllo-dough pie) to start, followed by a crêpe filled with wild mushrooms, served with roasted endive (though his efforts can be a little hit-or-miss). Meat lovers might sink their teeth into farmer's lamb with confit vegetables and mousseline potatoes. The wine list spotlights little-known producers alongside the big names—as befits this sister restaurant to Willi's Wine Bar. ✉ *15 rue des Petits-Champs* ☎ *01–42–97–53–85* ▭ *MC, V* ☾ *Closed Sun. and 2–3 wks in Aug. No lunch Sat.* Ⓜ *Palais-Royal.* ✛ *2:B5*

$$$$
MODERN
FRENCH
Champs-Elysées,
8ᵉ

Maison Blanche. The celebrated Pourcel twin brothers preside over this edgy "White House." Typical of the globe-trotting, southern French–inspired (and not always successful) fare are the vegetable pot-au-feu with white Alba truffle (a section of the menu is dedicated to vegetarian dishes), crisp-crusted scallop tart with crab and baby leeks, and French beef with an herb crust, mushrooms, and shallots slow cooked in Fitou wine. This is a place for the fat of wallet and trim of figure, though there is a €65 lunch menu. Desserts are divided into chocolate and fruit sections, the fruit options being the most playful. In keeping with the snow-white setting, staff can be rather frosty. ⊠15 av. Montaigne ☎01–47–23–55–99 ⚑Reservations essential ⊟AE, MC, V ⊘No lunch weekends Ⓜ Franklin-D.-Roosevelt. ⊹ 1:D6

$$$
BRASSERIE
Champs-Elysées,
8ᵉ

La Maison de l'Aubrac. Run by a former rugby player with his own cattle farm, this convivial 24-hour brasserie specializes in beef from the Aubrac, a volcanic region of central France renowned for the quality of its livestock. Beefy rugby enthusiasts come here for the he-man slabs of meat—from steak tartare enlivened with Espelette chili pepper to rump steak, faux-filet (aka sirloin in the United States), entrecôte, and rib of beef—and the regional specialties, such as *aligot* (cheesy mashed potatoes) served with sausage. If the food is straightforward, the wine list is not, with 1,000 different bottles to choose from. ⊠37 rue Marbeuf ☎01–43–59–05–14 ⊟AE, MC, V Ⓜ Franklin-D.-Roosevelt. ⊹ 1:E5

$$–$$$$
MODERN
FRENCH
Champs-Elysées,
8ᵉ

Market. Celebrated New York–based Alsatian chef Jean-Georges Vongerichten (Vong, Mercer Kitchen, and Jean-Georges) set up shop in this neighborhood to much fanfare, as this is his first restaurant in France. Put together with deceptively simple raw materials—burned pine and stone offset with African masks—the dining room makes a soigné if sometimes noisy arena for well-traveled and generally reliable dishes such as truffled pizza, quail with Thai spices, and sweet chestnut soufflé. Brunch is served from noon and 5 pm on weekends and there is a €45 dinner menu for those who get their orders in between 7 and 8 pm. ⊠15 av. Matignon ☎01–56–43–40–90 ⚑Reservations essential ⊟AE, DC, MC, V Ⓜ Franklin-D.-Roosevelt. ⊹ 1:F5

$–$$$
NORTH
AFRICAN
République, 10ᵉ

Le Martel. Of the scads of neighborhood couscous joints in Paris, a few have become fashionable thanks to their host's magnetic personality and their stylish setting; this converted bistro ranks among the more recent of that set. It's crowded, but the clientele of fashion designers, photographers, models, and media folk is as cool as it gets in this up-and-coming quartier. Everyone digs in to a mix of French standbys (such as artichokes with vinaigrette) and more exotic fare like lamb tagine with almonds, prunes, and dried apricots. ⊠3 rue Martel ☎01–47–70–67–56 ⊟MC, V ⊘Closed Sun. and Aug. No lunch Sat. Ⓜ Château d'Eau. ⊹ 2:E4

$–$$$
BRASSERIE
Montmartre, 18ᵉ

La Mascotte. Though everyone talks about the "new Montmartre," exemplified by a wave of chic residents and throbbingly cool cafés and bars, it's good to know that the old Montmartre is alive and well at the untrendy-and-proud-of-it Mascotte. This old-fashioned café-bras-

17

serie—which dates from 1889, the same year that saw the opening of the Eiffel Tower and the Moulin Rouge—is where you can find neighborhood fixtures such as the drag queen Michou (of the nearby club Chez Michou), who always wears blue. Loyalists come for the seafood platters, the excellent steak tartare, the warming *potée auvergnate* (pork stew) in winter, and the gossip around the *comptoir* (bar) up front. ⊠*52 rue des Abbesses* ☎*01–46–06–28–15* ▤*MC, V* Ⓜ*Abbesses.* ✣ *2:B1*

¢–$
CHINESE
Quartier Latin,
5ᵉ
☾

Mirama. Regulars at this popular and rather chaotic no-frills Chinese restaurant order the soup, a rich broth with a nest of thick noodles garnished with dumplings, barbecued pork, or smoked duck. Main courses are generous—the best are made with shellfish, and the Peking duck is also excellent. Service is brisk, so plan on having your coffee at a nearby café instead, but this place is quick, easy, and a far more reliable bet than the countless Asian *traiteurs* selling microwave-reheated food of suspect origins. ⊠*17 rue St-Jacques* ☎*01–43–29–66–58* ▤*MC, V* Ⓜ*St-Michel.* ✣ *4:C6*

$–$$
MODERN
FRENCH
Ile St-Louis, 4ᵉ
Fodor'sChoice
★

Mon Vieil Ami. "Modern Alsatian" might sound like an oxymoron, but once you've tasted the food here, you'll understand. The updated medieval dining room—stone walls, dark-wood tables, and small glass-panels dividers—provides a stylish milieu for the inventive cooking orchestrated by star Alsatian chef Antoine Westermann, which showcases heirloom vegetables (such as yellow carrots and pink-and-white beets) from star producer Joël Thiébault. Pâté *en croûte* (wrapped in pastry) with a knob of foie gras is hard to resist among the starters. Long-cooked, wine-marinated venison comes with succulent accompaniments of quince, prune, celery root, and chestnuts. This is not necessarily the place for a romantic dinner since seating is a little tight, but the quality of the food never falters. Call during opening hours (11:30–2:30 and 7–11) to book, since they don't answer the phone the rest of the time. ⊠*69 rue St-Louis-en-l'Ile* ☎*01–40–46–01–35* ▤*AE, DC, MC, V* ⊗*Closed Mon., Tues., 3 wks in Jan., and 3 wks in Aug.* Ⓜ*Pont Marie.* ✣ *4:E3*

$$$–$$$$
MODERN
FRENCH
Le Marais, 3ᵉ

Le Murano. If you love Baccarat's Cristal Room, you'll simply adore the swank Murano Urban Resort's restaurant in the achingly chic northern Marais. There is nothing subtle about the dining room, whose ceiling drips with white tubes of various lengths. Dress to the nines and arrive with plenty of attitude (or brace yourself with three test tubes of alcohol at the bar). The light, globe-trotting food neither distracts nor offends—try smoked salmon with pink *tarama* (cod roe), sautéed squid, and a signature dish of beer-marinated Japanese Kobe beef cooked *à la plancha* (on a grill). An oh-so-chic weekend brunch is served from noon until 5 PM. If you can survive the sneering once-over at the door, surprisingly good-humored dining room staff add to the experience. ⊠*13 bd. du Temple* ☎*01–42–71–20–00* ⌕*Reservations essential* ▤*AE, DC, MC, V* Ⓜ*Filles du Calvaire.* ✣ *2:G6*

$$$$
BISTRO
Trocadéro/Tour
Eiffel, 15ᵉ

L'Os à Moelle. Come for the early sitting at this little bistro on the edge of town and you'll often discover the dining room filled with English and Japanese tourists (the waiters speak English automatically). The €38, multicourse dinner menu accounts for the restaurant's popularity—yet lately quality seems to have been slipping, with chef Thierry Faucher also running Les Caves de l'Os à Moelle across the street and the recently opened Les Symples de l'Os à Moelle in the suburb of Issy les Moulineaux. Of six courses, at least four are likely to be fine—but not all his ideas work, such as warm oysters in herb butter that fail to preserve the taste of the sea. Waiters plunk even the higher-priced bottles of wine on the table without waiting for the customer to swill and slurp. Still, these problems are nothing that couldn't be fixed with a little more attention from the chef. ✉ *3 rue Vasco-de-Gama* ☎ *01–45–57–27–27* ⌚ *Reservations essential* 🚫 *MC, V* 🕐 *Closed Sun., Mon., 1 wk in July, and 3 wks in Aug.* Ⓜ *Balard.* ✛ *3:A6*

$$$–$$$$
BISTRO
Bastille/Nation,
12ᵉ

L'Oulette. Chef-owner Marcel Baudis's take on the cuisine of his native southwestern France is original and delicious, and service here is effusive—qualities that will help you overlook the out-of-the-way location and out-of-date design (though there is now a terrace for summer dining). The menu changes with the seasons: you might come across foie gras confit in spiced wine or monkfish studded with chorizo sausage in a spicy broth. Nearly everyone wisely opts for the *menu de saison* (€51) that includes a generous amount of wine; there is also a more elaborate €90 menu. The restaurant, in the rebuilt Bercy district, is a bit hard to find, so head out with your map. (Baudis also runs the Bistrot de l'Oulette, at 38 rue des Tournelles in the Marais.) ✉ *15 pl. Lachambeaudie* ☎ *01–40–02–02–12* 🚫 *AE, DC, MC, V* 🕐 *Closed weekends* Ⓜ *Dugommier.* ✛ *4:H5*

$
BISTRO
Les Gobelins,
13ᵉ

L'Ourcine. La Régalade–trained chef Sylvain Danière knows just what it takes to open a wildly popular bistro: choose an obscure location in a residential neighborhood, decorate it simply but cheerfully, work extremely hard, set competitive prices (€32 for three courses), and constantly reinvent your menu. The real key ingredient is talent, though, and Danière has plenty of it, as demonstrated by his winning trio of pork cheeks with lentils and foie gras, and a tart lime cream for dessert. Locals mingle with well-informed tourists from Texas or Toulouse in the red-and-cream dining room, and you can watch the chef hard at work in his small kitchen. ✉ *92 rue Broca* ☎ *01–47–07–13–65* 🚫 *MC, V* 🕐 *Closed Sun., Mon., and mid-July–mid-Aug.* Ⓜ *Les Gobelins.* ✛ *4:D6*

$–$$
BISTRO
Bastille/Nation,
11ᵉ

Le Passage des Carmagnoles. Feeling carnivorous? Search out this friendly spot near Place de la Bastille in an obscure passage. Though it bills itself as a wine bar, it has a full menu, including the celebrated andouillette sausage from the town of Vouvray. The initials AAAAA mean the sausage has the stamp of approval from the French andouillette aficionados' association. As the andouillette's pungent tripey aroma makes it an acquired taste, other, less fragrant dishes are available, such as rabbit with mustard, steak tartare flavored with mint, game in season, and even ostrich. The wine bar claim is far from unfounded, though; Le

17

Passage has many unusual bottles. ✉*18 passage de la Bonne Graine, enter by 108 av. Ledru-Rollin* ☎*01–47–00–73–30* ▭*AE, MC, V* ◷*Closed Sun.* Ⓜ*Ledru-Rollin.* ✛ *4:H3*

$–$$
BISTRO
Trocadéro/Tour
Eiffel, 16ᵉ

Le Petit Rétro. A diverse clientele (men in expensive suits at noon and well-dressed locals in the evening) frequents this little bistro with Art Nouveau tiles and bentwood furniture. You can't go wrong with the daily specials, which are written on a chalkboard presented by one of the friendly servers: perhaps crisp-skinned blood sausage with apple-and-honey sauce, blanquette de veau, and a crepe mille-feuille with orange and Grand Marnier. Arrive with an appetite, because the food is hearty. There are several prix-fixe menus to choose from, starting at €21.50 at lunch (for two courses). ✉*5 rue Mesnil* ☎*01–44–05–06–05* ▭*AE, MC, V* ◷*Closed weekends and 3 wks in Aug.* Ⓜ*Victor-Hugo.* ✛ *1:A5*

$$$$
HAUTE FRENCH
Champs-Elysées,
8ᵉ

Pierre Gagnaire. If you want to venture to the frontier of luxe cooking today—and if money is truly no object—dinner here is a must. Chef Pierre Gagnaire's work is at once intellectual and poetic, often blending three or four unexpected tastes and textures in a single dish. Just taking in the menu requires concentration (ask the waiters for help), so complex are the multi-line descriptions about the dishes' six or seven ingredients. The Grand Dessert, a seven-dessert marathon, will leave you breathless, though it's not as overwhelming as it sounds. The businesslike gray-and-wood dining room feels refreshingly informal, especially at lunch, but it also lacks the grandeur expected at this level. The uninspiring prix-fixe lunch (€105) and occasional ill-judged dishes (Gagnaire is a big risk taker, but also one of France's top chefs) linger as drawbacks, and prices keep shooting skyward, which makes Pierre Gagnaire an experience best saved for the financial elite. ✉*6 rue de Balzac* ☎*01–58–36–12–50* ⚑*Reservations essential* ▭*AE, DC, MC, V* ◷*Closed Sat. No lunch Sun.* Ⓜ*Charles-de-Gaulle-Etoile.* ✛ *1:D4*

$$–$$$
MODERN
FRENCH
Louvre/Tuileries,
1ᵉʳ

Pinxo. The word *pinxo* means "to pinch" in Basque, and this is how the food in this fashionable hotel restaurant is meant to be eaten—often with your fingers, and off your dining companion's plate (each dish is served in three portions for sharing). Freed from the tyranny of the *entrée-plat-dessert* cycle, you can nibble your way through such mini-dishes as marinated herring with Granny Smith apple and horseradish, and squid cooked *à la plancha* (on a grill) with ginger and chili peppers. Alain Dutournier, who also runs the more formal Le Carré des Feuillants and Au Trou Gascon, drew on his southwestern roots to create this welcoming modern spot; granted, some dishes work better than others, but it's hard not to love a place that serves fried Camembert croquettes with celery sticks as a cheese course. ✉*9 rue d'Alge, or through the Hôtel Plaza Paris Vendôme, at 4 rue du Mont Thabor* ☎*01–40–20–72–00* ▭*AE, DC, MC, V* ◷*Closed 2 wks in Aug.* ✛ *2:A6*

$$$$
HAUTE FRENCH
Bois de
Boulogne, 16ᵉ

Le Pré Catelan. Live a Belle Époque fantasy by dining beneath the chestnut trees on the terrace of this fanciful landmark *pavillon* in the Bois de Boulogne. Each of chef Frédéric Anton's dishes is a variation on a theme, such as *l'os à moelle*: bone marrow prepared two ways, one peppered and the other stuffed with porcini and cabbage, both braised in a concentrated meat jus. For a taste of the good life at a (relatively) gentle price, order the €75 lunch menu and soak up the opulent surroundings along with service that's as polished as the silverware. ⊠*Route de Suresnes* ☎*01–44–14–41–14* ✍*Reservations essential Jacket and tie* ▤*AE, DC, MC, V* ⊗*Closed Sun. and Mon., 2 wks in Feb., and 1 wk in Oct.–Nov. No dinner Sun. June–Sept.* Ⓜ*Porte Dauphine.* ✛ *1:A3*

$
MODERN
FRENCH
Quartier Latin,
5ᵉ

Le Pré Verre. Chef Philippe Delacourcelle knows his cassia bark from his cinnamon, thanks to a long stint in Asia, and he opened this lively bistro, with its purple-gray walls and photos of jazz musicians, to showcase his unique culinary style, rejuvenating archetypal French dishes with Asian and Mediterranean spices. So popular has it proved, especially with Japanese visitors, that the restaurant opened a branch in Tokyo in late 2007. His bargain prix-fixe menus (€13 at lunch for a main dish, glass of wine, and coffee; €26.50 for three courses at dinner) change constantly, but his trademark spiced suckling pig with crisp cabbage is a winner, as is his rhubarb compote with gingered white-chocolate mousse. Ask for advice in selecting wine from a list that highlights small producers. ⊠*8 rue Thénard* ☎*01–43–54–59–47* ▤*MC, V* ⊗*Closed Sun., Mon., and 3 wks in Aug.* Ⓜ*Maubert-Mutualité.* ✛ *4:D4*

$$$
SEAFOOD
Champs Elysées,
17ᵉ
Fodor'sChoice
★

Rech. Having restored the historic Paris bistros Aux Lyonnais and Benoît to their former glory, star chef Alain Ducasse has turned his piercing attention to this seafood brasserie founded in 1925. His wisdom lies in knowing what not to change: the original Art Deco chairs in the main floor dining room; seafood shucker Malec, who has been a fixture on this chic stretch of sidewalk since 1982; and the XXL éclair (it's supersized) that's drawn in the locals for decades. Original owner Auguste Rech believed in serving a limited selection of high-quality products, a principle that suits Ducasse perfectly, and from the compact open kitchen upstairs, young chef Baptiste Peupion turns out impeccable dishes such as octopus carpaccio with Genovese pesto, lobster ravioli, and astonishingly good clam chowder. Don't forget to save room for the whole farmer's Camembert, another Rech tradition. ⊠ 62 av. des Ternes ☎01–45–72–29–47 ▤*AE, DC, MC, V* ⊗*Closed Sun. and Mon.* ✛ *1:B3*

$$–$$$
BISTRO
Bastille/Nation,
11ᵉ

Le Repaire de Cartouche. In this split-level, dark-wood bistro between Bastille and République, chef Rodolphe Paquin applies a disciplined creativity to earthy French regional dishes. The menu changes regularly, but typical are a salad of *haricots verts* (green beans) topped with tender slices of squid, scallops on a bed of diced pumpkin, juicy lamb with white beans, game dishes in winter, and old-fashioned desserts like baked custard with tiny shell-shape madeleines. In keeping with cost-conscious times, he whips up a bargain three-course lunch menu for €17 that doesn't skimp on ingredients—expect the likes of homemade pâté to start, followed by fried red mullet or hangar steak with french fries, and chocolate tart. The wine list is very good, too, with some bargain wines from small producers. ⊠*8 bd. des Filles du Calvaire* ☎*01–47–00–25–86* ✍*Reservations essential* ▤*MC, V* ⊗*Closed Sun., Mon., and Aug.* Ⓜ*Filles du Calvaire.* ✛ *4:G1*

17

$$$
BISTRO
Louvre/Tuileries,
1er

Restaurant du Palais-Royal. This stylish modern bistro decorated in jewel tones serves food to match its stunning location under the arcades of the Palais-Royal, facing its magnificent gardens. Sole, scallops, and risotto—including a dramatic black squid-ink and lobster or an all-green vegetarian ver-

sion—are beautifully prepared, but juicy beef fillet with *pommes Pont Neuf* (thick-cut frites) is also a favorite of expense-account lunchers. Finish with an airy mille-feuille that changes with the seasons—berries in summer, chestnuts in winter—or a decadent baba doused with rum from Guadeloupe. Book in advance, especially in summer, when the terrace tables are hotly sought after. ⊠ *Jardins du Palais-Royal, 110 Galerie Valois* ☎ *01–40–20–00–27* ▤ *AE, DC, MC, V* ⊘ *Closed Sun.* Ⓜ *Palais-Royal.* ✛ *2:B6*

$$$
BISTRO
Quartier Latin,
5^e
Fodor's Choice
★

Ribouldingue. Find offal off-putting? Don't let that stop you from trying this new bistro near the ancient St-Julien-le-Pauvre church, where offcuts take pride of place on the compulsory €27 prix fixe. You can avoid odd animal bits completely, if you must, and by opting for dishes such as marinated salmon and veal rib with fingerling potatoes. Or go out on a limb with the *tétine de vache* (thin breaded and fried slices of cow's udder) and *groin de cochon* (the tip of a pig's snout). This adventurous menu is the brainchild of Nadège Varigny, daughter of a Lyonnais butcher. She runs the front of house while chef Caroline Moncel turns out the impeccable food—veal kidney with potato gratin is a house classic. Don't miss the unusual desserts, such as the tart ewe's-milk ice cream. ⊠ *10 rue St-Julien-le-Pauvre* ☎ *01–46–33–98–80* ▤ *MC, V* ⊘ *Closed Sun., Mon., and 3 wks in Aug.* Ⓜ *St-Michel.* ✛ *4:D3*

$
BRITISH
Montmartre, 9^e

Rose Bakery. On a street lined with French food shops selling produce, fresh fish, baguettes, and monastery cheeses, this British-run café-restaurant might easily go unnoticed, if it weren't for the frequent line out the door. Whitewashed walls, childlike art, and concrete floors provide the décor, and organic producers supply the ingredients for food so fresh and tasty it puts most Paris lunch spots to shame. French office workers and the area's Anglos fill the room at lunch to feast on seasonal salads, soups, and hot dishes such as risotto, followed by carrot cake, sticky toffee pudding, or comically large lemon tarts. The nostalgic can buy homemade granola, British marmalade, organic peanut butter, or baked beans to take home—and, should you find that you can't live without the food here, Rose Bakery has its own cookbook in English. Weekend brunch is popular, so plan to arrive early. ⊠ *46 rue des Martyrs* ☎ *01–42–82–12–80* ▤ *AE, MC, V* ⊘ *Closed Mon. and 2 wks in Aug. No dinner* Ⓜ *Notre-Dame-de-Lorette.* ✛ *2:C2*

$$$
ITALIAN
Bastille/Nation,
12^e

Sardegna a Tavola. Paris might have more Italian restaurants than you can shake a noodle at, but few smack of authenticity like this out-of-the-way Sardinian spot with peppers, braids of garlic, and cured hams hanging from the ceiling. Dishes are listed in Sardinian with French translation—*malloredus* is a gnocchi-like pasta; Sardinian ravioli are stuffed with cheese and mint. Perhaps best of all are the clams in a spicy broth with tiny pasta and the orange-scented prawns with tagliatelle. ⊠*1 rue de Cotte* ☎*01–44–75–03–28* ⊟*AE, MC, V* ☉*Closed Sun. No lunch Mon.* Ⓜ*Ledru-Rollin.* ✣ *4:H4*

$$$$
HAUTE FRENCH
Champs-Elysées,
7ᵉ

Les Saveurs de Flora. Alain Passard–trained Flora Mikula made her name at Les Olivades, a Provençal bistro in the chic residential 7ᵉ, before joining a gaggle of ambitious restaurateurs in this platinum-card area. Moving away from the bistro register, she's turning out refined food with southern twists in an unabashedly pink, boudoirlike setting. Standout dishes on the changing seasonal menu are three soft-boiled eggs with truffle, porcini, and foie gras, roasted scallops with herb butter, and a spectacular Grand Marnier soufflé. To take advantage of the superb cheese trolley, order from the pricier *carte (menu)*; a cheese plate is available on the €36 menu for a €2 supplement. Service, like the food, is generally impeccable, with the occasional minor slip-up. ⊠*36 av. George V* ☎*01–40–70–10–49* ⊟*AE, MC, V* ☉*Closed Sun. and Aug. No lunch Sat.* Ⓜ*Franklin-D.-Roosevelt.* ✣ *1:D5*

$$$–$$$$
HAUTE FRENCH
Opéra/Grands
Boulevards, 8ᵉ

Senderens. Iconic chef Alain Senderens waited until retirement age to make a rebellious statement against the all-powerful Michelin inspectors, "giving back" the three stars he had held for 28 years and renaming his restaurant (it was Lucas Carton). He also updated the décor, juxtaposing curvy, white, new furnishings and craterlike ceiling lights against the splendid Art Nouveau interior. The fusion menu spans the globe, though Senderens has also, happily for the patrons, reintroduced the occasional Lucas Carton signature dishes such as polenta with truffles in winter. Some dishes work, as in warm semismoked salmon with Thai spices and cucumber, and some fall flat, as in a too-rich starter of roast foie gras with fig salad and licorice powder. Senderens has also taken his passion for food-and-drink matches to extremes, suggesting a glass of wine, whiskey, sherry, or even punch to accompany each dish. Upstairs, Le Passage Bar serves sushi, tapas, and some of the same dishes as the main dining room. ⊠*9 pl. de la Madeleine* ☎*01–42–65–22–90* ⊟*AE, DC, MC, V* Ⓜ*Madeleine.* ✣ *1:H5*

$$–$$$
BISTRO
Invalides, 7ᵉ

Le Soleil. Louis-Jacques Vanucci made his name dishing up Parisian bistro classics at his restaurant in the Clignancourt flea market (Le Soleil, 109 avenue Michelet, in the suburb of St-Ouen) before opening this central Paris offshoot a few steps from the Champ de Mars with fellow chef Jean-Jacques Jouteux. Here, in a dining room reminiscent of a Provençal patio, the focus is on southern French cooking made with the flawless ingredients for which Vanucci is famed. A simple dish of sautéed baby squid with roasted garlic becomes sublime thanks to the freshness of the seafood and the plump, pink-skinned cloves. Be sure to save room for one of the desserts, each of which develops a theme such as "lemons from Nice" or "Riviera coffee." Befitting this chic area, service is polished and polite. ⊠*153 rue de Grenelle* ☎*01–45–51–54–12* ⊟*AE, MC, V* ☉*Closed Sun., Mon., and 5 wks in July/Aug.* Ⓜ*Ecole Militaire.* ✣ *3:E2*

17

A Cheese Primer

Their cuisine might be getting lighter, but the French aren't ready to relinquish their cheese. Nearly every restaurant, no matter how humble or haute, takes pride in its odorous offerings. Some present a single, lovingly selected slice, whereas the more prestigious restaurants wheel in a trolley of specimens aged on the premises. These may be labeled, but most often the cheese waiter will name and describe them. Cheese always comes after the main course and before—or instead of—dessert.

Among the best bistros for cheese are **Astier**, where a giant wicker basket of oozy wonders is brought to the table, and **Le Comptoir**, where a dazzling cheese platter is part of the five-course dinner prix fixe. A few *bars à fromages* are springing up—devoted to cheese the way *bars à vins* are dedicated to wine. La **Fromagerie 31**, *(64 rue de Seine, 01–43–26–50–31)* is a terrific example.

Armed with these phrases, you can wow the waiter and work your way through the most generous platter.

Avez-vous le Beaufort d'été? (Do you have summer Beaufort?)

Beaufort is similar to Gruyère, and the best Beaufort is made with milk produced during the summer, when cows munch on fresh grass. Aged Beaufort is even more reminiscent of a mountain hike.

Je voudrais un chèvre bien frais/ bien sec. (I'd like a goat cheese that's nice and fresh/nice and dry.)

France produces many goat cheeses, some so fresh they can be scooped with a spoon and some tough enough to use as doorstops. It's a matter of taste, but hard-core cheese eaters favor the drier specimens, which stick to the roof of the mouth and have a frankly goaty aroma.

C'est un St-Marcellin de vache ou de chèvre? (Is this St-Marcellin made with cow's or goat's milk?)

St-Marcellin is a more original choice than ubiquitous crottin de chèvre (poetically named after goats' turds). Originally a goat cheese, today it's more often made with cow's milk. The best have an oozy center, though some like it dry as a hockey puck.

C'est un Brie de Meaux ou de Melun? (Is this Brie from Meaux or Melun?)

There are many kinds of Brie; Brie de Meaux is the best known, with a smooth flavor and runny center, whereas the much rarer Brie de Melun is more pungent and saltier.

Je n'aime pas le Camembert industriel! (I don't like industrial Camembert!)

Camembert might be a national treasure, but most of it is industrial. Real Camembert has a white rind with rust-color streaks and a yellow center.

Avez-vous de la confiture pour accompagner ce brebis? (Do you have any jam to go with this sheep's cheese?)

In the Basque region berry jam is the traditional accompaniment for sharp sheep's-milk cheeses, like Ossau-Iraty.

C'est la saison du Mont d'Or. (It's Mont d'Or season.)

This potent mountain cheese, also known as Vacherin, is produced only from September to March. It's so runny that it's traditionally eaten with a spoon.

—*Rosa Jackson*

$$$–$$$$
MODERN
FRENCH
Champs-Elysées,
8ᵉ

Spoon, Food & Wine. Alain Ducasse's original fusion bistro has a silver screen lighted with sculptures and a long central table where strangers share a unique dining experience. The mix-and-match menu hasn't changed significantly since the restaurant first opened, but you can now order the SpoonSum sampler menu at lunch for €47 or a more elaborate €89 tasting menu at dinner. Fashion folk love this place for its many vegetable and pasta dishes and its irresistible desserts, particularly the TobleSpoon, a takeoff on Toblerone. If you've sampled the Spoon concept elsewhere in the world, don't expect the same here; each branch is tailored to a particular city's tastes, and what looks exotic in Paris (bagels and bubble-gum ice cream) might seem humdrum in New York. ⊠*14 rue de Marignan* ☎*01–40–76–34–44* ⌖*Reservations essential* ▭*AE, MC, V* ⊗*Closed weekends, Aug., and 1 wk at Christmas* Ⓜ*Franklin-D.-Roosevelt.* ✤*1:E5*

$$–$$$
BISTRO
Bastille/Nation,
12ᵉ

Le Square Trousseau. This beautiful Belle Époque bistro with a charming sidewalk terrace that faces a leafy square in summer has long been a favorite of the fashion set, though the chances of spotting a movie star or model have diminished in recent years. No one can resist dressed-up bistro dishes like peppered country pâté, slow-cooked lamb with baby vegetables, or baby chicken with mustard and bread-crumb crust. Wines might seem pricey but are lovingly selected from small producers—you can also buy them, along with superb Spanish ham, at the restaurant's small boutique–wine bar next door. If you're on a budget, try the lunch menu at €21 for two courses or €25 for three. ⊠*1 rue Antoine Vollon* ☎*01–43–43–06–00* ▭*MC, V* ⊗*Closed Sun. and Mon.* Ⓜ*Ledru-Rollin.* ✤*4:H3*

17

$$$$
FRENCH FUSION
Champs-Elysées,
8ᵉ

Stella Maris. A pretty Art Deco front window is the calling card for this pristine spot near the Arc de Triomphe. An expense-account crowd mixes with serious French gourmands here, to dine on the subtle cuisine of likable Japanese chef Tateru Yoshino, who trained with Joël Robuchon and rewrites his menu four times a year. You can find hints of Japan in dishes—made with organic ingredients—such as eel blanquette with grilled cucumber, salmon prepared four ways (in salt, marinated with dill, smoked, and panfried), and a unique take on the French classic *tête de veau,* with turtle jus. Put your trust in Yoshino by opting for the tasting menu (€90 or €130), or keep your budget in check with the €49 lunch menu. ⊠*4 rue Arsène-Houssaye* ☎*01–42–89–16–22* ⌖*Reservations essential* ▭*AE, DC, MC, V* ⊗*Closed Sun., Aug., and Christmas. No lunch Sat.* Ⓜ*Etoile.* ✤*1:C4*

$$$–$$$$
CARIBBEAN
Trocadero, 16ᵉ

La Table de Babette. Thirty years ago Babette de Rozières, who grew up in Guadeloupe, used all her savings to open a tiny creole restaurant in Paris. Now she occupies one of the city's most prestigious dining rooms: the restaurant formerly known as Jamin, where Joël Robuchon once reigned. If Babette isn't afraid to think big—she is also a star chef on French television—her cooking has lost none of its soul, and reasonably priced set menus are available to sample it. Caribbean cooking relies on sunny ingredients prepared simply, and you'll find classics such as chayote squash filled with crabmeat, *blaff* (a lemony fish stew), and mutton *colombo* (a Caribbean curry) on the carte. Try to save room for an exotic dessert, perhaps sweet-potato mousse with berry coulis. ⊠*32 rue de Longchamp* ☎*01–45–53–00–07* ▤*AE, MC, V* ⊘*Closed Sun. No lunch Sat.* Ⓜ*Trocadéro or Iéna.* ✛ *1:B6*

$$$$
MODERN
FRENCH
Trocadéro/Tour
Eiffel, 16ᵉ

La Table de Joël Robuchon. Chef David Alves keeps up the lofty standard set by star chef Joël Robuchon, with dishes like quail stuffed with foie gras, served with truffled potato purée. As at Robuchon's L'Atelier, you'll find a selection of small plates alongside more substantial dishes, but the seating arrangement is more conventional (no bar, just tables and chairs) and La Table accepts reservations—in fact, you should book weeks in advance for a seat in this small dining room that is somewhat disconcertingly decorated in gold leaf. ⊠*16 av. Bugeaud* ☎*01–56–28–16–16* ⚑*Reservations essential* ▤*MC, V* Ⓜ*Victor-Hugo.* ✛ *1:A5*

$$–$$$
BISTRO
Trocadéro/Tour
Eiffel, 16ᵉᵉ
Fodor's Choice
★

La Table Lauriston. Serge Barbey has developed a winning formula in his chic bistro near the Trocadero: top-notch ingredients, simply prepared and generously served. His trademark dish, a gargantuan rib steak, is big enough to silence even the hungriest Texan. To start, you can't go wrong with his silky foie gras au torchon—the liver is poached in a flavorful bouillon—or one of the seasonal salads, such as white asparagus in herb vinaigrette. Given the neighborhood you might expect a businesslike setting, but the dining room feels cheerful, with vividly colored walls and velvet-upholstered chairs. Don't miss his giant baba au rhum, which the waiters will douse in a choice of three rums. ⊠*129 rue de Lauriston* ☎*01–47–27–00–07* ⚑*Reservations essential* ▤*AE, DC, MC, V* ⊘*Closed Sun. and 3 wks in Aug. No lunch Sat.* Ⓜ*Trocadéro.* ✛ *1:A6*

$$$$
HAUTE FRENCH
Champs-Elysées,
8ᵉ

La Table du Lancaster. Operated by one of the most enduring families in French gastronomy (the Troisgros clan has run a world-famous restaurant in Roanne for three generations) this stylish boutique-hotel restaurant is the perfect setting for stellar cosmopolitan cuisine; try to sit in the stunning Asian-inspired courtyard with its red walls and bamboo. Often drawing on humble ingredients such as eel or pigs' ears, the food reveals fascinating flavor and texture contrasts, like silky sardines on crunchy melba toast or tangy frogs' legs in tamarind. A classic borrowed from the menu in Roanne is cod in a seaweed bouillon over white rice, a subtle and sensual dish. And don't miss the desserts, such as not one but two slices of sugar tart with grapefruit slices for contrast. On Sundays there is a special €85 lunch menu that includes a glass of champagne. ⊠*Hotel Lancaster, 7 rue de Berri* ☎*01–40–76–40–18* ⚑*Reservations essential* ▤*AE, DC, MC, V* ⊘*Closed Aug. No lunch Sat.* Ⓜ*George V.* ✛ *1:D4*

$$$$
HAUTE FRENCH
Champs-Elysées,
8ᵉ

Taillevent. Perhaps the most traditional—for many diners this is only high praise—of all Paris luxury restaurants, this *grande dame* basks in renewed freshness under brilliant chef Alain Solivérès, who draws inspiration from the Basque country, Bordeaux, and Languedoc for his daily-changing menu. Traditional dishes such as scallops meunière (with butter and lemon) are matched with contemporary choices such as a splendid spelt risotto with truffles and frogs' legs or panfried duck liver with caramelized fruits and vegetables. One of the 19th-century paneled salons has been turned into a winter garden, and contemporary paintings adorn the walls. The service is flawless, and the exceptional wine list is well priced. All in all, a meal here comes as close to the classic haute-cuisine experience as you can find in Paris. You must reserve dinner tables a month in advance. ✉ *15 rue Lamennais* ☎ *01–44–95–15–01* ✍ *Reservations essential Jacket and tie* ▭ *AE, DC, MC, V* ⊘ *Closed weekends and Aug.* Ⓜ *Charles-de-Gaulle–Etoile.* ✚ *1:D4*

$$
BISTRO
Bastille/Nation,
11ᵉ

Le Temps au Temps. This 26-seat bistro, whose tiny dining room is dominated by a chandelier decorated with paper butterflies, serves unusually creative market-inspired cooking that keeps the regulars coming back—typical of the ever-changing €32 prix fixe are spiced mackerel fillets perched on a marrow bone, or roasted skate wing in a curried broth. For dessert, expect the likes of dense chocolate terrine with homemade honey sorbet. There are a few seats at the bar for solo diners. Service is thoughtful and attentive. ✉ *13 rue Paul Bert* ☎ *01–43–79–63–40* ▭ *MC, V* ⊘ *Closed weekends and Aug.* Ⓜ *Faidherbe-Chaligny.* ✚ *4:H3*

$$–$$$$
BISTRO
Invalides, 7ᵉ

Thoumieux. You can find all the ingredients of a quintessential Parisian bistro here: red-velour banquettes, yellow walls, bustling waiters, and locals with their poodles. Little has changed since 1923—except the prices. Thoumieux has been owned by the same family for four generations, and their roots in the Corrèze region of southwest France show in the number of hearty duck-based dishes, including rib-sticking rillettes, duck confit, and one of the city's best cassoulets. Thoumieux has also resurrected such neglected dishes as *tripes à la mode de Caen* (tripe slow cooked with leeks and Calvados) and fricassee *de crêtes et de couilles de coq* (two extremes of the rooster). ✉ *79 rue St-Dominique* ☎ *01–47–05–49–75* ▭ *AE, MC, V* Ⓜ *Invalides.* ✚ *3:E1*

$–$$
BISTRO
Montparnasse,
6ᵉ

Le Timbre. Working in a tiny open kitchen, Manchester native Chris Wright could teach many a French chef a thing or two about *la cuisine française.* He uses only the finest suppliers to produce a constantly changing seasonal menu that keeps the locals coming back, and a spring meal might begin with lightly cooked vegetables atop tapenade on toast, and asparagus spears dabbed with an anise-spiked sauce, balsamic vinegar, and Parmesan. The signature mille-feuille is spectacular, but try not to miss *le vrai et le faux fromage,* perhaps a two-year-old British cheddar juxtaposed with a farmer's goat cheese from the Ardèche. (The joke is that the English cheese is the "real" cheese and the French cheese is fake—although French people might read it the other way.) ✉ *3 rue Ste-Beuve* ☎ *01–45–49–10–40* ▭ *MC, V* ⊘ *Closed Sun., Mon., Aug., and 10 days at Christmas.* Ⓜ *Vavin.* ✚ *4:A5*

$$$$
HAUTE FRENCH
Quartier Latin,
5ᵉ

La Tour d'Argent. La Tour d'Argent has had a rocky time lately with the loss of a Michelin star, the death of owner Claude Terrail, and a change of chef, but the kitchens are freshly renovated and there is no denying the splendor of its setting overlooking the Seine. If you don't want to splash out on dinner, treat yourself to the set-price lunch menu for a relatively accessible €70; this entitles you to succulent slices of one of the restaurant's numbered ducks (the great duck slaughter began in 1919 and is now well past the millionth mallard, as your numbered certificate will attest). The most celebrated dish, *canard au sang* (duck in a blood-based sauce), is available à la carte or for a €26 supplement. Don't be too daunted by the vast wine list—with the aid of the sommelier you can splurge a little (about €80) and perhaps taste a rare vintage Burgundy from the extraordinary cellars, which survived World War II. ⊠ *15–17 quai de la Tournelle* ☎ *01–43–54–23–31* ⚲ *Reservations essential Jacket and tie at dinner* ▭ *AE, DC, MC, V* ☉ *Closed Mon. and Aug. No lunch Tues.* Ⓜ *Cardinal Lemoine.* ✛ *4:E4*

$$$
BISTRO
Latin Quarter,
5ᵉ

Toustem. Not content with heading one of the most celebrated restaurants in St-Germain, Hélène Darroze has opened this bistro offshoot in a 13th-century building around the corner from Notre-Dame. Hip designer Matali Crasset has boldly juxtaposed a white, orange, and lime-green color scheme against the original Gothic woodwork, and if the result is slightly bizarre, it does feel inviting. Even more welcoming is the hearty southwestern food from the chalkboard menu, such as *macaronnade de foie gras* (pasta tossed with mushrooms, big chunks of panfried duck liver, and lashings of cream). Calorie-counters could stick with lighter fare like a multicolored tomato salad and seared tuna with sautéed peppers, which would leave room for one of the decadent layered desserts. It's a bit pricey for a bistro, but nothing as shocking as Darroze's eponymous haute cuisine restaurant. ⊠ *12 rue de l'Hôtel Colbert* ☎ *01–40–51–99–87* ▭ *AE, DC, MC, V* ☉ *Closed Sun. and Mon.* Ⓜ *St-Michel.* ✛ *3:D3*

$$$–$$$$
HAUTE FRENCH
Trocadéro/Tour
Eiffel, 15ᵉ

Le Troquet. A quiet residential street shelters one of the best-value bistros around: prix-fixe menus start at €24 at lunch and rise to €40 for a six-course tasting menu, but it's the quality, not quantity, that counts. Chef Christian Etchebest sends out a changing roster of dishes from the Basque and Béarn regions of southwestern France, and a typical meal might include vegetable soup with foie gras and cream, panfried scallops in crab sauce or *axoa de veau* (a Basque veal sauté), and a vanilla soufflé with cherry jam. Béarn red wine fills the glasses, and happy regulars fill the dining room. ⊠ *21 rue François-Bonvin* ☎ *01–45–66–89–00* ▭ *MC, V* ☉ *Closed Sun., Mon., 3 wks in Aug., 1 wk in May, and 1 wk at Christmas* Ⓜ *Ségur.* ✛ *3:E5*

$$–$$$
LATIN
AMERICAN
Bastille/Nation,
11ᵉ

Unico. An architect and a photographer, both Parisians born in Argentina, teamed up to open Bastille's hottest new restaurant—literally, since the Argentinean meat served here is grilled over charcoal—and good-looking young locals pile into the orange-tiled, vintage 1970s dining room to soak up the party vibe. Whichever cut of beef you choose (the ultimate being *lomo*, or fillet), it's so melt-in-your-mouth that the sauces served on the side seem almost superfluous. Dessert probably won't be necessary, but banana in dulce de leche could satisfy the strongest sweet craving. Be sure to order an Argentinean wine, the perfect accompaniment for this bold cuisine. ⊠ *15 rue Paul-Bert* ☎ *01–43–67–68–08* ▭ *MC, V* ☉ *Closed Sun and Mon.* Ⓜ *Faidherbe-Chaligny.* ✛ *4:H3*

$$–$$$$ **Le Vaudeville.** Le Vaudeville is filled with journalists, bankers, and locals
BRASSERIE *d'un certain âge* who come for the good-value assortment of prix-fixe
Opéra/Grands menus (including two courses for €20.50 after 10:30 PM) and highly
Boulevards, 2ᵉ professional service. Shellfish, house-smoked salmon, foie gras with
raisins, slow-braised lamb, and desserts such as the floating island
topped with pralines are particularly enticing. Enjoy the graceful 1920s
décor—almost the entire interior of this intimate dining room is done
in real or faux marble—and lively dining until 1 AM daily. ⊠ *29 rue
Vivienne* ☎ *01–40–20–04–62* ⊟ *AE, DC, MC, V* Ⓜ *Bourse*. ✥ *2:C5*

$–$$ **Villa Victoria.** The restaurant formerly known as Velly has changed own-
BISTRO ers and name, but the kitchen continues to turn out some of the best
Montmartre, 9ᵉ bistro food in the neighborhood. In a timeworn setting—including a
lovely Art Deco bar—happy regulars tuck into updated French fare
such as beef fillet in green mustard sauce with sautéed potatoes, or
turbot with blood sausage and grenadine. The chalkboard selection
changes constantly, and three courses are a bargain at €32, though
you can also order individual dishes at slightly stiffer à la carte prices.
Seating is elbow-to-elbow and the atmosphere is convivial, aided by the
well-priced wines. ⊠ *52 rue Lamartine* ☎ *01–48–78–60–05* ⊟ *MC, V*
⊘ *Closed Sun. and Aug.* Ⓜ *Notre-Dame-de-Lorette*. ✥ *2:C3*

$$$–$$$$ **Le Violon d'Ingres.** Following in the footsteps of Joël Robuchon and
HAUTE FRENCH Alain Senderens, Christian Constant has given up the star chase in
Invalides, 7ᵉ favor of more accessible prices and a packed dining room (book at
Fodor's Choice least a week ahead). In 2006 Constant began offering a single €48 set
★ menu (with several choices for each course), and put Stéphane Schmidt
in charge of the kitchen so he could dash between his four restaurants
in this street, making sure the hordes are happy. And why wouldn't
they be? The food is sophisticated and the atmosphere is lively; you
can even find signature dishes such as the almond-crusted sea bass with
rémoulade sauce (a buttery caper sauce), alongside game and scallops
(in season), and comforting desserts like *pots de crème* and chocolate
tart. The food is still heavy on the butter, but with wines starting at
around €20 this is a wonderful place for a classic yet informal French
meal. ⊠ *135 rue St-Dominique* ☎ *01–45–55–15–05* ⌕ *Reservations
essential* ⊟ *AE, DC, MC, V* ⊘ *Closed Sun. and Mon.* Ⓜ *Ecole Mili-
taire*. ✥ *3:D2*

$–$$ **Willi's Wine Bar.** More a restaurant than a wine bar, this British-owned
MODERN spot is a stylish haunt for Parisian and visiting gourmands who might
FRENCH stop in for a glass of wine at the oak bar or settle into the wood-beamed
Louvre/Tuileries, dining room. The selection of reinvented classic dishes changes daily
1ᵉʳ and might include roast cod with artichokes and asparagus in spring,
venison in wine sauce with roast pears and celery-root chips in fall, and
mango candied with orange and served with vanilla cream in winter.
The restaurant is prix fixe only, you can have appetizers at the bar. The
list of about 250 wines reflects co-owner Mark Williamson's passion
for the Rhône Valley and Spanish sherries. ⊠ *13 rue des Petits-Champs*
☎ *01–42–61–05–09* ⊟ *MC, V* ⊘ *Closed Sun.* Ⓜ *Bourse*. ✥ *2:B5*

17

$$
CHINESE
Bastille/Nation,
11ᵉ

Wok Cooking. Design-it-yourself Asian stir-fry in a minimalist room has made this spot a hit with the penny-wise hipsters around party-hearty Bastille. You select the type of noodle you want and load up at a buffet with meats, seafood, and vegetables; then join the line to negotiate your preferred seasoning with the chefs who man the woks. (A few gestures should be all you need.) The all-you-can-eat single-price tariff (€20) lets you walk to the wok as many times as you want. Otherwise, there are deep-fried spring rolls as starters and a signature dessert of caramelized fruit salad. It's mobbed on Friday and Saturday and doesn't serve lunch. ⊠ *25 rue des Taillandiers* ☎ *01–55–28–88–77* ▤ *MC, V* ⊘ *Closed Sun. No lunch* Ⓜ *Bréguet Sabin, Bastille, Ledru-Rollin.* ✛ *4:H2*

$–$$
JAPANESE
St-Germain, 6ᵉ

Yen. If you're having what is known in French as a *crise de foie* (liver crisis), the result of overindulging in rich food, this chic Japanese noodle house with a summer terrace and a VIP room upstairs is the perfect antidote. The blond-wood walls soothe the senses, the staff is happy to explain proper slurping technique, and the soba (buckwheat noodles), served in soup or with a restorative broth for dipping, will give you the courage to face another round of caramelized foie gras. The soba noodles are made fresh on the premises every day, showing Parisians that there is more to Japanese cuisine than sushi. Desserts come from Sadaharu Aoki, who is famous for his green-tea éclairs. ⊠ *22 rue St-Benoît* ☎ *01–45–44–11–18* ▤ *AE, DC, MC, V* ⊘ *Closed Sun. and 3 wks in Aug.* Ⓜ *St-Germain-des-Prés.* ✛ *4:A2*

$$$
MODERN
FRENCH
Quartier Latin,
6ᵉ

Ze Kitchen Galerie. William Ledeuil made his name at the popular Les Bouquinistes (a Guy Savoy baby bistro) before opening this contemporary bistro in a loftlike space. If the name isn't exactly inspired, the cooking shows creativity and a sense of fun: from a deliberately deconstructed menu featuring raw fish, soups, pastas, and *à la plancha* (grilled) plates, consider the roast and confit duck with a tamarind-and-sesame condiment and foie gras, or lobster with mussels, white beans, and Thai herbs. Worldly eaters might find the flavors subtle, but the food is adventurous for Paris. The menu changes monthly and there are several different prix-fixe options at lunch, starting at €27. ⊠ *4 rue des Grands-Augustins* ☎ *01–44–32–00–32* ▤ *AE, DC, MC, V* ⊘ *Closed Sun. No lunch Sat.* Ⓜ *St-Michel.* ✛ *4:C2*

¢–$
JAPANESE
Louvre/Tuileries,
1ᵉʳ

Zen. There is no shortage of Japanese restaurants in this area around the Louvre, but this recent addition is a cut above much of the competition. The white-and-lime-green space feels refreshingly bright and modern, and you can perch at one of the curvy counters or settle in at a table. The menu has something for every taste, from warming ramen soups (part of a €9.90 lunch menu that includes five pork dumplings) to sushi and sashimi prepared with particular care. For a change, try the donburi, a bowl of rice topped with meat or fish, or Japanese curry with breaded pork or shrimp. A sign of the chef's pride in his food is that he offers cooking classes some Sundays (in French). ⊠ *8 rue de l'Echelle* ☎ *01–42–61–93–99* ▤ *MC, V* Ⓜ *Pyramides or Palais Royal.* ✛ *2:B4*

Dining & Lodging Atlas

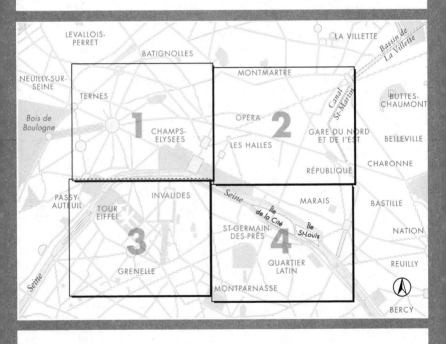

KEY	
□	Hotels
■	Restaurants
▣	Restaurant in Hotel
Ⓜ	Métro Stations

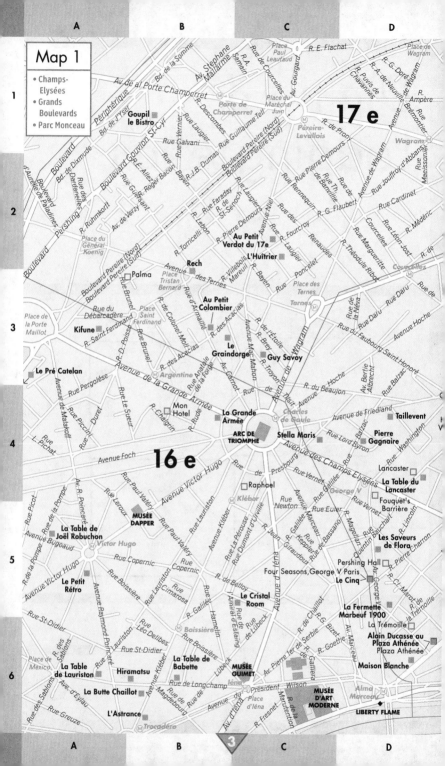

Map 1

- Champs-Elysées
- Grands Boulevards
- Parc Monceau

17 e

16 e

ARC DE TRIOMPHE

Goupil le Bistro

Au Petit Verdot du 17e

L'Huîtrier

Rech

Palma

Au Petit Colombier

Kifune

Le Graindorge

Guy Savoy

Le Pré Catelan

Mon Hotel

La Grande Armée

Stella Maris

Taillevent

Pierre Gagnaire

La Table de Joël Robuchon

MUSÉE DAPPER

Raphael

Lancaster

La Table du Lancaster

Fouquet's Barrière

Les Saveurs de Flora

Le Petit Rétro

Le Cristal Room

Four Seasons George V Paris

Pershing Hall

Le Cinq

La Fermette Marbeuf 1900

La Trémoille

La Table de Lauriston

Hiramatsu

La Table de Babette

MUSÉE GUIMET

Alain Ducasse au Plaza Athénée

Plaza Athénée

Maison Blanche

La Butte Chaillot

MUSÉE D'ART MODERNE

L'Astrance

LIBERTY FLAME

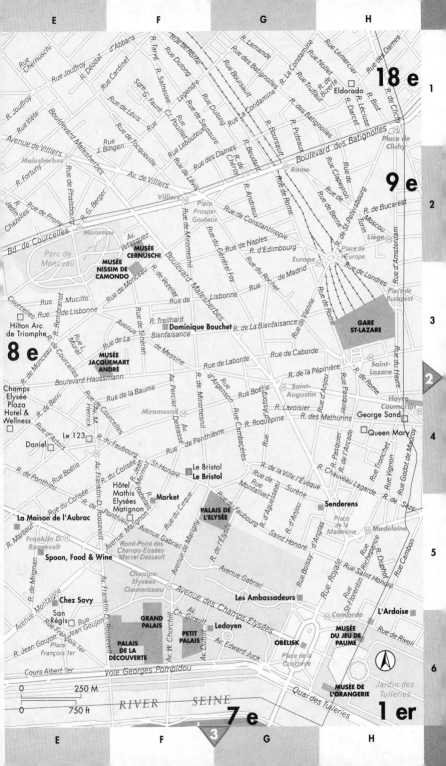

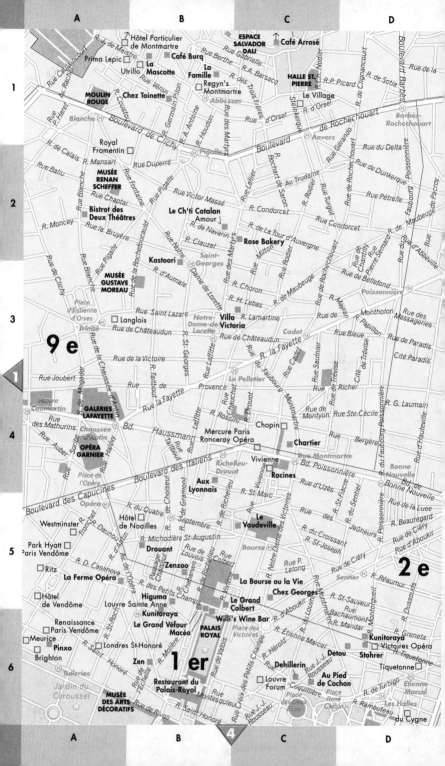

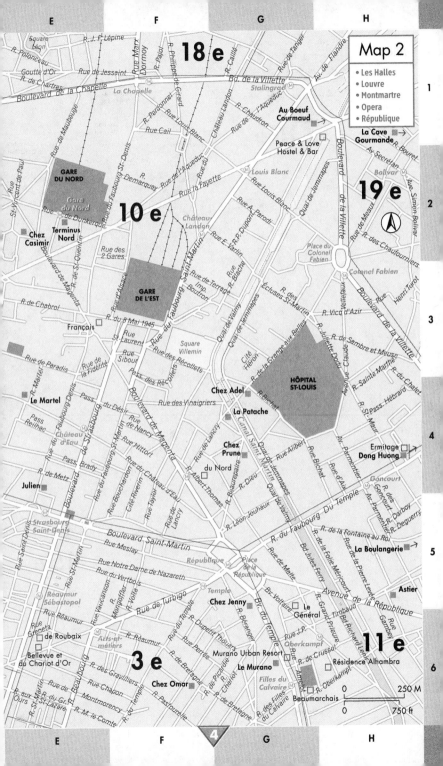

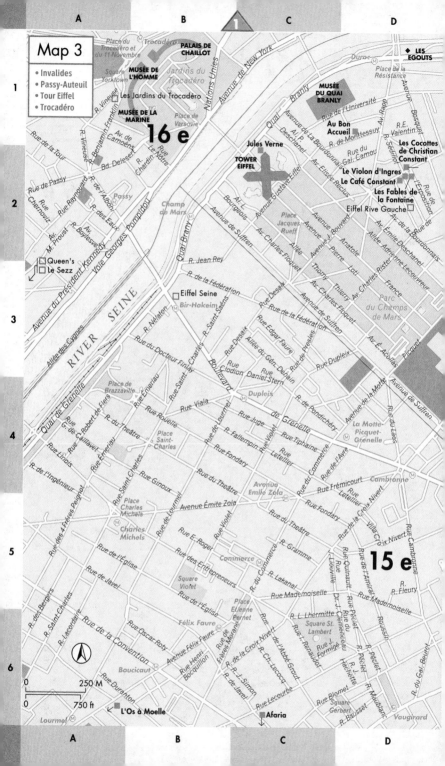

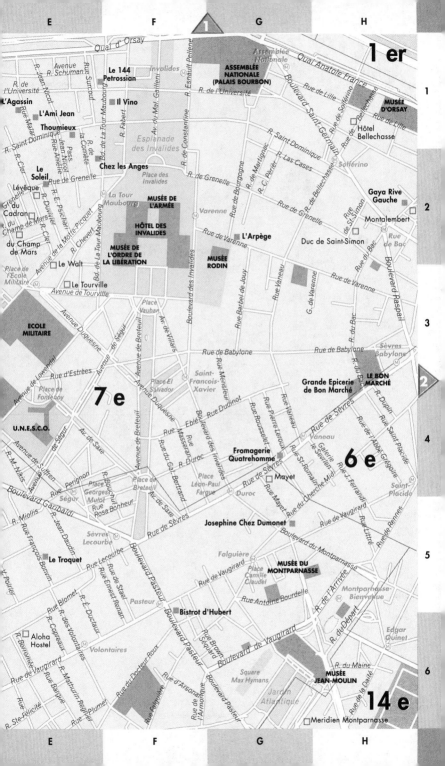

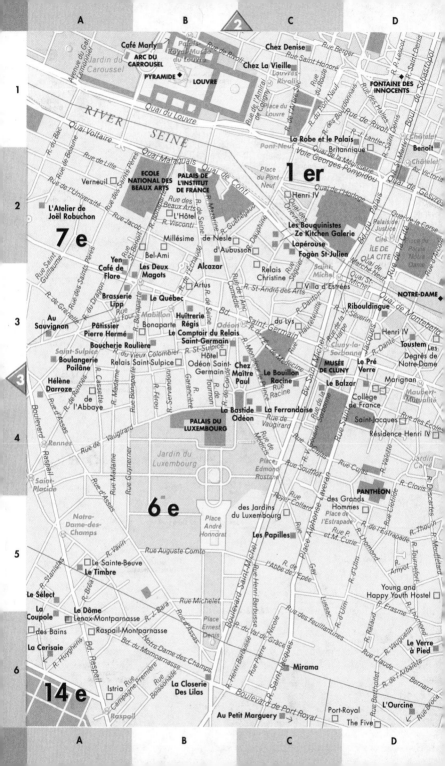

A B **2** C D

Café Marly
Palais-Royal Musée du Louvre
ARC DU CARROUSEL
Jardin du Carrousel
Chez Denise
Rue Berger
Rue Saint Honoré
Chez La Vieille
PYRAMIDE
LOUVRE
Louvre-Rivoli
FONTAINE DES INNOCENTS

RIVER SEINE
Quai du Louvre

La Robe et le Palais
Britannique
Pont-Neuf
Benôit

Henri IV
1 er
Verneuil
L'Atelier de Joël Robuchon
ECOLE NATIONAL DES BEAUX ARTS
PALAIS DE L'INSTITUT DE FRANCE

7 e

Place du Pont-Neuf

Palais de Justice
ÎLE DE LA CITÉ
Notre Dame

Les Bouquinistes
Ze Kitchen Galerie
Lapérouse
Fogón St-Julien
NOTRE-DAME

Millésime
de Nesle
d'Aubusson

Yen
Café de Flore
Bel-Ami
Les Deux Magots
Alcazar
Relais Christine
Villa d'Estrées

Brasserie Lipp
Artus
Le Québec

Au Sauvignon
Pâtissier Pierre Hermé
Bonaparte
Mabillon
Huîtrerie Régis
Le Comptoir du Relais Saint-Germain
du Lys
Ribouldingue
Henri IV
Toustem
Les Degrés de Notre-Dame

Boucherie Roulière
Boulangerie Poilâne
Relais Saint-Sulpice
Hôtel
Odéon Saint-Germain
Chez Maître Paul
Le Bouillon Racine
MUSÉE DE CLUNY
Cluny-la-Sorbonne
Le Pré Verre
Le Balzar
Marignan

Hélène Darroze
de l'Abbaye
La Bastide Odéon
La Ferrandaise
Collège de France
Saint-Jacques
Résidence Henri IV

3

PALAIS DU LUXEMBOURG

Jardin du Luxembourg

4

Rennes
Saint-Placide

6 e

Place André Honnorat

PANTHÉON
des Grands Hommes
Place de l'Estrapade

Natre-Dame-des-Champs

des Jardins du Luxembourg
Les Papilles

Rue Auguste Comte

5

Le Sainte-Beuve
Le Timbre

Le Sélect
La Coupole
Le Dôme
Lenox-Montparnasse
Raspail-Montparnasse
des Bains
La Cerisaie

Young and Happy Youth Hostel

Le Verre à Pied

14 e
Istria

La Closerie Des Lilas

Mirama

Au Petit Marguery
Port-Royal
The Five
L'Ourcine

A B C D

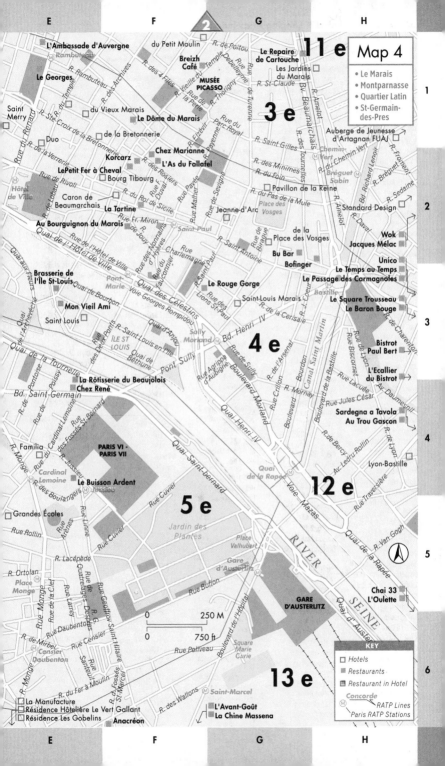

Where to Stay

Four Seasons Hotel George V Paris

WORD OF MOUTH

"If you want the best view of the Eiffel Tower, stay in the Plaza Athenee, and ask for Suite 666. It has a full-on unobstructed view. Imagine the sight at night!"

—travelhorizons

Updated
by Heather
Stimmler-Hall

If your Parisian fantasy involves staying in a historic hotel with the smell of fresh-baked croissants gently rousing you in the morning, here's some good news: you need not be Ritz-rich to realize it. With more than 1,450 hotels, the City of Light gives visitors stylish options in all price ranges.

In terms of location, there are more hotels on the Rive Droite (the Right Bank) offering luxury—in terms of formality—than on the Rive Gauche (the Left Bank), where the hotels are frequently smaller and richer in old-fashioned charm. The Rive Droite's 1er, 8^e, and 16^e arrondissements are still the most exclusive, and the prices there reflect that. Some of these palatial hotels charge more than €500 a night without batting an eye. Less expensive alternatives on the Rive Droite can be found in the fashionable Marais quarter (3^e and 4^e arrondissements). The hotbed of chic hotels on the Rive Gauche is the 6^e arrondissement; choices get cheaper in the 5e and 7e. Some excellent budget deals can be found slightly off the beaten track in the 9e and 13e arrondissements. Wherever possible, we've located budget hotels in more expensive neighborhoods—check out the handful of budget-priced sleeps in the shadow of Notre-Dame, St-Germain-des-Prés, and the Louvre.

Although historic charm is a given, space to stretch out is not. Even budget travelers can sleep under 200-year-old wooden beams, but if you're looking for enough room to spread out multiple suitcases, better book a suite in a four-star palace hotel. Indoor spaces—from beds to elevators—may feel cramped to those not used to life on a European scale. The new no-smoking law went into effect in all Parisian hotels in February 2007 (and all public spaces in January 2008). Enforcement may not be perfect for the first few years, but at least now you'll have a valid complaint if your room smells like stale smoke. Amenities have also improved, with virtually every hotel now equipped with cable TV (meaning CNN and BBC news in English), minibars, in-room safes, and wireless Internet access (though not always free). Another recent change is the increasing availability of air-conditioning, which can be saintly in August.

WHERE SHOULD I STAY?

	Neighborhood Vibe	Pros	Cons
St-Germain and Montparnasse (6e, 14e, 15e)	The center of café culture and the emblem of the Left Bank, the mood is leisurely, the attractions are well established, and the prices are high.	A safe, historic area with chic fashion boutiques, famous cafés and brasseries, and lovely side streets. Lively day and night.	Expensive. Noisy along the main streets. The area around the monstrous Tour Montparnasse is a soul-sucking tribute to commerce.
The Quartier Latin (5e)	The historic student quarter of the Left Bank, full of narrow, winding streets, and major parks and monuments such as the Panthéon.	Plenty of cheap eats and sleeps, discount book and music shops, and noteworthy open-air markets. Safe area for wandering walks.	Touristy. No métro stations on the hilltop around the Panthéon. Student pubs can be noisy in summer. Hotel rooms tend to be smaller.
Marais and Bastille (3e, 4e, 11e)	Cute shops, museums, and laid-back bistros line the narrow streets of the Marais, home to both the gay and Jewish communities. Farther east, ethnic eats and edgy shops.	Generally excellent shopping, sightseeing, dining, and nightlife in the super-safe Marais. Bargains aplenty at Bastille hotels. Several modern-design hotels, too.	The Marais's narrow sidewalks are always overcrowded, and rooms don't come cheap. It's noisy around the gritty boulevards of Place de la Bastille and Nation.
Montmartre and northeast Paris (18e, 19e)	The hilltop district is known for winding streets leading from the racy Pigalle district to the stark-white Sacré-Coeur Basilica.	Amazing views of Paris, romantic cobblestone streets, and the seductive stretch of shops around Moulin Rouge.	Steep staircases, few métro stations, and Pigalle can be too seedy to stomach, especially late at night, when it can also be unsafe.
Champs-Elysées and western Paris (8e, 16e, 17e)	The world-famous avenue is lively 24/7 with cinemas, high-end shops, and nightclubs, all catering to the moneyed jet set.	The home to most of the city's famous palace hotels, there's no shortage of luxurious sleeps here.	The high prices of this neighborhood, along with its Times Square tendencies, repel Parisians but lure pickpockets.
Around the Tour Eiffel (7e, 15e)	The impressive Eiffel Tower and monumental Palais de Chaillot at Trocadéro straddle the Seine River.	Safe, quiet, and relatively inexpensive area of Paris with green spaces and picture-perfect views at every turn.	With few shops and restaurants, this district is very quiet at night; long distances between métro stations.
Louvre, Les Halles, Ile de la Cité (1e, 2e, 8e)	The central Parisian district around the Tuileries gardens and Louvre museum is best known for shopping and sightseeing; Les Halles is a buzzing hub of commerce and mass transit.	Convenient for getting around Paris on foot, bus, or métro. Safe, attractive district close to the Seine and shops of all types. All the major métro and RER lines are right by Les Halles.	The main drag along Rue de Rivoli can be noisy with traffic during the day, and the restaurants cater mostly to tourists. Shops are tacky and fast food predominates around Les Halles.

18

PARIS LODGING PLANNER

Lodging Strategy

Where should we stay? With hundreds of Paris hotels, it may seem like a daunting question. But fret not—our expert writers and editors have done most of the legwork. The 100-plus selections here represent the best this city has to offer. Scan "Best Bets" on the following pages for top recommendations by price and experience. Or find a review quickly in the listings, which are arranged by arrondissement and then alphabetically.

Reservations

Make reservations as far in advance as possible, especially for May, June, September, and October. Calling works, but e-mail (or fax) may be the easiest way to make contact, since hotel staff are probably more likely to read English than understand it over the phone. Specify arrival and departure dates; room size (single or double), room type (standard, deluxe, or suite); the number of people in your party; and whether you want a bathroom with a shower or bathtub (or both). Ask if a deposit is required, and what happens if you cancel. Tourist offices can sometimes secure last-minute reservations, but they charge a small fee.

Checking In

Typical check-in and check-out times are 2 PM and noon, respectively, although some properties allow check-in as early as noon and require check-out as early as 11 AM. Many flights from North America arrive early in the morning, but having to wait six hours for a room after arriving jet-lagged at 8 AM isn't the ideal way to start a vacation. Alert the hotel of your early arrival; larger establishments can often make special early check-in arrangements, but don't expect more than baggage storage.

Hotel Quality

Note that the quality of accommodations can vary from room to room. If you don't like the room you're given, ask to see another. The French star ratings can be misleading: official stars are granted for specific amenities and services rather than for ambience, style, or overall comfort, so you may find that a two-star hotel eclipses a three-star establishment. Many hotels prefer to remain "under-starred" for tax reasons.

Children

Most hotels in Paris allow children to stay in their parents' room at no charge. Hotel rooms are often on the small side, so inquire about connecting rooms or suites. For more information about kid-friendly accommodations, consult the "With Kids?" feature in this chapter.

Breakfast

Almost all Parisian hotels charge extra for breakfast, with per-person prices ranging from €5 to more than €30. Continental breakfast—coffee, baguette, croissant, jam, and butter—is sometimes included in the hotel rate. We denote this with a CP, for Continental Plan. If you decide to eat elsewhere, inform the staff so breakfast won't be charged to your bill.

Hotel Features

Unless stated in the review, hotels are equipped with elevators, and all guest rooms have air-conditioning, TV, telephone, and a private bathroom. Remember that in France the first floor is the floor above the ground floor, or *rez-de-chaussée*. Note that we use "Ethernet" to designate the presence of genuine high-speed lines and mention wireless access where available (otherwise, expect escargot-pace Web surfing). The number of rooms listed at the end of each review reflects those with private bathrooms (which means they have a shower or a tub, but not necessarily both). Tubs don't always have fixed curtains or showerheads; how the French rinse themselves with the handheld nozzle without flooding the entire bathroom remains a cultural mystery. It's rare to find moderately priced places that expect guests to share toilets or bathrooms, but be sure you know what facilities you are getting when you book a budget hotel.

What It Costs

Often a hotel in a certain price category will have a few less-expensive rooms; it's worth asking about this possibility. In the off-season—mid-July, August, November, early December, and late January—rates can be considerably lower. Recognizing the recently painful dollar–euro exchange rate for Americans, guaranteed U.S. dollar rates are increasingly promoted. You should also inquire about specials and weekend deals, and you may be able to get a better rate per night if you are staying a week or longer. There is a nominal city *taxe de séjour* ranging between €0.20 and €1.20 per person, per night, based on the hotel's star rating. Sometimes this tax is included in the room price, sometimes not.

If you're staying in Paris for more than just a few days, you might want to look into the increasingly popular option of renting an apartment. Check out the Lodging Alternatives feature in this chapter. Not only does this often save in nightly costs, but with your own kitchen you can save money living like a local and cooking some of your own meals.

In this Chapter

18

What It Costs

	FOR TWO PEOPLE			
¢	$	$$	$$$	$$$$
under €75	€75–€100	€101–€150	€151–€225	over €225

Prices are for two people in a standard double room in high season, including tax (19.6%) and service charge.

BEST BETS FOR PARIS LODGING

Fodor's offers a selective listing of high-quality lodging experiences at every price range, from the city's best budget options to its most sophisticated grandedame hotel. Here, we've compiled our top recommendations by price and experience. The very best properties—those that provide a particularly remarkable experience in a price range—are designated with a Fodor's Choice symbol.

FODOR'S CHOICE ★

Eiffel Seine Hôtel, 15^e

Four Seasons Hôtel George V Paris, 8^e

Hôtel Familia, 5^e

Hôtel des Bains, 14^e

Les Degrés de Notre-Dame, 5^e

Hôtel Langlois, 9^e

Hôtel Odéon Saint-Germain, 6^e

Hôtel Plaza Athénée, 8^e

Hôtel d'Aubusson, 6^e

Hôtel S. Christopher's Inn (Hostel), 19^e

By Price

¢

St-Christopher's Inn (hostel), 19^e

Hôtel Henri IV, 1^e

Hôtel Marignan, 5^e

Hôtel Tiquetonne, 2^e

Port-Royal Hôtel, 5^e

$

Hôtel Familia, 5^e

Hôtel de Nesle, 6^e

Hôtel des Bains, 14^e

Hôtel Français, 10^e

Résidence Les Gobelins, 13^e

$$

Hôtel Amour, 9^e

Hôtel Eiffel Rive Gauche, 7^e

Hôtel Langlois, 9^e

Hôtel Prima Lepic, 18^e

Hôtel Vivienne, 2^e

$$$

Hôtel Mathis Elysées Matignon, 8^e

Hôtel Relais Saint-Sulpice, 6^e

Hôtel Résidence Henri IV, 5^e

Hôtel Odéon St-Germain, 6^e

Standard Design Hôtel, 11^e

$$$$

Four Seasons Hôtel George V Paris, 8^e

Hôtel Duc de Saint-Simon, 7^e

Hôtel Saint Merry, 4^e

Hôtel Plaza Athénée, 8^e

By Experience

MOST CHARMING

Hôtel Britannique, 1er

Hôtel d'Aubusson, 6^e

Hôtel des Jardins du Luxembourg, 5^e

Les Degrés de Notre-Dame, 5^e

HISTORIC

Hôtel de la Place des Vosges, 4^e

Hôtel Odéon St-Germain, 6^e

Hôtel Saint Merry, 4^e

Ritz, 1er

BEST DESIGN

Hôtel Bellechasse, 7^e

Mon Hotel, 16^e

Hôtel du Petit Moulin, 3^e

The Five Hôtel, 5^e

MOST CENTRAL

Hôtel Henri IV, 1er

Hôtel Louvre Forum, 1er

Hôtel Meurice, 1er

Hôtel Saint-Louis Marais, 4^e

BUSINESS TRAVEL

Four Seasons Hôtel George V Paris, 8^e

Hôtel Bel-Ami, 6^e

Hôtel Fouquet's Barrière, 8^e

Hôtel Westminster, 2^e

Les Jardins du Marais, 12^e

BEST VIEWS

Hôtel Brighton, 1er

Hôtel de Vendôme, 1er

Hôtel des Grands Hommes, 5^e

Hôtel du Cadran, 7^e

MOST ROMANTIC

Hôtel Bourg Tibourg, 4^e

Hôtel Caron de Beaumarchais, 4^e

Hôtel Daniel, 8^e

L'Hôtel, 6^e

Hôtel Raphael, 16^e

HOTEL LISTINGS (BY ARRONDISSEMENT)

1er ARRONDISSEMENT

It simply doesn't get any more central than the Louvre/Tuileries neighborhood. It's a five-minute walk to major sights such as the Louvre, les Jardins des Tuileries, Notre-Dame, and Sainte-Chapelle. Also nearby are two major shopping streets—Rue de Rivoli and Rue St-Honoré—and the Forum des Halles shopping mall. The central bus, RER, and métro stations will get you around the rest of Paris effortlessly.

$$$ Hôtel Brighton. Many of Paris's most prestigious palace hotels face the Tuileries or Place de la Concorde, but the Brighton breathes the same rarified air under the arcades for a fraction of the price. Smaller rooms with showers look onto a courtyard; street-facing chambers have balconies and a royal view of the gardens and the Rive Gauche. Extensive recent renovations updated all the rooms, with the newest ones featuring flat-screen TVs and heated towel racks. The least expensive rooms have windows under the arches along Rue de Rivoli, and the first-floor rooms have high ceilings. Pros: Central location in a prestigious neighborhood near major Paris sights. Cons: The busy street can make rooms with a view a bit noisy; variable quality in décor between rooms. ⊠*218 rue de Rivoli,* ☏*01–47–03–61–61* ⊕*www.paris-hotel-brighton.com* ⇝*61 rooms* ⸜*In-room: Wi-Fi, safe. In-hotel: laundry service, some pets allowed* ▤*AE, DC, MC, V* Ⓜ*Tuileries.* ✛ *2:A6*

$$$ Hôtel Britannique. Open since 1861 and just a stone's throw from the Louvre, the Britannique blends courteous English service with old-fashioned French elegance. Take the winding staircase to rooms done in a mix of attractive repro furniture and antiques. Wi-Fi and in-room flat-screen TVs lend an air of modernity. During World War I, the hotel served as headquarters for a Quaker mission. Pros: On a calm side street less than a block from the main métro/RER station; attentive staff. Cons: Smallish rooms; soundproofing between rooms could be better. ⊠*20 av. Victoria,* ☏*01–42–33–74–59* ⊕*www.hotel-britannique.fr* ⇝*38 rooms, 1 suite* ⸜*In-room: safe, Wi-Fi. In-hotel: bar, laundry service* ▤*AE, DC, MC, V* Ⓜ*Châtelet.* ✛ *4:1D*

$$ Hôtel du Cygne. Passed down from mother to daughter, "the Swan" is decorated with homey touches like hand-sewn curtains, country quilts, and white wooden furniture. Renovated bathrooms are in marble, and older ones have mosaic tiling. Book early for the larger rooms, which include Nos. 16, 26, 35, and 41. Ancient wooden beams run the length of the two stairwells, which makes for uneven stepping that challenges even the most agile guests. Pros: Spotless rooms and bathrooms; central location on a pedestrian street; good value. Cons: Old building with small rooms; not the most attractive area of central Paris; can be intimidating after dark. ⊠*3 rue du Cygne,* ☏*01–42–60–14–16* ⊕*www.hotelducygne.fr* ⇝*20 rooms* ⸜*In-room: no a/c, safe* ▤*MC, V* Ⓜ*Etienne Marcel, Les Halles.* ✛ *2:D6*

¢ Hôtel Henri IV. When tourists think of staying on one of the islands, it's usually Ile St-Louis, not Ile de la Cité they consider, but the overlooked isle shelters one of the city's most beloved budget-priced sleeps.

18

The 17th-century building that once housed King Henri IV's printing presses offers few comforts: the narrow staircase (five flights, no elevator) creaks and the ragged rooms show their age. Most bathrooms are in the hallway, and they may not be up to your standard of hygiene; pay a little extra and get a room with private shower, or reserve room No. 16, the only one with a tub. The payoff is a location overlooking the oasis-like Place Dauphine, just a few steps from the Pont Neuf and Sainte-Chapelle. Pros: Very quiet, central location; good value. Cons: Steep stairs and no elevator; no services or amenities; no e-mail or online reservations. ⊠*25 pl. Dauphine,* ☎*01–43–54–44–53* ⟲*20 rooms, 7 with bath* ⚷*In-room: no a/c, no phone, no TV* ▤*MC, V* ▯⊚▯*CP* Ⓜ*Cité, St-Michel, Pont Neuf.* ✛ *4:C2*

$$ **Hôtel Londres St-Honoré.** An appealing combination of character and comfort distinguishes this small, inexpensive hotel a five-minute walk from the Louvre. Exposed oak beams, statues in niches, and rustic stone walls give the place an old-fashioned air. Most rooms have floral bedspreads and standard hotel furniture, though bathrooms are refreshingly modern, with real hair dryers. Note that elevator service begins on the second floor, so some stairs are guaranteed. Pros: Within walking distance of major sites; good value for the neighborhood. Cons: Small elevator that doesn't go to ground floor; small beds; upper rooms can get very hot in summer (fans are available). ⊠*13 rue St-Roch,* ☎*01–42–60–15–62* ⊕*www.hotellondresthonore-paris.com* ⟲*21 rooms, 4 suites* ⚷*In-room: no a/c (some), safe, Wi-Fi. In-hotel: public internet, some pets allowed* ▤*AE, DC, MC, V* Ⓜ*Pyramides.* ✛ *2:A6*

$–$$ **Hôtel Louvre Forum.** This hotel near the Louvre, Les Halles, and Palais-Royal is a find, with modern, spotless rooms that are well equipped for the price. Furniture is of the Ikea genre, and the baths are simple white tile, but bonuses include a bright sitting area and a stone-cellar breakfast room, both with murals. Pros: Clean and comfortable with elevator; in the center of Paris. Cons: Rooms and elevator are small; not much character. ⊠*25 rue du Bouloi,* ☎*01–42–36–54–19* ⊕*www.paris-hotel-louvre-forum.com* ⟲*27 rooms* ⚷*In-room: safe, Wi-Fi. In-hotel: bar* ▤*AE, MC, V* Ⓜ*Louvre.* ✛ *2:C6*

$$–$$$ **Hôtel Louvre Sainte Anne.** This small but modern hotel between the Opéra and the Louvre has bright rooms decorated in a country theme, with little extras like heated towel racks. The two spacious triples on the top floor cost a bit extra but have small terraces with views of Sacré-Coeur. Breakfast is served in a stone-vaulted cellar, and the exceptionally friendly staff can recommend plenty of noteworthy nearby restaurants. Pros: Central location; free Wi-Fi; very helpful staff. Cons: Smallish rooms and dull décor; "Japanese" district can feel very un-Parisian. ⊠*32 rue Ste-Anne,* ☎*01–40–20–02–35* ⊕*www.louvre-ste-anne.fr* ⟲*20 rooms* ⚷*In-room: safe, Wi-Fi. In-hotel: room service, some pets allowed* ▤*AE, MC, V* Ⓜ*Pyramides.* ✛ *2:B5*

$$$$ **Hôtel Meurice.** The Meurice has welcomed royalty and celebrity since ☾ 1835, from the Duchess of Windsor to Salvador Dalí. In late 2007 the lobby, bar, and restaurant were given a swanky makeover by French designer Philippe Starck. Rooms have a gilded Louis XVI or Napoleonic Empire style, with antique furnishings covered in sumptuous French and Italian brocades. Most rooms have a Tuileries/Louvre or Sacré-Coeur view, but the massive Royal Suite takes in a 360-degree panorama. Bathrooms are marble, with two sinks and deep, spacious tubs. The health club includes grape-seed-based treatments, such as "cabernet sauvignon" massages; children are pampered with their own Meurice teddy bear and tot-size slippers and bathrobe. Pros: Views over the gardens; trendy public spaces; free high-speed Internet in rooms. Cons: On a noisy street; popularity makes the public areas not very discreet. ⊠*228 rue de Rivoli,* ☎*01–44–58–10–09* ⊕*www. meuricehotel.com* ⌑*160 rooms, 36 suites* ⌂*In-room: safe, Wi-Fi. In-hotel: 2 restaurants, room service, bar, gym, concierge, laundry service, public Internet, some pets allowed* ⊟*AE, DC, MC, V* Ⓜ*Tuileries, Concorde.* ⊹ *2:A6*

$$$$ Hôtel de Vendôme. With a discreet entrance on the posh Place Vendôme and a tiny jewel box of a lobby with inlaid marble and carved mahogany paneling, the Vendôme has all the comfort and luxury of the neighboring palace hotels without the ostentatious size. Rooms are done handsomely in French period styles from Louis XIV to Art Deco, with marble baths, antique furniture, and hand-carved wood detailing. Modern touches include flat-screen TVs, and a bedside console that controls the lights, curtains, and music. The British-style restaurant and bar, decorated in leather and wood, hosts a pianist Wednesday through Saturday and serves contemporary French-fusion fare. Pros: Luxurious décor and amenities in a boutique-hotel size; central location on a prestigious shopping square. Cons: Can feel a bit old-fashioned and stuffy; no spa or gym amenities that one would normally find at this price. ⊠*1 pl. Vendôme,* ☎*01–55–04–55–00* ⊕*www.hoteldevendome.com* ⌑*19 rooms, 10 suites* ⌂*In-room: safe, DVD (some), Wi-Fi. In-hotel: restaurant, room service, bar, concierge, laundry service, parking (fee), some pets allowed* ⊟*AE, DC, MC, V* Ⓜ*Concorde, Opéra.* ⊹ *2:A5*

$$$$ Renaissance Paris Vendôme. Hiding behind a classic 19th-century façade is a fresh, contemporary hotel with subtle 1930s influences. Under a huge atrium skylight, the lobby's polished black-marble floors, lacquered hardwood furnishings, neutral fabrics, and decadent antiques set the mood. The small library has free Wi-Fi and a wood-burning fireplace, and the intimate Bar Chinois is decorated with elaborate Chinese wallpaper. Imported woods and black slate accent the hotel's sauna, steam room, and countercurrent swimming pool. Rooms have flannel fabrics and fluffy white comforters, with such modern amenities as flat-screen TVs, CD and DVD players, and free high-speed Internet. The marble bathrooms feature Bulgari toiletries and heated towel racks. Contemporary French and Basque-style cuisine are served in the hotel's Pinxo Restaurant. Pros: Posh location; trendy restaurant frequented by locals; free Wi-Fi. Cons: As part of the Marriott group it can feel a bit corporate and lacking in character. ⊠*4 rue du Mont Thabor,* ☎*01–40–20–20–00* ⊕*www.renaissanceparisvendome.com* ⌑*82 rooms, 15 suites* ⌂*In-room: safe, DVD, VCR, Ethernet. In-hotel: res-*

18

taurant, room service, bar, pool, gym, concierge, laundry service, public Internet, parking (fee) ☐AE, DC, MC, V Ⓜ Tuileries. ✥ 2:A6

$$$$ **Ritz.** Ever since César Ritz opened the doors of his hotel in 1898, the ☾ mere name of this venerable institution has become synonymous with luxury. The famed Ritz Escoffier cooking school, where you can learn the finer points of *gateaux*, is here, as is the new Ritz Lounge Bar and the Hemingway Bar. There's also a Greek-temple-style subterranean spa and swimming pool. Guest rooms match this level of luxe; even the "humbler" spaces have every modern doodad, cleverly camouflaged with the décor of gleaming mirrors, chandeliers, and antiques. (Think marble baths with gold pull chains that summon the valet or maid.) The most palatial suites are named after famous Ritz residents: Coco Chanel, the Prince of Wales, and Elton John. Pros: Spacious swimming pool; selection of bars and restaurants; top-notch service. Cons: Can feel stuffy and old-fashioned; easy to get "lost" in the vast hotel; paparazzi magnet. ✉15 pl. Vendôme, ☎01–43–16–30–30 ⊕www. ritz.com ⬎106 rooms, 56 suites ♨In-room: safe, Ethernet, Wi-Fi. In-hotel: 3 restaurants, room service, bars, pool, gym, spa, concierge, children's programs (ages 6–12), laundry service, public Internet, parking (fee) ☐AE, DC, MC, V Ⓜ Opéra. ✥ 2:A5

2ᵉ ARRONDISSEMENT

Posh boutiques, 24-hour brasseries, and bustling boulevards define this lively neighborhood, at the center of which are the Opéra Garnier and the historic department stores of the Boulevard Haussmann. The Montorgueil market street is now also home to several trendy bars and vintage clothing shops, and the clubs and cinemas around the métro Grands Boulevards attract a boisterous nightlife crowd.

$ **Hôtel Bellevue et du Chariot d'Or.** This old Belle Époque time traveler is proud to keep its dingy chandeliers and faded gold trimming. Budget groups from France and the Netherlands come for the clean, sans-frills rooms; some units sleep four. Halls are lined with stamped felt that helps muffle sounds trickling up from the marble-floor lobby and bar. There may be some quirks, like the hefty old-fashioned room keys and the bathtub/showers without curtains, but you're just a few blocks from hipper addresses in the heart of the Marais. Pros: Large rooms great for families; Wi-Fi; easy walk to the Marais and Les Halles districts. Cons: A very busy, noisy street; not the most attractive part of central Paris; drab décor. ✉39 rue de Turbigo, ☎01–48–87–45–60 ⊕www.hotelbellevue75.com ⬎59 rooms ♨In-room: no a/c, Wi-Fi. In-hotel: bar ☐AE, DC, MC, V ◎CP Ⓜ Réaumur-Sébastopol, Arts et Métiers. ✥ 2:E6

$$$$ **Hôtel de Noailles.** With a nod to the work of postmodern designers like Putman and Starck, this style-driven boutique is both contemporary and cozy. Rooms are sleek and streamlined, with backlit, custom-built cabinets, glassed-in bathrooms, and fabric or faux-leather wall coverings. A spacious outdoor terrace is off the breakfast lounge. Pros: Just a block from the airport bus; easy walk to the Louvre and Opéra. Cons: Small elevator; no interesting views; some visitors have complained

about surly service. ✉*9 rue de Michodière,* ☎*01–47–42–92–90*
🌐*www.paris-hotel-noailles.com* ⇌*61 rooms* ♿*In-room: safe, Wi-Fi.
In-hotel: room service, bar, laundry service, some pets allowed* ▭*AE,
DC, MC, V* Ⓜ*Opéra.* ✛ *2:B5*

¢ **Hôtel Tiquetonne.** Just off the Montorgueil market and a short hoof from
Les Halles (and slightly seedy Rue St-Denis), this is one of the least
expensive hotels in the city center. The so-old-fashioned-they're-vin-
tage-cool rooms aren't much to look at and have few amenities, but
they're clean, and some are spacious. Cheaper rooms are available with
just a sink (toilets and pay showers are in each hall). Pros: Dirt-cheap
rooms in the center of town; in a newly trendy shopping and nightlife
area. Cons: Minimal service and no amenities; noise from the street.
✉*6 rue Tiquetonne,* ☎*01–42–36–94–58* ⇌*45 rooms, 33 with bath*
♿*In-room: no a/c, no TV. In-hotel: some pets allowed* ▭*AE, MC, V*
☾*Closed Aug. and last wk of Dec.* Ⓜ*Etienne Marcel.* ✛ *2:D6*

$ **Hôtel Vivienne.** The décor is a bit schizoid: some guest rooms have chan-
deliers, others have fuzzy brown rugs and busy bedspreads, and another
is fashionably minimalist. Rooms Nos. 39, 40, and 41 are blessed with
large rooftop balconies. The location near the Opéra Garnier and
Grands Boulevards department stores and the free Internet station in
the lobby make this a good bet in this price range. Pros: Good value
for central Paris; a block from the métro station; free Internet. Cons:
A noisy street and late-night bar across the road can make it hard to
keep windows open in summer; some rooms are small and ugly. ✉*40
rue Vivienne,* ☎*01–42–33–13–26* 🖶*01–40–41–98–19* ⇌*45 rooms,
35 with bath* ♿*In-room: no a/c, Wi-Fi. In-hotel: some pets allowed*
▭*MC, V* Ⓜ*Bourse, Richelieu-Drouot.* ✛ *2:C4*

18

$$$$ **Hôtel Westminster.** On one of the most prestigious streets in Paris between
the Opéra and Place Vendôme, this former inn was built in the mid-
19th century. Even now that Wi-Fi has arrived, the public areas and
rooms happily retain their period furniture, marble fireplaces, crystal
chandeliers, and piped-in classical music. Duke's piano bar is a pleasant, popular rendezvous spot, and the hotel's gourmet restaurant, Le
Céladon, serves outstanding French cuisine. The fitness center has a
Moorish-inspired steam room and views over Paris's rooftops. Pros:
Prestigious location; good-value promotional rates on the Web site;
popular jazz bar. Cons: Not trendy; some bad views of air shaft; location makes the price higher than expected. ✉*13 rue de la Paix,* ☎*01–
42–61–57–46* 🌐*www.hotelwestminster.com* ⇌*80 rooms, 21 suites*
♿*In-room: safe, Wi-Fi. In-hotel: restaurant, room service, bar, gym,
spa, concierge, laundry service, public Internet, parking (fee), some pets
allowed* ▭*AE, DC, MC, V* Ⓜ*Opéra.* ✛ *2:A5*

$$$$ **Park Hyatt Paris Vendôme.** Understated luxury with a contemporary Zen
vibe differentiates this Hyatt from its more classic neighbors between
the Place Vendôme and Opéra Garnier. Five Haussmann-era office
buildings have been converted into a showcase for polished beige lime-
stone, mahogany veneer surfaces, and bronze sculptures. The minimalist cool vibe in the rooms extends to the Japanese-inspired spalike

With Kids?

Just because you have children in tow doesn't mean your dream of a pampering vacation needs to go down the drain. Several top Paris hotels go out of their way to accommodate families. But ask questions before you go to ensure peace of mind: Do cribs come with linens? Are high chairs available? Is there a children's menu available? Can the hotel arrange for an English-speaking babysitter? Some hotels will even clear out the minibar, baby-proof a room, or provide baby-proofing materials if you alert them in advance. Here are some of the top picks for traveling with kids.

Glamorous grande-dames like the **Four Seasons Hôtel George V Paris** ($$$$, 8e) and **Plaza Athénée** ($$$$, 8e) give children four-star treatment with personalized T-shirts, child-size bathrobes, luxurious hotel-branded toys, and special menus. Space is at a premium in Paris hotels, and if you have more than two people in a standard room, you'll really start to feel the squeeze. The answer? A suite, where you can spread out in style. The **Hôtel Raphael** ($$$$, 16e) offers generously sized suites with ample room for kids to play. Parents

will find a friend in the concierge, who arranges for bilingual babysitters and priority access to amusement parks, and offers recommendations on kid-friendly restaurants and entertainment. For space on a budget, try the **Hôtel Marignan** ([cen]–$, 5e), where large rooms (some sleeping four or five), access to a communal kitchen, and a relaxed atmosphere make it a good choice for families. The **Hôtel Résidence Henri IV** ($$$–$$$$, 5e) is an apartment hotel offering rooms equipped with a two-burner stove, dorm-size fridge, sink, and basic dishware. Apartments have space for up to four guests.

The chain **Novotel** (☎800/221–4542 for reservations, 08–25–88–44–44 in France) is a good bet, as it allows two children under 16 to stay free in their parents' room; kids are offered free breakfast and gifts. Many Novotel hotels have playgrounds and children's corners with video games.

Renting a furnished apartment also is a convenient choice for families. Weekly rentals can be more economical than booking a room at a midlevel hotel (⇨ *Lodging Alternatives box*).

---

baths, under-floor heating, and spacious dressing area. Spa treatments feature French Carita products, and the entire hotel is Wi-Fi accessible. Pros: The latest hotel technology and stylish design; spa suites; popular bar and restaurant. Cons: As part of the Hyatt chain, can feel anonymous. ✉ *3–5 rue de la Paix*, ☎*01–58–71–12–34* ⊕*www.paris. vendome.hyatt.com* ⇨*132 rooms, 36 suites* ☖*In-room: safe, DVD (some), Ethernet. In-hotel: 2 restaurants, room service, bar, gym, spa, concierge, laundry service, public Internet, parking (no fee), some pets allowed* ⊟*AE, DC, MC, V* Ⓜ*Concorde, Opéra.* ✛ *2:A5*

3e ARRONDISSEMENT

The north end of the Marais is still an up-and-coming district of art galleries and hip cafés mixed with traditional bistros and unrenovated *hôtels particuliers* (town houses). At the south end are the Picasso Museum and easy access to the many other museums and shopping streets of the Marais. The busy Place République and the colorful Enfants Rouges covered market are to the northeast.

$$$–$$$$ Hôtel du Petit Moulin. French designer Christian Lacroix personally decorated each of the 17 rooms in this former bakery dating back to the reign of Henri IV. Opened as a hotel in 2005, the historic façade and elegant lobby retain the historic architectural elements, and the lounge, halls, and rooms are an explosion of styles and colors that define Lacroix's fashions: shag carpeting and clay tiles, pink pop-art walls and *toile de Jouy* fabric, antique furnishings and contemporary light fixtures. The result is a comfortable, discreet hotel without the flash of its trendy boutique competitors. Pros: Unique hotel with historical character and contemporary style in a trendy neighborhood. Cons: The nearest métro station is a few blocks away; rooms have minimal amenities; bar is not open to the public. ⊠*29–31 rue de Poitou,* ☎*01–42–74–10–10* ⊕*www.paris-hotel-petitmoulin.com* ⬐*12 rooms, 5 suites* ⚥*In-room: safe, Wi-Fi. In-hotel: room service, bar, laundry service, some pets allowed* ⊟*AE, MC, V* Ⓜ*Filles-du-Calvaire.* ✛ *4:F1*

$ Hôtel de Roubaix. Although this faded ghost hasn't updated its grandmotherly décor or creaky elevator in recent decades, it conveys an amiable coziness and charges unbeatable prices, especially given the location five minutes from the Marais and the Pompidou Center. Rooms are bright but basic, with large beds and walk-in showers. Pros: Centrally located on a not-so-busy side street; typical old-fashioned Parisian character; good value. Cons: Old and outdated décor; no bathtubs; no air-conditioning. ⊠*6 rue Greneta,* ☎*01–42–72–89–91* ⊕*www.hotel-de-roubaix.com* ⬐*53 rooms* ⚥*In-room: no a/c, Ethernet* ⊟*MC, V* ⦿*CP* Ⓜ*Réaumur-Sébastopol, Arts et Métiers.* ✛ *2:E6*

$$$$ Murano Urban Resort. As the epicenter of Parisian cool migrates eastward, it's no surprise that a design-conscious hotel has followed. On the trendy northern edge of the Marais, this cheeky hotel that dares to call itself a resort combines Austin Powers playfulness with serious 007-inspired gadgetry. A psychedelic elevator zooms guests to ultra-violet-lighted hallways, where they enter pristine white rooms via fingerprint sensor locks. White shag carpeting, black-slate bathrooms, pop-art furniture, and bedside control panels that change the color of the lighting keep guests amused—until it's time for cocktails. Stylish Parisians pack the hotel's vodka bar and sleek restaurant, where a live DJ holds court in the elevated booth. Two suites have private terraces with heated, countercurrent pools. Pros: High-tech amenities and funky style; very trendy bar attracts stylish locals; brunch served until 5 [pm] on Sunday. Cons: On the far edge of the Marais on a noisy, busy boulevard; dark hallways can make it difficult to find your room;

18

the white carpeting quickly shows wear and tear. ⊠*13 bd. du Temple,* ☎*01–42–71–20–00* ⊕*www.muranoresort.com* ⊷*43 rooms, 9 suites* ⌂*In-room: safe, DVD, Wi-Fi. In-hotel: restaurant, room service, bar, pool, gym, spa, concierge, laundry service, parking (fee), some pets allowed* ☐*AE, DC, MC, V* Ⓜ*Filles du Calvaire.* ✛ *2:G6*

WORD OF MOUTH

"I stayed a couple years ago at the Grand Hôtel Jeanne-d'Arc. It's in the Marais, tucked away on a quiet side street. It is not fancy to say the least, but it was convenient…There is a metro stop a block away…. I really liked the Marais. It is definitely not touristy. I think you get a good feel for what living in Paris would be like. But you're also not far from a lot of attractions." —Bostboy71

$$$$ **Pavillon de la Reine.** This enchanting countrylike château is hidden off the regal Place des Vosges behind a stunning garden courtyard. Gigantic beams, chunky stone pillars, original oils, and a weathered fireplace speak to the building's 1612 origins. The hotel has large doubles, duplexes, and suites decorated in either contemporary or 18th-century-style wall fabrics. Many rooms look out on the entry court or an interior Japanese-inspired garden. Pros: Beautiful garden courtyard; typically Parisian historic character; proximity to the Place des Vosges without the noise. Cons: Expensive for the Marais and the size of the rooms; the nearest métro is a few long blocks away. ⊠*28 pl. des Vosges,* ☎*01–40–29–19–19, 800/447–7462 in U.S.* ⊕*www.pavillon-de-la-reine.com* ⊷*30 rooms, 26 suites* ⌂*In-room: safe, Wi-Fi. In-hotel: room service, bar, concierge, laundry service, parking (no fee), some pets allowed* ☐*AE, DC, MC, V* Ⓜ*Bastille, St-Paul.* ✛ *4:G2*

4ᵉ ARRONDISSEMENT

The Marais and the neighboring Ile St-Louis are two of the most charming neighborhoods for shopping and architecture in Paris, although their old streets are better reached on foot than by métro (the central location helps). Between them is the busy Rue St-Antoine/Rue de Rivoli east–west shopping artery. The Marais is also known for its many museums, lively nightlife, and quirky but harmonious mix of the city's gay and Jewish communities.

$ **Grand Hôtel Jeanne-d'Arc.** You can get your money's worth at this hotel in an unbeatable location off the tranquil Place du Marché Ste-Catherine, one of the city's lesser-known pedestrian squares. The 17th-century building has been a hotel for more than a century, and although rooms are on the spartan side, they're well maintained, with spotless tiled bathrooms and cheery, if somewhat mismatched, colors (some rooms facing the back are more muted). The welcoming staff is informal and happy to recount the history of this former market quartier. Pros: Charming street close to major sites; good value for the Marais; lots of drinking and dining options nearby. Cons: Late-night revelers on the square can be noisy after midnight; minimal amenities; rooms have varying quality and size. ⊠*3 rue de Jarente,* ☎*01–48–87–62–11* ⊕*www.hoteljeannedarc.com* ⊷*36 rooms* ⌂*In-room: no a/c. In-hotel: some pets allowed, public Wi-Fi* ☐*MC, V* Ⓜ*St-Paul.* ✛ *4:G2*

$$$$ **Hôtel Bourg Tibourg.** Scented candles and subdued lighting announce the designer-du-jour Jacques Garcia's theatrical mix of haremlike romance and Gothic contemplation. Royal-blue paint and red velvet line the claustrophobic halls, and Byzantine alcoves hold mosaic-tile tubs. The rooms are barely bigger than the beds, and every inch has been upholstered, tasseled, and draped in a cacophony of stripes, florals, and medieval motifs. A pocket garden has room for three tables, leafy plants, and a swath of stars above. Pros: Quiet side street in central Paris; luxurious style at moderate prices; great nightlife district. Cons: Rooms are very small and ill equipped for those with large suitcases; no hotel restaurant. ⊠ *19 rue Bourg Tibourg,* ☎ *01–42–78–47–39* ⊕ *www.hotelbourg tibourg.com* ⥅ *29 rooms, 1 suite* ⌂ *In-room: safe, Wi-Fi. In-hotel: laundry service* ⊟ *AE, DC, MC, V* Ⓜ *Hôtel de Ville.* ✛ *4:E2*

$$–$$$ **Hôtel de la Bretonnerie.** This small hotel is in a 17th-century *hôtel particulier* (town house) on a tiny street in the Marais, a few minutes' walk from the Centre Pompidou and the bars and cafés of Rue Vieille du Temple. Choose either *chambres classiques* or *chambres de charme;* the latter are more spacious (and pricier), with more elaborate furnishings like Louis XIII–style four-poster canopy beds and marble bathtubs. Overall, the establishment is spotless, and the staff is welcoming. Breakfast is served in the vaulted cellar. Pros: Central location and comfortable décor at a moderate price; typical Parisian character; Wi-Fi. Cons: Quality and size of the rooms vary greatly; the in-your-face gay district location may not be to everyone's taste. ⊠ *22 rue Ste-Croix-de-la-Bretonnerie,* ☎ *01–48–87–77–63* ⊕ *www.bretonnerie.com* ⥅ *22 rooms, 7 suites* ⌂ *In-room: no a/c, safe, Wi-Fi. In-hotel: laundry service* ⊟ *MC, V* Ⓜ *Hôtel de Ville.* ✛ *4:E1*

$$–$$$ **Hôtel Caron de Beaumarchais.** The theme of this intimate hotel is the work of former next-door neighbor Pierre-Augustin Caron de Beaumarchais, supplier of military aid to American revolutionaries and author of *The Marriage of Figaro.* First-edition copies of his books adorn the public spaces, and the salons reflect the taste of 18th-century French nobility—down to the wallpaper and 1792 pianoforte. Richly decorated with floral fabrics and period furnishings, the rooms have original beams, hand-painted bathroom tiles, and gilt mirrors, as well as flat-screen TVs and Wi-Fi. Pros: Cozy, historic Parisian décor; central location within easy walking distance to major monuments. Cons: Small rooms; busy street of bars and cafés can be noisy. ⊠ *12 rue Vieille-du-Temple,* ☎ *01–42–72–34–12* ⊕ *www.carondebeaumarchais.com* ⥅ *19 rooms* ⌂ *In-room: safe, Wi-Fi. In-hotel: laundry service* ⊟ *AE, DC, MC, V* Ⓜ *Hôtel de Ville.* ✛ *4:F2*

$$$–$$$$ **Hôtel Duo.** The former Axial Beaubourg hotel doubled in size and changed its name in 2006. It now has a fresh, contemporary style with bold colors and dramatic lighting, particularly in the newer wing, and the original 16th-century beams add character to the older rooms. Amenities include a small fitness area, a sauna, and a stylish bar and breakfast lounge that fits in perfectly with the hip design vibe of the Marais district. Pros: Trendy Marais location; walking distance to major monuments; choice of two different room styles. Cons: Noisy

18

street; service not always delivered with a smile. ✉ *11 rue du Temple,* ☎ *01–42–72–72–22* ⊕ *www.duoparis.com* 🛏 *58 rooms* ♿ *In-room: safe, Wi-Fi. In-hotel: room service, bar, gym, laundry service* ▤ *AE, DC, MC, V* Ⓜ *Hôtel de Ville.* ✛ *4:E1*

$$ **Hôtel de la Place des Vosges.** Despite a lack of some expected comforts and an elevator that doesn't serve all floors, a loyal clientele swears by this small, historic hotel. The Louis XIII–style reception area and rooms with oak-beam ceilings, rough-hewn stone, and a mix of rustic finds from secondhand shops evoke the Old Marais. The lone top-floor room, the hotel's largest, has a Jacuzzi and a view over Rive Droit rooftops. Other, considerably smaller rooms are cheaper. Fans are provided in summer. Pros: Excellent location just off the 17th-century square; historic Parisian décor; good value rates for the amenities. Cons: No air-conditioning; most rooms are very small; street-facing rooms can be noisy. ✉ *12 rue de Birague,* ☎ *01–42–72–60–46* ⊕ *www.hotel placedesvosges.com* 🛏 *16 rooms* ♿ *In-room: no a/c, safe, Wi-Fi* ▤ *AE, DC, MC, V* Ⓜ *Bastille.* ✛ *4:G2*

$$–$$$ **Hôtel Saint Louis.** The location on the Ile St-Louis is the real draw of this modest hotel, which retains many of its original 17th-century stone walls and wooden beams. Tiny balconies on the upper levels have Seine views. Number 51 has a tear-shape tub and a peek at the Panthéon. Breakfast is served in the vaulted stone cellar. Pros: Romantic location on the tiny island Ile St-Louis; ancient architectural details; air-conditioning. Cons: The location makes the price high; métro stations are across the bridge; small rooms. ✉ *75 rue St-Louis-en-l'Ile,* ☎ *01–46– 34–04–80* ⊕ *www.hotelsaintlouis.com* 🛏 *19 rooms* ♿ *In-room: safe, Wi-Fi. In-hotel: some pets allowed* ▤ *MC, V* Ⓜ *Pont Marie.* ✛ *4:E3*

$$ **Hôtel Saint-Louis Marais.** Once an annex to a local convent, this 18th-century *hôtel particulier* has retained its stone walls and beams juxtaposed with red-clay tile floors and antiques. A wood-banistered stair leads to the small but proper rooms, decorated with basic red carpet and green bedspreads. One room is equipped with a kitchenette. The hotel is in Village St-Paul, a little tangle of medieval lanes just south of the well-traveled Marais, though it is not yet itself overrun by tourists. Pros: Quiet area of the Marais within walking distance of the islands and Bastille; historic Parisian character; Wi-Fi. Cons: No elevator; small rooms with outdated décor. ✉ *1 rue Charles V,* ☎ *01–48–87–87–04* ⊕ *www.saintlouismarais.com* 🛏 *19 rooms* ♿ *In-room: no a/c, safe, Wi-Fi. In-hotel: laundry service, public Internet, parking (fee), some pets allowed* ▤ *DC, MC, V* Ⓜ *Sully Morland, Bastille.* ✛ *4:G3*

$$$–$$$$ **Hôtel Saint Merry.** Due south of the Pompidou Center is this small and stunning Gothic hideaway, once the presbytery of the adjacent St-Merry church. Inside the 17th-century stone interior you can gaze through stained glass, relax on a church pew, or lean back on a headboard recycled from an old Catholic confessional. Room No. 9 is bisected by stone buttresses still supporting the church. The Saint Merry's lack of elevator and modern temptations like TV are in keeping with its ascetic past (and keeps the place monkishly quiet). Pros: Unique medieval charac-

ter; central location on a pedestrian street full of cafés and shops. Cons: No amenities; street-facing rooms can be too noisy to open windows in summer. ✉*78 rue de la Verrerie,* ☎*01–42–78–14–15* ⊕*www. hotelmarais.com* 🛏*11 rooms, 1 suite* ♿*In-room: no a/c, safe, no TV (some). In-hotel: room service, laundry service, some pets allowed* ▱*AE, MC, V* Ⓜ*Châtelet, Hôtel de Ville.* ✛ *4:E1*

$$$ **Hôtel du Vieux Marais.** A great value for the money in one of the most popular neighborhoods in Paris, this pleasingly minimalist hotel with a *fin-de-siècle* façade is on a quiet street in the heart of the Marais. Rooms are bright and impeccably clean, with contemporary oak furnishings, burgundy-leather seating, and velour curtains. Bathrooms are immaculately tiled in Italian marble, with walk-in showers or combination shower/tubs. If you prefer a bit of extra space, ask about special rates on the triple rooms. The staff is exceptionally friendly, and the lobby has Wi-Fi. Pros: Quiet side street location in central Paris; good value for the size and comfort. Cons: Some rooms are very small and face a dark inner courtyard; décor lacks character. ✉*8 rue du Plâtre,* ☎*01–42–78–47–22* ⊕*www.vieuxmarais.com* 🛏*30 rooms* ♿*In-room: safe, Wi-Fi* ▱*MC, V* Ⓜ*Hôtel de Ville.* ✛ *4:E1*

WORD OF MOUTH

"We are returning in October and just love where we stay, the Hotel Les Degres de Notre Dame. It is a lovely hotel, right near the Seine and Notre Dame, in the Latin Quartier. It is right near the Batobus stop, if you will be using that. It may not be as high end as you want, but we just love it. It certainly has an old world feel…I would splurge for the top floor room which I think has a full view of Notre Dame, rather than the view we had out of our bathroom window." —cat111719

5ᵉ ARRONDISSEMENT

The Latin Quarter is the historic center of Parisian learning, and a large student population still frequents the cheap eateries and chain clothing shops around the Sorbonne and the Musée Cluny. The narrow streets along the Seine hide many ancient churches and bookshops, and the hillside leading up to the Panthéon is full of casual bars and colorful food markets at Place Maubert and Rue Mouffetard.

$$–$$$ **Les Degrés de Notre-Dame.** On a quiet lane a few yards from the Seine,
Fodor'sChoice this diminutive budget hotel is lovingly decorated with the owner's
★ flea-market finds. Number 23 is the largest of the lower-priced rooms, whereas the more costly No. 24 has more space, wooden floors, and particularly appealing antique furnishings. The most expensive room, No. 501, occupies the entire top floor, with views of Notre-Dame and space for four guests. There's no elevator, but colorful murals of Parisian scenes decorate the winding stairwell. The shabby-chic Parisian character of the hotel and its French-Moroccan restaurant-bar make this unique establishment unforgettable. Pros: Within walking distance of Notre-Dame and Ile St-Louis; attractive location in quiet part of Latin Quarter; popular locals' restaurant. Cons: No air-conditioning; outdated décor; no elevator. ✉*10 rue des Grands Degrés,* ☎*01–55–*

18

42–88–88 ⊕*www.lesdegreshotel.com* ⇱*10 rooms* ⬙*In-room: no a/c,
safe. In-hotel: restaurant, bar, public Wi-Fi, no kids under 12* ▤*MC,
V* ⓘ❘*CP* Ⓜ*Maubert-Mutualité.* ✛ *4:D3*

$$$ **The Five Hôtel.** Small is beautiful at this tiny design hotel on a quiet
street near the Mouffetard market. Rooms combine cozy and high-
tech features such as fiber-optic fairy lights above the beds and in
the bathrooms, fluffy duvet comforters, original Chinese lacquer art-
works, and 400 satellite channels on flat-screen TVs. All rooms have
free Wi-Fi and L'Occitane toiletries. The ground-floor suite has a pri-
vate Jacuzzi patio. Pros: Stylish design; personalized welcome; quiet
side street. Cons: Rooms are too small for excessive baggage; the near-
est métro is a 10-minute walk. ⊠*3 rue Flatters,* ☏*01–43–31–74–21*
⊕*www.thefivehotel.com* ⇱*24 rooms* ⬙*In-room: safe, Wi-Fi. In-
hotel: laundry service, concierge, public Wi-Fi* ▤*AE, DC, MC, V*
Ⓜ*Gobelins.* ✛ *4:D6*

$ **Hôtel Collège de France.** Exposed-stone walls, wooden beams, and medi-
eval artwork echo the style of the Musée Cluny, two blocks from this
small, family-run hotel. Rooms convey a less elaborate, more stream-
lined aesthetic than the lobby and are relatively quiet owing to the
side-street location. Number 62, on the top floor, costs a bit more but
has a small balcony with superb views. Pros: Walking distance to major
Left Bank sights and the islands; free Wi-Fi, good value. Cons: Big dif-
ference between renovated and unrenovated rooms; no air-condition-
ing; thin walls between rooms. ⊠*7 rue Thénard,* ☏*01–43–26–78–36*
⊕*www.hotel-collegedefrance.com* ⇱*29 rooms* ⬙*In-room: no a/c,
safe, Wi-Fi. In-hotel: room service* ▤*AE, DC, MC, V* Ⓜ*Maubert-
Mutualité, St-Michel–Cluny–La Sorbonne.* ✛ *4:D4*

$–$$ **Hôtel Familia.** Owners Eric and Sylvie continue to update and improve
Fodor'sChoice their popular budget hotel without raising the prices. They've added
★ custom-made wood furniture from Brittany, new carpeting, and antique
tapestries and prints on the walls. The second and fifth floors have balconies (some with views of Notre-Dame), and all rooms are perfectly
soundproofed from traffic below. Pros: Attentive, friendly service; great
value; has all the modern conveniences. Cons: On a very busy street;
some rooms are very small; noise between rooms can be loud. ⊠*11 rue
des Ecoles,* ☏*01–43–54–55–27* ⊕*www.hotel-paris-familia.com* ⇱*30
rooms* ⬙ *In-hotel: laundry service, concierge, public Wi-Fi, parking
(fee)* ▤*AE, DC, MC, V* Ⓜ*Cardinal-Lemoine.* ✛ *4:E4*

$$ **Hôtel Grandes Ecoles.** Guests enter Madame Lefloch's country-style
domain through two massive wooden doors. Distributed among a trio
of three-story buildings, rooms have a distinct grandmotherly vibe with
flowery wallpaper and lace bedspreads, but are downright spacious for
this part of Paris. The Grandes Ecoles is legendary for its cobbled inte-
rior courtyard and garden, which becomes the second living room and
a perfect breakfast spot, weather permitting. Rooms in the "garden"
wing are coolest in summer. Pros: Large courtyard garden; close to Latin
Quarter nightlife spots; good value. Cons: Uphill walk from the métro;
outdated décor; few amenities. ⊠*75 rue du Cardinal Lemoine,75005*

☎*01–43–26–79–23* ⊕*www.hotel-grandes-ecoles.com* ↩*51 rooms* ♿*In-room: no a/c, no TV, Wi-Fi. In-hotel: room service, parking (fee), some pets allowed* ▭*MC, V* Ⓜ*Cardinal Lemoine.* ✠ *4:E5*

$$$$ **Hôtel des Grands Hommes.** The "great men" this hotel honors with its name rest in peace within the towering Panthéon monument across the street. The hotel's look combines urns and laurel-wreath motifs with plush fabrics and plaster busts of writers and statesmen. Superior rooms are larger and face the Panthéon, and top-floor rooms have balconies with tables and chairs. All rooms have period furnishings, handsome wallpapers, and interesting architectural details. The sister Hôtel Panthéon next door has similar services and prices with country-style furnishings. Pros: Close to Place de la Contrescarpe nightlife; major Latin Quarter sights within walking distance; comfortable and attractive. Cons: Closest métro is 10 minutes' walk to bottom of the hill; neighborhood can be loud with student revelers after dark; high price for the Latin Quarter. ✉*17 pl. du Panthéon,* ☎*01–46–34–19–60* ⊕*www.hoteldesgrandshommes.com* ↩*31 rooms* ♿*In-room: safe, Wi-Fi. In-hotel: laundry service, some pets allowed, public Wi-Fi* ▭*AE, DC, MC, V* Ⓜ*RER: Luxembourg.* ✠ *4:D5*

$$$ **Hôtel Henri IV Rive Gauche.** From the ashes of the legendary dive bar Polly Magoo rose this smart new hotel back in 2003; it's 50 paces from Notre-Dame and the Seine. The identical, impeccable rooms have beige and rose blossom–print linens and framed prints of architectural drawings. Street-side rooms get a bit of traffic noise, but views of the 15th-century Eglise St-Severin make up for it. The lobby has pleasing terra-cotta floor tiles, pale green walls, and a stone fireplace. (Note: Don't confuse this with other Henri IV hotels in the area.) Pros: Elegant, comfortable décor; central location close to major sights and RER station. Cons: On a busy street full of late-night bars; some rooms are very small. ✉*9–11 rue St-Jacques,* ☎*01–46–33–20–20* ⊕*www.hotel-henri4.com* ↩*23 rooms* ♿*In-room: safe, Wi-Fi. In-hotel: public Internet, some pets allowed* ▭*AE, DC, MC, V* Ⓜ*St-Michel.* ✠ *4:D3*

$$ **Hôtel des Jardins du Luxembourg.** Blessed with a personable staff and a smart, stylish look, this hotel on a calm cul-de-sac a block away from the Luxembourg Gardens is an oasis for contemplation. The welcoming hardwood-floor lobby with a fireplace leads to smallish rooms furnished with wrought-iron beds, contemporary bathrooms, and Provençal fabrics. Ask for one with a balcony, or request one of the larger ground-floor rooms with private entrance onto the street. A hot buffet breakfast is served in the cheerful dining room. It's an easy commute to either the airport or the Eurostar via the RER train that stops at the end of the street. Pros: Quiet street close to gardens and RER station; nice décor; hot buffet breakfast. Cons: Extra charge to use Wi-Fi; some very small rooms; air-conditioning not very strong. ✉*5 impasse Royer-Collard,* ☎*01–40–46–08–88* ⊕*www.les-jardins-du-luxembourg.com* ↩*26 rooms* ♿*In-room: safe, Wi-Fi. In-hotel: laundry service* ▭*AE, DC, MC, V* Ⓜ*RER: Luxembourg.* ✠ *4:C5*

18

¢–$ **Hôtel Marignan.** Paul Keniger, the energetic third-generation owner, has cultivated a convivial atmosphere for independent international travelers. Not to be confused with the hotel of the same name near the Champs-Elysées, the Marignan lies squarely between budget-basic and youth hostel (no TVs or elevator) and offers lots of communal conveniences—a fully stocked and accessible kitchen, free laundry machines, and copious tourist

information. Rooms are modest (some sleeping four or five) but generally large, and the bathrooms are clean. This is a good choice for families. The least expensive rooms share toilets and/or showers. Pros: Great value for the location; kitchen and laundry open to guests; Wi-Fi. Cons: No elevator; room phones only take incoming calls; has a bit of a youth-hostel atmosphere ⊠ *13 rue du Sommerard,* ☎ *01–43–54–63–81* ⊕ *www.hotel-marignan.com* ↩ *30 rooms, 12 with bath* ⚿ *In-room: no a/c, kitchen, no TV, Wi-Fi. In-hotel: laundry facilities* ▤ *MC, V* ⏏|*CP* Ⓜ *Maubert Mutualité.* ✛ *4:D4*

$$$–$$$$ **Hôtel Résidence Henri IV.** Sometimes travelers, especially those with children, need a home base where they can kick back and make their own meals, and this is a good option. The elegant rooms here have molded ceilings, marble mantelpieces, a pale color scheme, and kitchenettes equipped with two-burner stoves, dorm-size fridges, sinks, and basic dishware. Apartments have space for up to four guests. Free Wi-Fi is available in the lobby. The location on a quiet cul-de-sac by the Ecole Polytechnique is steps from the Panthéon and the Sorbonne. Pros: Kitchenettes in rooms; free Wi-Fi; close to Latin Quarter sights. Cons: No air-conditioning; closest métro is a few blocks away. ⊠ *50 rue des Bernadins,* ☎ *01–44–41–31–81* ⊕ *www.residencehenri4.com* ↩ *8 rooms, 5 apartments* ⚿ *In-room: no a/c, safe, kitchen. In-hotel: laundry service, some pets allowed, public Wi-Fi* ▤ *AE, DC, MC, V* Ⓜ *Maubert-Mutualité.* ✛ *4:D4*

$$ **Hôtel Saint-Jacques.** Nearly every wall in this bargain hotel is bedecked with faux-marble and trompe-l'oeil murals. As in many old, independent Paris hotels, each room is unique, but a general 19th-century theme of Second Empire furnishings and paintings dominates, with a Montmartre cabaret theme in the new breakfast room. Wi-Fi is available in the lounge bar. About half the rooms have tiny step-out balconies that give a glimpse of Notre-Dame and the Panthéon. Room 25 has a long, around-the-corner balcony, and No. 16 is popular for its historic ceiling fresco and moldings. Repeat guests get souvenir knickknacks or T-shirts. Pros: Unique Parisian décor; friendly service; close to Latin Quarter sights. Cons: No air-conditioning; very busy street makes it too noisy to open windows in summer; thin walls between rooms. ⊠ *35 rue des Ecoles,* ☎ *01–44–07–45–45* ⊕ *www.hotel-saintjacques.com*

⊷*38 rooms* ⚹*In-room: no a/c, safe, Wi-Fi. In-hotel: public Internet* ▭*AE, DC, MC, V* Ⓜ*Maubert-Mutualité.* ⊕ 4:D4

¢–$ **Port-Royal Hôtel.** The spotless rooms and extra-helpful staff at the Port-Royal are well above average for this price range. Just below the Rue Mouffetard market at the edge of the 13ᵉ arrondissement, it may be somewhat removed from the action, but the snug antiques-furnished lounge areas, garden courtyard, and rooms with wrought-iron beds, mirrors, and armoires make it worth the trip. Rooms at the lowest end of the price range are equipped only with sinks (an immaculate shared shower room is in the hallway). Pros: Excellent value for the money; attentive service; typical Parisian neighborhood close to two major markets. Cons: Not very central; on a busy street; few amenities. ✉*8 bd. de Port-Royal,* ☎*01–43–31–70–06* ⊕*www.hotelportroyal.fr* ⊷*46 rooms, 20 with bath/shower* ⚹*In-room: no a/c, no TV* ▭*No credit cards* Ⓜ*Les Gobelins.* ⊕ 4:G6

6ᵉ ARRONDISSEMENT

THE 6ᵉ IS A POPULAR Left Bank area, known for the chic boutiques around St-Germain-des-Prés. The streets are more tranquil near the elegant Jardin du Luxembourg, and the nightlife is liveliest around Odéon and Place St-André-des-Arts. In addition to the well-known boutique hotels, some excellent budget sleeps can be found here—but what you gain in location you lose in size and comfort.

$$$$ **Artus Hôtel.** One of the best things about the Artus, aside from the sleek look, is the fact that it's smack in the middle of Rue de Buci. This means you can breakfast at Paul, shop at the wonderful street market, then have an espresso at Bar du Marché. Contemporary rooms have dark-wood furnishings and whitewashed, wood-beamed ceilings that complement brightly colored walls and bedspreads. Bathrooms are in marble and chrome. The more spacious duplex suite under the roof, No. 140, has a small bathroom loft with a shower, makeup table, and freestanding bathtub; the street-facing top-floor suite has a patio with a table and chairs, perfect for people-watching. Pros: Attentive service; excellent location on a market street; stylish design. Cons: Rooms are small for the price; neighborhood is quite busy and at times noisy. ✉*34 rue de Buci,* ☎*01–43–29–07–20* ⊕*www.artushotel.com* ⊷*25 rooms, 2 suites* ⚹*In-room: safe, Wi-Fi. In-hotel: public Internet, room service, laundry service, some pets allowed* ▭*AE, DC, MC, V* ⦿*CP* Ⓜ*Mabillon.* ⊕ 4:B3

$$$$ **L'Hôtel.** Why do rock stars love this eccentric and opulent boutique hotel? Though sophisticated in every way, there's something just a bit naughty in the air. Is it its history as an 18th-century *pavillion d'amour* (inn for trysts)? Is it that Oscar Wilde permanently checked out in Room 16, back in 1900? Or is it Jacques Garcia's makeover—rooms done in yards of thick, rich fabrics in colors like deep red and emerald green? We say all of the above, plus the intimate bar and restaurant allows guests to mingle with the Parisian *beau monde*. A grotto holds a countercurrent pool and a steam room. Pros: Luxurious décor; elegant bar and restaurant; walking distance to the Orsay and the Lou-

18

vre. Cons: Some rooms very small for the price; closest métro station is a few blocks' walk. ✉*13 rue des Beaux-Arts,* ☎*01–44–41–99–00* ⊕*www.l-hotel.com* ⇆*16 rooms, 4 suites* ☆*In-room: safe, Wi-Fi. In-hotel: restaurant, room service, bar, pool, laundry service, some pets allowed* ⊟*AE, DC, MC, V* Ⓜ*St-Germain-des-Prés.* ✛ *4:B2*

Fodor'sChoice
★
$$$–$$$$

🏨 **Hôtel Odéon Saint-Germain.** The exposed stone walls and original wooden beams give this 16th-century building typical Left Bank character, and designer Jacques Garcia's generous use of striped taffeta curtains, velvet upholstery, and plush carpeting imbues the family-run hotel with the distinct luxury of St-Germain-des-Prés. Several small rooms decorated with comfy armchairs and Asian antiques make up the lobby, where guests can help themselves to a Continental buffet breakfast in the morning and an honesty bar throughout the day. Rooms are decorated in eggplant and caramel, with flat-screen TVs and designer toiletries. The ones overlooking the street have more space and double windows for soundproofing. Pros: Warm welcome; free Internet; luxuriously appointed, historic building in an upscale shopping district. Cons: Small rooms aren't convenient for those with extra-large suitcases. ✉*13 rue St-Sulpice,* St-Germain-des-Prés ☎*01–43–25–70–11* ⊕*www.paris-hotel-odeon.com* ⇆*22 rooms, 5 junior suites* ☆*In-room: safe, Ethernet, Wi-Fi. In hotel: room service, bar, public Internet, some pets allowed, laundry service* ⊟*DC, MC, V.* ✛ *4:B3*

$$$–$$$$

Hôtel de l'Abbaye. This hotel on a tranquil side street near St-Sulpice welcomes you with a cobblestone ante-courtyard and vaulted stone entrance. The lobby's salons have vestiges of the original 18th-century convent, with a breakfast room overlooking the spacious garden. Rooms are either a mix of floral and striped fabrics with period furnishings, or are contemporary minimalist with wood paneling and modern art. All have flat-screen TVs; upper-floor accommodations have oak beams and sitting alcoves. Duplexes (split-level suites) have lovely private terraces. Pros: Tranquil setting, upscale neighborhood; good value for price. Cons: Rooms differ greatly in size and style; some are quite small. ✉*10 rue Cassette,* ☎*01–45–44–38–11* ⊕*www.hotel-abbaye. com* ⇆*42 rooms, 4 suites* ☆*In-room: safe, Wi-Fi. In-hotel: room service, bar, laundry service, public Internet* ⊟*AE, MC, V* ⏁*CP* Ⓜ*St-Sulpice.* ✛ *4:A4*

$$$$
Fodor'sChoice
★

Hôtel d'Aubusson. The staff greets you warmly at this 17th-century town house and former literary salon. The showpiece is the stunning front lobby spanned by massive beams and headed by a gigantic fireplace. Decked out in rich burgundies, greens, or blues, the bedrooms are filled with Louis XV– and Regency-style antiques and Hermès toiletries; even the smallest rooms are a generous size by Paris standards. Behind the paved courtyard is a second structure with three apartments, which are ideal for families. The hotel's Café Laurent hosts jazz musicians three nights a week, and there is piano music in the lobby four nights a week. All returning guests (and new guests who book at least four nights) get special VIP treatment such as champagne and flowers on arrival. Pros: Central location near shops and market street; live jazz on weekends; personalized welcome. Cons: Some of the newer rooms lack character; busy street; bar can be noisy on weekends. ✉*33 rue Dauphine,* ☎*01–43–29–43–43* ⊕*www. hoteldaubusson.com* ⇆*49 rooms* ♿*In-room: safe, DVD (some), Wi-Fi. In-hotel: room service, bar, concierge, laundry service, public Internet, parking (fee), some pets allowed* ⊟*AE, DC, MC, V* Ⓜ*Odéon.* ✛ *4:C2*

$$$$ **Hôtel Bel-Ami.** Just a stroll from Café de Flore, the Bel-Ami hides its past as an 18th-century textile factory behind veneer furnishings and crisply jacketed staff. You're immediately hit by the Conran Shop–meets–espresso bar lobby, with club music and a sleek fireplace lounge to match. There's Wi-Fi throughout, and a fitness center with sauna and Tibetan massage treatment rooms. Rooms lean toward minimalist chic in soothing colors but are transformed often to keep up with the hotel's young and trendy clientele. It fills up fast when the fashion circus comes to town. Pros: Upscale, stylish hotel; central St-Germain-des-Prés location; spacious fitness center and spa. Cons: Some guests report loud noise between rooms; some very small rooms in lower price category. ✉*7–11 rue St-Benoît,* ☎*01–42–61–53–53* ⊕*www.hotel-bel-ami.com* ⇆*113 rooms, 2 suites* ♿*In-room: safe, Wi-Fi. In-hotel: room service, bar, gym, concierge, laundry service* ⊟*AE, DC, MC, V* Ⓜ*St-Germain-des-Prés.* ✛ *4:B2*

$$–$$$ **Hôtel Bonaparte.** The congenial staff makes a stay in this intimate hotel an extra-special treat. Old-fashioned upholsteries and 19th-century furnishings make the relatively spacious rooms feel comfortable and unpretentious. Services may be basic, but the location in the heart of St-Germain, about 30 steps from St-Sulpice, is fabulous. Light sleepers should request rooms overlooking the courtyard. Pros: Upscale shopping neighborhood; large rooms for the Left Bank. Cons: Outdated décor and some tired mattresses; air-conditioning not very strong. ✉*61 rue Bonaparte,* ☎*01–43–26–97–37* ⊕*www.hotelbonaparte.fr* ⇆*29 rooms* ♿*In-room: safe, refrigerator, Wi-Fi* ⊟*MC, V* ⍾*CP* Ⓜ*St-Sulpice.* ✛ *4:B3*

$$ **Hôtel du Lys.** To jump into an inexpensive Parisian fantasy, just climb the stairway to your room (there's no elevator) in this former 17th-century royal residence. Well maintained by Madame Steffen, the endearingly odd-shape guest rooms have tiny nooks, weathered antiques, and exposed beams. It may be modest, but it's extremely atmospheric. Breakfast is served in the lobby or in your room. Pros: Central location on a quiet side street; historic character. Cons: No elevator or air-conditioning; old-fashioned décor is decidedly outdated; perfunctory service. ✉*23 rue Serpente,* ☎*01–43–26–97–57* ⊕*www.hoteldulys.com* ⇆*22 rooms* ♿*In-room: no a/c, safe. In-hotel: some pets allowed* ⊟*MC, V* ⍾*CP* Ⓜ*St-Michel, Odéon.* ✛ *4:C3*

18

$$ **Hôtel Mayet.** This fresh, quirky hotel a few blocks from the Bon Marché department store feels a bit like an art-school dormitory: the identical rooms are decorated in battleship gray and maroon, with big aluminum wall clocks, chunky propeller-like ceiling fans, and metal storage containers. The basement breakfast room blasts you with primary colors, and a canvas by the graffitist André hangs in the entry. Pros: Funky, artistic atmosphere; free Wi-Fi; close to two main métro stations and an English bookshop.

Cons: Not very central; décor can feel almost dormlike; closed in August. ⊠3 rue Mayet, ☎01–47–83–21–35 ⊕www.mayet.com ⇘23 rooms △In-room: no a/c, Wi-Fi. In-hotel: public Internet, some pets allowed ⊟AE, DC, MC, V ⊙Closed Aug. and Christmas week ¹⊙¹CP Ⓜ Duroc. ✢ 3:G4

$$$ **Hôtel Millésime.** Step through the doors of this St-Germain-des-Prés hotel and you'll feel transported to the sunny south of France. Rooms are decorated in warm reds, yellows, and royal blues, with rich fabrics and sparkling tiled bathrooms. The centerpiece is the gorgeous Provençal courtyard with ocher walls and wrought-iron balconies (Room 15 has direct access). Friendly service and a bountiful buffet breakfast make this a great find. Pros: Upscale shopping location; young, friendly staff; well-appointed rooms. Cons: Ground floor rooms can be noisy; larger rooms are significantly more expensive. ⊠15 Rue Jacob, ☎01–44–07–97–97 ⊕www.millesimehotel.com ⇘20 rooms, 1 suite △In-room: safe, Wi-Fi. In-hotel: room service, bar, laundry service, public Internet, some pets allowed ⊟AE, MC, V Ⓜ St-Germain-des-Prés. ✢ 4:B2

$ **Hôtel de Nesle.** This one-of-a-kind budget hotel is like a quirky and enchanting dollhouse. Services are bare-bones—no elevator, phones, or breakfast—but the payoff is in the snug rooms cleverly decorated by theme. Sleep in Notre-Dame de Paris, lounge in an Asian-style boudoir, spend the night with Molière, or steam it up in Le Hammam. Decorations include colorful murals, canopy beds, and clay tiles. Most rooms overlook an interior garden, and the dead-end street location keeps the hotel relatively quiet. If you book one of the 11 rooms without a shower, you'll have to share the one bathroom on the second floor. Pros: Unique, fun décor; good value for chic location; small garden. Cons: No amenities or services; reservations by phone only. ⊠7 rue de Nesle, ☎01–43–54–62–41 ⊕www.hoteldenesleparis.com ⇘20 rooms, 9 with bath △In-room: no a/c, no phone, no TV. In-hotel: some pets allowed, public Internet ⊟MC, V Ⓜ Odéon. ✢ 4:C2

$$$ **Hôtel Relais Saint-Sulpice.** A savvy clientele frequents this fashionable little hotel sandwiched between St-Sulpice and the Luxembourg Gar-

dens. Eclectic art objects and furnishings, some with an Asian theme, oddly pull off a unified look. A zebra-print stuffed armchair sits beside an Art Deco desk, and an African mud cloth hangs above a neo-Roman pillar. The rooms themselves, set around an ivy-clad courtyard, are understated, with Provençal fabrics, carved wooden furnishings, and sisal carpeting. Downstairs there's a sauna and a glass-roofed breakfast salon. Room 11 has a terrific view of St-Sulpice. Pros: Chic location, close to two métro stations; bright breakfast room and courtyard, good value. Cons: Smallish rooms in the lower category; noise from the street on weekend evenings. ⊠ *3 rue Garancière,* ☎ *01–46–33–99–00* ⊕ *www.relais-saint-sulpice.com* ⊋ *26 rooms* ⚬ *In-room: safe, Wi-Fi. In-hotel: laundry service* ▭ *AE, DC, MC, V* Ⓜ *St-Germain-des-Prés, St-Sulpice.* ✣ *4:B3*

$$–$$$ **Hôtel Le Sainte-Beuve.** On a tranquil street between the Jardin du Luxembourg and Montparnasse's timeless cafés and brasseries is the pleasant Sainte-Beuve. The spacious lobby and breakfast area are bathed in light, showcasing a wood-fire hearth and Greek Revival columns. White and beige tones dominate the uncluttered rooms, with wooden period furnishings. Extras include bathrobes and a laptop that you can borrow for free (though you can't take it out of the hotel). Pros: Stylish décor; upscale location without tourist crowds; close to major métro lines. Cons: A good 10-minute walk to the Latin Quarter or St-Germain-des-Prés; small rooms and elevator. ⊠ *9 rue Ste-Beuve,* ☎ *01–45–48–20–07* ⊕ *www.paris-hotel-charme.com* ⊋ *22 rooms* ⚬ *In-room: safe, Wi-Fi. In-hotel: room service, bar, laundry service, some pets allowed* ▭ *AE, DC, MC, V* Ⓜ *Vavin.* ✣ *4:A5*

$$$$ **Relais Christine.** This exquisite property was once a 13th-century abbey, but don't expect monkish quarters. You enter from the impressive stone courtyard into a lobby and fireside honor bar decorated with rich fabrics, stone, wood paneling, and antiques. The cavernous breakfast room and adjacent fitness center feature vaulted medieval stonework. Spacious, high-ceilinged rooms offer a variety of classical and contemporary styles: Asian-theme wall fabrics, plain stripes, or rich aubergine paint. Split-level lofts sleep up to five people, and several ground-level rooms open onto a lush garden with private patios and heaters. Pros: Quiet location while still close to the action; historic character; luxuriously appointed rooms. Cons: Some guests report noise from doors on the street; no Wi-Fi; no on-site restaurant. ⊠ *3 rue Christine,* ☎ *01–40–51–60–80, 800/525–4800 in U.S.* ⊕ *www.relais-christine. com* ⊋ *33 rooms, 18 suites* ⚬ *In-room: safe, DVD (some), dial-up. In-hotel: room service, bar, concierge, laundry service, parking (no fee), some pets allowed* ▭ *AE, DC, MC, V* Ⓜ *Odéon.* ✣ *4:C2/3*

$$$$ **Villa d'Estrées.** The Napoleonic era meets North Africa in this moody den: the lobby is bedecked in scarlet drapery, tasseled lamps, and vintage photos of 19th-century sheiks. With only two rooms per floor, running into your neighbors is unlikely. The spacious rooms have boldly striped or patterned wall fabrics in deep red, sea-blue, black, tan, or beige, and are outfitted with king-size beds. Small but sumptuous baths are done in black marble tile. If you plan a longer stay and would be

18

better served by a guest room with kitchenette, check out the sister property across the street, the Hôtel Résidence des Arts. Pros: Centrally located on a tiny side street; luxurious décor; intimate atmosphere. Cons: No hotel facilities such as bar, fitness center, or restaurant; some complain about noise on the street from local bars and between rooms. ⊠*17 rue Gît-le-Coeur,* ☎*01–55–42–71–11* ⊕*www.paris-hotel-latin-quarter.com* ⌨*5 rooms, 5 suites* ⬧*In-room: safe, Wi-Fi. In-hotel: room service, laundry service, some pets allowed* ▤*AE, DC, MC, V* Ⓜ*St-Michel.* ✢ *4:C3*

7ᵉ ARRONDISSEMENT

The wide, tree-lined avenues of the 7ᵉ are home to several of the city's immense monuments, including the Tour Eiffel and Les Invalides. In between are mostly residential streets dotted with embassies and other government buildings. Evenings tend to be quiet, and shopping streets are sparse, with the exception of the charming Rue Cler food market and its many cafés.

$$$$ 🏨 **Le Bellechasse.** French designer Christian Lacroix helped decorate all 34 rooms of Le Bellechasse, which is just around the corner from the popular Musée d'Orsay. Guests enter a refreshingly bright lobby of black slate floors, white walls, and mismatched velour and leather armchairs. Floor-to-ceiling windows overlook the elegant patio courtyard. Each room design is unique, but all have an eclectic mix of fabrics, textures, and colors, as well as Lacroix's whimsical characters screened on the walls and ceilings. Most guest rooms have an open-concept bathroom, with the bathtub and sink in a corner and a separate toilet. Four rooms have doors leading to the patio courtyard. Pros: Central location near top Paris museums; unique style; spacious and bright; Anne Semonin toiletries. Cons: Street-facing rooms can be a bit noisy. ⊠*8 rue de Bellechasse,* ☎*01—45-50-22-31* ⊕*www.lebellechasse. com* ⌨*34 rooms* ⬧*In-room: safe, Wi-Fi, Ethernet. In-hotel: room service, bar, laundry service* ▤*AE, DC, V, JCB.* ✢ *3:H1*

$–$$ **Grand Hôtel Lévêque.** The Tour Eiffel is around the corner, but the real draw here is the bustling pedestrian street market, one of the city's finest, just outside the hotel's front door. Staff are friendly and helpful, and the bistro-style breakfast room next to the reception desk has hot- and cold-drink machines. Rooms have simple furnishings and ceiling fans. Pros: Prime location on a popular market street; budget singles if you don't mind shared shower. Cons: Décor in need of refreshing; air-conditioning only available from June to September. ⊠*29 rue Cler,* ☎*01–47–05–49–15* ⊕*www.hotel-leveque.com* ⌨*50 rooms, 45 with bath/shower* ⬧*In-room: safe, dial-up* ▤*AE, MC, V* Ⓜ*Ecole Militaire.* ✢ *3:E2*

$$$ **Hôtel du Cadran.** The charming Madame Chaine and her gracious staff go out of their way to ensure that you enjoy your stay at this comfortable hotel near the Rue Cler market. A fireplace and grandfather clock lend warmth to the lobby, and rooms have a contemporary feel with Wi-Fi and Roger & Gallet toiletries; some have views of the Tour Eiffel, and No. 108 has its own tiny garden patio. Ask about last-minute deals. Pros: Easy walk to Eiffel Tower, Invalides, and the market;

updated décor. Cons: Small rooms; prices at the high end for this area. ✉ *10 rue du Champ de Mars,* ☎ *01–40–62–67–00* ⊕ *www.cadran hotel.com* 🛏 *42 rooms* ♿ *In-room: safe, DVD (some), Wi-Fi. In-hotel: bar, laundry service* ☰ *AE, DC, MC, V* Ⓜ *Ecole Militaire.* ✛ *3:E2*

$ **Hôtel du Champ de Mars.** Françoise and Stéphane Gourdal's hotel just off Rue Cler has an appealing down-home feel, with a vibrant Provençal-inspired lobby and huge picture windows overlooking the street. Country-style wood furnishings, custom wall stenciling, and crisp fabric chair covers decorate each room. The two on the ground floor open onto a leafy private courtyard. Wireless Internet access is available in the lounge. Pros: Cozy country décor; good value; walking distance to Eiffel Tower and Invalides. Cons: Smallish rooms; no air-conditioning. ✉ *7 rue du Champ de Mars,* ☎ *01–45–51–52–30* ⊕ *www.hotel-du-champ-de-mars.com* 🛏 *25 rooms* ♿ *In-room: no a/c, safe, Wi-Fi* ☰ *MC, V* Ⓜ *Ecole Militaire.* ✛ *3:E2*

$$$$ **Hôtel Duc de Saint-Simon.** If it's good enough for the notoriously choosy Lauren Bacall, you too may fall for the Duc's charms. Its hidden location between Boulevard St-Germain and Rue de Bac is just one of many pluses. Four of the antiques-filled rooms have spacious terraces overlooking the courtyard. The 16th-century basement lounge is a warren of stone alcoves with a zinc bar and plush seating. To keep the peace, parents are discouraged from bringing children along. Pros: Upscale neighborhood close to St-Germain-des-Prés; historic character. Cons: Rooms in the annex are smaller and have no elevator; no air-conditioning; some worn décor. ✉ *14 rue St-Simon,* ☎ *01–44–39–20–20* ⊕ *www.hotelducdesaintsimon.com* 🛏 *29 rooms, 5 suites* ♿ *In-room: no a/c (some), safe, Wi-Fi. In-hotel: bar, laundry service, parking (fee), no kids* ☰ *AE, DC, MC, V* Ⓜ *Rue du Bac.* ✛ *3:H2*

$$ **Hôtel Eiffel Rive Gauche.** On a quiet street near the Tour Eiffel, this bright and welcoming hotel is a good budget find. The rooms are small but comfortable, with modern wood furnishings and orange and gold walls. Many of them open directly onto the Tuscan-style patio with its verdigris railings and terra-cotta tiles. Fans are available in the summer. The owner, Monsieur Chicheportiche, is a multilingual encyclopedia of Paris. Pros: Close to the Eiffel Tower; bright and cheery décor; fans in the summer. Cons: No air-conditioning; some noise between rooms; big difference in room sizes. ✉ *6 rue du Gros Caillou,* ☎ *01–45–51–24–56* ⊕ *www.hotel-eiffel.com* 🛏 *30 rooms* ♿ *In-room: no a/c, safe. In-hotel: laundry service, public Internet* ☰ *MC, V* Ⓜ *Ecole Militaire.* ✛ *3:D2*

$$$ **Hôtel Le Tourville.** This is a rare find: a cozy upscale hotel that doesn't cost a fortune. Each room has crisp, milk-white damask upholstery set against pastel or ocher walls, a smattering of antique bureaus and lamps, original artwork, and fabulous old mirrors. The junior suites have hot tubs, and the superior room has its own private garden terrace. The staff couldn't be more helpful. Pros: Close to the Eiffel Tower and Invalides; attentive service; soundproofed windows. Cons: No shower curtains for the bathtubs; air-conditioning works only during summer months. ✉ *16 av. de Tourville,* ☎ *01–47–05–62–62* ⊕ *www.*

18

hoteltourville.com 🛏*27 rooms, 3 suites* ♿*In-room: safe (some), Wi-Fi. In-hotel: room service, bar, laundry service, some pets allowed* ▭*AE, DC, MC, V* Ⓜ*Ecole Militaire.* ✛ *3:E3*

$$ Hôtel Verneuil. The Verneuil is on a narrow street near the Seine and the rooms are petite, but each is painstakingly decorated. The white-cotton quilts on the beds and the framed, pressed flowers on the walls make you feel like you've arrived *chez grand-mère.* Fans of Serge Gainsbourg can pilgrimage to his former home directly across the street. Pros: Quiet location near St-Germain-des-Prés; good value for the trendy address; spacious bathrooms. Cons: Small rooms; some stairs to get to the elevator; a few blocks to the nearest métro. ✉*8 rue de Verneuil,* ☎*01–42–60–83–14* ⊕*www.hotelverneuil.com* 🛏*26 rooms* ♿*In-room: no a/c (some), safe, Wi-Fi. In-hotel: room service, bar, laundry service, public Internet, some pets allowed* Ⓜ*RER: Musée d'Orsay.* ✛ *4:A2*

$$$$ Le Walt. Wood floors and rich fabrics in chocolate and plum tones accent this family-run boutique hotel in the chic district between the Tour Eiffel and Les Invalides. The small lobby opens to a dining room and bar overlooking a private patio where breakfast is served in summer. Rooms are decorated with contemporary furnishings and oil-portrait headboards. The slightly larger sister hotel, Le Marquis, offers similar services and style a few blocks down the street. Pros: Contemporary yet cozy style; close to métro and major monuments; air-conditioning and Wi-Fi. Cons: On a very busy street; no restaurant in the hotel; some complain about the noise of doors closing in hallways. ✉*37 av. de la Motte Picquet,* ☎*01–45–51–55–83* ⊕*www.lewaltparis. com* 🛏*25 rooms* ♿*In-room: safe, Wi-Fi. In-hotel: room service, bar, laundry service, parking (fee), some pets allowed* ▭*AE, DC, MC, V* Ⓜ*Ecole Militaire.* ✛ *3:E2*

8ᵉ ARRONDISSEMENT

For those seeking the city's glitz and glamour, it's hard to beat the 8e arrondissement. From the late-night cafés, shops, and cinemas of the lively Champs-Elysées to the couture boutiques and clubs of Avenue George V and Avenue Montaigne, there are plenty of opportunities to whip out the platinum card. Foodies will find bliss in the gourmet shops around Place de la Madeleine. Prices come down to earth a bit on the quiet side streets.

$$$$ Champs-Elysees Plaza Hotel and Wellness. Discreet, contemporary elegance, just steps from hustle and bustle of the Champs Elysees is what you'll find at this gracious, thoroughly welcoming 7-floor townhouse. No detail has been overlooked, from sumptuous fabrics in plums, browns, and grays—Marie Antoinette would have lusted after these silks for her dresses—to Hermès toiletries, fresh flowers, and jazz on the in-room stereo. Rooms and bathrooms are more than spacious, and higher floors have lovely views of the city. Great care has been taken to make the gym, hammam, and sauna areas fresh and welcoming, with plants and mirrors, and spaces that aren't claustrophobic. Pros: Extremely comfortable spaces, attentive service, central location. Cons: Neighborhood is too chichi to have much character, small (but charming) elevator. ⊠*35 rue de Berrii75008* ☏*01–53–53–20–20* ⊕*www.champselyseeplaza.com* ⤻*6 rooms, 29 suites* ⬙*In-room: Wi-Fi, safe, refrigerator. In-hotel: restaurant, bar gym, spa, public internet, laundry service, concierge, room service* ▭*AE, MC, V* Ⓜ*George V, St-Philippe-du-Roule.*

$$$$ **Four Seasons Hôtel George V Paris.** The George V is as poised and polished as the day it opened in 1928: the original Art Deco detailing and 17th-century tapestries have been restored, the bas-reliefs regilded, and the marble-floor mosaics rebuilt tile by tile. Rooms are decked in fabrics and Louis XVI trimmings but have homey touches like selections of CDs and French books. Le Cinq restaurant is one of Paris's hottest tables, and the business center has six fully equipped working stations with computers and printers. The low-lighted spa and fitness center pampers guests with 11 treatment rooms, walls covered in *toile de Jouy* fabrics, and an indoor swimming pool evoking Marie-Antoinette's Versailles. A relaxation room is available for guests who arrive before their rooms are ready. Even children get the four-star treatment, with personalized T-shirts and portable DVD players to distract them at dinnertime. Pros: In the couture shopping district; courtyard dining in the summer; guest-only indoor swimming pool. Cons: Several blocks from the nearest métro; lacks the intimacy of smaller boutique hotels. ⊠*31 av. George V,* ☏*01–49–52–70–00, 800/332–3442 in U.S.* ⊕*www.fourseasons.com/paris* ⤻*184 rooms, 61 suites* ⬙*In-room: safe, kitchen (some), DVD, Ethernet, Wi-Fi. In-hotel: 2 restaurants, room service, bar, pool, gym, spa, concierge, children's programs (ages 1–12), laundry service, airport shuttle, some pets allowed* ▭*AE, DC, MC, V* Ⓜ*George V.* ✛ *1:D5*

*Fodor's*Choice ★ ☺

18

$$$$ **Hôtel Le Bristol.** The Bristol ranks among Paris's most exclusive hotels and has the prices to prove it. Some of the spacious and elegant rooms have authentic Louis XV and Louis XVI furniture and marble bathrooms in pure 1920s Art Deco; others have a more relaxed 19th-century style. The public *salons* are stocked with old-master paintings and sculptures, and sumptuous carpets and tapestries. The huge interior garden restaurant and monthly fashion shows in the bar draw the posh and wealthy. A lounge bar and a casual brasserie overlook the Faubourg St-Honoré. Pros: Large interior garden, luxury shopping street. Cons: A few blocks from the nearest métro, old-fashioned atmosphere may not be for everyone. ⊠*112 rue du Faubourg St-Honoré,* ☏*01–53–43–43–00* ⊕*www.lebristolparis.com* ⤻*162 rooms, 73 suites* ⬙*In-room: safe, DVD, Ethernet. In-hotel: restaurant, room service, bar, pool, gym, spa, concierge, laundry service, public Wi-Fi, parking (no fee), some pets allowed* ▭*AE, DC, MC, V* Ⓜ*Miromesnil.* ✛ *1:F4*

$$$$ Hôtel Daniel. A contemporary antidote to the minimalist trend, the Daniel is decorated in sumptuous fabrics and antique furnishings from France, North Africa, and the Far East. The lobby feels like a living room, with deep sofas covered in colorful satin pillows, dark hardwood floors, and delicate Chinese floral wallpaper. Rooms have *toile de Jouy* fabrics, free Wi-Fi, and flat-screen TVs. Little luxuries include lavender sachets and padded hangers in the closets, and glass jars of sea salts in the marble or Moroccan-tile bathrooms. Room No. 601, under the mansard roof, has a huge claw-foot bathtub. Pros: Intimate, homey atmosphere, free Wi-Fi, close to the Champs-Elysées. Cons: Across from a noisy bar, no fitness center. ⊠*8 rue Frédéric Bastiat,* ☎*01–42–56–17–00* ⊕*www.hoteldanielparis.com* ⌁*17 rooms, 9 suites* ⌂*In-room: safe, DVD, Wi-Fi. In-hotel: restaurant, room service, bar, laundry service, parking (fee), some pets allowed* ▭*AE, DC, MC, V* Ⓜ*St-Philippe-du-Roule.* ⊹ *1:E4*

$$$$ Hôtel Fouquet's Barrière. This contemporary luxury hotel opened in 2006 above the legendary Fouquet's Brasserie at the corner of the Champs-Elysées and Avenue George V. The design, by Jacques Garcia, is more refined retro than opulent, with a rich neutral palette in silk, mahogany, velvet, and leather. The hotel competes with Parisian palaces by offering 24-hour butler service, plasma TV screens hidden behind mirrors and above bathtubs, and multimedia desks with integrated scanner, printer, and color copier. Le Diane restaurant offers a more feminine atmosphere than the brasserie, and the teak- and red-walled spa claims to have the largest indoor pool in Paris. Pros: Many rooms overlooking the Champs-Elysées; bathroom televisions; main métro line right outside. Cons: The anonymous décor lacks Parisian character; busy street can be noisy; expensive part of town. ⊠*46 av. George V,* ☎*01–40–69–60–00* ⊕*www.fouquets-barriere.com* ⌁*107 rooms, 40 suites* ⌂*In-room: safe, DVD, Ethernet, Wi-Fi. In-hotel: 2 restaurants, room service, bar, pool, gym, spa, laundry service, concierge, public Wi-Fi, parking (fee), some pets allowed* ▭*AE, DC, MC, V* Ⓜ*George V.* ⊹ *1:D4*

$$$$ Hôtel Lancaster. Contemporary flourishes like perfume-bottle lamp bases and a Japanese garden give this former Spanish nobleman's town house a refreshing, modern atmosphere. Not everything is contemporary, though: room keys and doorbells are vintage, and there are more than 1,000 antiques and 18th-century paintings throughout the hotel. Free Wi-Fi and iPod docking stations in every room cater to high-tech travelers. Rooms are elegant—the Emile Wolf Suite has a baby grand—with a mix of antiques and updated fabrics, marble bathrooms, and walk-in closets. The fitness room has a splendid view of Sacré-Coeur. Pros: Sunday brunch with organic farm products; free Wi-Fi. Cons: Street-facing rooms can be noisy; size of rooms varies greatly. ⊠*7 rue de Berri,* ☎*01–40–76–40–76, 877/757–2747 in U.S.* ⊕*www.hotel-lancaster.fr* ⌁*46 rooms, 11 suites* ⌂*In-room: safe, DVD, Wi-Fi. In-hotel: restaurant, room service, bar, gym, laundry service, parking (fee), some pets allowed* ▭*AE, DC, MC, V* Ⓜ*George V.* ⊹ *1:D4*

Fodor's Choice
★
🕐
$$$$

Hôtel Plaza Athénée. Prime-time stardom as Carrie Bradshaw's Parisian pied-à-terre in the final episodes of *Sex and the City* boosted the street cred of this 1911 palace hotel. Its revival as the city's lap of luxury, however, owes more to the meticulous attention of the renowned chef Alain Ducasse, who oversees everything from the hotel's flagship restaurant and restored 1930s Relais Plaza brasserie to the quality of the breakfast croissants. Rooms have been redone in Regency, Louis XVI, or Art Deco style, with remote-control air-conditioning, mini hi-fi/CD players, and even a pillow menu. The trendy bar has as its centerpiece an impressive Bombay glass *comptoir* glowing like an iceberg. Pros: On a luxury shopping street; stylish clientele and locals at the bar and restaurants; special attention to children. Cons: Vast difference in style of rooms; easy to feel anonymous in such a large hotel. ⊠*25 av. Montaigne,* ☎*01–53–67–66–65, 866/732–1106 in U.S.* ⊕*www. plaza-athenee-paris.com* ⇌*145 rooms, 43 suites* ⌂*In-room: safe, DVD, Ethernet. In-hotel: 3 restaurants, room service, bar, concierge, laundry service, some pets allowed* ☰*AE, DC, MC, V* Ⓜ*Alma-Marceau.* ✢ *1:D6*

$$$

Hôtel Queen Mary. This cheerfully cozy hotel is two blocks from Place de la Madeleine and Paris's famous department stores. Sunny yellow walls, plush carpeting, and fabrics in burgundy, gold, and royal blue soften the regal architectural detailing and high ceilings. Rooms are handsomely appointed with large beds and such thoughtful extras as trouser presses, Roger & Gallet toiletries, and decanters of sherry. Guests mingle in the bar during happy hour and, in good weather, enjoy breakfast in the garden courtyard. Pros: Close to high-end shopping streets and department stores; large beds; extra-attentive service. Cons: Some rooms are quite snug; ones on the ground floor can be noisy. ⊠*9 rue Greffulhe,* ☎*01–42–66–40–50* ⊕*www.hotelqueenmary.com* ⇌*35 rooms, 1 suite* ⌂*In-room: safe, Wi-Fi. In-hotel: room service, bar, laundry service, some pets allowed* ☰*MC, V* Ⓜ*Madeleine, St-Lazare, Havre Caumartin.* ✢ *1:H4*

$$$$

Hôtel San Régis. On a quiet side street near tony Avenue Montaigne, this discreet hotel walks softly but wields huge snob appeal (the same family that opened it once owned the Tour d'Argent and the George V). All guest rooms and suites have carefully chosen antiques, embroidered silks and brocades, and richly patterned Pierre Frey wall fabrics; bathrooms are done in Italian marble, with Hermès toiletries. Top-floor suites have balcony views of the Tour Eiffel, Grand Palais, Opéra Garnier, and Madeleine. The elegant wood-paneled Boiseries Lounge leads to the tiny English Bar and a dining room that serves traditional French cuisine. Pros: On a quiet street; authentic old Parisian feel; personalized service. Cons: Old-fashioned décor can feel outdated; no fitness facilities. ⊠*12 rue Jean-Goujon,* ☎*01–44–95–16–16* ⊕*www.hotel-sanregis.fr* ⇌*33 rooms, 11 suites* ⌂*In-room: safe, Wi-Fi. In-hotel: restaurant, room service, bar, laundry service, public Internet* ☰*AE, DC, MC, V* Ⓜ*Franklin-D.-Roosevelt.* ✢ *1:E6*

18

$$$$ Pershing Hall. Formerly an American Legion hall, this circa-2001 boutique hotel quickly became a must-stay address for the dressed-in-black pack. Designed by Andrée Putman, Pershing Hall champions masculine minimalism, with muted surfaces of wood and stone and cool attitudes to match. Rooms have stark white linens, triptych dressing mirrors, slender tubelike hanging lamps, and tubs perched on round marble bases. The only trace of lightheartedness is the free minibars. All deluxe rooms and suites face the courtyard dining room, whose west wall is a six-story hanging garden with 300 varieties of plants. The lounge bar serves drinks, dinner, and DJ-driven music until 2 AM. Pros: In prime shopping and nightlife district; bar and restaurant frequented by hip locals; in-room DVD players. Cons: Bar noise can be heard in some rooms; expensive neighborhood. ⊠ *49 rue Pierre-Charron,* ☎ *01–58–36–58–00* ⊕ *www.pershinghall.com* ⌔ *20 rooms, 6 suites* ⌂ *In-room: safe, DVD, Ethernet, Wi-Fi. In-hotel: restaurant, room service, bar, spa, concierge, laundry service, some pets allowed* ⊟ *AE, DC, MC, V* Ⓜ *George V, Franklin-D.-Roosevelt.* ✛ *1:D5*

$$$$ 🏨 **Hôtel Mathis Elysées Matignon.** Completely remodeled in 2007, each room in this boutique hotel has been lovingly decorated with antiques and artworks. Leopard-print carpets, rich aubergine, slate, and mustard walls, and baroque mirrors make for an eclectic look. Room 43 has a sexy boudoir style, and the top-floor suite has a modern pop-art look. The Mathis's restaurant is owned separately from the hotel, but shares an entrance. Pros: A block from the Champs-Elysées and Faubourg St-Honoré; large choice in décor of rooms; free Wi-Fi. Cons: Some noise from street and bar downstairs; small closets; few services. ⊠ *3 rue de Ponthieu, ,* ☎ *01–42–25–73–01* ⊕ www.paris-hotel-mathisely-sees.com ⌔ *23 rooms* ⌂ *In-room: safe, Wi-Fi. In-hotel: room service, concierge, laundry service, some pets allowed* ⊟ *AE, DC, MC, V* Ⓜ*. Franklin-D.-Roosevelt.* ✛ *4:B3*

$$$$ La Trémoille. La Trémoille offers business travelers a trendy home base, with Haussmann-era marble fireplaces and plaster moldings that have been given a shot of style by contemporary armoires, furniture upholstered in fake fur, and funky mohair curtains. Unique to this hotel is the "hatch," a butler closet by each door where meals and laundry can be delivered without disturbing the guests. The Louis II restaurant and piano lounge bar features French Mediterranean cuisine and a trendy-but-cozy setting of black lacquer tables, silver beaded curtains, and beige and eggplant fabrics. Pros: Piano bar frequented by locals; spa and fitness facilities. Cons: A few blocks from the nearest métro; expensive neighborhood. ⊠ *14 rue de La Trémoille,* ☎ *01–56–52–14–00* ⊕ *www.hotel-tremoille.com* ⌔ *88 rooms, 5 suites* ⌂ *In-room: safe, DVD, Ethernet, Wi-Fi. In-hotel: restaurant, room service, bar, gym, spa, concierge, laundry service, parking (fee), some pets allowed* ⊟ *AE, DC, MC, V* Ⓜ*Alma-Marceau.* ✛ *1:D6*

9ᵉ ARRONDISSEMENT

Ideal if you're seeking good deals near Montmartre and central Paris, the 9ᵉ arrondissement has several distinctly different neighborhoods. To the southwest is the busy Opéra district with the historic department stores of the Grands Boulevards. To the north, at the foot of Montmartre, are the neon-lighted sex shops and clubs of the infamous Pigalle district. In between are the pleasant residential districts of Nouvelle Athènes and Rue des Martyrs.

$$ **Hôtel Amour.** The hipster team behind this designer boutique hotel just off the trendy Rue des Martyrs already count among their fiefdoms some of the hottest hotels, bars, and nightclubs in Paris. But despite the cool factor and the funky rooms individually decorated by Parisian avant-garde artists, the prices remain democratically bohemian. Of course, there are few amenities, but there is a 24-hour retro brasserie and garden terrace in the back where locals come to hang out in warmer weather. The hotel is not designed for children; vintage nudie magazines decorate, and the sex shops of Pigalle are blocks away. Pros: Hip clientele and locals at the brasserie; close to Montmartre; garden dining in summer. Cons: Few amenities; a few blocks from the nearest métro; close to red-light district. ⊠*8 rue Navarin,* ☎*01–48–78–31–80* ⊕*www.hotelamour.com* ↩*20 rooms* ♻*In-room: no a/c, no phone, no TV. In-hotel: restaurant, bar, public Wi-Fi, room service, laundry service, some pets allowed* ▤*AE, DC, MC, V* Ⓜ*Pigalle.* ✛ *2:B2*

$–$$ **Hôtel Chopin.** The Chopin recalls its 1846 birth date with a creaky-floored lobby and aged woodwork. The basic but comfortable rooms overlook the Passage Jouffroy's quaint toy shops and bookstores or the rooftops of Paris, but none face the busy nearby streets. The best rooms end in "7" (No. 407 overlooks the Grévin Wax Museum's ateliers), whereas those ending in "2" tend to be darkest and smallest (but cheapest). Pros: Unique location; close to major métro station; great nightlife district. Cons: Neighborhood can be noisy; some rooms are dark and cramped; few amenities. ⊠*10 bd. Montmartre, 46 passage Jouffroy,* ☎*01–47–70–58–10* ⊟*01–42–47–00–70* ↩*36 rooms* ♻*In-room: no a/c, safe* ▤*AE, MC, V* Ⓜ*Grands Boulevards.* ✛ *2:C4*

$$$ **Hôtel George Sand.** This family-run boutique hotel where the 19th-century writer George Sand once lived is fresh and modern, while preserving some original architectural details. Rooms have tea/coffee-making trays and high-tech comforts such as complimentary high-speed Internet and cordless phones. Bathrooms are decked out in yacht-inspired wood flooring, with Etro toiletries. Pros: Next door to two department stores; historic atmosphere; free Internet. Cons: Noisy street; some rooms are quite small. ⊠*26 rue des Mathurins,* ☎*01–47–42–63–47* ⊕*www.hotelgeorgesand.com* ↩*20 rooms* ♻*In-room: safe, Ethernet, Wi-Fi. In-hotel: room service, laundry service* ▤*AE, MC, V* Ⓜ*Havre Caumartin.* ✛ *1:H4*

$$ **Hôtel Langlois.** After starring in *The Truth About Charlie* (a remake of *Charade*), this darling hotel gained a reputation as one of the most atmospheric budget sleeps in the city. Rates have crept up, but the former circa-1870 bank retains its beautiful wood-paneled reception area and wrought-iron elevator. The individually decorated and spacious rooms are decked out with original glazed-tile fireplaces and period art. Some rooms, such as Nos. 15, 21, and 41, have enormous retro bathrooms.

Fodor's Choice
★

18

Pros: Excellent views from the top floor; close to department stores and Opéra Garnier; historic décor. Cons: Noisy street; off the beaten path; some sagging furniture. ⊠*63 rue St-Lazare,* ☎*01–48–74–78–24* ⊕*www.hotel-langlois.com* ⟿*24 rooms, 3 suites* ⌂*In-hotel: public Internet, some pets allowed* ⊟*AE, MC, V* Ⓜ*Trinité.* ✛ *2:A3*

$$$ **Hôtel Royal Fromentin.** At the border of Montmartre's now tamed red-light district sits this former cabaret with much of its deco wood paneling and theatrical trappings intact. Prices are at the low end of its category. The hotel has dark, rich décor, with green walls, red armchairs, an antique caged elevator, and vaudeville posters in the stained-glass-ceilinged lounge. Reproduction furniture, antique prints and oils, and busy modern fabrics fill out the larger-than-average rooms. Some windows face Sacré-Coeur. Guests receive a complimentary book illustrating the history of absinthe, which is once again served in the hotel's historic bar. Pros: Spacious rooms for the price; historic absinthe bar; close to Sacré-Coeur. Cons: Some guests may find neighborhood peep shows and sex shops disturbing; far from the center of Paris. ⊠*11 rue Fromentin,* ☎*01–48–74–85–93* ⊕*www.hotelroyalfromentin.com* ⟿*47 rooms* ⌂*In-room: no a/c, Wi-Fi. In-hotel: bar, laundry service, some pets allowed* ⊟*AE, DC, MC, V* Ⓜ*Blanche.* ✛ *2:B1*

$$$ **Mercure Paris Ronceray Opéra.** On one of Haussmann's Grands Boulevards between a historic covered shopping passage and the Grévin Wax Museum, the Ronceray Opéra is convenient for exploring Montmartre, browsing department stores, or enjoying the area's revival in local nightlife. The Drouot auction house and Hard Rock Cafe are also nearby. The hotel's original 19th-century architecture has been preserved in the elegant Rossini bar and ballroom, where breakfast is served under crystal chandeliers. Comfortably modern rooms glow with wood-paneled walls, warm red fabrics, and marble baths. Rooms 319 and 419 have views of Sacré-Coeur. Pros: Unique location; historic architecture; central nightlife district. Cons: Décor in rooms lacks character of public areas; noisy neighborhood. ⊠*10 bd. Montmartre, Passage Jouffroy,* ☎*01–42–47–13–45* ⊕*www.mercure.com* ⟿*128 rooms, 2 suites* ⌂*In-room: no a/c (some), safe, Wi-Fi. In-hotel: room service, bar, laundry service, some pets allowed* ⊟*AE, DC, MC, V* Ⓜ*Grands Boulevards.* ✛ *2:C4*

10ᵉ ARRONDISSEMENT

As one of the latest up-and-coming districts of Paris, the multicultural 10^e attracts many students, artists, and young professionals, particularly around the Canal St-Martin to the east and the Rue du Faubourg St-Denis to the west. In between are two of the city's busy train stations, Gare de l'Est and Gare du Nord, home of the Eurostar. Nightlife is concentrated around the Bonne Nouvelle métro station.

$$ **Hôtel Français.** This Haussmann-era budget hotel faces historic Gare de l'Est and is two blocks from Gare du Nord and the popular Canal St-Martin district. The décor isn't memorable, but it's still rare to find air-conditioning, elevators, hair dryers, free Wi-Fi, and trouser presses in rooms of this price, so fussing over the color of the curtains seems

CLOSE UP

Lodging Alternatives

APARTMENT RENTALS

If you want a home base that's roomy enough for a family and comes with cooking facilities, consider a furnished rental. These can save you money, especially if you're traveling with a group. Home-exchange directories sometimes list rentals as well as exchanges. You can also look on the **Paris Tourism Office** Web site (www. parisinfo.com) for reputable agency listings. Policies differ from company to company, but you can generally expect a minimum required stay anywhere from three to seven days; a refundable deposit (expect to pay $200–$500) payable on arrival; sometimes an agency fee; and weekly or biweekly maid service.

The following is a list of good-value residence hotels and apartment services, each with multiple properties in Paris: **Ah! Paris** (☎ 01–40–28–97–96 ⊕ www.ahparis.com). **Citadines Résidences Hôtelières** (☎ 08–25–33– 33–32 ⊕ www.citadines.fr) is a chain of apartment-style hotel accommodations. They're modern and somewhat generic, but offer many services and good value for short stays. **Lodgis Paris** (☎ 01–70–39–11–11 🖷 01–

70–39–11–15 ⊕ www.lodgis.com). **Paris Vacation Apartments** (☎ 06– 12–44–64–78 🖷 01–42–64–20–03 ⊕ www.parisvacationapartments.com). **Rothray** (☎ 01–48–87–13–37 🖷 01– 42–78–17–72 ⊕ www.rothray.com).

Agencies based in the United States can also help you find an apartment in Paris: **New York Habitat** (✉ 307 7th Ave., Suite 306, New York, NY ☎ 01–42–36–78–70 in France, 212/255–8018 in U.S. 🖷 212/627– 1416 in U.S. ⊕ www.nyhabitat.com). **Rendez-vous à Paris** (✉ 1220 North Market Street, Suite 606, Wilmington, DE ⊕ www.rendez-vousaparis.com). **Rentals in Paris** (☎ 516/977–3318 🖷 516/977–3318 ⊕ www.rentals-in-paris.com). **Villanet** (✉ 1251 N.W. 116th St., Seattle, WA ☎ 206/417– 3444 or 800/964–1891 🖷 206/417– 1832 ⊕ www.rentavilla.com).

HOSTED ROOMS

The Paris Tourism Office (⊕ www. parisinfo.com) lists bed-and-breakfast agencies, and **Hôtes Qualité Paris** (⊕ www.hotesqualiteparis.fr) unites the listings for several agencies in one place, searchable in English by neighborhood or price (€45–€150 per couple, breakfast included).

18

pointless. Some rooms overlook the charming "indoor patio" breakfast room. The busy neighborhood isn't very attractive, but the métro station across the street is a direct line to Notre-Dame, the Latin Quarter, St-Germain-des-Prés, and the marché aux puces. Pros: Convenient for Eurostar travelers; many amenities for the price; air-conditioning. Cons: Noisy street; unattractive neighborhood. ✉ *13 rue du 8 Mai 1945,* ☎ *01–40–35–94–14* ⊕ *www.hotelfrancais.com* ⇄ *71 rooms* ♿ *In-room: safe, Wi-Fi. In-hotel: room service, bar, parking (fee), some pets allowed* ☰ *AE, MC, V* Ⓜ *Gare de l'Est.* ✢ *2:E3*

¢ **Hôtel du Nord.** Behind the rustic façade of this budget hotel that's just around the corner from Place de la République is a charming little lobby with clay-tile floors, exposed stone walls, and wooden beams. There are few perks, but the hotel does have bikes available free to guests, perfect for a ride down to the nearby Marais district or a cruise along the tree-lined Canal St-Martin. Pros: Bike rental; close to East Paris nightlife districts. Cons: Few amenities; busy Place de la République is quite noisy. ⊠47 *rue Albert Thomas,* ☎01–42–01–66–00 ⊕*www.hotel-dunord-leparivelo.com* ⌫24 *rooms* ☌*In-room: no a/c. In-hotel: bicycles* ▤*MC, V* Ⓜ*République.* ✛ *2:F4*

11ᵉ ARRONDISSEMENT

This East Paris neighborhood became a popular new district for artists and "bourgeois bohemians" in the late 1990s with its laid-back bars, cheap clubs, and funky boutiques along Rue Oberkampf and Rue Méilmontant. There are no museums or monuments, but the relaxed atmosphere, relatively low prices, and proximity to the Bastille and Marais make it popular.

$$$–$$$$ Le Général Hôtel. Designer Jean-Philippe Nuel's sleek hotel was one of Paris's first budget design hotels. The daring interior splashes fuchsia on the walls, though rooms are more subdued in cream, chocolate, and chestnut. Clever elements include clear-plastic desk chairs and silver rubber duckies to float in the tubs. The fifth- and sixth-floor rooms facing the street have balconies with chimney-pot views to the west. One of the hotel's two seventh-floor suites has a bathtub right in the bedroom. Pros: Free Wi-Fi, coffee/tea-making facilities in the room; in popular nightlife district. Cons: Smallish rooms; not within easy walking distance of major tourist sights. ⊠*5–7 rue Rampon,* ☎*01–47–00–41–57* ⊕*www.legeneralhotel.com* ⌫*45 rooms, 2 suites* ☌*In-room: safe, Wi-Fi. In-hotel: bar, laundry service, gym, public Internet, some pets allowed* ▤*AE, DC, MC, V* Ⓜ*République.* ✛ *2:G5*

$$ Hôtel Beaumarchais. This bold hotel straddles the fashionable Marais district in the 3ᵉ and the hip student and artist neighborhood of Oberkampf in the 11ᵉ. Brightly colored vinyl armchairs, an industrial metal staircase, and glass tables mark the lobby, which hosts monthly art exhibitions. Out back, a small courtyard is decked in hardwood, a look you'll rarely see in Paris. The rooms hum with primary reds and yellows, some with Keith Haring prints. Kaleidoscopes of ceramic fragments tile the bathrooms. Pros: Free Ethernet; popular nightlife district; bright and colorful. Cons: Smallish rooms; off the beaten tourist track. ⊠*3 rue Oberkampf,* ☎*01–53–36–86–86* ⊕*www.hotelbeaumarchais.com* ⌫*31 rooms* ☌*In-room: safe, Ethernet, Wi-Fi. In-hotel: some pets allowed* ▤*AE, MC, V* Ⓜ*Filles du Calvaire, Oberkampf.* ✛ *2:G6*

$ Hôtel Résidence Alhambra. The white façade, rear garden, and flower-filled window boxes brighten this lesser-known neighborhood between the Marais and Rue Oberkampf. Rooms are smallish (splurge for a triple, just €116), with modern furnishings and run-of-the-mill bedspreads and drapes. Some overlook the flowery courtyard. There is a free Internet station in the lobby, and five métro lines are around the corner at Place de la République. Pros: Free Ethernet; popular nightlife district; bright and colorful. Cons: Small doubles; long walk to the center of town; no air-conditioning. ⊠*13 rue de Malte,* ☎*01–47–00–35–52* ⊕*www.hotelalhambra.fr* ⟟*58 rooms* ⚐*In-room: no a/c. In-hotel: public Internet, some pets allowed* ▤*AE, DC, MC, V* Ⓜ*Oberkampf.* ✢ *2:H6*

$$$ **Les Jardins du Marais.** Behind an unassuming façade on a narrow street, this rambling hotel's nine historic buildings (including Gustave Eiffel's old workshop) surround a spacious sculpture-garden courtyard. Complete renovations have transformed this former budget residence hotel, introducing neutral linens and Art Deco furnishings (similar to those in the owner's other property, the Hilton Arc de Triomphe) while keeping some of the wet bars and tea/coffee-making facilities. Every room overlooks the garden, where meals are served in summer. In cooler weather you can still enjoy garden views from the glass conservatory restaurant and bar. Pros: Historic building; easy walk to the Marais and Bastille; all rooms face garden courtyard. Cons: Often booked by groups; big difference between room décor and public areas; some rooms in these odd old buildings have a pillar in the center. ⊠*74 rue Amelot,* ☎*01–40–21–20–00* ⊕*www.homeplazza.com* ⟟*201 rooms, 64 suites* ⚐*In-room: safe, Wi-Fi. In-hotel: restaurant, room service, bar, parking (fee)* ▤*AE, DC, MC, V* Ⓜ*St-Sébastien-Froissart.* ✢ *4:H1*

$$$ **Standard Design Hôtel.** It was about time for a design hotel to open in this alternative hipster corner of the Bastille district. Its sleek black façade and black-and-white interior reflect the mood of its fashion-forward clientele, and the fairly affordable rates don't clash with the neighborhood's funky boutiques and retro bistros. In-room stylings include black duvets, flat-screen TVs, and white lacquered furnishings. A bright breakfast room is on the top floor. Massage and manicures are available in the guest rooms. Pros: Trendy design style; free Wi-Fi; funky shopping and nightlife district. Cons: Can be noisy; some rooms very small; have to borrow hair dryer from the front desk. ⊠*29 rue des Taillandiers,* ☎*01–48–05–30–97* ⊕*www.standard-hotel.com* ⟟*36 rooms* ⚐*In-room: Wi-Fi. In-hotel: room service, public Internet, public Wi-Fi* ▤*AE, DC, MC, V* Ⓜ*Bastille.* ✢ *4:H2*

12ᵉ ARRONDISSEMENT

The Bastille district remains a beacon for night owls with its cinemas, late-night bars, and nightclubs spread along the Rue de Lappe and Rue du Faubourg St-Antoine. During the day people come for the two colorful markets on the north end of Place de la Bastille and at Place d'Aligre. The Viaduc des Arts, home to craft boutiques, artisans, and art galleries, stretches from the Opéra Bastille to the Gare de Lyon.

$$ **Hôtel Lyon-Bastille.** This cozy, family-run hotel is just a block from the Gare de Lyon and has been open since 1903. Its turn-of-the-20th-century pedigree shows up in its curves and alcoves, and tall French windows let in plenty of light. The rooms have been done up in pale blues and lilacs, and have satellite TV and free Wi-Fi. The Marché Aligre

18

and Viaduc des Arts artisan boutiques are just a few blocks away. Pros: Easy access to major métro and train lines; free Wi-Fi; friendly welcome. Cons: Outdated décor; noisy traffic area; tiny elevator. ⊠3 *rue Parrot*, ☎01–43–43–41–52 ⊕*www.hotellyonbastille.com* ♥47 *rooms, 1 suite* ⚓*In-room: safe, Wi-Fi. In-hotel:* ⊟*AE, DC, MC, V* Ⓜ*Gare de Lyon.* ✢ *4:H4*

13ᵉ ARRONDISSEMENT

The 13ᵉ is often dismissed as a "new" district of high-rise apartments—which is true in the Chinatown area east of Place d'Italie—but the historic Gobelins district blends seamlessly with the Mouffetard market and Jardin des Plantes of the neighboring 5ᵉ, without the steep prices. The 13ᵉ is also home to the charming Butte-aux-Cailles hilltop and the contemporary Rive Gauche district along the Seine.

$$$ **Hôtel La Manufacture.** Just behind Place d'Italie and a short stroll from both the Jardin des Plantes and Rue Mouffetard, La Manufacture's lesser-known location makes you feel like a *vrai* (real) Parisian. The lobby has oak floors, subtle lighting, a wooden bar, and a breakfast room with patio chairs and gingham-covered benches. Rooms are decorated in clean lines and natural colors; options include triples and eight sets of connecting rooms for families. The most expensive top-floor rooms are more spacious and have Tour Eiffel or Panthéon views. Pros: Easy access to major métro and bus lines; safe nontouristy district; bright breakfast room. Cons: Street noise; a long stroll to the center of Paris; small rooms. ⊠*8 rue Philippe de Champagne*, ☎01–45–35–45–25 ⊕*www.hotel-la-manufacture.com* ♥57 *rooms* ⚓*In-room: Ethernet. In-hotel: bar, laundry service, some pets allowed* ⊟*AE, DC, MC, V* Ⓜ*Place d'Italie.* ✢ *4:E6*

$$ **Résidence Hôtelière Le Vert Galant.** In a little-known neighborhood west of Place d'Italie awaits a sincere welcome from Madame Laborde, the proprietress. More like her own house, this plain but proper hotel encloses a peaceful green garden. Eight of the rooms have kitchenettes, which can reduce dining-out costs, unless the hotel's pricey L'Auberge Etchegorry restaurant lures you in. Victor Hugo was known to take a glass or two at this outstanding Basque dining spot. Pros: Quiet location with a garden; kitchenettes in some rooms; safe residential district. Cons: Not very central; no air-conditioning; some noise between rooms. ⊠*41–43 rue Croulebarbe*, ☎01–44–08–83–50 ⊕*www.vert-galant.com* ♥15 *rooms* ⚓*In-room: no a/c, safe, kitchen (some), Wi-Fi. In-hotel: restaurant, laundry service, parking (fee)* ⊟*AE, DC, MC, V* Ⓜ*Les Gobelins.* ✢ *4:E6*

$ **Résidence Les Gobelins.** Wicker furniture and sunny colors warm up this small, simple hotel on a quiet side street between Place d'Italie and the Quartier Latin, not far from the market street Rue Mouffetard. Some rooms overlook a small flower-filled garden, as does the lounge–breakfast room. Jamaican expat Jennifer Poirier runs the Résidence with her French husband, Philippe. Their wholehearted welcome is a big part of this hotel's draw. Pros: Close to major métro and bus lines; friendly welcome. Cons: Twenty-minute walk to the center of Paris; few amenities; no air-conditioning. ✉*9 rue des Gobelins,* ☎*01–47–07–26–90* ⊕*www.hotelgobelins.com* ⇄*32 rooms* ⚥*In-room: no a/c* ▭*AE, MC, V* Ⓜ*Les Gobelins.* ✛ *4:E6*

14ᵉ ARRONDISSEMENT

Once the stomping ground of artists and writers, Montparnasse is still a lively area of Paris, separated from the more upscale 6ᵉ arrondissement by the busy Boulevard du Montparnasse. Although the area around the hulking Tour Montparnasse, train station, and commercial center looks a bit like Times Square, with billboards and cinemas, the area around the cemetery has more of a Parisian village atmosphere, particularly on the Rue Daguerre market street near Denfert-Rochereau.

$ **Hôtel des Bains.** In a charming neighborhood, this hidden find has taste-
FodorśChoice fully decorated rooms, satellite TV, and air-conditioning. Prices are
★ excellent, especially for the family-friendly two-room suites (€105–€155), one with a terrace, in a separate building off the courtyard garden. Local artists contributed different pieces to each room. Pros: Close to Luxembourg Gardens and St-Germain-des-Prés; garden courtyard; typical Parisian character. Cons: Décor may seem a bit outdated; streets can be noisy; some rooms very small. ✉*33 rue Delambre,* ☎*01–43–20–85–27* ⊕*www.hotel-des-bains-montparnasse.com* ⇄*35 rooms, 8 suites* ⚥*In-room: safe. In-hotel: parking (fee), some pets allowed* ▭*MC, V* Ⓜ*Vavin, Edgar Quinet.* ✛ *4:A6*

$$$ **Hôtel Istria.** This small, family-run hotel on a quiet side street was a Montparnasse artists' hangout in the 1920s and '30s. It has a flower-filled courtyard and simple, clean, comfortable rooms with Japanese wallpaper and light-wood furnishings. Breakfast is served in a vaulted cellar. Pros: Close to major métro and train stations; quiet courtyard-facing rooms. Cons: No air-conditioning; some rooms very small; not centrally located. ✉*29 rue Campagne-Première,* ☎*01–43–20–91–82* ⊕*www.istria-paris-hotel.com* ⇄*26 rooms* ⚥*In-room: no a/c, safe. In-hotel: laundry service, public Internet, public Wi-Fi* ▭*AE, MC, V* Ⓜ*Raspail.* ✛ *4:A6*

$$$ **Hôtel Lenox-Montparnasse.** Parisians know this hotel near the Luxembourg Gardens for its monthly live-music concerts in the cozy bar. Tourists appreciate the extra amenities such as free Wi-Fi. The largest (and best) rooms have fireplaces and exposed beams; in the standard-size rooms, there's barely a suitcase-width between the wall and the foot of the bed. Pros: Close to Montparnasse and St-Germain-des-Prés; lively music bar; free Wi-Fi. Cons: Standard rooms very small; noisy street. ✉*15 rue Delambre,* ☎*01–43–35–34–50* ⊕*www.paris-hotel-lenox.com* ⇄*46 rooms, 6 suites* ⚥*In-room: safe, Wi-Fi. In-hotel: bar, room service, laundry service, public Internet, parking (fee)* ▭*AE, DC, MC, V* Ⓜ*Vavin.* ✛ *4:A6*

$$$ **Hôtel Raspail-Montparnasse.** Rooms are named after the artists who made Montparnasse the art capital of the world in the 1920s and '30s—Picasso, Chagall, and Modigliani. Pay a bit extra—and reserve well in advance—for one of the three deluxe corner rooms, which have windows facing the Tour Eiffel. All are soundproofed, but none completely

18

drown out the hum of traffic below. Pros: Convenient location for métro and bus; many markets and cafés nearby; friendly staff. Cons: Traffic noise; some smallish rooms. ⊠ *203 bd. Raspail,* ☎ *01–43–20–62–86* ⊕ *www.charming-hotel-paris.com* ⤳ *38 rooms* ⌂ *In-room: safe, Wi-Fi. In-hotel: room service, bar, laundry service, parking (fee), public Internet* ▤ *AE, DC, MC, V* Ⓜ *Vavin.* ✥ *4:A6*

15ᵉ ARRONDISSEMENT

If your ideal Paris hotel is within walking distance of the Iron Lady, the 15ᵉ won't disappoint. There are few other monuments or sights, but this residential district has plenty of bistros, boutiques, cafés, and, beneath the elevated métro line, a popular street market.

$$$
Fodor's Choice
★

Eiffel Seine Hôtel. Opened in 2006, this stylish budget hotel mixes contemporary amenities and custom Art Nouveau décor. Directly across from the Eiffel Tower's métro station, it's hard to believe this independently owned hotel doesn't cost twice as much. Thoughtful extras include the hearty buffet breakfast, free Wi-Fi, and free public parking. Pros: Next door to the Eiffel Tower; easy métro access; free Wi-Fi. Cons: Not an easy walk to the center of town, some street noise. ⊠ *3 bd. de Grenelle,* ☎ *01–45–78–14–81* ⊕ *www.paris-hotel-eiffelseine. com* ⤳ *45 rooms* ⌂ *In-room: safe, Wi-Fi. In-hotel: room service, laundry service, concierge, public Wi-Fi, parking (no fee)* ▤ *AE, DC, MC, V* Ⓜ *Bir Hakeim.* ✥ *3:B3*

16ᵉ ARRONDISSEMENT

The 16ᵉ arrondissement is so large that it has two postal codes. Considered one of the poshest residential districts in Paris, it's a good destination for travelers interested in sightseeing during the day and getting a good night's sleep in a safe, quiet neighborhood. Museums are concentrated on the northern end around Trocadéro, and luxury shopping streets are found closer to the Arc de Triomphe. Nature lovers may want to stay close to the Bois de Bologne, the city's largest park.

$$$$
☾

Hôtel Raphael. This discreet palace hotel was built in 1925 to cater to travelers spending a "season" in Paris, so every space is generously sized for long, lavish stays. The closets, for instance, have room for ball gowns and plumed hats. Guest rooms, most with king-size beds and 6-foot-tall windows, are decorated with 18th- and early-19th-century antiques, Oriental rugs, silk damask wallpaper, and ornately carved wood paneling. Bathrooms are remarkably large, and most have clawfoot tubs. The roof terrace, home to a restaurant in summer, has panoramic views of the city. Parents will find a friend in the concierge, who arranges for bilingual babysitters and priority access to amusement parks, and offers recommendations on kid-friendly restaurants and entertainment. Pros: A block from the Champs-Elysées and Arc de Triomphe; rooftop garden terrace; cozy hotel bar frequented by locals. Cons: Old-fashioned Parisian décor won't impress fans of minimalism; the neighborhood can have a majestic yet cold atmosphere. ⊠ *17 av. Kléber,* ☎ *01–53–64–32–00* ⊕ *www.raphael-hotel.com* ⤳ *52 rooms, 38 suites* ⌂ *In-room: safe, DVD (some), VCR (some), Wi-Fi. In-hotel:*

CLOSE UP

The Hostel Scene

No matter what your age, you can save on lodging costs by staying at hostels. Most of Paris's hostels and *auberges de jeunesse* (student hostels) are bargains at €19–€30 a night for a bed in shared rooms (usually three to six beds) or €50–€80 for a private double, with free showers and a baguette-and-coffee wake-up call. In summer you should reserve in writing a month in advance (deposits are often taken via credit card for reservations); if you don't have a reservation, it's a good idea to check in as early as 8 AM. Note that some youth hostels have age restrictions, and be sure to check if there's a night curfew and/or lockouts during the day. You might also want to pack your earplugs.

Paris's major public hostels are run by the **Féderation Unie des Auberges de Jeunesse (FUAJ)**. For about €20, a bed, sheets, shower, and breakfast are provided; there are usually three or four beds to a room. **Maisons Internationales des Jeunes Etudiants (MIJE)** has the plushest hostels for guests ages 18–30.

There are also private hostels with accommodations that run from pleasant, if spartan, double rooms to dormlike arrangements. New on the Paris scene is the purpose-built 275-bed hostel **St. Christopher's Inn** (⊠

68 Quai de la Seine, 75019 ☎*01–40–34–34–40* ⊕ *www.st-christophers. co.uk*). Another large hostel is the **Auberge de Jeunesse d'Artagnan FUAJ** (⊠*80 rue Vitruve,75020* ☎*01–40–32–34–56* 🖶*01–40–32–34–55* ⊕*www.fuaj.org*). In the Marais, the nonprofit organization **MIJE** (⊠ *Le Fauconnier, 11 rue de Fauconnier; Fourcy, 6 rue Fourcy; Maubuisson, 12 rue des Barres*, ☎*01–42–74–23–45* 🖶*01–42–74–08–93* ⊕*www.mije. com*)lists17th-century properties. Smaller independent hostels include the **Peace & Love Hostel & Bar** (⊠*245 rue de La Fayette* ☎*01–46–07–65–91* ⊕*www.paris-hostels. com*);**Le Village** (⊠*20 rue d'Orsel*, ☎*01–42–64–22–02* 🖶*01–42–64–22–04* ⊕*www.villagehostel.fr*); and **Young and Happy Youth Hostel** (⊠*80 rue Mouffetard*, ☎*01–45–35–09–53* 🖶*01–47–07–22–24* ⊕*www. youngandhappy.fr*)

Membership in any Hostelling International (HI) association, open to travelers of all ages, allows you to stay in HI-affiliated hostels at member rates; a one-year membership is $28 for adults. Hostels run about €10–€25 per night. Members have priority if the hostel is full; they're also eligible for discounts. For more information contact Hostelling International (⊕ *www.hiusa.org*).

18

---

2 restaurants, room service, bar, gym, concierge, laundry service, some pets allowed ⊟*AE, DC, MC, V* Ⓜ*Kléber.* ✛ *1:C4*

$$$–$$$$ **Les Jardins du Trocadéro.** This hotel near the Trocadéro and the Tour Eiffel blends old-style French elegance (period antiques, Napoleonic draperies, classical plaster busts) with modern conveniences (DVDs, flat-screen TVs, free Wi-Fi). Wall paintings of genies and dressed-up monkeys add a fanciful dash. Beds are large—either kings or queens—and have hypoallergenic bedding and mattresses. Marble bathrooms have whirlpool tubs. Pros: Hillside views over the Eiffel Tower; free Wi-Fi; upscale residential district. Cons: Not an easy walk to the center of town; some rooms are rather small and cramped; room service doesn't always speak English. ⊠*35 rue Benjamin-Franklin*, ☏*01–53–70–17–70, 800/246–0041 in U.S.* ⊕*www.jardintroc.com* ⇗*20 rooms* ᴥ*In-room: safe, DVD (some), Wi-Fi. In-hotel: restaurant, room service, bar, laundry service, parking (fee)* ⊟*AE, DC, MC, V* Ⓜ*Trocadéro.* ✛ *3:A1*

$$ **Queen's Hôtel.** One of only a handful of hotels in the tony residential district near the Bois de Boulogne, the Queen's is a small, comfortable, old-fashioned place with a high standard of service. Its bills itself a *hôtel-musée*, because it contains works by contemporary French artists such as René Julian and Maurice Friedman, whose paintings hang in the rooms and public areas. Guest rooms pair contemporary and older furnishings and have large mirrors and spotless tiled bathrooms, many with jetted tubs. Pros: Unique artsy atmosphere; charming shopping street; friendly welcome. Cons: Not so convenient for getting around the city on foot; vast difference in quality of room décor. ⊠*4 rue Bastien-Lepage*, ☏*01–42–88–89–85* ⊕*www.queens-hotel.fr* ⇗*21 rooms, 1 suite* ᴥ*In-room: safe, Wi-Fi. In-hotel: some pets allowed* ⊟*AE, DC, MC, V* Ⓜ*Michel-Ange Auteuil.* ✛ *3:A3*

$$$$ **Le Sezz.** Created by French furniture designer Christophe Pillet, Le Sezz mixes rough, stacked stone walls with flashes of bright color and tall glass sculptures. One-way glass walls separate the sleeping areas from the bathrooms, many of which have tubs big enough for two. The owner has pushed the trend of scaled-down reception desks even further by not having one at all. All the paperwork is done in advance, so you can go directly to your room without having to stand around the lobby. A champagne bar and *Espace Bien-Être* ("well-being center," or spa) cater to jet-setters. Pros: Sexy designer décor; huge bathtubs; quiet location. Cons: Residential district far from the center; the hotel bar is a bit too quiet; services are limited for a hotel in this price range. ⊠*6 av. Frémiet*, ☏*01–56–75–26–26* ⊕*www.hotelsezz. com* ⇗*13 rooms, 14 suites* ᴥ*In-room: safe, DVD, Wi-Fi. In-hotel: room service, bar, concierge, laundry service, public Internet* ⊟*AE, DC, MC, V* Ⓜ*Passy.* ✛ *3:A3*

$$$ **Mon Hotel.** Contemporary design and modern comforts, just two blocks from the Arc de Triomphe and Champs Elysées, are big draws for this stylish boutique hotel. The lobby is dramatic, whereas the rooms are more comforting with chamois wall coverings, neutral tones, and black-and-white portraits of famous personalities. High-tech amenities include MP3 docking stations and Nespresso machines, and more than 1,000 satellite TV stations. Pros: Free Wi-Fi; unique contemporary décor; convenient for walking to the Champs-Elysées. Cons: Some rooms have limited closet space; no extra beds for children; inconvenient for walking to the center of Paris. ⊠*1 rue Argentine*, Champs-Elysées, ☏*01–45–02–76–76* ⊕*www.monhotel.fr* ⇗*37 rooms* ᴥ*In-room: safe, Wi-Fi. In-hotel: room service, bar, spa* ⊟*AE, MC, V* Ⓜ*Argentine.* ✛ *1:B4*

17ᵉ ARRONDISSEMENT

In the 17ᵉ you can find both an upscale residential district, between the Arc de Triomphe and the pretty Parc Monceau, and a more artsy, bohemian flavor in the former working-class districts of Batignolles and Place de Clichy. Still relatively undiscovered by tourists, it's an area of Paris with many excellent hotel deals.

¢–$ **Hôtel Eldorado.** The unpretentious Eldorado, just west of Montmartre, is perfect for guests who are happy lying low without room phones, TVs, or an elevator. Each room has its individual distressed-chic charms—leopard spots and zebra stripes, knickknacks from Africa and the Far East, flea-market antiques, and club chairs. Many rooms face the garden courtyard, where artsy bohemian types from the hotel's wine bistro hang out on summer nights. Rooms No. 16 and No. 17 have their own little balconies. Ask for a room in the back building for a quiet night's sleep. Pros: Budget décor with character; leafy garden courtyard; hipster locals' hangout. Cons: Far from the center of Paris; few amenities; courtyard can be noisy in summer. ✉ *18 rue des Dames,* ☎ *01–45–22–35–21* ⊕ *www.eldoradohotel.fr* 📞 *33 rooms, 23 with bath* ♿ *In-room: no a/c, no phone, no TV. In-hotel: restaurant* ▤ *AE, DC, MC, V* Ⓜ *Place de Clichy.* ✛ *1:H1*

$$ **Hôtel Palma.** This modest hotel in a small 19th-century building between the Arc de Triomphe and Porte Maillot is an exceptional deal considering its rather aristocratic neighbors. Cheerful and homey rooms have hand-painted wood furnishings, floral-motif fabrics, and tile bathrooms. Ask for one on an upper floor with a view across Rive Droite rooftops. There's air-conditioning on the sixth (top) floor only. Pros: Close to the Champs-Élysées; cozy décor; quiet location. Cons: A bit off the beaten track; no air-conditioning on lower floors; no Wi-Fi. ✉ *46 rue Brunel,* ☎ *01–45–74–74–51* ⊕ *www.hotelpalma-paris.com* 📞 *37 rooms* ♿ *In-room: no a/c (some), dial-up. In-hotel: some pets allowed* ▤ *AE, MC, V* Ⓜ *Argentine.* ✛ *1:A3*

18ᵉ ARRONDISSEMENT

Home to the Moulin Rouge and the scene of Audrey Tatou's flights of fancy in the film *Amélie*, Montmartre inspires visitors with its narrow, cobbled streets and sweeping cityscape from the steps of Sacré-Coeur. The trade-offs for this old-village atmosphere are steep staircases and a location far from the heart of Paris.

$ **Ermitage Hôtel.** It's a bit of a hike from the nearest métro, but this family-run hotel in a Napoléon III–era building is friendly and filled with mirrored armoires, chandeliers, and other antiques. There's a private terrace for the two ground-level rooms, and all rooms have funky flowery décor. The building is only two stories high, and the highest-tech item is the fax machine. Pros: Family-run atmosphere; charming Parisian neighborhood. Cons: Not close to the métro station; no amenities; minuscule bathrooms. ✉ *24 rue Lamarck,* ☎ *01–42–64–79–22* ⊕ *www.ermitagesacrecoeur.fr* 📞 *12 rooms* ♿ *In-room: no a/c, no TV. In-hotel: public Internet, some pets allowed* ▤ *No credit cards* ⦿ *CP* Ⓜ *Lamarck Caulaincourt.* ✛ *2:H4*

18

$$ Hôtel Prima Lepic. An impressive value, the Prima Lepic stands out among dozens of mediocre traps in this tourist zone. Elements from the original 19th-century building remain, such as vintage tiling in the entry and white iron furniture in the breakfast area. The bright rooms are full of spring colors and florals; the so-called Baldaquin rooms have reproduction canopy beds. Larger rooms are suitable for families but have little natural light. Pros: Charming décor; surrounded by boutiques and cafés. Cons: No air-conditioning; thin walls; not convenient for getting to the center of town on foot. ⊠29 rue Lepic, ☎01–46–06–44–64 ⊕www.hotel-paris-lepic.com ⟿38 rooms ⌂In-room: no a/c, safe, Wi-Fi. In-hotel: laundry service ⊟AE, DC, MC, V Ⓜ Blanche. ✛ 2:A1/B1

$–$$ Hôtel Regyn's Montmartre. Lots of folks book the tiny Regyn's for the out-of-*Amélie* Place des Abbesses location; they're also pleased to find bright, warm colors and rooms with modern bathrooms, hair dryers, radios, and Wi-Fi. Ask to stay on one of the two top floors for great views of either the Tour Eiffel or Sacré-Coeur. Overall, courteous service and a relaxed charm make this an attractive low-budget choice. Pros: Métro station right outside; great views over Paris. Cons: No air-conditioning; some street noise; tiny elevator. ⊠18 pl. des Abbesses, ☎01–42–54–45–21 ⊕www.paris-hotels-montmartre. com ⟿22 rooms ⌂In-room: no a/c, safe, Wi-Fi. In-hotel: some pets allowed ⊟AE, MC, V Ⓜ Abbesses. ✛ 2:B1

$ Hôtel Utrillo. This very likable hotel is on a quiet side street at the foot of Montmartre, near colorful Rue Lepic. The tired old décor is slowly being replaced by a more contemporary style with bold colors and artworks. Two rooms (Nos. 61 and 63) have views of the Tour Eiffel. In the lobby are two free Internet stations, and the sauna is a luxury at this price. Pros: Family-run feel; some Eiffel Tower views; free Internet. Cons: No air-conditioning; some street noise. ⊠7 rue Aristide-Bruant, ☎01–42–58–13–44 ⊕www.hotel-paris-utrillo.com ⟿30 rooms ⌂In-room: no a/c, Wi-Fi. In-hotel: public Internet, some pets allowed ⊟MC, V Ⓜ Abbesses, Blanche. ✛ 2:B1

Side Trips from Paris

Chartres Cathedral

WORD OF MOUTH

"Last summer at Versailles, the regular State Rooms were crowded with a river of people. So we took the tour of the Private Apartments and, wow, was it great! We got to see how Louis XV really lived his life . . . the dog room, the library, his famous desk, and also the theater he had build for his sons—even his commode. The group was very small and the person (who spoke in English) was so informative. As for the State Rooms, opt for the helpful audioguides."

—Hypatia2A

www.fodors.com/forums

SIDE TRIPS FROM PARIS PLANNER

Train vs. Car

Traveling to Chartres, Disney-land Paris, and Versailles from Paris is easy. Although each side trip is within an hours' drive, we *strongly* recommend taking the train from the city rather than renting a car. If Disneyland is your destination and you don't plan to visit Paris, there are shuttle buses that will take you directly from the airports to the park.

Tour Options

Cityrama (01–44–55–60–00 www.cityrama.fr) organizes guided excursions to Chartres (€57–€65) from April through October, and half- and full-day trips to Versailles (€40–€88). **Paris Vision** (01–42–60–30–01 www.parisvision.com) also runs half- and full-day trips to Versailles (€40–€88).

Planning Tips

The château of Versailles is closed on Monday.

Disneyland Paris gets extremely crowded on summer weekends, so try to plan your trip during the week.

Getting Out of Town

Versailles: Three train routes travel between Paris and Versailles (25–40 minutes each way, round-trip fare €6). The RER-C to Versailles Rive-Gauche takes you closest to the château (600 yards away via Avenue de Sceaux). An all-inclusive pass for round-trip train fare plus château admission costs €23.45 (€28.75 on weekends). The other trains run from Paris's Gare St-Lazare to Versailles Rive-Droite (closer to the Trianons and town market but a kilometer from the château via Rue du Maréchal-Foch and Avenue de St-Cloud) and from Paris's Gare Montparnasse to Versailles-Chantiers (1 km [½ mi] from the château via Rue des Etats-Généraux and Avenue de Paris). From Versailles-Chantiers some trains continue on to Chartres.

Chartres: Trains depart hourly from Paris's Gare Montparnasse to Chartres (50–70 minutes, round-trip fare about €25). The cathedral is a ¼ uphill walk from the station.

Disneyland Paris: There's a shuttle bus to the park from Charles de Gaulle (56 km [35 mi]) and Orly (50 km [31 mi]) airports. Trip time is 45 minutes; the fare is €21 one way. Disneyland's train station (Marne-la-Vallée–Chessy) is right outside the park. Trains run every 10–20 minutes from RER-A stations in central Paris. Trip time is 40 minutes; the fare is €16 round-trip.

DINING & LODGING PRICE CATEGORIES (IN EUROS)				
¢	$	$$	$$$	$$$$
Restaurants				
Under €11	€11–€17	€17–€23	€23–€30	Over €30
Hotels				
Under €50	€50–€80	€80–€120	€120–€190	over €220

Restaurant prices are per person for a main course at dinner, including tax (19.6%) and service; note that if a restaurant offers only prix-fixe (set-price) meals, it has been given the price category that reflects the full prix-fixe price. Hotel prices are for a standard double room in high season, including tax (19.6%) and service charge

Updated by
Simon Hewitt

With so much to see in Paris, it can seem hard to justify taking a side trip. But just outside the city is the rest of the fabled region known as Ile-de-France, where along with gorgeous countryside and quiet towns you'll find spectacular Versailles, the immense Chartres cathedral, and a little region unto itself where a mouse named Mickey is king.

Plan to spend an entire day at **Versailles**, enjoying the gorgeously manicured gardens—one of the largest parks in Europe—as well as touring the palace, which includes the Hall of Mirrors, as well as Marie Antoinette's private retreat in the northwest part of the royal park. **Chartres** is a charming town that makes a lovely day or half-day side trip from Paris. Its main attraction is Cathédrale de Chartres, an impressive Gothic cathedral that has world-renowned stained-glass windows. **Disneyland Paris** arrived in 1992, and the magic was slow to take effect. The resort opened with the uninspiring name of EuroDisney and further baffled the French, for whom no meal is complete without wine, with its ban on alcohol. After that ban was lifted in the park's sit-down restaurants and the park's name changed, Disneyland Paris became France's leading tourist attraction, drawing sellout crowds of Europeans wanting a taste of the American Dream—and of American families stealing a day from their Louvre schedule. A second park, Walt Disney Studios, opened in 2002.

19

VERSAILLES

16 km (10 mi) west of Paris via A13.

EXPLORING

Fodor'sChoice
★

It's hard to tell which is larger at **Château de Versailles**—the world-famous château that housed Louis XIV and 20,000 of his courtiers, or the mass of tour buses and visitors standing in front of it. The grandest palace in France remains one of the marvels of the world and its full story is covered in the special photo feature on the château in this chapter, "Gilt Trip: A Tour of Versailles." But this edifice was not just

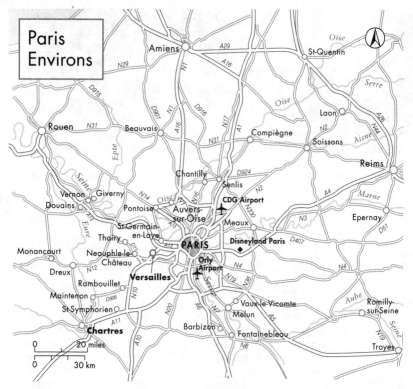

Paris Environs

home to the Sun King, it was to be the new headquarters of the French government capital (from 1682 to 1789 and again from 1871 to 1879). To accompany the palace, a new city—in fact, a new capital—had to be built from scratch. Tough-thinking town planners took no prisoners, dreaming up vast mansions and avenues broader than the Champs-Élysées. If you have any energy left after exploring Louis XIV's palace and park, a tour of Versailles—a textbook 18th-century town—offers a telling contrast between the majestic and the domestic.

From the front gate of the palace turn left onto the Rue de l'Independence-Américaine and walk over to Rue Carnot past the stately Écuries de la Reine, once the queen's stables, now the regional law courts, to octagonal Place Hoche. Down Rue Hoche to the left is the powerful Baroque facade of **Notre-Dame**, built from 1684 to 1686 by Jules Hardouin-Mansart as the parish church for Louis XIV's new town.

Around the back of Notre-Dame, on Boulevard de la Reine (note the regimented lines of trees), are the elegant Hôtel de Neyret and the **Musée Lambinet,** a sumptuous mansion from 1751, furnished with paintings, weapons, fans, and porcelain. ⊠*54 bd. de la Reine* ☎*01–39–50–30–32* ✆*€5.30* ☉*Tues.–Thurs. and weekends 2–6, Fri. 2–5.*

Take a right onto Rue Le Nôtre, then go left and right again into Passage de la Geôle, a cobbled alley, lined with quaint antiques shops, which climbs up to **Place du Marché-Notre-Dame,** whose open-air morning market on Tuesday, Friday, and Sunday is famed throughout the region (note the four 19th-century timber-roof halls).

Cross Avenue de St-Cloud and head to **Avenue de Paris;** its breadth of 120 yards makes it wider than the Champs-Élysées, and its buildings are just as grand and even more historic. Cross the avenue and return toward the château. Avenue de Paris leads down to Place d'Armes, a vast sloping plaza usually filled with tourist buses. Facing the château are the Trojan-size royal stables.

The **Grandes Écuries** (*Grand Stables*), to the right, house the **Musée des Carrosses** (Carriage Museum), open April through October, weekends only (€2), and the **Manège,** where you can see 28 white horses and their riders, trained by the equine choreographer Bartabas, practicing every morning. ⊠*1 av. de Paris* ☎*01–39–02–07–14* ☜*€8* ⊗*Tues.–Fri. 9–noon, weekends 11–2.*

Turn left from the Grandes Écuries, cross Avenue de Sceaux and Avenue de Paris, pass the imposing chancellery on the corner, and take Rue de Satory—a cute pedestrian shopping street—to the domed **Cathédrale St-Louis,** with its twin-towered facade, built from 1743 to 1754 and enriched with a fine organ and paintings.

Rue d'Anjou leads down to the 6-acre **Potager du Roi,** the lovingly restored, split-level royal fruit-and-vegetable garden created in 1683 by Jean-Baptiste de La Quintinye. ⊠*Entrance at 4 rue Hardy* ☎*01–39–24–62–62* ⊕*www.potager-du-roi.fr* ☜*€6.50* ⊗*Apr.–Oct., daily 10–6; Nov.–Mar., weekdays 2–5.*

WHERE TO STAY & EAT

$$–$$$ ✕**Au Chapeau Gris.** This bustling wood-beamed restaurant just off Avenue de St-Cloud, overlooking elegant Place Hoche, offers hearty selections of meat and fish, ranging from boeuf rossini with wild mushrooms to salmon and scallops marinated in lime and the top-price lobster fricasseed in Sancerre. The wine list roams around the vineyards of Bordeaux and Burgundy, while desserts include crème brûlée with lemon zest, and apricot and caramel tart. The €28 prix-fixe menu makes a filling lunchtime option. ⊠*7 rue Hoche* ☎*01–39–50–10–81* ☐*AE, MC, V* ⊗*Closed Wed. No dinner Tues. and late July–late Aug.*

★ **$$$$** ⊡**Trianon Palace.** A modern-day Versailles, this deluxe hotel is in a turn-of-the-20th-century, creamy white creation of imposing size, filled with soaring rooms (including the historic Salle Clemenceau, site of the 1919 Versailles Peace Conference), palatial columns, and with a huge garden close to the château. Once faded, the hotel, now part of the Westin chain, is aglitter once again with a health club (the pool idles beneath a glass pyramid) and a refurbished lobby with Murano chandeliers and high-back, green-leather armchairs. Try to avoid the newer annex, the Pavillon Trianon, and insist on the main building (ask for one of the even-numbered rooms, which look out over the woods near the Trianons; odd-numbered rooms overlook the modern

Continued on page 399

GILT TRIP
A TOUR OF VERSAILLES

Louis XIV's Hall of Mirrors

A two-century spree of indulgence in the finest bling-bling of the age by the consecutive reigns of three French kings produced two of the world's most historic artifacts: gloriously, the Palace of Versailles and, momentously, the French Revolution.

Less a monument than an entire world unto itself, Versailles is the king of palaces. The end result of 380 million francs, 36,000 laborers, and enough paintings, if laid end to end, to equal 7 miles of canvas, it was conceived as the ne plus ultra expression of monarchy by Louis XIV. As a child, the king had developed a hatred for Paris (where he had been imprisoned by a group of nobles known as the Frondeurs), so, when barely out of his teens, he cast his cantankerous royal eye in search of a new power base. Marshy, inhospitable Versailles was the stuff of his dreams. Down came dad's modest royal hunting lodge and up, up, and along went the minion-crushing, Baroque palace we see today.

Between 1661 and 1710, architects Louis Le Vau and Jules Hardouin Mansart designed everything his royal acquisitiveness could want, including a throne room devoted to Apollo, god of the sun (Louis was known as *le roi soleil*). Convinced that his might depended on dominating French nobility, Louis XIV summoned thousands of grandees from their own far-flung châteaux to reside at his new seat of government. In doing so, however, he unwittingly triggered the downfall of the monarchy. Like an 18th-century Disneyland, Versailles kept its courtiers so richly entertained they all but forgot the murmurs of discontent brewing back home.

As Louis XV chillingly fortold, "After me, the deluge." The royal commune was therefore shocked—shocked!—by the appearance, on October 5, 1789, of a revolutionary mob from Paris ready to sack Versailles and imprison Louis XVI. So as you walk through this awesome monument to splendor and excess, give a thought to its historic companion: the French Revolution. A tour of Versailles's grand salons inextricably mixes pathos with glory.

19

CROWNING GLORIES: TOP SIGHTS OF VERSAILLES

Seducing their court with their self-assured approach to 17th- and 18th-century art and decoration, a trinity of French kings made Versailles into the most vainglorious of châteaux.

Versailles from the outside

Galerie des Glaces (Hall of Mirrors). Of all the rooms at Versailles, none matches the magnificence of the Galerie des Glaces (Hall of Mirrors). Begun by Mansart in 1678, this represents the acme of the Louis Quatorze (Louis-XIV) style. Measuring 240 feet long, 33 feet wide, and 40 feet high, it is ornamented with gilded candlesticks, crystal chandeliers, and a coved ceiling painted with Charles Le Brun's homage to Louis XIV's reign.

Detail of the ceiling

In Louis's day, the Galerie was laid with priceless carpets and filled with orange trees in silver pots. Nighttime galas were illuminated by 3,000 candles, their blaze doubled in the 17 gigantic mirrors that precisely echo the banner of windows along the west front. Lavish balls were once held here, as was a later event with much greater world impact: the signing of the Treaty of Versailles, which put an end to World War I on June 28, 1919.

Hall of Mirrors

The Grands Appartements (State Apartments). Virtual stages for ceremonies of court ritual and etiquette, Louis XIV's first-floor state salons were designed in the Baroque style on a biceps-flexing scale meant to one-up the lavish Vaux-le-Vicomte château recently built for Nicolas Fouquet, the king's finance minister.

Inside the Apollo Chamber

Flanking the Hall of Mirrors and retaining most of their bombastic Italianate Baroque decoration, the Salon de la Guerre (Salon of War) and the Salon de la Paix (Salon of Peace) are ornately decorated with gilt stucco, painted ceilings, and marble sculpture. Perhaps the most extravagant is the Salon d'Apollon (Apollo Chamber), the former throne room.

Hall of Battles

Appartements du Roi (King's Apartments). Completed in 1701 in the Louis-XIV style, the king's state and private chambers comprise a suite of 15 rooms set in a "U" around the east facade's Marble Court. Dead center across the sprawling cobbled forecourt is Louis XIV's bedchamber—he would awake and rise (just as the sun did, from the east) attended by members of his court and the public. Holding the king's chemise when he dressed soon became a more definitive reflection of status than the possession of an entire province. Nearby is Louis XV's magnificent Cabinet Intérieur (Office of the King), shining with gold and white boiseries; in the center is the most famous piece of furniture at Versailles, Louis XV's roll-top desk, crafted by Oeben and Riesener in 1769.

Louis XIV

IN FOCUS GILT TRIP: A TOUR OF VERSAILLES

King's Apartments

Chambre de la Reine (Queen's Bed Chamber). Probably the most opulent bedroom in the world, this was initially created for Marie Thérèse, first wife of Louis XIV, to be part of the Queen's Apartments. For Marie Antoinette, however, the entire room was glammed up with silk wall-hangings covered with Rococo motifs that reflect her love of flowers. Legend has it that the gardens directly beyond these windows were replanted daily so that the queen could enjoy a fresh assortment of blossoms each morning. The bed, decked out with white ostrich plumes *en panache*, was also redone for Louis XVI's queen. Nineteen royal children were born in this room.

VINTAGE BOURBON

Versailles was built by three great kings of the Bourbon dynasty. Louis XIV (1638–1715) began its construction in 1661. After ruling for 72 years, Louis Quatorze was succeeded by his great grandson, Louis XV (1710–74), who added the Royal Opera and the Petit Trianon to the palace. Louis XVI (1754–93) came to the throne in 1774 and was forced out of Versailles in 1789, along with Marie Antoinette, both guillotined three years later.

19

Queen's Bed Chamber

Petits Appartements (Small Apartments). As styles of decor changed, Louis XIV's successors felt out of sync with their architectural inheritance. Louis XV exchanged the heavy red-and-gilt of Italianate Baroque for lighter, pastel-hued Rococo. On the top floor of the palace, on the right side of the central portion, are the apartments Louis XV commissioned to escape the wearisome pomp of the first-floor rooms. Here, Madame de Pompadour, mistress of Louis XV and famous patroness of the Rococo style, introduced grace notes of intimacy and refinement. In so doing, she transformed the daunting royal apartments into places to live rather than pose.

Parc de Versailles. Even Bourbon kings needed respite from Versailles's endless confines, hence the creation of one of Europe's largest parks, designed to surround the palace. The 250-acre grounds (☎ 01–30–83–77–88 for guided tour) are the masterpiece of André Le Nôtre, presiding genius of 17th-century classical French landscaping. Le Nôtre was famous for his "green geometries": ordered fantasies of clipped yew trees, multicolored flower beds (called parterres), and perspectival allées cleverly punctuated with statuary, laid out between 1661 and 1668. The architectonic effect is best admired from inside the palace, views about which Le Nôtre said, "Flowers can only be walked on by the eyes."

Ultimately, at the royal command, rivers were diverted—to flow into more than 600 fountains—and entire forests were imported to ornament the park, which is centered around the mile-long Grand Canal. As for the great fountains, their operation costs a fortune in these democratic days, and so they perform only on Saturday and Sunday afternoons (🕐 3:30–5:30) from mid-April through mid-October; admission during this time is €6. The park is open daily 7 AM–8 PM or dusk.

LIGHTING UP THE SKY

The largest fountain in Versailles' château park, the Bassin de Neptune, becomes a spectacle of rare grandeur during the Fêtes de Nuit (☎ 01-30-83-78-88 for details), a light-and-fireworks show held on ten nights (usually Saturday) between late July and early September. Starting at 10:30 PM, with upwards of 200-plus actors costumed in knee-breeches and curled wigs, the 90-minute show is well worth the ticket admission of €16 to €48.

Dauphin's Apartments

Bassin de Neptune

Chapel and Opéra Royal: In the north wing of the château are three showpieces of the palace. The solemn white-and-gold Chapelle was completed in 1710—the king and queen attended daily mass here seated in gilt boxes. The Opéra Royal (Opera House), entirely constructed of wood painted to look like marble, was designed by Jacques-Ange Gabriel for Louis XV in 1770. Connecting the two, the 17th-century Galeries have exhibits retracing the château's history.

Opéra Royal

VERSAILLES: FIRST FLOOR, GARDENS & ADJACENT PARK

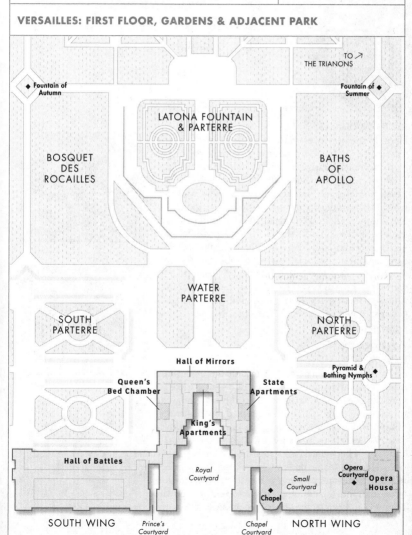

TO ↗
THE TRIANONS

◆ Fountain of
Autumn

Fountain of ◆
Summer

LATONA FOUNTAIN
& PARTERRE

BOSQUET
DES
ROCAILLES

BATHS
OF
APOLLO

WATER
PARTERRE

SOUTH
PARTERRE

NORTH
PARTERRE

Hall of Mirrors

Pyramid &
Bathing Nymphs ◆

Queen's
Bed Chamber

State
Apartments

King's
Apartments

Hall of Battles

Royal
Courtyard

Opera
Courtyard

Opera
House

Small
Courtyard

◆ Chapel

SOUTH WING

Prince's
Courtyard

Chapel
Courtyard

NORTH WING

LET THEM EAT CRÊPE:
MARIE ANTOINETTE'S ROYAL LAIR

Was Marie Antoinette a luxury-mad butterfly flitting from ball to costume ball? Or was she a misunderstood queen who suffered a loveless marriage and became a prisoner of court etiquette at Versailles? Historians now believe the answer was the latter and point to her private retreats at Versailles as proof.

R.F.D. VERSAILLES?

Here, in the northwest part of the royal park, Marie Antoinette (1755–93) created a tiny universe of her own: her comparatively dainty mansion called Petit Trianon and its adjacent "farm," the relentlessly picturesque Hameau ("hamlet"). In a life that took her from royal cradle to throne of France to guillotine, her happiest days were spent at Trianon. For here she could live a life in the "simplest" possible way; here the queen could enter a salon and the game of cards would not stop; here women could wear simple gowns of muslin without a single jewel. Toinette only wanted to be queen of Trianon, not queen of France. And considering the horrible, chamber-pot-pungent, gossip-infested corridors of Versailles, you can almost understand why.

TEEN QUEEN

From the first, Maria-Antonia (her actual name) was ostracized as an outsider, "l'Autrichienne"—the Austrian. Upon arriving in France in 1770—at a mere 15 years of age—she was married to the Dauphin, the future King Louis XVI. But shamed by her initial failure to deliver a royal heir, she grew to hate overcrowded Versailles and soon escaped to the Petit Trianon. Built between 1763 and 1768 by Jacques-Ange Gabriel for Madame de Pompadour, this bijou palace was a radical statement: a royal residence designed to be casual and unassuming. Toinette refashioned the Trianon's interior in the sober Neoclassical style.

Hameau

Queen's House

Temple of Love

Petit Trianon

"THE SIMPLE LIFE"

Just beyond Petit Trianon lay the storybook Hameau, a mock-Norman village inspired by the peasant-luxe, simple-life daydreams caught by Boucher on canvas and by Rousseau in literature. With its water mill, thatched-roof houses, pigeon loft, and vegetable plots, this make-believe farm village was run by Monsieur Valy-Busard, a farmer, and his wife, who often helped the queen—outfitted as a Dresden shepherdess with a Sèvres porcelain crook—tend her flock of perfumed sheep.

Marie Antoinette

19

As if to destroy any last link with reality, the queen built nearby a jewel-box theater (open by appointment). Here she acted in little plays, sometimes essaying the role of a servant girl. Only the immediate royal family, about seven or so friends, and her personal servants were permitted entry; disastrously, the entire officialdom of Versailles society was shut out—a move that only served to infuriate courtiers. This is how fate and destiny close the circle. For it was here at Trianon that a page sent by Monsieur de Saint-Priest found Marie-Antoinette on October 5, 1789, to tell her that Paris was marching on an already half-deserted Versailles.

Was Marie Antoinette a political traitor to France whose execution was well merited? Or was she the ultimate fashion victim? For those who feel that this tragic queen spent—and shopped—her way into a revolution, a visit to her relatively modest Petit Trianon and Hameau should prove a revelation.

FACTS & FANCIES

Sharing a joint ticket—€9—with the Petit Trianon is the Grand Trianon, also found in the northwest sector of Versailles's park. Created by Hardouin Mansart in 1687, it was used as a retreat for Louis XIV but restored in the early 19th century, with Empire-style salons. Both Trianons are open Tuesday–Sunday noon–5:30. As for the Hameau, the grounds are open to the public, but its rooms are now undergoing a 10-year renovation.

TAKING ON VERSAILLES (WITHOUT LOSING YOUR HEAD)

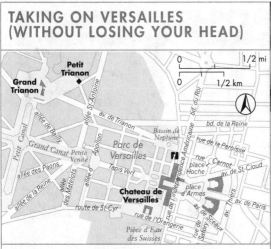

Statue of King Louis XIV

TOURING THE PALACE

The army of 20,000 noblemen, servants, and sycophants who moved into Louis XIV's huge Château de Versailles is matched today by the battalion of 3 million visitors a year. You may be able to avoid the crowds (and lines for tours) if you arrive here at 9 AM. The main entrance is near the top of the courtyard to the right; there are different lines depending on tour, physical ability, and group status. Frequent guided tours in English visit the private royal apartments. More detailed hour-long tours explore the opera house or Marie Antoinette's private parlors. You can go through the grandest rooms—including the Hall of Mirrors and Marie Antoinette's stunningly opulent bed chamber—without a group tour. To figure out the system, pick up a brochure at the information office or ticket counter.

TOURING THE PARK

If the grandeur of the palace begins to overwhelm, the Parc de Versailles is the best place to come back down to earth. The distances of the park are vast—the Trianons themselves are more than a mile from the château—so you might want to climb aboard a horse-drawn carriage (€7, ⊕ www.calechesversailles.com), take the electric train (🚃 5.80 round-trip, ⊕ www.train-versailles.com), or rent a bike from Petite-Venise (🚃 €5.20 per hr or €26 for 6 hrs, ☎ 01–39–66–97–66), the building at the top of the Grand Canal, where you can also hire a rowboat (🚃 €8.50 per hr). You can also drive to the Trianons and canal through the Grille de la Reine (🚃 €5.50 per car).

PICNIC IN THE PARK

If you don't opt for a luncheon at La Flotille restaurant (by the Grand Canal), take a cue from the locals, picnicking in grand fashion, as only the French know how. The brochures request that you don't picnic on the lawns, but they don't mention the groves scattered throughout the woods.

⊠ Place d'Armes, Versailles

⊕ www.chateauversailles.fr

☎ 01-30-83-78-00

🎟 €13.50; Petit and Grand Trianons (joint ticket) €9; Parc de Versailles free; Sunday fountain show €6; Fêtes de Nuit €16–€48.

🚪 Main palace Apr.-Oct., Tues.-Sun. 9-6:30; Nov.-Mar., Tues.-Sun, 9-5:30. Trianons Tues.—Sun. noon—6. Park daily dawn—dusk.

Ⓜ RER Line C from Paris to Versailles Rive Gauche station or SNCF trains from Paris's Gare St-Lazare and Gare Montparnasse.

annex). Unfortunately, fabled chef Gérard Vié departed in 2007, and the hotel's restaurant had not reopened at this writing. Pros: Palatial glamour; wonderful setting right by château. Cons: Uncertain status of new restaurant; lack of a personal touch after recent changes of ownership. ✉1 bd. de la Reine ☎01–30–84–51–20 ⊕www.trianonpalace.fr ➪165 rooms, 27 suites ⌂In-room: safe, refrigerator, Wi-Fi. In-hotel: 2 restaurants, room service, bar, pool, gym, public Wi-Fi, parking (no fee), some pets allowed ⊟AE, DC, MC, V ⊺⊙|BP.

NIGHTLIFE & THE ARTS

Directed by Bartabas, the **Académie du Spectacle Equestre** (☎01–39–02–07–14 ⊕www.acadequestre.com) stages hour-long shows on weekend afternoons of horses performing to music—sometimes with riders, sometimes without—in the converted 17th-century Manège (riding school) at the Grandes Écuries opposite the palace. The **Centre de Musique Baroque** (⊕www.cmbv.com) often presents concerts of Baroque music in the château opera and chapel. The **Mois Molière** (☎01–30–97–84–48) in June heralds a program of concerts, drama, and exhibits inspired by the famous playwright.

SHOPPING

Aux Colonnes (✉14 rue Hoche) is a highly rated confiserie (candy shop) with a cornucopia of chocolates and candies; it's closed Monday. **Les Délices du Palais** (✉4 rue du Maréchal-Foch) has all the makings for an impromptu picnic (cold cuts, cheese, salads); it's also closed Monday. **Legall** (✉Pl. du Marché) has a huge choice of cheeses—including one of France's widest selections of goat cheeses; it's closed Sunday afternoon and Monday.

CHARTRES

88 km (55 mi) southwest of Paris.

19

EXPLORING

If Versailles is the climax of French secular architecture, perhaps Chartres is its religious apogee. All the descriptive prose and poetry that have been lavished on this supreme cathedral can only begin to suggest the glory of its 12th- and 13th-century statuary and stained glass, somehow suffused with burning mysticism and a strange sense of the numinous. Chartres is more than a church—it's a nondenominational spiritual experience. If you arrive in summer from Maintenon across the edge of the Beauce, the richest agrarian plain in France, you can see Chartres's spires rising up from oceans of wheat. The whole town—with its old houses and picturesque streets—is worth a leisurely exploration. From Rue du Pont-St-Hilaire there's an intriguing view of the rooftops below the cathedral. Ancient streets tumble down from the cathedral to the river, lined most weekends with bouquinistes selling old books and prints. Each year on August 15 pilgrims and tourists flock here for the Procession du Voeu de Louis XIII, a religious procession through the streets commemorating the French monarchy's vow to serve the Virgin Mary.

Worship on the site of the **Cathédrale Notre-Dame,** better known as Chartres Cathedral, goes back to before the Gallo-Roman period; the crypt contains a well that was the focus of druid ceremonies. In the late 9th century Charles II (known as the Bald) presented Chartres with what was believed to be the tunic of the Virgin Mary, a precious relic that went on to attract hordes of pilgrims. The current cathedral, the sixth church on the spot, dates mainly from the 12th and 13th centuries and was erected after the previous building, dating from the 11th century, burned down in 1194. A well-chronicled outburst of religious fervor followed the discovery that the Virgin Mary's relic had miraculously survived unsinged. Princes and paupers, barons and bourgeois gave their money and their labor to build the new cathedral. Ladies of the manor came to help monks and peasants on the scaffolding in a tremendous resurgence of religious faith that followed the Second Crusade. Just 25 years were needed for Chartres Cathedral to rise again, and it has remained substantially unchanged since.

The lower half of the facade survives from the earlier Romanesque church: this can be seen most clearly in the use of round arches rather than the pointed Gothic type. The **Royal Portal** is richly sculpted with scenes from the life of Christ—these sculpted figures are among the greatest created during the Middle Ages. The taller of the two spires (380 feet versus 350 feet) was built at the start of the 16th century, after its predecessor was destroyed by fire; its fanciful Flamboyant intricacy contrasts sharply with the stumpy solemnity of its Romanesque counterpart (access €3, open daily 9:30–noon and 2–4:30). The **rose window** above the main portal dates from the 13th century, and the three windows below it contain some of the finest examples of 12th-century stained-glass artistry in France.

As spiritual as Chartres is, the cathedral also had its more earthbound uses. Look closely and you can see that the main nave floor has a subtle slant. This was built to provide drainage as this part of the church was often used as a "hostel" by thousands of overnighting pilgrims in medieval times.

Your eyes will need time to adjust to the somber interior. The reward is seeing the gemlike richness of the stained glass, with the famous deep Chartres blue predominating. The oldest window is arguably the most beautiful: **Notre-Dame de la Belle Verrière** (Our Lady of the Lovely Window), in the south choir. The cathedral's windows are being gradually cleaned—a lengthy, painstaking process—and the contrast with those still covered in the grime of centuries is staggering. It's worth taking a pair of binoculars along with you to pick out the details. If you wish to know more about stained-glass techniques and the motifs used, visit the small exhibit in the gallery opposite the north porch. For even more detail, try to arrange a tour (in English) with local institution Malcolm Miller, whose knowledge of the cathedral's history is formidable. (He leads tours twice a day Monday through Saturday; the cost is €10. You can reach him at the telephone number below.) The vast black-and-white labyrinth on the floor of the nave is one of the few to have survived from the Middle Ages; the faithful were expected to travel along its entire length (some 300 yards) on their knees. Guided tours of the **Crypte** start from the Maison de la Crypte opposite the south porch. You can also see a 4th-century Gallo-Roman wall and some 12th-century wall paintings. ⊠*16 cloître Notre-Dame* ☎*02–37–21–75–02* ⊕*www.chartres-tourisme. com* ✉*Crypt €3* ☉*Cathedral 8:30–7:30, guided tours of crypt Easter–Oct., daily at 11, 2:15, 3:30, and 4:30; Nov.–Easter, daily at 11 and 4:15.*

GET ENLIGHTENED

Vitrail (stained glass) being the key to Chartres's fame, you may want to visit the **Galerie du Vitrail** (⊠*17 cloître Notre-Dame* ☎*02–37–36–10–03* ⊕*www.galerie-du-vitrail.com*), which specializes in the noble art. Pieces range from small plaques to entire windows, and there are books on the subject in English and French.

The **Musée des Beaux-Arts** *(Fine Arts Museum)* is in a handsome 18th-century building just behind the cathedral that used to serve as the bishop's palace. Its varied collection includes Renaissance enamels, a portrait of Erasmus by Holbein, tapestries, armor, and some fine (mainly French) paintings from the 17th, 18th, and 19th centuries. There's also a room devoted to the forceful 20th-century landscapes of Maurice de Vlaminck, who lived in the region. ⊠*29 cloître Notre-Dame* ☎*02–37–90–45–80* ✉*€2.40* ☉*Wed.–Sat. and Mon. 10–noon and 2–5, Sun. 2–5.*

The Gothic church of **St-Pierre** (⊠*Rue St-Pierre*), near the Eure River, has magnificent medieval windows from a period (circa 1300) not represented at the cathedral. The oldest stained glass here, portraying Old Testament worthies, is to the right of the choir and dates from the late 13th century.

Exquisite 17th-century stained glass can be admired at the church of **St-Aignan** (⊠*Rue des Grenets*), around the corner from St-Pierre.

19

WHERE TO STAY & EAT

$$–$$$

Fodor'sChoice

★

✕**Moulin de Ponceau.** Ask for a table with a view of the River Eure, with the cathedral looming behind, at this 16th-century converted water mill. Better still, on sunny days you can eat outside, beneath a parasol on the stone terrace by the water's edge—an idyllic setting. Choose from a regularly changing menu of French stalwarts such as rabbit terrine, trout with almonds, and tarte tatin, or splurge on "la trilogie" of scallops, foie gras, and langoustine. ⊠*21 rue de la Tannerie* ☎*02–37–35–30–05* ▤*AE, MC, V* ☉*Closed 2 wks in Feb. No dinner Sun.*

$$–$$$

✕**La Vieille Maison.** Just 100 yards from the cathedral, in a pretty 14th-century building with a flower-decked patio, this restaurant is a fine choice for either lunch or dinner. Chef Bruno Letartre changes his menu regularly, often including such regional specialties as asparagus, rich duck pâté, and superb homemade foie gras along with fish, seafood, and game in season. Prices, though justified, can be steep, but the €20 lunch menu served on summer weekdays is a good bet. ⊠*5 rue au Lait* ☎*02–37–34–10–67* ⊕*www.lavieillemaison.fr.st* ▤ *MC, V* ☉*Closed Mon. No dinner Sun. No lunch Tues.*

★ $$–$$$ ╳▥**Le Grand Monarque.** Set on Chartres's main town square not far from the cathedral, this is a delightful option with decor that remains seductively and warmly redolent of the 19th century. Built originally as a coaching inn (and today part of the Best Western chain), the hotel has numerous rooms, many attractively set with brick walls, wood antiques, lush drapes, and modern bathrooms; the best are in a separate turn-of-the-20th-century building overlooking a garden, while the most atmospheric are tucked away in the attic. Downstairs, the stylishly decorated Georges restaurant serves such delicacies as pheasant pie and scallops with lentils and has prix-fixe menus starting at €29.50. It's closed Monday and there's no dinner Sunday, but the hotel's Madrigal brasserie is open daily. Pros: Old-fashioned charm; good restaurant. Cons: Best rooms are in an annex; stiff uphill walk to cathedral. ⊠*22 pl. des Épars,* ☎*02–37–18–15–15* 🖷*02–37–36–34–18* ⊕*www. bw-grand-monarque.com* ⬎*55 rooms* ⭗*In-room: no a/c (some), refrigerator, Wi-Fi. In-hotel: restaurant, bar, public Wi-Fi, parking (fee), some pets allowed* ▤*AE, DC, MC, V* ⭕❙*BP.*

DISNEYLAND PARIS

🕑 *38 km (24 mi) east of Paris via A4.*

EXPLORING

Disneyland Paris (originally called Euro Disney) is probably not what you've traveled to France to experience. But if you have a child in tow, the promise of a day here may get you through an afternoon at Versailles or Fontainebleau. If you're a dyed-in-the-wool Disney fan, you'll want to make a beeline for the park to see how it has been molded to appeal to the tastes of Europeans (Disney's "Imagineers" call it their most lovingly detailed park). And if you've never experienced this particular form of Disney showmanship, you may want to put in an appearance if only to see what all the fuss is about. When it opened, few turned up to do so; today the place is jammed, and Disneyland Paris is here to stay—and grow, with **Walt Disney Studios** opened alongside it in 2002.

Disneyland Park, as the original theme park is styled, consists of five "lands": Main Street U.S.A., Frontierland, Adventureland, Fantasyland, and Discoveryland. The central theme of each land is relentlessly echoed in every detail, from attractions to restaurant menus to souvenirs. The park is circled by a railroad, which stops three times along the perimeter. **Main Street U.S.A.** goes under the railroad and past shops and restaurants toward the main plaza; Disney parades are held here every afternoon and, during holiday periods, every evening.

Top attractions at **Frontierland** are the chilling Phantom Manor, haunted by holographic spooks, and the thrilling runaway mine train of Big Thunder Mountain, a roller coaster that plunges wildly through floods and avalanches in a setting meant to evoke Utah's Monument Valley. Whiffs of Arabia, Africa, and the West Indies give **Adventureland** its exotic cachet; the spicy meals and snacks served here rank among the best food in the park. Don't miss the Pirates of the

Caribbean, an exciting mise-en-scène populated by eerily human-like, computer-driven figures, or Indiana Jones and the Temple of Doom, a breathtaking ride that re-creates some of this hero's most exciting moments.

Fantasyland charms the youngest park-goers with familiar cartoon characters from such classic Disney films as *Snow White, Pinocchio, Dumbo,* and *Peter Pan.* The focal point of Fantasyland, and indeed Disneyland Paris, is Le Château

PUTTING THE PARIS IN DISNEYLAND PARIS

The following are quirks unique to Mickey's European pied-à-terre. Wine is served in the park (they changed their no-alcohol policy in the 1990s) and there's no Mickey walking around—he was too mobbed by kiddies; now he stays in one spot, and you line up to see him.

de la Belle au Bois Dormant (Sleeping Beauty's Castle), a 140-foot, bubblegum-pink structure topped with 16 blue- and gold-tipped turrets. Its design was allegedly inspired by illustrations from a medieval *Book of Hours*—if so, it was by way of Beverly Hills. The castle's dungeon conceals a 2-ton, scaly, green dragon that rumbles in its sleep and occasionally rouses to roar—an impressive feat of engineering, producing an answering chorus of shrieks from younger children. **Discoveryland** is a futuristic eye-knocker for high-tech Disney entertainment. Robots on roller skates welcome you on your way to Star Tours, a pitching, plunging, sense-confounding ride based on the *Star Wars* films. In Le Visionarium, a simulated space journey is presented by 9-Eye, a staggeringly realistic robot. One of the park's newest attractions, the Jules Verne–inspired **Space Mountain Mission 2,** pretends to catapult *exploronauts* on a rocket-boosted, comet-battered journey through the Milky Way.

Walt Disney Studios opened next to the Disneyland Park in 2002. The theme park is divided into four "production zones." Beneath imposing entrance gates and a 100-foot water tower inspired by the one erected in 1939 at Disney Studios in Burbank, California, **Front Lot** contains shops, a restaurant, and a studio re-creating the atmosphere of Sunset Boulevard. In **Animation Courtyard,** Disney artists demonstrate the various phases of character animation; Animagique brings to life scenes from *Pinocchio* and *The Lion King;* while the Genie from *Aladdin* pilots flying carpets over Agrabah. **Production Courtyard** hosts the Walt Disney Television Studios; Cinémagique, a special-effects tribute to U.S. and European cinema; and a behind-the-scenes Studio Tram tour of location sites, movie props, studio decor, and costuming, ending with a visit to Catastrophe Canyon in the heart of a film shoot. **Back Lot** majors in stunts. At Armageddon Special Effects you can confront a flaming meteor shower aboard the Mir space station, then complete your visit at the giant outdoor arena with a Stunt Show Spectacular involving cars, motorbikes, and Jet Skis. ☎*01–60–30–60–30* ⊕*www. disneylandparis.com* ✉*€46, €120 for 3-day Passport; includes admission to all individual attractions within Disneyland or Walt Disney Studios, but not meals; tickets for Walt Disney Studios are also valid*

19

for admission to Disneyland during last 3 opening hrs of same day ☉*Disneyland mid-June–mid-Sept., daily 9 am–10 pm; mid-Sept.–mid-June, weekdays 10–8, weekends 9–8; Dec. 20–Jan. 4, daily 9–8; Walt Disney Studios daily 10–6* ☰*AE, DC, MC, V.*

WHERE TO STAY & EAT

¢–$$$ ✕**Disneyland Restaurants.** Disneyland Paris is peppered with places to eat, ranging from snack bars and fast-food joints to five full-service restaurants—all with a distinguishing theme. In addition, Walt Disney Studios, Disney Village, and Disney Hotels have restaurants open to the public. But since these are outside the park, it's not recommended that you waste time traveling to them for lunch. Disneyland Paris has relaxed its no-alcohol policy and now serves wine and beer in the park's sit-down restaurants, as well as in the hotels and restaurants outside the park. ☎*01–60–45–65–40* ☰*AE, DC, MC, V.*

$$$–$$$$ 🏨**Disneyland Hotels.** The resort has 5,000 rooms in six hotels, all a short distance from the park, ranging from the luxurious Disneyland Hotel to the not-so-rustic Camp Davy Crockett. Free transportation to the park is available at every hotel. Packages including Disneyland lodging, entertainment, and admission are available through travel agents in Europe. ⌖*Centre de Réservations, B.P. 100, cedex 4, 77777 Marne-la-Vallée* ☎*01–60–30–60–30, 407/934–7639 in U.S.* ⊕*www.disneyland-paris.com* ☞*All hotels have at least 1 restaurant, café, indoor pool, health club, sauna, bar, Wi-Fi* ☰*AE, DC, MC, V* 🍽*FAP.*

NIGHTLIFE & THE ARTS

Nocturnal entertainment outside the park centers on **Disney Village,** a vast pleasure mall designed by American architect Frank Gehry. Featured are American-style restaurants (crab shack, diner, deli, steak house), including **Billybob's Country Western Saloon** (☎*01–60–45–70–81*). Also in Disney Village is **Buffalo Bill's Wild West Show** (☎*01–60–45–71–00 for reservations*), a two-hour dinner extravaganza with a menu of sausages, spare ribs, and chili; performances by a talented troupe of stunt riders, bronco busters, tribal dancers, and musicians; plus some 50 horses, a dozen buffalo, a bull, and an Annie Oakley–style sharpshooter, with a golden-maned "Buffalo Bill" as emcee. A re-creation of a show that dazzled Parisians 100 years ago, it's corny but great fun. There are two shows nightly, at 6:30 and 9:30; the cost is €60 for adults, €40 for children under 12.

UNDERSTANDING PARIS

Books & Movies

Vocabulary

BOOKS & MOVIES

Books

Fiction. Think of writers in Paris, and the romanticized expat figures of the inter-war "lost generation" often come to mind: Ernest Hemingway (*The Sun Also Rises*), F. Scott Fitzgerald, Ezra Pound, and Gertrude Stein just to name a few. Further back in time are classics like Charles Dickens's *A Tale of Two Cities*, set during the Revolution, and Henry James's novels *The American* and *The Ambassadors*, both tales of Americans in Europe. The expats of the Second World War set the scene for future Americans in Paris: James Baldwin's life in the city in the 1950s informed novels such as *Giovanni's Room*, and the denizens of the so-called Beat Hotel (Allen Ginsberg, William Burroughs, and Henry Miller) squeezed in some writing among their less salubrious activities. The Canadian writer Mavis Gallant, who published many stories in *The New Yorker*, also began her tenure in Paris in the '50s; her collection *Paris Stories* is a delight.

Recent best sellers with a Paris setting include, of course, Dan Brown's *The Da Vinci Code*, as well as Diane Johnson's *Le Divorce* and *Le Mariage*, Anita Brookner's *Incidents in the Rue Laugier*, and Patrick Suskind's *Perfume: The Story of a Murderer*. Paul LaFarge's *Haussmann, or the Distinction* spins historical detail about the ambitious city planner into a fascinating period novel. For literary snacking, *Paris in Mind* pulls together excerpts from books by American authors.

For Children. Who doesn't remember Miss Clavel and her 12 young students in two straight lines? Ludwig Bemelmans's beloved *Madeleine* series about the namesake heroine is also illustrated with the author's drawings of Paris landmarks such as the Opéra and the Jardins du Luxembourg. *Eloise in Paris*, by Kay Thompson, also has illustrations, these by Hilary Knight (look for his take on Christian Dior). The *Anatole* books by Eve Titus are classics, starring a Gallic mouse. Playful, bright illustrations drive Maira Kalman's *Ooh-la-la (Max in Love)*; the singsong language, smattered with French, is perfect for reading aloud. Joan MacPhail Knight wrote a pair of books about an American girl visiting France in the late 1800s: *Charlotte in Giverny* and *Charlotte in Paris*.

History. Recent studies devoted to the capital include Philip Mansel's *Paris Between Empires: Monarchy and Revolution*; Jill Harsin's *Barricades: War on the Streets in Revolutionary Paris*; and Johannes Willms's *Paris: Capital of Europe*, which runs from the Revolution to the Belle Époque. Simon Schama's *Citizens* is a good introduction to the French Revolution. Alistair Horne's *Seven Ages of Paris* skips away from standard historical approaches, breaking the city's past into seven eras and putting a colorful spin on the Renaissance, the Revolution, Napoléon's Empire, and other periods.

Biographies and autobiographies of French luminaries and Paris residents can double as satisfying portraits of the capital during their subjects' lifetimes. Works on Baron Haussmann are especially rich, as the 19th-century prefect so utterly changed the face of the city. For a look at American expatriates in Paris between the wars, pick up *Sylvia Beach and the Lost Generation*, by Noel R. Fitch. Tyler Stovall's *Paris Noir: African-Americans in the City of Light* examines black American artists' affection for Paris during the 20th century; *Harlem in Montmartre*, by William A. Shack, homes in on expat jazz culture. Walter Benjamin's *The Arcades Project* uses the 19th century as a point of intersection for studies on advertising, Baudelaire, the Paris Commune, and other subjects.

Memoirs, Essays & Observations. Ernest Hemingway's *A Moveable Feast*, the tale of his 1920s expat life in Paris as a struggling writer, grips from its opening lines. Gertrude Stein, one of Hemingway's friends, gave her own version of the era in *The Autobiography of Alice B. Toklas.* In *The Secret Paris of the '30s,* Brassaï put into words the scenes he captured in photographs. Joseph Roth gave an exile's point of view in *Report from a Parisian Paradise.* Art Buchwald's funny yet poignant *I'll Always Have Paris* moves from the postwar GI Bill days through his years as a journalist and adventurer. Stanley Karnow also drew on a reporter's past in *Paris in the Fifties.* Henry Miller's visceral autobiographical works such as *The Tropic of Cancer* reveal a grittier kind of expat life. Janet Flanner's incomparable *Paris Journals* chronicle the city from the 1940s through 1970, and no one has yet matched A. J. Liebling at table, as described in *Between Meals.*

More recent accounts by Americans living in Paris include Edmund White's *Our Paris: Sketches with Memory* (White is also the author of a brief but captivating wander through the city in *The Flaneur*), Alex Karmel's *A Corner in the Marais: Memoir of a Paris Neighborhood,* Thad Carhart's *The Piano Shop on the Left Bank,* and the very funny *Me Talk Pretty One Day,* by David Sedaris. Adam Gopnik, a *New Yorker* writer who lived in Paris in the 1990s, intersperses articles on larger French issues with descriptions of daily life with his wife and son in *Paris to the Moon.* Gopnik also edited the anthology *Americans in Paris,* a collection of observations by everyone from Thomas Jefferson to Cole Porter.

Works in Translation. Many landmarks of French literature have long been claimed as classics in English as well—Victor Hugo's great 19th-century novels, including *The Hunchback of Notre-Dame* and *Les Misérables,* spin elaborate descriptions of Paris. Other 19th-century masterpieces include Gustave Flaubert's *Sentimental Education,* set against the capital's 1848 uprisings, and Honoré de Balzac's *Human Comedy,* a series of dozens of novels, many set in Paris.

Marcel Proust's masterpiece *À la Recherche du Temps Perdu* (*In Search of Lost Time*) describes fin-de-siècle Paris's parks, glittering aristocratic salons, and dread during the Great War. Colette was another great chronicler of the Belle Époque; her short works include *Chéri* and the Claudine stories.

Simone de Beauvoir's *The Prime of Life,* the second book in her autobiographical trilogy, details her relationship with the existentialist philosopher Jean-Paul Sartre in the context of 1930s and '40s Paris, when the Rive Gauche cemented its modern bohemian reputation in its cafés and jazz clubs.

Movies

Drama. One of the most talked-about movies of 2006 was Sofia Coppola's lavish *Marie Antoinette*; it might not have been a box office hit, but it's an interesting take on life at Versailles. Previous to that, the film version of *The Da Vinci Code* (2006), starring Tom Hanks and Audrey Tautou, was talked about for months preceding its release, although some were disappointed. The heist film *Ronin* (1998) pairs Robert De Niro and Jean Reno with a hyperkinetic chase through the streets of Paris, and in *Frantic* (1987) Harrison Ford plays an American doctor visiting Paris when his wife disappears and director Roman Polanski shoots the city to build suspense and dread. The Palais-Royal gets an equally tense treatment in the Audrey Hepburn–Cary Grant thriller *Charade* (1963); the 2002 remake, *The Truth About Charlie,* doesn't hold a candle to the original. In *Before Sunset* (2004), Ethan Hawke meets Julie Delpy in Paris in the sequel to *Before Sunrise.*

French Films. One of the biggest hits out of France was *Amélie* (2001), which follows a young woman determined to change people's lives. There's a love angle, *bien sûr,* and the neighborhood of Montmartre is practically a third hero, although Parisians sniffed that it was a sterilized version of the raffish quartier.

Jean-Luc Godard's *Breathless* (1960) and François Truffaut's *The 400 Blows* (slang for "raising hell"; 1959) kicked off the New Wave cinema movement. Godard eschewed traditional movie narrative techniques, employing a loose style—including improvised dialogue and hand-held camera shots—for his story about a low-level crook (Jean-Paul Belmondo) and his girlfriend (Jean Seberg). Truffaut's film is a masterwork of innocence lost, a semiautobiographical story of a young boy banished to juvenile detention.

Catherine Deneuve is practically a film industry in and of herself. Her movies span the globe; those shot in Paris range from *Belle de Jour* (1967)—Luis Buñuel's study of erotic repression—to *Le Dernier Métro* (1980), a World War II drama.

Classic film noir and contemporary crime dramas are also highlights of French cinema: for a taste, rent *Rififi* (1955), with its excruciatingly tense 33-minute heist scene; *Le Samouraï* (1967), in which Alain Delon plays the ultimate cool assassin; or Robert Bresson's *Pickpocket* (1959). *La Casque d'Or* (1952) looks back to the underworld of the early 1900s, with Simone Signoret as the title irresistible blond. French director Luc Besson introduced a sly female action hero with *Nikita* (1990), in which Jean Reno chills as the creepy "cleaner" you don't want making house calls.

Filmed during the Occupation, *The Children of Paradise* (1945) became an allegory for the French spirit of resistance: the love story was set in 1840s Paris, thereby getting past the German censors. Other romantic films with memorable takes on Paris include *Cyrano de Bergerac* (1990), with Gérard Depardieu as the large-schnozzed hero; the comedy

When the Cat's Away (1996); the talk-heavy films of Eric Rohmer; *Camille Claudel* (1988), about the affair between Rodin and fellow sculptor Claudel; and the gritty *The Lovers on the Bridge* (1999), the flaws balanced by the bravado of Juliette Binoche waterskiing on the Seine surrounded by fireworks. *The Red Balloon* (1956) is also a love story of a sort: a children's film of a boy and his faithful balloon.

Musicals. Love in the time of Toulouse-Lautrec? Elton John songs? Baz Luhrmann's *Moulin Rouge* (2001) whirls them together and wins through conviction rather than verisimilitude. John Huston's 1952 film of the same name is also well worth watching. Gene Kelly pursues Leslie Caron through postwar Paris in *An American in Paris* (1951); the Gershwin-fueled film includes a stunning 17-minute dance sequence. Caron reappears as the love interest—this time as a young girl in training to be a courtesan—in *Gigi* (1958). *Funny Face* (1957) stars Fred Astaire and Audrey Hepburn, and there's an unforgettable scene of Hepburn descending the staircase below the *Winged Victory* in the Louvre.

VOCABULARY

One of the trickiest French sounds to pronounce is the nasal final n sound (whether or not the n is actually the last letter of the word). You should try to pronounce it as a sort of nasal grunt—as in "huh." The vowel that precedes the n will govern the vowel sound of the word, and in this list we precede the final n with an h to remind you to be nasal.

Another problem sound is the ubiquitous but untransliterable eu, as in bleu (blue) or deux (two), and the very similar sound in je (I), ce (this), and de (of). The closest equivalent might be the vowel sound in "put," but rounded. The famous rolled r is a glottal sound. Consonants at the ends of words are usually silent; when the following word begins with a vowel, however, the two are run together by sounding the consonant. There are two forms of "you" in French: vous (formal and plural) and tu (a singular, personal form). When addressing an adult you don't know, vous is always best.

ENGLISH	FRENCH	PRONUNCIATION

BASICS

Yes/no	Oui/non	wee/nohn
Please	S'il vous plaît	seel voo play
Thank you	Merci	mair-**see**
You're welcome	De rien	deh ree-**ehn**
Excuse me, sorry	Pardon	pahr-**don**
Good morning/ afternoon	Bonjour	bohn-**zhoor**
Good evening	Bonsoir	bohn-**swahr**
Goodbye	Au revoir	o ruh-**vwahr**
Mr. (Sir)	Monsieur	muh-**syuh**
Mrs. (Ma'am)	Madame	ma-**dam**
Miss	Mademoiselle	mad-mwa-**zel**
Pleased to meet you	Enchanté(e)	ohn-shahn-**tay**
How are you?	Comment allez-vous?	kuh-mahn-tahl-ay **voo**
Very well, thanks	Très bien, merci	tray bee-ehn, mair-**see**
And you?	Et vous?	ay voo?

NUMBERS

one	un	uhn
two	deux	deuh
three	trois	twah
four	quatre	**kaht**-ruh
five	cinq	sank
six	six	seess
seven	sept	set
eight	huit	wheat
nine	neuf	nuf
ten	dix	deess
eleven	onze	ohnz
twelve	douze	dooz
thirteen	treize	trehz
fourteen	quatorze	kah-torz
fifteen	quinze	kanz
sixteen	seize	sez
seventeen	dix-sept	deez-**set**
eighteen	dix-huit	deez-**wheat**
nineteen	dix-neuf	deez-**nuf**
twenty	vingt	vehn
twenty-one	vingt-et-un	vehnt-ay-**uhn**
thirty	trente	trahnt
forty	quarante	ka-**rahnt**
fifty	cinquante	sang-**kahnt**
sixty	soixante	swa-**sahnt**
seventy	soixante-dix	swa-sahnt-**deess**
eighty	quatre-vingts	kaht-ruh-**vehn**
ninety	quatre-vingt-dix	kaht-ruh-vehn-**deess**
one hundred	cent	sahn
one thousand	mille	meel

COLORS

black	noir	nwahr
blue	bleu	bleuh
brown	brun/marron	bruhn/mar-**rohn**
green	vert	vair
orange	orange	o-**rahnj**
pink	rose	rose
red	rouge	rouge
violet	violette	vee-o-**let**
white	blanc	blahnk
yellow	jaune	zhone

DAYS OF THE WEEK

Sunday	dimanche	dee-**mahnsh**
Monday	lundi	luhn-**dee**
Tuesday	mardi	mahr-**dee**
Wednesday	mercredi	mair-kruh-**dee**
Thursday	jeudi	zhuh-**dee**
Friday	vendredi	vawn-druh-**dee**
Saturday	samedi	sahm-**dee**

MONTHS

January	janvier	zhahn-vee-**ay**
February	février	feh-vree-**ay**
March	mars	marce
April	avril	a-**vreel**
May	mai	meh
June	juin	zhwehn
July	juillet	zhwee-**ay**
August	août	ah-**oo**
September	septembre	sep-**tahm**-bruh
October	octobre	awk-**to**-bruh
November	novembre	no-**vahm**-bruh
December	décembre	day-**sahm**-bruh

USEFUL PHRASES

Do you speak	Parlez-vous	par-lay **voo**
English?	anglais?	**ahn**-glay
I don't speak . . . French	Je ne parle pas . . . français	zhuh nuh parl pah frahn-**say**
I don't understand	Je ne comprends pas	zhuh nuh kohm-**prahn** pah
I understand	Je comprends	zhuh kohm-**prahn**
I don't know	Je ne sais pas	zhuh nuh say **pah**
I'm American/ British	Je suis américain/ anglais	zhuh sweez a-may-ree-**kehn**/ ahn-**glay**
What's your name?	Comment vous appelez-vous?	ko-mahn voo za-pell-ay-**voo**
My name is . . .	Je m'appelle . . .	zhuh ma-**pell** . . .
What time is it?	Quelle heure est-il?	kel air eh-**teel**
How?	Comment?	ko-**mahn**
When?	Quand?	kahn
Yesterday	Hier	yair
Today	Aujourd'hui	o-zhoor-**dwee**
Tomorrow	Demain	duh-**mehn**
Tonight	Ce soir	suh **swahr**
What?	Quoi?	kwah
What is it?	Qu'est-ce que c'est?	kess-kuh-**say**
Why?	Pourquoi?	**poor**-kwa
Who?	Qui?	kee
Where is . . .	Où est . . .	oo ay
the train station?	la gare?	la gar
the subway station?	la station de métro?	la sta-**syon** duh may-**tro**
the bus stop?	l'arrêt de bus?	la-**ray** duh **booss**
the post office?	la poste?	la post
the bank?	la banque?	la bahnk
the . . . hotel?	l'hôtel . . .?	lo-**tel**
the store?	le magasin?	luh ma-ga-**zehn**
the cashier?	la caisse?	la **kess**
the . . . museum?	le musée . . .?	luh mew-**zay**

the hospital?	l'hôpital?	lo-pee-**tahl**
the elevator?	l'ascenseur?	la-sahn-**seuhr**
the telephone?	le téléphone?	luh tay-lay-**phone**
Where are the restrooms? (men/women)	Où sont les toilettes? (hommes/femmes)	oo sohn lay twah-**let** (**oh**-mm/**fah**-mm)
Here/there	Ici/là	ee-**see**/la
Left/right	A gauche/à droite	a goash/a draht
Straight ahead	Tout droit	too drwah
Is it near/far?	C'est près/loin?	say pray/lwehn
I'd like . . .	Je voudrais . . .	zhuh voo-**dray**
a room	une chambre	ewn **shahm**-bruh
the key	la clé	la clay
a newspaper	un journal	uhn zhoor-**nahl**
a stamp	un timbre	uhn **tam**-bruh
I'd like to buy . . .	Je voudrais acheter . . .	zhuh voo-**dray** **ahsh**-tay
cigarettes	des cigarettes	day see-ga-**ret**
matches	des allumettes	days a-loo-**met**
soap	du savon	dew sah-**vohn**
city map	un plan de ville	uhn plahn de **veel**
road map	une carte routière	ewn cart roo-tee-**air**
magazine	une revue	ewn reh-**vu**
envelopes	des enveloppes	dayz ahn-veh-**lope**
writing paper	du papier à lettres	dew pa-pee-**ay** a **let**-ruh
postcard	une carte postale	ewn cart pos-**tal**
How much is it?	C'est combien?	say comb-bee-**ehn**
A little/a lot	Un peu/beaucoup	uhn peuh/bo-**koo**
More/less	Plus/moins	plu/mwehn
Enough/too (much)	Assez/trop	a-say/tro
I am ill/sick	Je suis malade	zhuh swee ma-**lahd**
Call a . . .	Appelez un . . .	a-play uhn
doctor	docteur	dohk-**tehr**
Help!	Au secours!	o suh-**koor**
Stop!	Arrêtez!	a-reh-**tay**
Fire!	Au feu!	o fuh
Caution!/Look out!	Attention!	a-tahn-see-**ohn**

DINING OUT

A bottle of . . .	une bouteille de . . .	ewn boo-**tay** duh
A cup of . . .	une tasse de . . .	ewn tass duh
A glass of . . .	un verre de . . .	uhn vair duh
Bill/check	l'addition	la-dee-see-**ohn**
Bread	du pain	dew pan
Breakfast	le petit-déjeuner	luh puh-**tee** day-zhuh-**nay**
Butter	du beurre	dew burr
Cheers!	A votre santé!	ah vo-truh sahn-**tay**
Cocktail/aperitif	un apéritif	uhn ah-pay-ree-**teef**
Dinner	le dîner	luh dee-**nay**
Dish of the day	le plat du jour	luh plah dew **zhoor**
Enjoy!	Bon appétit!	bohn a-pay-**tee**
Fixed-price menu	le menu	luh may-**new**
Fork	une fourchette	ewn four-**shet**
I am diabetic	Je suis diabétique	zhuh swee dee-ah-bay-**teek**
I am vegetarian	Je suis végé-tarien(ne)	zhuh swee vay-zhay-ta-ree-**en**
I cannot eat . . .	Je ne peux pas manger de . . .	zhuh nuh **puh** pah mahn-**jay** deh
I'd like to order	Je voudrais commander	zhuh voo-**dray** ko-mahn-**day**
Is service/the tip included?	Est-ce que le service est compris?	ess kuh luh sair-**veess** ay comb-**pree**
It's good/bad	C'est bon/mauvais	say bohn/ mo-**vay**
It's hot/cold	C'est chaud/froid	say sho/frwah
Knife	un couteau	uhn koo-**toe**
Lunch	le déjeuner	luh day-zhuh-**nay**
Menu	la carte	la cart
Napkin	une serviette	ewn sair-vee-**et**
Pepper	du poivre	dew **pwah**-vruh

Plate	une assiette	ewn a-see-**et**
Please give me . . .	Donnez-moi . . .	doe-nay-**mwah**
Salt	du sel	dew sell
Spoon	une cuillère	ewn kwee-**air**
Sugar	du sucre	dew **sook**-ruh
Waiter!/Waitress!	Monsieur!/ Mademoiselle!	muh-**syuh**/ mad-mwa-**zel**
Wine list	la carte des vins	la cart day vehn

MENU GUIDE

| FRENCH | ENGLISH |

GENERAL DINING

Entrée	Appetizer/Starter
Garniture au choix	Choice of vegetable side
Plat du jour	Dish of the day
Selon arrivage	When available
Supplément/En sus	Extra charge
Sur commande	Made to order

PETIT DÉJEUNER (BREAKFAST)

Confiture	Jam
Miel	Honey
Oeuf à la coque	Boiled egg
Oeufs sur le plat	Fried eggs
Oeufs brouillés	Scrambled eggs
Tartine	Bread with butter
Poissons/Fruits de Mer (Fish/Seafood)	
Anchois	Anchovies
Bar	Bass
Brandade de morue	Creamed salt cod
Brochet	Pike
Cabillaud/Morue	Fresh cod
Calmar	Squid
Coquilles St-Jacques	Scallops

Crevettes	Shrimp
Daurade	Sea bream
Ecrevisses	Prawns/Crayfish
Harengs	Herring
Homard	Lobster
Huîtres	Oysters
Langoustine	Prawn/Lobster
Lotte	Monkfish
Moules	Mussels
Palourdes	Clams
Saumon	Salmon
Thon	Tuna
Truite	Trout

VIANDE (MEAT)

Agneau	Lamb
Boeuf	Beef
Boudin	Sausage
Boulettes de viande	Meatballs
Brochettes	Kabobs
Cassoulet	Casserole of white beans, meat
Cervelle	Brains
Chateaubriand	Double fillet steak
Choucroute garnie	Sausages with sauerkraut
Côtelettes	Chops
Côte/Côte de boeuf	Rib/T-bone steak
Cuisses de grenouilles	Frogs' legs
Entrecôte	Rib or rib-eye steak
Épaule	Shoulder
Escalope	Cutlet
Foie	Liver
Gigot	Leg
Porc	Pork
Ris de veau	Veal sweetbreads

Rognons	Kidneys
Saucisses	Sausages
Selle	Saddle
Tournedos	Tenderloin of T-bone steak
Veau	Veal

METHODS OF PREPARATION

A point	Medium
A l'étouffée	Stewed
Au four	Baked
Ballotine	Boned, stuffed, and rolled
Bien cuit	Well-done
Bleu	Very rare
Frit	Fried
Grillé	Grilled
Rôti	Roast
Saignant	Rare

VOLAILLES/GIBIER (POULTRY/GAME)

Blanc de volaille	Chicken breast
Canard/Caneton	Duck/Duckling
Cerf/Chevreuil	Venison (red/roe)
Coq au vin	Chicken stewed in red wine
Dinde/Dindonneau	Turkey/Young turkey
Faisan	Pheasant
Lapin/Lièvre	Rabbit/Wild hare
Oie	Goose
Pintade/Pintadeau	Guinea fowl/Young guinea fowl
Poulet/Poussin	Chicken/Spring chicken

LÉGUMES (VEGETABLES)

Artichaut	Artichoke
Asperge	Asparagus
Aubergine	Eggplant
Carottes	Carrots

Champignons	Mushrooms
Chou-fleur	Cauliflower
Chou (rouge)	Cabbage (red)
Laitue	Lettuce
Oignons	Onions
Petits pois	Peas
Pomme de terre	Potato
Tomates	Tomatoes

FRUITS/NOIX (FRUITS/NUTS)

Abricot	Apricot
Amandes	Almonds
Ananas	Pineapple
Cassis	Black currants
Cerises	Cherries
Citron/Citron vert	Lemon/Lime
Fraises	Strawberries
Framboises	Raspberries
Pamplemousse	Grapefruit
Pêche	Peach
Poire	Pear
Pomme	Apple
Prunes/Pruneaux	Plums/Prunes
Raisins/Raisins secs	Grapes/Raisins

DESSERTS

Coupe (glacée)	Sundae
Crème Chantilly	Whipped cream
Gâteau au chocolat	Chocolate cake
Glace	Ice cream
Tarte tatin	Caramelized apple tart
Tourte	Layer cake

DRINKS

A l'eau	With water
Avec des glaçons	On the rocks
Bière	Beer
Blonde/brune	Light/dark
Café noir/crème	Black coffee/with steamed milk
Chocolat chaud	Hot chocolate
Eau-de-vie	Brandy
Eau minérale	Mineral water
gazeuse/non gazeuse	carbonated/still
Jus de . . .	. . . juice
Lait	Milk
Sec	Straight or dry
Thé	Tea
au lait/au citron	with milk/lemon
Vin	Wine
blanc	white
doux	sweet
léger	light
brut	very dry
rouge	red

Paris Essentials

PLANNING TOOLS, EXPERT INSIGHT, GREAT CONTACTS

There are planners and there are those who, excuse the pun, fly by the seat of their pants. We happily place ourselves among the planners. Our writers and editors try to anticipate all the issues you may face before and during any journey, and then they do their research. This section is the product of their efforts. Use it to get excited about your trip to Paris, to inform your travel planning, or to guide you on the road should the seat of your pants start to feel threadbare.

GETTING STARTED

We're really proud of our Web site: Fodors.com is a great place to begin any journey. Scan Travel Wire for suggested itineraries, travel deals, restaurant and hotel openings, and other up-to-the-minute info. Check out Booking to research prices and book plane tickets, hotel rooms, rental cars, and vacation packages. Head to Talk for on-the-ground pointers from travelers who frequent our message boards. You can also link to loads of other travel-related resources.

▌ RESOURCES

ONLINE TRAVEL TOOLS

ALL ABOUT PARIS

Besides the tourist office Web sites, *⊕en. parisinfo.com* and *⊕www.PIDF.com*, there are several other helpful government-sponsored sites. The Paris mayor's office site, *⊕www.paris.fr*, covers all kinds of public cultural attractions, student resources, park and market info, and more. On the French Ministry of Culture's site, *⊕www.culture.fr*, you can search by theme (contemporary art, cinema, music, theater, etc.) or by region (Paris is in the Ile-de-France). The Réunion des Musées Nationaux (RMN), a consortium of public museums, hosts a group site for 32 national institutions: *⊕www.rmn.fr*. Fourteen of these museums are in Paris proper, including the Louvre, the Musée Rodin, and the Musée d'Orsay. The site has visitor info and an exhibition calendar for current and upcoming shows.

A useful Web site for checking Paris addresses is the phone and address directory, Les Pages Jaunes (*⊕www. pagesjaunes.fr*). Input a specific address, and you get not just a street map but a photo.

For food-related info, make a beeline for Patricia Wells's site, *⊕www.patriciawells. com*. It covers Wells's recent restaurant reviews (mostly for places in Paris), other food-related news, and a terrific glossary of French food terms. Dininginfrance. com (*⊕www.dininginfrance.com*) has a special section on Paris, with a selection of recent newspaper and magazine articles published on the capital's food scene.

Secrets of Paris (*⊕www.secretsofparis. com*) is a free online newsletter of tips on dining, nightlife, accommodations, and sightseeing off the beaten path put together by Fodor's updater Heather Stimmler-Hall.

Paris-Anglo.com (*⊕www.paris-anglo. com*) includes directories of cooking schools, galleries, language classes, and more, plus a biweekly column on various *la vie parisienne* topics. Though not entirely dedicated to Paris, the journal *France Today* (*⊕www.francetoday.com*) often covers Paris-related news, arts events, and the like. The excellent *Paris Notes* newsletter is an all-in-one resource for Paris-centric news, with a cultural events calendar and in-depth articles on everything from current trends to overlooked historic sights. It's published 10 times a year; the Web site (*⊕www.paris-notes.com*) includes article archives, plus special sections on hotels, restaurants, and architecture.

And of course there are all sorts of Paris-related blogs that can be great sources of information and travel inspiration. Some of our faves are Paris Daily Photo (*⊕www.parisdailyphoto.com*), a fun blog with cool photos from around the city, and Metropole Paris (⊕www.metropoleparis.com), a weekly online magazine since 1996, about Paris news, events, and musings by longtime expat Ric Erickson. French Word-a-Day (⊕*www.frenchword-a-day.typepad.com*) is an engaging slice-of-life, with a vocab bonus.

VISITOR INFORMATION

The Maison de la France is the international arm of the French tourism ministry; through its newsletters, brochures, and Web site you can pick up plenty of information on Paris attractions, special events, promotions, and more.

Once you're in Paris, you can turn to the branches of the tourist information office. The longtime main tourist office that was on the Champs-Elysées moved to Rue des Pyramides (near the Opéra) in 2004, and a half dozen visitor bureaus are stationed at the city's most popular tourist sights. It's often easier to visit one of these branches in person than to call the hotline, because on the phone you'll have to wait through long stretches of generic recorded information at €0.34 per minute. Most are open daily; the Gare de Lyon and Opéra–Grands Magasins branches, however, are open Monday through Saturday. The tourism bureaus have friendly, efficient, and multilingual staff. You can gather info on special events, local transit, hotels, tours, excursions, and discount passes. The branch in the Carrousel du Louvre specializes in information on the Ile-de-France (the region around Paris).

Contacts **Maison de la France** (☎514/288–1904 or 310/271–6665 in U.S. ⊕www.franceguide.com).

Local Tourism Information **Espace du Tourisme d'Ile-de-France** (⊠Carrousel du Louvre, 99 rue de Rivoli, ☎08-92-68-30-00 ⊕www.pidf.com Ⓜ Palais-Royal Musée du Louvre). **Office du Tourisme de la Ville de Paris Pyramides** (⊠25 rue des Pyramides, ☎08-92-68-30-00 €0.34 per minute Ⓜ Pyramides). **Office du Tourisme de la Ville**

de Paris Gare du Lyon (⊠Arrivals, 20 bd. Diderot, Ⓜ Gare du Lyon). **Office du Tourisme de la Ville de Paris Gare du Nord** (⊠18 rue de Dunkerque, Ⓜ Gare du Nord). **Office du Tourisme de la Ville de Paris Opéra–Grands Magasins** (⊠11 rue Scribe, Ⓜ Opéra). **Office du Tourisme de la Ville de Paris Tour Eiffel** (⊠Between east and north legs of Eiffel Tower Ⓜ Champs de Mars/Tour Eiffel).

▌ THINGS TO CONSIDER

GOVERNMENT ADVISORIES

As different countries have different worldviews, look at travel advisories from a range of governments to get more of a sense of what's going on out there. And be sure to parse the language carefully. For example, a warning to "avoid all travel" carries more weight than one urging you to "avoid nonessential travel," and both are much stronger than a plea to "exercise caution." A U.S. government travel warning is more permanent (though not necessarily more serious) than a so-called public announcement, which carries an expiration date.

The U.S. Department of State's Web site has more than just travel warnings and advisories. The consular information sheets issued for every country have general safety tips, and other useful details.

General Information & Warnings **Consular Affairs Bureau of Canada** (⊕www.voyage.gc.ca). **U.S. Department of State** (⊕www.travel.state.gov).

GEAR

You'll notice it right away: in Paris the women dress well to go shopping, to go to the cinema, to have a drink; the men look good when they're fixing their cars. The Parisians are a people who still wear hats to the races and well-cut clothes for fine meals; you will not see them in sweats unless they're doing something *sportif*. So, don't wear shorts, sweats, or sneakers if you want to blend in. Good food in good settings deserves good clothing—not necessarily a suit and tie, but a long-sleeve shirt and pants for him, something nice for her. Trendy nightclubs usually refuse entrance to men who are wearing sandals.

Be sure to bring rain gear, a comfortable pair of walking shoes, and a sweater or shawl for cool churches and museums. You can never tell about the weather, so a small, foldable umbrella is a good idea. If you'd like to scrutinize the stained glass in churches, bring a pair of small binoculars. A small package of tissues is always a good idea for the occasional rustic bathroom in cafés, airports, and train stations. An additional note: if you're the kind of person who likes a washcloth in the bathroom, bring your own; they're not something you'll find in Paris hotels.

PASSPORTS & VISAS

All citizens of Canada and the United States, even infants, need only a valid passport to enter France for stays of up to 90 days. If you lose your passport, call the nearest embassy or consulate and the local police immediately.

PASSPORTS & VISAS

A passport verifies both your identity and nationality—a great reason to have one. Another reason is that you need a passport now more than ever. At this writing, U.S. citizens must have a passport when traveling by air between the United States and several destinations for which other forms of identification (e.g., a driver's license and a birth certificate) were once sufficient. These destinations include Mexico, Canada, Bermuda, and all countries in Central America and the Caribbean (except the territories of Puerto Rico and the U.S. Virgin Islands). Soon enough you'll need a passport when traveling between the United States and such destinations by land and sea, too.

U.S. passports are valid for 10 years. You must apply in person if you're getting a passport for the first time; if your previous passport was lost, stolen, or damaged; or if your previous passport has expired

> ## WORD OF MOUTH
>
> "The vast majority of tourists will be wearing jeans and walking shoes, so the most important consideration is: how would you be most comfortable? Do you like to dress casually, or do you like being a bit more fashionable? It can get warm in the summer, so a sundress or skirt would probably be cooler, but there's certainly no reason to wear heels." –travelhorizons

and was issued more than 15 years ago or when you were under 16. All children under 18 must appear in person to apply for or renew a passport. Both parents must accompany any child under 14 (or send a notarized statement with their permission) and provide proof of their relationship to the child.

■ **TIP→** Before your trip, make two copies of your passport's data page (one for someone at home and another for you to carry separately). Or scan the page and e-mail it to someone at home and/or yourself.

There are 13 regional passport offices, as well as 7,000 passport acceptance facilities in post offices, public libraries, and other governmental offices. If you're renewing a passport, you can do so by mail. Forms are available at passport acceptance facilities and online.

The cost to apply for a new passport is $97 for adults, $82 for children under 16; renewals are $67. Allow six weeks for processing, both for first-time passports and renewals. For an expediting fee of $60 you can reduce this time to about two weeks. If your trip is less than two weeks away, you can get a passport even more rapidly by going to a passport office with the necessary documentation. Private expediters can get things done in as little as 48 hours, but charge hefty fees for their services.

VISAS

A visa is essentially formal permission to enter a country. Visas allow countries to keep track of you and other visitors—and generate revenue (from application fees). You *always* need a visa to enter a foreign country; however, many countries, like France, routinely issue tourist visas on arrival, particularly to U.S. citizens. When your passport is stamped or scanned in the immigration line, you're actually being issued a visa.

U.S. Passport Information **U.S. Department of State** (☎877/487–2778 ⊕http://travel.state.gov/passport).

U.S. Passport & Visa Expediters **A. Briggs Passport & Visa Expeditors** (☎800/806–0581 or 202/338–0111 ⊕www.abriggs.com). **American Passport Express** (☎800/455–5166 or 800/841–6778 ⊕www.americanpassport.com). **Passport Express** (☎800/362–8196 ⊕www.passportexpress.com). **Travel Document Systems** (☎800/874–5100 or 202/638–3800 ⊕www.traveldocs.com). **Travel the World Visas** (☎866/886–8472 or 301/495–7700 ⊕www.world-visa.com).

TRIP INSURANCE

What kind of coverage do you honestly need? Do you even need trip insurance at all? Take a deep breath and read on.

We believe that comprehensive trip insurance is especially valuable if you're booking a very expensive or complicated trip (particularly to an isolated region) or if you're booking far in advance. Who knows what could happen six months down the road? But whether you get insurance has more to do with how comfortable you are assuming all that risk yourself.

Comprehensive travel policies typically cover trip cancellation and interruption, letting you cancel or cut your trip short because of a personal emergency, illness, or, in some cases, acts of terrorism in your destination. Such policies also cover evacuation and medical care. Some also cover you for trip delays because of bad weather or mechanical problems as well as for lost or delayed baggage. Another type of coverage to look for is financial default—that is, when your trip is disrupted because a tour operator, airline, or cruise line goes out of business. Generally you must buy this when you book your trip or shortly thereafter, and it's available to you only if your operator isn't on a list of excluded companies.

If you're going abroad, consider buying medical-only coverage at the very least. Neither Medicare nor some private insurers cover medical expenses anywhere outside the United States besides Mexico and Canada (including time aboard a cruise ship, even if it leaves from a U.S. port). Medical-only policies typically reimburse you for medical care (excluding that related to preexisting conditions) and hospitalization abroad, and provide for evacuation. You still have to pay the bills and await reimbursement from the insurer, though.

Expect comprehensive travel insurance policies to cost about 4% to 7% or 8% of the total price of your trip (it's more like 8%–12% if you're over age 70). A medical-only policy may or may not be cheaper than a comprehensive policy. Always read the fine print of your policy to make sure that you are covered for the risks that are of most concern to you. Compare several policies to make sure you're getting the best price and range of coverage available.

BOOKING YOUR TRIP

Unless your cousin is a travel agent, you're probably among the millions of people who make most of their travel arrangements online. But have you ever wondered just what the differences are between an online travel agent (a Web site through which you make reservations instead of going directly to the airline, hotel, or car-rental company), a discounter (a firm that does a high volume of business with a hotel chain or airline and accordingly gets good prices), a wholesaler (one that makes cheap reservations in bulk and then resells them to people like you), and an aggregator (one that compares all the offerings so you don't have to)? Is it truly better to book directly on an airline or hotel Web site? And when does a real live travel agent come in handy?

ONLINE

You really have to shop around. A travel wholesaler such as Hotels.com or Hotel-Club.net can be a source of good rates, as can discounters such as Hotwire or Priceline, particularly if you can bid for your hotel room or airfare. Indeed, such sites sometimes have deals that are unavailable elsewhere. They do, however, tend to work only with hotel chains (which makes them just plain useless for getting hotel reservations outside of major cities) or big airlines (so that often leaves out upstarts like jetBlue and some foreign carriers like Air India). Also, with discounters and wholesalers you must generally prepay, and everything is nonrefundable. And before you fork over the dough, be sure to check the terms and conditions, so you know what a given company will do for you if there's a problem and what you'll have to deal with on your own.

■TIP➔ **To be absolutely sure everything was processed correctly, confirm reservations made through online travel agents, discounters, and wholesalers directly with your hotel before leaving home.**

Booking engines like Expedia, Travelocity, and Orbitz are actually travel agents, albeit high-volume, online ones. And airline travel packagers like American Airlines Vacations and Virgin Vacations—well, they're travel agents, too. But they may still not work with all the world's hotels.

An aggregator site will search many sites and pull the best prices for airfares, hotels, and rental cars from them. Most aggregators compare the major travel-booking sites such as Expedia, Travelocity, and Orbitz; some also look at airline Web sites, though rarely the sites of smaller budget airlines. Some aggregators also compare other travel products, including complex packages—a good thing, as you can sometimes get the best overall deal by booking an air-and-hotel package.

WITH A TRAVEL AGENT

If you use an agent—brick-and-mortar or virtual—you'll pay a fee for the service. And know that the service you get from some online agents isn't comprehensive. For example Expedia and Travelocity don't search for prices on budget airlines like jetBlue, Southwest, or small foreign carriers. That said, some agents (online or not) *do* have access to fares that are difficult to find otherwise, and the savings can more than make up for any surcharge.

A knowledgeable brick-and-mortar travel agent can be a godsend if you're booking a cruise, a package trip that's not available to you directly, an air pass, or a complicated itinerary including several overseas flights. What's more, travel agents that specialize in a destination may have exclusive access to certain deals and insider information on things such as charter flights. Agents who specialize in types of travelers (senior citizens, gays and lesbians, naturists) or types of trips (cruises, luxury travel, safaris) can also be invaluable. And complain about the surcharges all you like, but when things don't work out the way you'd hoped, it's nice to have an agent to put things right.

■TIP→ Remember that Expedia, Travelocity, and Orbitz are travel agents, not just booking engines. To resolve any problems with a reservation made through these companies, contact them first.

Agent Resources American Society of Travel Agents (☎ 703/739–2782 ⊕ www. travelsense.org).

■ ACCOMMODATIONS

Most hotels and other lodgings require you to give your credit-card details before they will confirm your reservation. If you don't feel comfortable e-mailing this information, ask if you can fax it (some places even prefer faxes). However you book, get confirmation in writing and have a copy handy when you check in.

Be sure you understand the hotel's cancellation policy. Some places allow you to cancel without any kind of penalty— even if you prepaid to secure a discounted rate—if you cancel at least 24 hours in advance. Others require you to cancel a week in advance or penalize you the cost of one night. Small inns and bed-and-breakfasts are most likely to require you to cancel far in advance. Most hotels allow children under a certain age to stay in their parents' room at no extra charge, but others charge for them as extra adults; find out the cutoff age for discounts.

■TIP→ Assume that hotels operate on the European Plan (EP, no meals) unless we specify that they use the Breakfast Plan (BP, with full breakfast), Continental Plan (CP, Continental breakfast), Full American Plan (FAP, all meals), Modified American Plan (MAP, breakfast and dinner) or are all-inclusive (AI, all meals and most activities).

For more information about lodgings in Paris, see the Where to Stay chapter.

■ AIRLINE TICKETS

Most domestic airline tickets are electronic; international tickets may be either electronic or paper. With an e-ticket the only thing you receive is an e-mailed receipt citing your itinerary and reservation and ticket numbers. The greatest advantage of an e-ticket is that if you lose your receipt, you can simply print out another copy or ask the airline to do it for you at check-in. You usually pay a surcharge (up to $50) to get a paper ticket, if you can get one at all. The sole advantage of a paper ticket is that it may be easier to endorse over to another airline if your flight is canceled and the airline with which you booked can't accommodate you on another flight.

■TIP→ Discount air passes that let you travel economically in a country or region must often be purchased before you leave home. In some cases you can get them only through a travel agent.

You can save on air travel within Europe if you plan on traveling to and from Paris aboard Air France. If you sign up for Air France's Euro Flyer program, you can buy coupons that enable you to travel to any Air France destination. Rates are calculated by season: each coupon purchased November–March costs $90; coupons purchased April–October cost $120. You can purchase a minimum of three or a maximum of nine coupons, and all must be used within two months. You can purchase these coupons only in the United States, and you must ask for them specifically. These coupons are a great deal if you're planning on traveling from city to city and don't want to worry about the cost of one-way travel.

Air Pass Info Air France (☎ 800/237–2747 ⊕ www.airfrance.us). **All Asia Pass** (Cathay Pacific ☎ 800/233–2742 ⊕ www.cathaypacific. com). **FlightPass** (EuropebyAir ☎ 888/321–4737 ⊕ www.europebyair.com).

▌ RENTAL CARS

When you reserve a car, ask about cancellation penalties, taxes, drop-off charges (if you're planning to pick up the car in one city and leave it in another), and surcharges (for being under or over a certain age, for additional drivers, or for driving across state or country borders or beyond a specific distance from your point of rental). All these things can add substantially to your costs. Request car seats and extras such as GPS when you book.

Rates are sometimes—but not always—better if you book in advance or reserve through a rental agency's Web site. There are other reasons to book ahead, though: for popular destinations, during busy times of the year, or to ensure that you get certain types of cars (vans, SUVs, exotic sports cars).

▌TIP➔ **Make sure that a confirmed reservation guarantees you a car. Agencies sometimes overbook, particularly for busy weekends and holiday periods.**

Unless you have a special, compelling reason, do yourself a favor and **avoid driving in Paris**. The pleasures of walking and the thorough, reliable public transit system should see you through most situations—and why mar your day with the stress of navigating narrow, one-way streets while surrounded by breakneck drivers in mosquito-size cars? You're better off driving only on trips out of the city, and even then, you'll probably be happier if you take the train.

If you must drive in Paris, an International Driver's Permit (IDP) is not required, but it is recommended. It can be used only in conjunction with a valid driver's license. Check the AAA Web site for more info as well as for IDPs ($10) themselves.

Thanks to competition among Internet sites, rental rates start as low as $35 a day and $200 a week for an economy car with air-conditioning, manual transmission, and unlimited mileage. This does not include tax on car rentals, which is 19.6% or, if you pick up a car at the airport, the airport tax. Make reservations before you go; you can generally get a much better deal. Note that driving in Paris is best avoided, and parking is very difficult to find. You're better off renting a car only when you want to take excursions out of the city.

Renting a car through a local French agency has a number of disadvantages, the biggest being price, as they simply cannot compete with the larger international companies. These giants combine bilingual service, the security of name recognition, extensive services (such as 24-hour hotlines), and fully automatic vehicles. However, there are a couple of exceptions. Easycar, an Internet-only rental service, has gained a solid reputation in the budget rental sector. Rentacar Prestige can be useful if you're interested in luxury cars (convertible BMWs) or large family vans (a Renault Espace, for example).

Drivers in France must be over 18 years old, but there is no top age limit (if your faculties are intact). To rent a car, however, you must be 21 or older and have a major credit card. If you're under 25, there's a €17-per-day supplementary charge.

▌ VACATION PACKAGES

Packages *are not* guided excursions. Packages combine airfare, accommodations, and perhaps a rental car or other extras (theater tickets, guided excursions, boat trips, reserved entry to popular museums, transit passes), but they let you do your own thing. During busy periods packages may be your only option, as flights and rooms may be sold out otherwise. Packages will definitely save you time. They can also save you money, particularly in peak seasons, but—and this is a really big "but"—you should price each part of the package separately to be sure. And be aware that prices advertised on Web sites and in newspapers rarely include service charges or taxes, which can up your costs by hundreds of dollars.

■TIP➡ **Some packages and cruises are sold only through travel agents. Don't always assume that you can get the best deal by booking everything yourself.**

Each year consumers are stranded or lose their money when packagers—even large ones with excellent reputations—go out of business. How can you protect yourself? First, always pay with a credit card; if you have a problem, your credit-card company may help you resolve it. Second, buy trip insurance that covers default. Third, choose a company that belongs to the United States Tour Operators Association, whose members must set aside funds to cover defaults. Finally, choose a company that also participates in the Tour Operator Program of the American Society of Travel Agents (ASTA), which will act as mediator in any disputes. You can also check on the tour operator's reputation among travelers by posting an inquiry on one of the Fodors.com forums.

Organizations

American Society of Travel Agents (ASTA ☎703/739–2782 or 800/965–2782 ⊕www. astanet.com). **United States Tour Operators Association** (USTOA ☎212/599–6599 ⊕www.ustoa.com).

❚ GUIDED TOURS

Guided tours are a good option when you don't want to do it all yourself. And not all guided tours are an if-it's-Tuesday-this-must-be-Belgium experience. A knowledgeable guide can take you places that you might never discover on your own, and you may be pushed to see more than you would have otherwise. Tours aren't for everyone, but they can be just the thing for trips to places where making travel arrangements is difficult or time-consuming (particularly when you don't

speak the language). Whenever you book a guided tour, find out what's included and what isn't. Also, in most cases prices in tour brochures don't include fees and taxes. And remember that you'll be expected to tip your guide (in cash) at the end of the tour.

BIKE & SEGWAY TOURS

Cycling is a wonderful way to get a different view of Paris and work off all those three-course "snacks." A number of companies organize bike tours around Paris and its environs (Versailles, Chantilly, and Fontainebleau); these tours always include bikes, helmets, and an English-speaking guide. Costs start at around €25 for a half day; reservations are recommended.

Fat Tire Bike Tours is the best-known anglophone group. In addition to a general orientation bike tour, they organize a nighttime cycling trip that includes a boat cruise on the Seine. Maison Roue Libre runs both city-center and countryside tours; request an English guide when you call. Paris à Vélo, C'est Sympa offers thematic tours; the Paris Wakes Up tour, for instance, is a unique spin through Montmartre at 6 AM.

Information Fat Tire Bike Tours (✉24 rue Edgar Faure, 15e ☎01–56–58–10–54 ⊕www. FatTireBikeToursParis.com). **Maison Roue Libre** (✉1 passage Mondétour, 1er ☎01–44–76–86–43 ⊕www.rouelibre.fr). **Paris à Vélo, C'est Sympa** (✉37 bd. Bourdon, 4e ☎01–48–87–60–01 ⊕www.parisvelosympa.com).

BOAT TOURS

There are several boat tour companies operating cruises of one hour to a half day of sightseeing (and even dining) on the Seine. See the In-Focus on the Seine for more information. Canauxrama organizes leisurely tours year-round in flat-bottom barges along the Canal St-Martin in east Paris. There are four daily departures; the trips last about 2½ hours and have live commentary in French and English. Reservations are required. Paris

Canal runs 2½-hour trips with live bilingual commentary between the Musée d'Orsay and the Parc de La Villette from April to mid-November. Reservations are required. Yachts de Paris organizes romantic 2½-hour "gourmand cruises" (for about €165) year-round. Yachts set off every evening at 7:45; you'll be served a three-course meal.

Information Canauxrama (☎01–42–39–15–00 ⊕www.canauxrama.com). **Paris Canal** (☎01–42–40–96–97 ⊕www.pariscanal.com). **Yachts de Paris** (☎01–44–54–14–70 ⊕www.yachtsdeparis.fr).

BUS TOURS

The two largest bus-tour operators are Cityrama, with 90-minute double-decker tours for €22, and Paris Vision, a two-hour luxury coach tour for €20. Both have headsets for commentary in more than a dozen languages. For a more intimate—albeit expensive—tour of the city, Paris Vision also runs minibus excursions with a multilingual tour operator from €55. Paris L'OpenTour gives tours in a London-style double-decker bus with English or French commentary over individual headsets. You can catch the bus at any of 50 pickup points; tickets cost €26 for one day, €29 for unlimited use for two days. Les Cars Rouges also has hop-on–hop-off tours on double-decker London-style buses, but with only 10 stops. A ticket good for two consecutive days costs €22.

For a more economical and commentary-free trip, take a regular Parisian bus for a mere €1.40 per ticket. A special Montmartrobus (€1.40) runs from the Anvers métro station to the top of Montmartre's winding streets. The RATP's Balabus goes from Gare du Lyon to the Grand Arche de la Défense, passing by dozens of major sights on the way. The Balabus runs from mid-April through September; tickets are €1.50 each, with one to three tickets required, depending on how far you travel.

Information Les Cars Rouge (☎01–53–95–39–53 ⊕www.carsrouges.com). **Cityrama** (✉4 pl. des Pyramides, 1ᵉʳ ☎01–44–55–61–00 ⊕www.ecityrama.com). **Paris L'OpenTour** (☎01–42–66–56–56 ⊕www.paris-opentour.com). **Paris Vision** (✉214 rue de Rivoli, 1ᵉʳ ☎01–42–60–30–01 ⊕www.parisvision.com). **RATP** (☎08–92–68–41–14 €0.35 per minute ⊕www.ratp.fr).

MINIBUS TOURS

Paris Trip and Paris Major Limousine organize tours of Paris and environs by limousine, Mercedes, or minibus (for 4–15 passengers) for a minimum of four hours. Chauffeurs are bilingual. The price varies from €260 to €400.

Information Paris Major Limousine (✉6 pl. de la Madeleine, 8ᵉ ☎01–44–52–50–00 ⊕www.1st-limousine-services.com). **Paris Trip** (✉2 Cité de Pusy, 17ᵉ ☎01–56–79–05–23 ⊕www.paris-trip.com).

SPECIAL-INTEREST & WALKING TOURS

Has it been a while since Art History 101? Paris Muse can help guide you through the city's museums; with its staff of art historians (all native English-speakers) you can crack the Da Vinci code or gain a new understanding of hell in front of Rodin's sculpted gates. Rates run from €60 to €120, including museum admission.

If you'd like a bit of guidance flexing your own artistic muscles, catch a themed photography tour with Paris Photo Tours. Run by the transplanted Texan Linda Mathieu, these relaxed tours are perfect for first-time visitors and anyone hoping to improve their vacation photography abilities.

Sign up with Chic Shopping Paris to smoothly navigate the city's shopping scene. You can choose a set tour, such as Shabby Chic (vintage–secondhand places) or Made in France (unique French products), or ask for an itinerary tailor-made to your interests. Tours start at €100.

Edible Paris, the brainchild of food writer and Fodor's updater Rosa Jackson, is a customized itinerary service for food-oriented visitors. Submit a wish list of your interests and guidelines for your tastes, and you'll receive a personalized itinerary, maps, and restaurant reservations on request. Prices start around US$200. If you'd like a behind-the-scenes look at food in the capital, contact Culinary Concepts; Stephanie Curtis's tours will take you to Rungis, the gigantic professional food market on the outskirts of Paris, at €120 per person. The Rungis trip starts at 5 AM and needs to be booked a month in advance with a minimum of three people. Or try the bread, cheese, and wine walking tour for €120, which takes you into cheese and wine cellars and to the wood-burning ovens at the celebrated Poîlane bakery.

The team at Paris Walking Tours offers a wide selection of tours, from neighborhood visits to museum tours and theme tours such as Hemingway's Paris, and the Marais, Montmartre, and Latin Quarter itineraries. The guides are very knowledgeable, taking you into less trammeled streets and divulging interesting stories about even the most unprepossessing spots. A two-hour group tour costs €10. For a more intimate experience, Context Paris offers specialized in-depth tours of the city's art and architecture by English-speaking architects and art historians. Prices range from €30 per person for a two-hour general tour, to €60 pp for a three-hour Medieval Architecture tour; private tours range from €170 per group (maximum five people) for a two-hour Introductory Paris walk, to €1,100 for a four-hour gourmet lunch and history of French gastronomy tour.

Black Paris Tours offers tours exploring the places made famous by African-American musicians, writers, artists, and political exiles. Tours include a four- to five-hour walking-bus-métro tour (€90) that offers first-time visitors a city orientation and a primer on the history of African-Americans in Paris. For those interested in getting behind the scenes at the Château de Versailles, French Links has more than 150 fully customizable themed tours, including Jewish Paris, Normandy Beaches, and Champagne Houses, from $658 per half day. Secrets of Paris offers a Naughty Paris themed tour for ladies, with visits to female-friendly adult toy and racy lingerie boutiques, erotic art galleries, the city's sexiest cocktail bars, and recommendations for naughty cabarets and couples-only clubs.

A list of walking tours is also available from the Caisse Nationale des Monuments Historiques, in the weekly magazine *Pariscope*, and in *L'Officiel des Spectacles*, which lists walking tours under the heading *"Conférences"* (most are in French, unless otherwise noted). The magazines are available at the press kiosk.

Information **Black Paris Tours** (☏01–46–37–03–96 ⊕www.tomtmusic.com). **Caisse Nationale des Monuments Historiques** (✉Bureau des Visites/Conférences, Hôtel de Sully, 62 rue St-Antoine, 4ᵉ ☏01–44–61–21–70). **Chic Shopping Paris** (☏06–14–56–23–11 ⊕www.chicshoppingparis.com). **Context Paris** (☏06–13–09–67–11 ⊕www.contextparis.com). **Culinary Concepts** (✉10 rue Poussin, ☏01–45–27–09–09 stecurtis@aol.com). **Edible Paris** (⊕www.edible-paris.com). **French Links** (☏01–45–77–33–63 ⊕www.frenchlinks.com) **Paris Muse** (☏06–73–77–33–52 ⊕www.parismuse.com). **Paris Photo Tours** (☏01–44–75–83–80 ⊕http://parisphototours.com). **Paris Walking Tours** (☏01–48–09–21–40 ⊕www.paris-walks.com). **Secrets of Paris** (☏01–43–36–69–85 ⊕www.secretsofparis.com)

TRANSPORTATION

Addresses in Paris are fairly straight-forward: there's the number, the street name, and the zip code designating one of Paris's 20 *arrondissements* (districts); for instance, Paris 75010 (the last two digits, "10") indicates that the address is in the 10th. The large 16^e arrondissement has two numbers assigned to it: 75016 and 75116. For the layout of Paris's arrondissements, see the What's Where map in the *Experience* chapter.

The arrondissements are laid out in a spiral, beginning from the area around the Louvre (1er arrondissement), then moving clockwise through the Marais, the Quartier Latin, St-Germain, and then out from the city center to the outskirts to Ménilmontant/Père-Lachaise (20e arrondissement). Occasionally you may see an address with a number plus *bis*—for instance, 20 bis, rue Vavin. This indicates the next entrance or door down from 20 rue Vavin. Note that in France you enter a building on the ground floor, or *rez-de-chaussée* (RC or 0), and go up one floor to the first floor, or *premier étage*. General address terms used in this book are *av.* (avenue), *bd.* (boulevard), *carrefour* (crossway), *cours* (promenade), *passage* (passageway), *pl.* (place), *quai* (quay/wharf/pier), *rue* (street), and *sq.* (square).

■ BY AIR

Flying time to Paris is 7 hours from New York, 9½ hours from Chicago, and 11 hours from Los Angeles. Flying time from London to Paris is 1½ hours.

The French are notoriously stringent about security, particularly for international flights. Don't be surprised by the armed security officers patrolling the airports, and be prepared for very long check-in lines. Peak travel times in France are between mid-July and September, during the Christmas–New Year's holi-

NAVIGATING PARIS

Paris is a walker's city, but public transportation is excellent when your feet get tired. The métro and bus systems are extensive and easy to use.

There are many landmarks in Paris to orient yourself—churches, the Opéra, the Eiffel Tower, etc. Choose one near your hotel, for example, and if you get lost, it'll be easy to get back on track.

As with any city that's not laid out in a numbered grid, it can be confusing to find what you're looking for—especially in a foreign language; don't hesitate to ask for help. Most people are happy to give assistance, especially if you try out some French (like bonjour).

days in late December and early January, and during the February school break. During these periods airports are especially crowded, so allow plenty of extra time. Never leave your baggage unattended, even for a moment. Unattended baggage is considered a security risk and may be destroyed.

Airline and Airport Links.com (⊕www. airlineandairportlinks.com) has links to many of the world's airlines and airports.

Airline Security Issues Transportation Security Administration (⊕www.tsa.gov) has answers for almost every question that might come up.

AIRPORTS

The major airports are Charles de Gaulle (CDG, also known as Roissy), 26 km (16 mi) northeast of Paris, and Orly (ORY), 16 km (10 mi) south of Paris. Both are easily accessible from Paris. Whether you take a car or bus to travel from Paris to the airport on your departure, always allot an extra hour because of the often horrendous traffic tie-ups in the airports themselves (especially in peak sea-

GETTING STARTED / BOOKING YOUR TRIP / **TRANSPORTATION** / ON THE GROUND

sons and at peak hours): at the airports, you'll often need to take the interairport buses to shuttle you from one terminal to another, and if this bus is held up because of traffic (often the case), serious nail biting can result.

Airport Information **Charles de Gaulle/ Roissy** (☎01–48–62–22–80 in English ⊕www.adp.fr). **Orly** (☎01–49–75–15–15 ⊕www.adp.fr).

GROUND TRANSPORTATION

By bus from CDG/Roissy: Roissybus, operated by the RATP (Paris Transit Authority), runs between Charles de Gaulle and the Opéra every 20 minutes from 6 AM to 11 PM; the cost is €8.60. The trip takes about 45 minutes in regular traffic, about 90 minutes in rush-hour traffic.

By shuttle from CDG/Roissy: The Air France shuttle service is a comfortable option to get to and from the city—you don't need to have flown the carrier to use it. Line 2 goes from the airport to Paris's Charles de Gaulle Etoile and Porte Maillot from 5:45 AM to 11 PM. It leaves every 15 minutes and costs €13, which you can pay on board. Passengers arriving in Terminal 1 need to take Exit 34; Terminals 2A, 2B, and 2D, Exit 6; Terminal 2C, Exit 5, Terminals 2E and 2F, Exit 3. Line 4 goes to Montparnasse and the Gare de Lyon from 7 AM to 9 PM. Buses run every 30 minutes and cost €13. Passengers arriving in Terminal 1 need to look for Exit 34, Terminals 2A and 2C need to take Exit C2, Terminals 2B and 2D, Exit B1, and Terminals 2E and 2F, Exit 3.

A number of van services serve both Charles de Gaulle and Orly airports. Prices are set so there are no surprises even if traffic is a snail-pace nightmare. To make a reservation, call or fax your flight details at least one week in advance to the shuttle company and an air-conditioned van with a bilingual chauffeur will be waiting for you upon your arrival. Confirm the day before. These vans sometimes pick up more than one party, though, so you may have to share the shuttle with other passengers. Likewise, when taking people to the airport these shuttles usually pick up a couple of groups of passengers. This adds at least 20 minutes to the trip.

By taxi from CDG/Roissy: Taxis are generally the least desirable mode of transportation into the city. If you're traveling at peak hours, journey times (and prices) are unpredictable. At best, the journey takes 30 minutes, but it can be as long as one hour.

By train from CDG/Roissy: The least expensive way to get into Paris from CDG is the RER-B line, the suburban express train, which runs from 5 AM to 11:30 PM daily. Each terminal has an exit where the free RER shuttle bus (a white-and-yellow bus with the letters ADP in gray) passes by every 7–15 minutes to take you on the short ride to the nearby RER station: at Terminals 2A and 2C, it's Exit 8; at Terminals 2B and 2D, Exit 6; at Terminal 2E, Exit 2.06; and at Terminal 2F, Exit 2.08. Or you can walk easily from many terminals to the train station—just look for the signs. Trains to central Paris (Les Halles, St-Michel, Luxembourg) depart every 15 minutes. The fare (including métro connection) is €8.30, and journey time is about 45 minutes.

By bus from Orly: Air France buses run from Orly to Les Invalides and Montparnasse; these run every 15 minutes from 6 AM to 11 PM. (You need not have flown on Air France to use this service.) The fare is €9, and journey time is between 30 and 45 minutes, depending on traffic. To find the bus, take Exit K if you've arrived in Orly South, or Exit D from Orly West. RATP's Orlybus is yet another option; buses leave every 15 minutes for the Denfert-Rochereau métro station in Montparnasse; the cost is €6.10. For a cheaper bus ride, take Jet Bus, which shuttles you from the airport to Villejuif Louis Aragon station, on métro line 7, for under €5.80. It operates daily from 6 AM to 10 PM; at

Orly South look for Exit H, quai 2; from Orly West head for Exit C. The downside is that the Villejuif Louis Aragon station is far from the city center.

By train from Orly: The cheapest way to get into Paris is to take the RER-C to station Pont de Rungis–Aéroport d'Orly, and then catch the free shuttle bus from the terminal to the train station. Trains to Paris leave every 15 minutes. Passengers arriving in either the South or West Terminal need to use Exit G. The fare is €5.95, and journey time is about 35 minutes. Another slightly faster option is to take RATP's monorail service, Orlyval, which runs between the Antony RER-B station and Orly Airport daily every four to eight minutes from 6 AM to 11 PM. Passengers arriving in the South Terminal should use Exit K; take Exit W if you've arrived in the West Terminal. The fare to downtown Paris is €9.30 and includes the RER transfer.

TRANSFERS BETWEEN AIRPORTS

To transfer between Paris's airports, there are several options. See the "By Train" options above: the RER-B travels from CDG to Orly with Paris in the middle, so to transfer, just stay on. Travel time is about 50–70 minutes and costs €17.90. The Air France Bus line 3 also runs between the airports for €16 one way, every 30 minutes, with about 50 minutes travel time. Taxis are available but expensive: from €60 to €80, depending on traffic.

Contacts Air France Bus (☎08-92-35-08-20 recorded information in English, €0.34 per minute ⊕www.cars-airfrance.com). **Airport Connection** (☎01-43-65-55-55 🖷01-43-65-55-57 ⊕www.airport-connection.com). **Paris Airports Services** (☎01-55-98-10-80 🖷01-55-98-10-89 ⊕www.parisairportservice.com). **RATP (including Roissybus, Orlybus, Orlyval)** (☎08-92-68-77-14, €0.34 per minute ⊕www.ratp.com).

TRAVEL TO CENTRAL PARIS.		
From	Orly	CDG
Taxi	20 mins–45 mins; €30–€50	45 mins–75 mins; €40–€70
Bus	30 mins–45 mins; €5.80–€9	45 mins–90 mins; €8.60–€13
Airport Shuttle	45 mins–90 mins; €22–€45	1 hrs–2 hrs; €22–€45
RER	25 mins–40 mins; €9.10	45 mins–1 hrs; €8.10

FLIGHTS

As one of the premier destinations in the world, Paris is serviced by a great many international carriers and a surprisingly large number of U.S.-based airlines. Air France (which partners with Delta) is the French flag carrier and offers numerous direct flights (often several per day) between Paris's Charles de Gaulle Airport and New York City's JFK Airport; Newark, New Jersey; Washington's Dulles Airport; and the cities of Boston, Atlanta, Cincinnati, Miami, Chicago, Houston, San Francisco, Los Angeles, Toronto, Montréal, and Mexico City. Most other North American cities are served through Air France partnerships with Delta and Continental Airlines. American-based carriers are usually less expensive but offer, on the whole, fewer nonstop direct flights. United Airlines has nonstop flights to Paris from Chicago, Denver, Los Angeles, Miami, Philadelphia, Washington, and San Francisco. American Airlines offers daily nonstop flights to Paris's Charles de Gaulle Airport from numerous cities, including New York City's JFK, Miami, Chicago, and Dallas/Fort Worth. Northwest has a daily departure to Paris from its hub in Detroit. In Canada, Air France and Air Canada are the leading choices for departures from Toronto and Montréal; in peak season departures are often daily. The relatively new carrier Zoom offers discount flights from Toronto and Montréal twice weekly. From London,

Air France, British Airways, and British Midland are the leading carriers, with up to 15 flights daily in peak season. In addition, direct routes link Manchester, Edinburgh, and Southampton with Paris. Ryanair, easyJet, and BMI Baby offer direct service from Paris to Dublin, London, Glasgow, Amsterdam, Cardiff, and Brussels, to name just a few. Tickets are available on the Web only and need to be booked well in advance to get the best prices—a one-way ticket from Paris to Dublin costs a mere €30, for example.

Airline Contacts Air Canada (☎888/247–2262 in U.S. and Canada, 00–800–8712–7786 in France ⊕www.aircanada.com). **Air France** (☎800/237–2747 in U.S., 08–25–86–48–64 ⊕www.airfrance.com). **American Airlines** (☎800/433–7300, 01–55–17–43–41 in Paris, 08–10–87–28–72 elsewhere in France ⊕www.aa.com). **British Airways** (☎800/247–9297 in U.S., 08–25–82–54–00 in France ⊕www.britishairways.com). **Continental Airlines** (☎800/523–3273 for U.S. and Mexico reservations, 800/231–0856 for international reservations, 01–71–23–03–35 in France ⊕www.continental.com). **Delta Airlines** (☎800/221–1212 for U.S. reservations, 800/241–4141 for international reservations, 08–11–64–00–05 in France ⊕www.delta.com). **Northwest Airlines** (☎800/225–2525, 00–890–710–710 in France ⊕www.nwa.com). **United Airlines** (☎800/864–8331 for U.S. reservations, 800/538–2929 for international reservations, 08–10–72–72–72 in France ⊕www.united.com). **USAirways** (☎800/428–4322 for U.S. and Canada reservations, 800/622–1015 for international reservations, 08–10–63–22–22 in France ⊕www.usairways.com). **Zoom** (☎866/359–9666 in North America, 0800–213–266 in France ⊕www.flyzoom.com).

Discount Airlines BMI Baby (☎01–41–91–87–04 in France ⊕www.bmibaby.com). **easyJet** (☎08–26–10–26–11 in France ⊕www.easyjet.com). **Ryan Air** (☎08–92– 23–23–75 in France ⊕www.ryanair.com).

Within Europe Air France (☎0845/242–9242 in U.K., 08–25–86–48–64 in France ⊕www.airfrance.com). **British Airways**

(☎0870/850–9850 in U.K., 08–25–82–54–00 in France ⊕www.britishairways.com). **British Midland** (☎0870/607–0222 in U.K., 01–55–69–83–06 in France ⊕www.flybmi.com).

▌BY BOAT

Linking France and the United Kingdom, a boat or ferry trip across the Channel can range from 35 minutes (via hovercraft) to 95 minutes (via ferryboat). Trip length also depends on departure point: popular routes link Boulogne and Folkestone, Le Havre and Portsmouth, and, the most booked passage, Calais and Dover.

P&O European Ferries links Portsmouth and Dover, England, with Calais (75 minutes). P&O has up to three sailings a day. Seafrance operates up to 15 sailings a day from Dover to Calais; the crossing takes 70 or 90 minutes, depending on the ship.

The driving distance from Calais to Paris is 290 km (180 mi). The fastest routes to Paris from each port are via N43, A26, and A1 from Calais and the Channel Tunnel; and via N1 from Boulogne.

Information P&O European Ferries (☎0870/598–0333 ⊕www.poportsmouth.com). **Seafrance** (☎0870/443–1653 ⊕www.seafrance.net).

▌BY BUS

ARRIVING & DEPARTING PARIS

The excellent national train service in France means that long-distance bus service in the country is practically nonexistent; regional buses are found where train service is spotty. Local bus information to the rare rural areas where trains do not have access can be obtained from the SNCF *(see By Train, below)*.

The largest international operator is Eurolines France, whose main terminal is in the Parisian suburb of Bagnolet (a half-hour métro ride from central Paris, at the end of métro line 3). Eurolines runs international routes to more than 1,500 cities in Europe.

It's possible to take a bus (via ferry) to Paris from the United Kingdom; just be aware that what you save in money will almost certainly cost you in time—the bus trip takes about seven hours as opposed to the three it takes on the Eurostar train line (Victoria Station–Gare du Nord). In general, the price of a round-trip bus ticket is 50% less than that of a plane ticket and 25% less than that of a train ticket, so if you have the time and the energy, this is a good way to cut the cost of travel. Eurolines also offers a 15-day (€169–€329) or 30-day (€229–€439) pass if you're planning on doing the grand European tour. Ask about one of the Circle tours that depart from Paris (for example, via London, Amsterdam, then back to Paris again). Eurolines operates a service from London's Victoria Coach Station, via the Dover–Calais ferry, to Paris's Porte de Bagnolet. There's an 8 AM departure that arrives in Paris at 4 PM, a 10 AM departure that arrives at 7:30 PM, and the overnight trips at 8:30 PM, which arrives in Paris at 6:30 AM, and the 11 PM departure, which arrives at 8:15 AM. Fares are €60 round-trip (an under-25 youth pass is €45). Other Eurolines routes include Amsterdam (7 hours, €72), Barcelona (15 hours, €170), and Berlin (10 hours, €150). There are also international-only arrivals and departures from Avignon, Bordeaux, Lille, Lyon, Toulouse, and Tours.

Eurolines accepts all major credit cards but does not accept traveler's checks.

Reservations for an international bus trip are essential. Be sure to check the Eurolines Web site for special discounts or incentives. Avoid buying your ticket at the last minute, when prices are highest.

IN PARIS

With dedicated bus lanes now in place throughout the city—allowing buses and taxis to whiz past other traffic mired in tedious jams—taking the bus is an appealing option. Although nothing can beat the métro for speed, buses offer great city views, and the new ones are equipped with air-conditioning—a real perk on those sweltering August days.

Paris buses are green and white; route number and destination are marked in front, major stopping places along the sides. Brown bus shelters contain time-tables and route maps; note that buses must be hailed at these larger bus shelters, as they service multiple lines and routes. Smaller stops are designated simply by a pole bearing bus numbers.

More than 200 bus routes run throughout Paris, reaching virtually every nook and cranny of the city. On weekdays and Saturday, buses run every five minutes (as opposed to the 15- to 20-minute wait you'll have on Sunday and national holidays). One ticket will take you anywhere within the city; once you get off at any point, that ticket is no longer valid.

A map of the bus system is on the flip side of every métro map, in all métro stations, and at all bus stops. Maps are also found in each bus. A recorded message announces the name of the next stop. To get off, press one of the red buttons mounted on the silver poles that run the length of the bus, and the *arrêt demandé* (stop requested) light directly behind the driver will light up. Use the rear door to exit.

The Balabus, an orange-and-white public bus that runs between mid-April and September, gives an interesting 50-minute tour around the major sights. You can use your Paris-Visite, Carte Orange, or Mobilis pass *(⇨ by Métro)*, or one to three bus tickets, depending on how far you ride. The route runs from La Défense to the Gare de Lyon.

The RATP has also introduced aboveground tram lines: two (T-1 and T-2) operate in the suburbs, and the new T-3 tram, which connects the 13e, 14e, and 15e arrondissements, running from the Porte d'Ivry (Chinatown) to the Parc Mont-souris, Porte d'Orléans, and the Paris Expo–Porte de Versailles. Trams take the same tickets as buses and the métro, with one ticket good for the entire line.

Regular buses accept métro tickets. Your best bet is to buy a *carnet* of 10 tickets for €11.10 at any métro station, or you can buy a single ticket on board (exact change appreciated) for €1.50. If you have individual tickets, you should be prepared to punch your ticket in the red-and-gray machines at the entrance of the bus. You need to show (but not punch) weekly, monthly, and Paris-Visite/Mobilis tickets to the driver. Tickets can be bought on buses, in the métro, or in any bar–tabac store displaying the lime-green métro symbol above its street sign.

Most routes operate from 7 AM to 8:30 PM; some continue to midnight. After 8:30 PM you must either take the métro or one of the 35 Noctilien lines (indicated by a separate signal at bus stops). These bus lines operate every 10–60 minutes (12:30 AM–5:30 AM) between Châtelet, major train stations, and various nearby suburbs; they can be stopped by hailing them at any point on their route. The Noctilien uses the same tickets as the métro and regular bus.

Bus Information Eurolines (☎08–92–89–90–91 in France, 08705–808080 in U.K. ⊕www.eurolines.fr or www.eurolines-pass.com). **Noctilien** (⊕www.noctilien.fr). **RATP** (☎08–92–68–77–14 €0.35 per minute ⊕www.ratp.com).

▌ BY CAR

We can't say it too many times: unless you have a special, compelling reason, do yourself a favor and **avoid driving in Paris.** But if you've decided to do it anyway, there are some things to know. France's roads are classified into five types; they are numbered and have letter prefixes: *A* (*autoroute,* expressways), *N* (*route nationale*), *D* (*route départmentale*), and the smaller *C* or *V.* There are excellent links

between Paris and most French cities. When trying to get around Ile-de-France, it's often difficult to avoid Paris—just try to steer clear of rush hours (7–9:30 and 4:30–7:30). A *péage* (toll) must be paid on most expressways outside Ile-de-France: the rate varies but can be steep. Certain booths allow you to pay with a credit card.

The major ring road encircling Paris is called the *périphérique,* with the *périphérique intérieur* going counterclockwise around the city, and the *périphérique extérieur,* or the outside ring, going clockwise. Up to five lanes wide, the périphérique is a major highway from which *portes* (gates) connect Paris to the major highways of France. The names of these highways function on the same principle as the métro, with the final destination as the determining point in the direction you must take.

Heading north, look for Porte de la Chapelle (direction Lille and Charles de Gaulle Airport); east, for Porte de Bagnolet (direction Metz and Nancy); south, for Porte d'Orléans (direction Lyon and Bordeaux); and west, for Porte d'Auteuil (direction Rouen and Chartres) or Porte de St-Cloud.

GASOLINE

There are gas stations throughout the city, but they can be difficult to spot; you'll often find them in the underground tunnels that cross the city and in larger parking garages. Gas is expensive and prices vary enormously, ranging from about €1.35 to €1.70 per liter. If you're on your way out of Paris, save money by waiting until you've left the city to fill up. All gas stations accept credit cards.

PARKING

Finding parking in Paris is tough. Both meters and parking-ticket machines use parking cards (*cartes de stationnements*), which you can purchase at any café posting the red TABAC sign; they're sold in three denominations: €10, €20, or €30. Parking in the capital runs €2 per hour. Insert your card into the nearest meter, choose the approximate amount of time you expect to stay, and receive a green receipt. Place it on the dashboard on the passenger side; make sure the receipt's clearly visible to the meter patrol. Parking tickets are expensive, and there's no shortage of blue-uniformed parking police. Parking lots, indicated by a blue sign with a white P, are usually underground and are generally expensive (charging €1.20 to €3 per hour, or €9 to €23 per day). One bright spot: you can park for free on Sunday, national holidays, and in certain residential areas in August. Parking meters with yellow circles indicate the free parking zone during August.

ROAD CONDITIONS

Chaotic traffic is a way of life in Paris. Some streets in the city center can seem impossibly narrow; street signs are often hard to spot; jaded city drivers often make erratic, last-minute maneuvers without signaling; and motorcycles often weave around traffic. Priority is given to drivers coming from the right, so watch for drivers barreling out of small streets on your right. Traffic lights are placed to the left and right of crosswalks, not above, so they may be blocked from your view by vehicles ahead of you.

There are a few major roundabouts at the most congested intersections, notably at *L'Etoile* (around the Arc de Triomphe), the Place de la Bastille, and the Place de la Concorde. Watch oncoming cars carefully and stick to the outer lane to make your exit. The *périphériques* (ring roads) are generally easier to use, and the quais that parallel the Seine can be a downright pleasure to drive when there's no traffic. Electronic signs on the périphériques and highways post traffic conditions: *fluide* (clear) or *bouchon* (jammed).

Some important traffic terms and signs to note: *sortie* (exit), *sens unique* (one way), *stationnement interdite* (no parking), *impasse* (dead end). Blue rectangular signs indicate a highway; triangles carry illustrations of a particular traffic hazard; speed limits are indicated in a circle, with the maximum speed circled in red.

ROADSIDE EMERGENCIES

If your car breaks down on an expressway, pull your car as far off the road as quickly as possible, set your emergency indicators, and, if possible, take the emergency triangle from the car's trunk and put it at least 30 yards behind your car to warn oncoming traffic; then go to a roadside emergency telephone. These phones put you in direct contact with the police, automatically indicating your exact location, and are available every 3 km (2 mi). If you have a breakdown anywhere else, find the nearest garage or contact the police. There are also 24-hour assistance hotlines valid throughout France (available through rental agencies and supplied to you when you rent the car), but do not hesitate to call the police in case of any roadside emergency, for they are quick and reliable and the phone call is free.

Emergency Services Police (☎ 17).

RULES OF THE ROAD

You must always carry vehicle registration documents and your personal identification. The French police are entitled to stop you at will to verify your ID and your car—such spot checks are frequent, especially at peak holiday times. In France you drive on the right and give priority to drivers coming from the right (this rule is called *priorité à droite*).

You must wear your seat belt, and children under 12 may not travel in the front seat. Children under 10 need to be in a car seat or specific child-restraining device, always in the back seat. Speed limits are designated by the type of road you're driving on: 130 kph (80 mph) on expressways (*autoroutes*), 110 kph (70 mph) on divided highways (*routes nationales*), 90 kph (55 mph) on other roads (*routes*), 50 kph (30 mph) in cities and towns (*villes et villages*). These limits are reduced by 10 kph (6 mph) in rainy, snowy, and foggy conditions. Drivers are expected to know these limits, so signs are generally posted only when there are exceptions to these rules. Right-hand turns are not allowed on a red light.

The use of handheld cellular phones while driving is forbidden; the penalty is a €60 fine. Alcohol laws have become quite tough—a 0.05% blood alcohol limit (a lower limit than in the United States).

▌ BY MÉTRO

Taking the métro is the most efficient way to get around Paris. Métro stations are recognizable either by a large yellow *M* within a circle or by the distinctive curly green Art Nouveau railings and archway bearing the full title (Métropolitain). *See the Métro map, on the inside back cover of this book.*

Fourteen métro and five RER (Réseau Express Régional, or the Regional Express Network) lines crisscross Paris and the suburbs, and you are seldom more than 500 yards from the nearest station. The métro network connects at several points in Paris with the RER, the commuter trains that go from the city center to the suburbs. RER trains crossing Paris on their way from suburb to suburb can be great time-savers, because they make only a few stops in the city (you can use the same tickets for the métro and the RER within Paris).

It's essential to know the name of the last station on the line you take, as this name appears on all signs. A connection (you can make as many as you like on one ticket) is called a *correspondance*. At junction stations, illuminated orange signs bearing the name of the line terminus appear over the correct corridors for each correspondance. Illuminated blue signs marked *sortie* indicate the station exit. Note that tickets are valid only inside the gates, or *limites*.

Access to métro and RER platforms is through an automatic ticket barrier. Slide your ticket in and pick it up as it pops out. **Keep your ticket during your journey**; you'll need it to leave the RER system and in case you run into any green-clad ticket inspectors, who will impose a hefty fine if you can't produce your ticket.

Métro service starts at 5:30 AM and continues until 1 AM Sunday through Thursday, and until 2 AM on Friday and Saturday, when the last train on each line reaches its terminus. Some lines and stations in Paris are a bit risky at night, in particular lines 2 and 13, and the mazelike stations at Les Halles and République. But in general, the métro is relatively safe throughout, providing you don't travel alone late at night or walk around with your wallet hanging out of your back pocket.

All métro tickets and passes are valid not only for the métro but also for all RER, tram, and bus travel within Paris. Métro tickets cost €1.50 each; a *carnet* (10 tickets for €11.10) is a better value. The *Carte Navigo* replaced the weekly Carte Orange in March 2008, and is available only to residents or those who can prove they work in the region. Visitors can still purchase the one-day (Mobilis) and two- to five-day (Paris-Visite) tickets for unlimited travel on the entire RATP (Paris transit authority) network: métro, RER, bus, tram, funicular (Montmartre), and Noctilien (night bus). The Mobilis and Paris-Visite passes are valid starting any day of the week. Paris-Visite also gives you discounts on a few museums and attractions, too. Mobilis tickets cost €5.60. Paris-Visite is €8.50 (one day), €14 (two days), €19 (three days), and €27.50 (five days) for Paris only.

TICKET/PASS	PRICE
Single Fare	€1.50
Daily Mobilis Pass	€5.60

TICKET/ PASS	PRICE
Paris Visit One-Day Pass	€8.50
10-Ticket Carnet	€11.10
Paris Visit Two-Day Pass	€14
Paris Visit Three-Day Pass	€19
Paris Visit Five-Day Pass	€27.50

Métro Information Any RATP window in the Metro sells tickets and provides maps, but if you're looking to purchase RATP souvenirs, you can find them at the main office near the Gare de Lyon. **RATP** (⊠54 quai de la Rapée, 12ᵉ ⊕ www.ratp.fr), open daily 9–5.

▌ BY TAXI

Taxi rates are based on location and time. Daytime rates, denoted A (7 AM–7 PM), within Paris are €0.82 per kilometer (½ mi), and nighttime rates, B, are €1.10 per kilometer. Suburban zones and airports, C, are €1.33 per kilometer. There's a basic hire charge of €2.10 for all rides, a €1 supplement per piece of luggage, and a €0.70 supplement if you're picked up at an SNCF (the French rail system) station. Waiting time is charged at €26.28 per hour. The easiest way to get a taxi is to ask your hotel or a restaurant to call one for you, or go to the nearest taxi stand (you can find one every couple of blocks)—they're marked by a square, dark blue sign with a white T in the middle. ▌TIP➔ **People waiting for cabs often form a line but will jump at any available taxi; be firm and don't let people cut in front of you.** A taxi is available when the entire sign is lighted up, and taken when just the little bulb at the bottom of the sign is lighted. They'll accept a fourth passenger for an average supplement of €2.75. It's

customary to tip the driver about 10% (⇨*Tipping*).

Taxi Companies Airport Taxi (☎01–48–40–17–17). **Taxis Bleus** (☎0891–70–10–10). **Taxi G7** (☎01–47–39–47–39).

▌ BY TRAIN

The SNCF, France's rail system, is fast, punctual, comfortable, and comprehensive. There are various options: local trains, overnight trains with sleeping accommodations, and the high-speed TGV, or Trains à Grande Vitesse (averaging 255 kph [160 mph] on the Lyon/southeast line and 300 kph [190 mph] on the Lille and Bordeaux/southwest lines).

The TGVs, the fastest way to get around the country, operate between Paris and Lille/Calais, Paris and Lyon/Switzerland/Provence, Paris and Angers/Nantes, Paris and Tours/Poitiers/Bordeaux, Paris and Brussels, and Paris and Amsterdam. As with other mainline trains, a small supplement may be assessed at peak hours.

Paris has six international rail stations: Gare du Nord (northern France, northern Europe, and England via Calais or Boulogne); Gare St-Lazare (Normandy, England via Dieppe); Gare de l'Est (Strasbourg, Luxembourg, Basel, and central Europe); Gare de Lyon (Lyon, Marseille, Provence, Geneva, Italy); Gare d'Austerlitz (Loire Valley, southwest France, Spain); and Gare Montparnasse (Brittany, Aquitaine, TGV-Atlantique service to the west and south of France, Spain). Until 2005 there were smoking and no-smoking cars on the trains, including the TGVs, but smoking is now prohibited on all trains in France.

There are two classes of train service in France: *première* (first class) or *deuxième* (second class). First-class seats have 50% more legroom and nicer upholstery than those in second class, and the first-class cars tend to be quieter. First-class seats on the TGV have computer connections.

First-class fares are nearly twice as much as those for second-class seats.

Fares are cheaper if you avoid traveling at peak times (around holidays and weekends), purchase tickets at least 15 days in advance (look for the *billet Prem's*), or find your destination among the last-minute offers online every Tuesday.

You can call for train information or reserve tickets in any Paris station, irrespective of destination, and you can access the multilingual computerized schedule information network at any Paris station. You can also make reservations and buy your ticket while at the computer. Go to the Grandes Lignes counter for travel within France and to the Billets Internationaux desk if you're heading out of the country. Note that calling the SNCF's 08 number costs €0.35 per minute; to save this cost, either go to the nearest station and make the reservations in person or visit the SNCF Web site, ⊕ www.sncf.fr.

If you plan to travel outside Paris by train, consider purchasing a France Rail Pass, which allows three days of unlimited train travel in a one-month period. If you travel solo, first class will run you $304 and second class is $258; you can add up to six days on this pass for $44 a day for first class, $37 a day for second class. For two people traveling together on a Saver Pass, the cost is $259, and in second class it's $222; additional days (up to six) cost $37 each for first class, $31 each for second class. Other options include the France Rail 'n Drive Pass (combining rail and rental car).

France is one of 17 countries in which you can use EurailPasses, which provide unlimited first-class rail travel in all the participating countries for the duration of the pass. If you plan to rack up the miles, get a standard pass. These are available for 15 days ($744), 21 days ($965), one month ($1,198), two months ($1,691), and three months ($2,087). If your travels will be more limited, the Eurail Selectpass gives you first-class travel over a two-month period in three to five bordering countries in 22 Eurail network countries. The Selectpass starts at $471 for five days of travel within three countries. Another option is the 2-Country Pass, which covers rail travel in and between pairs of bordering countries over a two-month period. Unlike most Eurail passes, 2-Country Passes are available for first- or second-class travel. Costs begin at $371 (first class) and $296 (second class) for four days of travel; up to six extra days can be purchased.

In addition to standard EurailPasses, there are the Eurail Youthpass (for those under age 26, with second-class travel), the Eurail Saver Pass (which gives a discount for two or more people traveling together), the Eurail Flexipass (which allows a certain number of travel days within a set period), and the Euraildrive Pass (train and rental car).

■ TIP➔ **Remember that you must purchase your Eurail passes at home before leaving for France. You can purchase Eurail passes through the Eurail Web site as well as through travel agents.**

Another option is to purchase one of the discount rail passes available for sale only in France from SNCF.

When traveling together, two people (who don't have to be a couple) can save money with the Prix Découverte à Deux. You'll get a 25% discount during périodes bleus (blue periods: weekdays and periods not on or near any holidays). Note that you have to be with the person you said you would be traveling with.

Reduced fares are available if you're a senior citizen (over 60), for children under 12, and up to four accompanying adults, and if you're under 26.

If you purchase an individual ticket from SNCF in France and you're under 26, you automatically get a 25% reduction (a valid ID such as an ISIC card or your passport is necessary). If you're going to be using the train quite a bit during your stay in France and if you're under 26, consider buying the Carte 12–25 (€49), which offers unlimited 50% reductions for one year (provided that there's space available at that price; otherwise you'll just get the standard 25% discount).

If you don't benefit from any of these reductions and you plan on traveling at least 200 km (132 mi) round-trip and don't mind staying over a Saturday night, look into the Prix Découverte Séjour. This ticket gives you a 25% reduction.

■ TIP➜ A rail pass does not guarantee you a seat on the train you wish to ride. You need to book seats ahead even if you have a pass.

Seat reservations are required on TGVs and are a good idea on trains that may be crowded—particularly in summer and during holidays on popular routes. You also need a reservation for sleeping accommodations.

THE CHANNEL TUNNEL

Short of flying, taking the Channel Tunnel is the fastest way to cross the English Channel: 35 minutes from Folkestone to Calais, 60 minutes from motorway to motorway, or 2 hours and 15 minutes from London's St. Pancras Station to Paris's Gare du Nord. The Belgian border is just a short drive northeast of Calais. High-speed Eurostar trains use the same tunnels to connect London's St. Pancras Station directly with Midi Station in Brussels in around 2 hours.

There's a vast range of prices for Eurostar—round-trip tickets range from €415 for first class (with access to the Philippe Starck–designed Première Class lounge) to €70 for second class, depending on when you travel. It's a good idea to make a reservation if you're traveling with your car on a Chunnel train; cars without reservations, if they can get on at all, are charged 20% extra.

British Rail also has four daily departures from London's Victoria Station, all link-ing with the Dover–Calais/Boulogne ferry services through to Paris. There's also an overnight service on the Newhaven–Dieppe ferry. Journey time is about eight hours. Credit-card bookings are accepted by phone or in person at a British Rail Travel Centre.

Information Rail Europe (☎800/257–2887 in U.S. ⊕ www.raileurope.com). **SNCF** (✉88 rue St-Lazare, Paris ☎08–92–35–35–35 €0.35 per minute ⊕ www.Voyages-sncf.fr).

Channel Tunnel Car Transport Eurotunnel (☎0870/535–3535 in U.K., 070/223210 in Belgium, 03–21–00–61–00 in France ⊕ www. eurotunnel.com).

French Motorail/Rail Europe (☎0870/241–5415 ⊕ www.raileurope.co.uk/frenchmotorail).

Channel Tunnel Passenger Service BritRail Travel (☎866/274–8724 in U.S. ⊕ www. britrail.com).

Eurostar (☎08–36–35–35–39 in France, 0870/518–6186, in U.K. ⊕ www.eurostar. co.uk). **Rail Europe** (☎888/382–7245 in U.S., 0870/584–8848 in U.K. inquiries and credit-card bookings ⊕ www.raileurope.com).

GETTING STARTED / BOOKING YOUR TRIP / **TRANSPORTATION** / ON THE GROUND

ON THE GROUND

▮ COMMUNICATIONS

INTERNET

If you use a major Internet provider, getting online in Paris shouldn't be difficult. Call your Internet provider to get the local access number in Paris. Many hotels have business services with Internet access, in-room modem lines, or high-speed wireless access. ▮TIP➜ **You will, however, need an adapter for your computer for the European-style plugs**. If you're traveling with a laptop, carry a spare battery and adapter. Never plug your computer into any socket before asking about surge protection.

A few of the more conveniently located Internet cafés are listed below.

Access Numbers in Paris AOL (☎08–60–91–99–99). **Compuserve** (☎08–60–00–73–10).

Cybercafes (🌐www.cybercafes.com) lists more than 4,000 Internet cafés worldwide. **La Baguenaude** (✉30 rue Grande-Truanderie, 1ᵉʳ, Beaubourg/Les Halles ☎01–40–26–27–74 🌐http://perso.wanadoo.fr/baguenaude. cafe). **Cybersquare** (✉1 pl. République, 3ᵉ, République ☎01–48–87–82–36 🌐www.cyber-square-paris.com). **Milk** (✉53 rue de la Harpe, 5ᵉ, Quartier Latin ☎01–44–07–38–89 🌐 www. milklub.com). **Sputnik** (✉14 rue Butte-aux-Cailles, 13ᵉ, Les Gobelins ☎01–45–65–19–82).

PHONES

The good news is that you can now make a direct-dial telephone call from virtually any point on earth. The bad news? You can't always do so cheaply. Calling from a hotel is almost always the most expensive option; hotels usually add huge surcharges to all calls, particularly international ones. In some countries you can phone from call centers or even the post office. Calling cards usually keep costs to a minimum, but only if you purchase them locally. And then there are mobile phones (➪*below*), which are sometimes

more prevalent—particularly in the developing world—than landlines; as expensive as mobile phone calls can be, they are still usually a much cheaper option than calling from your hotel.

The country code for France is 33. The first two digits of French numbers are a prefix determined by zone: Paris and Ile-de-France, 01; the northwest, 02; the northeast, 03; the southeast, 04; and the southwest, 05. Pay close attention to numbers beginning with 08. Calls that begin with 08 followed by 00 are toll-free, but calls that begin with 08 followed by 36—like the information lines for the SNCF, for example—cost €0.35 per minute. Numbers that begin with 06 are reserved for cell phones.

Note that when dialing France from abroad, you should drop the initial 0 from the telephone number (all numbers listed in this book include the initial 0, which is used for calling numbers *from within* France). To call a telephone number in Paris from the United States, dial 011–33 plus the phone number, but minus the initial 0 listed for the specific number in Paris. In other words, the local number for the Louvre is 01–40–20–51–51. To call this number from New York City, dial 011–33–1–40–20–51–51. To call this number from within Paris, dial 01–40–20–51–51. To call France from the United Kingdom, dial 00–33, then dial the number in France minus the initial 0 of the specific number.

CALLING CARDS

French pay phones are operated by *télécartes* (phone cards), which you can buy from post offices, tabacs, magazine kiosks, and any métro station. The ones you insert into pay phones have a "puce" microchip—a small silver square—that you can see on the card. There are as many phone cards these days as bakeries, so to be safe, request the *télécarte inter-*

national, which, despite its name, allows you to make either local or international calls and offers greatly reduced rates. Instructions are in English, and the cost is €9 for 60 units and €18 for 120 units. You may also request the simple *télécarte,* which allows you to make calls in France (the cost is €10 for 50 units, €18 for 120 units). You can use your credit card in much the same way as a télécarte, but there's a minimum €20 charge. You have 30 days after the first call on your credit card to use the €20 credit.

There are also international calling cards available that work on any phone (including your hotel phone) because you dial a free number and punch in a code; these do not have the "puce" microchip. Telephone cards are sold that enable you to make long-distance and international calls from any phone. Don't hesitate to invest in one if you plan on making calls from your hotel, as hotels often accumulate service charges and also have the most expensive rates.

CALLING OUTSIDE FRANCE
Good news—telephone rates are actually decreasing in France because the France Telecom monopoly now has some stringent competition. As in most countries, the highest rates fall between 8 AM and 7 PM and average out to a hefty €0.22 per minute to the United States, Canada, and the closer European countries, including Germany and Great Britain. Rates are greatly reduced from 7 PM to 8 AM, costing an average of €0.10 per minute.

To make a direct international call out of France, dial 00 and wait for the tone; then dial the country code (1 for the United States and Canada, 44 for the United Kingdom, 61 for Australia, and 64 for New Zealand) and the area code (minus any initial 0) and number.

To call with the help of an operator, dial the toll-free number 08–00–99–00 plus the last two digits of the country code. Dial 08–00–99–00–11 for the United States and Canada, 08–00–99–00–44

for England, and 08–00–99–00–61 for Australia.

Access Codes **AT&T Direct** (☎08–00–99–00–11, 08–00–99–01–11, 800/222–0300 for information). **MCI WorldPhone** (☎08–00–99–00–19, 800/444–4444 for information). **Sprint International Access** (☎08–00–99–00–87, 800/793–1153 for information).

CALLING WITHIN FRANCE
For telephone information in France, you need to call one of the dozen or so six-digit renseignement numbers that begin with 118. Some of the better-known ones are 118–008 for the Pages Jaunes, or 118–711 for France Telecom. The number 118–247 is a bilingual option, run in partnership with the Paris tourism office. The average price for one of these calls is about €1.

Since all local numbers in Paris and the Ile-de-France begin with a 01, you must dial the full 10-digit number, including the initial 0. A local call costs €0.11 for every three minutes.

To call from region to region within France, dial the full 10-digit number, including the initial 0.

Public telephone booths can almost always be found in post offices, métro stations, bus stops, and in most cafés, as well as on the street.

MOBILE PHONES
If you have a multiband phone (some countries use different frequencies than what's used in the United States) and your service provider uses the world-standard GSM network (as do T-Mobile, Cingular, and Verizon), you can probably use your phone abroad. Roaming fees can be steep, however: 99¢ a minute is considered reasonable. And overseas you normally pay the toll charges for incoming calls. It's almost always cheaper to send a text message than to make a call, since text messages have a very low set fee (often less than 5¢).

If you just want to make local calls, consider buying a new SIM card (note that your provider may have to unlock your phone for you to use a different SIM card) and a prepaid service plan in the destination. You'll then have a local number and can make local calls at local rates. If your trip is extensive, you could also simply buy a new cell phone in your destination, as the initial cost will be offset over time.

■TIP➜ **If you travel internationally frequently, save one of your old mobile phones or buy a cheap one on the Internet; ask your cell phone company to unlock it for you, and take it with you as a travel phone, buying a new SIM card with pay-as-you-go service in each destination.**

Cell phones are called *portables* and most Parisians have one. British standard cell phones work in Paris, but for North Americans only triband phones work. If you'd like to rent a cell phone for your trip, reserve one at least four days before your departure, as most companies will ship it to you before you travel. Cellular Abroad rents cell phones packaged with prepaid SIM cards that give you a French cell-phone number and calling rates. Planetfone rents GSM phones, which can be used in more than 100 countries, but the per-minute rates are expensive.

Contacts Cellular Abroad (☏800/287–5072 ⊕www.cellularabroad.com). **Mobal** (☏888/888–9162 ⊕www.mobalrental.com) rents mobiles and sells GSM phones (starting at $49) that will operate in 140 countries. Per-call rates vary throughout the world. **Planet Fone** (☏888/988–4777 ⊕www.planetfone.com).

■ CUSTOMS & DUTIES

You're always allowed to bring goods of a certain value back home without having to pay any duty or import tax. But there's a limit on the amount of tobacco and liquor you can bring back duty-free, and some countries have separate limits for perfumes; for exact figures, check with your customs department. The values of so-called "duty-free" goods are

included in these amounts. When you shop abroad, save all your receipts, as customs inspectors may ask to see them as well as the items you purchased. If the total value of your goods is more than the duty-free limit, you'll have to pay a tax (most often a flat percentage) on the value of everything beyond that limit.

If you're coming from outside the European Union (EU), you may import the following duty-free: (1) 200 cigarettes or 100 cigarillos or 50 cigars or 250 grams of tobacco; (2) 2 liters of wine and, in addition, (a) 1 liter of alcohol over 22% volume (most spirits) or (b) 2 liters of alcohol under 22% volume (fortified or sparkling wine) or (c) 2 more liters of table wine; (3) 50 ml of perfume and 250 ml of toilet water; (4) 200 grams of coffee, 100 grams of tea; and (5) other goods to the value of about €182 (€91 for ages 14 and under).

If you're arriving from an EU country, you may be required to declare all goods and prove that anything over the standard limit is for personal consumption. But there is no limit or customs tariff imposed on goods carried within the EU except on tobacco (800 cigarettes, 200 cigars, 1 kg of tobacco) and alcohol (10 liters of spirits, 90 liters of wine, with a maximum of 60 liters of sparkling wine, 110 liters of beer).

Any amount of euros or foreign currency may be brought into France, but foreign currencies converted into euros may be reconverted into a foreign currency only up to the equivalent of €769.

Information in Paris Direction des Douanes (☏01–40–40–39–00 ⊕www.douane.gouv.fr).

U.S. Information U.S. Customs and Border Protection (⊕www.cbp.gov).

■ ELECTRICITY

The electrical current in Paris is 220 volts, 50 cycles alternating current (AC); wall outlets take continental-type plugs, with two round prongs.

Consider making a small investment in a universal adapter, which has several types of plugs in one lightweight, compact unit. Most laptops and mobile phone chargers are dual voltage (i.e., they operate equally well on 110 and 220 volts), so require only an adapter. These days the same is true of small appliances such as hair dryers. Always check labels and manufacturer instructions to be sure. Don't use 110-volt outlets marked FOR SHAVERS ONLY for high-wattage appliances such as hair dryers.

■ EMERGENCIES

The French National Health Care system has been organized to provide fully equipped, fully staffed hospitals within 30 minutes of every resident in Paris. A sign of a white cross within a rectangular blue box appears on all hospitals. This guidebook does not list the major Paris hospitals, as the French government prefers an emergency operator to make the judgment call and assign you the best and most convenient option for your emergency. Note that if you're able to walk into a hospital emergency room by yourself, you are often considered "low priority," and the wait can be interminable. So if time is of the essence, it's best to call the fire department (☎ 18); a fully trained team of paramedics will usually arrive within five minutes. You may also dial for a Samu ambulance (☎ 15); there's usually an English-speaking physician available who will help you assess the situation and either dispatch an ambulance immediately or advise you about your best course of action. Be sure to check with your insurance company before your trip to verify that you are covered for medical care in other countries.

In a less urgent situation, do what the French do and call SOS Doctor or SOS Dental services; like magic, in less than an hour a certified, experienced doctor or dentist arrives at the door, armed with an old leather doctor case filled with the essentials for diagnosis and treatment (at an average cost of €65). The doctor or dentist may or may not be bilingual but, at worst, will have a rudimentary understanding of English. This is a very helpful 24-hour service to use for common symptoms of benign illnesses that need to be treated quickly for comfort, such as high fever, toothache, or upset stomachs (which seem to have the unfortunate habit of announcing themselves late at night).

The American Hospital and the Hertford British Hospital both have 24-hour emergency hotlines with bilingual doctors and nurses who can provide advice. For small problems go to a pharmacy, marked by a green neon cross. Pharmacists are authorized to administer first aid and recommend over-the-counter drugs, and they can be very helpful in advising you in English or sending you to the nearest English-speaking pharmacist.

Call the police (☎ 17) if there has been a crime or an act of violence. On the street, some French phrases that may be needed in an emergency are *Au secours!* (Help!), *urgence* (emergency), *samu* (ambulance), *pompiers* (firemen), *poste de station* (police station), *médecin* (doctor), and *hôpital* (hospital).

A hotline of note is SOS Help for English-language crisis information, open daily 3 PM–11 PM.

Doctor & Dentist Referrals SOS Dentiste (☎01–43–37–51–00). **SOS Médecin** (☎01–47–07–77–77).

Foreign Embassies United States Consulate ⊠2 rue St-Florentin, 1er, Paris ☎01–43–12–22–22 in English ⊙Weekdays 9–1 Ⓜ Concorde.

General Emergency Contacts **Ambulance** (☎15). **Fire Department** (☎18). **Police** (☎17). These numbers are toll-free and can be dialed from any phone.

Hospitals & Clinics **The American Hospital** (✉63 bd. Victor-Hugo, Neuilly ☎01–46–41–25–25). **The Hertford British Hospital** (✉3 rue Barbès, Levallois-Perret ☎01–46–39–22–22).

Hotline **SOS Help** (☎01–46–21–46–46).

Pharmacies **Dhéry** (✉Galerie des Champs, 84 av. des Champs-Elysées, 8e ☎01–45–62–02–41) is open 24 hours. **Pharmacie des Arts** (✉106 bd. Montparnasse, 14e ☎01–43–35–44–88) is open daily until midnight. **Pharmacie Internationale** (✉5 pl. Pigalle, 9e ☎01–48–78–38–12) is open daily until midnight. **Pharmacie Matignon** (✉2 rue Jean-Mermoz, at Rond-Point de Champs-Elysées, 8e ☎01–45–62–79–16) is open daily until 2 AM.

HOLIDAYS

With 11 national holidays (*jours fer-iés*) and five weeks of paid vacation, the French have their share of repose. In May there's a holiday nearly every week, so be prepared for stores, banks, and museums to shut their doors for days at a time. If a holiday falls on a Tuesday or Thursday, many businesses *font le pont* (make the bridge) and close on that Monday or Friday as well. Some exchange booths in tourist areas, small grocery stores, restaurants, cafés, and bakeries usually remain open. Bastille Day (July 14) is observed in true French form. Celebrations begin on the evening of the 13th, when city firemen open the doors to their stations, often classed as historical monuments, to host their much-acclaimed all-night balls and finish the next day with the annual military parade and air show.

Note that these dates are for the calendar year 2009: January 1 (New Year's Day); April 12–13 (Easter Sunday/Monday); May 1 (Labor Day and Ascension); May 8 (VE Day); May 21–22 (Pentecost Sunday/Monday); July 14 (Bastille Day); August 15 (Assumption); November 1 (All Saints' Day); November 11 (Armistice); December 25 (Christmas).

▌ HOURS OF OPERATION

On weekdays banks are open generally 9–5 (note that the Banque de France closes at 3:30), and some banks are also open Saturday 9–5. In general, government offices and businesses are open 9–5. *See Mail, below, for post office hours.*

Most museums are closed one day a week—usually Monday or Tuesday—and on national holidays. Generally, museums and national monuments are open from 10 to 5 or 6. A few close for lunch (noon–2) and are open only in the afternoon on Sunday. Many of the large museums have one *nocturne* (nighttime) opening per week, when they are open until 9:30 or 10. Pharmacies are generally open Monday–Saturday 8:30–8. Nearby pharmacies that stay open late, for 24 hours, or Sunday, are listed on the door.

Generally, large shops are open from 9:30 or 10 to 7 or 8 Monday to Saturday and remain open through lunchtime. Many of the large department stores stay open until 10 Wednesday or Thursday. Smaller shops and many supermarkets often open earlier (8 AM) but take a lengthy lunch break (1–3) and generally close around 8 PM; small food shops are often open Sunday morning 9–1. There is typically a small corner grocery store that stays open late, usually until 11, if you're in a bind for basic necessities like diapers, bread, cheese, and fruit. Note that prices are substantially higher in such outlets than in the larger supermarkets. Many shops close all day Sunday, except in the Marais, where shops that stand side by side on Rue des Francs Bourgeois, from antiques dealers to chic little designers, open their doors to welcome hordes of Sunday browsers. The Bastille, the Quartier Latin, the Champs-Elysées, Ile St-Louis, and the Ile de la Cité also have shops that open Sunday.

∎ MAIL

Post offices, or PTT, are scattered throughout every arrondissement and are recognizable by a yellow LA POSTE sign. They're usually open weekdays 8–7, Saturday 8–noon. Airmail letters or postcards usually take at least five days to reach North America. When shipping home antiques or art, request assistance from the dealer, who can usually handle the customs paperwork for you or recommend a licensed shipping company.

Airmail letters and postcards to the United States and Canada cost €0.85 for 20 grams, €1.70 for 50 grams, and €2.30 for 100 grams. Stamps can be bought in post offices and cafés displaying a red TABAC sign.

If you're uncertain where you'll be staying, have mail sent to American Express (if you're a card member) or to "poste restante" at any post office.

Main Branches **Main office** (✉52 rue du Louvre, 1er), open 24 hours, 7 days a week. **Champs-Elysées office** (✉10 rue Balzar, 8e), Monday to Saturday, open until 7 PM.

SHIPPING PACKAGES

Sending overnight mail from Paris is relatively easy. Besides DHL, Federal Express, and UPS, the French post office has an overnight mail service called Chronopost that has special prepaid boxes for international use (and also boxes specifically made to mail wine). All agencies listed can be used as drop-off points, and all have information in English.

Express Services **DHL** (✉6 rue des Colonnes, 2e ☎08-20-20-25-25 ⊕www.dhl. com ✉59 av. Iéna, 16e ☎08-20-20-25-25). **Federal Express** (✉63 bd. Haussmann, 8e ☎01-40-06-90-16 ⊕www.fedex.com/fr). **UPS** (✉34 bd. Malesherbes, 8e ☎08-21-23-38-77 ✉107 rue Réaumur, 2e ☎08-00-87-78-77 ⊕www.ups.com).

∎ MONEY

Although a stay in Paris is far from cheap, you can find plenty of affordable places to eat and shop, particularly if you avoid the obvious tourist traps. Prices tend to reflect the standing of an area in the eyes of Parisians; the touristy area where value is most difficult to find is the 8e arrondissement, on and around the Champs-Elysées. Places where you can generally be certain to shop, eat, and stay without overpaying include the St-Michel/Sorbonne area on the Left Bank; the mazelike streets around Les Halles and the Marais in central Paris; in Montparnasse south of the boulevard; and in the Bastille, République, and Belleville areas of eastern Paris.

In cafés, bars, and some restaurants you can save money by eating or drinking at the counter instead of sitting at a table. Two prices are listed—*au comptoir* (at the counter) and *à salle* (at a table)—and sometimes a third for the terrace. A cup of coffee, standing at a bar, costs from €1.50; if you sit, it will cost €2 to €7. A glass of beer costs from €2 standing and from €2.50 to €7 sitting; a soft drink costs between €2 and €5. A ham sandwich will cost between €3 and €6.

Expect to pay €7–€10 for a short taxi ride. Museum entry is usually between €3.50 and €9.50, though there are hours or days of the week when admission is reduced or free.

Prices throughout this guide are given for adults. Substantially reduced fees are almost always available for children, students, and senior citizens.

ATMS & BANKS

Your own bank will probably charge a fee for using ATMs abroad; the foreign bank you use may also charge a fee. Nevertheless, you can usually get a better rate of exchange at an ATM than you will at a currency-exchange office or even when changing money in a bank. And extracting funds as you need them is a safer option than carrying around a large amount of cash.

ATMs are one of the easiest ways to get euros. Although transaction fees may be higher abroad than at home, banks usually offer excellent wholesale exchange rates through ATMs. You may, however, have to look around for Cirrus and Plus locations; it's a good idea to get a list of locations from your bank before you go. Note, too, that you may have better luck with ATMs if you're using a credit card or debit card that is also a Visa or MasterCard rather than just your bank card.

■**TIP➜** To get cash at ATMs in Paris, your PIN must be four digits long. If yours has five or more, remember to change it before you leave. If you're having trouble remembering your PIN, do not try more than twice, because at the third attempt the machine will eat your card, and you will have to go back the next morning to retrieve it.

CREDIT CARDS

Throughout this guide, the following abbreviations are used: **AE**, American Express; **DC**, Diners Club; **MC**, MasterCard; and **V**, Visa.

It's a good idea to inform your credit-card company before you travel, especially if you're going abroad and don't travel internationally very often. Otherwise, the credit-card company might put a hold on your card owing to unusual activity—not a good thing halfway through your trip. Record all your credit-card numbers—as well as the phone numbers to call if your cards are lost or stolen—in a safe place, so you're prepared should something go wrong. Both MasterCard and Visa have general numbers you can call (collect if you're abroad) if your card is lost, but you're better off calling the number of your issuing bank, since MasterCard and Visa usually just transfer you to your bank; your bank's number is usually printed on your card.

If you plan to use your credit card for cash advances, you'll need to apply for a PIN at least two weeks before your trip. Although it's usually cheaper (and safer) to use a credit card abroad for large purchases (so you can cancel payments or be reimbursed if there's a problem), note that some credit-card companies *and* the banks that issue them add substantial percentages to all foreign transactions, whether they're in a foreign currency or not. Check on these fees before leaving home, so there won't be any surprises when you get the bill.

■**TIP➜** Before you charge something, ask the merchant whether he or she plans to do a dynamic currency conversion (DCC). In such a transaction the credit-card processor (shop, restaurant, or hotel, not Visa or MasterCard) converts the currency and charges you in dollars. In most cases you'll pay the merchant a 3% fee for this service in addition to any credit-card company and issuing-bank foreign-transaction surcharges.

Dynamic currency conversion programs are becoming increasingly widespread. Merchants who participate in them are supposed to ask whether you want to be charged in dollars or the local currency, but they don't always do so. And even if they do offer you a choice, they may well avoid mentioning the additional surcharges. The good news is that you *do* have a choice. And if this practice really gets your goat, you can avoid it entirely thanks to American Express: with its cards, DCC simply isn't an option.

Reporting Lost Cards American Express (☎800/528–4800 in U.S., 336/393–1111 collect from abroad ⊕www.americanexpress. com). **Diners Club** (☎800/234–6377 in U.S., 303/799–1504 collect from abroad ⊕www. dinersclub.com). **MasterCard** (☎800/627–8372 in U.S., 636/722–7111 collect from abroad ⊕www.mastercard.com). **Visa** (☎800/847–2911 in U.S., 410/581–9994 collect from abroad ⊕www.visa.com). [cmt] Omit Discover in all guides outside the US, Bahamas, Caribbean, and Mexico[/cmt]

CURRENCY & EXCHANGE

In 2002 the single European Union (EU) currency, the euro, became the official currency of the 12 countries participating in the European Monetary Union (with the notable exceptions of Great Britain, Denmark, and Sweden). The euro system has eight coins: 1 and 2 euros, plus 1, 2, 5, 10, 20, and 50 cents. All coins have one side that has the value of the euro on it, whereas the opposite side is adorned with each country's own unique national symbol. There are seven colorful notes: 5, 10, 20, 50, 100, 200, and 500 euros. Notes have the principal architectural styles from antiquity onward on one side and the map and the flag of Europe on the other and are the same for all countries. Also be aware that because of their high nickel content, euro coins can pose problems for people with an allergic sensitivity to the metal.

If you've brought some rumpled francs from home this trip, you can still exchange them. You have until midnight February 17, 2012, to change notes at the Banque de France. A fixed rate of exchange was established: 1 euro equaling 6.55957 French francs. After this date, however, you may as well frame those remaining francs and hang them on the wall for posterity, not prosperity.

At this writing, 1 euro equaled approximately U.S.$1.59 and 1.62 Canadian dollars.

The easiest way to get euros is through ATMs; you can find them in airports, train stations, and throughout the city. ATM rates are excellent because they are based on wholesale rates offered only by major banks. ■TIP→ **It's a good idea to bring some euros with you from home so you don't have to wait in line at the airport.** At exchange booths always confirm the rate with the teller before exchanging money. You won't do as well at exchange booths in airports or rail and bus stations, in hotels, in restaurants, or in stores. Of all the banks in Paris, the Banque de France has the best rates.

WORST-CASE SCENARIO

All your money and credit cards have just been stolen. In these days of real-time transactions, this isn't a predicament that should destroy your vacation. First, report the theft of the credit cards. Then get any traveler's checks you were carrying replaced. This can usually be done almost immediately, provided that you kept a record of the serial numbers separate from the checks themselves. If you bank at a large international bank like Citibank or HSBC, go to the closest branch; if you know your account number, chances are you can get a new ATM card and withdraw money right away. **Western Union** (☎ 800/325–6000 ⊕ www.westernunion. com) sends money almost anywhere. Have someone back home order a transfer online, over the phone, or at one of the company's offices, which is the cheapest option. The U.S. State Department's **Overseas Citizens Services** (⊕ www. travel.state.gov/travel ☎ 202/501–4444) can wire money to any U.S. consulate or embassy abroad for a fee of $30. Just have someone back home wire money or send a money order or cashier's check to the state department, which will then disburse the funds as soon as the next working day after it receives them.

▮ RESTROOMS

Use of public toilet facilities in cafés and bars is usually reserved for customers, so you may need to buy a little something first. Bathrooms are often downstairs and are unisex, which may mean walking by a men's urinal to reach the cubicle. Turkish-style toilets—holes in the ground with porcelain pads for your feet—are still found (though they are becoming scarcer). Stand as far away as possible when you press the flushing mechanism to avoid water damage to your shoes. In certain cafés the lights will not come on in the bathroom until the cubicle door is locked. These lights work on a three-minute timer to save electricity. Simply press the button again if the lights go out. Clean public toilets are available in fast-food chains, department stores, and public parks. You can also find free toilet units on the street, and there are free bathrooms in the larger métro stations, town halls, and in all train stations.

There are restroom attendants in train and métro stations and some of the nicer restaurants and clubs, so always bring some coins to the bathroom. Attendants in restaurants and the like are in charge of cleaning the bathrooms and perhaps handing you a clean towel; slip some small change into the prominently placed saucer.

Find a Loo **The Bathroom Diaries** (⊕www. thebathroomdiaries.com) is flush with unsanitized info on restrooms the world over—each one located, reviewed, and rated.

▮ SAFETY

Paris is one of the safest big cities in the world, but as in any big city be streetwise and alert. Certain neighborhoods are more seedy than dangerous, thanks to the night trade that goes on around Les Halles and St-Denis and on Boulevard Clichy in Pigalle. Some off-the-beaten-path neighborhoods—particularly the outlying suburban communities around Paris—may warrant extra precaution. When in doubt, stick to the boulevards and well-lighted, populated streets, but keep in mind that even the Champs-Elysées is a haven for pickpockets.

The métro is quite safe overall, though some lines and stations, in particular lines 2 and 13, get dodgy late at night. Try not to travel alone late at night, memorize the time of the last métro train to your station, ride in the first car by the conductor, and just use your common sense. If you're worried, spend the money on a taxi. Pickpocketing is the main problem, day or night. Be wary of anyone crowding you unnecessarily or distracting you. Pickpockets often work in groups; on the métro they usually strike just before a stop so that they can leap off the train as it pulls into the station. Be especially careful if taking the RER from Charles de Gaulle/Roissy airport into town; disoriented or jet-lagged travelers are vulnerable to sticky fingers. Pickpockets often target laptop bags, so keep your valuables on your person.

A tremendous number of protest demonstrations are held in Paris—scarcely a week goes by without some kind of march or public gathering. Most protests are peaceful, but it's best to avoid them. The CRS (French riot police) carefully guard all major demonstrations, directing traffic and preventing violence. They are armed and use tear gas when and if they see fit.

Report any thefts or other problems to the police as soon as possible. There are three or four police stations in every arrondissement in Paris and one police station in every train station; go to the police station in the area where the event occurred. In the case of pickpocketing or other theft, the police will give you a Déclaration de Perte ou de Vol (receipt for theft or loss). Police reports must be made in person, but the process is generally quite streamlined. In the case of theft, valuables are usually unrecoverable, but identity documents have been known to resurface. You may need a receipt of theft or loss to replace stolen train or plane tickets, passports, or traveler's checks; the receipts may also be useful for filing insurance claims.

Although women traveling alone sometimes encounter troublesome comments and the like, *dragueurs* (men who persistently profess their undying love to hapless female passersby) are a dying breed in this increasingly politically correct world. Note that smiling automatically out of politeness is not part of French culture and can be quickly misinterpreted. If you encounter a problem, don't be afraid to show your irritation. Completely ignoring the *dragueur* should be discouragement enough; if the hassling doesn't let up, don't hesitate to move quickly away.

■TIP➔ **Distribute your cash, credit cards, IDs, and other valuables between a deep front pocket, an inside jacket or vest pocket, and a hidden money pouch. Don't reach for the money pouch once you're in public.**

▌TAXES

All taxes must be included in affixed prices in France. Prices in restaurants and hotel prices must by law include taxes and service charges. ■TIP➔ **If these appear as additional items on your bill, you should complain.**

V.A.T. (value-added tax, known in France as TVA), at a standard rate of 19.6% (33% for luxury goods), is included in the price of many goods, but foreigners are often entitled to a refund. To be eligible for V.A.T. refund, the item (or items) that you have purchased must have been bought in a single day in a participating store (look for the "Tax-Free" sticker on the door) and must equal or exceed €182. The V.A.T. for services (restaurants, theater, etc.) is not refundable.

When making a purchase, ask for a V.A.T. refund form and find out whether

the merchant gives refunds—not all stores do, nor are they required to. Have the form stamped like any customs form by customs officials when you leave the country or, if you're visiting several European Union countries, when you leave the EU. After you're through passport control, take the form to a refund-service counter for an on-the-spot refund (which is usually the quickest and easiest option), or mail it to the address on the form (or the envelope with it) after you arrive home. You receive the total refund stated on the form, but the processing time can be long, especially if you request a credit-card adjustment.

Global Refund is a Europe-wide service with 225,000 affiliated stores and more than 700 refund counters at major airports and border crossings. Its refund form, called a Tax Free Check, is the most common across the European continent. The service issues refunds in the form of cash, check, or credit-card adjustment.

V.A.T. Refunds Global Refund (☎800/566–9828 ⊕www.globalrefund.com).

▌ TIME

The time difference between New York and Paris is six hours (so when it's 1 PM in New York, it's 7 PM in Paris). The time difference between London and Paris is one hour.

The European format for abbreviating dates is day/month/year, so 7/5/06 means May 7, not July 5.

▌ TIPPING

Bills in bars and restaurants must by law include service (despite what entrepreneurial servers may tell you), but it is customary to round your bill with small change unless you're dissatisfied. The amount varies—from €0.20 for a beer to €1–€2 after a meal. In expensive restaurants it's common to leave an additional 5% on the table.

Tip taxi drivers and hairdressers 10% of the bill. Give theater ushers €0.50. In some theaters and hotels cloakroom attendants may expect nothing (watch for signs that say *pourboire interdit*—tipping forbidden); otherwise, give them €0.75. Washroom attendants usually get €0.30, though the sum is often posted.

If you stay more than two or three days in a hotel, leave something for the chambermaid—about €1.50 per day. Expect to pay €1.50 (€0.75 in a moderately priced hotel) to the person who carries your bags or hails a taxi for you. In hotels providing room service, give €1 to the waiter (unless breakfast is routinely served in your room). If the chambermaid does pressing or laundering for you, give her €1.50–€2 on top of the bill. If the concierge has been helpful, leave a tip of €8–€16.

Service-station attendants get nothing for pumping gas or checking oil but €0.75 or €1.50 for checking tires. Train and airport porters get a fixed sum (€1–€1.50) per bag. Museum guides should get €1.50–€3 after a guided tour. It's standard practice

to tip long-distance bus drivers about €2 after an excursion.

TIPPING GUIDELINES FOR PARIS	
Bellhop	€1–€2, depending on the level of the hotel
Hotel Concierge	€5 or more, if he or she performs a service for you
Hotel Doorman	€1–€2 if he helps you get a cab
Hotel Maid	€1–€2 a day (either daily or at the end of your stay, in cash)
Hotel Room-Service Waiter	€1–€2 per delivery, even if a service charge has been added
Taxi Driver	10%, or just round up the fare to the next euro amount
Tour Guide	10% of the cost of the tour
Valet Parking Attendant	€1–€2, but only when you get your car
Waiter	Just small change (up to a euro or two) to round out your bill. Service is included
Restroom attendant	Restroom attendants in more expensive restaurants expect small change or €1

INDEX

PHOTO CREDITS

NOTES

NOTES

ABOUT OUR WRITERS

When writer-editor Jennifer Ditsler-Ladonne decided it was time to leave her longtime home, Manhattan, there was only one place to go: Paris. Her insatiable curiosity—which earned her a reputation in New York for knowing just the right place to get just the right anything—has found the perfect home in the inexhaustible streets of Paris. If you're looking for rare medieval arcana or Paris's wild edible mushrooms, she's the person to call, as we did for our shopping update.

Since moving to Paris from New York in 2004, journalist/photographer Linda Hervieux has explored most corners of city while covering assignments ranging from the French presidential election to the search for the perfect hot chocolate. Her writing has appeared in publications including the New York Daily News, the New York Times, the International Herald Tribune, and Fodors.com. Paris is perfect base to pursue two of her favorite hobbies: studying art history at the Louvre school and mastering the French language, a battle that never ends.

Simon Hewitt headed to Paris straight from studying French and art history at Oxford. It was a return to base; his grandmother was French, as is his daughter, Anaïs. He has been working for Fodor's since 1987 and is a Fodor's correspondent for Art & Auction.

Rosa Jackson's love affair with French cooking began at age four, when she spent her first year in Paris before returning to the Canadian north. Early experiments with éclairs and croissants led her to enroll in the Paris Cordon Bleu, where she learned that even great chefs make mistakes. A France-based food writer for more than a decade, Rosa also creates personalized food itineraries via www.edible-paris.com, teaches cooking in Nice, and has her own food blog (http://rosajackson.blogspot.com). She has eaten in hundreds of Paris restaurants—and always has room for dessert.

Lisa Pasold first fell in love with Paris architecture and atmosphere in 1989 while dragging her suitcase up seven flights of stairs to a chambre de bonne. She writes about travel, food, and architecture for such newspapers as the Chicago Tribune and the Globe and Mail. She has also published two books of poetry, Weave and A Bad Year for Journalists. As a travel writer, she has been thrown off a train in Belarus and mushed huskies in the Yukon, but her favorite place to explore remains the fabulous tangle of streets that surround her Paris home.

Nicole Pritchard is a resident Parisienne-about-town and writes about topics related to nightlife, fashion and beauty, and celebrity culture. She has worked in the fashion industry for several years, and recently graduated with a master's degree in international business from one of Paris's grandes écoles. She's often spotted at Café de Flore, Hôtel Costes, and various fashion soirées.

Heather Stimmler-Hall came to Paris as a university student in 1995 and was almost immediately put to work by family and friends back home who were asking for hotel recommendations. A decade later she's made a career out of reading between the lines of glossy hotel brochures and talking even the grumpiest receptionist into letting her poke around their rooms. She's reviewed hundreds of hotels for international magazines and newspapers such as the Times of London, ELLE, France magazine, easyJet in-flight magazine, and her own monthly e-newsletter, www.secretsofparis.com. Although she's not too jaded to appreciate the city's gorgeous five-star palace and design-boutique hotels, what really gets her excited are the hidden budget hotels with a uniquely Parisian character.